RESEARCH METHODS FOR LEISURE AND TOURISM

Visit the *Research methods for Leisure and Tourism*, 4TH edition Companion Website at **www.pearsoned.co.uk/veal** to find valuable **student** learning material including:

- Annotated links to relevant sites on the web
- Interactive media resources, including video cases, flash animations and extra cases
- A full compendium of part bibliographies for you to print out and take with you to the library
- Online tutorials for SPSS, Excel and Nvivo
- Additional practice datasets

We work with leading authors to develop the
strongest educational materials in leisure and tourism,
bringing cutting-edge thinking and best learning
practice to a global market.

Under a range of well-known imprints, including
Financial Times Prentice Hall, we craft high quality print and
electronic publications which help readers to understand
and apply their content, whether studying or at work.

To find out more about the complete range of our
publishing, please visit us on the World Wide Web at:
www.pearsoned.co.uk

Research Methods for Leisure and Tourism

A Practical Guide

Fourth edition

A. J. Veal

University of Technology, Sydney

**Financial Times
Prentice Hall
is an imprint of**

Harlow, England • London • New York • Boston • San Francisco • Toronto • Sydney • Singapore • Hong Kong
Tokyo • Seoul • Taipei • New Delhi • Cape Town • Madrid • Mexico City • Amsterdam • Munich • Paris • Milan

Pearson Education Limited
Edinburgh Gate
Harlow
Essex CM20 2JE
England

and Associated Companies throughout the world

Visit us on the World Wide Web at:
www.pearsoned.co.uk

First published 1992
Second edition published 1997
Third edition published 2006
Fourth edition published 2011

ISBN: 978-0-273-71750-8

British Library Cataloguing-in-Publication Data
A catalogue record for this book is available from the British Library

10 9 8 7 6 5 4 3 2 1
14 13 12 11

Typeset in 10/12.5pt Book Antiqua by 35
Printed and bound by Ashford Colour Press, Gosport

Summary contents

List of figures		xx
List of tables		xxvi
List of case studies		xxvii
Guided Tour		xxviii
Preface		xxx
Acknowledgements		xxxii

I	Preparation	1
1.	Introduction to research: what, why and who?	3
2.	Approaches to leisure and tourism research	27
3.	Starting out – research plans and proposals	51
4.	Research ethics	101
5.	The range of research methods	121
6.	Reviewing the literature	153

II	Data collection	179
7.	Secondary data sources	181
8.	Observation	207
9.	Qualitative methods: introduction and data collection	231
10.	Questionnaire surveys: typology, design and coding	255
11.	Experimental research	317
12.	Case study method	341
13.	Sampling: quantitative and qualitative	355

III   Data analysis   373
14.   Analysing secondary data   375
15.   Analysing qualitative data   391
16.   Analysing survey data   417
17.   Statistical analysis   459

IV   Communicating results   503
18.   Preparing a research report   505

       References   525
       Index   547

Detailed chapter contents

List of figures	xx
List of tables	xxvi
List of case studies	xxvii
Guided Tour	xxviii
Preface	xxx
Acknowledgements	xxxii

I	**Preparation**	**1**
1	**Introduction to research: what, why and who?**	**3**
	Introduction	3
	What is research?	4
	Research defined	4
	Scientific research	5
	Social science research	5
	Descriptive, explanatory and evaluative research	5
	Why study research?	8
	In general	8
	Research in policy-making, planning and management processes	9
	Who does research?	14
	Academics	15
	Students	16
	Government, commercial and non-profit organisations	16
	Managers	17
	Consultants	18
	Who pays?	18
	Research outputs	19
	Academic journal articles	20
	Professional journal articles	21
	Conference papers/presentations	21
	Books	21
	Policy/planning/management reports	21
	Terminology	23

Summary	24
Test questions	24
Exercises	25
Resources	25

2 Approaches to leisure and tourism research — 27

Introduction	27
Disciplinary traditions	27
Approaches, dimensions, issues, terminology	30
Ontology, epistemology, methodology	30
Positivist, post-positivist, interpretive and critical approaches/paradigms	30
Descriptive, explanatory and evaluative research	33
Qualitative and quantitative research	34
Theoretical and applied research	37
Reflexivity	38
Empirical and non-empirical research	38
Induction and deduction	39
Experimental and naturalistic methods	42
Objectivity and subjectivity	44
Primary and secondary data	44
Self-reported and observed data	45
Validity, reliability and trustworthiness	46
Summary	47
Test questions	48
Exercises	48
Resources	49

3 Starting out – research plans and proposals — 51

Introduction: the research process	51
Planning a research project	51
1. Select a topic	53
2. Review the literature	60
3. Devise conceptual framework	62
4. Decide research question(s)	72
5. List information requirements	75
6. Decide research strategy	75
7. Obtain ethics clearance	78
8. Conduct research	79
9. Communicate findings	80
10. Store data	80
The research process in the real world	81
Case studies	81
Research proposals	92
Introduction	92
Self-generated research proposals	92
Responsive proposals – briefs and tenders	96

Summary   99
Test questions   99
Exercises   100
Resources   100

4   Research ethics   101

Introduction   101
Institutional oversight of research ethics   102
Ethics in the research process   103
Ethical issues in research   106
   Social benefit   106
   Researcher competence   107
   Free choice   108
   Informed consent   109
   Risk of harm to the subject   112
   Honesty/rigour in analysis, interpretation and reporting   116
   Authorship and acknowledgements   117
Access to research information   118

Summary   118
Test questions   119
Exercises   119
Resources   120

5   The range of research methods   121

Introduction – horses for courses   121
The range of major research methods   122
   Scholarship   122
   Just thinking   123
   Existing sources – using the literature   123
   Existing sources – secondary data   124
   Observation   124
   Qualitative methods   125
   Questionnaire-based surveys   126
   Experimental method   128
   Case study method   128
Subsidiary/cross-cutting techniques   129
   Coupon surveys/conversion studies   129
   En route/intercept/cordon surveys   129
   Time-use surveys   129
   Experience sampling method (ESM)   131
   Panel studies   132
   Longitudinal studies   132
   Media reader/viewer/listener surveys   133
   Action research   133
   Historical research   134
   Content analysis   135

Delphi technique   135
Projective techniques   135
Perceptual mapping   136
Repertory grid   136
Use of scales   137
Psychographic/lifestyle research   138
Q methodology   139
Conjoint analysis   140
Quantitative modelling   141
Network analysis   141
Meta-analysis   142

Multiple methods   142
Triangulation   142
Community study as method   143
Counting heads   145

Choosing methods   145
The research question or hypothesis   146
Previous research   146
Data availability/access   146
Resources   146
Time and timing   147
Validity, reliability and generalisability   147
Ethics   147
Uses/users of the findings   147

Summary   148
Test questions   149
Exercises   150
Resources   150

6   Reviewing the literature   153

Introduction – an essential task   153
The value of bibliographies   154
Searching: sources of information   155
Library catalogues   155
Specialist indexes and databases   156
Searching on the Internet   157
Google Scholar   157
Published bibliographies   157
General leisure and tourism publications   158
Reference lists   158
Beyond leisure and tourism   159
Unpublished research   159

Obtaining copies of material   159
Compiling and maintaining a bibliography   160
Reviewing the literature   161
Types of literature review   161
Reading critically and creatively   164
Summarising   166

Referencing the literature 167
    The purpose of referencing 167
    Recording references 167
Referencing and referencing systems 170
    The author/date or Harvard system 170
    Footnote or endnote system 172
    Comparing two systems 174
Referencing issues 175
    Second-hand references 175
    Excessive referencing 175
    Latin abbreviations 176

Summary 176
Test questions 177
Exercises 177
Resources 177

II Data collection 179

7 Secondary data sources 181

Introduction – measurement 181
Measuring leisure and tourism activity 181
    Counting heads 183
Introduction to secondary data sources 186
    Advantages and disadvantages of using secondary data 187
    Types of secondary data 187
Administrative/management data 188
    Tourist arrivals and departures 188
    Management data 188
National leisure participation surveys 189
    The national leisure survey phenomenon 189
    Validity and reliability 192
    Sample size 192
    Main question – participation reference period and duration 193
    Age range 194
    Social characteristics 195
    The importance of participation surveys 195
    National time-use surveys 195
Tourism surveys 197
    International and domestic tourism surveys 197
    Sample size 197
    Definitions 197
Economic data 199
    Household expenditure 199
    Satellite accounts 200
The population census 200

The modern population census   200
Uses of census data   202
Documentary sources   202
Opportunism   203

Summary   203
Test questions   204
Resources   204

8   Observation   207

Introduction   207
Types of observational research: quantitative and
qualitative   208
Possibilities   208
Children's play   208
Informal recreation/tourism areas visit numbers:
counting heads   209
Informal recreation/tourism areas: spatial/functional
patterns of use   210
Visitor profiles   212
Deviant behaviour   212
Mystery shopping   214
Complementary research   214
Everyday life   215
Social behaviour   216
Main elements of observational research   216
Step 1:   Choice of site(s)   217
Step 2:   Choice of observation point(s)   217
Step 3:   Choice of observation time-period(s)   217
Step 4:   Continuous observation or sampling?   217
Step 5:   Count frequency   218
Step 6:   What to observe   218
Step 7:   Division of site into zones   220
Step 8:   Recording information   220
Step 9:   Conducting the observation   222
Step 10: Analysing data   222
Use of technology   225
Automatic counters   225
GPS   226
Aerial photography   226
Still photography   226
Video   227
Time-lapse photography   227

Just looking   227
Summary   227
Test questions   228
Exercises   229
Resources   229

9 Qualitative methods: introduction and data collection   231

Introduction   231
    The nature of qualitative methods   231
    History and development   232
Merits, functions, limitations   235
The qualitative research process   237
The range of qualitative methods – introduction   238
In-depth interviews   239
    Nature   239
    Purposes and situations   240
    Checklist   241
    The interviewing process   242
    Recording   245
Focus groups   245
    Nature   245
    Purposes   245
    Methods   245
Participant observation   246
    Nature   246
    Purposes   246
    Methods   246
Analysing texts   247
    Nature   247
    Novels and other literature   248
    Mass media coverage   248
    Film   248
    Material culture   249
Biographical research   249
    Nature   249
    Biography/autobiography   249
    Oral history   250
    Memory work   250
    Personal domain histories   250
Ethnography   250
Validity and reliability, trustworthiness   251

Summary   252
Test questions   252
Exercises   253
Resources   253

10 Questionnaire surveys: typology, design and coding   255

Introduction   255
    Definitions and terminology   255
    Roles   256

Merits	257
Limitations	258
Interviewer-completion or respondent-completion?	260
Types of questionnaire survey	261
The household questionnaire survey	**262**
Nature	262
Conduct	262
Omnibus surveys	263
Time-use surveys	263
National surveys	264
The street survey	**264**
Nature	264
Conduct	265
Quota sampling	265
The telephone survey	**266**
Nature	266
Conduct	266
Representativeness and response levels	267
National surveys	268
The mail survey	**268**
Nature	268
The problem of low response rates	268
Mail and user/site/visitor survey combos	272
E-surveys	**272**
Nature and conduct	272
Advantages and disadvantages	273
User/on-site/visitor surveys	**274**
Nature	274
Conduct	274
The uses of user surveys	275
User/site/visitor and mail/e-survey combo	277
Captive group surveys	**278**
Nature	278
Conduct	278
Questionnaire design	**279**
Introduction – research problems and information requirements	279
Example questionnaires	280
General design issues	280
Types of information	287
Activity/events/places questions	287
Respondent characteristics	291
Attitude/opinion questions	298
Market segments	300
Ordering of questions and layout of questionnaires	300
Coding	**303**
Pre-coded questions	303
Open-ended questions	303
Recording coded information	304

Validity of questionnaire-based data 306
   Threats to validity 306
   Checking validity 306
Conducting questionnaire surveys 310
   Planning fieldwork arrangements 310
   Conducting a pilot survey 313

Summary 314
Test questions 315
Exercises 315
Resources 316

11   Experimental research 317

Introduction 317
Principles of experimental research 318
   Components 318
   The classic experimental design 318
Validity 319
   Threats to validity 320
   Field experiments versus laboratory experiments 321
Quasi-experimental designs 321
   Types of quasi-experimental design 321
   Experiments and projects 322
Experimental methods in leisure and tourism research 322
   Discrete choice experiments (DCEs) 323
   Policy/management experimental projects 326
   Experimenting with research methods 329
   Psychological/perceptual studies 332
   Sport-related experiments 332
   Children's play 335
   Other examples 337

Summary 338
Test questions 339
Exercises 339
Resources 339

12   Case study method 341

Introduction 341
Definitions 342
   What is the case study method? 342
   What the case study method is not 342
   Scale 343
Validity and reliability 344
Merits of the case study approach 346
Design of case studies 346
   Defining the unit of analysis 346

Selecting the case(s) 347
Data gathering 347
Analysis 348
Case studies in practice 349

Summary 352
Test questions 353
Exercises 353
Resources 353

13 **Sampling: quantitative and qualitative** 355

Introduction 355
The idea of sampling 355
Samples and populations 356
Representativeness 357
Sampling for household surveys 357
Sampling for telephone surveys 358
Sampling for site/user/visitor surveys 359
Sampling for street surveys and quota sampling 360
Sampling for mail surveys 360
Sampling for complex events and destination studies 361
Sample size 361
Level of precision – confidence intervals 362
Detail of proposed analysis 365
Budget 366
Confidence intervals applied to population estimates 367
Sample size and small populations 367
Weighting 368
Sampling for qualitative research 369

Summary 370
Test questions 371
Exercises 371
Resources 372
Appendix 13.1: Suggested appendix on sample size and confidence intervals 372

III **Data analysis** 373

14 **Analysing secondary data** 375

Introduction 375
Case studies of secondary data analysis 375
Children's play safety 375
International data on inequality, leisure and tourism 376
Estimating demand for a leisure facility 376
Tourism trend analysis 376

Facility utilisation   376
Facility catchment area   376

Summary   389
Exercises   389
Resources   389

15   Analysing qualitative data   391

Introduction   391
   Data collection and analysis   391
   Data storage and confidentiality   392
   Case study example   393
Manual methods of analysis   396
   Introduction   396
   Reading   396
   Emergent themes   397
   Mechanics   397
   Analysis   399
Qualitative analysis using computer software –
introduction   400
   Interview transcripts   401
NVivo   401
   Introduction   401
   Starting up   401
   Creating a project   401
   Saving   402
   Attributes   403
   Cases and their attributes   403
   Importing documents   403
   Linking cases and documents   405
   Setting up a coding system   405
   Modelling   407
   Coding text   407
   Project summary   407
   Analysis   407

Summary   413
Test questions   414
Exercises   414
Resources   415

16   Analysing survey data   417

Introduction   417
Survey data analysis and types of research   418
   Descriptive research   418
   Explanatory research   418
   Evaluative research   419
   Overlaps   420
   Reliability   420

Spreadsheet analysis   420
Statistical Package for the Social Sciences (SPSS)   422
Preparation   425
    Cases and variables   425
    Specifying variables   425
    Starting up   430
    Entering information about variables – Variable View
    window   430
    Saving work   432
    Entering data – Data View window   432
SPSS Statistics procedures   433
    Starting an analysis session   433
    Descriptives   433
    Frequencies   435
    Checking for errors   437
    Multiple response   437
    Recode   439
    Mean, median and mode – measures of central tendency   441
    Presenting the results: statistical summary   441
    Crosstabulation   443
    Weighting   445
    Graphics   446
The analysis process   450

Summary   450
Test questions   451
Exercises   451
Resources   451
Appendix 16.1:   *SPSS* frequencies output file   453

17   Statistical analysis   459

Introduction   459
The statistics approach   460
    Probabilistic statements   460
    The normal distribution   460
    Probabilistic statement formats   461
    Significance   463
    The null hypothesis   464
    Dependent and independent variables   464
Statistical tests   465
    Types of data and appropriate tests   465
    Chi-square   466
    Comparing two means: the t-test   471
    A number of means: one-way analysis of variance (ANOVA)   475
    A table of means: factorial analysis of variance (ANOVA)   477
    Correlation   480
    Linear regression   484
    Multiple regression   489
    Cluster and factor analysis   492
    In conclusion   494

	Summary	495
	Test questions and exercises	496
	Resources	496
Appendix 17.1:	Details of example data file used – variable details and data	497
Appendix 17.2:	Statistical formulae	502

IV   Communicating results **503**

18   Preparing a research report **505**

Introduction	505
Written research reports	505
Getting started	506
Report components	506
Main body of the report – technical aspects	511
Main body of the report – structure and content	516
In conclusion	521
Other media	521
Oral presentations	521
Use of PowerPoint-type software	522
Summary	523
A final comment	524
Test questions/exercises	524
Resources	524
References	525
Index	547

Supporting resources

Visit **www.pearsoned.co.uk/veal** to find valuable online resources

Companion Website for students
- Annotated links to relevant sites on the web
- Interactive media resources, including video cases, flash animations and extra cases
- A full compendium of part bibliographies for you to print out and take with you to the library
- Online tutorials for SPSS, Excel and Nvivo
- Additional practice datasets

For instructors
- Customisable PowerPoint slides, including key figures and tables from the main text
- A fully updated Instructor's Manual, including sample answers for all question material in the book
- Testbank of question material

Also: The Companion Website provides the following features:
- Search tool to help locate specific items of content
- E-mail results and profile tools to send results of quizzes to instructors
- Online help and support to assist with website usage and troubleshooting

For more information please contact your local Pearson Education sales representative or visit **www.pearsoned.co.uk/veal**

List of figures

1.1	Types of research	6
1.2	Why study research?	8
1.3	Examples of policies, plans and management	10
1.4	The rational-comprehensive model of planning/management	10
1.5	Examples of planning/management tasks and associated research	12
1.6	Who does research?	15
1.7	Managers and research	17
1.8	Who pays?	19
1.9	Research report formats	20
2.1	Disciplines and examples of research questions	29
2.2	Terminology: approaches, dimensions and issues	31
2.3	Research methods used in USA leisure journals, 1992–2002	36
2.4	*Leisure Studies* contents, 1982–2006	37
2.5	Circular model of the research process	40
3.1	Elements in the research process	52
3.2	Examples of research topics from different sources	53
3.3	Reasons for re-visiting theories/propositions/observations from the literature	55
3.4	Purposes of research	58
3.5	Roles of the literature in research	60
3.6	Development of a conceptual framework	64
3.7	Exploration of relationships between concepts – example	64
3.8	Concept map example	65
3.9	Examples of concepts – definition and operationalisation	66
3.10	Examples of operationalisation of concepts	68
3.11	Conceptual framework as quantifiable model	69
3.12	Concept map: holiday/leisure facility choice	70
3.13	Concept map: performance monitoring	71
3.14	Conceptual framework: market research study	71
3.15	Conceptual framework: customer service quality study	72
3.16	The research question vs the hypothesis	73

3.17	Information needs for the market research study (Figure 3.14)	76
3.18	Research strategy components	76
3.19	Example of research programme diagrammatic representation	79
3.20	Example of research project timetable	79
3.21	The research process in the real world	82
3.22	Facility use study conceptual framework	85
3.23	Facility use study: list of concepts, definitions and operationalisation	85
3.24	Facility use study: information needs and likely sources	86
3.25	Facility use study: research questions	87
3.26	Facility use study: research strategy	88
3.27	Recreation services project: concept map	89
3.28	Recreation services project: concepts – definitions and operationalisation	90
3.29	Recreation services project: information requirements and research strategy	91
3.30	Research proposal checklist: self-generated research	93
3.31	Research proposal checklist – responsive research	98
4.1	Ethics in the research process	104
4.2	Information for research participants: checklist	110
4.3	Example of a consent form	111
4.4	Ethics guidelines for anonymous questionnaire-based surveys	113
4.5	Personally identifiable data	115
5.1	The range of major methods	122
5.2	Qualitative data collection methods	126
5.3	Types of questionnaire-based survey	128
5.4	Subsidiary, cross-cutting and multiple techniques/methods	130
5.5	Action research process	134
5.6	Repertory grid example	136
5.7	Scales for leisure/tourism-related topics	138
5.8	Examples of psychographic/lifestyle categories	139
5.9	A simple network	141
5.10	Triangulation	144
5.11	Considerations in selecting a research method	145
6.1	The roles of the literature in research	154
6.2	Sources of information	155
6.3	Types of literature review	161
6.4	Questions to ask when reviewing the literature	165
6.5	Making sense of the literature	167
6.6	Standard/generic reference formats	168
6.7	Examples of references	169
6.8	Reference systems: features, advantages, disadvantages	174
7.1	Measuring leisure and tourism activity	182
7.2	Counting heads: sources and methods – leisure	184
7.3	Counting heads: sources and methods – tourism	185

7.4	Advantages and disadvantages of using secondary data	187
7.5	Types of secondary data	188
7.6	Management data	189
7.7	National leisure participation survey details	191
7.8	National tourism survey details	198
7.9	Household expenditure survey leisure items	199
7.10	Census data: levels of availability	201
7.11	Census data available	201
7.12	Documentary sources	202
8.1	Types of observational research	208
8.2	Situations for observational research	209
8.3	Visitor movement patterns in a museum	211
8.4	Pattern of conflict at the Bathurst Bike Races, Easter Saturday, 1985	213
8.5	Steps in an observation project	216
8.6	Counts of site use	219
8.7	Mapping observed data: use of a park	219
8.8	Flows within a site	220
8.9	Examples of observation recording sheets	221
8.10	Park usage pattern	223
9.1	Sequential and recursive approaches to research	238
9.2	Qualitative methods: summary	239
9.3	Questions, responses and interview types	240
9.4	Example of a checklist for in-depth interviewing	242
9.5	Interviewing interventions – Whyte	244
10.1	The use of questionnaire surveys compared with other methods – examples	258
10.2	Interviewer-completion compared with respondent-completion	260
10.3	Types of questionnaire survey – characteristics	261
10.4	Factors affecting mail survey response	268
10.5	Mail survey follow-ups	270
10.6	Mail survey response pattern	271
10.7	Types of e-survey	273
10.8	Questionnaire design process	279
10.9	Question-wording: examples of good and bad practice	284
10.10	Open-ended vs pre-coded questions – example	285
10.11	Example of range of replies resulting from an open-ended question	286
10.12	Range of information in leisure/tourism questionnaires	288
10.13	Economic status, occupational and socio-economic groupings	292
10.14	Household type and visitor group type	295
10.15	Life-cycle stages	296
10.16	Housing information	297
10.17	Opinion or attitude question formats	299
10.18	Filtering: examples	302

10.19	Coding open-ended questions – example	304
10.20	Completed questionnaire	305
10.21	Data from 15 questionnaires	307
10.22	Questionnaire surveys: threats to validity	308
10.23	Fieldwork planning tasks	311
10.24	Pilot survey purposes	314

11.1	Classic experimental design	319
11.2	Threats to validity of experiments	320
11.3	Quasi-experimental designs	322
11.4	Types and contexts of experiments in leisure and tourism research	323
11.5	Cultural events: attributes, values and preferences	325
11.6	Experimental model of policy projects	327
11.7	Survey respondent groups – Hammitt and McDonald	331

| 12.1 | The case study method: demographic and geographic levels | 343 |
| 12.2 | Case study research: theory and policy | 345 |

| 13.1 | Normal curve and confidence intervals | 363 |
| 13.2 | Selected qualitative sampling methods | 370 |

14.1	Inequality and leisure and tourism	379
14.2	Estimating likely demand for a leisure facility	381
14.3	Tourism trends – quarterly arrivals and moving average	386
14.4	Facility utilisation	387
14.5	Catchment/market area	388

15.1	Circular model of the research process in quantitative and qualitative contexts	392
15.2	Outline conceptual framework for qualitative study of activity choice	393
15.3	Interview transcript extracts	395
15.4	Developed conceptual framework for qualitative study of activity choice	398
15.5	'Crosstabulation' of qualitative data	399
15.6	NVivo procedures covered	402
15.7	Create NVivo project – procedure	403
15.8	Attributes – procedure	404
15.9	Cases and attributes – procedure	405
15.10	Importing internal documents – procedure	406
15.11	Linking documents and cases – procedure	406
15.12	Setting up a coding system – procedure	408
15.13	Modelling – procedure	409
15.14	Coding text – procedure	410
15.15	Activity Choice project summary	411
15.16	Queries – procedure	412
15.17	Matrix coding query – procedure	413

16.1	Research types and analytical procedures	418
16.2	Survey data: spreadsheet analysis	421
16.3	Questionnaire survey data: steps in spreadsheet analysis	423
16.4	Survey analysis – overview	424
16.5	Variable names, labels and values	426
16.6	Starting a *SPSS Statistics* session	430
16.7	Blank Variable View and Data View windows	431
16.8	Variable View window with variable names, labels, etc.	432
16.9	Data View window with data from 15 questionnaires	433
16.10	Starting a *SPSS* analysis session	434
16.11	Descriptives	434
16.12	Frequencies for one variable	436
16.13	Multiple response – procedure	438
16.14	Recode procedures and output	440
16.15	*Means* procedures and output	442
16.16	Campus Life Survey 2010: statistical summary	443
16.17	Crosstabs – procedure	444
16.18	Data types and graphics	446
16.19	Graphics procedure and output	447
17.1	Drawing repeated samples and the normal distribution	462
17.2	Dependent and independent variables	465
17.3	Types of data and statistical test	466
17.4	Alternative expressions of hypotheses	467
17.5	Procedure for the Chi-square test	468
17.6	Distribution of Chi-square assuming the null hypothesis is true	469
17.7	Presentation of Chi-square test results	471
17.8	Chi-square and t distributions	472
17.9	Comparing means: t-test: paired samples – procedure	473
17.10	Comparing means: t-test: independent samples – procedure	474
17.11	Comparing ranges of means – procedure	475
17.12	Comparing means and variances	476
17.13	One-way analysis of variance – procedure	478
17.14	A table of means – procedure	479
17.15	Factorial analysis of variance – procedure	480
17.16	Relationships between variables	481
17.17	Correlation	483
17.18	Correlation matrix – procedure	485
17.19	Regression line	486
17.20	Regression analysis – procedure	487
17.21	Regression line: curve fit – procedure	488
17.22	Regression: curve fit, non-linear – procedure	490
17.23	Multiple regression – procedure	491
17.24	Structural equation modelling	492
17.25	Simple manual factor analysis	493
17.26	Plots of 'clusters'	494
17.27	Dendrogram	494

18.1   Types of research report   507
18.2   Report style and components   508
18.3   Example report contents page   510
18.4   Main body of report: technical aspects   511
18.5   Dot-point list example   512
18.6   Table and commentaries   514
18.7   Conventional academic article structure   517
18.8   Report as narrative – structure   519

List of tables

7.1	Participation rates in sports, England, 2002, 2008–9	193
7.2	Time use: Britain and Australia	196
8.1	Observed use of a park	223
8.2	Estimating visit numbers from count data	224
10.1	Attendance at arts events, England, 2003	290
13.1	Confidence intervals related to sample size	364
13.2	Necessary sample sizes to achieve given confidence intervals	365
13.3	Sample size and population size: small populations	368
13.4	Interview/usage data from a site/visitor survey	369
13.5	Weighting	369
14.1	Inequality and leisure and tourism data	378
14.2	Cinema attendance by age	382
14.3	Study town and national age structure compared	382
14.4	Estimating demand for cinema attendance	383
14.5	Tourist arrivals 2004–9	385
14.6	Facility utilisation data	387

List of case studies

2.1	Research approaches in leisure journals	36
2.1	Tennis vs golf – inductive and deductive approaches	41
3.1	Operationalisation of concepts	68
3.2	Conceptual framework for a holiday/leisure facility choice study	69
3.3	Facility use: research design process	83
3.4	Evaluating public recreation services: research design process	88
3.5	Example of a successful self-generated research proposal	94
4.1	Examples of ethical issues in leisure and tourism research	105
6.1	Lifestyle and leisure literature review	162
8.1	Observation of museum visitor behaviour	211
8.2	Observing riots	213
9.1	Early qualitative research: *English Life and Leisure*	233
10.1	Example questionnaires	281
11.1	Discrete choice experiments: examples	324
11.2	Policy/management-related experimental studies	327
11.3	Experiments with research methods: examples	330
11.4	Psychological/perceptual experiments	333
11.5	Sport-related experiments	334
11.6	Children's play experiments	335
12.1	*English Life and Leisure*	349
12.2	Euro Disneyland	350
12.3	Nike, advertising and women	351
12.4	*Leisure, Lifestyle and the New Middle Class*	352
14.1	*The Spirit Level* and leisure and tourism	377
14.2	Estimating likely demand for a leisure facility	380
14.3	Tourism trend analysis	385
14.4	Facility utilisation	386
14.5	Facility catchment or market area	388
15.1	Activity choice qualitative study	393

Guided Tour

Each **part opener** summarises the main themes of each chapter and how they relate to other parts within the book.

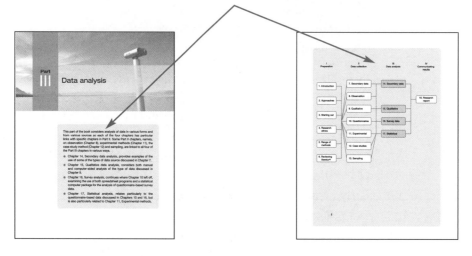

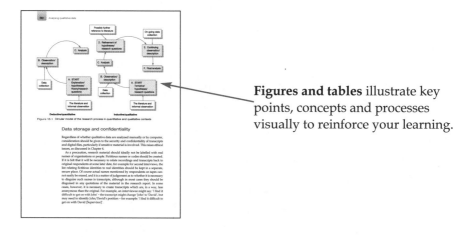

Figures and tables illustrate key points, concepts and processes visually to reinforce your learning.

Located the end of every chapter the **Test questions** will help you review your understanding and knowledge of the chapter.

Exercises will help you to test your understanding of each chapter and can be used for self testing, class exercises or debates.

Chapter summaries provide the key concepts and issues along with a concise checklist of the topics and issues covered.

Each chapter includes a list of **Resources** directing you to a variety of websites, journals and books in order to help you with additional study and research.

The title also includes a large number of **case studies**. These will provide a range of material fir seminars and private study by illustrating real life applications and implications of the topics covered in the chapter.

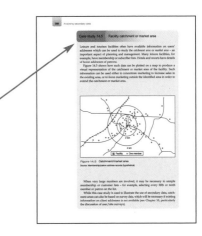

Preface

The first edition of *Research Methods for Leisure and Tourism* was published in 1992, the second in 1997 and the third in 2006. In this fourth edition, in addition to a general updating of sources, a number of changes have been made, including:

- division of the book into four parts: I Preparation; II Data collection; III Data analysis; and IV Communicating results – this has involved splitting some chapters into two, while noting that the spilt between data collection and data analysis is somewhat forced for some types of qualitative method;

- expansion of material on three topics to form three new chapters on:
  - research ethics;
  - the case study method; and
  - experimental methods;

- addition of a spreadsheet (Excel) analysis section in addition to SPSS in the survey analysis chapter;

- updating of SPSS statistical package material to version 18 and NVivo to version 8;

- provision of a bank of test questions on the book's website.

A number of other changes have been made in the light of my own and others' experience in using the book in teaching undergraduate and graduate students. I am most grateful for the helpful comments received on the proposal for the new edition from anonymous reviewers contacted by the publisher, and have done my best to respond to most of them. I am also grateful to my UTS colleagues, notably Dr. Simon Darcy, for on-going support in the development of the book.

The new chapter on experimental methods merits some comment. In the third edition of the book experimental methods were discussed in a single page, noting that they were used in psychology and sport/human movement areas and in some research on children's play behaviour. On delving into the subject more deeply, I realised that this is far too limited a view and that experimental methods in leisure and tourism research, while used in only a minority of publications, are nevertheless quite common. If we adopt an inclusive definition, covering quasi-experimental methods, we find that numerous policy-related projects designed to increase participation in sport and culture, for its own sake or to achieve specific social goals, are experimental, although often subject to criticism for their lack of rigour. There is also a considerable body of research experimenting with and evaluating different research methods. And there are specific research techniques which are experimental in nature or have experimental features, including discrete choice experiments, Q methodology, multi dimensional scaling, action research and the use of visual stimuli to elicit responses.

When a new edition of a textbook is being considered, publishers typically send the proposal to teachers who use the existing edition of the book and others with appropriate expertise who provide anonymous comment on the existing and proposed new edition. A comment from one reviewer regarding data analysis software used in the book calls for a particular response. It was suggested that the selection of packages might be related to an exclusive arrangement with software publishers. This is not the case: I simply utilise software packages with which I am familiar and which have been available to the students in the universities where I have taught. I can vouch for the usefulness of the packages used but I have not conducted a 'consumer test' of available packages so am not in a position to compare the packages used with others available.

Regarding presentational style: although I have not been entirely consistent about it, I have, in the interests of readability, reduced the amount of overt referencing in the body of the text. In general, references to examples of the use of various methods and techniques are provided in case studies or in the resources at the end of each chapter. Further, in within-text references I frequently use full names rather than just surnames, in an attempt to remind the reader that researchers are real people.

Readers may wish to consult the online material available at www.pearsoned.co.uk/veal, which includes:

- copies of all diagrams, tables and some dot-point lists in PowerPoint files;
- copies of statistical and qualitative data-sets used in the book, plus others;
- extended versions of some case studies;
- some sections of the text from the third edition not included in this edition;
- the bank of test questions as noted above;
- *errata* – which will be corrected in reprints following discovery;
- updates to Resource website addresses as information comes to hand.

The aims of the book remain unchanged: to provide a 'how to do it' text and also to offer an understanding of how research findings are generated in order to assist students and practising managers to become knowledgeable consumers of the research of others.

A. J. Veal
University of Technology, Sydney
November 2010

Acknowledgements

We are grateful to the following for permission to reproduce copyright material:

Figures

Figure 10.11 from *Port Hacking Visitor Use Study*, Centre for Leisure and Tourism Studies, University of Technology, Sydney (Robertson, R. W., and Veal, A. J. 1987); Figure 11.7 from Response bias and the need for extensive mail questionnaire follow-ups among selected recreation samples, *Journal of Leisure Research*, 14(3), pp. 207–16 (Hammitt, W. E., and McDonald, C. D. 1982); Figures 16.7, 16.8 and 16.9 screenshots from PASW Statistics Data Editor, reprint courtesy of International Business Machines Corporation, © SPSS, Inc., an IBM Company; Figure 17.24 adapted from *Principles and Practice of Structural Equation Modelling*, 2nd ed., Guilford Press (Kline, R. B. 2005).

In some instances we have been unable to trace the owners of copyright material, and we would appreciate any information that would enable us to do so.

Part

1

Preparation

This part of the book contains six chapters;

- Chapters 1 and 2, Introduction to research: what, why and who? and Approaches to leisure and tourism research, set the context for research generally and for the background to research in the fields of leisure and tourism.

- Chapter 3, Starting out: research plans and proposals, considers the all-important process of designing a research project and provides a framework for the various components of research discussed in the rest of the book.

- Chapter 4 introduces the topic of the ethical conduct of research, which relates to moral as well as legal and administrative issues.

- Chapter 5, The range of research methods, provides an overview of the range of social science research methods and techniques used in leisure and tourism contexts, which are discussed in more detail in the rest of the book.

- Chapter 6 discusses the fundamental task of reviewing the literature, that is, examining existing published and unpublished research relevant to the project in hand.

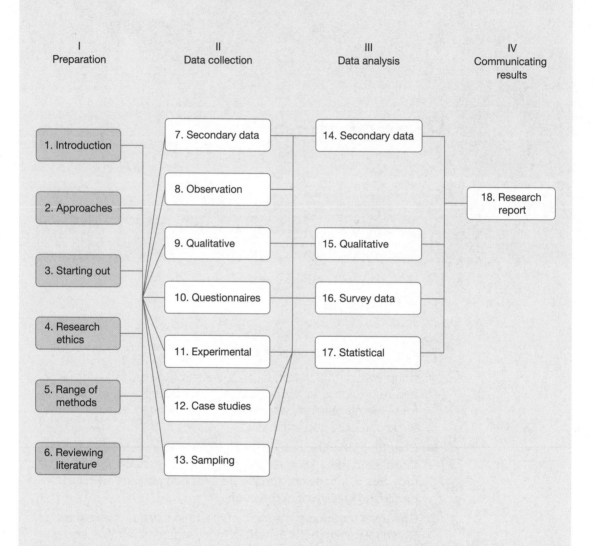

I Preparation	II Data collection	III Data analysis	IV Communicating results
1. Introduction	7. Secondary data	14. Secondary data	
2. Approaches	8. Observation		18. Research report
3. Starting out	9. Qualitative	15. Qualitative	
4. Research ethics	10. Questionnaires	16. Survey data	
5. Range of methods	11. Experimental	17. Statistical	
6. Reviewing literature	12. Case studies		
	13. Sampling		

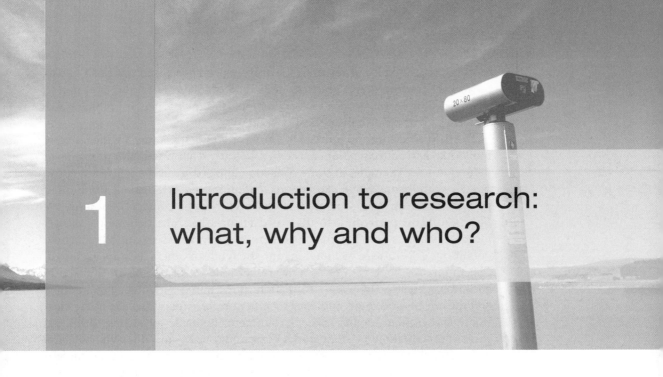

1 Introduction to research: what, why and who?

Introduction

Information, knowledge and understanding concerning the natural, social and economic environment have become the very basis of cultural and material development in contemporary societies and economies. The recent controversies over the research basis of the global climate change predictions offer a dramatic demonstration of this. An understanding of how information and knowledge are generated and utilised and an ability to conduct or commission research relevant to the requirements of an organisation can therefore be seen as key skills for managers in any industry sector and a key component of the education of the modern professional. Research is, however, not just a set of disembodied skills; it exists and is practised in a variety of social, political and economic contexts. The purpose of this book is to provide an introduction to the world of social research in the context of leisure and tourism, as industries, public policy concerns and fields of academic inquiry and reflection. The aim is to provide a practical guide to the conduct of research and an appreciation of the role of research in the policy-making, planning and management processes of the leisure and tourism industries and to foster a critical understanding of existing theoretical and applied research.

The focus of the book is leisure and tourism. While research methodology can be seen as universal, various fields of research – including leisure and tourism studies – have developed their own methodological emphases and bodies of experience. In some fields of enquiry scientific laboratory experiments are the norm, while in others social surveys are more common. While most of the principles of research are universal, a specialised text such as this reflects the traditions and practices in its field of focus and draws attention to examples of relevant applications of methods and the particular problems and issues which arise in such applications.

The field of leisure and tourism is a large one, encompassing a wide range of individual and collective human activity. It is an area fraught with problems of definition – for example, in some contexts the word *recreation* is used synonymously with *leisure*, while in others recreation is seen as a distinct and limited part of leisure or even separate from leisure. In some countries the term *free time* is used in preference to the word leisure. In some definitions *tourism* includes *business travel*, while in others such travel is excluded. In some definitions *day-trips* are included in tourism, while in others they are excluded. The aim in this book is to be *inclusive* rather than *exclusive*. Leisure is taken to encompass such activities as: recreation; play; games; involvement in sport and the arts, as spectator, audience member or participant; the use of the electronic and printed media; live entertainment; hobbies; socialising; drinking; gambling; sightseeing; visiting parks, coast and countryside; do-it-yourself; arts and craft activity; home-based and non-home-based activity; commercial and non-commercially-based activity; and doing nothing in particular. Tourism is seen primarily as a leisure activity involving travel away from a person's normal place of residence, but also encompassing such activities as business travel, attending conventions and visiting friends and relatives, if for no other reason than that such travellers invariably engage in leisure activities in addition to the business or personal activity which is the prime motivator for travel. Since the book covers leisure *and* tourism day-tripping is included, whether it is viewed as part of recreation or tourism. Leisure and tourism are seen as activities engaged in by individuals and groups, but also as service industries which involve public sector, non-profit and commercial organisations.

Most of the book is concerned with *how* to do research, so the aim of this opening chapter is to introduce the 'what, why and who' of research. What is it? Why study it? Who does it?

What is research?

Research defined

What is research? The sociologist Norbert Elias defined research in terms of its aims, as follows:

> The aim, as far as I can see, is the same in all sciences. Put simply and cursorily, the aim is to make known something previously unknown to human beings. It is to advance human knowledge, to make it more certain or better fitting . . . The aim is . . . discovery. *(Elias, 1986: 20)*

Discovery – making known something previously unknown – could cover a number of activities, for instance the work of journalists or detectives. Elias, however, also indicates that research is a tool of 'science' and that its purpose is to 'advance human knowledge' – features which distinguish research from other investigatory activities.

Scientific research

Scientific research is conducted within the rules and conventions of science. This means that it is based on logic and reason and the systematic examination of evidence. Ideally, within the scientific model, it should be possible for research to be *replicated* by the same or different researchers and for similar conclusions to emerge (although this is not always possible or practicable). It should also contribute to a cumulative body of knowledge about a field or topic. This model of scientific research applies most aptly in the physical or natural sciences, such as physics or chemistry. In the area of *social science*, which deals with people as individuals and social beings with relationships to groups and communities, the pure scientific model must be adapted and modified, and in some cases largely abandoned.

Social science research

Social science research is carried out using the methods and traditions of social science. Social science differs from the physical or natural sciences in that it deals with *people* and their social behaviour, and people are less predictable than non-human phenomena. People can be aware of the research being conducted about them and are not therefore purely passive subjects; they can react to the results of research and change their behaviour accordingly. While the fundamental behaviour patterns of non-human phenomena are constant and universal, people in different parts of the world and at different times behave differently. The social world is constantly changing, so it is rarely possible to produce exact replications of research at different times or in different places and obtain similar results.

Descriptive, explanatory and evaluative research

Elias's term *discovery* can be seen as, first, the process of finding out – at its simplest, therefore, research might just *describe* what exists. But to 'advance human knowledge, to make it more certain or better fitting' requires more than just the accumulation of information, or facts. The aim is also to provide *explanation* – to explain why things are as they are, and how they might be. In this book, we are also concerned with a third function of research, namely *evaluating* – that is judging the degree of success or value of policies or programmes. Three types

1. Descriptive research	finding out, describing what is
2. Explanatory research	explaining *how* or *why* things are as they are (and using this to predict)
3. Evaluative research	evaluation of policies and programmes.

Figure 1.1 Types of research

of research can be identified corresponding to these three functions, as shown in Figure 1.1. In some cases particular research projects concentrate on only one of these, but often two or more of the approaches are included in the same research project.

1. Descriptive research

Descriptive research is very common in the leisure and tourism area, for three reasons: the relative newness of the field, the changing nature of the phenomena being studied, and the frequent separation between research and action.

Since leisure and tourism are relatively new fields of study there is a need to map the territory. Much of the research therefore seeks to discover, describe or map patterns of behaviour in areas or activities which have not previously been studied in the field or for which information needs to be updated on a regular basis. It might therefore be described as *descriptive*. In some texts this form of research is termed *exploratory*, which is also appropriate, but because the other categories of research, explanatory and evaluative, can also at times be exploratory, the term descriptive is used here. Explanation of what is discovered, described or mapped is often left until later or to other researchers.

Leisure and tourism phenomena are subject to constant change. Over time, for example:

● the popularity of different leisure activities changes;

● the leisure preferences of different social groups (for example young people or women) change; and

● the relative popularity of different tourism destinations changes.

A great deal of research effort in the field is therefore devoted to tracking – or monitoring – changing patterns of behaviour. Hence the importance in leisure and tourism of secondary data sources, that is data collected by other organisations, such as government statistical agencies, as discussed in Chapter 7. A complete understanding and explanation of these changing patterns would be ideal, so that the future could be predicted, but this is only partially possible, so providers of leisure and tourism services must be aware of changing social and market conditions whether or not they can be fully explained or understood; they are therefore reliant on a flow of descriptive research to provide up-to-date information.

Descriptive research is often undertaken because that is what is commissioned. For example, a company may commission a *market profile* study or a local council may commission a *recreation needs* study from a research team – but the actual use of the results of the research, in marketing or planning, is a separate exercise with which the research team is not involved: the research team may simply be required to produce a descriptive study.

2. *Explanatory research*

Explanatory research moves beyond description to seek to explain the patterns and trends observed, for example:

- A particular type of activity or destination falling in popularity and an explanation is called for.

- Particular tourism developments gain approval against the wishes of the local community: why or how does this happen?

- The arts are patronised by some social groups and not others: what is the explanation for this?

Such questions raise the thorny issue of *causality*: the aim is to be able to say, for example, that there has been an increase in A because of a corresponding fall in B. It is one thing to discover that A has increased while B has decreased; but to establish that the rise in A has been *caused* by the fall in B is often a much more demanding task. To establish causality, or the likelihood of causality, requires the researcher to be rigorous in the collection, analysis and interpretation of data. It also generally requires some sort of theoretical framework to relate the phenomenon under study to wider social, economic and political processes. The issue of causality and the role of theory in research are discussed further in later chapters.

Once causes are, at least partially, understood the knowledge can be used to *predict*. This is clear enough in the physical sciences: we know that heat causes metal to expand (explanation) – therefore we know that if we apply a certain amount of heat to a bar of metal it will expand by a certain amount (prediction). In the biological and medical sciences this process is also followed, but with less precision: it can be predicted that if a certain treatment is given to patients with a certain disease then it is *likely* that a certain proportion will be cured. In the social sciences this approach is also used, but with even less precision. For example, economists have found that demand for goods and services, including leisure and tourism goods and services, responds to price levels: if the price of a product or service is reduced then sales will generally increase. But this does not always happen because there are so many other factors involved – such as variation in quality or the activities of competitors. Human beings make their own decisions and are far less predictable than non-human phenomena. Nevertheless prediction is a key aim of much of the research that takes place in the area of leisure and tourism.

3. *Evaluative research*

Evaluative research arises from the need to make judgements on the success or effectiveness of policies or programmes – for example whether a particular leisure facility or programme is meeting required performance standards or whether a particular tourism promotion campaign has been cost-effective. In the private sector the level of profit is the main criterion used for such evaluations, although additional ratios may also be used. In the public sector, where facilities or services are not usually intended to make a cash profit, research is required to assess community benefits and even, in some cases such as parks, to assemble data as elementary as levels of use. Evaluative research is highly developed in some areas of public policy, for example education, but is less well developed in the field of leisure and tourism (Shadish *et al.*, 1991).

Why study research?

In general

Why study research? Research and research methods might be studied for a variety of reasons, as summarised in Figure 1.2:

- First, it is useful to be able to *understand* and *evaluate* research reports and articles which one might come across in an academic or professional context. It is also advantageous to understand the basis and limitations of such reports and articles.

- Second, many readers of this book may engage in research in an academic environment, where research is conducted for its own sake, in the interests of the pursuit of knowledge – for example for a thesis.

- Third, most readers will find themselves conducting or commissioning research for professional reasons, as managers. It is therefore particularly appropriate to consider the role of research in the policy-making, planning and management process.

---

1. Understanding research reports, etc.
2. To conduct academic research projects
3. Management tool in:
    - policy-making
    - planning
    - managing
    - evaluating

Figure 1.2 Why study research?

Of course, for many readers of this book, the immediate challenge is to complete a research-related project as part of an undergraduate or postgraduate programme of study. This book should, of course, assist in this task, but it is a means to an end, not an end in itself. Research projects conducted as part of a curriculum are seen as a learning process to equip the student as a professional consumer, practitioner and/or commissioner of research in professional life.

Research in policy-making, planning and management processes

All organisations, including those in the leisure and tourism industries, engage in policy-making, planning and managing processes to achieve their goals. A variety of terms is used in this area and the meanings of terms vary according to the context and user. In this book:

- *policies* are considered to be the statements of principles, intentions and commitments of an organisation;

- *plans* are detailed strategies, typically set out in a document, designed to implement policies in particular ways over a specified period of time;

- *management* is seen as the process of implementing policies and plans.

Although planning is usually associated in the public mind with national, regional and local government bodies, it is also an activity undertaken by the private sector. Organisations such as cinema chains, holiday resort developers or sport promoters are all involved in planning, but their planning activities are less public than those of government bodies. Private organisations are usually only concerned with their own activities, but government bodies often have a wider responsibility to provide a planning framework for the activities of many public and private sector organisations. Examples of policies, plans and management activity in leisure and tourism contexts are given in Figure 1.3.

Both policies and plans can vary enormously in detail, complexity and formality. Here the process is considered only briefly in order to examine the part played by research. Of the many models of policy-making, planning and management processes that exist, the *rational-comprehensive* model, a version of which is depicted in Figure 1.4, is the most traditional, 'ideal' model. It is beyond the scope of this book to discuss the many alternative models which seek to more accurately reflect real-world decision-making, but guidance to further reading on this issue is given at the end of the chapter.[1] Suffice it to say here, that these alternatives are often 'cut-down' versions of the rational-comprehensive model, emphasising some aspects of this model and de-emphasising, or omitting, others. Thus some reflect the view that it is virtually impossible to be completely *comprehensive* in assessing alternative policies;

---

[1]Earlier editions of this book contained a different version of the rational-comprehensive model with nine steps: the current version arose out of work presented in Veal (2010a, Chapters 7–8).

Level	Leisure centre	Tourist commission	Arts centre	National park
Policy	Maximise use by all age groups	Extend peak season	Encourage contemporary composers	Increase non-government revenue
Plan	Two-year plan to increase visits by older people by 50 per cent	Three-year plan to increase shoulder season visits by promoting new festivals	Three-year plan to commission new work by contemporary composers	Three-year plan to implement user-pays programme
Management	Implement daily morning keep-fit sessions for older people	Choose marketing themes	Select composers and commission and produce works	Implement user-pays programme

Figure 1.3 Examples of policies, plans and management

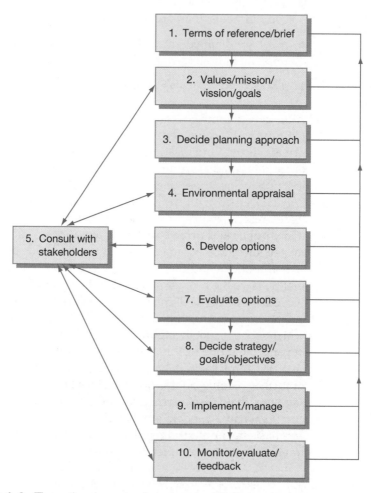

Figure 1.4 The rational-comprehensive model of planning/management

some reflect the fact that political interests often intervene before 'rational' or 'objective' decisions can be made; while others elevate community/stakeholder consultation to a central rather than supportive role. In nearly all cases the models are put forward as an *alternative* to the rational-comprehensive model, so the latter, even if rejected, remains the universal reference point.

In most of these models a research role remains – sometimes curtailed and sometimes enhanced. It is rare that all of the steps shown in Figure 1.4 are followed through in the real world. And it is also rare for research to inform the process in all the ways discussed below. The steps depicted provide an agenda for discussing the many roles of research in policy-making, planning and management processes. Two examples of how the process might unfold in leisure and tourism contexts are given in Figure 1.5.

1. *Terms of reference/brief*: The 'terms of reference' or 'brief' for a particular planning or management task sets out the scope and purpose of the exercise. Research can be involved right at the beginning of this process in assisting in establishing the terms of reference. For example, existing research on levels of sports participation in a community may result in a government policy initiative to do something about the level of sports participation; or research on environmental impacts of tourism growth may prompt a government to develop a sustainable tourism plan.

2. *State values/mission/goals*: Statements of the missions or goals of the organisation may already be in place if the task in hand is a relatively minor one, but if it is a major undertaking, such as the development of a strategic plan for the whole organisation, then the development of statements of mission and goals may be involved. It is very much a task for the decision-making body of an organisation (such as the board or the council) to determine its mission and/or goals; research may be directly involved when consultation with large numbers of stakeholders is involved, as discussed under step 5.

3. *Decide planning approach*: Like research, a range of different methodologies and approaches is available for policy-making and planning. In Veal (2010a: Chapter 7) a range of such methods and approaches is discussed, including: adopting fixed standards of provision; providing opportunity; resource-based planning; meeting demand; meeting the requirements/requests of stakeholders; meeting unmet needs; providing benefits; and increasing participation. The method/approach selected will determine the type of research to be carried out during the policy-making/planning process: for example, a needs-based approach will require a definition of need and a method for collecting information on needs, while resource-based planning will require identification of the range of heritage, cultural and/or environmental resources to be included and processes for data gathering and evaluation.

4. *Environmental appraisal*: An environmental appraisal involves the gathering of relevant information on the context of the task in hand. Information may relate to the organisation's internal workings or to the outside world,

Steps in the planning/ management process (see Figure 1.4)	Young people and sport in a local community		Sustainable tourism in a tourism destination	
	Policy/Planning/ management	Associated Research	Policy/Planning/ management	Associated Research
1. Terms of reference	Increase young people's participation in sport	Existing research indicates 40 per cent participation rate	Develop local sustainable tourism strategy	Physical survey indicates road capacity reached
2. Set values/ mission/ goals	Increase participation level to 60 per cent over five years	–	Develop policy to increase tourism volume by 50 per cent over ten years within acceptable environmental impact parameters	Study of likely increases in tourism demand over ten years
3. Decide planning approach	Needs-based, demand-based, etc.: for discussion, see Veal (2010a: Chapter 7)	As below	Demand-based, stakeholder-based, etc.: for discussion, see Veal (2010a: Chapter 7)	As below
4. Environmental appraisal	Consider existing supply – demand	Existing programmes and infrastructure fully used	Examine current environmental impacts of tourism and future scenarios	Extensive physical surveys (traffic + other environmental issues) + develop- ment of future tourism demand scenarios
5. Consult stakeholders	Consult sporting clubs, schools, young people	Survey indicates support among all groups and confirms feasibility	Consult community and tourism industry provider groups	Survey + meetings with community and tourism industry provider groups
6. Develop options	1. Publicity campaign 2. Free vouchers 3. Build more community facilities 4. Provide support to clubs/ schools 5. Train leaders/ coaches/ teachers	Review of experience of each option in other regions, based on published accounts and a survey	1. Road-building/ traffic manage- ment programme 2. Local public transport solution 3. Alternative accommodation development strategies	Survey of experience of similar destinations in similar stages of the tourism life- cycle

Figure 1.5   Examples of planning/management tasks and associated research

Steps in the planning/ management process (see Figure 1.4)	Young people and sport in a local community		Sustainable tourism in a tourism destination	
	Policy/Planning/ management	Associated Research	Policy/Planning/ management	Associated Research
7. Evaluate options/	Evaluate options 1–5	Each option costed; on basis of survey evidence, estimate made of cost-effectiveness of each option.	Evaluate options 1 and 2 against range of options in 3	Options 1 and 2 costed and evaluated against a range of accommodation development strategies (option 3)
8. Decide strategy/ goals/objectives	Options 3 and 4 adopted	Options 3 and 4 recommended	Options selected in light of evaluative research	Options ranked in order of effectiveness and net environmental impact
9. Implement – manage	Implement options 3 and 4	–	Implement public transport and three-star accommodation option	–
10. Monitor/ evaluate/ feedback	Assess success in terms of increased participation. Continue programme: increase resources for training coaches/leaders	Survey indicates participation increase to 45 per cent after one year, but shortage of coaches/leaders	Assess success in terms of tourism numbers and traffic congestion. Develop peak public holiday traffic management plan	Annual surveys of traffic conditions and tourism numbers undertaken. Persistent peak public holiday congestion problems noted

Figure 1.5 (*continued*)

including actual and potential clients, and the activities of governments and competitors and physical resources. Such information may be readily to hand and may just need collation, or it may require extensive research.

5. *Consult with stakeholders*: Consultation with *stakeholders* is considered vital by most organisations and, indeed, is a statutory requirement in many forms of public sector planning. Stakeholders can include employees, clients, visitors, members of the general public, members of boards and councils and neighbouring or complementary organisations. Research can be a significant feature of such consultation, especially when large numbers of individuals or organisations are involved.

6. *Develop options*: In order to develop a plan or strategy, consideration must be given to what policy options are available to pursue the goals of the

organisation, their feasibility, their likely contribution to the achievement of the goals and the best way to implement them. Research can be involved in the process of *identifying* alternative policy or planning options, for example, by providing data on the extent of problems or on stakeholder preferences.

7. *Evaluate options*: Deciding on a strategy involves selecting a course or courses of action from among all the options identified. This choice process may involve a complex procedure requiring research to *evaluate* the alternatives. Typical formal evaluation techniques include cost–benefit analysis, economic impact analysis and environmental and social impact analysis (see Shadish *et al.*, 1991; Veal, 2010a: Chapters 12, 13), and the use of the *importance-performance* technique (Martilla and James, 1977; Harper and Balmer, 1989) or *conjoint analysis* (Claxton, 1994).

8. *Decide strategy/goals/objectives*: Evaluation processes rarely produce a single best solution or course of action. Thus, for example, option A may be cheaper than option B, but option B produces better outcomes. Final decisions on which strategy to pursue must be taken by the governing body of the organisation – the board or council – based on political and/or personal values. A strategy should involve clear statements of what the strategy is intended to achieve (goals), with measurable outcomes and time-lines (objectives).

9. *Implement – manage*: Implementing a plan or strategy is the field of management. Research can be involved in day-to-day management in investigating improved ways of deploying resources and in providing continuous feedback on the management process – for example in the form of customer surveys. However, the line between such research and the monitoring and evaluation process is difficult to draw.

10. *Monitor/evaluate*: Monitoring progress and evaluating the implementation of strategies is clearly a process with which research is likely to be involved. The process comes full circle with the feedback step. The data from the monitoring and evaluation step can be fed back into the planning or management cycle and can lead to a revision of any or all of the decisions previously made. The monitoring and evaluation process may report complete success, it may suggest minor changes to some of the details of the policies and plans adopted, or it could result in a fundamental re-think, going 'back to the drawing board'.

Who does research?

This book is mainly concerned with how to conduct research, but it also aims to provide an understanding of the research process which will help the reader to become a knowledgeable, critical consumer of the research carried out by others. In reading reports of research, it is useful to bear in mind *why* the

Group	Motivation/purpose
Academics	Part of the job description. Knowledge for its own sake and/or to engage with industry/profession and/or benefit society
Students	Coursework students: projects as learning medium and/or part of professional training Research students: adding to knowledge and training/qualification for a research/academic career
Government, commercial and non-profit organisations	Research to inform policy, monitor performance and aid in decision-making. Relevant to the idea of 'evidence-based policy'
Managers	Research to inform practice, monitor performance and aid in decision-making
Consultants	Research under contract to government, commercial and non-profit organisations

Figure 1.6   Who does research?

research has been done and to a large extent this is influenced by *who* did the research and *who paid* for it to be done. Who does research is important because it affects the nature of the research conducted and hence has a large impact on what constitutes the *body of knowledge* which students of leisure and tourism must absorb and which leisure and tourism managers draw on.

Leisure and tourism research is undertaken by a wide variety of individuals and institutions, as listed in Figure 1.6. The respective roles of these research actors are discussed in turn below.

Academics

Academics are members of the paid academic staff of academic institutions, including professors, lecturers, tutors and research staff – in North American parlance: *the faculty*. In most academic institutions professors and lecturers are expected, as part of their contract of employment, to engage in both research and teaching. Typically a quarter or third of an academic's time might be devoted to research and writing. Promotion and job security depend partly (some would say mainly) on the achievement of a satisfactory track record in published research. Publication can be in various forms, as discussed under 'outputs' below.

Some research arises from academic interest and some arises from immediate problems being faced by the providers of leisure or tourism services. Much published academic research tends to be governed by the concerns of the various theoretical disciplines, such as sociology, economics or psychology, which may or may not coincide with the day-to-day concerns of the leisure or tourism industries. In fact part of the role of the academic researcher is to 'stand apart' from the rest of the world and provide disinterested analysis, which may be critical and may not be seen as particularly supportive by those working in the industry. However, what some see as overly critical and unhelpful, or just plain irrelevant, others may see as insightful and constructive.

There are nevertheless applied disciplines which focus specifically on aspects of the policy, planning and management process, such as planning, management, marketing or financial management. While academic research in these areas can also be critical rather than immediately instrumental, it is more likely to be driven by the sorts of issues which concern the industry. Generally academics become involved in funded research of a practically orientated nature when their own interests coincide with those of the agency concerned. For instance an academic may be interested in ways of measuring what motivates people to engage in certain outdoor recreation activities and this could coincide with an outdoor recreation agency's need for research to assist in developing a marketing strategy. Some academics specialise in applied areas – such as marketing or planning – so they are very often in a better position to attract funding from industry sources.

Students

PhD and Master's degree students are major contributors to research. In the past, theses (or dissertations to use the term more common in North America) were available only in hard copy at the library of the university which produced them. Later a photocopy service became available notably from the University of Michigan, followed by micro-fiche copies, but increasingly in recent years they have become available in digital form and university libraries generally subscribe to various thesis databases (see Chapter 6).

In the science area research students often work as part of a team, under the direction of a supervisor who may determine what topics will be researched by individual students within a particular research programme. In the social sciences this approach is less common, with students having a wider scope in their selection of research topic.

PhD theses are the most significant form of student research, but research done by Master's degree and graduate diploma students and even undergraduates in the form of projects and honours theses can be a useful contribution to knowledge. Leisure and tourism are not generally well endowed with research funds, so even, for example, a small survey conducted by a group of undergraduates on a particular leisure activity or in a particular locality, or a thorough review of an area of literature, may be of considerable use or interest to others.

Government, commercial and non-profit organisations

Government, commercial and non-profit organisations conduct or commission research to inform policy, monitor performance or aid in decision-making.

A term coined to describe this relationship between policy and research is *evidence-based policy* (Pawson, 2006). Some large organisations have their own in-house research organisations – for example, the Office of National Statistics in the UK, the Australian Bureau of Statistics in Australia and the US Forest Service Experiment Stations in the USA. Commercial organisations in leisure and tourism tend to rely on consultants for their social, economic and market research, although equipment manufacturers, for instance in sport, may conduct their own scientific research for product development.

Research reports from these organisations can be important sources of knowledge, especially of a more practically oriented nature. For example, in nearly every developed country some government agency takes responsibility for conducting nation-wide surveys of tourism patterns and leisure participation rates, as shown by Cushman *et al.* (2005a). This is descriptive research which few other organisation would have the resources or incentive to undertake.

Managers

Professionals in leisure and tourism who recognise the full extent of the management, policy-making and planning process see research as very much part of their responsibilities. Managers may find themselves carrying out research on a range of types of topic, as indicated in Figure 1.7. Since most of the readers of this book will be actual or trainee managers, this is an important point to recognise.

Successful management depends on good information. Much information – for example sales figures – is available to the manager as a matter of routine and does not require *research*. However, the creative utilisation of such data – for example to establish market trends – may amount to research. Other types of information can only be obtained by means of specific research projects. In some areas of leisure and tourism management even the most basic information must be obtained by research. For example, while managers of theatres

---

Current customers
Market research: potential customers/community
Environmental appraisal
Organisational performance
- Sales
- Efficiency
- Staff performance/motivation
Competitors
Products
- Existing
- New

Figure 1.7 Managers and research

or resorts routinely receive information on the level of use of their facilities from sales figures or bookings, this is not the case for the manager of an urban park or a beach. To gain information on the number of users of this type of facility it is necessary to conduct a specific data gathering exercise. Such data gathering may not be very sophisticated and some would say that it does not qualify as *research*, being just part of the management information system, but in the sense that it involves *finding out*, sometimes *explaining*, and the deployment of specific techniques and skills, it qualifies as research for the purposes of this book.

Most managers need to carry out – or commission – research if they want information on their users or customers: for example, where they come from (the 'catchment area' of the facility) or their socio-economic characteristics. Research is also a way of finding out about customers' evaluations of the facility or service. It might be argued that managers do not themselves need research skills since they can always commission consultants to carry out research for them. However, managers will be better able to commission good research and evaluate the results if they are familiar with the research process themselves. It is also the case that few managers in leisure and tourism work in an ideal world where funds exist to commission all the research they would like; often the only way managers can get research done is to do it using their own and colleagues' 'in-house' skills and time.

Consultants

Consultants offer their research and advisory services to government and commercial and non-profit organisations. Some consultancy organisations are large, multi-national companies involved in accountancy, management and project development consultancy generally, and who often establish specialised units covering the leisure and/or tourism field. Examples are PricewaterhouseCoopers and Ernst and Young. But there are also many smaller, specialised organisations in the consultancy field. Some academics operate consultancy companies as a 'side-line', either because of academic interest in a particular area or to supplement incomes or both. Self-employed consultancy activity is common among practitioners who have taken early retirement from leisure or tourism industry employment.

Who pays?

Most research requires financial support to cover the costs of paying full-time or part-time research assistants, to pay for research student scholarships, to pay interviewers or a market research firm to conduct interviews, or to cover travel costs or the costs of equipment. Research is funded from a variety of sources, as indicated in Figure 1.8:

- Unfunded
- University internal funds
- Government-funded research councils
- Private trusts
- Industry – public, commercial or non-profit

Figure 1.8 Who pays?

- *Unfunded*: Some research conducted by academics requires little or no specific financial resources over and above the academic's basic salary – for example, theoretical work and the many studies using students as subjects.

- *University internal funds*: Universities tend to use their own funds to support research which is initiated by academic staff and where the main motive is the 'advancement of knowledge'. Most universities and colleges have research funds for which members of their staff can apply.

- *Government-funded research councils*: Governments usually establish organisations to fund scientific research – for example, the UK Economic and Social Research Council or the Australian Research Council. These or similar bodies often also provide scholarships for research students.

- *Private trusts*: Many private trusts or foundations also fund research – for example, the Ford Foundation and the Leverhulme Trust. Trusts have generally been endowed with investment funds by a wealthy individual or from a public appeal.

- *Industry*: Funds may come from the world of practice – for instance, from a government department or agency, from a commercial company or from a non-profit organisation such as a governing body of a sport. In this case the research will tend to be more practically oriented. Government agencies and commercial and non-profit organisations fund research to solve particular problems or to inform them about particular issues relevant to their interests.

Research outputs

Research for leisure and tourism planning/management is presented in many forms and contexts. Some of these are listed in Figure 1.9 and discussed briefly below. The formats are not all mutually exclusive: a number of them may arise in various aspects in a single research project.

Academic journal articles
Professional journal articles
Conference presentations/papers
Books
Policy/planning/management reports
- Position statements
- Market profiles
- Market research
- Market segmentation/lifestyle/psychographic studies
- Feasibility studies
- Leisure/recreation needs studies
- Tourism strategies/marketing plans
- Forecasting studies

Figure 1.9   Research report formats

Academic journal articles

Publication of research in academic journals is considered to be the most prestigious form in academic terms because of the element of *refereeing* or *peer review*. Articles submitted to such journals are assessed (refereed) on an anonymous basis by two or three experts in the field, as well as the editors. Editorial activity is overseen by a board of experts in the field, whose names are listed in the journal. Some of the main refereed journals in the leisure and tourism area are:

- *Journal of Leisure Research* (USA),
- *Leisure Sciences* (USA),
- *Society and Leisure* (Canada),
- *Annals of Leisure Research* (Australia),
- *Annals of Tourism Research* (UK),
- *Tourism Management* (UK),
- *Leisure Studies* (UK),
- *Journal of Travel Research* (USA).

Academic research and publication is, to a large extent, a 'closed system'. Academics are the editors of the refereed journals and serve on their editorial advisory boards and referee panels. They therefore determine what research is acceptable for publication. Practitioners thus very often find published academic research irrelevant to their needs – this is hardly surprising since much of it is not designed for the practitioner but for the academic world. The student training to become a professional practitioner in the leisure or tourism field should not therefore be surprised to come across scholarly writing on leisure and tourism which is not suitable for direct practical application to policy, planning and management. This does not mean that it is irrelevant, but simply that it does not necessarily focus explicitly on immediate practical problems.

Professional journal articles

Journals published by professional bodies for their members rarely publish original research, but may publish summaries of research of immediate relevance to practitioners.

Conference papers/presentations

Some academic conferences publish the papers presented in a hard-copy or online set of *proceedings*. In some cases such papers have been peer reviewed and have a similar status to academic journals but this is rare in leisure and tourism. Typically research presented at conference, will also be published in journals or book form.

Books

Academic books can be divided into *textbooks*, like this one, and *monographs*, which may present the results of a single empirical research project or research programme, may be largely theoretical or may be a mixture of the two. Textbooks are not expected to present original research but may provide summaries and guides to research. Edited books with chapters contributed by a number of authors may be closer to the textbook model, or, if they contain original research, may be closer to the monograph model.

Policy/planning/management reports

Research conducted by commercial bodies is usually confidential but that conducted by government agencies is generally available to the public, increasingly via the Internet. Such reports can invariably be found on the websites of national agencies, such as sports councils or tourism commissions and government departments, and local councils. Such reports can take a variety of forms:

● *Position statements*: are similar to the *environmental appraisals* discussed above in relation to the rational-comprehensive planning model. They are compilations of factual information on the current situation with regard to a topic or issue of concern, and are designed to assist decision-makers to become knowledgeable about the topic or issue and to take stock of such matters as current policies, provision levels and demand. For example, if a local council wishes to develop new policies for heritage conservation in its area, a position statement might be prepared listing what actual and potential heritage properties and attractions currently exist, their ownership, quality, nature and state of preservation, existing policies, rules and regulations and types of use.

- *Market profiles*: are similar to position statements, but relate specifically to current and potential consumers and suppliers of a product or service. If an organisation wishes to start a project in a particular tourism or leisure market it will usually require a profile of that market sector. How big is the market? What are its growth prospects? Who are the customers? What sub-sectors does it have? How profitable is it? Who are the current suppliers? Such a profile will usually require considerable research and can be seen as one element in the broader activity of market research.

- *Market research*: is a more encompassing activity. Research on the actual or potential market for a product or service can take place in advance of a service being established but also as part of the on-going monitoring of the performance of an operation. Market research seeks to establish the scale and nature of the current market – the number of people who use or are likely to use the product or service and their characteristics and expenditure – and actual and potential customer requirements and attitudes.

- *Market segmentation/lifestyle/psychographic studies*: traditionally market researchers attempted to classify consumers into sub-markets or segments on the basis of their product preferences, including leisure activities and holiday behaviour, and their socio-demographic characteristics such as age, gender, occupation and income. Later they sought to classify people using not only these background social and economic characteristics but also their attitudes, values and behaviour. Such lifestyle segments may be developed as part of any survey-based research project, but there are also commercially developed systems which survey companies may apply to a range of market research projects. Examples are discussed in Chapter 5 (p. 138).

- *Feasibility studies*: investigate not only current consumer characteristics and demands, as in a market profile, but also future demand and such aspects as the financial viability and environmental impact of proposed development or investment projects. The decision whether or not to build a new leisure facility or launch a new tourism product is usually based on a feasibility study (Kelsey and Gray, 1986).

- *Leisure/recreation needs studies*: are a common type of research in leisure planning. These are comprehensive studies, usually carried out for local councils, examining levels of provision and use of leisure facilities and services, levels of participation in leisure activities, and views and aspirations of the population concerning their own leisure preferences and desired provision. In some cases a needs study also includes a leisure or recreation 'plan', which makes recommendations on future provision; in other cases the plan is a separate document. It has been argued that so-called leisure needs studies are not *needs* studies at all, since they do not investigate what people need, but what they *want*, would *like to do* or *might do* in the future (Veal, 2009).

- *Tourism strategies/tourism marketing plans*: are the tourism equivalent of the leisure/recreation needs study, but rather than referring to the *needs* of the local population, tourism strategies or marketing plans refer to the tourism *demands* of non-local populations to be accommodated in a destination area. Such tourism studies usually consider the capacity of the host area to meet the demands of a projected volume of tourism, in terms of accommodation, transport, existing and potential attractions and acceptable levels of environmental impacts.

- *Forecasting studies*: form a key input to many plans. They might provide, for example, projections of demand for a particular leisure activity or for a particular type of tourist accommodation over a ten-year period. Forecasting is intrinsically research-based and can involve predicting the likely effects of future population growth and change, the effects of changing tastes, changing levels of income or developments in technology. Leisure and tourism forecasting have become substantial fields of study in their own right.

Terminology

Like any field of study and practice, research methods has its own distinct terminology, some of which is familiar to the wider community and some of which is not. Most terms and expressions will be introduced and defined in the appropriate chapters which follow; but some are common to the whole research process and some key ones are described here.

Subject is used to refer to people providing information or being studied in a research project. For example, if a social survey involves interviews with a sample of 200 people it involves 200 *subjects*. Some researchers prefer to use the term *participant*, believing that subject implies subjective, suggesting a hierarchical relationship between the researcher and the researched. The term *case* is sometimes used, particularly when the phenomenon being researched is not individual people – for example, organisations, countries, destinations, sports.

Variable refers to a characteristic, behaviour pattern or opinion which varies from subject to subject. Thus, for example, age, income, level of holiday-taking or music preferences are all variables. An *independent* variable is one which is controlled by forces outside the context of the study, and influences *dependent* variables within the scope of the study. Thus, for example, in a study of outdoor recreation the weather would be an independent variable while the number of people who visit a park is a dependent variable. In another context, such as the study of climate, the weather could be a dependent variable influenced by such independent variables as the behaviour of the sun and the temperature of the oceans.

Summary

This chapter addresses the 'What?' of research in defining and introducing the concept of research and describes three types of research with which this book is concerned: descriptive, explanatory and evaluative. The 'Why?' of research is discussed primarily in the context of policy-making, planning and management, since the majority of the users of the book will be studying for a vocational qualification. The links between research and the various stages of policy-making, planning and management are discussed using the rational-comprehensive model as a framework, and attention is drawn to the variety of forms that research reports can take in the management environment. 'Who?' conducts research is an important and often neglected aspect of research: in this chapter, the respective research roles of academics, students, governmental and commercial organisations, consultants and managers are discussed. Finally, there is an introduction to the various formats in which research results may be published, from academic journal articles to a variety of management-related reports.

Test questions

1. What is the difference between research and journalism?

2. Outline the differences between *descriptive*, *explanatory* and *evaluative* research.

3. What are the broad differences between policy-making, planning and management, as presented in this chapter?

4. Summarise the potential role of research in three of the ten steps in the 'rational-comprehensive' model of the policy-making/planning/management process presented in this chapter.

5. Name three of the 12 formats which research reports might take, as put forward in this chapter and outline their basic features.

6. Outline three of the six topics, as put forward in this chapter, on which managers might conduct or commission research.

7. Why does academic research often appear to be irrelevant to the needs of practitioners?

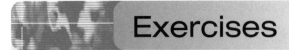

Exercises

1. Choose a leisure or tourism organisation with which you are familiar and outline ways in which it might use research to pursue its objectives.

2. Choose a leisure or tourism organisation and investigate its research activities. What proportion of its budget does it devote to research? What research has it carried out? How are the results of the research used, by the organisation or others?

3. Take an edition of a leisure or tourism journal, such as *Leisure Studies* or *Annals of Tourism Research*, and ascertain, for each article: why the research was conducted; how it was funded; and who or what organisations are likely to benefit from the research and how.

4. Repeat exercise 3, but using an edition of a journal outside the leisure/tourism field, for example a sociology journal or a physics journal.

5. Using the same journal edition as in 3 above, examine each article and determine whether the research is descriptive, explanatory or evaluative.

Resources

- *Tracking change in leisure participation*: Veal (2006).

- *Models of planning and policy-making*: introductory discussions: Parsons (1995: 248ff), Veal (2010a: Chapter 7–8), for a more advanced discussion, see Treuren and Lane (2003).

- *Tourism research methods*: see Smith (1995) for a quantitative, geographical approach. Ryan (1995) for coverage of similar ground to this book. Dann, Nash and Pearce (1988) and Pearce and Butler (1993) for a number of methodological papers and, for a mine of information on all aspect of tourism research, see the comprehensive collection of papers edited by Ritchie and Goeldner (1994).

- *Research in the planning process*: Kelsey and Gray (1986), Veal (1994).

- *Evaluative research*: Henderson and Bialeschki (2002), Pollard (1987), Shadish *et al.* (1991), Veal (2010a: Chapters 12, 13).

- *Evidence-based policy*: Solesbury (2002), Pawson (2006).

- *Segmentation/psychographics/lifestyle:* Wells (1974), Veal (1993), Chisnall (1991).

- *Feasibility studies*: Kelsey and Gray (1986).

- *Leisure/recreation needs studies*: Veal (2009, 2010b).

- *Tourism strategies/marketing plans*: Middleton *et al.* (2009: Chapter 10).

- *Leisure and tourism forecasting*: see Archer (1994), Veal (1987, 1994, 2010a: Chapter 11), Kelly (1987), *Henley Centre for Forecasting* (Quarterly).

- *Terminology*: Blackshaw and Crawford (2006).

2 Approaches to leisure and tourism research

Introduction

The aim of the chapter is to introduce a range of disciplines and paradigms within which leisure and tourism research is conducted. The chapter examines:

● *Disciplinary traditions:* reviews of a number of academic disciplines and their approaches to leisure and tourism research, including sociology, economics, geography, psychology, social psychology, history and philosophy.

● *Terminology: approaches, dimensions, issues:* examination of a number of mainly dichotomous concepts which characterise research approaches and methods.

Disciplinary traditions

The bulk of published leisure and tourism research has arisen, not from the demands of the leisure and tourism industries, but from the interests of academics who owe allegiance to a particular discipline. Here we examine, very briefly, the contributions by academic disciplines that have been particularly significant in the field, namely:

- sociology and cultural studies,

- economics,

- geography/environmental studies,

- psychology/social psychology,

- history and anthropology,

- political science.

Disciplines are characterised by the particular aspect or dimension of the universe with which they are concerned, the theories which they develop for explanation and the distinctive techniques they use for conducting research. Some commentators refer to leisure studies and tourism studies as disciplines, but since, arguably, they do not meet the criteria for a free-standing discipline, in this book they are seen as multi-disciplinary, cross-disciplinary or inter-disciplinary *fields of study*:

- *Multi-disciplinary* means that research from a number of disciplines is used – for example, the economics and the sociology of leisure/tourism.

- *Cross-disciplinary* means that issues, theories, concepts and methods which are common to more than one discipline are involved – for example, the *cross-disciplinary dimensions* discussed later in this chapter.

- *Inter-disciplinary* refers to sub-fields of research which do not fit neatly into any particular discipline – for example, time-budget research.

When reading in the area of leisure and tourism studies it should be noted that not all commentators keep the wide mix of disciplines consistently in mind. For example, when making comments on 'leisure studies' they may in fact be discussing only 'the sociology of leisure'.

We should also note other fields of study which are generally longer-established than leisure/tourism studies and which are sometimes referred to as disciplines, sometimes as 'applied disciplines' and sometimes as fields of study. The first of these is cultural studies, which sits somewhere between sociology and the humanities but, because of its particular history in relation to leisure studies, is best treated together with sociology, as above. Other fields are management, marketing, planning and education. However, despite the importance of these fields of study for professional practitioners in the leisure and tourism sectors, they are not examined separately in this chapter because for research purposes they generally draw, to varying degrees, on the methods associated with the six disciplines listed above.

The relationships between leisure and tourism research and the six disciplines are summarised in Figure 2.1, which presents examples of descriptive, explanatory and evaluative research topics/questions addressed by each discipline and the main research methods/techniques used. A more detailed discussion of disciplinary contributions and traditions is provided on the book's website and further relevant reading is indicated in the Resources section.

Descriptive	Explanatory	Evaluative
Sociology		
• What proportions of the population and of various age, gender, ethnic and socio-economic groups participate in specified leisure activities? • What are the trends in numbers of tourists visiting a particular destination over the last ten years?	• Why do members of middle-class, highly educated, groups make greater use of cultural facilities than members of other groups? • What factors influence rises and falls in tourist visits to a particular tourist destination?	• To what extent have policies designed to boost women's participation in sport been successful? • How successful has a training programme been in increasing locals' employment in the tourism industry?
Geography/environment		
• What is the spatial area from which most users of a particular leisure facility travel? • What impacts does a particular island tourist resort have on the environment?	• What is the relative importance of distance and travel time in affecting use of a particular leisure facility? • How do the different styles of tourism (back-packer, package tour, touring) impact on the environment?	• How effective is the local council in meeting the leisure demands of all neighbourhoods in its area? • How effective is the tourism strategy in protecting the environment from the impacts of tourism?
Economics		
• What proportion of household expenditure is devoted to leisure/tourism goods and services? • What proportion of the labour force works in the leisure and tourism industries?	• What is the relationship between level of income and expenditure on leisure and tourism? • What is the relationship between travel cost and level of visits to a leisure/tourism facility?	• What are the costs and benefits of hosting the Olympic Games? • What has been the economic impact of developing tourism at destination X?
Psychology/social psychology		
• What satisfactions do people obtain from engaging in a leisure activity or going on holiday? • What is the level of stress among teenagers?	• To what extent is Maslow's hierarchy of need relevant to leisure/tourism? • Does leisure activity/going on holiday relieve stress? If so, how lasting is this?	• How effective has a youth sports programme been in enhancing participants' self-esteem? • How effective has a marketing policy been in enhancing visitor satisfaction?
History/anthropology		
• How has the balance between work and leisure time changed since 1900? • What is the history of the 'Grand Tour'?	• What has been the influence of marketing and materialism on changes in the work/life balance since 1950? • What has caused the growth in gambling over the past 20 years?	• How successful have public policies to increase physical activity been over the past 30 years? • Over the past 30 years, have governments helped or hindered the development of tourism?
Political/policy science		
• What are the leisure/tourism policies of the major political parties? • What proportion of publicly owned leisure facilities are managed by commercial contract?	• How has changing political philosophy affected leisure and tourism policies in the last two changes of government? • How is power exercised in leisure/tourism contexts?	• How effective are policies directed at 'inclusion' in increasing leisure participation? • How effective have joint public–private partnerships been in leisure/tourism development?

Figure 2.1 Disciplines and examples of research questions

Approaches, dimensions, issues, terminology

Here we discuss a number of approaches, dimensions, issues and associated terminology which recur in the research literature and discourses on research, and of which at least a basic understanding is necessary if the literature and the discourses are to be understood. They are listed in Figure 2.2. Those terms which arise in pairs, X and Y, are often presented in the literature as X *versus* Y. But X and Y are not always opposed to one another, they are often complementary, so here the form X *and* Y is used. It is impossible to analyse all the terms and concepts in detail in this introductory chapter, especially given that definitions vary in the literature. Additional sources are provided in the Resources section of the chapter.

Ontology, epistemology, methodology

Ontology, epistemology and methodology are frequently encountered in discussions of research approaches, particularly in sociology:

● *Ontology* refers to the nature of reality assumed by the researcher – in the positivist paradigm (see below) the researcher assumes that the 'real world' being studied is as seen by the researcher, while in interpretive and similar approaches the researcher's perspective is not privileged: emphasis is placed on the varying views and realities as perceived by the people being studied.

● *Epistemology* refers to the relationship between the researcher and the phenomenon being studied – again the distinction is most sharply drawn between the positivist and interpretive stance, with the former seeking to adopt an objective, distanced stance, while the interpretive researcher is more subjective and engaged with the subjects of the study.

● *Methodology* refers to the ways by which knowledge and understanding are established. For example, the method used in the classic positivist approach is the controlled experiment (as discussed below), which is only possible in a limited number of leisure and tourism research contexts. The quantitative and qualitative divide, as discussed below, also offers distinctive methodologies. Ideally the choice of method in a study should be closely influenced by the ontological and epistemological perspectives used.

Positivist, post-positivist, interpretive and critical approaches/paradigms

The positivism, post-positivism and interpretive and critical approaches refer to *paradigms* in the social sciences which are ways of looking at the theoretical/research world:

Pairs/groups of terms	Brief definition	Associated terms
Ontology	Way of looking at the world.	Paradigm, philosophy
Epistemology	Relationship between researcher and the subject of research.	
Method	Ways of gathering and analysing data.	Technique
Positivist	Hypotheses are tested using objectively collected factual data which, if successful, produces scientific laws.	Scientific method, logical empiricist, functionalist, objectivist
Post-positivist	Hypotheses found to be consistent (or not) with the data deemed to be 'not falsified', establishing *probable* facts or laws.	
Interpretive	People provide their own accounts or explanation of situation/behaviour.	Phenomenology, phenomenography, symbolic interaction, intersubjectivity, ethnography, subjectivist
Critical	Research influenced by beliefs/values critical of the status quo in society.	Standpoint
Constructivist	People construct their own views of reality and the researcher seeks to discover this.	Social constructivism
Descriptive	Seeks to describe what is.	Exploratory
Explanatory	Seeks to explain relationships between phenomena.	Predictive
Evaluative	Seeks to test policy/management outcomes against benchmarks.	
Qualitative	Research in which words (and possibly images, sounds) are the medium.	
Quantitative	Research in which numbers are the main medium.	
Theoretical	Research which results in general propositions about how things/people behave.	Pure
Applied	Use of research to address particular policy/management issues.	Evidence-based
Experimental	Research where the researcher seeks to control all variables.	Controlled experiment
Naturalistic	Research where subjects are researched in their 'natural' environment where the researcher's control is minimal.	Real-life context
Reflexive	The process of examining the relationship between the researcher and the subject of the research.	Intersubjective
Empirical	Research involving data – quantitative or qualitative or both.	
Non-empirical	Research involving only theory and the literature.	Theoretical
Inductive	Hypotheses/explanations/theory are generated from examination of the data.	Exploratory
Deductive	Data collected to test a priori hypotheses.	Hypothetical-deductive, confirmatory
Primary data	Data gathered by the researcher for the current project.	
Secondary data	Use of existing data gathered by other people/organisations for other purposes.	
Self-reported	Subjects' own accounts of activity/behaviour.	
Observed	Researcher's observation of subjects' activity/behaviour.	Unobtrusive
Validity	The research accurately identifies/measures what is intended.	
Reliability	Repetition of the research would produce similar findings.	
Trustworthiness	Trust which can be placed in qualitative research.	

Figure 2.2 Terminology: approaches, dimensions and issues

- *Positivism* is a framework of research, similar to that adopted by the natural scientist, in which the researcher sees the phenomena to be studied from the outside, with behaviour to be explained on the basis of data and observations objectively gathered by the researcher, using theories and models developed by the researcher. The classic positivist approach uses the *hypothetical-deductive* model, which uses a deductive process (as discussed below) to test a pre-established hypothesis. If successful, this results in the establishment of 'laws' – for example, Newton's laws of motion. Many commentators are highly suspicious of such attempts to translate natural science approaches into the social sciences, arguing that it is inappropriate to draw conclusions about the causes and motivations of *human* behaviour on the basis of the type of evidence used in the natural sciences. Anthony Giddens (1974: 2) pointed out that in the social sciences by the 1970s the term 'positivist' had almost become a term of abuse.

- *Post-positivism* is distinguished from the classic positivist approach by some writers (for example Guba and Lincoln, 2006) as an approach in which hypotheses found to be consistent with the data are deemed to be 'not falsified'; researchers do not claim to have discovered the 'truth' but to have established *probable* facts or laws which are useful until such time as they are supplanted by new theories/laws which provide a fuller or more comprehensive explanation of the available data.

- *Interpretive* approaches to research place reliance on people providing their own explanations of their situation or behaviour. The interpretive researcher tries to 'get inside' the minds of subjects and see the world from their point of view. This of course suggests a more flexible approach to data collection, usually involving qualitative methods and generally an inductive approach. A number of variations exist within this category, as indicated in the 'associated terms' column in Figure 2.2, and these are discussed in Chapter 9.

- *Critical* approaches to research are influenced by particular sets of beliefs or values which are critical of the *status quo* in society: the most common in leisure and tourism are neo-Marxist perspectives, which are critical of the capitalist system, and various feminist perspectives, which are critical of the economic, social and political inequality between men and women. There are numerous other perspectives which researchers may adopt or causes with which they may be associated. One term used for research shaped by such commitments is *standpoint research* (Humberstone, 2004), while Karla Henderson (2009) has used the term '*just* research' to refer to research which is not just *about* diversity and inclusiveness but is committed to it. Critical researchers reject the notion of 'objectivity' (as discussed below) but will generally make their own values explicit in the conduct and reporting of their research. They would argue that the so-called 'objectivity' often claimed for or attributed to certain research approaches, notably the positivistic approach, is invalid because for those researchers who are not critical of the *status quo*, their values are, by implication, supportive or tolerant of it.

Along with parallel debates on quantitative and qualitative research, there is much debate in the leisure and tourism studies literature on the relative merits, suitability and appropriateness of the above alternative approaches to research. However, since leisure and tourism researchers are generally all using a combination of theory and empirical evidence to draw conclusions about leisure and tourism phenomena, the question arises as to how great the underlying, as opposed to surface, differences are between these approaches. Allen Lee (1989) has explored this issue and, using the terms 'subjectivist' and 'objectivist', argues that a subjectivist case study in organisation studies has similarites to the classic scientific experiment.

In the 1990s numerous commentators, in calling for more interpretive and qualitative research, referred to positivist, and quantitative, approaches as dominant in leisure and tourism studies. Since the 1990s, with the wide range of research approaches evident in published research, particularly outside North America, this is hard to substantiate (Veal, 1994). While positivism can be said to be still dominant in tourism, interpretive research is becoming increasingly common there also, although commentary on this is difficult to disentangle from discussions of qualitative versus quantitative research methods (e.g. see Phillimore and Goodson, 2004b).

Descriptive, explanatory and evaluative research

In Chapter 1 the differences between descriptive, explanatory and evaluative research were discussed and it is appropriate to raise the issue again here:

- *Descriptive* research aims to describe, as far as possible, what is. The focus is not on explanation. Another term which might be used here is *exploratory*, although exploratory research could also extend to attempts at explanation.

- *Explaining* the patterns in observed or reported data usually involves establishing that one phenomenon is caused by another, and the aim of research is to identify these causal relationships. For example, where descriptive research might show that a tourism destination is losing market share, explanatory research would seek to establish whether this was caused by, for example, price movements or the service quality.

- *Evaluative* research seeks to assess the success of policy or management action – for example, the effects of a marketing campaign.

These issues raise the question of *causality*: whether A or B is the cause. Labovitz and Hagendorn (1971: 4) state that there are '. . . at least four widely accepted scientific criteria for establishing causality. These criteria are association, time priority, nonspurious relation and rationale':

- *Association* is a 'necessary condition for a causal relation' – that is, A and B must be associated in some way – for example, A increases when B decreases.

There are two characteristics of an association that generally strengthen the conclusion that one variable is at least a partial cause of another. The first is magnitude, which refers to the size or strength of the association . . . The second . . . is consistency. If the relation persists from one study to the next under a variety of conditions, confidence in the causal nature of the relation is increased. *(Labovitz and Hagendorn, 1971: 5)*

● *Time priority* means that for A to be the cause of B then A must take place before B.

● *Nonspurious relationships* are defined as associations between two variables that 'cannot be explained by a third variable' (Labovitz and Hagendorn, 1971: 9). This means that it must be established that there is no third factor, C, which is affecting both A and B.

● *Rationale* means that statistical or other evidence is not enough; the conclusion that A causes B is not justified simply on the basis of an observed relation; it should be supported by some plausible, theoretical or logical explanation to suggest how it happens.

These matters are taken up again in Chapter 3 and the chapters in Part III.

Qualitative and quantitative research

Much leisure and tourism research involves the collection, analysis and presentation of statistical information. Sometimes the information is innately quantitative – for instance the numbers of people engaging in a list of leisure activities in a year, the number of tourists visiting a particular holiday area or the average income of a group of people. Sometimes the information is qualitative in nature but is presented in quantitative form – for instance numerical scores obtained by asking people to indicate levels of satisfaction with different services, where the scores range from 1, 'very satisfied', to 5, 'very dissatisfied'.

The *quantitative* approach to research involves numerical data. It relies on numerical evidence to draw conclusions or to test hypotheses. To be sure of the reliability of the results it is often necessary to study relatively large numbers of people and to use computers to analyse the data. The data can be derived from questionnaire surveys, from observation involving counts, or from administrative sources, such as ticket sales data from a leisure facility or data collected by immigration authorities at airports on the number of tourist arrivals from different origins.

There can be said to be three approaches to quantitative research:

● *Type A: hypothetical-deductive* quantitative research conforms to the hypothetical-deductive model discussed under positivism above. Invariably statistical methods and tests, such as the chi-square tests, t-tests, analysis of variance, correlation or regression outlined in Chapter 17, are used. This model is implicit in many discussions of quantitative methods.

- *Type B: statistical* quantitative research makes use of statistical methods but is not necessarily hypothetical-deductive. It can be descriptive, exploratory and/or deductive.

- *Type C: inductive* quantitative research is based on numerical data, but makes little or no use of statistical tests: its most sophisticated statistical measure is usually the percentage and sometimes means/averages. This type of quantitative research is very common in the British tradition of leisure and tourism research. For example, in reading the British journal *Leisure Studies*, it is notable that, whereas there are many articles which present numerical information, very few utilise the types of statistical tests and techniques discussed in Chapter 17. This is in marked contrast to the leading American *Journal of Leisure Research*, where a substantial proportion of the articles that include numerical data make use of such tests, so are of type A or B. Type C research is more informal than type B or type A and is closer in approach to qualitative methods.

The *qualitative* approach to research is generally not concerned with numbers but typically with information in the form of words, conveyed orally or in writing. In addition to words, images and sounds may also be involved. Definitions offered in the literature often go beyond this minimalist definition to include types of methods which are often associated with qualitative research but, arguably, are not exclusive to the approach. Thus, for example, Denzin and Lincoln (2006: 3) include in their definition the proposition that qualitative research practices 'transform the world', when clearly any type of research *may* achieve this. Similarly, they state that qualitative research involves a 'naturalistic' (see below) approach, when clearly qualitative methods may be deployed in non-naturalistic settings (for example, a laboratory) and quantitative research may take place in 'naturalistic' settings (for example, quantitative observation at a leisure/tourism site).

Qualitative research methods generally make it possible to gather a relatively large amount of information about the research subjects, which may be individuals, places or organisations. But the collection and analysis processes typically place a practical limit on the number of subjects which can be included. The approach involves obtaining a full and rounded account and understanding of the leisure or tourist behaviour, attitudes and/or situation of a few individuals, as opposed to the more limited amount of information which might be obtained in a quantitative study of a large sample of individuals. No claim is therefore made that the sample studied in a qualitative study is representative of a larger population, so that the findings cannot be generalised statistically to the wider population although, as Gregory Szarycz (2009) observes, this principle is often breached in the reporting; Sherry Dupuis (1999: 54) makes the same observation.

The methods used to gather qualitative information include observation, informal and in-depth interviewing, participant observation and analysis of texts. Research studying groups of people using non-quantitative, anthropological approaches, is referred to as *ethnographic* research or *ethnographic fieldwork*. Such methods were initially developed by anthropologists, but have been adapted by sociologists for use in their work.

The use of qualitative methods in leisure and tourism research has increased significantly in recent years. Case study 2.1 shows that quantitative methods remain strong in American journals, but that theoretical and qualitative methods are now dominant in the British journal *Leisure Studies*.

Case study 2.1   Research approaches in leisure journals

Every so often content analyses are undertaken of academic journals regarding such topics as the subject matter and disciplinary basis of articles and the research methods used. Selected results from a number of such studies are summarised here.

Figure 2.3 presents results from Karla Henderson's content analysis of American leisure studies journals over the period 1992–2002 and Figure 2.4 presents data for one of the British journals, *Leisure Studies*, over the period 1982–2006. While all the journals include international contributions, the great majority are from authors based in the country of publication, so the journal contents indicated in the two diagrams reflect the research traditions of North America and Britain respectively. The difference between the empirical and quantitative tradition of North America and the more theoretical and qualitative traditions of Britain are clear. The *Leisure Studies* data covers 25 years in five-year periods, showing the trend towards qualitative methods, with the latter representing the largest empirical approach in the last period.

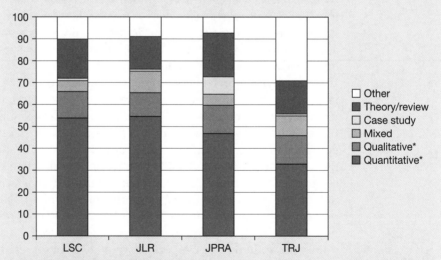

Figure 2.3   Research methods used in USA leisure journals: 1992–2002

Data source: Henderson (2006: 5)

LSC = *Leisure Sciences*, JLR = *Jnl of Leisure Research*, JPRA = *Jnl of Park & Recreation Admin.*,
TRJ = *Therapeutic Recreation Jnl*[†]
* Categories: Quantitative = 'Questionnaires'; Qualitative = 'Interviews' (in-depth, structured, telephone) and 'Group' (focus group, Delphi, nominal group)
[†] In *Therapeutic Recreation Jnl* Other is dominated by experimental method.

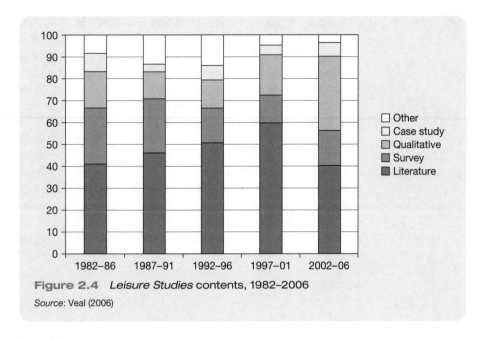

Figure 2.4 *Leisure Studies* contents, 1982–2006

Source: Veal (2006)

The question of the differences between, and respective merits of, quantitative and qualitative methods is arguably the most discussed methodological issue in leisure and tourism research. The discussion is led by proponents of qualitative methods who generally portray themselves as pioneering a novel approach in the face of opposition from proponents of 'traditional' quantitative methods. While the debate between protagonists of qualitative and quantitative research can become somewhat partisan, it is now widely accepted that the two approaches complement one another. Leading proponents of qualitative methods, Egon Guba and Yvonne Lincoln (1998: 195) have stated: 'From our perspective, both qualitative and quantitative methods may be appropriate with any research paradigm'.

Quantitative research is often based on initial qualitative work and it is possible that the two approaches are moving closer together in one respect, as computers are now being used to analyse qualitative data.

Qualitative methods are considered specifically in Chapters 9 and 15, but also arise in Chapters 7, 8, 12 and 13.

Theoretical and applied research

Theoretical research seeks to draw conclusions about the class of phenomena being studied which can be applied to that class of phenomena as a whole, not just the cases or subjects included in the study. Indeed, some theoretical research is non-empirical (see below), so it does not involve the direct study of cases or subjects, but relies on the existing research literature.

Applied research, however, is less universal in its scope: it does not nece-ssarily seek to create wholly *new* knowledge about the world but to apply existing theoretical knowledge to particular problems or issues. Such problems or issues my arise in particular policy, planning or management situations. Policy studies, planning and management are themselves fields of study which have developed a body of theory. Because they are related to areas of practice they can be seen as *applied disciplines*. In these fields, therefore, there can be such a thing as *applied theory*. The rational-comprehensive model of management portrayed in Figure 1.4 is an example of a context for considering the differ-ence between theoretical and applied research: research which might seek to develop or elaborate the model in general would be theoretical whereas research which simply used the model as a framework for examining a prob-lem in a particular organisation would be called applied. In some discussions of this dimension the term 'pure' is used rather than 'theoretical'.

Reflexivity

A reflexive approach to research involves explicit consideration of the relation-ship between the researcher and the researched. This is the only section in the chapter which does not involve two or more terms since, as Charlotte Davies (1997: 3) points out, all research involves a degree of reflexivity. Thus, for example, in small particle physics the very act of measurement can only be achieved by the researcher causing physical interference with the particle being measured and this becomes the focus of the research methodology. In questionnaire-based research, interaction between the researcher and the respondent is in the form of the asking of questions: different wording of the questions and the manner in which they are posed affect the answers given. Reflexivity is most often considered in the context of qualitative research and the deeper the involvement of the researcher with the research subjects the more relevant it becomes, the most extreme being participant observation. Thus reflexivity may be related to physical relation-ships, to culture or power or to a variety of forms of social interaction. In social research, reflexivity is sometimes referred to as intersubjectivity (Glancy, 1993).

In methodologies closer to the classic scientific model, the aim is generally to minimise the impact of the researcher on the research subjects and description of measures taken to achieve this are confined to the 'methods' section of the research report, although it may be revisited in the conclusions, particularly if the results are less than clear-cut and might be improved in future by changes in the research design. But in interpretive studies involving methods such as participant observation, discussion of the relationship between the researcher and the researched can be a major part of the analysis and reporting process.

Empirical and non-empirical research

The dichotomy here should probably be between *purely* empirical research, if such a thing exists, and *purely* theoretical research. Empirical research involves the collection and/or analysis of data, which may be quantitative or qualitative, primary or secondary. The research is informed by observations or information from the 'real world'. It is, however, rare for any research project to be exclusively empirical – it is usually informed by some sort of theory or conceptual framework (see Chapter 3), however implicit.

It is possible for the researcher to become carried away with data and their analysis and to forget the theory which should make them *meaningful*. In such cases the disparaging term 'mindless empiricism' is sometimes used to describe this situation. Similarly, theoretical research with no reference to information about the 'real world', however contested the description of that might be, is likely to be of limited value. Typically – and ideally – theoretical and empirical research coexist and enhance each other; indeed, most research projects have complementary theoretical and empirical components.

Reviews of the contents of the main leisure or tourism journals reveal the existence of both sorts of research (see 'theory/review' versus the rest in Figure 2.3 and 'literature' versus the rest in Figure 2.4). While the empirical studies provide some of the building blocks of a great deal of research and knowledge, non-empirical contributions are needed to review and refine ideas and to place the empirical work in context. A book like this inevitably devotes more space to empirical methods, because they involve more explicit, technical processes which can be described and taught. It cannot however be too strongly stressed that a good review of the literature or a thoughtful piece of writing arising from deep, insightful, inspirational thinking about a subject can be worth a hundred, unthinking, surveys!

Induction and deduction

Induction and deduction refer to alternative approaches to explanation in research. It has been noted that research involves *finding out* and *explaining*. Finding out might be called the 'what?' of research. Explaining might be called the 'how?' and the 'why?' of research.

Finding out involves description and gathering of information. Explaining involves attempting to understand that information: it goes beyond the descriptive. Appropriate research methods can facilitate both these processes. Description and explanation can be seen as part of a circular model of research as illustrated in Figure 2.5.

The research process can work in two ways:

● *Deductive:* The process starts at point A1 and moves via observation/ description (B) to analysis/testing (C) which confirms or disproves the hypothesis (D1). The process is *deductive*: it involves *deduction*, where the process is based on prior logical reasoning and available evidence from observation or the research literature resulting in a hypothesis to be tested.

● *Inductive*: The process may begin with a question, at point A2, or it may begin with observation/description, at point B in the diagram; it then moves from analysis (C) to answering, or failing to answer, the question. The process is *inductive*: the explanation is *induced* from the data; the data come first and the explanation later.

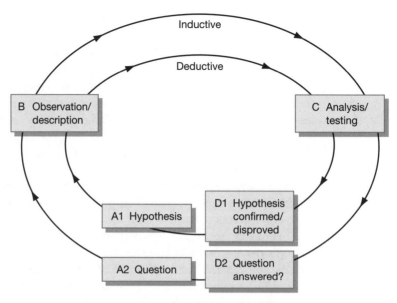

Figure 2.5 Circular model of the research process

The concept of a *hypothesis* arises in the deductive process. A hypothesis is a proposition about how something might work or behave – an explanation which may or may not be supported by data, or possibly by more detailed or rigorous argument. A hypothesis may be suggested from informal observation and experience of the researcher or from examination of the existing research literature. As we shall see in Chapter 3, not all research projects involve the use of hypotheses which are associated with the classic positivistic or *hypothetical-deductive* model as discussed above.

The terms *theory* or *model* could also be included at point D1. When more elaborate hypotheses or a number of inter-related hypotheses are involved, the term theory or model may be used. A theory or model can be similar to a hypothesis, in being propositional, or it may have been subjected to empirical validation – that is, testing against data. A research project may involve a single circuit or a number of circuits of the process, possibly in both directions. Theory and models can also arise out of the inductive process if, for example, the question was a 'why?' question.

Case study 2.2 illustrates the concepts of induction and deduction using an example of the relative popularity of two leisure activities.

In practice data are rarely collected without at least an informal explanatory model in mind – otherwise how would the researcher know what data to collect? So there is always an element of deduction in any research. And it is not possible to develop hypotheses and theories without at least some initial information on the topic in hand, however informally obtained; so there is always an element of induction. Thus most research is partly inductive and partly deductive.

There is a tendency, particularly among writers on qualitative methods, to associate quantitative methods with a deductive approach and qualitative

Case study 2.2   Tennis vs golf – inductive and deductive approaches

The relative popularity of tennis and golf could be studied using an inductive or deductive approach to research and explanation.

A. Inductive

A descriptive survey shows that more people play tennis than play golf. This is just a piece of information; we cannot explain why this is so without additional information and analysis. If the research also reveals that it costs more to play golf than to play tennis then we could offer the explanation that relative popularity is related to price.

However, qualitative information from the survey might also indicate that more people consider tennis as being fun to play than consider golf to be fun. This suggests that tennis is intrinsically more attractive than golf for many people and its popularity is not related to price but to intrinsic enjoyment.

On the other hand, the research might indicate that there are more tennis courts available than golf courses in the particular community being studied, suggesting that, if there were more golf courses available, then golf would be more popular – implying that popularity is related to availability of facilities.

In this example, a series of possible explanations is being *induced* from the data. In its most fully developed form the explanation amounts to a theory. In this case a theory of sports participation might be developed relating levels of participation to costs of participation, intrinsic satisfactions and supply of facilities, perceived attractiveness of the activity and facilities and so on.

B. Deductive

On the basis of reading and existing theory on leisure activities generally, the following two hypotheses are put forward.

Hypothesis 1: if sport A is more expensive to play than sport B, then sport B will be more popular than sport A.

Hypothesis 2: if more facilities are available for sport B than for sport A then sport B will be more popular than sport A.

To test these hypotheses a research project is designed to collect information on:

- the levels of participation in the two sports – tennis and golf;
- the costs of participating in the two sports;
- the availability of facilities for the two sports in the study area.

The two hypotheses would then be tested using the data collected. The data collection and outcomes are limited by the hypotheses put forward. In this example the idea of 'intrinsic motivation', which featured in the inductive approach, was not identified. In this case the research is guided from the beginning by the initial hypotheses. The process is deductive.

methods with inductive approaches. But quantitative research can be, and often is, inductive. For example:

- *Factor analysis*, as discussed in Chapter 17, is a highly quantitative data manipulation technique which seeks to identify a manageable number of meaningful 'factors' from a large number of variables, such as might be generated from a questionnaire. The technique can be used as an *exploratory* (i.e. inductive) tool, to discover what, if any, factors might exist in the data, and as a *confirmatory* (i.e. deductive) tool, to confirm the existence of hypothesised factors.

- *Structural equation modelling* (SEM), as discussed in Chapter 17, is also a highly quantitative technique; in his book on the technique, Rex Kline notes that computer programs used to analyse data for SEM require the researcher to provide in advance specifications of the model to be tested and observes:

  > These *a priori* specifications reflect the researcher's hypotheses, and in total they make up the model to be evaluated in the analysis. In this sense SEM could be viewed as confirmatory [i.e. deductive]. That is, the model is given at the beginning of the analysis, and one of the main questions to be answered is whether it is supported by the data. But, as often happens in SEM, the data may be inconsistent with the model, which means that the researcher must either abandon the model or modify the hypotheses on which it is based. The former option is rather drastic. In practice, researchers more often opt for the second choice, which means the analysis now has a more exploratory [i.e. inductive] nature as revised models are tested with the same data. *(Kline, 2005: 10)*

Whether hypotheses or theories containing the explanation are put forward at the start of a research project or arise as a result of exploratory data analysis, they represent the key creative part of the research process. Data collection and analysis can be fairly mechanical but interpretation of data and the development of explanations requires at least creativity and, at best, inspiration!

Experimental and naturalistic methods

The experiment is the classic scientific research method: the popular image of the scientist is someone in a white coat in a laboratory, conducting experiments. In the experimental method of research the scientist aims to control the environment of the subject of the research and measure the effects of controlled change. Knowledge based on the experimental method progresses on the basis that, in a controlled experimental situation, any change in A must have been brought about by a change in B because everything except A and B have been held constant. The experimental researcher therefore aims to produce conditions such that the research will fulfil the requirements for causality discussed above.

In the world of human beings, with which the social scientist deals, there is much less scope for experiment than in the world of inanimate objects or animals with which natural scientists deal. Some situations do exist where experimentation with human beings in the field of leisure or tourism can take place. For example, it is possible to experiment with:

- variations in design or location of children's play equipment;

- willing subjects in game-playing or decision-making tasks under different conditions or responding to 'stimuli', such as photographs or videos;

- sporting/human movement activity where subjects can be asked to engage in particular forms of physical exercise and their physical and psychological reactions can be measured;

- management situations, for instance varying prices or advertising strategies in relation to leisure or tourism services.

But many areas of interest to the leisure or tourism researcher are not susceptible to controlled experiment. For instance, the researcher interested in the effect of people's level of income on their behaviour cannot take a group of people and vary their incomes in order to study the effects of income on leisure participation or tourism behaviour – it would be difficult to find people on executive salaries willing voluntarily to spend a year living on a student grant in the interests of research! Furthermore, unlike the natural scientist experimenting with rats, it is not possible to find two groups of humans identical in every respect except for their level of income. Even more fundamentally, it is of course not possible to vary people's social class or race. In order to study these phenomena it is necessary to use *non-experimental* methods: that is, it is necessary to study differences between people as they exist.

So, for example, in order to study the effects of income on leisure participation patterns or touristic behaviour it is necessary to gather information on the leisure and travel behaviour patterns of a range of people with different levels of income. But people differ in all sorts of ways, some of which may be related to their level of income and some not. For example, two people with identical income levels can differ markedly in terms of their personalities, their family situation, their physical health, and so on. So, in comparing the behaviour of two groups of people, it is difficult to be sure which differences arise as a result of income differences and which as a result of other differences. The results of the research are therefore likely to be less clear-cut than in the case of the controlled experiment.

One term used for studying people in their normal environment, that is, not in a laboratory, is *naturalistic*. In a fully naturalistic study the researcher would be as unobtrusive as possible so as not to interfere in any way with the normal behaviour of the research subjects. Unlike the laboratory experiment, where as many variables as possible are controlled, the naturalistic researcher would be taking a *holistic* or *systematic* view, in which all relevant known and unknown variables are in operation simultaneously. As Egon Guba and Yvonna Lincoln

(1998: 8) put it, in naturalistic research: 'first, no manipulation on the part of the inquirer is implied and, second, the inquirer imposes no a priori units on the outcome'.

Some observational methods seek to achieve this. Interviews of various types may begin to interfere with the normal or 'natural' behaviour of the subject: the asking of a question can be seen as a sort of loosely controlled experiment. But interviews which take place in a subject's home or at a leisure site or holiday destination are more naturalistic than a focus group session in the office of a market research company which is closer to the experiment end of the experimental–naturalistic continuum. For some types of naturalistic research project, quite extensive interaction may be required between the researcher and the subjects being researched in order to gain an understanding of behaviour in the subject's normal/natural environment.

The experimental method is dealt with in Chapter 11. The survey and qualitative methods discussed in Chapters 7–10 can all be seen as naturalistic but varying in their degrees of naturalism.

Objectivity and subjectivity

As indicated in Chapter 1 and in the discussion of the experimental method above, the classical stance of the researcher in the natural science research model is as an objective observer. Experiments are set up to prove or disprove a hypothesis. If the data from the experiment are consistent with the hypothesis, the latter is accepted as reflecting the real world until such time as new evidence emerges which is inconsistent with the hypothesis, which is then rejected or modified. In practice, absolute objectivity is impossible since the researcher's selection of one research topic rather than any one of a thousand others suggests a value position: the researcher's choice implies that the selected topic is, in some way, more important than the others. If the research has been funded from a trust or government grant-giving body the application will invariably have been required to demonstrate the 'social benefits' of the research. When moving into the social science area it becomes even more difficult to maintain the classic objective stance: thus much research on leisure is conducted because the researcher is convinced of the value of leisure activity to society as a whole or to particular groups within society. In the case of tourism there may be a belief in the economic benefits it can bring to host communities or, in some cases, concern about its negative consequences or unequal sharing of costs and benefits. Nevertheless, researchers typically seek to be as objective as possible and to report honestly on the results of empirical enquiry, as discussed in Chapter 4.

Primary and secondary data

In planning a research project it is advisable to consider whether it is necessary to go to the expense of collecting new information (*primary* data, where the researcher is the first user) or whether existing data (*secondary* data, where the researcher is the secondary user) will do the job. Sometimes existing information is in the form of research already completed on the topic or a related topic; sometimes it arises from non-research sources, such as administration. A fundamental part of any research project is therefore to scour the existing published – and unpublished – sources of information for related research. Existing research might not obviate the need for the originally proposed research, but it may provide interesting ideas and points of comparison with the proposed research.

Even if the research project is to be based mainly on new information it will usually be necessary also to make use of other, existing, information – such as official government statistics or financial records from a leisure or tourism facility or service. Such information is generally referred to as *secondary data*, as opposed to the *primary data*, which is the new data to be collected in the proposed research. The topic of secondary data is dealt with in Chapters 7 and 14.

Self-reported and observed data

The best, and often the only, sources of information about people's leisure or tourism behaviour or attitudes are individuals' own reports about themselves. Much leisure and tourism research therefore involves asking people about their past behaviour, attitudes and aspirations, by means of an interviewer-administered or respondent-completed questionnaire (Chapter 10) or by means of informal, in-depth, semi-structured or unstructured interview (Chapter 9). In some cases information can be gathered from written sources such as diaries, letters or biographies.

There are some disadvantages to this approach, mainly that the researcher is never sure just how honest or accurate people are in responding to questions. In some instances people may deliberately or unwittingly distort or 'bend' the truth – for instance, in understating the amount of alcohol they drink or overstating the amount of exercise they take. In other instances they may have problems of recall – for instance, in remembering just how much money they spent on a recreational or holiday trip some months ago – or even yesterday! In biomedical research, which relies a great deal on subjects/patients accurately reporting such things as symptoms and behaviour, study of the design and practice of such data collection has come to be referred as the 'science of self-report' (Stone *et al.*, 2000).

For some types of information an alternative to relying on self-report is for the researcher to *observe* behaviour. For instance, to find out how children use a playground or how adults make use of a resort area or a park it would probably be better to watch them than to try to ask them about it. Patterns of movement and crowding can be *observed*. Sometimes people leave behind evidence of their behaviour – for instance, the most popular exhibits at a museum will be the ones where the carpet is most worn, and the most used beaches are likely to be those where the most litter is dumped. Generally these techniques are referred to as *observational* or *unobtrusive* techniques and are dealt with in Chapter 8.

Clearly observation does not provide direct information on motives, attitudes and aspirations or past behaviour.

Validity, reliability and trustworthiness

The quality of research and the trust which can be placed in it depends on the methods used and the care with which they have been deployed. Two dimensions are generally considered in this context: validity and reliability.

Validity is the extent to which the information presented in the research truly reflects the phenomena which the researcher claims it reflects. *External validity* refers to generalisability or representativeness: to what extent can the results be generalised to a population wider than the particular sample used in the study? This will depend on how the members of the sample are selected, as discussed in Chapter 13. *Internal validity* refers to how accurately the characteristics of the phenomena being studied are represented by the variables used and the data collected – sometimes referred to as *measurement* or *instrument* (for example, questionnaire) *validity* – and the extent to which the study identifies and measures all the relevant variables.

Leisure and tourism research is fraught with difficulties in this area, mainly because empirical research is largely concerned with people's behaviour and with their attitudes, and for information on these the researcher is, in the main, reliant on people's own reports in the form of responses to questionnaire-based interviews and other forms of interview. These instruments are subject to a number of imperfections, which means that the validity of leisure and tourism data can rarely be as certain as in the natural sciences. For example, data on the number of people who have participated in an activity at least once over the last month (a common type of measure used in leisure research) covers a wide range of different types of involvement, from the person who participates for two hours every day to the person who accidentally engaged in the activity just once for a few minutes. So the question of what is a *participant* can be complex. More detailed questioning to capture such complexity can be costly to undertake on a large scale and can try the patience of interviewees, thus increasing the risk that responses will be inaccurate or incomplete.

Reliability is the extent to which research findings would be the same if the research were to be repeated at a later date or with a different sample of subjects. Again it can be seen that the model is taken from the natural sciences where, if experimental conditions are appropriately controlled, a replication of an experiment should produce identical results wherever and whenever it is conducted. This is rarely the case in the social sciences, because they deal with human beings in differing and ever changing social situations. While a single person's report of his or her behaviour may be accurate, when it is aggregated with information from other people, it presents a snap-shot picture of a group of people, which is subject to change over time, as the composition of the group changes, or as *some* members of the group change their patterns of behaviour. Further, identical questions asked of people in different locations, even within the same country or region, are likely to produce different results, because of the varying social and physical environment. This means that the social scientist, including the leisure and tourism researcher, must be very cautious when making general, theoretical, statements on the basis of empirical research. While measures can be taken to ensure a degree of generalisability, strictly speaking, any research findings relate only to the subjects involved, at the time and place the research was carried out.

There is a considerable literature on validity and reliability, particularly related to experimental research and the use of scales (see Chapter 5); sources are indicated in the Resources section at the end of the chapter.

It has been noted that the use of validity and reliability as criteria for assessing the quality of research arose from the positivist tradition and that they are therefore not always fully appropriate for non-positivist research approaches. In qualitative research in particular, the concepts of *trustworthiness* and authenticity have been introduced by Guba and Lincoln (1998) to replace validity and reliability. Trustworthiness has four components: credibility (paralleling internal validity), transferability (external validity), dependability (reliability) and confirmability (objectivity). Authenticity includes: fairness and ontological, educative, analytic and tactical authenticity. Because qualitative studies do not follow a regimented process, a detailed explanation of the research process is advisable, as Karla Henderson (2006: 231) has put it: 'A thorough reporting of the process and the results of qualitative data collection and analysis is the key to justifying and assuring that trustworthiness exists in the study.'

Summary

The aim of this chapter is to provide an introduction to the disciplinary context and traditions of leisure and tourism research and to introduce some of the general dimensions and concepts associated with social science research. It begins with a brief overview of the contributions of individual disciplines to leisure and tourism research, covering: sociology, geography, economics, psychology/social psychology, history and anthropology and political science. The review indicates that most of the disciplines contributing to leisure and tourism research now make use of a wide variety of research methods. The second half of the chapter covers a range of generic social science concepts and issues which arise in the literature and with which the leisure and tourism researcher should be familiar. They are: ontology, epistemology and methodology; positivist, post-positivist, interpretive and critical approaches; descriptive, explanatory and evaluative research as discussed in Chapter 1; qualitative and quantitative research; theoretical and applied research; empirical and non-empirical research; induction and deduction; experimental and non-experimental research; primary and secondary data; self-reported and observed data; and validity and reliability.

Test questions

1. What are the basic differences between theoretical and applied research?

2. What are the basic differences between empirical/non-empirical research?

3. What are the basic differences between the inductive and deductive approach to research?

4. What are the basic differences between descriptive and explanatory research?

5. What are the basic differences between the positivist and interpretive approach to research?

6. What are the basic differences between experimental and non-experimental research?

7. What is the basic difference between primary and secondary data?

8. What is the basic difference between self-reported and observed data?

9. What are the basic differences between qualitative and quantitative research?

10. What are validity and reliability?

Exercises

1. Examine any issue of either *Leisure Studies* or *Annals of Tourism Research* and classify the articles into disciplinary areas. Contrast the key questions which each article is addressing.

2. Using the same journal issue as in exercise 1, determine whether the articles are: (a) empirical or non-empirical; (b) deductive or inductive; (c) positivist or interpretive.

3. Using either *Leisure Studies* or *Annals of Tourism Research*, take an issue of the journal at two-yearly intervals over 10 or 12 years and summarise the apparent change over time in the topics addressed and methods used in the articles.

Resources

- Disciplines: tourism: Tribe (1997), Leiper (2000).

- Reflexivity: Davies (1997); Dupuis (1999), Donne (2006), Howe (2009); inter-subjectivity: Glancy (1993).

- Qualitative versus quantitative research: Kelly (1980), Henderson (1990), Borman *et al.* (1986), Bryman and Bell (2003: Chapters 21 and 22), Godbey and Scott (1990), Kamphorst *et al.*, (1984), Krenz and Sax (1986) and Veal (1994).

- Experimental method in leisure research: Havitz and Sell (1991).

- The science of self-report: Stone *et al.* (2000).

- Validity/reliability: Burns (1994: 206–28), Vaske (2008: 66–75), Riddick and Russell (2008: 149–53, 179–81).

- Trustworthiness: Lincoln and Guba (1985), Guba and Lincoln (1998); in tourism: DeCrop (2004), Henderson (2006: 225–36).

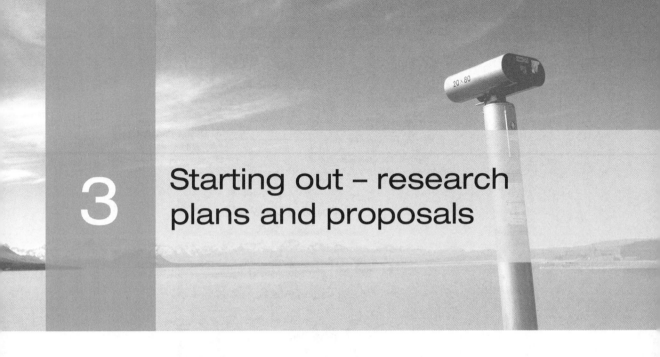

3 Starting out – research plans and proposals

Introduction: the research process

This chapter examines:

● stages in the planning of research projects;

● the formulation and presentation of research proposals and tenders.

Planning a research project

A research plan or proposal must summarise how a research project is to be conducted in its entirety; consequently preparation of a plan or proposal involves examination of the whole research process from beginning to end. In this chapter, therefore, a certain amount of cross-referencing is required to later chapters, where elements of the process are dealt with in detail.

The research process can be envisaged in a number of ways, but for the purposes of discussion in this chapter it is divided into ten main elements, as shown in Figure 3.1. The enormous variety of approaches to research means that all research projects do not follow precisely the sequence as set out in the

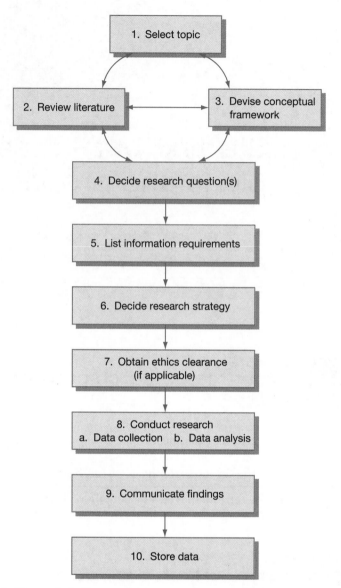

Figure 3.1 Elements in the research process

diagram. In particular, the first four elements depicted – selecting the topic, reviewing the literature, devising a conceptual framework and deciding the key research questions – rarely happen in the direct, linear way that the numbered sequence implies. There is generally a great deal of 'to-ing and fro-ing' between the elements. Hence, in Figure 3.1, these elements are depicted on a circle, implying that a number of circuits may be necessary before proceeding to element 5. To illustrate the process in operation, two case studies are presented in summary at the end of this section and in more detail on the book's website, where additional examples can also be found. Each of the ten elements in Figure 3.1 is discussed in turn below.

1. Select a topic

How do research topics arise? They may arise from a range of sources, including: the researcher's personal interests; reading research literature; a policy or management problem; an issue of social concern; a popular or media issue; published research agendas; and/or brainstorming, which may draw on a number of the above sources. Examples of topics arising from these sources are shown in Figure 3.2.

Source of topic	Examples of topics
Personal interest (usually combined with one or more of the next five sources)	<ul><li>A particular sport – trends in participation, participants' motivations/satisfactions</li><li>Leisure access and needs of a particular ethnic or age group</li><li>Tourism conflicts in a particular (home) locality</li><li>A particular professional group – its ethos, history and future.</li></ul>
The literature	<ul><li>Does Csikzentmihayli's (1990) idea of 'flow' apply to participation in sport X, or to tourist trips to destination Y?</li><li>How do MacCannell's (1976) ideas on 'signs' relate to 'sun, sea, sand, sex' holidays, as opposed to sight-seeing holidays?</li><li>What is known about the leisure activity of 'taking a holiday', as opposed to the activity of choosing a tourism destination?</li></ul>
Policy/management	<ul><li>Why are visits to leisure facility X declining?</li><li>What market segments should be used to develop a strategy for promoting sport X, arts venue Y, or tourism destination Z?</li><li>What are the leisure needs of community X?</li></ul>
Social	<ul><li>The impact of growing tourism on a local environment</li><li>Leisure needs of single parents</li><li>The role of sport in a third-world community.</li></ul>
Popular/media	<ul><li>Are recreational drugs harmful?</li><li>Are city streets less safe than they used to be?</li><li>Who goes to 'rave' parties and what do they get out of them?</li></ul>
Published research agendas	<ul><li>Both of the following examples include a wide range of potential research topics:<ul><li>*An Australian Leisure Research Agenda* (Lynch and Brown, 1995)</li><li>'Tourism research: policy and managerial priorities for the 1990s and beyond' (Ritchie, 1994).</li></ul></li></ul>
Brainstorming	<ul><li>Conduct a 'brainstorm' session on any of the above topics/sources – a means of exploring the potential of all of the above.</li></ul>
Opportunism	<ul><li>Government-collected leisure participation data provides the opportunity to undertake some demand forecasting</li><li>Membership of a sporting club or a visit to a tourist destination offers an opportunity to conduct participant participation.</li></ul>

Figure 3.2 Examples of research topics from different sources

Personal interest

Personal interest can give rise to a research project in a number of ways. For example, the researcher may be personally involved in a sport or other leisure activity, may be a member of a particular social group, based on gender, ethnicity or occupation, or may live in or have visited a particular tourism location and so be personally aware of certain local issues or problems. Using personal interest as a focus for research has advantages and disadvantages. The advantage lies in the knowledge of the phenomenon which researchers already have, the possibility of access to key individuals and information sources, and the high level of motivation which is likely to be brought to the research. Pirkko Markula and Jim Denison (2005) suggest that personal experience is a way into the process of exploring potential topics for research in sport, but clearly it can also apply in other forms of leisure and tourism The disadvantage is that the researcher may be unduly biased and may not be able to view the situation 'objectively'; familiarity with the subject of the research may result in too much being taken for granted so that the researcher can't 'see the wood for the trees'.

While a particular personal interest in the research topic may be referred to in writing up a research project – generally in a foreword or preface rather than in the main body of the report – it is often not mentioned in formal reports of research, such as journal articles. On the other hand, for some types of qualitative or 'standpoint' research, as discussed in Chapter 2, the researcher's personal relationship with the subjects of the research may be an important aspect of the methodology.

Personal interest may be a component in the process of selecting a research topic, but does not alone generally provide a sufficient rationale or focus for a research project; it is necessary to develop additional criteria for selection of a specific topic from among the other sources discussed below.

The research literature

The research literature is the most common source of topics for academic research. A researchable topic derived from reading of the literature can take a variety of forms. It may arise from an informal scanning of the literature which stimulates a spark of interest in a topic, or it may arise from a more critical and focused reading. Much reported research is very specific to time and place, so that even a widely accepted theory might be subject to further testing and exploration. Thus it my be that a certain theory or theoretical proposition has never been tested empirically, or it merits further empirical testing for a variety of reasons, as set out in Figure 3.3.

A topic may, however, be inspired not by theory, but by other material from the literature. For example, a particular research technique might be of interest, and the aim is then to find a suitable setting to explore the use of the technique. An historical account could inspire a researcher to explore the history of an area or an activity or a group of people.

Clearly, therefore, identifying a topic from the literature requires a special, *questioning, exploratory* approach to reading research literature: the aim is to

Type of reason	The theory/proposition/ observation history	Example
Geographical	May have been tested only in one country/region	Theory established using US data could be tested in another country. Behaviour patterns of urban residents – are they replicated in rural areas?
Social	May have been established on the basis of the experience of one social group only	Theory based on men's experience – does it apply to women? Theory tested on middle-class subjects – does it apply to working-class people?
Temporal	May be out of date	Theory on youth culture established in the 1980s – is it still valid?
Contextual	May have been established in fields other than leisure/tourism	Foucault's (1979) theories on power are based on studies in a hospital – are they relevant in the tourism industry?
Methodological	May have been tested using only one methodology	Conclusions from a qualitative study could be tested quantitatively.

Figure 3.3 Reasons for re-visiting theories/propositions/observations from the literature

identify not just what the literature *says*, but also what it does *not* say or the *basis* for assertions made. The process of critically reviewing the literature is discussed further below under element 2 of the research process, and in Chapter 6. If the research literature is to be the main source of ideas for a research topic then the first two elements of the research process – (1) selecting a topic and (2) reviewing the literature – are effectively combined.

A policy or management issue/problem

Policy or management topics are often specified by a leisure or tourism organisation, but students or academics interested in policy or management issues can also identify such topics. For example: tourism forecasting is conducted not only by, and at the behest of, government and commercial tourism bodies but also by academics; and surveys of users of leisure or tourist facilities or cost–benefit analyses of programmes and projects can be conducted by interested academics as well as leisure or tourism service organisations. The difference between industry-sponsored and academically initiated research is that:

- The results of academically initiated research will often be made public, will generally be presented so as to highlight their more general implications rather than the particular application to the facility or programme being studied, and will be concerned as much with the *methodology* of the study as with its substantive findings.

● Results from industry-sponsored research, on the other hand, may often not be made public, the wider implications of the research might not be examined and the methodology, while it must be sound, will often not be of particular interest to the sponsoring organisation.

In some cases academics involved with one or more industry-sponsored projects, the results of which have been reported to the sponsoring organisation, may publish academic articles highlighting particular features for a wider readership.

Research sponsored by government bodies lies somewhere in between these two situations: the results of the research may be very specific, but will often not be confidential.

It is common for policy or management topics to be outlined by an organisation in a *brief* or set of *terms of reference* for a funded research or consultancy project. Research organisations – usually consultants – are invited to respond in the form of a competitive *tender* to conduct the project. This type of procedure has its own set of practices and conventions, as discussed later in the chapter under *Briefs and tenders*.

Social concern

Social concern – of the researcher and/or sections of society at large – can give rise to a wide-range of research topics. For example, concern for certain deprived or neglected groups in society can lead to research on the leisure needs or behaviour of members of such groups. Concern for the environment can lead to research on the environmental impact of tourism in sensitive areas. Often such research is closely related to policy or management issues, but the research may have a more limited role, seeking to highlight problems rather than necessarily seeking to devise solutions.

Popular/media

A popular issue can inspire research that seeks to explore popular beliefs or perceptions, especially where it is suspected that these may be inaccurate or contestable. 'Popular' usually means 'as portrayed in the media'. For example, this might be seen as the motivation for much research on media portrayals of such phenomena as sporting crowd violence and 'alienated youth' (Rowe, 1995: 4) or a major controversial leisure or tourism development.

Published research agendas

From time to time public agencies, professional bodies or individual academics publish 'research agendas', based on an assessment, often made by a committee, of the research needs of a field of study. The following are some examples:

- Lynch and Brown (1999): a review and summary of research agendas for leisure/recreation in Britain, Australia and North America;

- Ritchie (1994) and Faulkner *et al.* (2003): agendas for the field of tourism;

- Brownson *et al.* (2008): the process of developing a research agenda for the promotion of physical activity;

- Carlsen *et al.* (2008): a research agenda developed for Edinburgh festivals, but which provides a framework for events generally.

Often the aim of the body initiating the agenda is to implement the published research agenda itself, but in other cases the idea is for researchers in the field generally – including students – to respond by adopting topics in the agenda for their own research. Students looking for research topics know that if their topic is selected from such a published list, then there will be at least a few people 'out there' who will be interested in the results!

Brainstorming

Brainstorming involves a group of two or more people bouncing ideas off one another in discussion in pursuit of inspiration or solutions to a problem. Typically this might be done with the aid of a white-board or flip-chart to write down ideas as they emerge. It can be seen as a separate source of ideas for a research topic or a way of refining ideas from any or all of the sources discussed above.

Opportunism

Sometimes an idea for research is prompted for opportunistic reasons: a data source becomes available. The various government surveys and other data collected for policy and administrative purposes and used for limited and internal policy-related or administrative purposes present constant opportunities for secondary analysis, and this is discussed further in Chapter 7. Membership of an organisation or a visit to a tourist destination or an event may provide the opportunity for participant observation and the availability of organisational or personal archives may provide an opportunity for historical research. In all these cases, as well as considering the nature and quality of the available data, one or more of the above rationales have to be brought into play to see if conducting a project using the data can be justified

Selecting the topic

What makes a viable research topic? There is no single, or simple, answer to this question. In general it is not the topic itself which is good or bad but the way the research is conceptualised (see element 3 of the research process) and how the research question or questions are framed (element 4). A key question is whether the topic has already been researched by someone else – hence the need for a review of the literature, as discussed in element 2. But even when a topic has already been researched there is invariably scope for further research – sometimes this is pointed out by the original researcher in concluding comments.

Thus the first four elements of the research process – select topic, review literature, conceptualise, define research questions – form an iterative, often untidy, process, which is invariably difficult and challenging and sometimes frustrating. But it is essential to get this stage right or the rest of the research effort may be wasted.

The purpose of research

The *purposes* of a research project can shape the choice of topic and the subsequent research design. Three types of purpose are discussed here, namely: knowledge for its own sake; ideological/political purposes; and policy/management purposes; and their key features are summarised in Figure 3.4. These purposes or motivations for research are often not explicitly stated in research reports, but are generally implicit. They affect the choice of topic and the overall shaping of the research process.

Knowledge for its own sake. The classic purpose of research is to 'add to knowledge' for its own sake, or for the general good as judged by the researcher.

Type of purpose/motivation	Features
Pursue knowledge for its own sake	Academic/scientific criteria – but may combine with others below

Ideologically driven:
• Conservative
• Reformist, e.g.
  social-democratic
  environmental
• Radical/critical, e.g.
  neo-liberal
  neo-Marxist
  radical-feminist
  anti-globalist
	• defence/acceptance of the status quo
	
	• a more egalitarian society
	• sustainability
	
	• defence/extension of the market
	• demonstration of class conflict/exploitation
	• demonstration of patriarchy/women's oppression
	• demonstrate undesirable features of global market trends

Policy/management: • Critical • Instrumental	• Critiques current policy/management – may reflect one or more radical/critical stances above • Accepts broad philosophy of organisational milieu being studied

Figure 3.4 Purposes of research

Some researchers continue to be driven by this goal in all or some of their research, and work in an institutional environment, typically a university, where it can be pursued. Much unfunded research undertaken by academics in their own time is of this nature. But even in such a 'pure' situation, other, less noble, although not necessarily illegitimate, purposes may be involved – for example personal career advancement.

Ideological/political. Many academic researchers are motivated in whole or in part by an ideological or political agenda. It could be said that *all* are so motivated, and in certain areas of the social sciences this is a valid point. Many social scientists might be described as *reformist*, in that they are motivated by a general desire for a more equitable or just society and their research will tend to be at least be consistent with such a goal, if not centrally concerned with it. Thus, for example, much leisure research is concerned with equality and inequality of access to leisure opportunities and much tourism research is concerned with unjust exploitation of host communities. Similarly, in both fields, environmental protection and sustainability is often an implicit or explicit concern.

If none of these concerns is apparent, but the research is dealing with social issues, the implicit stance may be taken as *conservative* – implying contentment with the political, social and/or economic *status quo*. In contrast some researchers are guided by one or more of a number of ideological positions which seek fundamental change in society and might be described as *radical* or *critical*. In Chapter 2 the concept of *standpoint research* was noted. On the right of the political spectrum is radical 'New Right' thinking which endorses market processes and seeks their extension and might be termed *neo-liberal*. There is relatively little research in leisure studies with this outlook, although it is implicit in some tourism research which is concerned with the economic development of tourism.

By contrast, there are researchers who, in the words of Yvonna Lincoln (2005: 165), are 'committed to seeing social science used for democratic and liberalizing social purposes'. Researchers on the left with, for example, neo-Marxist beliefs, are often explicit about the political purpose of research. Thus neo-Marxists John Clarke and Chas Critcher state: 'the study of leisure for its own sake . . . is an irrelevancy. The purpose of studying any particular element of the social order is to . . . understand the ways in which one particular element is shaped by other structures . . .' (Clarke and Critcher, 1985: xiii) and in the epilogue to their book they discuss how 'socialism as a movement might benefit from an active appreciation of leisure' (p. 232). Researchers with radical feminist beliefs seek to combat patriarchal power: for example, Betsy Wearing seeks to develop the concept of leisure as 'a potential site for resistance to and subversion of hegemonic masculinity' (Wearing, 1998: xvi). In tourism, Philip Pearce (2005: 15) notes that 'some scholars want to see researchers generate more powerful emancipatory perspectives on social life'.

Policy/management. The purpose of policy or management-related research seems obvious enough: to address policy or management problems. But the stance adopted can vary and can be affected by the ideological positions outlined above. Some research might be seen as *critical*, in that it steps outside the policy or management milieu of the public or private sector organisations being studied and adopts a reformist or leftist stance when it critiques processes such as privatisation or 'managerialism' or seeks to demonstrate the inequitable outcomes of certain policies or management practices. Research which seeks to make private sector operations more efficient or profitable and generally accepts the broad philosophical stance of the field being studied can be seen as *instrumental*.

2. Review the literature

Introduction

The process of reviewing the existing research literature is sufficiently important for a complete chapter to be devoted to it in this book (Chapter 6). 'Reviewing the literature' is a somewhat academic term referring to the process of identifying and engaging with previously published research relevant to the topic of interest. The process can play a number of roles, as listed in Figure 3.5 and discussed further in Chapter 6.

In many cases the review undertaken in the early stages of the research has to be seen as a preliminary or interim literature review only, since time does not always permit a thorough literature review to be completed at the start of a project. Part of the research programme itself may be to explore the literature further. Having investigated the literature as thoroughly as possible, it is usually necessary to proceed with the research project in the hope that all relevant material has been identified. Exploration of the literature will generally continue for the duration of the project. Researchers always run the risk of coming across some previous – or contemporaneous – publication which will completely negate or upstage their work just as they are about to complete it. But that is part of the excitement of research! In fact, unlike the situation in the natural sciences, the risk of this happening in the leisure and tourism field is minimal, since research in this area can rarely be replicated exactly. In the natural sciences research carried out in, say, California can reproduce exactly the findings of research carried out in, say, London. In leisure and tourism research, however, this is not the case – a set of research procedures carried out in relation to residents of California could be expected to produce very different results from identical procedures carried out in London – or even

---

- Entire basis of the research
- Source of ideas on topics for research
- Source of information on research already done by others
- Source of methodological or theoretical ideas
- Basis of comparison
- Source of information that is an integral/supportive part of the research

---

Figure 3.5 Roles of the literature in research

New York – simply because leisure and tourism research is involved with unique people in varying social settings.

Conducting the review

Where possible, attempts should be made to explore not just published research – the *literature* – but also unpublished and on-going research. This process is very much hit and miss. Knowing what research is on-going or knowing of completed but unpublished research usually depends on having access to informal networks, although some organisations produce registers of on-going research projects. Once a topic of interest has been identified it is often clear, from the literature, where the major centres for such research are located and to discover, from direct approaches or from websites, annual reports or newsletters, what research is currently being conducted at those centres. This process can be particularly important if the topic is a 'fashionable' one. However, in such cases the communication networks are usually very active which eases the process. In this respect papers from conferences and seminars are usually better sources of information on current research than books and journals, since the latter have long gestation periods, so that the research reported in them is generally based on work carried out two or more years prior to publication.

As discussed in Chapter 6, a review of the literature should be concluded with a *summary* which provides an overview of the field, its substantive and methodological merits and deficiencies or gaps, and an indication of how such conclusions are related to the research task in hand.

What discipline?

In an academic context, especially for undergraduate or graduate projects, it is helpful to consider what *discipline(s)* the project relates to. In some cases this is obvious because the project is linked to a particular disciplinary unit – for example, marketing. In other cases the project is a capstone exercise in a degree course which may draw on one or more of any of the subjects studied in the course. Often, the fact that a topic does not have an obvious disciplinary label results in student researchers failing to draw on available disciplinary theories and frameworks and failing to take the opportunity to demonstrate the knowledge they have gained during the course of their studies. For example, if the research topic is to do with the subject of *golf*, searching library catalogues and databases using the keyword 'golf' will undoubtedly produce a certain amount of useful material. But consideration of whether the focus of the study is to be on golf management, golf marketing, the social context of golf or the motivations of golf players opens up the possibility of applying generic theories and relating the research to comparable studies on other phenomena in the area of management, planning, sociology and psychology respectively. An important question to ask is, therefore: what disciplinary field(s) is this research related to? What theories and ideas can be drawn from the literature in this discipline or these disciplines?

3. Devise conceptual framework

The idea of a conceptual framework

The development of a conceptual framework is arguably the most important part of any research project and also the most difficult. And it is the element which is the weakest in many research projects. A *conceptual framework* involves *concepts* involved in a study and the *hypothesised relationships between them*.

In this discussion the term conceptual framework has been used to cover a wide range of research situations. Thus such a term can be used in applied research when the framework adopted might relate to such activities as planning or marketing. In such cases, ideas for conceptual frameworks may readily be found in the planning or marketing literature. When the research is more academically oriented, the term *theoretical framework* might equally well be used. Miles and Huberman, in their book on *Qualitative Data Analysis*, describe conceptual frameworks as follows:

> A conceptual framework explains, either graphically or in narrative form, the main things to be studied – the key factors, constructs or variables – and the presumed relationships among them. Frameworks can be rudimentary or elaborate, theory-driven or commonsensical, descriptive or causal. *(Miles and Huberman, 1994: 18)*

Different types of research – descriptive, explanatory or evaluative – tend to call for different styles of conceptual framework. *Descriptive research* rarely requires an elaborate conceptual framework, but clear definitions of the concepts involved are required. In some cases this can nevertheless be a considerable undertaking: for example, considerable thought is required when the descriptive task is to discover people's time use and a taxonomy and associated coding system must devised for every conceivable form of leisure and non-leisure activity (see Burton, 1971), or when the task is to gather data on the many types of tourist expenditure and activity. Both *explanatory* and *evaluative* research call for well-developed conceptual frameworks which form the basis for the explanation or evaluation work required from the research.

One reaction to this discussion of conceptual frameworks is to observe that the approach seems inconsistent with the apparently more inductive approach, as discussed in Chapter 2, in which theory is derived from the data rather than data being used to test pre-existing theory. In particular, it seems inconsistent with the more apparent approaches such as grounded theory and informal, flexible approaches used in qualitative research. However, as Miles and Huberman indicate, conceptual frameworks are just as vital for qualitative research as for quantitative – arguably more so. In the context of qualitative research, Karla Henderson uses the term 'working hypothesis' to indicate that an initial framework may lack detail and may be subject to change as the research unfolds:

> A researcher conducting an inductive qualitative study should have a broad research question, conceptual framework, or working hypothesis in mind when beginning a project and, subsequently, as data collection begins. . . . however, a researcher

must be willing to let the working hypothesis metamorphose as the study progresses. *(Henderson, 2006: 79)*

In fact, a conceptual framework need not be a straitjacket: it can be a flexible, evolving device. As discussed in Chapter 9, in qualitative research, theory development and data collection and analysis are often intertwined, rather than being sequential. But the researcher rarely starts with an absolutely blank conceptual framework – there is usually some sort of rudimentary framework drawn from the literature or other sources. At the minimum there will be an initial list of relevant concepts with which the researcher is concerned and without which it is difficult to know what questions to ask or what issues to explore. In some cases the researcher may start with a framework from the literature which is seen as unsatisfactory in some way: the aim of the research then is not to validate the framework but to do the opposite and replace it with an improved – and possibly very different – model. The conceptual framework drawn up at the beginning of the research project can be seen as the 'first draft'; as data gathering and analysis proceeds, further drafts will emerge, incorporating new insights arising from the research. The developing conceptual framework becomes the focus of the research process.

The concepts identified and the framework within which they are set determines the whole course of the study. In exploring the conceptual framework for the study the researcher is asking: what's going on here? What processes are at work or likely to be at work? Sometimes the framework is developed from individual reflection or 'brainstorming' and sometimes it arises from the literature; indeed, an existing framework from the literature might well be used and merely adapted for application in a new situation. Where a number of areas of literature has been reviewed to provide the basis for the research, the skill is to draw the theoretical ideas together into a common framework – even if the aim is to show the incompatibility between two or more perspectives. Such links of course should be clearly and fully explained in the exposition of the framework.

Devising a conceptual framework

The development of a conceptual framework can be thought of as involving four elements, as depicted in Figure 3.6. The element 'Identification of concepts' should, perhaps, be the starting point, but this is rarely the case: the tendency is to think about relationships first, and then identify and define the concepts involved, as this becomes necessary. In fact the exercise is generally *iterative* – that is, it involves going backwards and forwards, or round and round, between the various elements until a satisfactory solution is reached. The four elements are discussed in turn below.

1. *Explore/explain the relationships.* Relationships may represent power relationships, influencing factors, money or information flows or simply a sequence of elements in a process. The postulated relationships correspond to the theory – however tentative – which underpins the conceptual framework. Explaining a conceptual framework may be a lengthy and complex process,

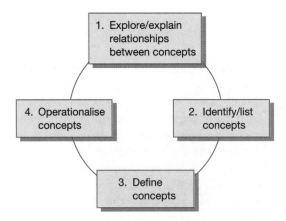

Figure 3.6   Development of a conceptual framework

especially when links with the literature are involved. The example in Figure 3.7 is very simple. It shows how the ideas develop from a simple statement (Stage A) to a more complex statement or series of statements (Stage C). In the example, the statements are expressed in the form of hypotheses; they could alternatively be expressed as questions, for example: 'To what extent is the decision influenced by income?'

One aid to the development of a conceptual framework is to use the device of a *concept map*, sometimes referred to as a *mental map* or *relevance tree*. While some concept maps are more self-evident than others, a concept map *is* only an

Stage	Statements/hypotheses (*concepts are in italics*)
A	*Participation* in a leisure or tourism activity arises as a result of an individual (or household/family) decision-making process.
B	Whether or not a person participates could depend on a variety of *events and circumstances*, for example: • the *availability of and access to facilities* may be good or bad; • *advertising and promotion* may vary in quantity and influence; • the *cost* of participation may be high or low; • a *chance event*, such as meeting up with a group of friends, may trigger *participation*.
C	Whether or not individuals participate will also depend on their *characteristics*, such as: • *age* • *income* • *personality* and • *past experience* in participating in that or similar experiences.

Figure 3.7   Exploration of relationships between concepts – example

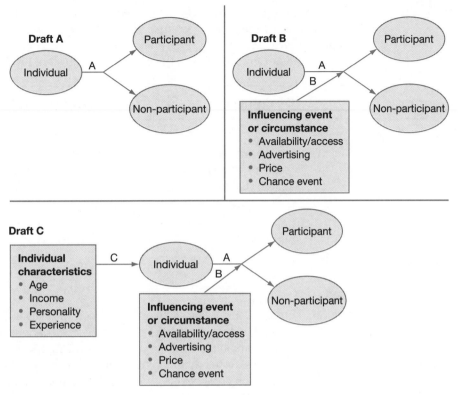

Figure 3.8 Concept map example

(Related to stages in Figure 3.7)

optional aid – a full narrative discussion and explanation always forms the core of the conceptual framework. A concept map merely illustrates or summarises the discussion.

Concept mapping can be seen as a form of visual 'brainstorming' and can be done alone or as part of a group exercise. The idea is to write down, on a piece of paper or a board or flip-chart, all the concepts which appear to be relevant to a topic, in any order which they come to mind. Then begin to group the concepts and indicate linkages between them. This is likely to involve a process of trial and error. Figure 3.8 illustrates diagrammatically the framework described in words in Figure 3.7. Three versions of the concept map correspond to the three stages in Figure 3.7.

The concept map then, depicts *concepts* – usually depicted in boxes or circles – and the *relationships* between concepts, which are usually represented by lines between the concepts, with or without directional arrows. Different types of concept might be represented by different shaped boxes. The concepts and their relationships are explained in the accompanying text (Figure 3.7). The key relationships identified at stages A, B and C in the process are labelled accordingly.

2. *Identify/list concepts*. Concepts are general representations of the phenomena to be studied – the 'building blocks' of a study. Concepts emerge in the discussion of relationships and the concept mapping process: here we formally identify, recognise and list them. They might involve types of individuals (e.g. manager, customer), groups of individuals (e.g. gang, community) or organisations (e.g. firm, government) of their characteristics or actions. The first column of Figure 3.9 lists the concepts encountered in Figures 3.7 and 3.8.

Concept*	Definition	Operationalisation
1. Participant		
a. In leisure	Person who engages in relatively freely chosen activity during leisure time.	Participation in activity identified as 'leisure' at least once in preceding year.
b. In tourism	Person who travels away from home for leisure purposes.**	Travel for leisure purposes at least 40km from home with at least one overnight stay in preceding 3 months.
2. Influencing event or circumstance		
a. Availability of/access to:		
• Leisure facilities	Preferred leisure facilities at affordable price available in home community.	Range of facilities within day-trip range at or below a various 'benchmark' costs, e.g. £10, £20, £30 a head.
• Tourism opportunities	Holiday services at preferred destination available at affordable price.	Range of two-week holidays of different sorts available at a range of 'benchmark' costs, related to household income.
b. Advertising/ promotion	Leisure/tourism advertising/promotion to which individual is exposed.	Individual's recall of a specified list of advertisements/promotions in past three months.
c. Cost (of participation)	Total cost of leisure/tourism experience.	Costs of ranges of activities as indicated in 2a and 2b above.
d. Chance event	Unplanned occurrence which affects decision to participate.	Events which individual claims affected recent decisions to participate: experience, advice from friend/relative, item read or seen in the media.
3. Individual characteristics	Individual attributes (which influence leisure/tourism decisions), for example:	
	a. Age	a. Age last birthday
	b. Income	b. Annual household income before tax
	c. Personality	c. Results of Myer-Briggs test
	d. Past leisure/tourism experience	d. Leisure: activities undertaken in past six months (from checklist); Tourism: trips taken in past five years.

Figure 3.9   Examples of concepts – definition and operationalisation

* Concepts appearing in Figure 3.8, Draft C.
** NB some definitions of tourism include other purposes, such as business.
† The words in brackets apply specifically to this study.

3. *Define concepts.* Concepts must be clearly defined for research purposes. Dictionary definitions or definitions from the research literature may be used, but it is often necessary to be selective or adaptive. Figure 3.9 column 2 includes suggested definitions for the concepts listed. Definitions might be very rudimentary in the early stages of the exercise and become more detailed and complex with time: as we talk about 'X' we have to clarify 'exactly what we mean' by 'X'.

4. *Operationalise concepts.* The terminology used to describe the process of *operationalisation* depends on whether a concept is quantitative or qualitative in nature or in its treatment:

● Quantitative: operationalisation involves deciding *how the concept might be measured.*

● Qualitative: operationalisation process involves deciding how the concept might be *identified, described or assessed* when conducting qualitative research, such as in-depth interviews.

Examples of operationalisation of concepts are shown in Figure 3.9 column 3. Most of the concepts listed lend themselves to quantification and measurement, at least in part, but concepts 2a, 2b and 2d have qualitative characteristics and could be treated either way. The question of measurement is discussed more fully in Part II of the book, particularly in Chapter 7.

To some extent operationalisation involves thinking ahead as to how information might, in practice, be gathered about a concept: it is an indication of the practical implications of the definition. Often arbitrary or pragmatic choices have to be made in order to 'operationalise' the project. For example, should 'leisure participation' involve 'regular' participation to be counted as 'participation' or is 'once a year' adequate? Or, what distance should someone have to be travelling away from home to be classified as a 'tourist' – 40km or 50km or 25km? These may be arbitrary decisions, or decisions based on the need to gather data which is comparable to other, existing, data.

Case study 3.1 presents an example of a discussion of the operationalisation of concepts from the literature.

Models

A theoretical framework might also be called a *model*, particularly when the research is quantitative in nature. For example the relationship between holiday-taking and a person's social and economic circumstances could be expressed in quantitative modelling terms as shown in Figure 3.11. A survey of holiday-taking would identify various groups with different levels of income and holiday frequency, and statistical analysis could be used to 'calibrate' the equation, that is find values for the 'parameters' a and b, so that the level of holiday-taking of a particular group could be predicted once the average income of that group was known. In Figure 3.11 hypothetical parameters of 0.1 and 0.05 are presented to illustrate the approach and an example is given of how

Case study 3.1   Operationalisation of concepts

Figure 3.10 summarises the discussion of the operationalisation of concepts used by Patrick West (1989) in a study of the use of parks by ethnic minorities in Detroit. The study sought to discover whether black and white Detroit residents had different pattens of use of city parks and regional parks and whether black residents' use of parks was constrained by ethnic sub-cultural tastes, marginality (limitations of income or transport) or racial discrimination. Figure 3.10 presents the information in tabular form, but in the article it is presented in narrative form over two pages.

Concept	Definition	Operationalisation
City park	Park within the city	All parks within Detroit city boundaries
Regional park	Park outside the city	All parks located in three counties surrounding Detroit city
Race	Ethnic/racial identity	Subjects' response to self-identification question with the following categories: black, Hispanic, white, other
Marginality	Limitations on participation due to a. limited income or b. access to transportation	*Objective indicators*: a. annual income and b. automobile ownership *Subjective indicators*: subjects' reported perception of barriers to park use: a. 'expense', b. transportation
Sub-cultural preferences	Unconstrained preference for use or non-use of parks	Coded responses to open-ended question on non-use of parks or reasons for not using parks more often, such as 'no interest' or 'prefer to do other things'
Inter-racial constraints	Actual or subjective feelings of racial discrimination resulting in feelings of being 'uncomfortable' or 'unwelcome' in parks	Coded responses to open-ended questions on reasons for use/non-use of parks and specific questions on experience of 'negative reactions of other people' in parks

Figure 3.10 Examples of operationalisation of concepts
Source: West (1989)

Conceptual framework/theory	The frequency of holiday-taking of a particular group is positively related to the group's average level of income
Concepts/variables	H = average number of holiday trips per year N = annual income in £000s
Relationship/equation	$H = a + bN$
Example of calibrated equation (value of a and b found from survey-based research)	$H = 0.1 + 0.05N$
Use of the equation for prediction (assume N = £30k)	$H = 0.1 + 0.05 \times 30 = 0.1 + 1.5 = 1.6$ trips a year

Figure 3.11 Conceptual framework as quantifiable model

such an equation might be used to estimate or predict holiday expenditure of groups with given income levels, now or in the future. The technicalities of the statistical process are not pursued further here, but are touched on again in Chapter 17, when the technique of regression is discussed. More complex models could be developed, including, perhaps, people age, occupation, the price of travel, exchange rates, and so on. Indeed, such models are used to predict future tourism demand to and from different countries and regions.

Examples of conceptual frameworks in leisure and tourism studies

Leisure participation. The example conceptual framework presented in Figure 3.8 relates to leisure participation decision-making, including the decision to take a holiday. A more elaborate version of a framework related to this topic is presented in Case study 3.2 and other examples in the research literature are indicated in the Resources section.

Case study 3.2	Conceptual framework for a holiday/leisure facility choice study

In a 1992 paper entitled 'Tourist motivation: life after Maslow', Christine Witt and Peter Wright (Witt and Wright, 1992) seek to move tourist motivation theory beyond reliance on Maslow's famous 'hierarchy of needs'. They review a range of other motivation theories and note that most deal with what people need, but do not involve consideration of how such needs will be met and therefore have limited usefulness in the context of tourism studies. They suggest the use of *expectancy theory*, developed largely in the context of work motivation. Expectancy theory models the individual's *expectations* regarding the likelihood that a course of action satisfying his or her needs and the extent to which the need will be satisfied. When applied to holiday destination

▶

choice, the model involves consideration of the importance of certain holiday attributes (such as warm climate, interesting surroundings) in satisfying an individual's needs and the individual's assessment of the extent to which a certain destination has these attributes and is therefore likely to satisfy his or her needs. Feedback processes suggest that each holiday experienced will contribute to the development of the individual's understanding and knowledge of destination attributes and their relationships with his or her needs. Witt and Wright develop a diagrammatic representation of the model, which serves as a conceptual framework not for a single research project but for research projects on destination choice in general.

The model developed could also apply to non-holiday leisure experiences, so the version presented in Figure 3.12 is relates not just to holiday destinations but to holiday destinations and leisure facilities.

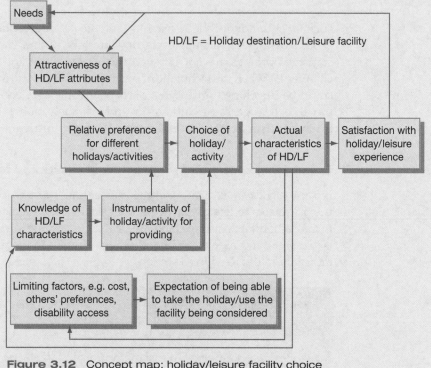

Figure 3.12   Concept map: holiday/leisure facility choice

Source: Based on Witt and Wright (1992: 50)

Management/policy research. In many cases research is part of a specific management task, of the sort discussed at the end of Chapter 1 and listed in Figure 1.6. In these cases the conceptual framework for the research may be part of a wider task. Often the 'research question' is clear from the beginning, because it is to resolve the management problem or task. Planning, marketing or management frameworks from the applied literature may be used as the basis for the research framework. Three examples are given in Figures 3.13–15.

Figure 3.13 presents a generic concept map of research which might be conducted for *performance evaluation*, as indicated in step 8 of the rational-comprehensive model of the management process shown in Figure 1.4. Typically, the progress towards achievement of objectives in a corporate plan or strategy is measured by *key performance indicators* (KPIs), which must often be obtained by some sort of research. Thus, for example, an objective to increase event visitor numbers would have associated with it a KPI which would call for

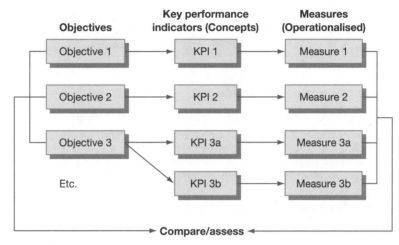

Figure 3.13   Concept map: performance monitoring

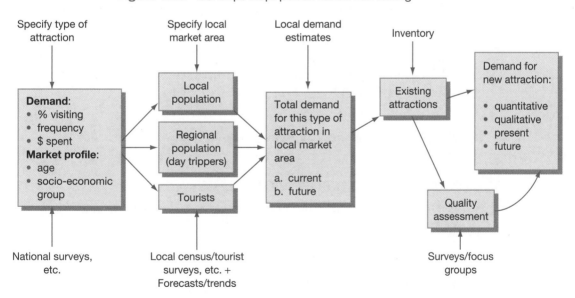

Aim: to assess the size and nature of the market for a potential new tourist/leisure attraction.

Strategy (concepts are indicated in italic): 1. to obtain information on the general level of *demand* for *this type of attraction* in the community at large, and the *market profile* of visitors to existing similar attractions, using national or regional data; 2. to estimate the *current level of demand* and *future level of demand* for this type of attraction in the specified *market area*, based on *local demand*, *day-trip demand* and *tourist demand*; 3. to assess *existing provision* of this type of attraction in the locality and the likely *market share* which the new attraction might attract; 4. to conduct a consumer study of *quality* of existing provision to guide developers on the design of the proposed new attraction.

Figure 3.14   Conceptual framework: market research study

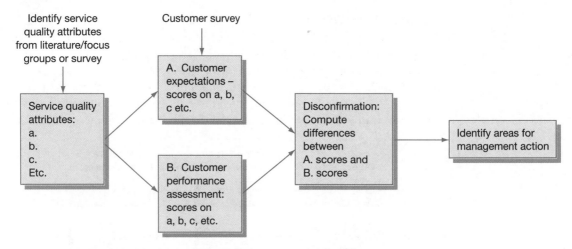

Aim: To assess customers' satisfaction with a leisure/tourism facility/service.

Strategy (concepts in italic): Use the SERVQUAL approach to customer service quality measurement (see Parasuraman *et al.*, 1985; Howat *et al.*, 2003), which compares customers' *expectations* concerning various *attributes of service quality* with customers' assessment of actual *performance* of the service in regard to those attributes. The *difference* or *disconfirmation* between the two assessments provides information for managers on areas of service quality which require *management action*.

Figure 3.15   Conceptual framework: customer service quality study

periodic measurement of the number of event visitors. Figure 3.14 concerns a market research study for a proposed new facility or attraction, while Figure 3.15 concerns a customer service quality study using the SERVQUAL approach. The latter is similar to what is sometimes referred to as the *importance-performance* approach (see the Resources section).

Further examples of conceptual frameworks are presented in the case studies at the end of the chapter.

4. Decide research question(s)

Research question, problem or hypothesis?

The focus of a research project might be expressed as a *question*, a *problem* or a *hypothesis*.

● A question requires an answer.

● A problem requires a solution.

● A hypothesis is expressed as a statement, which must be proved 'true' (consistent with the evidence), or 'false' (not consistent with the evidence).

The differences and relationships between the question-based approach and the hypothesis-based approach are illustrated in Figure 3.16, which uses the *problem* of declining visitor numbers at a leisure/tourism site as an illustrative

Research question	Hypothesis
A. Simple version	
1. *Pose research question:* Why have visitor levels declined in the last two years at site X?	1. *State hypothesis:* Visitor levels declined in the last two years at site X because of the attraction of newer, better value sites.
2. *Conduct research*	2. *Conduct research*
3. *Answer:* Because of the attraction of newer, better value sites.	3. *Result:* Consistent with the evidence.
B. More detailed version	
1. *Pose research question:* Why have visitor levels declined in the past two years at site X?	1. *Develop hypotheses* Brainstorm/review literature/make enquiries as to range of possible reasons for decline in attendances.
2. *Develop research strategy* Brainstorm/review literature/make enquiries as to range of possible reasons for decline in visits. Compile list of possible reasons: a. attraction of newer, better value facilities b. declining income in local catchment c. downturn in tourist numbers d. decline in quality of the facility e. increase in prices.	2. *Formulate/state hypotheses:* Visit levels have declined because of: a. attraction of newer, better value facilities b. declining disposable income in local catchment c. downturn in tourist numbers d. decline in quality of the facility, or e. increase in prices . . . or a combination of the above.
3. *Conduct research:* Collect evidence/data to discover which reasons are plausible.	3. *Conduct research* Collect evidence/data and test all five hypotheses.
4. *Answer:* Because of the attraction of newer, better value sites.	4. *Results:* a. Consistent with evidence; b. Not consistent; c. Not consistent; d. Not consistent; e. Not consistent.

Figure 3.16   The research question vs the hypothesis

example. Two versions are offered, version A, the simple version, and the more complex version B, involving exploration of a range of possible answers in the question form and testing a range of hypotheses in the hypothesis form. In each case the left hand column uses the question form and the right hand uses the hypothesis form.

The hypothesis format is more common in the natural sciences while the research question format is more common in the social sciences. The latter lends itself to descriptive and inductive research, while the former is more appropriate for explanatory and deductive research, as discussed in Chapter 2. For most of the book the research question format is assumed, but the hypothesis format is integral to certain forms of statistical analysis and so is used in Chapter 17.

Specific starting point

In some cases the research *topic* selected by the researcher is quite specific from the beginning and is initially expressed in the form of a question: the subsequent literature review and the conceptual framework are then the process by which this specific issue is analysed and placed in the context of existing knowledge. This is demonstrated in the example used in Figure 3.16 on declining visitor numbers at a site.

Decision-making models

The conceptual framework can involve *decision-making models* as presented in Figure 3.12 – that is, the research is designed to explore the causal factors and processes involved in people's decisions to visit a site or destination in order to discover how others might be persuaded to visit, or how existing visitors might be persuaded to visit again. The literature review would involve a review of similar existing models and a review of existing research on the various factors which influence people to choose a destination or visit a leisure site.

Area of interest

In other cases the topic is initially quite vague: it is an area of interest without a very specific focus. In such cases the literature review and the process of developing a conceptual framework help to focus the topic and determine what exactly should be researched. The aim is to focus the research on one or more very specific questions which can be answered by the research. This is inevitably an iterative process; a question that looks simple and answerable, once subject to thought, reading and analysis, often develops into many questions which become conceptually too demanding to deal with in one project or which cannot be managed in the time and with the resources available. In such a situation a smaller part of the problem must be isolated for research. This does not mean that the complex, 'big picture' must always be ignored – there is always a case, when writing up a research project, for setting it in its wider context and explaining how and why the particular focus was adopted.

Research questions or objectives?

Often research projects have a set of practical *objectives* but these should not be confused with research *questions*. Nor should objectives be confused with the list of *tasks* necessary to conduct the research – as discussed under *research strategy* below. Thus, for example, to say: 'The purpose of this research is to conduct a survey of a group of clients . . .' is to confuse ends with means. The survey, in this case, is being conducted for a purpose, to answer the research question(s), not as an end in itself. Of course, a research question can be embedded in an objective; thus it is possible to say:

The objective of this research is to answer the following question: Why are attendances falling?

The one possible exception to this rule is the sort of research project which is aimed at establishing a database for a range of possible future uses. For example, the national statistics office of most countries conducts the population census every five or ten years as a service to a multitude of users who use the data for a wide range of purposes – so 'conducting a census of the population' could be said to be the objective of the research project. But even in this case, most of the possible future uses are known: the project assumes at least a prior range of policy-oriented research questions, related to trends in ageing, educational needs, health matters, and so on. Few leisure or tourism researchers find themselves in this sort of 'open-ended' data collection situation: data should generally not be collected for their own sake or in the hope that they 'might come in useful'.

Primary and secondary questions

In most situations the idea of *primary* and *subsidiary* questions is helpful. The subsidiary questions are necessary steps towards answering the primary question. For example, in Figure 3.14, a number of unknowns are indicated in the diagrams, which could be turned into subsidiary research questions. Thus, in Figure 3.14 the 'market profile' could be translated into the subsidiary question: 'What is the profile of existing visitors to this type of attraction?' Compiling an inventory of existing competing local attractions presupposes the subsidiary question: 'What are the existing competing local attractions for the proposed development?'

5. List information requirements

The research question(s) and the conceptual framework should give rise to a list of *information requirements*. In some cases the information requirements are quite clear and the likely sources of information are straightforward. For example, in the case of the market research study in Figure 3.14, each of the concepts suggests the need for data to determine its nature or to measure it. This is illustrated in Figure 3.17, which indicates the information needs for the market research study. It also suggests some likely sources for this information. But some types of information can be obtained from a variety of sources, so the decision regarding the source of the information is a separate issue and is discussed further below. The information needs are only indicated in abbreviated form in Figure 3.17: for example, a 'market profile' for a particular type of attraction could involve more than just age and socio-economic group. This is clearly linked to the idea of 'operationalising' concepts, as discussed above.

6. Decide research strategy

Development of a *research strategy* involves making decisions on a number of aspects of the research process, as listed in Figure 3.18.

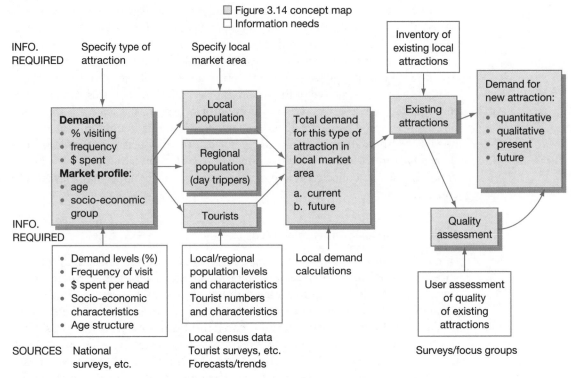

Figure 3.17   Information needs for the market research study (Figure 3.14)

---

a. Identify project elements/stages
b. Decide information gathering techniques to be used
c. Decide data analysis techniques to be used
d. Decide budget
e. Draw up timetable

Figure 3.18   Research strategy components

a. Project elements/stages

Often a research project will involve a number of different elements, or 'sub-projects' – for example, gathering of primary and secondary data or data gathering in different locations or in different time-periods. This is clearly illustrated in the project shown in Figure 3.14, where there is an initial 'sub-project' to establish the nature of the market, a second sub-project to assess the nature and scale of the local market base, then a third sub-project to estimate demand for the proposed attraction. A project may be devised in stages, particularly when one part is dependent on the findings from another. For example, stage 1 might involve some fieldwork in a particular location and, depending on the outcomes of stage 1, stage 2 might involve more in-depth work in the same location or conducting work in a second location.

b. Information gathering techniques to be used

It is at this stage that alternative information gathering techniques are considered. While the *operationalisation of concepts* and the identification of *information needs* processes may already have indicated certain types of information source, it is here that the detail is determined. For each item in the list of information needs, a range of sources may be possible. Judgement is required to determine just what techniques to use, particularly in the light of time and resources available, or likely to be made available.

A further review of the literature can be valuable at this stage, concentrating particularly on techniques used by previous researchers, and asking such questions as whether their chosen methods were shown to be limiting or even misguided and whether lessons can be learned from past errors.

The range of information gathering methods which are most likely to be considered at this stage are those covered in the following chapters of this book, namely:

● utilisation of existing information, including published and unpublished research and secondary data (Chapters 6 and 7);

● observation (Chapter 8);

● qualitative methods: including ethnographic methods, participant observation, informal and in-depth interviews, group interviews or focus groups (Chapter 9);

● questionnaire-based surveys: including household face-to-face surveys, street surveys, telephone surveys, user/site surveys, postal surveys (Chapter 10);

● experimental methods (Chapter 11);

● the case study approach (Chapter 12).

These individual techniques are not discussed further here since they are covered in general terms in Chapter 4 and in detail in subsequent chapters, as indicated. Where the process of information gathering involves going out into the field – for instance to conduct interviews or to undertake observation – the planning of *fieldwork* needs to be considered. In the case of experimental research the proposed programme of experiments would be considered here. If the proposed research does not involve primary data collection, then this will not be a consideration. Where extensive data collection is involved, then the organisation of fieldwork may be complex, involving recruitment and training of field staff (e.g. interviewers or observers), obtaining of permissions, including ethics committee clearance in universities (as discussed below), and organisation of data processing and analysis.

c. Approach to data analysis

Data analysis may be simple and straightforward and may follow fairly logically from the type of information collection technique to be used. This is particularly the case when the research is descriptive in nature. In some cases, however, the analysis of data may be complex and particular thought needs to be given to the time and the skills which will be required to undertake the analysis. Consideration must be given to the format of the data which will be collected and just how its analysis will answer the research questions posed. The planned analysis procedures have implications for data collection. For example, Case study 3.2 involves comparison of holiday-takers and non-holiday-takers, implying that an adequate sample of the two groups would need to be collected and ways would need to be found to compare their characteristics, patterns of holiday-taking, local leisure participation and perceptions. Where qualitative data are to be collected, for example using in-depth interviews, thought must be given as to how the results of the interviews will be analysed. Details of analysis methods which are appropriate and possible for different data collection techniques are discussed in subsequent chapters, but it must be borne in mind that when planning a project, full consideration should be given to the time and resources required not only to the *collection* of data but also to its *analysis*.

d. Budget and e. Timetable

In some situations key aspects of the budget and timetable are fixed. For example, students generally have only their own labour available and are typically required to submit a report by a specified date. Research consultants usually have an upper budgetary limit and a fixed completion date. In other situations, for example when seeking a grant for research from a grant-giving body, or permission to conduct an 'in-house' project, the proposer of the research is called upon to recommend both budget and timetable. Whatever the situation, the task is never easy, since there is rarely enough time or money available to conduct the ideal research project, so compromises invariably have to be made.

The research strategy and timetable can be represented in various graphical formats; examples are shown in Figures 3.19 and 3.20.

7. Obtain ethics clearance

Ethical behaviour is important in research, as in any other field of human activity. Certain ethical considerations, concerned with such matters as plagiarism and honesty in reporting of results, arise in all research, but additional issues arise when the research involves human subjects, in both the biological and social sciences. The principles underlying 'research ethics' are universal – they concern things like honesty and respect for the rights of individuals.

Professional groups, such as market researchers, have established explicit 'codes of ethics' to which members are obliged to adhere. Most universities now have codes of ethics enforced by ethics committees. Typically, undergraduate and graduate projects are covered by a generic code of behaviour,

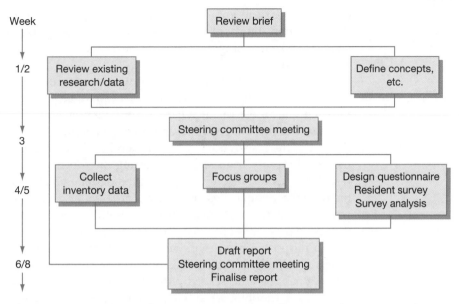

Figure 3.19 Example of research programme diagrammatic representation

Week:	1	2	3	4	5	6	7	8
Review literature								
Secondary data analysis								
Conduct survey								
Analyse survey								
Focus groups								
Meetings with clients	–			–		–		–
Write up report								

Figure 3.20 Example of research project timetable

but research proposals for theses and funded research by academics which involve humans or animals must be individually submitted for approval by the University Ethics Committee before the research can proceed.

Research ethics are considered in more detail in Chapter 4.

8. Conduct research

Element 8 is divided into two components: (a) data collection and (b) data analysis. These two components have not been presented as two sequential elements because in some research approaches, particularly qualitative methods, they are often intertwined; in other cases there are multiple data collection/ analysis tasks in a single research project, with some being contingent on the results of others.

Actually conducting the research is what the rest of the book is about, so it is not discussed in detail here. However, it cannot be stressed enough, that good research will rarely result if care is not taken over the preparatory processes discussed in this chapter. In a more positive vein, good preparation can ease the rest of the research process considerably. Often inexperienced researchers move too rapidly from stage 1, selecting the topic, to stage 8, conducting the research. This can result in the collection of data which is of doubtful use, and the researcher being presented with a problem of making sense of information which has been labouriously collected, but does not fit into any framework. If the above process is followed, then every item of information collected should have a purpose, since it will have been collected to answer specific questions or test specific hypotheses. This does not of course mean that the unexpected will not happen and 'serendipitous' findings may not arise, nor is it intended to ignore methodologies in which the framework – strategy – data collection/ analysis relationships are iterative in nature: it is intended to ensure that the core intellectual structure of the research is 'front of mind'.

It might be thought that inductive research, grounded theory and various forms of qualitative research require less preparation, but in practice this is rarely the case. As discussed in Chapter 9, in qualitative research it is certainly true that there is often a more fluid, evolutionary structure to the research design, but a sound preparatory base is still vital.

9. Communicate findings

The question of writing up of research results is not discussed in detail here because the whole of the final chapter of the book is devoted to this topic. Unlike the conduct of the empirical components of research, which inexperi- enced researchers invariably rush into too quickly, beginning the writing up of results is often delayed too long, so that insufficient time is left to complete it satisfactorily. An outline of the research process, as presented here, can itself be part of the problem, in that it implies that the writing up process comes right at the end. In fact, the writing of a research report can begin almost as soon as the project begins, since all the early stages, such as the review of the literature and the development of the conceptual framework, can be written up as the project progresses.

10. Store data

Data, in the form of questionnaires, images and audio and video tapes/disks, in various hard-copy and electronic formats must be securely stored during the conduct of a project and for a period of time after its conclusion. Particular ethical and legal issues arise in the case of personally identifiable data and these are discussed in Chapter 4. These matters are generally affected by legislation relating to privacy and rights of access to personal records. Some data may also be subject to freedom of information legislation.

Research organisations, such as universities, generally have policies on the minimum length of time for which hard-copy materials, such as questionnaires, and electronic data must be stored after completion of research projects, typically five years. Given the length of time sometimes taken for results to be published, this is seen as a necessary precaution in case errors are detected in published results which may need to be checked back to original data sources – for example, the errors can arise from mis-coding of questionnaires or in transferring of data from questionnaires or other sources into electronic form. Given that researchers may move on from institutions before the minimum storage time-period elapses, it is clearly necessary for institutions to have organised archiving and disposal systems. Of course, the ease of electronic storage means that this form of the data will generally be stored indefinitely. Re-analysis of data at a later stage and replication of research for comparative purposes often arises. In the case of longitudinal research, as discussed in Chapter 5, this is intrinsic to the method. This means that the data as stored should be easily accessible and readable by the original researcher and possibly others.

The research process in the real world

As noted in the introduction, the research process rarely proceeds in the ordered way depicted in Figure 3.1 and in the above discussion. The ten-element process is an idealised framework which underpins the actual process. It is also the sort of process which has to be outlined when planning the allocation of time in a project and when seeking funding. The idea that the process might not be entirely uni-directional is indicated by the fact that the first four elements are shown as connected in a circular process. Figure 3.21 shows some additional examples of iterative components of the process, and additional events which might occur during the course of research and cause revisions of any element. In some more inductive research processes iteration between the data and the research questions and conceptual framework is intrinsic to the approach and this can be conveyed verbally and diagrammatically in research proposals. This is particularly the case with qualitative methods, as discussed in Chapter 9.

Case studies

Two case studies are presented to demonstrate the first six elements of the research process shown in Figure 3.1. They are presented in somewhat

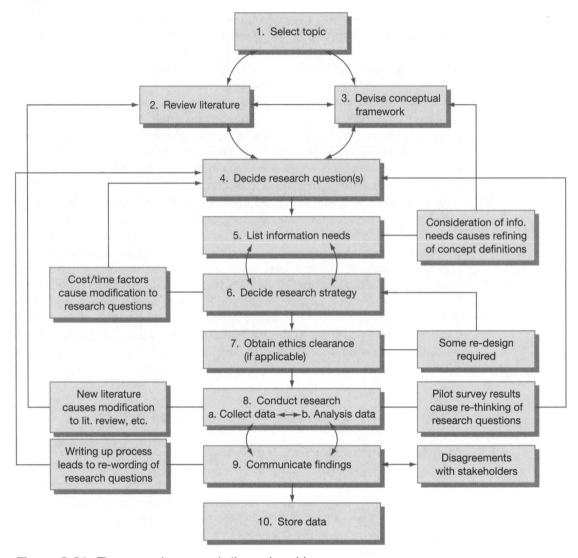

Figure 3.21 The research process in the real world

abbreviated form here, with longer versions available on the book's website. Using the terms introduced in Chapter 1:

● Case study 3.3, is *explanatory* research with evaluative features and arises from a hypothetical management problem; it seeks to find an explanation for a decline in the number of visitors to a leisure or tourism facility.

● Case study 3.4 is *evaluative* in nature, considering the relationship between a local council's objectives for leisure services and how its performance might be assessed.

Case study 3.3   Facility use: research design process

(Note: an extended version of this Case study is presented on the book's website.)

This case study outlines the sequence of six elements in the research process which lead up to the preparation of a responsive research proposal. The outline is presented in a summary form to illustrate the process.

1. Select topic

The topic has been presented by the management of a museum, but it could also apply to other types of leisure/tourism facilities. While attendances from tourists have been rising, attendances by members of the local community have been declining over a number of years and the management would like to know why.

2. Summary of literature review relevant to museum visitation

The literature to be reviewed covers museums and leisure/tourism facility management generally. There is an extensive research literature on museum visitors and part of the proposed research will therefore involve a detailed examination of this literature. At this planning stage three sources have been drawn on to provide a starting point for the study. The first two suggest that the decline could be related to trends in the general community, while the third suggests that the problem may lie with the management of the facility.

- Bennett and Frow (1991) show that gallery and museum users are over-whelmingly drawn from the more highly educated, higher income social groups.
- Rojek (2000: 22–4), suggests that the phenomenon of 'fast leisure' might be a characteristic of the postmodern age.
- The literature on customer service and service quality may therefore offer ideas on how to research the problem of declining attendances. The SERVQUAL model has been applied in leisure and tourism contexts (Williams, 1998; Howat *et al.*, 1996), as discussed in Figure 3.15, and relates customers' *expectations* concerning aspects of their experience with the *actual experience.*

3. Conceptual framework/theoretical discussion: models of facility visitation

The three literature resources examined above can be said to reflect different, but possibly complementary, models of leisure facility visiting/demand.

▶

Model 1 – Social class, etc. and demand: segmentation. The socio-economic characteristics of the catchment area population may have changed over recent years, resulting in a decline in numbers in the groups from which museum visitors are traditionally drawn. This suggests a simple model of changing *visitor demand*, based on the proposition that the changing level of visitor demand is determined by changes in the size of *target demographic demand segments* between the current time-period and some earlier time.

Model 2 – Perceived time-squeeze: fast leisure: Whether or not there have been changes in the size of the target demographic segments, Rojek's 'fast leisure' phenomenon could also be at work. Although it is difficult to assess this, if people *feel* that they are rushed, perhaps because of longer paid working hours and more demanding domestic commitments, this may affect their leisure behaviour and they may be able to articulate this change in a survey response.

Model 3 – Service quality. The SERVQUAL model relates visitors' *expectations* concerning aspects of a visit to the *actual experience*. It involves initial identification of *key service dimensions* (KSDs) which are seen as critical to management and visitors. Discrepancies between expectations and experience on the various KSDs – the pattern of *disconfirmation* – provides a guide to management on where action may be necessary. Current users may be first-time visitors or regular visitors who are tolerant of poor quality aspects of their visit, so *lapsed* visitors may be of more interest.

A concept map summarising the above discussion is presented in Figure 3.22. Figure 3.23 presents definitions of the concepts involved in the conceptual framework and indications as to how they might be operationalised.

4. Decide research questions

The primary research question and the subsidiary research questions arising from the conceptual framework are presented in Figure 3.24.

5. List information needs: what do we need to know?

Information needed to answer each of the subsidiary questions is listed in Figure 3.25 together with possible sources for the information.

6. Decide research strategy: studying the market

From the above process a number of elements of a possible research strategy emerge, as indicated in Figure 3.26. The feasibility of such a strategy will need to be evaluated in relation to available time and resources.

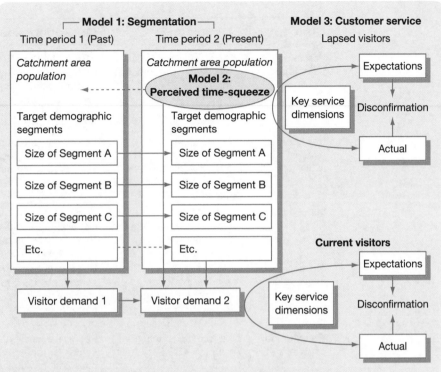

Figure 3.22 Facility use study conceptual framework

Concept*	Definition	Operationalisation*	IR**
Catchment area	Geographical area from which most visitors are drawn	Area where **70% of visitors live**	a.
Target demographic segments (TDS)	Demographic/socio-economic groups living in the catchment area and most likely to visit museums	• Segment A: **Managerial/ professional group** • Segment B: **35–44 age-group** • **etc.** (e.g. as indicated by ABS report 4114.0)	b., c.
Visitor demand	Current number of visits to the museum	Number of **visits in a calendar year** (see Figure 7.1 for alternative measures of leisure)	c.

Figure 3.23 Facility use study: list of concepts, definitions and operationalisation

* Items in bold are key operationalisation decisions.
** Information Requirements: see Figure 3.24.

Concept*	Definition	Operationalisation*	IR**
Perceived time-squeeze	Individual's subjective feeling of being pressed for time	ABS method: Individual response to question as to whether person **feels 'pressed for time'** – Always/ often, Sometimes, Rarely/never (e.g. as in ABS report 4153.0)	d., e.
Key service dimensions (KSD)	Those aspects of a service or visit considered important by visitors and/or management	List of key service dimensions **determined by focus groups** with visitors and management	f.
Lapsed visitors	Persons who have visited the museum but no longer do so	Lapsed visitors = persons who last visited the museum **more than 12 months ago**, but live within the catchment area	h.
Visitor expectations re KSD	The level of service/quality of experience visitors expect to find in regard to KSD	Response, using **Likert scales**, in regard to statements on the importance/expectations of each KSD	g., h.
Visitor actual experience	Level of satisfaction with the KSD	Response, using **Likert scales**, in regard to satisfaction with each KSD	g., h.
Disconfirmation	Discrepancy between expectations and actual experience re KSD	*Difference between expectation and satisfaction scores* for each KSD	g., h.

Figure 3.23   (*continued*)

Item	Information required	Likely sources
a. Catchment area	Data on where visitors to the museum travel from: 70% cut-off	User survey (new survey or museum's past survey if available)
b. Target demographic segments (TDS)	Data on demographic/socio-economic groups with high museum visit rates – for this museum (if available) or museums in general	ABS report No. 4114.0 or museum's past survey if available
c. Change in period 1 to 2 in: • TDS population numbers in catchment area • visitor demand at museum	For period 1 and period 2: • catchment area TDS numbers • annual visitor numbers in periods 1 and 2	• population census • museum's own data

Figure 3.24   Facility use study: information needs and likely sources

Item	Information required	Likely sources
d. Catchment area TDS and time-squeeze	Information on subjective feelings of catchment area TDS members	Survey of catchment area TDS
e. Time-squeeze effects on museum-visiting	Information on museum-visiting patterns of catchment area TDS members	Survey of catchment area TDS
f. List of key service dimensions (KSD)	Information on customers' and managers' views on important aspects of a museum visit	Focus groups of customers and managers
g. Current visitors' evaluation of expectations and actual experience re KSDs	Current visitors' scores on KSD expectation and actual experience scales	User survey
h. Lapsed visitors' evaluation of expectations and actual experience re KSDs	Lapsed visitors' scores on KSD expectation and actual experience scales	Catchment area social survey

Figure 3.24 (*continued*)

Primary question	Why are attendances at the museum falling?
Subsidiary questions General	a. What is the catchment area of the facility, from which most visitors are drawn?
Model 1	b. What are the target demographic segments (TDS) which are attracted to museums/this museum?
	c. What was the relationship between visitor demand and population in the TDSs living in the catchment area, between time-period 1 and time-period 2?
Model 2	d. Are people in the TDSs living in the catchment area feeling 'time-squeezed'?
	e. If the answer to d. is 'yes' – is this likely to be affecting museum visiting?
Model 3	f. What are the 'key service dimensions' (KSD) for the museum?
	g. What are *current* visitors' expectations, actual experience and disconfirmation with regard to the KSDs?
	h. What are *lapsed* visitors' expectations, actual experience and disconfirmation with regard to the KSDs?

Figure 3.25 Facility use study: research questions

Data collection method	Subjects	Purpose
Focus groups	Managers and users	Establish KSDs
On-site questionnaire-based survey	Current visitors	Establish catchment area of the facility Establish Target Demographic Segments (TDSs) Model 3: collect SERVQUAL data
Secondary data: population census	Catchment area population	Establish size of TDSs in catchment area – years 1, 2
Household survey	Catchment area population	Model 2: to establish extent of perceived time-squeeze Model 3: collect SERVQUAL data from lapsed users.

Figure 3.26   Facility use study: research strategy

Case study 3.4	Evaluating public recreation services: research design process

1. Topic

The topic is the evaluation of the performance of a public leisure or recreation service, such as that which might be provided by a local council.

2. Literature review

Hatry and Dunn (1971) suggest the following objectives for a public recreation service:

> Recreation services should provide for all citizens, to the extent practicable, a variety of adequate, year-round leisure opportunities which are accessible, safe, physically attractive, and provide enjoyable experiences. They should, to the maximum extent, contribute to the mental and physical health of the community, to its economic and social well-being and permit outlets that will help decrease incidents of antisocial behaviour such as crime and delinquency. *(Hatry and Dunn, 1971:13)*

Other literature will be examined in the course of the proposed study, but, meanwhile, from this statement a number of concepts, which constitute criteria for effectiveness, can be isolated:

- adequacy
- enjoyableness
- accessibility
- (un)crowdedness
- variety

- safety
- physical attractiveness
- crime avoidance
- health
- economic well-being.

3. Conceptual framework

The first criterion mentioned by Hatry and Dunn is adequacy and this is interpreted as the provision of a range of facilities and services which attract high levels of attendance. Achieving this is dependent on providing and managing services which: offer enjoyable experience and are accessible, uncrowded, varied, safe and physically attractive. The resultant high levels of usage, which could be termed effect 1, should lead to certain further social benefit outcomes, namely: a low/reduced level of crime; a high/enhanced level of health; and a high/enhanced level of economic well-being, which could be termed effect 2. These relationships are illustrated in the concept map, Figure 3.27. A list of concepts and their definitions and operationalisation is presented in Figure 3.28.

4. Research Questions

Main question

To what extent is the organisation achieving its goals in recreation provision?

Subsidiary questions

To what extent is the organisation achieving its goals with regard to: (a) adequacy; (b) enjoyableness; (c) accessibility; (d) (un)crowdedness; (e) variety;

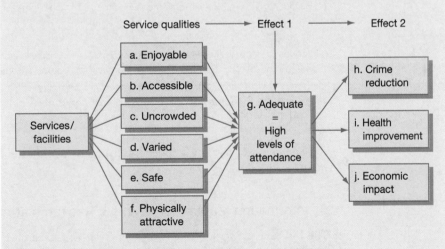

Figure 3.27 Recreation services project: concept map

Concept	Definition	Operationalisation
Service quality		
a. Enjoyableness	Providing pleasure for users/participants	User satisfaction
b. Accessibility	Facilities within x minutes and y kilometres travelling for all of the community	Persons living within x minutes and y kilometres of facilities
c. (Un)crowdedness	Facilities not perceived as crowded by users	Crowdedness indices (waiting times, ratios of use to capacity, user perceptions)
d. Variety	Range of different activities on offer	Number of different activities catered for
e. Safety	Accident-free environment	Number of accidents
f. Physical attractiveness	Facilities which appear attractive to users and interested non-users (e.g. neighbours)	Index of facility attractiveness (user and non-user perceptions)
Effect 1		
g. Adequacy of service/levels of use/ participation	Services which meet community demand; provision of access to all	Level of attendance; number of participants and non-participants; persons living within x minutes and y kilometres of facilities; crowdedness indices (waiting times, ratios of use to capacity, user perceptions)
Effect 2		
h. Crime avoidance	Services which help reduce crime by providing creative outlets for energies	Reported crime rates in community
i. Health	Facilities/services which promote health (e.g. through exercise)	Illness measures
j. Economic well-being	Facilities/services which contribute to jobs, income, etc.	Business income; jobs; property values

Figure 3.28 Recreation services project: concepts – definitions and operationalisation

(f) safety; (g) physical attractiveness; (h) crime avoidance; (i) health; (j) economic well-being?

5. Information requirements and 6. Research strategy

The information requirements arising from the research questions and the resultant research strategy are summarised in Figure 3.29.

Research question	Information requirements	Research strategy	
		Data source*	Data item
To what extent is the organisation achieving its goals with regard to the following?			
a. Enjoyableness	User satisfaction	A or B	User satisfaction
b. Accessibility	Measure of community accessibility to facilities	C	Spatial analysis for each residential zone: % of persons living within x mins and y km of facilities
c. (Un)crowdedness		D A	Ratios of use to capacity User perceptions of crowding, waiting times
d. Variety	Measure of variety	D	Number of different activities catered for
e. Safety	Measure of safety	D	Number of accidents per facility/type of facility
f. Physical attractiveness	Measure of facility attractiveness	i A ii B	Index of perceived facility attractiveness for: i. users, ii. non-users
g. Level of use	Use levels of facilities	i D ii B	Number of visits per facility and per facility type per annum for i. formal (ticketed) and ii. informal (e.g. parks) facilities
h. Level of crime	Measure of crime levels	C	Level of crime of various types (violence, vandalism, etc.) at beginning and end of planning period
i. Community health	Measure of community health	C	Level of community health of various types (physical, mental) at beginning and end of planning period
j. Economic well-being	Measure of economic well-being	C	Level of economic well-being (employment, business investment, property values, etc.) at beginning and end of planning period

Figure 3.29 Recreation services project: information requirements and research strategy

*A. On-site user surveys, B. Household/community survey, C. Secondary data: (population census, community crime statistics, community health statistics, economic data), D. Management data.

Research proposals

Introduction

Research proposals of two broad kinds are discussed here.

- *Self-generated* – proposals of the sort prepared by students seeking approval for research for a project or thesis on a topic of their own choosing or by academics seeking funds for a research project of their own devising.

- *Responsive* – proposals prepared by consultants responding to research briefs prepared by potential clients, sometimes simulated in the teaching environment with student projects for real or hypothetical client organisations.

Planners and managers seeking 'in-house' resources to conduct research fall somewhere between the two situations described.

In each case the proposal is a written document, which may or may not be supported by an oral presentation, and which must be convincing to the person or persons who will decide whether the research should go ahead. The writers of a research proposal are faced with the difficult task of convincing the decision-makers of:

- the value of the research;

- the soundness of the proposed approach;

- the valuable and original insights which they will bring to the project; and

- their personal capability to conduct the research.

In some cases the decision-makers will be experts in the field, while in other cases they may be non-experts, so care must be taken to ensure that the proposal is understandable to all concerned. Clarity of expression and succinctness are often the key qualities looked for in these situations.

Self-generated research proposals

Academic research proposals, for student theses/projects or for academics seeking funding, must not only describe what research is to be done and how, but also provide a rationale for the choice of topic. The topic and its treatment must be seen to be appropriate, in terms of scale and complexity, to the particular level of project involved, be it an undergraduate project, a PhD thesis or a funded project involving a team of researchers over a number of years.

In general the academic research proposal must cover the material dealt with in this chapter. In some cases considerable work will already have been completed before the proposal is submitted. This could apply in the case of a PhD proposal, which might be based on as much as a year of preparatory work, or a proposal from an experienced academic who has been working in a particular field for a number of years. In such cases, the proposal may present considerable completed work on elements 1 to 6 of the research process as discussed above. The funding being sought may only be required to conduct the fieldwork part of the research and write up the results – elements 7 to 9 of the process. In other cases little more than the selection of the topic may have been completed and the proposal outlines a programme of funding to undertake elements 2 to 9 of the process. Some proposals contain a preliminary review of the literature with a proposal to undertake more as part of the project. Some proposals are very clear about the conceptual framework to be used, while in other cases only speculative ideas are presented. While bearing in mind, therefore, that there can be substantial differences between proposals of various types, the checklist in Figure 3.30 is offered as a guide to the contents of a proposal. A summary of a successful self-generated proposal is provided in Case Study 3.5.

Item	Element of Figure 3.1	Chapter
1. Background and justification for selection of topic	1	3
2. (Preliminary) review of the literature	2	3
3. Conceptual/theoretical framework/theoretical discussion	3	3
4. Statement of research questions or hypotheses	4	3
5. Outline of data/information requirements and research strategy	5, 6	3
6. Details of information collection methods: structured by the research strategy, but including:	6	
• outline of any additional literature to be reviewed		6
• summary of any secondary data sources to be used		7
• outline of empirical tasks to be conducted – qualitative and/or quantitative, including, as appropriate:		7–12
• sample/subject selection methods (Chapter 13)		13
• justification of sample sizes		13
• measures to ensure quality		7–12
7. Consideration of ethical implications	7	4
8. Details of data analysis methods	6	9, 11, 12, 14–17
9. Timetable or work/tasks	6e	3
10. Budget, where applicable, including costing of each element/stage/task	6	3
11. Report/thesis chapter outline or indication of number and type of publications	9	18
12. Other resources, researcher skills/experience/'track record' (necessary when seeking funds)	6d	3

Figure 3.30 Research proposal checklist: self-generated research

Case study 3.5	Example of a successful self-generated research proposal

This is a summary of Frawley *et al.* (2009), a research grant application to the University of Technology, Sydney, Faculty of Business Internal Grants programme. Results of the research can be found in Veal and Frawley (2009).

'Sport For All' and major sporting events

Introduction: Sport for All

'Sport for All' is a collective term used to describe a range of policies adopted by governments to promote active participation in sport in the community. The origins of the Sport for All movement lie with the Council of Europe in the 1960s but it is now espoused by governments worldwide and by the International Olympic Committee (IOC).

One among many measures adopted by governments to promote Sport for All is to support participation in, and the hosting of, major sporting events, such as the Olympic Games and the Commonwealth Games. Among the claimed public benefits of such events is inspiring people to themselves participate in sport, a process referred to as the 'trickle down' effect.

Research questions

Three issues are addressed in the proposed research:

1. Effectiveness of the 'trickle down' effect. Whether this effect actually works and, if so, whether it is cost-effective, is unknown. The evidence available on the effectiveness of the policy is at best anecdotal. The proposed research is concerned with the question of whether or not the trickle-down effect works.

2. Cost-effectiveness of the 'trickle down' effect. Public expenditure costs of supporting the Olympic Games have been related to the number of medals won, but if the 'trickle down' effect works, part of these costs should be set against the values of the social benefits of increased community participation in sport.

3. Administrative support to ensure the 'trickle down' effect. It seems likely that in some cases the trickle-down effect could work without intervention by sporting organisations or government – for example, in the case of people taking up individual activities which require little infrastructure. In other cases, such as team sports, increased participation may depend on sporting organisations' activities.

Existing research

There is a small but growing literature on the 'legacy' of major sporting events in host countries, particularly the Olympic Games, but very little of it is concerned with the mass sport participation legacy (De Moragas *et al.*, 2003). Exceptions are:

- Cashman (1999), who lists mass sport participation as just one of nine types of legacy;
- Hogan and Norton (2000), who note the lack of federal government emphasis on mass participation compared with elite sport;
- a 2001 review by the Australian Sports Commission which concluded that the evidence is not clear on whether the trickle-down effect was in operation in Australia following the Sydney 2000 Olympic Games;
- an analysis by the Australian Bureau of Staistics (Vanden Heuvel and Conolly, 2001) which suggested that a trickle-down effect following the Sydney 2000 Olympic Games could not be discounted;
- a preliminary analysis by Veal and Frawley (2009) which suggests a mixed picture among Olympic and non-Olympic sports, with some showing increases in participation in Australia after 2000, some a decline and some being stable;
- a study by Hindson *et al.* (1994) relating to New Zealand's participation in the 1992 Barcelona Summer Olympic Games and the Albertville Winter Olympic Games, which indicated very little impact on participation; and
- a report by Sust (1995) on a specific program developed in Barcelona around the time of the 1992 Olympics to encourage children's participation in sport.

The above research, while for the most part soundly based, is deficient in a number of respects:

- it tends to deal with only the immediate post-Sydney Olympics period, giving no indication of the sustainability of any detected changes in participation levels;
- it tends to deal with sport as a whole, but not individual Olympic and non-Olympic sports;
- there is no consideration of state/region-specific or city-specific participation levels;
- there has been little research on sporting club and sporting organisations' activities;
- there has been no consideration of costs of supporting major sporting events compared with the potential benefits of increased participation;
- Australian work has concentrated almost entirely on the Sydney 2000 Olympics.

The proposed research is designed to overcome the first four of these deficiencies. Additional funding may be sought to address the last two items.

Research plan (6)

- The study draws on data from the annual Exercise, Recreation and Sport Surveys (ERASS) conducted by the Standing Committee on Recreation and Sport (SCORS), over the period 2001–5 and the 1999, 2000 and 2002 Australian Bureau of Statistics Participation in Sport and Physical Activities (PSPA) surveys to examine whether, in regard to sport participation as a whole, there is evidence for a sustained 'trickle down' effect in Australia, before and after the Sydney 2000 Olympics, from 1998 to 2003.

- Using the same data sources, participation in individual Olympic and non-Olympic sports will be examined over the same period to determine whether there is evidence for a trickle-down effect for individuals sports.

- The published ERASS and PSPA reports contain state-specific data, but special tabulations will be obtained of state data broken down by metropolitan/non-metropolitan area, which yield data on capital cities – particularly Sydney, where the 2000 Games took place. While sample size limits the detail of this analysis, analysis will be undertaken using NSW and Sydney data to determine whether there is stronger evidence for any 'trickle down' effect in the host state/city.

- On the basis of item 3, five Olympic sports will be selected to examine the activities of governing bodies and clubs in regard to marketing and promotion activities before, during and after the Sydney 2000 Olympics. For each sport, this will involve examination of annual reports, interviews with officials of national (some Sydney-based and some Canberra-based) and state sporting governing bodies and interviews with managers of selected sport clubs.

Responsive proposals – briefs and tenders

A *brief* is an outline of the research which an organisation wishes to have undertaken. Consultants wishing to be considered to undertake the project must submit a written, costed proposal or *tender*. Usually briefs are prepared by an organisation with a view to a number of consultants competing to obtain the contract to do the research. In some cases potential consultants are first asked, possibly through an advertisement, to indicate their *expression of interest* in the project. This will involve a short statement of the consultants' capabilities, their track record of previous consultancies and the qualifications and experience of staff available. In some cases public bodies maintain a register of accredited consultants with particular interests and capabilities, who may be invited to tender for particular projects. In the light of such statements of interest or information in the register, a *shortlist* of consultants is sent the full brief and invited to submit a detailed proposal. In very large projects some financial compensation may be provided to shortlisted candidates to cover the costs of the work undertaken to prepare a more detailed tender. The successful tender is not usually selected on the basis of price alone (the budget is in any case often a fixed sum indicated in the brief) but on the quality of the submitted proposal and the track record of the consultants.

Briefs vary in the amount of detail they provide. Sometimes they are very detailed, leaving little scope for consultants to express any individuality in their proposals. In other cases they are very limited and leave a great deal of scope to consultants to indicate proposed methods and approaches. Client organisations experienced in commissioning research can produce briefs which are clear and 'ready to roll'. In other situations it is necessary to clarify the client's meanings and intentions. For example, a client might ask for a study of the 'leisure needs' of a community – in which case it would be necessary to clarify what the client means by 'leisure' – for example, whether home-based leisure, holidays, entertainment, restaurants or nightclubs are to be included. If a client asks for the 'effectiveness' of a programme to be assessed it may be necessary to clarify whether a statement of objectives or a list of performance criteria for the programme already exists, or whether that must be developed as part of the research.

Paradoxically, problems can arise when client organisations are over-specific about their requirements. For example an organisation may ask for a 'user survey' or 'visitor survey' to be conducted. It is not easy to decide what should be included in such a survey without information on the management or policy issues which the resultant data are intended to address. Is the organisation concerned about declining attendances? Is it wanting to change its 'marketing mix'? Is it concerned about the particular mix of clientele being attracted? Is it concerned about future trends in demand? It would be preferable in such a situation for the client to indicate the nature of the management issue and leave the tenderer to suggest the most suitable research approach to take, which might or might not include a survey.

Sometimes there is a hidden agenda which the potential researcher would do well to become familiar with before embarking on the research. For example, research can sometimes be used as a means to defuse or delay difficult management decisions in an organisation. An example would be where a leisure or tourism service is suffering declining attendances because of poor maintenance of facilities and poor staff attitudes to customers; this is very clear to anyone who walks in the door, but the management decides to commission a 'market study', in the hope that the answer to their problem can be found 'out there' in the market – when in fact the problem is very much 'in here', and their money might be better spent on improving maintenance and staff training than on research!

A situation where the client's requirements may seem vague is when the research is not related to immediate policy needs but to possible future needs or simply to satisfy curiosity. For example, a manager of a leisure or tourism facility might commission a visitor survey (perhaps because there is spare money in the current year's budget) without having any specific policy or management problems in mind. In that case the research will need to specify hypothetical or potential policy or management issues and match the data specifications to them.

What should a proposal contain? The first and golden principle is that it should *address the brief.* It is likely that the brief will have been discussed at great length in the commissioning organisation; every aspect of the brief is likely to be of importance to some individual or section in the organisation, so *all* aspects of the brief should be considered in the proposal. So, for example, if the brief lists, say, four objectives, it would be advisable for the proposal to indicate very clearly how each of the four objectives will be met. A proposal must therefore indicate the following:

● What is to be done?

● How it is to be done?

● When it will be done?

● What it will cost?

● Who will do it?

A typical responsive proposal might include elements as shown in Figure 3.31. An example of a brief and successful responsive proposal is provided on the book's website.

	Element	Chapter
1. Brief summary of key aspects of the proposal, including any unique approach and particular skills/experience of the consultants		
2. Re-statement of the key aspects of the brief and interpretation/ definition of key concepts		
3. Conceptual framework/theoretical discussion	3	3
4. Research strategy – methods/tasks	6	3
5. Details of information collection methods – structured by the research strategy, but including:	5, 6	
● outline of any additional literature to be reviewed	2	6
● summary of any secondary data sources to be used		7
● outline of fieldwork to be conducted – qualitative and/or quantitative		7–12
● sample/subject selection methods		13
● sample sizes and their justification		13
● measures to ensure quality		
6. Timetable of tasks, including interim reporting/meetings with clients/draft and final report submission	6	3
7. Budget: costing of each element/stage/task	6	3
8. Chapter outline of report and, if appropriate, details of other proposed reporting formats – e.g. interim reports, working papers, articles	9	18
9. Resources available, staff, track record		3

Figure 3.31 Research proposal checklist – responsive research

Summary

This chapter covers the process of planning a research project and preparing a research proposal. It is structured around eight 'elements':

1. selecting the topic;
2. reviewing the literature;
3. devising a conceptual framework;
4. deciding the research questions;
5. listing information needs;
6. deciding a research strategy;
7. obtaining ethics clearance (where relevant);
8. conducting the research;
9. reporting the findings; and
10. storing the data.

The term 'elements' is used rather than 'stages' or 'steps', since the ten elements do not always occur in the precise order indicated. In particular, the first elements listed take place in a variety of orders, often in an iterative process. The overview of the research process is followed by a discussion of research proposals – self-generated proposals, where the researcher initiates the research, and responsive proposals, which are prepared in response to a research brief from a commissioning organisation.

Test questions

1. In this chapter, it is suggested that a research topic might arise from eight different sources – what are the eight sources?

2. What is a concept?

3. What is meant by 'operationalisation' of a concept?

4. What is a conceptual framework?

5. What is the difference between a research question and a hypothesis?

6. What are the differences between a self-generated research proposal and a responsive research proposal and what implications do they have for the content of the two types of proposal?

Exercises

1. Select three articles from an issue of a leisure or tourism journal and identify the basis of their choice of research topic.

2. Select any article from a copy of a leisure or tourism journal and: (a) identify the key concepts used in the article; and (b) draw a simple concept map to show how the concepts are related.

3. Draw a concept map for a possible research project on either: (a) the effects of American culture on British leisure; or (b) the effects of the aging of the population on trends in tourism in Western countries.

4. Write a case study, similar in structure and length to Case study 3.3 on a topic of your own choice.

Resources

The best reading material for this chapter would be examples of successful research grant applications and proposals written in response to tenders. Completed research reports, whether academic or non-academic, vary in the amount of detail they provide about the development of the process.

- Approaches to tourism research: see Pizam (1994), Ryan (1995).

- Concepts in tourism: see Chadwick (1994).

- Selection of a research topic: see Chapter 2 of Howard and Sharp (1983).

- Stages in the research process: most general and specific research methods texts deal with the stages in the research process, for example: Gratton and Jones (2004: 32), Jennings (2001: 23–4), Kraus and Allen (1998: 108–9), Long (2007: 17), Mitra and Lankford (1999: 19), Riddick and Russell (2008: 14), Saunders *et al.* (2000: 5), Vaske (2008: 5).

- Influences on choice of topic/method, micro-politics/disputes in research: Punch (1994).

- Concept mapping: Brownson *et al.* (2008).

- Conceptual frameworks: Miles and Huberman (1994: 18–22).

- Examples of conceptual frameworks: leisure: Veal (1995), Brandenburg *et al.* (1982), Marans and Mohai (1991); tourism: Echtner and Ritchie (1993), Witt and Wright (1992).

- Importance-performance analysis: Veal (2010a: Ch. 13).

4 Research ethics

Introduction

Ethical behaviour is important in research, as in any other field of human activity. Ethical considerations, concerned with such matters as plagiarism and honesty in reporting of results, arise in all research, but additional issues arise when the research involves human and animal subjects, in both the biological and social sciences. Increasingly, ethical issues also arise in relation to research which may have an impact on the physical environment. The underlying principles of research ethics are universal: they concern things like honesty and respect for the rights of individuals and animals and the integrity of eco-systems. The issue came to the fore at the end of World War II when details were revealed of horrific experiments which had been conducted on prisoners in the German Nazi concentration camps, and certain medical experiments conducted in the United States in the 1960s and 1970s without the consent of the subjects (Loue, 2002). These events raised questions not only about the ethical conduct of research but also the use of findings from research conducted unethically. The result has been the establishment of international, national, professional and institutional codes of research ethics and their oversight by regulatory organisations.

An example of a code of research ethics is the document on the responsible conduct of research published in 2007 by a consortium of Australian organisations, which covered:

- honesty and integrity;

- respect for human research participants, animals and the environment;

- good stewardship of public resources used to conduct research;

- appropriate acknowledgment of the role of others in research;

- responsible communication of research results. (NHMRC *et al.*, 2007: 13).

In this chapter we consider:

- the institutional oversight of research ethics;

- ethics in the research process;

- ethical issues in research, including:
  - researcher competence;
  - subjects' freedom to participate or not;
  - informed consent;
  - risk of harm to subjects;
  - honesty/rigour in analysis, interpretation and reporting;
  - authorship and acknowledgements;
  - access to research information.

Institutional oversight of research ethics

Most universities now have their own codes of research ethics enforced by ethics committees. Typically, undergraduate and graduate projects are covered by a generic code of behaviour, but research proposals for student theses and funded and unfunded research by academics which involve human or animal subjects must be individually submitted for approval by the University Ethics Committee.

Codes of research ethics have intrinsic value in protecting the rights of humans and animals involved in research, but they also serve a professional and organisational function. Researchers may be subject to litigation and can lose professional indemnity if they are not seen to have adhered to the appropriate code of ethics. A related consideration is the question of public relations and the standing of organisations responsible for the research within the community. Some practices may be ethical, but still give offence, so the value of the data collected using such practices must be weighed against the ill-will which may be generated.

In universities and other research institutions research projects involving human or animal subjects are subject to approval by an ethics committee. Some universities have established ethics committees to cover the whole of the university, although usually there are at least two committees, covering human and animal-related research respectively. In some cases committees are faculty- or division-based. Typically the approval process involves the completion of an 'Application for Ethics Approval Form' which must provide full details of the rationale for the research, the methods to be used and qualifications of the researchers involved. The *National Ethics Application Form* of the Australian National Health and Medical Research Council (NHMRC, nd), which is a model for the use of Australian research institutions, runs to over 450 items of information.

When ethics committees are faculty/division-specific a researcher would expect committee members to be familiar with the research methods being used, but with university-wide committees there is a possibility that committee members might not be familiar with research methods being used by colleagues from very different disciplines, especially those using novel methods. This is believed by some to be the case with some qualitative methods which reflect a very different epistemology from the positivist approach of the natural sciences. This issue is argued by Yvonna Lincoln (2005) who notes 'increased scrutiny' from research committees in the United States 'largely in response to failures in biomedical research', but spilling over into the social sciences and resulting in '. . . multiple rereviews of faculty proposals for qualitative research projects and . . . rereviews and denials of proposed student research (particularly dissert- ation research) that utilise action research . . . methods, research in the subjects' own settings (e.g. high schools), and/or research which is predominantly qualitative in nature' (Lincoln, 2005: 167).

Ethics in the research process

Research ethics can be examined in regard to three dimensions: the nature of the ethical issue, the stage or component of the research process where the issues arise and whether the research subject is anonymous or identified.

Regarding the nature of the ethical issue, most codes of ethics and ethical practice are based on the 'golden rule' which relates to all human conduct and is endorsed by most religions, that is, that you should treat others as you your- self would wish to be treated. More specifically, the general principles usually invoked in codes of research ethics are that:

- the research should be *beneficial to society*;
- researchers should be suitably *qualified* and/or *supervised* to conduct the research;
- subjects should take part *freely*;
- subjects should take part only on the basis of *informed consent*;
- no *harm* should befall the research subjects;
- data should be *honestly* and *rigorously analysed, interpreted* and *reported*.

Ethical issue	Design/ organisation	Collection	Analysis/ interpretation	Storing data during project	Reporting	Storing data after project
Social benefit	●					
Researcher competence	●					
Subjects' freedom of choice		●				
Subjects' informed consent		●				
Risk of harm to subjects – anonymous		●				
Risk of harm to subjects – identifiable		●	●	●	●	●
Honesty/rigour in analysis/interpretation			●			
Honesty/rigour in reporting					●	

Figure 4.1   Ethics in the research process

These issues arise in different stages/components of the research process, as summarised in Figure 4.1.

Regarding anonymous versus personally identifiable data, in much primary empirical leisure and tourism research, for example on-site questionnaire-based surveys and much observational research, data are collected and stored anonymously: the researcher never knows the names of the subjects, so names are not recorded in any form. However, in some cases the names and contact details of individual subjects are known to the researcher and may be recorded in hard-copy or electronically as part of the data from the research.

The way these three dimensions relate to one another is shown in Case study 4.1. It can be seen that the question of identifiable subjects relates only to the storage and reporting of results components of the research. The ethical issues are discussed in turn below. Some examples of leisure and tourism research raising ethical issues are presented in Case study 4.1 and referred to in the discussion.

With regard to the design and conduct of research many codes of ethics deal with practices in laboratories, but this discussion is largely concerned with ethical conduct in the field – that is, with people in their own living environment, including leisure and tourism locations. As far as the reporting of results and storage of data are concerned, the same ethical principles apply, regardless of the methods involved.

Case study 4.1	Examples of ethical issues in leisure and tourism research

A. Deception in recreation/tourism survey research

In a celebrated case in outdoor recreation/tourism research, George Moeller and his colleagues (1980a) used incognito interviewers, posing as campers, to investigate campers' attitudes towards pricing using informal interviewing techniques. They discovered different results from those collected by formal interviews conducted by identified interviewers. It was believed that the views expressed to the incognito interviewers, which were more relaxed about possible price increases, were more truthful than views expressed to 'official' interviewers. However, the ethics of this practice raised considerable controversy in the *Journal of Leisure Research* (see Christensen, 1980, Moeller *et al.*, 1980b, LaPage, 1981).

B. Status of the participant observer in an outdoor adventure setting

Keith Donne (2006) conducted research for a PhD thesis as a participant observer at a watersports outdoor adventure centre involving a study of young people aged 14–16 years, who used the centre, and the professional instructors who worked at the centre. Among ethical issues he identifies during the experience were the following:

- In order to gain access to facilities involving contact with children it was necessary for the researcher to undergo an official police check to ensure that he had no prior criminal record.

- Donne describes the role he chose to play at the centre. Centre staff – mainly instructors – knew he was conducting research but it was necessary for him to indicate an appropriate level of expertise in watersports since he knew that 'appearing too knowledgeable could have resulted in confrontational situations' with the staff, while 'any pretence of incompetence' could have identified him as a liability He had personal skills in sailing and windsurfing, was a qualified kayak and canoe instructor and had competed at high level in canoe slalom. He decided to pose as 'an enthusiastic learner with a basic understanding and competence'. This mild level of deception was considered justified in the interests of successfully conducting the research.

- Early on Donne recognised two instructors at the centre whom he had taught in the past and who would be aware of his skill level and he had to take them into his confidence regarding his 'enthusiastic learner' role.

- When one of the centre instructors, who had been reluctant to be interviewed for the research, challenged Donne to a canoe race, he accepted but then regretted having done so because it placed him in a dilemma as to whether he should deliberately lose the race to secure the instructor's cooperation with the research.

C. Exposure by association in autobiographical research on elite sport coaching

Robyn Jones *et al.* (2006) discuss the example of a doctoral thesis on the relationship between an elite athlete (the researcher) and his coach, using the autobiographical method. The relationship between the two had deteriorated over time, with negative views expressed about the coach in the thesis. While a pseudonym was used for the coach, the author of the thesis was clearly identified and so, for people familiar with the athletics scene, the coach could be identified 'by association'. This was pointed out by one of the thesis examiners. The paper, involving the student and thesis supervisors, describes how the problem was dealt with in the final, approved, version of the thesis.

Ethical issues in research

Social benefit

Research on nuclear and chemical weaponry has given rise to the proposition that research should only be supported if its social benefits can be demonstrated. Such an assessment is, of course, subjective. Thus, during the Cold War, it was argued that research on nuclear weapons could be defended on the grounds that peace was maintained as long as each side – the West and the communist bloc – matched each other's weapons, in terms of technological sophistication as well as quantity, so that neither side would risk attacking the other: the principle of mutually assured destruction (MAD). In contemporary leisure and tourism research the issues are not as dramatic, but can arise in relation to funding sources: for example, should research funding be accepted from tobacco companies or from companies with questionable environmental practices?

Push polls

In 1995 the US National Council on Public Polls issued the following media release about:

> . . . a growing and thoroughly unethical political campaign technique, commonly called 'push polls', masquerading as legitimate political polling. . . . A 'push poll' is a

telemarketing technique in which telephone calls are used to canvass vast numbers of potential voters, feeding them false and damaging 'information' about a candidate under the guise of taking a poll to see how this 'information' affects voter preferences. In fact, the intent is to 'push' the voters away from one candidate and toward the opposing candidate. This is clearly political telemarketing, using innuendo and, in many cases, clearly false information to influence voters; there is no intent to conduct research.

These telemarketing techniques damage the electoral process in two ways. They injure candidates, often without revealing the source of the information. Also, the results of a 'push poll', if released, give a seriously flawed and biased picture of the political situation. *(National Council on Public Polls, 1995)*

Push polling typically takes place in marginal electorates where a successful telephone campaign can have a significant impact on the election outcome. A typical push poll question would of the following format: 'Given that candidate X could increase income tax by 50%, whereas candidate Y is committed to no increases in income tax, how does this affect your voting intentions?' The results of the poll are of less interest than the planting of the false or misleading information about candidate X in the listener's mind.

Push polling occurs in the political realm and would rarely be relevant to leisure and tourism, but it highlights the ethical dimension of the use of the 'leading question', which is discussed further in Chapter 10.

Researcher competence

Research ethics guidelines require that those undertaking research have appropriate levels of training, qualifications and experience, including familiarisation with ethical issues.

Occasionally cases in which unqualified individuals are found to have been practising as doctors and even surgeons attract media publicity. The community is shocked that unqualified people should be undertaking such important work and the individuals are duly prosecuted. Such cases represent the extreme of public ethical concern because of the level of risk of harm involved. But the issue of professional competence, while less clear-cut in other areas, is nevertheless applicable. In leisure and tourism research a researcher who is not competent, through training and/or experience, to conduct research runs the risk of:

- wasting the resources of the funding organisation;

- wasting the time of subjects;

- abusing the goodwill of subjects;

- misleading the users of the research results; and/or

- damaging the reputation of the research organisation.

Free choice

It seems obvious that subjects should not be coerced to become involved in research projects, but there are some grey areas. Some of these are institutional and some are intrinsic to the design and nature of the research.

Captive groups

In universities, students are often used as subjects in research. In some places students are *required* to be available for a certain amount of experimental or survey work conducted by academic staff, and in some cases they receive study credit for this involvement. Although, no doubt, students can opt out of such activities, there is moral pressure on them to conform and possibly fear of sanctions if they do not. Clearly it is unethical for the university to allow such undue moral pressure to be brought to bear.

Other captive group cases involve classes of schoolchildren or members of organisations, whose participation is agreed to by the person in charge. Again, while opting out may be possible, in practice it may be difficult and the subject may be, to all intents and purposes, coerced. As a consequence education authorities generally place strict controls on the amount and type of research which may be carried using schoolchildren. Research in prisons and mental and other hospitals raises similar questions about genuine freedom of choice on the part of the subject.

Children

Research involving children raises particular ethical issues. At what age are children able to give informed consent to being involved in research? How does this relate to parents' and carers' rights and obligations? If children below a certain age are not deemed to be able to give consent on their own behalf, in what circumstances, if any, is it appropriate for carers to give consent on the child's behalf? Are there situations where the risk of physical or emotional harm is greater for children than for adults involved with similar research processes?

In general it is believed that particular care should be taken in conducting research involving children because they typically see adults – including researchers – as figures of authority. Thus they may be less likely than adults to exercise their right to non-cooperation. This is not only a human rights issue but can also raise validity issues if children see questions as some sort of performance test and/or feel a need to please the questioner by answering or behaving in certain ways.

Where institutions are involved, such as play centres or schools, those organisations will have their own guidelines, particularly in regard to the requirements for parental permission.

Official surveys

The principle of freedom of choice is constantly infringed by governments: it is an offence, for example, not to complete the population census forms or to refuse cooperation with a number of other official surveys. In these cases, the 'social benefit' argument relating to the need for accurate and complete data is considered to outweigh the citizen's right to refuse to give information.

Observation

In the case of some types of research where large numbers of subjects are involved – for example, studies of traffic flows, pedestrian movements or crowd behaviour – choice on the part of the subject is impossible. In many observational research situations, if the subjects knew that they were being observed they might well modify their behaviour, and so invalidate the research. This would apply particularly in situations where antisocial, and even illegal, behaviour may be involved. These considerations might apply in research ranging from people's interpersonal behaviour in a gym through to research on the milieu of prostitution, gambling or drinking.

Participant observation

The problem of freedom to participate arises particularly in research using participant observation where, as discussed in Chapter 9, the researcher is a participant in the phenomenon being studied. Examples are presented in Case study 4.1. The whole basis of such research may rely on the researcher being accepted and trusted by the group being investigated: this may not be forthcoming if it is known that the participant is a researcher. If the researcher does 'come clean', there is the risk – even the likelihood – of the subjects modifying their behaviour, thus invalidating the research. To what extent is it ethical for researchers to disguise their identity to the people they are interacting with and studying – in effect to lie about their identity? When researchers are involved with groups engaging in illegal and/or antisocial activities, for example drug-taking or some youth gangs, where do their loyalties lie? In some research methodologies a different approach is adopted and fully informed interaction between researcher and subjects is embraced and becomes part of the analysed and reported research.

If it is accepted that the research of this type is permissible, despite the lack of freedom of consent, then the issue of confidentiality in reporting, as discussed below, becomes even more critical.

Informed consent

In experimental research, where there is a risk, however remote, of physical harm to the subject (for example where allergies might be involved, or a risk of muscle strains, or even of heart attack), it is clearly necessary for subjects to be fully aware of the risks involved in order to be able to give their 'informed consent' to participate. The level of risk of harm is a matter of judgement, and often only the researcher is fully aware of the extent of risk involved in any given research procedure. This raises the question of the extent to which the subject can ever be 'fully informed'. Subjects can never be as fully informed as

1. Name of organisation conducting the research
2. Purpose of the research
3. Sponsoring/funding organisation, if applicable
4. Participants and how they are being selected
5. What is required from participants:
   - nature of involvement (interviews, focus groups, etc.)
   - time required for each session
   - number of sessions
   - time-period over which sessions will take place
6. Any risks to the participant
7. Voluntary nature of participation
8. Right of participant to refuse to answer any questions or withdraw at any stage without giving reasons
9. Privacy and security of data
10. Ways in which data will be used
11. Contact details for research project supervisor

Figure 4.2   Information for research participants: checklist

the researcher. A judgement has to be made about what is reasonable. In the traditional science laboratory setting, verbal and written explanations of the nature of the research are given to the potential subjects and they are asked to sign a document indicating their agreement to being involved in the research. A checklist regarding the sort of information which should be provided to potential participants is provided in Figure 4.2 and an example of a consent form is provided in Figure 4.3. In the case of a single, anonymous questionnaire-based survey verbal consent is generally considered adequate, but if names are recorded, and lengthy and/or repeated interviews or other types of activity are involved, then written consent is advisable.

A researcher could of course 'go through the motions' of following this procedure but abuse it by providing misleading information about the level of risk – itself an unethical practice. Hence the need for clear guidelines and monitoring of these matters.

Physical or mental risks of harm do not generally arise in leisure and tourism research, but they are only one aspect of being informed. There may be a moral dimension also. For example, some people may object to being involved in research which is being conducted for certain public, political or commercial organisations. So being informed also involves being informed about the purpose of the research and the nature of the sponsor or beneficiary.

In some cases the status of the researcher is ambivalent: for example, when students engaged in a project as part of their learning process in a university course conduct the project on behalf of a real client organisation, or when part-time students conduct research for a university assignment using their fellow employees as subjects or conduct research on competitors. It is clearly unethical for students to identify themselves only as students and not to identify to their informants the organisation which will be the beneficiary of the research.

University of xxxxxxx
School of Leisure and Tourism

Holiday history research project

CONSENT FORM

I confirm that I have read and understood the research project
information sheet for the 'Holiday history research project' and
have had any questions answered to my satisfaction.   _____

I understand that my participation in the study is entirely voluntary
and I may cease to take part at any time without giving reasons.   _____

I agree to take part in the study as described in the information sheet. _____

I agree to interviews/discussion sessions being recorded.   _____

I agree that anonymous quotations from interviews/discussions may
be used in publications.   _____

Name: _____   Date: _____

Signature: _____

Researcher's name: _____   Date: _____

Signature: _____

Figure 4.3 Example of a consent form

But again there are some grey areas. In some cases the research would be invalidated if subjects knew its purpose in detail. For example, responses could be affected if the subjects knew that a suvey was being carried out to see how respondents reacted to interviewers of differing race or gender. In some attitudinal research, for example on potentially sensitive topics such as race or sex, it may be thought that responses would be affected if respondents were told too much about the research and therefore placed 'on their guard'. Clearly such deception raises ethical issues, and judgements have to be made about whether the value of the research justifies the use of mild deception.

In some cases the provision of detailed information to informants, and obtaining their written consent is neither practicable nor necessary. Thus the typical leisure or tourism survey:

- is anonymous,

- involves only a short interview (e.g. 3 or 4 minutes),

- involves fairly innocuous, non-personal questions,

- takes place at a facility/site with the agreement of the management or authorities.

In this type of situation most respondents are not interested in detailed explanations of the research. Most adults are familiar with the survey process and their main concern is that if they are to take part the interview should not take up too much of their time! Potential respondents can become impatient with attempts to provide detailed explanations of the research and would prefer to 'get on with it'. Often questions about the purpose of the survey, if they arise at all, do so later during the interview process, when the respondent's interest has been stimulated. A suggested set of guidelines for such survey situations is provided in Figure 4.4.

Risk of harm to the subject

There may be a risk of harm to the subject in the collection of data, in its storage and handling and in publication. Such risks obviously need to be eliminated or minimised, for the sake of the subjects, the researcher and sponsoring organisations and, indeed, the whole research process.

Data collection process

The risk of harm in data collection arises particularly in medical/biological research, where a subject's physical health may be put at risk by an experimental procedure. The risk of injury may arise in sport-related experimenting and testing: for example, in cases of excessive exertion. Assuming there is appropriate screening and selection of subjects, for example checking on health status, this risk should be minimised by appropriate briefing of subjects and clear explanation and implementation of informed consent procedures discussed below.

Risks of harm can also arise in psychological research, where stress and distress can be caused, and in socio-psychological research where interpersonal relationships could be damaged, although this is very rare in leisure/tourism research. In social research, where most leisure and tourism research falls, the risk of harm in the data collection process is almost non-existent.

Anxiety during the data collection process may arise if the subject has concerns about how the data are to be used. This may relate to themselves and their own privacy, which relates to data storage, handling and publication, as discussed below. The harm which may potentially arise if privacy is breached could vary from mild embarrassment to disruption of relationships with friends, colleagues or employers, to loss of reputation and/or position. Concerns may also relate to moral principles, for example the use of data by certain types of corporation or governments, which relates to the 'fully informed' issue discussed above. In this case the potential harm is the affront to the subject's moral principles. Both concerns relate to the right of the subject to refuse to answer questions and/or withdraw from the process at any stage.

Data storage and handling

Data storage and handling involve not only hard-copy materials, such as questionnaires, but also digital material, such as audio and video recordings, transcripts

1. Interviewers should be identified with a badge including their given name and the name of the organisation involved (the host/client organisation or university).
2. Interviewers should be fully briefed about the project so that they can answer questions if asked.
3. If a respondent-completion ('handout') questionnaire is used, a brief description of the purpose of the project should be provided on the questionnaire (typically two or three lines so that it takes just a few seconds to read), with contact telephone numbers of supervisors for those requiring more information.
4. Interviewers approaching potential respondents should introduce themselves and seek cooperation using wording such as the following: 'We are conducting a survey of users of ----, would you mind answering a few questions?'
5. Telephone numbers of supervisors should be available and can be given to respondents if required.
6. A short printed handout may be available with more information for those respondents who are interested.
7. Respondents should not be pressured if they refuse to answer a question or wish to terminate the interview at any time.

Figure 4.4 Ethics guidelines for anonymous questionnaire-based surveys

and coded data files. Typically hard-copy data may be kept for several years as the project progresses and the publication process unfolds, and for a minimum period of time after the completion of the project specified by research organisations, typically about five years. Digital data today are likely to be stored indefinitely. The term 'handling' is used as well as storage because, while data may be stored securely in a formal sense, there are issues about who has access to it at the various stages (e.g. coding, data computer entry, transmission) and whether they are aware of and adhere to confidentiality commitments.

Hard-copy data should be protected by an appropriately secure form of storage and digital data by password-protected access.

The risk of harm to the subject due to the way data are stored and handled is affected by whether the information is provided entirely anonymously or the subject's name and/or contact details are known to the researcher and/or recorded. There is an in-between situation which can be termed *partial anonymity*. These three situations are discussed in turn below.

1. *Anonymous subjects:* Even in an anonymous situation, informants may be reluctant to give certain types of information to 'a complete stranger'. Where such sensitivity is encountered, the usual approach is to stress the voluntary and anonymous nature of the information-giving process, while respecting the respondent's right to refuse to provide certain types of information.

2. *Partial anonymity:* Often research participants are not randomly drawn from the population but are members of a community or organisation. While the community or organisation may not be named in the publication, as discussed below, it may be in the stored data, and it is possible that individuals or groups could be identified by their position – e.g. the president, secretary, coach, head teacher, team captain. Participants may therefore have concerns about the security of the data, particularly if they have revealed information about themselves or expressed views about others which they would like to be kept confidential.

Much digital information is anonymous because of use of identification numbers rather than names, but somewhere, there will be a list linking names and identification numbers, so the security and confidentially of that list becomes important.

In addition to written information, observational research may involve photography and video material which may involve invasion of people's privacy if they are recognised, even in the most innocent-seeming activities.

3. *Identified subjects:* Privacy is a valued right in Western society and such rights are generally enshrined in laws, which vary in detail between jurisdictions. People can be offended and suffer stress if their affairs are made public or divulged to certain third parties. There is therefore an obligation on the researcher to ensure confidentiality of any personally identifiable data which have been collected.

Situations where personally identifiable data inevitably arise and the nature of the resultant confidentiality issues are summarised in Figure 4.5, together with suggested means to reduce risk.

Some routine methods for maintaining individuals' privacy, such as keeping lists of names separate from actual data and use of pseudonyms are indicated, but these measures may not always prevent research subjects from being offended in ways discussed further below. An important principle, but one that is difficult to prescribe in detail, is that the researcher should be aware of research subjects' sensitivities, whether they be personal, professional, cultural or organisational.

In some research projects the naming of individuals is inevitably involved – for example where the number of subjects is small and they are key figures associated with particular high profile organisations or communities. Where interviews are conducted with such individuals, care must be taken to adopt the journalist's practice of checking whether information is being given 'on the record' or 'off the record'. Thus, in interviews, particularly where sensitive matters arise, it is wise to ask named informants whether they are prepared to be quoted.

In reporting results, the use of false names or numbers to identify individuals, organisations, events, places and communities is the obvious solution. However, this is not always sufficient. The use of false names may protect identities from the world at large, but for those 'in the know', the places and the people involved in the research project may be all too easily identifiable – the partial anonymity situation discussed above. Particular care should be taken when dealing with members of close-knit communities: the researcher should be aware of cultural and interpersonal sensitivities within such communities. Such issues are further highlighted in certain types of qualitative research where the research methodology involves gaining the trust and confidence of research subjects. It would be unethical to betray such trust and confidence.

Research method	Who is identified?	Identifying information	Why identify?	Issues re storage or publication?	Methods to reduce risk
Postal surveys – quantitative	Sampled members of general public or of organisations	Names + addresses	Intrinsic to method	Storage	List of names and addresses kept separate from questionnaires and destroyed at end of data collection.
Telephone surveys – quantitative	Sampled members of general public or of organisations	Telephone numbers	Intrinsic to method + quality control	Storage	List of names and addresses kept separate from questionnaires and destroyed at end of data collection.
Interviews – qualitative – individuals	Private individuals	Name + possibly telephone no./ address	Intrinsic to method	Both	Use of pseudonyms; be aware of sensitivities.
Interviews – qualitative – individuals in organisational roles	Individuals in identifiable public offices (e.g. mayor) or corporate roles (e.g. managing director)	Names, positions, organisation/place/ contact details	Intrinsic to method	Both	Use pseudonyms for individuals, place or organisation, but not always possible. Clarify 'on record'/'off record'; be aware of sensitivities.
Interviews – qualitative – small groups	Members of small groups (e.g. a village, a club or a small business)	Names (possibly addresses, tel. nos., surnames may not be involved)	Intrinsic to method	Both, but mainly publication	Use of pseudonyms for individuals, group and place, but not always possible. Clarify 'on record'/'off record'; be aware of sensitivities.
Ethnographic – variety of subjects and qualitative methods	Individuals, separately or as members of a group	Names (possibly addresses, tel. nos., surnames may not be involved)	Intrinsic to method	Mainly publication	Use of pseudonyms, but issue may lie in betraying confidence/trust. Be aware of sensitivities.
Longitudinal research: a. quantitative b. qualitative	Same subjects are contacted to be studied at intervals over a number of weeks, months, years	Names, addresses, tel. nos.	Intrinsic to method	a. Storage b. Both	a. Keep names, etc. separate from data. b. Storage: as for a. Publication: use pseudonyms.

Figure 4.5   Personally identifiable data

Occasionally this issue can be carelessly exacerbated by the author's own list of 'acknowledgements' if it clearly identifies people, organisations and places!

When data are confidential, measures must be taken to protect that confidentiality through ensuring the security of the raw data, such as interview tapes/transcripts/questionnaires. Specific freedom of information and privacy laws invariably cover the storage of and access to personally identifiable data, including allowing individuals access to their own records and the right to have inaccuracies corrected.

Data can be stored with code-numbers or false names, with a key to the code-numbers or names being kept securely in a place apart from the data.

Mail surveys are an in-between case. If returned questionnaires do not have any identification, then there is no way of identifying non-respondents in order to send reminders. Sending reminders to *everyone* is costly and an irritation to those who have already responded. One solution is to place an identifying number on the provided return *envelope* rather than on the questionnaire, with an assurance that the number will not be transferred to the questionnaire. In some situations a third party, such as a legal firm, is used to receive the questionnaires and pass them on to the researcher in anonymous form.

Confidentiality issues often arise with regard to the relationship between the researcher and the organisation funding the research. In particular, if the funding organisation 'owns' the data, the researcher may wish to protect the confidentiality of informants by *not* passing on to the sponsoring organisation any information which could identify informants by name.

Publication

Many of the considerations discussed above in relation to data storage and handling also apply in the case of publication of results. Any undertaking given to individuals or organisations in regard to anonymity should be respected and steps should be taken to avoid inadvertent breaches of confidentiality. Typically issues do not arise at the publication stage with individuals in quantitative research, particularly if they were anonymous from the start. But if the subjects were drawn from a particular geographical community or an organisation, unintended embarrassment could arise. General readers would generally not be able to make the identification, or would not be concerned if they could. But people in the academic or policy community familiar with the research may be able to make the identification, as might interested residents or members of the organisation. So the researcher must be prepared, in ethical terms, for the possibility of such identification and take this into account when writing the research report.

Honesty/rigour in analysis, interpretation and reporting

The falsification of research results is clearly unethical. There have been some notorious cases in the natural sciences where experimental results have been falsified.

A common practice in quantitative research is to exclude 'outliers' from the analysis. Thus, for example, if a survey of physical recreation found that all respondents participated three times a week or less except for two who participated ten times a week, these two might be termed 'outliers' and excluded from the analysis because they would distort averages. This is generally seen as ethical as long as it is stated in the research report that it has taken place. The same principle could of course apply in qualitative research, although identifying an 'outlier' would be a more complex task.

Researchers are concerned about reporting 'negative findings' or non-findings. This typically does not arise with descriptive research – what is, is – or in evaluative research – the performance of the programme/organisation is as found. The difficulty arises with explanatory research when no apparent 'explanation' is found. But negative findings are of interest and use if the research has been carefully designed. Thus if the interest is in the effect on variable X of 15 different independent variables and none of them is found to have a significant influence, then this would generally be of interest, in that it suggests that other variables must be at work. In the case of qualitative research, of course, the fact that the 15 variables are not influential in one study does not preclude them being influential in another study, since the findings would not be generalisable.

In some cases, negative findings are the result of a limited sample size: there may be an effect, but the small sample size makes it impossible to be confident about it – it is statistically insignificant. With a larger sample it may have been found to be a small, but still significant, relationship. But such findings may be relevant for later studies when considering required sample sizes and may be taken into account in meta-analysis (see Chapter 5), which aggregates the findings of many similar studies. This may seem like purely practical rather than ethical matters but, arguably, there is an ethical obligation to report all the findings of research which might contribute to the development of knowledge.

Authorship and acknowledgements

Authorship

A clear ethical principle is that all those involved with a research project should receive appropriate acknowledgement of their contribution in any publication. Acknowledgement of funding sources, named informants or collaborators and anonymous research subjects may be made in a footnote or in a preface or acknowledgements section. Difficulties can arise in the case of claims for joint authorship, especially in academic research where careers are dependent on such matters. Judgements have to be made as to whether a research assistant, who may be a research student, has simply undertaken routine work for payment or whether he or she has contributed intellectually to the research.

Typically in team research situations, the name of the leader of the team, or 'principal investigator' is placed first in the list of authors but, where the leadership is shared, names may appear in alphabetical order or may be rotated in different publications in a research programme.

Plagiarism

Plagiarism – the use of others' data or ideas without due acknowledgement and, where appropriate, permission – is clearly unethical and is also covered by copyright and intellectual property laws.

Access to research information

Some of the controversies surrounding climate research in recent years have highlighted the issue of rights of access to research information. We have already referred to individuals' rights of access to personal information about them held by public and other corporate bodies, as covered by freedom of information and privacy legislation. But such legislation also covers the public rights of access to information held by public bodies, for example on decision-making processes, a right which is regularly pursued by journalists. While the provisions of legislation vary between jurisdictions, the common principle is that information held by public bodies is *not secret* unless publication would threaten individual privacy, commercial property rights or national security or the costs of compiling information and making it publicly available would be prohibitive. In theory, such provisions apply to research data gathered with the support of public funds and/or held by public research institutions and have implications for the way date sets are stored and the length of time for which they are kept. As noted above, since most research data in the social sciences are held in digital form, they are, for the most part, potentially storable indefinitely.

It might be thought that if the results of research have been published, there should be no further interest in the raw data but, as Montford (2010: 134, 379–83) discusses, in the natural sciences *replication* is a key criterion in assessing validity but, as data sets become increasingly complex and expensive to compile, the only way of checking and replicating some types of published research is through access to the authors' original data. Some scientific journals are therefore requiring public (website) archiving of data-sets and of the computer code used to analyse them as a condition of publication.

Summary

This chapter considers the ethical, and legal, dimensions of conducting research. It is noted that in universities and other research organisations the responsible and ethical conduct of research is regulated by codes of conduct and ethics committees. In this chapter we consider mainly issues arising in research involving human subjects. In the biological and physical sciences consideration is also given to the involvement with animals, and increasingly environmental dimensions are considered. Ethical considerations arise in all components of the research process, including design, data collection, data storage and handling, analysis and interpretation and publication. A number of questions must be answered satisfactorily for a research project to be judged to be ethical. Is the research likely to be of social benefit? Are the researchers involved competent to conduct the research? Are the individuals involved participating voluntarily, without compulsion? Are the individuals taking part fully informed about the purposes and nature of the research – have they given 'informed consent'? Is the risk of harm to subjects at an acceptably low level? Has the analysis and interpretation of data and reporting of the results been undertaken honestly and rigorously? Have all those involved been suitably acknowledged or, where appropriate, included among the authors?

Test questions

1. What are the main ethical issues which arise in research?

2. What is 'informed consent' and what measures must be taken to ensure it?

3. What are the 'grey areas' where participation in research may not be voluntary?

4. What are the main possible sources of harm to participants in social science research?

5. What is plagiarism?

Exercises

1. In conducting interviews with 15-year-olds on leisure activities, a few of the respondents let you know that they take illegal drugs and indicate indirectly who supplies them. Do you tell anyone or maintain confidentiality? Do you include the finding, anonymously, in your research report?

2. Read Christensen's (1980) critique of Moeller *et al.* (1980a) and the response of Moeller *et al.* (1980b) and discuss.

Resources

Websites

Research ethics guidelines:

- Market Research Society (UK): www.mrs.org.uk/standards/codeconduct.htm
- Social Research Association (UK): www.the-sra.org.uk/documents/pdfs/ethics02.pdf
- NHMRC/ARC/Universities Australia guidelines: www.nhmrc.gov.au/_files_nhmrc/file/publications/synopses/r39.pdf
- University of Technology, Sydney: for undergraduate and postgraduate students: www.gsu.uts.edu.au/policies/hrecguide.html.

Publications

- Research ethics and the social sciences: Israel and Hay (2006).
- Research ethics guidelines: Saunders *et al.* (2000: 459–62, 2007).
- Research ethics, ethics committees and qualitative research: Lincoln (2005).
- Research ethics in leisure/tourism: Fleming and Jordan (2006); in tourism: Ryan (2005).
- A particular case in leisure research: Moeller *et al.* (1980a, 1980b) and Christensen (1980).

5 The range of research methods

Introduction – horses for courses

In this chapter the range of alternative research methods and criteria for their use are examined in broad terms, as an introduction to the methods and techniques to be covered in more detail in subsequent chapters. The chapter has four main sections:

- *major methods*: a range of major methods used in leisure and tourism research, including the roles of scholarship, 'just thinking', the use of the research literature, secondary data, observation, particular qualitative methods and questionnaire-based surveys, experiments and case studies;

- *subsidiary and cross-cutting methods*: approaches and techniques which are subsidiary to one or more of the major methods, in that they are a variation on or an application of the major method or cut across a number of the major methods;

- *multiple methods*: including triangulation and the case-study method;

- *choice of method*: the process of selecting a research method for a particular purpose.

Choosing appropriate research methods is clearly vital. In this book we espouse the principle that every technique has its place; the important thing is for researchers to be aware of the limitations of any particular method and to take these into account when reporting research results. In this book a *horses for courses* approach is adopted; techniques are not intrinsically *good* or *bad*, but are considered to be *appropriate* or *inappropriate* for the task in hand. Further, it is maintained that it is not a question of good or bad techniques which should be considered, but good or bad *use* of techniques.

The range of major research methods

The range of major methods to be examined is listed in Figure 5.1. These are discussed in turn below.

Scholarship

Although the dividing line between *scholarship* and *research* generally can be difficult to draw, it is useful to consider the differences between the two. Scholarship involves being well-informed about a subject and also thinking

Method	Brief description
Scholarship	Being well-read about a topic and thinking deeply and creatively about it.
Just thinking	The thinking part of scholarship.
Existing sources – using the literature	Identifying, summarising and evaluating the research literature – part of all research but can be the sole method used in a project.
Existing sources – secondary data	Re-use of data originally collected by another organisation for other purposes.
Observation	Direct looking at behaviour, or use of still or video cameras.
Qualitative methods	Range of methods where the data gathered is in the form of words (or images/sounds), as opposed to quantitative methods, where data are in the form of numbers.
Questionnaire-based surveys	Methods using a formal, printed schedule of questions to gather data – the main quantitative method in leisure/tourism research.
Experimental method	The researcher controls the environment of the phenomenon being studied, holding all variables constant except those which are the focus of the research.
Case study method	The focus of the research is on one or a small number of cases, and typically a number of data-gathering and analysis methods is used.

Figure 5.1 The range of major methods

critically and creatively about a subject and the accumulated knowledge on it. Scholarship therefore involves *knowing the literature*, but also being able to synthesise it, analyse it and critically appraise it. Scholarship is traditionally practised in the role of teacher, but when the results of scholarship are published they effectively become a contribution to research.

Research involves the generation of new knowledge. Traditionally this has been thought of as involving the gathering and presentation of new data – empirical research – but clearly this is not a necessary condition for a contribution to be considered research. New insights, critical or innovative ways of looking at old issues, or the identification of new issues or questions – the fruits of scholarship – are also contributions to knowledge. Indeed, the development of a new framework or *paradigm* for looking at a field can be far more significant than a minor piece of empirical work using an outmoded paradigm.

Just thinking

There is no substitute for thinking! Creative, informed thinking about a topic can be the only process involved in the development and presentation of a piece of research, although it will usually also involve consideration of the literature, as discussed below.

But even when data collection is involved, the difference between an *acceptable* piece of research and an *exceptional* or *significant* piece of research is usually the quality of the creative thought that has gone into it. The researcher needs to be creative in:

● identifying and posing the initial questions or issues for investigation;

● conceptualising the research and developing a research strategy;

● analysing data;

● interpreting and presenting findings.

Texts on research methods, such as this, can provide a guide to mechanical processes, but creative thought must come from within the individual researcher – in the same way that the basics of drawing can be taught but *art* comes from within the individual artist.

Existing sources – using the literature

There is virtually no research that can be done which would not benefit from some reference to the existing literature, and for most research such reference is essential. It is possible for a research project to consist only of a review of the literature: in comparatively new areas of study, such as leisure and tourism, especially when they are multidisciplinary as leisure and tourism studies are, there is a great need for the consolidation of existing knowledge which can come from good literature reviews.

The review of the literature often plays a key role in the formulation of research projects; it indicates the state of knowledge on a topic and is a source of, or stimulant for, ideas, both substantive and methodological.

A review of the literature can be important even when it uncovers no literature on the topic of interest. To establish that *no* research has been conducted on a particular topic, especially when the topic is considered to be of some importance to the field, can be a research finding of some significance in its own right. The literature review process is discussed in detail in Chapter 6.

Existing sources – secondary data

Clearly, if information is already available which will answer the research questions posed, then it would be wasteful of resources to collect new information for the purpose. As discussed in Chapter 7, large quantities of information are collected and stored by government and other organisations as routine functions of policy-making, management and evaluation, including sales figures and visitor numbers, income and expenditure, staffing, accident reports, crime reports and travel, leisure participation and health data. Such data are referred to as *secondary* data, because their primary use is administrative and research is only a secondary use. Even when such data are not ideal for the research at hand, they can often provide answers to some questions more quickly and at less cost than the collection of new data.

Secondary data need not be quantitative. Historians, for example, use diaries, official documents or newspaper reports as sources – such sources may be seen as secondary, since they were not initially produced for research purposes, but for historians themselves some of them are described as primary sources. In policy research such documents as the annual reports or minutes of meetings of organisations might be utilised.

In some cases data have been collected for research as opposed to administrative purposes but may not have been fully analysed, or they may have been analysed only in one particular way for a particular purpose, or even not analysed at all. Secondary analysis, or re-analysis, of research data is a potentially fruitful, but widely neglected, activity.

Observation

The technique of observation is discussed in Chapter 8. Observation has the advantage of being unobtrusive – indeed, the techniques involved are sometimes referred to as *unobtrusive* techniques (Kellehear, 1993). Unobtrusive techniques involve gathering information about people's behaviour without their knowledge. While in some instances this may raise ethical questions (see Chapter 4), it clearly has certain advantages over techniques where subjects are aware of the researcher's presence and may therefore modify their behaviour, or where reliance must be placed on subjects' own recall and description of their behaviour, which can be inaccurate or distorted.

Observation may be the only possible technique to use in certain situations: for example, when researching illicit activity, which people may be reluctant to talk about, or when researching the behaviour of young children (for example their play patterns) who may be too young to interview.

Observation is capable of presenting a perspective on a situation which is not apparent to the individuals involved. For example, the users of a crowded part of a recreation or tourist area may not be aware of the uncrowded areas available to them – the uneven pattern of use of the site can only be assessed by observation.

Observation is therefore an appropriate technique to use when knowledge of the presence of the researcher is likely to lead to unacceptable modification of subjects' behaviour, and when mass patterns of behaviour not apparent to individual subjects is of interest.

Qualitative methods

As discussed in Chapter 2, qualitative methods stand in contrast to *quantitative* methods. The main difference between the two groups of techniques is that quantitative methods involve numbers – quantities – whereas qualitative methods rely on words, and sometimes images, as the unit of analysis. In the case of qualitative techniques the information collected does not generally lend itself to statistical analysis and conclusions are not based on such analysis.

In consequence there is a tendency for qualitative techniques to involve the gathering of large amounts of relatively detailed information about relatively few cases (people, organisations, facilities, programmes, locations) and for quantitative techniques to involve the gathering of relatively small amounts of data on relatively large numbers of cases. It should be emphasised, however, that this is just a *tendency*. It is possible, for example, for a quantitative research project to involve the collection of, say, 500 items of data on only 20 people and for a qualitative research project to involve the collection of relatively little information on, say, 200 people. Conversely, some questionnaire-based surveys designed to collect quantitative data can involve questionnaires many pages long, which take an hour or more to administer and can collect hundreds of items of data from each respondent. The difference in the two approaches lies in the nature of information collected and the way it is analysed.

In what situations are qualitative techniques used? They tend to be used when one or more of the following situations apply:

- when the focus of the research is on meanings and attitudes (although these can also be studied quantitatively);

- when the situation calls for exploratory theory building rather than theory testing;

- when the researcher accepts that the concepts, terms and issues must be defined by the subjects themselves and not by the researcher in advance;

- when interaction between members of a group is of interest.

Data collection methods	Alternative names/variations	Description
In-depth interviews	Informal, semi-structured or unstructured interviews	One-on-one interviews with small numbers of individuals, interviewed at length, possibly on more than one occasion, typically using a checklist of topics rather than a formal questionnaire.
Focus groups	Group interviews	Discussions with groups of people (typically 6–12) led by a facilitator.
Observation	Unobtrusive techniques	The phenomenon of interest is examined by the naked eye or by use of still or video camera.
Participant observation		The researcher becomes a participant in the phenomenon being studied.
Biographical methods	Auto-ethnography	Research subjects are invited to provide their own accounts of events, etc., in written or recorded oral form.
Analysis of texts	Content analysis,* hermeneutics	Analysis and interpretation of the content of published or unpublished texts. May also involve audio-visual materials (images, TV, film, music, radio).
Ethnography	Field research (in anthropology)	Studying groups of people using a mixture of the above methods.

Figure 5.2 Qualitative data collection methods

* Can also be quantitative.

Qualitative techniques are not appropriate when the aim of the research is to make general statements about large populations, especially if such statements call for quantification.

Figure 5.2 summarises a range of types of qualitative data collection method and these are discussed in more detail in Chapter 9.

Questionnaire-based surveys

A questionnaire is a printed or electronic list of questions. In a questionnaire-based survey the same questionnaire is used to interview a sample of respondents. The term questionnaire-*based* survey is used because such surveys can take two formats:

- *interview format*, in which an interviewer, in a face-to-face situation or via telephone, reads out the questions from the questionnaire and records the answers;

- *respondent-completion format*, in which the respondent reads the questions and writes answers on the questionnaire or on-screen, and no interviewer is involved.

In many discussions of research methods in the literature 'questionnaires' and 'interviews' are presented as alternatives; this is clearly misleading, since interviews may be conducted using a questionnaire. A more accurate distinction would be made between 'questionnaires' and 'informal, in-depth or unstructured interviews', as discussed above.

Questionnaire-based surveys are probably the most commonly used method in leisure and tourism research. This is partly because the basic mechanics are relatively easily understood and mastered, but also because so much leisure and tourism research calls for the sorts of general, quantified statement referred to above. Thus, for example, governments want to know how many people engage in sport; managers want to know what proportion of customers are dissatisfied with a service and marketers want to know how many people are in a particular market segment. All these examples come from practical policy/management situations, which emphasises that most of the resources for survey research come from the public or private sector of the leisure/ tourism industries. Academic papers are very often a secondary spin-off from research which has been sponsored for such specific, practical purposes.

Unlike qualitative techniques, where the researcher can begin data collection in a tentative way, return to the subjects for additional information and gradually build the data and concepts and explanation, questionnaire-based surveys require researchers to be very specific about their data requirements from the beginning, since they must be committed irrevocably to a questionnaire.

A further key feature of questionnaire-based surveys is that they depend on respondents' own accounts of their behaviour, attitudes or intentions. In some situations – for example in the study of 'deviant' behaviour or in the study of activities which are socially approved (e.g. playing sport) or disapproved of (e.g. smoking or drinking) – this can raise some questions about the validity of the approach, since accuracy and honesty of responses may be called into question.

Questionnaire-based surveys are used when quantified information is required concerning a specific population and when individuals' own accounts of their behaviour and/or attitudes are acceptable as a source of information. Questionnaire surveys nevertheless may be used to gather qualitative as well as quantitative data by the inclusion of open-ended questions, as discussed in Chapter 10 – although this is not a view shared by all researchers (see, for example, Sherry Dupuis (1999: 45)). In one of the earliest questionnaire-based studies of leisure in Australia, in describing their methodology, the authors (Scott and U'Ren, 1962: xiii) indicated that the questionnaire-based interviews lasted up to three hours, with most taking between one and one and a half hours and in interviewing, 'verbatim replies were recorded'.

Type	Alternative name	Description
Household survey	Community survey or social survey	People are selected on the basis of where they live and are interviewed in their home.
Street survey	Quota survey or intercept survey	People are selected by stopping them in the street, in shopping malls, etc.
Telephone survey		Interviews are conducted by telephone.
Online survey	Web-based survey	Respondents complete screen-based questionnaire online.
Mail survey	Postal survey	Questionnaires are sent and returned by mail.
Site or user survey	Visitor survey, customer survey, intercept survey	Users of a leisure or tourism facility or site are surveyed on-site.
Captive group survey		Members of groups such as classes of school children, members of a club or employees of an organisation are surveyed.

Figure 5.3 Types of questionnaire-based survey

Questionnaire surveys in the leisure and tourism field can be divided into six types, as shown in Figure 5.3 and considered in more detail in Chapters 10 and 16.

Experimental method

The experimental method is the traditional approach of the natural sciences and involves the researcher controlling the environment in order to study the effects of specified variables, typically in a laboratory setting. The principles of the method were discussed in Chapter 2 and are addressed in more detail in Chapter 11.

Case study method

A case study involves the study of an example – a case – of the phenomenon being researched. The aim is to seek to understand the phenomenon by studying single examples. Cases can consist of individuals, communities (the community study method as discussed above), organisations and whole countries. Invariably multiple methods are used, including historical/documentary research, the use of secondary data, interviews and, in the case of communities, questionnaire-based or qualitative surveys. The case study method and its use in leisure and tourism studies is discussed further in Chapter 12.

Subsidiary/cross-cutting techniques

The somewhat inelegant term 'subsidiary and cross-cutting' is used to describe a number of techniques which are subsidiary to one or more of the major methods discussed above, in that they are a variation on or an application of the major method (e.g. Delphi technique, which uses questionnaires) or cut across a number of major methods (e.g. action research, which can use any or all of the major methods). The techniques discussed here are listed in Figure 5.4 and discussed in turn below, and an indication is given of how they relate to the pattern of the book. The brief descriptions presented here do not provide a basis for implementing the various techniques, but they indicate their general nature and possibilities. Guides to further information are provided in the Resources section.

Coupon surveys/conversion studies

In marketing research use can be made of information from the responses of the public to advertising coupons – that is, where the public is invited in an advertisement to write or telephone for information on a product. The data can be used to indicate the level of interest in the product on offer (compared with other products or with the same product in previous periods) and also to indicate the geographical spread of the interested public. The question then arises as to the extent to which people who respond to such advertising actually become customers. Thus conversion studies are designed to examine the extent to which enquirers *convert* to become customers (Woodside and Ronkainen, 1994).

En route/intercept/cordon surveys

In tourism research, surveys of tourists while travelling are sometimes referred to as *en route* surveys (Hurst, 1994). Such surveys may be conducted in aeroplanes, at airports or while travelling by car (when travellers are waved into lay-bys for survey purposes with the assistance of police). In this book this type of survey, which invariably involves a questionnaire, is considered to be a special case of site or user surveys, as discussed in Chapter 10. Since respondents are 'intercepted' at or near a destination, site or attraction the term *intercept survey* is sometimes used, and if all approaches to the destination, site or attraction are covered, the term *cordon* survey may be used.

Time-use surveys

There is a long tradition in leisure studies of investigating people's allocation of time between such categories as paid work, domestic work, sleep and leisure

Technique	Brief description
Subsidiary and cross-cutting techniques/methods	
Coupon surveys/ conversion studies	Analysis of returns from 'special offer', 'two for the price of one', etc. vouchers /advertisements
En route/intercept/ cordon surveys	Survey conducted with visitors entering, leaving or travelling to or from a site /destination
Time-use surveys	Survey in which respondents complete a detailed 1–2-day diary of activities.
Experience sampling method (ESM)	Subjects are 'beeped' or contacted electronically several times a day to record activities/feelings, etc. as they go about day-to-day activities.
Panel studies	A sample of individuals recruited to a 'panel' who may take part in several surveys over a period of time.
Longitudinal studies	The same sample of subjects are repeatedly surveyed, typically over a number of years.
Media reader/viewer/ listener surveys	Media report on surveys which readers/listeners have been invited to take part in, typically online or via automated phone-in.
Action research	Research committed to social outcomes, typically involving collaboration with a client organisation.
Historical research	Research on past events.
Content analysis	Quantitative study of printed/written documents or static/moving images (see also qualitative methods).
Delphi technique	Process in which a sample of experts responds to questions about future events in repeated rounds ideally to achieve consensus.
Projective techniques	Subjects are asked to respond to hypothetical scenarios.
Perceptual mapping	Subjects provide graphic representation of components of a problem/issue, typically collaborative.
Repertory grid	Pairs of contrasting descriptors for the phenomenon being studied are elicited from respondents to form constructs, and scores on the constructs are analysed to form a perceptual picture.
The use of scales	Development and use of batteries of 'stimulus items' (statements/questions, features, etc.) to be responded to via Likert-type scales.
Psychographic/lifestyle studies	Research which gathers data on a wide range of attitudes, values and socio-demographic characteristics and analyses them to determine distinctive psychographic/lifestyle groups or market segments.
Q methodology	Process in which subjects rank scale items (as above) depicted on cards.
Conjoint analysis	A process for studying people's choice processes by asking people to express preferences for hypothetical products with different combinations of attributes.
Quantitative modelling	Quantitative method in which relationships between two or more variables are assessed statistically.
Network analysis	Study of links between individuals and/or organisations involved in an activity.
Meta-analysis	Examination and summary of a number of studies on the same topic, typically with a key outcome measure such as a correlation coefficient.
Multiple methods	
Triangulation	Two or more methods used to focus on the same phenomenon, providing confirmation or differing insights.
Community studies	Comprehensive study of a geographical or other community using a variety of data sources.
Counting heads	A management task involving various research approaches, needed in situations where usage/visitor numbers are not available from ticket sales.

Figure 5.4   Subsidiary, cross-cutting and multiple techniques/methods

(Szalai, 1972; Pentland *et al.* 1999). The approach has not been widely used in tourism research, when people are away from home, although Douglas Pearce (1988) has suggested its use and noted a few examples. Time-use – or time-budget – research is basically a special case of the household survey and some reference is made to it in that context in Chapter 10.

Experience sampling method (ESM)

The experience sampling method (ESM) was pioneered by Mihaly Csikszentmihalyi and his colleagues at the University of Chicago in 1977 (Csikszentmihalyi and Larson, 1977) and can be seen as a development of the time-budget survey/diary method. Alternative names for the technique are *ecological momentary assessment* (EMA) (Smyth and Stone, 2003) and *ambulatory assessment*.

An ESM study typically takes place over a few days, during which, on about eight occasions each day, study participants are alerted by some electronic device – a pager in the early examples, later by watches programmed to 'beep' at certain times and most recently by mobile telephone. When alerted, or as soon as practically possible thereafter, the study participant completes a short questionnaire in a booklet carried with the participant at all times or, in recent versions, responds to questions via text-message. Information is gathered on activities being undertaken, where and with whom, and attitudes and feelings. The method has the advantage of recording activities and feelings in real time and in the 'natural' environment of the subject, rather than relying on recall at a later date in a different environment. While the amount of information which can be elicited in any one episode is limited, the cumulative amount of information gathered, together with any information included in a preliminary conventional questionnaire, can be substantial.

The early study by Csikszentmihalyi and Larson (1977) was of adolescents' daily behaviour patterns, while one of the more recent studies using the method explored adult stress levels related to work and leisure patterns and family interactions (Schneider *et al.*, 2004).

The research approach made possible by ESM has been characterised as *idiographic*, based on the Greek word *idios*, meaning specific to an individual (Conner *et al.*, 2009). This is in contrast to *nomothetic* research, based on the Greek word *nomos*, meaning law, which seeks to establish general scientific laws of behaviour based on studies of a number of individuals. However, unlike qualitative research, which is often idiographic, ESM is generally quantitative in nature since it gathers data from individuals on repeated occasions.

Further developments in this type of electronically aided research are:

● the electronically activated recorder (EAR) in which the subject wears a small microphone and recording device which is automatically activated for short periods (for example for 30 seconds, 12 times per hour) thus providing a record of the environments the subject experiences and conversational interaction with people – this has been used in psychological research to track social interaction (Mehl *et al.*, 2001) but there are no known examples in leisure or tourism;

● digital tracking using global positioning systems.

The details of the method are not pursued further in this book, but references to examples of its use are provided in the Resources section.

Panel studies

Market research companies often maintain *panels* of individuals for some of their surveys. Panels are made up of a representative cross-section of the public who agree to be on call for a series of surveys over a period of time. Often some financial reward is paid to panel members, but this cost is off-set by the savings in not having to continually select and contact new samples of respondents. While managing such panels presents particular problems, the range of survey methods which can be used with panels – by telephone, by mail or by face-to-face interview – is the same as for normal one-off samples (LaPage, 1994). Panel studies can therefore be seen as a particular form of household questionnaire survey.

Longitudinal studies

Longitudinal studies involve surveying the same sample of individuals periodically over a number of years (Young *et al.*, 1991). Such studies are of course expensive because of the need to keep track of the sample members over the years, and the need to have a large enough sample at the beginning to allow for the inevitable attrition to the sample over time. They are, however, ideal for studying social change and the combined effects of social change and ageing. While longitudinal studies are a recognised technique in the social sciences, and leisure and tourism activity may feature in some studies, there are no known examples specifically focused on leisure or tourism.

Studies of communities can be seen as longitudinal if comparable data are collected at intervals over an extended period of time, even if the same individuals are not interviewed each time; in this case the constant is the community – physical, social and economic – rather than individuals. Such a study was conducted by Donald Getz (1993) in relation to the changing impact of tourism in Spey Valley, Scotland, between 1978 and 1992. He undertook surveys of adults and schoolchildren. While tracking down the children for repeat interviewing in 1992 would have been of interest, it also made sense for Getz to conduct a new survey of schoolchildren with the same age-range as those interviewed in 1978. Chang Huh and Christine Vogt (2008) adopted a similar approach in relation to the impact of tourism on coastal tourism over time.

Media reader/viewer/listener surveys

Newspapers, magazines and radio and television stations often run opinion poll type surveys among their readers, viewers or listeners, often web-based. At the local level the public's views on an issue may be canvassed by the inclusion of some sort of form in a newspaper, which readers may fill in and return, and radio and television stations often run 'phone in' polls on topical issues. The results of these exercises have entertainment value, but should not generally be taken seriously. This is mainly because there is no way of knowing whether either the original population (the readers/listeners/viewers who happen to read, hear or view the item) or the sample of respondents are representative of the population as a whole. In most cases they are decidedly unrepresentative, in that the audiences and readership of particular media outlets tend to have particular socio-economic characteristics and only those with pronounced views, one way or the other, are likely to become involved in the process. These exercises should not, of course be confused with surveys sponsored by the media but conducted by reputable survey companies, such as Newspoll or AC Nielsen.

Action research

The common image of research is as a detached process reporting objectively on what is discovered. When a researcher is personally committed to the topic under investigation, whether that be self-interest-related, such as the fortunes of a company, or a social cause, like saving the environment, efforts are still generally made to abide by the rules of science, for ethical reasons or because of the general belief that sound research is more likely to be effective in supporting a cause. Some types of research can, nevertheless, be deliberately designed to involve the researcher in the topic and are intended to be overtly part of the process of bringing about change – such research is termed 'action research'. Typically, action research is also distinguished by being conducted on behalf of, and in association with, one or more organisations, or stakeholders. Indeed, some definitions envisage the action research process as happening within a corporate organisation, with the researcher 'embedded' in the organisation for the duration of the project.

The action research process shown in Figure 5.5 indicates that researchers are involved in the 'action' stages of the process as well as the research stage and there may be various feedback loops in the process as research is conducted to assist the campaign for change and to evaluate outcomes.

There are similarities with the normal research process within an organisation, where step 3 is an internal resource allocation and implementation process. It can also be seen as a quasi-experimental process. Action research is not constrained as to methods or techniques. There is a tendency to see it as a form of qualitative research, but in their introductory text of the subject Davydd Greenwood and Morten Levin state:

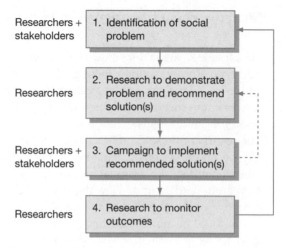

Figure 5.5 Action research process

> . . . it is wrong to think of action research as 'qualitative' research, yet a great many conventional researchers and far too many action researchers make this error. . . . An action research process must use qualitative, quantitative and/or mixed-method techniques wherever and whenever the conditions and subject an action research team deals with require. *(Greenwood and Levin, 2007: 98)*

Action research is less usual in the leisure and tourism context than in some areas of social policy, such as housing or ethnic affairs. One of the earliest studies in the leisure domain was the *Leisure and the Quality of Life* study which was conducted in Britain the 1970s and involved a wide range of leisure-provision projects in four locations (Department of the Environment, 1977). While the study was government-funded, the projects were initiated and overseen by locally established community groups, supported by research teams. The similarity between action research and the experimental method was demonstrated by the fact that the four local projects were referred to as 'experiments', while one of the research papers published as part of the project report was entitled: 'The action research background to the leisure experiments' (Batty, 1977).

Historical research

History is of course a major discipline with its own approaches to research. Historical research arises in the leisure and tourism research environment in at least two contexts: biographical research, discussed as a qualitative approach in Chapter 9, and in case study research, discussed below. It can also be seen as a form of secondary data analysis, since historians are invariably dependent on documents contemporary to a period, which were compiled for purposes other than historical research. As a discipline, history is part of the humanities, although in the context of leisure and tourism research it clearly extends into the social sciences when history is presented as a partial explanation for contemporary phenomena. Compared with the social science literature, in historical literature there is tendency for the question of method to be played down or taken for granted. While historical accounts are generally conducted in a scholarly manner, with detailed reference to sources, just how the source material has been used and analysed is not always clear: thus there is rarely a 'methods' section in historically based articles (see, for example, two recent examples in *Leisure Studies*: Philips, 2004; and Snape, 2004). Historical methods are not pursued in this book, but some sources are indicated in the Resources section.

Content analysis

In some fields of inquiry the focus of research is textual – for example, the content of organisations' annual reports, politicians' speeches or advertising messages. The analysis and interpretation of the content of published or unpublished texts is referred to as *content analysis*, often when the analysis is quantitative, or *hermeneutics*, when the analysis is of a more qualitative nature. The technique has not traditionally been widely used in leisure and tourism studies, but with the development of postmodernism and the widening of the scope of *text* to include a wide variety of cultural products such as company documents, advertising material, websites and letters, the approach is attracting increasing attention. The analyses in Case study 2.1, which involve counts of the popularity of different research methods used in leisure and tourism research journals, can be seen as exemplifying content analysis. Some examples of quantitative studies are listed in the Resources section and qualitative approaches are discussed in Chapter 9.

Delphi technique

The Delphi technique (named after the classical Greek 'Delphic oracle') is a procedure involving the gathering and analysing of information from a panel of experts on future trends in a particular field of interest. The experts in the field (e.g. leisure or tourism) complete a questionnaire indicating their views on the likelihood of certain developments taking place in future; these views are then collated and circulated to panel members for further comment, a process which might be repeated a number of times before the final results are collated. The technique is used in some areas of business and technological forecasting, and has been used to a limited extent in leisure and tourism. In this book the technique is not examined explicitly, but to some extent it involves questionnaire design and analysis, as covered in Chapters 10 and 16. A thorough state-of-the-art review has recently been provided by Donohue and Needham (2009).

Projective techniques

Projective techniques might be termed 'what if?' techniques, in that they involve subjects responding to hypothetical – projected – situations. For example, subjects might be asked to indicate how they might spend a particular sum of money if given a free choice, or how they might spend additional leisure time if it were made available, or they might be invited to respond to photographs of particular locations (Ryan, 1995: 124). While the technique can become elaborate and specialised, in this book it is considered to be an extension of questionnaire-based surveys and possibly of focus-group interviews.

Perceptual mapping

One of the issues in leisure and sport planning and marketing is the extent to which the public are well-informed about available facilities and services. This is partly related to information coming through the media, formal marketing activities and personal networks, but can also relate to people's spatial perception of the neighbourhood, city or region in which they live. For example, people are likely to be familiar with their immediate neighbourhood and the route to their place of work or school, but are likely to be less familiar with areas on the other side of town. This can apply particularly to people without cars, notably young people and the elderly. Information on people's 'perceptual space' can be elicited by inviting them to draw 'perceptual maps' of their city. This can also be applied in the planning and marketing of tourism within destinations (Pearce, 2005: 99–104).

Repertory grid

The repertory grid technique was developed by psychologist George Kelly in the 1950s and is used from time to time in leisure and tourism research. It can be seen as a formalisation and quantification of perceptual mapping. Research subjects are asked to indicate a range of qualities of the phenomenon being studied and then the opposite of that quality – for example, friendly: threatening; cool: uncool; expensive: cheap. A number of these *constructs* are elicited – typically up to about 20 – and entered into a grid, as shown in Figure 5.6. Subjects then indicate on the grid where the study object fits on each construct: for example, for the first construct, whether it is closer to the friendly end or the

Friendly						Threatening
Cool						Uncool
Expensive						Cheap
Etc.						

Figure 5.6 Repertory grid example

threatening end. This information can be scored and analysed using graphic and/or statistical analyses such as factor analysis (see Chapter 17) at the individual level and/or collectively.

Use of scales

A scale is a numerical index used to measure constructs or variables which are generally not intrinsically quantitative. Typically subjects are asked to respond to questions using rating scales and the scores are combined to produce a scale or index of the phenomenon of interest. In Chapter 10 the development and use of customised scales in questionnaires is discussed, but it is quite common for researchers to make use of standardised scales which have been developed by others. The advantage of the use of existing scales is that researchers are not continually 'reinventing the wheel' by devising their own measure of a particular phenomenon. Widely used scales have generally been subject to considerable testing to ensure validity – that is that they measure what they are intended to measure. Further, the use of common measures facilitates comparability between studies. The disadvantage is, of course, that any fault in the scale validity may be replicated across many studies and a fixed scale may not fully reflect different socio-economic environments or change over time.

The use of such scales is widespread, particularly in psychology and related disciplines, but they have not been widely utilised in the mainstream of leisure and tourism research. Some examples are as follows:

- Robyn McGuiggan (2000) makes use of the Myers–Briggs Type Indicator, one of most well-known scales used to assess personality, in a study of the relationship between personality and leisure activity preferences.

- The Leisure Satisfaction Scale (LSS) was developed by Beard and Ragheb (1980) and applied in a tourism context by Ryan and Glendon (1998).

- The Paragraphs About Leisure (PAL) scale, developed by Howard Tinsley and his associates (see Driver *et al.*, 1991), is concerned with a range of psychological benefits derived from participation in leisure activities.

- The Recreation Experience Preference (REP) scale, developed by Bev Driver and associates (also see Driver *et al.*, 1991), is similar to the PAL but focused particularly on outdoor natural area facilities.

- Researchers in the area of sport and exercise often make use of scales related to physical and mental health, such as that developed by Ware *et al.* (1994).

Despite the considerable amount of psychologically influenced research using scales in such areas as destination choice and tourist satisfaction (see Woodside *et al.*, 2000 and Mazanec *et al.*, 2001), the use of specialised standardised scales has not emerged prominently in tourism research.

The *Marketing Scales Handbook*, published in a number of volumes by the American Marketing Association (Bruner and Hensel, 1992), lists hundreds of

Listed in Bruner and Hensel (1992)

72	Cooking enjoyment	261	Sports activeness
74	Co-viewing TV (parent/child)	262	Sports enthusiasm
147	Involvement (television)	268	Time management
186	Pleasure	269–70	Time pressure
193	Pricing issues (air travel)	274	Venturesomeness
219	Restriction of TV viewing	277	Volunteerism (benefits)
226	Safety (air travel)	278	Volunteerism (family/job constraints)
227	Satisfaction (air travel)	279	Volunteerism (willingness)

Listed in Bruner et al. (2001)

2	Affect (music)	323	Sensation seeking
48	Attitude toward conservation activity	330–33	Services evaluation (airline features)
154	Experiential response to music	345	Service quality (health club)
180	Imaginal response to music	368	Shopping orientation (recreation)
186	Impulse buying (music)	403–6	Ad. avoidance in various media
217	Involvement (televised soccer match)	436	Attitude toward sex in advertising
239	Need to reexperience music	443	Attitude toward the ad. (humour)
259	Pressure to be thin	938	Work involvement
285	Quality of service (stadium)	939	Work/family conflict
307	Satisfaction (with health club)		

Figure 5.7 Scales for leisure/tourism-related topics

scales used in marketing research, most relating to generic topics, such as consumer motivation and attitudes, but others relating to specific settings. A selection of relevance to leisure and tourism is listed in Figure 5.7.

Further examples of the use of scales in leisure and tourism research are listed in the Resources section.

Psychographic/lifestyle research

Psychographic research, as discussed in Chapter 2, gathers data on a wide range of attitudes and socio-demographic characteristics of people and analyses the data to establish groupings or market segments with common characteristics, typically using statistical techniques such as factor and cluster analysis, as discussed in Chapter 17. A number of commercial survey/consultant organisations offer their own psychographic/lifestyle systems to clients to classify survey respondents into segments seen as more meaningful than those based on the usual age, gender and social class.

VALS*	ACORN†	
1. Survivor 2. Sustainer 3. Belonger	1. Wealth achievers	A. Wealthy executives B. Affluent greys (older people) C. Flourishing (well-off) families
4. Emulator 5. Achiever 6. I-Am-Me	2. Urban prosperity	D. Prosperous professionals E. Educated urbanites (young urban professionals) F. Aspiring singles (mainly urban area students)
7. Experiential 8. Socially conscious 9. Integrated	3. Comfortably off	G. Starting out (young couples) H. Secure families I. Settled suburbia (older couples in suburbs) J. Prudent pensioners
	4. Moderate means	K. Asian communities L. Post-industrial families (older skilled) M. Blue-collar roots (manual workers)
	5. Hard-pressed	N. Struggling (low-income) families O. Burdened singles (elderly and single parents) P. High-rise hardship Q. Inner city adversity

Figure 5.8 Examples of psychographic/lifestyle categories

* Values, Attitudes and Lifestyles: Strategic Business Insights (2009).
† A Classification of Residential Neighbourhoods: CACI Ltd (2006).

- The VALS typology (Values, Attitudes and Life Styles), developed in the United States, classifies people into nine segments, as shown in Figure 5.8. This system has been widely used in market research, including tourism research (e.g. Shih, 1986).

- The ACORN (A Classification of Residential Neighbourhoods) was developed in Britain by the commercial survey company CACI, and is based on socio-demographic data from census collection areas (see Chapter 7) so, since it does not contain attitude data it must be classified as a lifestyle rather than a psychographic system. It has five segments divided into 17 sub-segments as shown in Figure 5.8 and has been used in leisure research, notably in the annual Sport England Active People Survey, as discussed in Chapter 7.

Q methodology

Q methodology was developed in the 1930s by physicist/psychologist William Stephenson to examine people's subjective opinions of phenomena. It involves five steps:

1. Definition of the 'concourse', the scope of the phenomenon to be studied – typically in the form of a set of attitude statements (see Chapter 10), but sometimes photographs.

2. Development of the 'Q-sample' or 'Q-set' of stimulus items – typically a set of cards, each containing one of the statements/photographs.

3. Selection of the 'person-sample', 'P-sample or 'P-set' – the sample of individuals to be involved in the study.

4. Q-sorting – individuals sort the cards into piles arranged along a spectrum – for example, from strongly agree to strongly disagree, scored as in a Likert scale (see Chapter 10). Subjects are required to arrange cards on a provided template in the shape of a bell-shaped 'normal curve' (as shown in Figure 17.1a).

5. Analysis and interpretation – this involves factor analysis of the data (see Chapter 17) to discover themes.

Computer software packages, such a 'PQ Method' are available to analyse the data. Examples of applications in leisure and tourism studies are indicated in the Resources section and some further technical detail of the method is discussed in Chapter 17.

Conjoint analysis

Conjoint analysis is a methodology used to explore people's decision-making processes, including choices of products, such as holiday types, holiday desti-nations, leisure activities or particular leisure facilities. In particular, it seeks to discover how various features of products are evaluated by the consumer and how this evaluation influences choices. One way of doing this would be to examine people's actual selections against the attributes of a range of existing products, and there is research which adopts this approach, but it is a complex, 'messy' and possibly expensive, process. Furthermore, such research will be constrained by the available products and their features and will not include people for whom existing choices are not attractive and have therefore been rejected. In conjoint analysis subjects are asked to express their preferences among a range of hypothetical products with varying combinations of features. The more distinct features are considered and the more levels or categories exist for each feature, the more combinations there will be for consideration. For example, four features, each with four levels/categories, produces 256 different combinations. Selecting combinations for inclusion in a study and analysing the results is the complex mathematical task undertaken by conjoint analysis. The detail is beyond the scope of this book, but further reading is indicated in the Resources section and the approach is discussed again in Chapter 12 under the heading of Discrete choice experiments (DCEs).

Quantitative modelling

The techniques discussed so far are distinguished primarily by their data collection procedures and in some cases by both their data collection and analysis procedures. Quantitative modelling is distinguished by an approach to theory and data analysis: the data used are quantitative, but may have been collected by one or more of a variety of methods (e.g. observation, question-naires, documentary records, experiment). The idea of quantitative modelling was discussed briefly in Chapter 3, where it is noted that hypotheses concerning the relationships between variables may be expressed and tested in the form of models/equations (see Figure 3.11). This approach to research is considered further in Chapter 17, particularly in connection with linear and multiple regression.

Network analysis

Many human activities operate through networks involving nodes and links between them, including transport systems, electricity supply systems and telecommunications. A science has developed around this idea and has been used to optimise the design of networks. Figure 5.9 shows a simple network represented in analogue and digital format, with the numbers indicating the size of the flows between the nodes (e.g. traffic flows, financial flows, com-munication). Although it is not possible to pursue this here, it is clear that this situation lends itself to mathematical analysis, although analysis can be confined to graphical format and can involve qualitative approaches. In terms of data collection, the method involves the identification of the relevant nodes (organisations, destinations) in the system and measuring the extent of links between them. The approach has similarities to the notion of *sociometry* as used in psychotherapy and education research (see Oppenheim, 2000: 254–9; Dayton, 2005).

Tourism clearly involves networks, in terms of traffic flows and the structure of the industry and its interdependencies and a research literature is developing in the field (Scott *et al.* 2008). Everyday leisure activity also involves networks, among individuals and groups. The phenomenon of the social networking

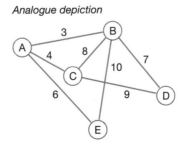

Analogue depiction

Digital depiction

	A	B	C	D	E
A	0	3	4	0	6
B	3	0	8	7	10
C	4	8	0	9	0
D	0	7	9	0	0
E	6	10	0	0	0

Figure 5.9   A simple network

website is the latest manifestation of this and, indeed, when network analysis is applied at the individual and small group level it is referred to as *social network analysis*. Numerous surveys of leisure facility and service users over many years have illustrated the importance of friendship networks when they have discovered that 'word of mouth' is a far more significant source of information for most people than any form of advertising. Social network analysis is not common in leisure studies, but has been explored by Patricia Stokowski (1994, Stokowski and Lee, 1991).

Meta-analysis

One approach to research combines features of a literature review and secondary data analysis and involves a quantitative appraisal of the findings of a number of research projects on the same topic. The technique, known as *meta-analysis* (Glass *et al.*, 1981), is suitable for the sort of research where findings are directly comparable from one study to another – for example, when the key findings are expressed in terms of correlation and regression coefficients between particular variables (see Chapter 17). In a meta-analysis, the reported findings of a large number of individual research projects in the same area provide the basis for further exploration and analysis of the area. Typically, because many studies are involved and must be compared on a common basis, only relatively simple relationships can be examined.

A less formal approach to cross-project appraisal is the *consensus study* in which a group of researchers reviews the accumulated research on a topic and seek to reach a consensus on the state of knowledge. This is discussed further in Chapter 6.

Examples of meta-analysis in the leisure and tourism area are given in the Resources section.

Multiple methods

Many research methods involve the use of more than one method or technique. Three multi-method situations are discussed here: triangulation, the community study, counting heads (see Figure 5.4). The case study method is also a multi-method approach, but this is considered a primary method in this book and so is discussed separately above and in Chapter 12.

Triangulation

Triangulation gets its name from the land surveying method of fixing the position of an object by measuring it from two different positions, with the object being the third point of the triangle. In research, the triangulation method involves the use of more than one research approach in a single study to gain a broader or more complete understanding of the issues being investigated. The methods used are often complementary in that the weaknesses of one approach are complemented by the strengths of another. Triangulation often utilises both qualitative and quantitative approaches in the same study. Duffy (1987: 131) has identified four different ways that triangulation can be used in research, namely:

● analysing data in more than one way;

● using more than one sampling strategy;

● using different interviewers, observers and analysts in the one study;

● using more than one methodology to gather data.

If triangulation methods are to be used in a study the approaches taken will depend on the imagination and the experience of the researcher. However, it is important that the research question is clearly focused and not confused by the methodology adopted, and that the methods are chosen in accordance with their relevance to the topic. In particular the *rationale* for using triangulation should be outlined in reporting the research. In particular the possible weaknesses of one method and the ways in which the additional method has been used to overcome such a weakness should be explained. This is clearly relevant to the issue of validity and reliability discussed in Chapter 2.

Often triangulation is claimed in a study because more than one data source and/or analytical method has been used to address different aspects of the research question, or even different research questions. However, it is when the different data/methods address the *same* question that true triangulation can be said to have occurred. Figure 5.10 presents an example where four data collection methods are used to address two research questions. A research report on a project where triangulation is claimed should therefore compare and contrast the findings from the multiple methods. Whether the multiple methods produce similar or different findings should then be an issue for discussion.

Community study as method

As long ago as 1954 Conrad Arensberg presented a case for viewing the community study as a distinct research method, describing it as a naturalistic, comparative method in which

> . . . a problem (or problems) in the nature, interconnections, or dynamics of behavior and attitudes is explored against or within the surround of other behavior and attitudes of the individuals making up the life of a particular community. *(Arensberg, 1954: 110)*

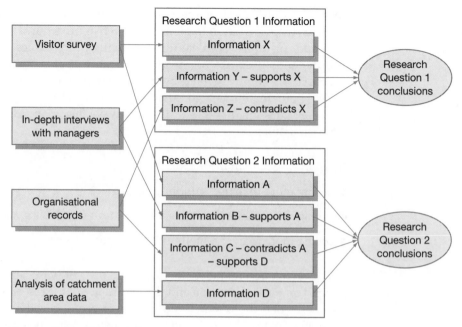

Figure 5.10 Triangulation

The key requirement of a community study is, of course, the existence of an identifiable community and this is generally geographical.

Community studies have been a feature of leisure studies from the beginning:

● In the United States, one of the most famous community studies, of 'Middletown', was conducted by Robert and Helen Lynd in 1929 and included three chapters on the use of leisure, while the first major study of leisure, entitled *Leisure: a Suburban Study*, by George Lundberg and his associates (1934), was a study of Westchester County in suburban New York.

● In the UK, a study of High Wycombe formed part of the earliest major study of leisure conducted in the late 1940s by Rowntree and Lavers (1951) (see Case studies 9.1 and 12.1).

● In Australia, one of the earliest examples of leisure research, *Leisure: a Social Enquiry* by Scott and U'Ren (1962), was of the leisure participation of residents of a Melbourne suburban housing estate.

A more recent community study was Derek Wynne's study of the leisure behaviours and lifestyles of residents of a new housing estate near London (Wynne, 1998 – see Case study 12.4).

Community studies arise in tourism in the study of relatively small host communities: for example, Jacqueline Waldren's (1996, 1997) study of the Mediterranean island of Mallorca.

In effect, community studies are case studies, so the methodological considerations relevant to case studies as discussed in Chapter 12 are also applicable to community studies.

Counting heads

In virtually all leisure and tourism contexts there is a requirement for information on visitor numbers for planning and management purposes. This calls for what is colloquially referred to as 'counting heads' or, in seated venues, counting 'bums on seats'. In many cases the required information is generated automatically by the ticket sales process. But there are situations where ticket numbers are not available, for example: urban parks, beaches, some museums and galleries and public events and tourist destinations with informal access (e.g. by private vehicle). In other cases, data are available from multiple sources – for example a tourist destination with a variety of modes of access or a festival with a combination of free and ticketed events. In these situations a variety of data collection methods may be available from which one or more methods may be selected. The methods/sources can be divided into administrative, survey-based and direct counts. Thus assembling data concerning one site or destination involves consideration of methods addressed in a number of the chapters in Part II, particularly Chapters 7, 8 and 10. This issue is addressed initially in Chapter 7 and information provided in Figures 7.2 and 7.3 and cross-referenced in Chapters 8 and 10.

Choosing methods

The process of choosing appropriate research methods for a research task is part of the whole process of planning and designing a research project, as discussed in Chapter 3. Here a number of considerations which should be borne in mind are discussed, as listed in Figure 5.11.

---

1. The research question or hypothesis

2. Previous research

3. Data availability/access

4. Resources

5. Time

6. Validity, reliability, trustworthiness

7. Generalisability

8. Ethics

9. Uses/users of the findings

Figure 5.11   Considerations in selecting a research method

The research question or hypothesis

Much of the decision on how to research a topic is bound up in the basic research question or hypothesis. As discussed in Chapter 3, the 'research question' can take a variety of forms, but generally it will point the researcher in the direction of certain data sources – for example, in relation to employees, customers or organisations. Certain types of data also suggest certain types of analysis.

Previous research

If the proposed research is closely keyed into the literature and previous research, then the methods used in that research are likely to influence the choice of methods. The aim may be to replicate the methodology used in previous studies to achieve comparability, to improve on the methods used, or to deliberately adopt a contrasting methodology.

Data availability/access

In some cases an obvious existing data source presents itself, and may even have prompted the research in the first place – termed *opportunistic* research in Chapter 2. For example:

● a set of archives of an organisation can provide the basis for historical research;

● official data which have been published but only superficially analysed could be analysed in more depth;

● access to a sample of people, such as the workforce or customer-base of a company, members of a club or members of an informal interest group can be seen as an opportunity too good to miss.

In other cases *lack* of access shapes the research – for example, ethical or practical issues may preclude some research on children, so data may have to be gathered from parents.

Resources

Clearly the resources of staff and money will have a major effect on the type and scale of the research to be conducted.

Time and timing

Time and timing is always a limitation. Most research projects have a time limit. Timing in relation to external events or routines is also often a factor: for example, research using the current year's attendance data must be completed quickly if it is to be used to influence next year's strategic planning; and empirical research on events, such as a sporting events or arts festivals, is constrained by their timing.

Validity, reliability and generalisability

As discussed in Chapter 2:

- *validity* is the extent to which the data collected truly reflect the phenomenon being studied;

- *reliability* is the extent to which research findings would be the same if the research were to be repeated at a later date, or with a different sample of subjects.

It is also noted in Chapter 2 that these concepts are sometimes replaced in qualitative research by the concept of *trustworthiness*.

As discussed in Chapter 2, generalisability refers to the extent to which the results of the research findings apply to other subjects, other groups, and other conditions. The extent to which this is required as an outcome of the research will influence the choice of method.

Ethics

Ethical issues also limit choices of research method. Reference has already been made to ethical issues surrounding research on children: further examples of ethical issues are discussed in Chapter 4.

Uses/users of the findings

The uses and users of the research are often taken for granted, but they are an important factor in shaping research. If substantial investment will depend on the results of the research, then a more extensive and thorough-going project will be required than if the research is to used only to generate ideas. When life and death issues are at stake – for example in medical research on the effects of a treatment for a disease – much more precision is needed in the results than if, for example, a company merely wishes to know the socio-economic characteristics of its customers.

Summary

This chapter complements Chapter 3 in setting out in brief the range of research methods available to the leisure and tourism researcher. It reinforces the message of Chapter 3, that research methods should ideally be selected on the basis of their suitability to answer the research questions posed, not on the basis of some prior preference for a particular method. Initially the 'major' research methods are reviewed, namely:

● scholarship;

● 'just thinking';

● the use of existing information – the literature and secondary data;

● observation;

● qualitative methods;

● questionnaire-based surveys;

● case study method;

● experimental method.

The first two are included to emphasise that research is not just about deploying techniques, but also involves being well-informed about the field and *thinking* about the problems and issues being researched in theoretical and practical terms. The other major methods foreshadow subsequent chapters which deal with them in detail.

The middle section of the chapter briefly introduces a number of approaches and techniques which are subsidiary to one or more of the major methods, in that they are a variation on or an application of the major method, or cut across a number of the major methods. The approaches and techniques covered are:

● coupon surveys/conversion studies;

● en route/intercept surveys;

● time-use surveys;

● experience sampling method;

● panel studies;

● longitudinal studies;

● media reader/viwer/listener surveys;

● action research;

● historical research;

● content analysis;

● the Delphi technique;

● projective techniques;

- perceptual mapping;
- repertory grid;
- the use of scales;
- psychographic/lifestyle research;
- Q methodology;
- conjoint analysis;
- quantitative modelling;
- network analysis;
- meta-analysis.

In the next section of the chapter consideration is given to 'multiple methods', with a discussion of the concept of *triangulation*, the *community study* as method and *counting heads*.

Finally factors to be considered in selecting research methods are examined.

Test questions

1. What is 'scholarship'?

2. Define each of the following:
   a. coupon surveys/conversion studies
   b. en route/intercept surveys
   c. time-use surveys
   d. experience sampling method (ESM)
   e. panel studies
   f. longitudinal studies
   g. media reader/viewer/listener surveys
   h. action research
   i. historical research
   j. content analysis
   k. the Delphi technique
   l. projective techniques
   m. perceptual mapping
   n. repertory grid
   o. the use of scales
   p. psychographic/lifestyle research
   q. Q methodology
   r. conjoint analysis
   s. quantitative modelling
   t. network analysis
   u. meta-analysis.

3. What is triangulation and why is it used in research?

4. What does counting heads involve?

Exercises

Exercises involving the major methods and subsidiary and cross-cutting methods arise in the subsequent chapters.

Resources

Websites

- Time use: Centre for Time Use Research, USA: www.timeuse.org, International Association for Time Use Research: www.iatur.org.

- Experience sampling method: Society for Ambulatory Assessment: www.ambulatory-assessment.org; software sites: www.experience-sampling.org, http://myexperience.sourceforge.net, www.cfs.purdue.edu/mfri/pages/PMAT/

- Q methodology: www.qmethod.org/about.php

- Longitudinal: UK Longitudinal Studies Centre: www.iser.essex.ac.uk/survey/ulsc, Australian Longitudinal Study of Women's Health: www.alswh.org.au.

Publications

- Major methods: see the Resources sections of Chapters 6–12.

- Action research: Reason and Bradbury (2001), McNiff and Whitehead (2002), Greenwood and Levin (2007); see White (2004) for statement of 'action' dimension of feminist leisure research.

- Community studies: Wynne (1986, 1998), Waldren (1996, 1997).

- Conjoint analysis: Cosper and Kinsley (1984), Claxton (1994), Jones (1991).

- Counting heads: Gartner and Hunt (1988); see Chapter 8.

- Coupon surveys/conversion studies: Woodside and Ronkanen (1994), Perdue and Botkin (1988).

- The Delphi technique: general and tourism: Donohue and Needham (2009), Green *et al.* (1990); leisure: Moeller and Shafer (1994).

- En route surveys: Gartner and Hunt (1988), Hurst (1994).

- Experience sampling method (ESM): Csikszentmihayli and Larson (1977), Hektner *et al.* (2006), Mannell and Kleiber (1997: 100–5), Schimmack and Diener (2003), Smyth and Stone (2003), Schneider *et al.* (2004), Connor *et al.* (2009).

- Historical research: Storey (2004), Williams (2003).

- Longitudinal studies: in the social sciences: Young *et al.* (1991), Getz (1993); in tourism: Huh and Vogt (2008); the Australian Longitudinal Study on Women's Health includes questions on leisure and a number of publications has resulted, for example: Brown *et al.* (2009); an up-to-date list of papers emerging from the project can be found on the project website listed above.

- Mental maps – see perceptual mapping.

- Meta-analysis: general: Shelby and Vaske (2008); outdoor recreation economic values: Shrestha and Loomis (2003); contingent valuation and cultural resources: Noonan (2003).

- Methodological debate: see Kelly (1980), Henderson (2006), Rojek (1989), Borman *et al.* (1986), Krenz and Sax (1986), Bryman and Bell (2003): 465–78 – Chapter 21: 'Breaking down the quantitative/qualitative divide', Dupuis (1999).

- Network analysis: Stokowski (1994), Scott *et al.* (2008), sociometry Oppenheim (2000: 254–5).

- Panel surveys: LaPage (1994), Kasprzyk *et al.* (1989), Rose (2000).

- Perceptual mapping: Pearce (2005: 99–104), Walmsley and Jenkins (1991); Young (1999), Guy *et al.* (1990).

- Projective techniques: Semeonoff (1976), Oppenheim (2000, Ch. 12).

- Psychographic/lifestyle research: O'Brien and Ford (1988); Strategic Business Insights (2009), CACI Ltd (2006)

- Q methodology: principles: McKeown and Thomas (1988); applications: neighbourhood leisure and the elderly: Annear *et al.* (2009); motivation to visit zoos: Sickler and Fraser (2009).

- Quantitative modelling: Smith (1995: 140–3), Frechtling (1996: 172–9), Crouch and Louviere (2001), Hanley *et al.* (2003).

- Repertory grid: Kelly (1955); in leisure/tourism: Botteril (1989), Stockdale (1984), Potter and Coshall (1988).

- Scales:
  - outdoor recreation: Beard and Ragheb (1980), Driver *et al.* (1991);
  - tourism: Ryan and Glendon (1998), Hung and Petrick (2010);
  - physical and mental health: Ware *et al.* (1994), Brown, *et al.* (2001);
  - leisure/tourism and the Myers–Briggs personality indicator: McGuiggan (2000, 2001), Allen (1982);

- - Perceived Leisure Control Scale and Perceived Leisure Competence Scale: Witt and Ellis (1987);
  - Life Satisfaction Index: Neugarten *et al.* (1961);
  - Locus of Control Scale: Levenson (1974);
  - Leisure Boredom Scale : Iso-Ahola and Weissinger (1990);
  - marketing: Bruner and Hensel, (1992).

- Textual analysis: Prior (2003); television coverage of sport: Billings and Tyler Eastman (2002); sport: Rowe (2004); corporate advertising: Carty (1997) – see Case study 12.3; destination images: Litvin and Mouri (2009).

- Time-budget studies: Szalai (1972), Pentland *et al.* (1999), Zuzanek and Veal (1998); in tourism: Pearce (1988); for children regarding physical activity: Ridley *et al.* (2006).

- Triangulation: Bryman and Bell (2003: 482–4), in tourism: Hartmann (1988), Oppermann (2000).

6 Reviewing the literature

Introduction – an essential task

The aim of this chapter is to explain the importance, for any research project, of reviewing previous research and being aware of existing writing – the literature – on a topic. In addition the chapter indicates general sources of information on leisure and tourism studies literature, sets out the mechanics of compiling bibliographies and recording bibliographical references and considers the *process* of reviewing the literature for research purposes.

Reviewing existing research or writing on a topic is a vital step in the research process. The field of leisure and tourism studies comprises relatively new areas of academic enquiry which are wide-ranging and multidisciplinary in nature. Research is not so plentiful in the field that we can afford to ignore research which has already been completed by others. As discussed briefly in Chapters 3 and 5, the literature can serve a number of functions, as indicated in Figure 6.1.

The aim of research of an academic nature is to add to the body of human knowledge. In most societies that body of knowledge is generally in written form – the literature. To presume to add to the body of knowledge it is necessary to be familiar with what knowledge exists and to indicate precisely how the proposed or completed research relates to it. In research which is of a consultancy or policy nature, where the *primary* aim is not to add to knowledge but to use research to assist directly in the solution of policy, planning or management problems, a familiarity with existing knowledge in the area is still vital. Much time and valuable resources can be wasted in 're-inventing the

- The entire basis of the research
- Source of ideas on topics for research
- Source of information on research already done by others
- Source of methodological or theoretical ideas
- Source of comparison between your research and that of others
- Source of information that is an integral or supportive part of the research – for example, statistical data on the study area population

Figure 6.1 The roles of the literature in research

wheel' to devise suitable methodologies to conduct a project, or in conducting projects with inadequate methodologies, when reference to existing work could provided information on tried and tested approaches.

Identifying relevant literature is often a demanding task. It involves a careful search for information on relevant published and, if necessary, unpublished work; obtaining copies of relevant items and reading and them; making a list of useful items to form a *bibliography*; and assessing and summarising aspects which are salient for the research proposal or the research report in hand.

The value of bibliographies

This chapter focuses on reviewing the literature in relation to planned research projects, but the development of a bibliography can be a useful end in itself. It might be thought that modern electronic search methods have made the compilation and publication of bibliographies on specific topics obsolete, but this is not the case. While electronic databases are continually developing, they are still incomplete, especially with regard to:

- older published material;

- 'ephemeral' material, such as conference papers and reports and working papers not published by mainstream publishers;

- chapters from edited collections of papers;

- relevant content which is not mentioned in abstracts or keywords.

More importantly, electronic data-bases do not provide an *evaluation* of material: they rarely distinguish between a substantial research paper and a lightweight commentary with no original content. Further, not all databases are full-text, so electronic systems will only be able to identify items on the basis of their titles or, in some cases, key words and abstracts. A database may not indicate, for example, whether a report on 'recreation activities' includes data on a specific activity, such as golf, or whether a report on 'holiday patterns' mentions a specific form of holiday, such as back-packing. A great deal of useful work can therefore still be done in compiling bibliographies on specific topics, thus helping to consolidate the 'state of the art' and saving other researchers a great deal of time and trouble in searching for material.

Examples of published bibliographies in the leisure and tourism area are listed in the Resources section at the end of the chapter and considerable scope exists for the development of similar bibliographies on other topics. A number of websites list online bibliographies, again as indicated in the Resources section.

Searching: sources of information

Where can the researcher look for information on existing published research on a topic? In this section a number of sources is examined, as listed in Figure 6.2.

Library catalogues

Modern libraries have computerised catalogues which are accessible via terminals within the library and also from remote locations via the Internet. These online catalogues include information on:

- the library's own physical holdings;

- online materials, including e-books, online versions of journals and database sites such as national governmental statistical offices;

- in some cases, access to other university and public library catalogues.

Many of the online materials, like lending rights, are available only to registered library members, such as students or academic staff.

- Library catalogues
- Specialist indexes and databases
- Searching the Internet
- Google Scholar
- Published bibliographies
- General leisure/tourism books
- Reference lists
- Beyond leisure and tourism

Figure 6.2 Sources of information

Searches can be made on the basis of the titles of publications or using key words assigned to them by the library. This can be very helpful as a starting point in establishing a bibliography. But it is *only* a starting point, particularly for the researcher with a specialist interest.

If search words such as *leisure, tourism, sport* or *the arts* are used, the typical computerised catalogue will produce an enormous number of references, running to thousands, and far too many to be manageable. But if more specialised terms, such as *female golfers* or *Asian backpackers* are entered, the catalogue will produce few references, sometimes none at all. Whether a large or small number of references is produced, a proportion will be of a 'popular' nature, concerned with, for example, how to play golf, biographies of golfers, or backpacker guides to budget accommodation in Europe. Such material may be of interest to some researchers, but will be of little use if the researcher is interested in such aspects as levels of participation in golf, the socio-economic characteristics of golfers or trends in the numbers of backpackers.

Neither can a library catalogue indicate, for instance, whether a general report on *sport* or *recreation* or *tourism* includes any reference to a specific leisure activity or a particular type of tourism. And of course the catalogue will not identify publications which, while they deal with one topic, provide a suitable methodology for studying other topics. Such material can only be identified by actually reading – or at least perusing – original texts.

Catalogues of a library's physical holdings do not contain references to individual articles in journals, individual chapters in books which are collections of readings, or individual papers in collections of conference papers. But integrated within library online catalogues is access to Internet sources provided by specialist organisations, such as EBSCO, Informaworld and Ingenta, and online services provided by journal publishers.

Specialist indexes and databases

Specialist indexes and databases are online resources generally accessed via subscribing libraries. Examples in the leisure and tourism area are as follows:

- The most extensive and well-established index and electronic database of leisure and tourism publications is *Leisure Tourism Database*, published by the UK organisation CAB International, previously as the quarterly *Leisure, Recreation and Tourism Abstracts*, but now available online to subscribing libraries. It contains over 100,000 abstracts sourced from over 6000 periodicals and other publications, including details of books and book chapters. The basic format is publication details and abstracts, but some items are available in full text.

- SPORTDiscus is the most comprehensive reference and full-text source, for some 500 sport and sports medicine journals, dating back to 1985.

- The ISI Web of Knowledge (formerly Social Sciences Citation Index) is a comprehensive listing of papers from thousands of social science journals, cross-referenced by author and subject. In addition, items of literature referred to by authors in papers are themselves listed and cross-referenced, so that further writings of any cited author can be followed up. Unfortunately many leisure and tourism journals are not included in the database, but the index nevertheless includes references to a considerable amount of leisure and tourism material.

The advantage of using this type of database is that they ensure a level of reliability by dealing mainly with peer-reviewed material as discussed later in this chapter.

Searching on the Internet

Direct searching on the Internet using a search engine such as 'Google' has rapidly become second nature to computer users. Such searches are clearly effective when searching for organisational websites, but are a rather blunt tool for searching for published material compared with the specialist sources discussed above. Extreme caution should be exercised in using Internet sources. Some key specialist websites are listed in the Resources section.

Google Scholar

The Google Scholar website stores bibliographical information related to authors. It does not contain a complete bibliography for the individuals listed, but just those items which have been referenced – or 'cited' – by other authors. It therefore has a similar structure to the ISI Web of Knowledge mentioned above. For example, entering the name of the well-known leisure and tourism author John L. Crompton produces a long list of Crompton's publications, arranged in order of number of citations. The first is his article in *Annals of Tourism Research* on 'Motivations for pleasure vacations' which had, in March 2010, 661 citations. Clicking on the article title provides details of the article and clicking on the citation number brings up a list of the 661 publications in which the article has been cited. This is an effective way of identifying other papers on a topic – in this case vacation motivation. The database can also be searched using key words.

Published bibliographies

Reference has already been made to the value of bibliographies on particular topics. Libraries usually have a separate section for bibliographies and it may be worth browsing in that section, especially when the topic of interest is interdisciplinary. While many bibliographies have been published in hard-copy form over the years (see the Resources section for examples), the trend recently has been to publish these resources online.

General leisure and tourism publications

The researcher should be aware of publications which contain information on specific activities or aspects of leisure or tourism. For example, Chapter 7 discusses national leisure participation and tourism surveys which contain information on as many as a hundred leisure activities, on tourism flows of different types and a number of background items such as age and income. They are therefore a source of basic statistical information on many topics of interest.

General introductory books on leisure or tourism may have something to say on the topic of interest or may provide leads to other sources of information via the index and bibliography. In addition, in specialist encyclopaedias most entries include bibliographic references. Examples of specialist encyclopaedias include:

- Jenkins and Pigram (2003) *Encyclopedia of Leisure and Outdoor Recreation;*
- Weaver (2000) *Encyclopedia of Tourism;*
- Jafari (2000) *Encyclopedia of Tourism;*
- Brukner *et al.* (2003) *Encyclopedia of Exercise, Sport and Health;*
- Sherrow (1996) *Encyclopedia of Women and Sports;*
- Levinson and Christensen (1996) *Encyclopedia of World Sport: From Ancient Times to the Present;*
- Pendergast and Pendergast (1999) *St. James Encyclopedia of Popular Culture.*

Searching through such texts, using the contents pages or the index, can be a somewhat 'hit and miss' process, but can often be rewarded with leads which could not be gained in any other way. Even scanning through the contents pages of key journals, such as *Leisure Studies* or *Annals of Tourism Research*, may produce relevant material which would not be identified by conventional searches.

Reference lists

Most importantly, the lists of references in the books and articles identified in initial searches will often lead to useful material. Researchers interested in a particular topic should be constantly on the alert for sources of material on that topic in anything they are reading. Sometimes key items are encountered when they are least expected. The researcher should become a 'sniffer dog' obsessed with 'sniffing out' anything of relevance to the topic of interest. In a real-world research situation this process of identifying as much literature as possible can take months or even years. While a major effort should be made to identify material at the beginning of any research project, it will also be an on-going exercise, throughout the course of the project.

Beyond leisure and tourism

Lateral thinking is also an aid to the literature search task. The most useful information is not always found in the most obvious places. Some commentators have remarked on how many researchers fail to look beyond immediate *leisure* or *tourism* material. Leisure and tourism are interdisciplinary areas of study, not disciplines in their own right – they do not have a set of research methods and theories uniquely their own. Much is to be gained from looking outside the immediate area of leisure or tourism studies. For example, if the research involves measurement of *attitudes* then certain *psychological* literature will be of interest; if the research involves the study of leisure or tourism *markets* then general *marketing* journals may be useful sources and if the research involves the leisure activities of the *elderly* then *gerontology* journals should be consulted.

Unpublished research

Where possible, attempts should be made to explore not just published research – the *literature* – but also unpublished and on-going research. This process is very much hit and miss. Knowing what research is on-going or knowing of completed but unpublished research usually depends on having access to informal networks, although some organisations produce registers of on-going research projects. Once a topic of interest has been identified it is often clear, from the literature, where the major centres for such research are located and to discover, from direct approaches or from websites, annual reports or newsletters, what research is currently being conducted at those centres. This process can be particularly important if the topic is a 'fashionable' one. However, in such cases the communication networks are usually very active which eases the process. In this respect papers from conferences and seminars are usually better sources of information on current research than books and journals, since the latter have long gestation periods, so that the research reported in them is generally based on work carried out two or more years prior to publication.

Obtaining copies of material

If material is not available in a particular library it can often be obtained through the *inter-library loan* service. This is a system through which loans of books and reports can be made between one library and another. In the case of journal articles the service usually involves the provision of a digital copy. In theory any item published in a particular country should be available through this system since it is connected with national copyright libraries – such as the

British Lending Library in Boston Spa or the National Library in Australia – where copies of all published items must be lodged by law. Practices vary from library to library, but in academic libraries the service is often available to postgraduate students but undergraduate students may only access it through a member of academic staff.

For researchers working in metropolitan areas the other obvious source of material is specialist libraries, particularly of government agencies. For example, in London, Sports England and the English Tourist Board libraries are major resources for leisure and tourism researchers. In metropolitan areas and some other regions there is also often a cooperative arrangement between municipal reference libraries such that particular libraries adopt particular specialist areas – so it can be useful to discover which municipal library service specialises in leisure and/or tourism.

The full texts of journals are increasingly available via the Internet sources discussed above, in libraries which subscribe to the appropriate services. This means that copies of complete articles can be downloaded and printed out, not just the reference.

Compiling and maintaining a bibliography

What should be done with the material once it has been identified? Firstly a record should be made of everything which appears to be of relevance. The researcher is strongly advised to start a file of every item of literature used. This can be of use not only for the current research project but also for future reference – a personal bibliography can be built up over the years. Such record keeping can be done using cards, but is best done on a computer, using a word-processor or a database program, which can also store keywords. This has the attraction that when there is a need to compile a bibliography on another topic in future, a start can be made from your personal bibliography by getting the computer to copy designated items into a new file. In this way the researcher only ever needs to type out a reference once! Specialist packages, such as *Endnote* and *Pro-Cite*, which store reference material in a standard format, but will automatically compile bibliographies in appropriate formats to meet the requirements of different report styles and the specifications of different academic journals.

It takes only seconds to copy out the *full details* of a reference when it is first identified. It is advisable to have a stock of blank cards, notebook or computer always at hand for such purposes. If this practice is adopted, hours of time and effort can be saved in not having to chase up details of references at a later date. Not only should the details be recorded accurately, as set out below, but also a note should be made on the card or in the database about the availability of the material – for example, the library catalogue reference, or the fact that the item is *not* in the library, or that a photocopy or electronic copy has been taken.

Reviewing the literature

Reviewing the literature on a topic can be one of the most rewarding – and one of the most frustrating – of research tasks. It is a task where a range of skills and qualities needs to be employed – including patience, persistence, insight and lateral thinking.

Types of literature review

The review of the literature can play a number of roles in a research project, as outlined above, and this leads to a number of approaches to conducting a review, as listed in Figure 6.3.

Inclusive bibliography

The *inclusive* approach to reviewing the literature seeks to identify everything that has been written on a particular topic. The compilation of such a bibliography may be a significant achievement in itself, independent of any research project with which it may be connected. It becomes a resource to be drawn on in the future by others. Such a bibliography does not amount to a 'review' of the literature if there is no accompanying commentary, although classification of entries into categories (e.g. books, articles, government reports) or time-periods can be seen as the beginning of such a process. In some cases bibliographies merely list the reference details; in other cases they include abstracts of the contents – in which case they are referred to as *annotated* bibliographies. A number of examples of comprehensive bibliographies are listed in the Resources section.

- Inclusive bibliography
- Inclusive/evaluative
- Exploratory
- Instrumental
- Content analysis/hermeneutics

Figure 6.3   Types of literature review

Inclusive/evaluative review/consensus studies

The *inclusive/evaluative* approach takes the inclusive approach a stage further by providing a commentary on the literature in terms of its coverage and its contribution to knowledge and understanding of the topic. When this type of exercise is undertaken by a panel of researchers appointed by a governmental or other organisation, it may be referred to as a 'consensus study'. The most well-known study of this type in recent years has been the series of reports by the United Nations Intergovernmental Panel on Climate Change which evaluated the results of thousands of scientific publications to draw conclusion regarding climate change and its causes (UNIPCC, 2007). A more modest team-based exercise was the study commissioned by the World Leisure Organisation in 2006 (Jackson, 2006). Individual or small-team authored examples include:

- a review of the tourism forecasting literature by Calantone *et al.* (1987);

- an assessment of the health benefits of contact with nature in parks conducted for Parks Victoria and the International Park Strategic Partners Group by Maller *et al.* (2002);

- a review of the literature on the concept of *lifestyle* (Veal, 1993, 2000 – see Case study 6.1).

Case study 6.1   Lifestyle and leisure literature review

A review of the literature on the concept of lifestyle (see Veal, 1993, 2000) arose because, in the mid-1980s, the author was required to teach a course to a postgraduate class on 'leisure and lifestyle'. A preliminary scan of the literature revealed that the term 'lifestyle' was widely used in leisure and tourism research but was generally ill-defined, defined differently by different authors or was not defined at all. Further detailed investigation identified some 400 references making substantial use of the term and indicated that the concept of lifestyle had a number of histories and associated meanings in different disciplines and study areas. These included:

- *Weberian* – early sociological formulation by Max Weber;
- *sub-cultural* – ways of life associated with different sub-cultural groups (e.g. youth sub-cultures);
- *psychological* – outlook on life established in the first few years of life;
- *market research/psychographics* – quantitative analysis of values, attitudes and socio-economic characteristics;
- *spatial research* – ways of life associated with a type of residential location (e.g. suburban, rural);

- *leisure styles* – groupings of types of leisure;
- *socialist lifestyles* – ways of life approved of and planned for by East European communist regimes of the 1960s and 1970s.

As a result of examining this body of literature, it was suggested that, in seeking a generic definition for the concept of lifestyle, a number of dimensions should be considered, namely:

- *activities/behaviour* – including leisure, tourism, consumption, work and home activity patterns;
- *values and attitudes* – political, moral, aesthetic;
- *individuals versus groups* – whether a 'lifestyle' is only a group phenomenon;
- *group interaction* – whether interaction among individuals adopting particular lifestyles is required to develop and reinforce a lifestyle;
- *coherence* – whether a lifestyle requires some sort of internal aesthetic or moral coherence;
- *recognisability* – whether a lifestyle must be recognised by others to exist;
- *choice* – whether adoption of a *lifestyle* involves choice on the part of an individual, compared with a 'way of life' which might be imposed.

The contribution of this review was to identify the variety of independent uses and definitions of the concept, arising from its multidisciplinary antecedents, and to analyse the concept in terms of its constituent elements.

A common variation on the inclusive/evaluative type of review might be termed *literature analysis* and involves a quantitative analysis of temporal trends in the content and/or authorship of the literature in a particular field or in a particular journal. For example, Riley and Love (2000) present an analysis of the contents of four tourism journals since their inception to show the changing proportion of articles using qualitative methodology through the 1970s and 1990s. Burdge (1989) analysed the contents of two leisure studies journals over the 1970s and 1980s to show the changing disciplinary mix of the contributing authors. See also Case study 2.1.

An even more formalised quantitative approach to analysing the literature is known as *meta-analysis* and involves a systematic, quantitative appraisal of the findings of a number of projects focused on the same topic as discussed in Chapter 5. The technique is suitable for the sort of research where findings are directly comparable from one study to another – for example when the key research findings are expressed in terms of correlation or regression coefficients (see Chapter 17). In this approach the reported findings of the research themselves become the subject of research and the number of reported projects can become so large that it is necessary to *sample* from them in the same way that individuals are sampled for empirical research. Examples are listed in the Resources section.

Exploratory review

The *exploratory* approach is more focused and seeks to discover existing research which might throw light on a specific research question or issue. This is very much the classic literature review which is the norm for academic research and best fits the model of the research process outlined in Chapter 3. Comprehensiveness is not as important as the focus on the particular question or issue. The skill in conducting such a review lies in keeping the question or issue in sight, while 'interrogating' the literature for ideas and insights which may help shape the research. The reviewer needs to be open to useful new ideas, but must not be side-tracked into areas which stray too far from the question or issue of interest.

Instrumental review

An example of the *instrumental* approach is the brief review in Case study 3.3. Here the focus of the research is a management issue and the literature is used as a source of suitable ideas on how the research might be tackled. The criterion for selection of literature is not to present a picture of the state of knowledge on the topic, but merely to identify a useful methodology for the project in hand.

Content analysis and hermeneutics

Content analysis and *hermeneutics* are techniques which involve detailed analysis of the contents of a certain body of literature or other documentary source as *texts*. The text becomes a focus of research in its own right rather than being merely a report of research. The texts might be, for example, novels, politicians' speeches or the contents of advertising. Content analysis tends to be quantitative, involving, for example, counting the number of occurrences of certain phrases. Hermeneutics tends to be qualitative in nature, the term being borrowed from the traditional approach to analysis and interpretation of religious texts. The essence of this approach is discussed in Chapter 9, in relation to the analysis of in-depth interview transcripts.

Reading critically and creatively

Reviewing the literature for *research* purposes involves reading the literature in a certain way. It involves being concerned as much with the methodological aspects of the research (which are not always well reported) as the substantive content. That is, it involves being concerned with *how* the conclusions are arrived at as well as with the conclusions themselves. It involves being critical

a. Individual items

- What is the (empirical) basis of this research?
- How does the research relate to other research writings on the topic?
- What theoretical framework is being used?
- What geographical area does the research refer to?
- What social group(s) does the research refer to?
- When was the research carried out and is it likely still to be empirically valid?

b. In relation to the literature as a whole

- What is the *range* of research that has been conducted?
- What *methods* have generally been used and what methods have been neglected?
- What, in summary, does the existing research tell us?
- What, in summary, does the existing research *not* tell us?
- What contradictions are there in the literature – either recognised or unrecognised by the authors concerned?
- What are the *deficiencies* in the existing research, in substantive or methodological terms?

Figure 6.4 Questions to ask when reviewing the literature

– questioning rather than accepting what is being read. The task is as much to ascertain what is *not* known, as it is to determine what *is* known. This is different from reading for other purposes, such as some essay-writing. In the latter instance a particular substantive critical issue may be being explored, but the research basis or overall scope of the literature being discussed may not be an issue.

As material is being read, a number of questions might be asked, as set out in Figure 6.4. The questions relate to both individual items and to the body of literature as a whole.

It can be helpful to be conscious of the appropriate way in which the contents of an item of literature should be reported. A number of styles of reporting are used, including:

- Smith believes . . . thinks . . . is of the opinion . . .

- Smith argues . . .

- Smith establishes . . .

- Smith observes . . .

- Smith speculates . . .

- Smith puts forward the possibility that . . .

- Smith concludes . . . .

An author's opinion or beliefs may be important if the author is someone who deals in opinions and beliefs, such as a politician or cleric, but we generally expect more than just statements of belief from academic literature. An academic may be influenced by particular ideological or religious beliefs – for example a well-known theorist in the field of leisure, Josef Pieper, author of *Leisure, the Basis of Culture*, was a Catholic priest and this is not irrelevant to his work, but if his work had been merely a statement of faith it would not have been as influential as it has been in the development of leisure theory. A review of the literature should convey accurately the basis of the material presented, whether it be opinion, the result of argument or presentation of empirical evidence, informal observation or speculation. The type of literature being summarised is therefore important: newspaper and popular and professional magazine articles are not subject to the same checks and balances as academic journal articles; and reports emanating from leisure or tourism organisations or from politically motivated organisations cannot always be relied on to tell 'the truth, the whole truth and nothing but the truth'. Of course such material may appear in a literature review, but its status and the way it is reported and interpreted should be treated with caution and subtlety.

Care should be taken when referring to textbooks. Textbooks, such as this one, may contain some original contributions from the author, but will mostly contain summaries of the state of knowledge in a field, with some material attributed to specific sources and some not. Generally, in a research report, particularly a thesis, original scholarly sources rather than textbooks should be referred to where possible.

As regards the substantive content of the literature, a major challenge for a reviewer is to find some framework to classify and analyse it. In the case of an inclusive literature review, literature might be classified chronologically, by geographical origin or by discipline. For other types of review, themes or issues are likely to be more important. Reviewing the literature in this way can be similar to the development of a conceptual framework for a research project, as discussed in Chapter 3. Some sort of diagrammatic, concept map, approach, as indicated in Figure 6.5, may be helpful. Such a diagram might be devised before starting a review, or may be developed, inductively, as the review progresses.

Summarising

A review of the literature should draw *conclusions* and *implications for the proposed research programme*. It is advisable to complete a review by presenting a *summary* which addresses the second set of questions in Figure 6.4. This summary should lead logically to the research project in hand. It should make clear to the reader just how the proposed research relates to the existing body of literature – whether it is seeking to: add to the body of knowledge in a unique way; fill a gap in knowledge; update existing knowledge; correct or contradict some aspect of existing knowledge; or simply use ideas from the literature as a source of ideas or comparison. When a large amount of literature with similar

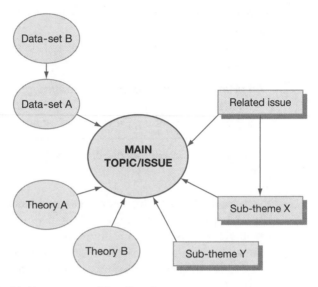

Figure 6.5   Making sense of the literature

format is being reviewed it may be helpful to summarise it in a tabular quasi-meta-analytical form, using headings such as: geographical area covered, sample size, independent variables used, year of survey.

Referencing the literature

The purpose of referencing

What is the purpose of referencing? Firstly, referencing is evidence of the writer's scholarship: it indicates that the particular research report is related to the existing body of knowledge. This is not only of importance to teachers marking student assignments or theses – it is part and parcel of the development of knowledge. Secondly, references enable the reader of the research report to check sources – either to verify the writer's interpretation of previous research or to follow up areas of interest.

Recording references

A number of standard or conventional formats exist for recording references to the literature. The conventions have been established by leading academic organisations and publishers. Guides are produced by organisations such as the American Psychological Association (1983) and the Australian Government Publishing Service (see Snooks and Co., 2002), to which the reader is referred

---

- **A book or report:**
  Author(s), Initials (Year) *Title of Book or Report in Italic*. Place of publication: Publisher.

- **An article from a periodical (journal/magazine/newspaper):**
  Author(s), Initials (Year) Title of article. *Title of Periodical in Italic*, Volume number (Issue number), Page number span.

Figure 6.6 Standard/generic reference formats

for more detail. The formats presented here do not conform to any one standard approach but offer a style which, if followed consistently, would be acceptable in most academic contexts. In what follows, the word *text* refers to the main body of the research report or article.

The general format recommended for recording references is as shown in Figure 6.6.

In some systems the date is put at the end, but when using the *author/date* or *Harvard* system, as discussed below, the date should follow the author name as indicated.

Note that the part of the reference which is in *italic* is the title which would be found in a library catalogue. Thus what is found in a library catalogue is the name of the periodical, not the title of the article, so it is the *title of the periodical* that is in italic. In the case of a chapter from a book, the title of the book is found in the catalogue, not the title of the chapter, so the *title of the book* is in italic.

Note that the *publisher* of a book is not the same as the *printer* of the book. For example, for this book the *publisher* is Financial Times/Prentice Hall (or Pearson Education), but the *printer* is Ashford Colour Press (see p. iv). References do not need to refer to the printer. And note that it is *not* necessary to refer to the publisher in the case of periodicals.

Some examples of reference formats are set out in Figure 6.7 to illustrate the principles.

Particular note should be made that, in the book chapter example, the main reference is to the author(s) of the chapter, not to the editor(s) of the book.

Internet references are becoming increasingly common. One of the problems with this medium is that some sources disappear or their website address (URL) changes over time, so that it is difficult for the reader to follow them up. For individual publications it is often advisable to give the index or 'list of publications' address rather than the often long and complex address of the individual publication. The general principle to be followed is that an Internet reference should include all the details which would normally apply to hard-copy items, *plus* the website URL *and* the date accessed. The place of publication is not always clear from the website, but can generally be found with a little effort. If accessing a journal article via the Internet, it is not necessary to give the website address unless the journal is known to be only published electronically. Published style guides are now available for referencing in relation to this evolving medium, for example, *The Columbia Guide to Online Style* (Walker and Taylor, 1998).

1. A book	Ryan, C. (1991) *Recreational Tourism: A Social Science Perspective*. London: Routledge.
2. An edited book	Ritchie, J. R. B. and Goeldner, C. R. (eds) (1994) *Travel, Tourism, and Hospitality Research: A Handbook for Managers and Researchers*. 2nd edn, New York: John Wiley and Sons.
3. A chapter from an edited book	Gunn, C. A. (1994) A perspective on the purpose and nature of tourism research methods. In J. R. B. Ritchie and C. R. Goeldner (eds) *Travel, Tourism, and Hospitality Research: A Handbook for Managers and Researchers*. 2nd edn, New York: John Wiley and Sons, 3–12.
4. A published conference report (NB in the example, the printed proceedings were published two years after the conference was held)	Ruskin, H. and Sivan, A. (eds) (1995) *Leisure Education: Towards the 21st Century, Proceedings of the International Seminar of the World Leisure and Recreation Commission on Education, Jerusalem, August, 1993*. Provo, Utah: Brigham Young University Press.
5. A published conference paper	Veal, A. J. (1995) Leisure studies: frameworks for analysis. In H. Ruskin and A. Sivan (eds) *Leisure Education: Towards the 21st Century, Proceedings of the International Seminar of the World Leisure and Recreation Commission on Education, Jerusalem, August, 1993*. Provo, Utah: Brigham Young University Press, 124–136.
6. A government agency report, authored and published by the same agency	Sport England (1999) *Best Value Through Sport: Case Studies*. London: Sport England.
7. A journal article	Ravenscroft, N. (1993) Public leisure provision and the good citizen. *Leisure Studies*, 12(1), 33–44.
8. A newspaper article with named author	Hornery, A. (1996) Market researchers facing major hurdles. *Sydney Morning Herald*, 11 April, p. 26.
9. A newspaper item without a named author	*Sydney Morning Herald* (1996) Our green future, 7 June, p. 12.
10. An Internet source	Veal, A. J. (2003) *Education, Training and Professional Development in Leisure: A Bibliography*. On-line Bibliography 10, Sydney: School of Leisure and Tourism Studies, University of Technology, Sydney, available at: www.business.uts.edu.au/lst/research/bibs.html (accessed Jan 2005).

Figure 6.7 Examples of references

Some guidelines suggest that newspaper articles should be referenced with the title of the article rather than, as here, with the author or the name of the newspaper. The important point to note is that, once a style is adopted, it should be consistent throughout the report.

Referencing and referencing systems

There are two commonly used referencing systems: the 'author/date' system, sometimes referred to as the 'Harvard' system, and the 'footnote' or 'endnote' system. These two systems are discussed in turn below.

The author/date or Harvard system

Basic features

In the author/date, or Harvard, system, references to an item of literature are made in the text by using the author's name and the year of the publication; at the end of the paper or report, references are listed in alphabetical order. Thus, a sentence in a report might look something like this:

> Research on women and leisure in the 1970s and 1980s included work in Britain by Deem (1986), in Canada by Bella (1989), in the United States by Bialeschki and Henderson (1986), and in Australia by Anderson (1975).

Note that authors' initials are not used in these references (unless there are two authors with the same surname). At the end of the report a list of references is provided, arranged in alphabetical order, as follows.

References

Anderson, R. (1975) *Leisure: An Inappropriate Concept for Women?* Canberra: AGPS.

Bella, L. (1989) Women and leisure: beyond androcentrism. In E. L. Jackson and T. L. Burton (eds) *Understanding Leisure and Recreation*, State College, PA: Venture, 151–80.

Bialeschki, M. D. and Henderson, K. (1986) Leisure in the common world of women. *Leisure Studies*, 5(3), 299–308.

Deem, R. (1986) *All Work and No Play? The Sociology of Women's Leisure*. Milton Keynes: Open University Press.

Style variation

The style of presentation can be varied; for instance, the above statement could be made drawing less explicit attention to specific authors:

> Interest in research on women and leisure was widespread in the 1970s and 1980s in the English speaking world, as work from authors in Britain, Canada, the United States and Australia indicates (Bella, 1989; Bialeschki and Henderson, 1986; Deem, 1986; Anderson, 1975).

Specifics and quotations

When referring to *specific points* from an item of literature, rather than making a general reference to the whole item, as above, page references should be given to the specific point of interest. This is particularly important when referring to a specific point from a substantial publication like a book, for example:

> Aitchison (2003: 135–58) makes the link between gender issues and leisure management practices.

When *quoting* directly from a source, page references should also be given:

> Iso-Ahola makes the point that: 'To survive as an academic field, scholars must supply evidence that their methods of investigation are valid and reliable rather than "soft" ' (1980: 49).

A longer quotation would be indented in the page and handled like this:

> Iso-Ahola argues the case for scientific research in the leisure area and states:
>
> > To survive as an academic field, scholars must supply evidence to the effect that their methods of investigation are valid and reliable rather than 'soft'. This becomes increasingly important in obtaining grants from sources inside and outside academic institutions (Iso-Ahola, 1980: 49).

Advantages and disadvantages

The author/date system is an 'academic' style. Its disadvantage is therefore that referencing is very 'up-front', even obtrusive, in the text. It is not an appropriate style for some practically orientated reports, particularly where the readership is not academic. Large numbers of references using this style tend to 'clutter up' the text and make it difficult to read. The system also has the disadvantage that it does not incorporate footnotes (at the foot of the page) or endnotes (at the end of the chapter). However, one view is that footnotes and endnotes are undesirable anyway – that if something is worth saying it is worth saying in the text. If notes and asides are nevertheless considered necessary it is possible to establish a footnote system for this purpose in addition to using the author/date system for references to the literature only. This of course becomes somewhat complex. If footnotes or endnotes are considered necessary then it is probably best to use the footnote style for everything, as discussed below.

The advantages of the author/date system are that it saves the effort of keeping track of footnote or endnote numbers; it indicates the date of publication to the reader; the details of any one item of literature have to be written out only once; and it results in a tidy, alphabetical list of references at the end of the document.

Footnote or endnote system

Basic features

The *footnote* style involves the use of numbered references in the text and a list of corresponding numbered references at the foot of the page, at the end of each chapter or at the end of the report or book. The term footnote originates from the time when the notes were invariably printed at the foot of each page – and this can be seen in older books. However, printing footnotes at the bottom of the page came to be viewed as too complex to organise and too expensive to set up for printing, so it was generally abandoned in favour of providing a list of notes at the end of each chapter or at the end of the book. Consequently *endnotes* are now more common. Ironically, the advent of word-processing has meant that the placing of footnotes at the bottom of the page can now be done automatically by computer. Most word-processing packages offer this feature, automatically making space for the appropriate number of footnotes on each page and keeping track of their numbering and so on. Publishers have, however, generally adhered to the practice of placing the notes all together at the end of the chapter or book.

The actual number reference in the text can be given in brackets (1) or as a superscript: [1]. Using the footnote system, the paragraph given above appears as follows:

Research on women and leisure in the 1970s and 1980s included Deem's[1] work in Britain, Bella's[2] work in Canada, Bialeschki and Henderson's[3] work in the United States and Anderson's[4] work in Australia.

The list of notes at the end of the report appear in the numerical order in which they appear in the text:

Notes
1 Deem, R. (1986) *All Work and No Play? The Sociology of Women's Leisure.* Milton Keynes: Open University Press.
2 Bella, L. (1989) Women and leisure: beyond androcentrism. In E. L. Jackson and T. L. Burton (eds) *Understanding Leisure and Recreation.* State College, PA.: Venture, 151–80.

3 Bialeschki, M. D. and Henderson, K. (1986) Leisure in the common world of women. *Leisure Studies*, 5(3), 299–308.

4 Anderson, R. (1975) *Leisure: An Inappropriate Concept for Women?* Canberra: AGPS.

It can be seen that this format is less obtrusive in the text than the author/date system. In fact it can be made even less obtrusive by using only one footnote, as follows:

Research on women and leisure in the 1970s and 1980s included work by researchers in Britain, Canada, the United States and Australia.[1]

At the end of the report the reference list then appears as follows:

Notes

1 In Britain: Deem, R. (1986) *All Work and No Play? The Sociology of Women's Leisure*. Milton Keynes: Open University Press.

In Canada: Bella, L. (1989) Women and leisure: beyond androcentrism. In E. L. Jackson and T. L. Burton (eds) *Understanding Leisure and Recreation*, State College, PA.: Venture, 151–80.

In the USA: Bialeschki, M. D. and Henderson, K. (1986) Leisure in the common world of women. *Leisure Studies*, 5(3), 299–308.

In Australia: Anderson, R. (1975) *Leisure: An Inappropriate Concept for Women?* Canberra: AGPS.

Multiple references

It should never be necessary to write a reference out in full more than once in a document. Additional references to a work already cited can be made using *op. cit.* or references back to previous footnotes. For example, the above paragraph of text might be followed by:

Deem pioneered the study of women and leisure in Britain.[2]

The footnote would then say:

2 Deem, *op. cit.*   **or**   2 See footnote 1.

Specifics, quotations

Page references for specific references or quotations are given in the footnote rather than the text. So the Iso-Ahola quotation given above would look like this:

Iso-Ahola makes the point that: 'To survive as an academic field, scholars must supply evidence to the effect that their methods of investigation are valid and reliable rather than "soft" '.[4]

The footnote would then say:

> 4 Iso-Ahola, S. E. (1980) Tools of social psychological inquiry. Chapter 3 of *The Social Psychology of Leisure and Recreation*, Dubuque: Wm. C. Brown, p. 49.

Further quotations from the same work might have footnotes as follows:

> 5 Iso-Ahola, *op. cit.* p. 167.

Advantages and disadvantages of the footnote/endnote system

One of the advantages of the footnote system is that it is less obtrusive than the author/date system and it can accommodate authors' notes in addition to references to the literature, as discussed above. A disadvantage of the system is that it does not result in a tidy, alphabetical list of references. This diminishes the convenience of the report as a source of literature references for the reader. Some writers therefore resort to producing a bibliography in addition to the list of references. This results in extra work, since it means that references have to be written out a second time (but see 'Comparing two systems' below). Keeping track of footnotes or endnotes and their numbering is much less of a disadvantage than it used to be, since this can now be taken care of by the word-processing program.

Comparing two systems

The features, advantages and disadvantages of the two systems, author/date and footnote/endnote, are summarised in Figure 6.8.

Feature	Harvard/Author–date	Footnote/Endnote
Reference in text	Author (date)	Number, e.g.: [1]
Reference format	Author (date) *Title*. Publishing details.	1. Author *Title*. Publishing details, date
Reference list format	Alphabetical list at end of report	Numbered list at: <ul><li>foot of pages, or</li><li>end of chapters, or</li><li>end of report</li></ul>
Advantages	<ul><li>alphabetical bibliography</li><li>easy to use</li><li>date of publication conveyed in text</li></ul>	<ul><li>unobtrusive in text</li><li>can add other notes/comments</li></ul>
Disadvantages	<ul><li>obtrusive in text</li><li>can't add notes</li></ul>	<ul><li>can be difficult to use without computer</li><li>no alphabetical bibliography</li></ul>

Figure 6.8   Reference systems: features, advantages, disadvantages

One way of combining the advantages of both systems is for the list of notes in a footnote/endnote system to consist of author/date references and then to provide an alphabetical list of references at the end of the report. So the list of footnotes for the above paragraph would then appear as follows:

Notes
[1] Deem, 1986.
[2] Bella, 1989.
[3] Bialeschki and Henderson, 1986.
[4] Anderson, 1975.

An alphabetical bibliography would then follow which would be the same as for the author/date system. This approach is particularly useful when making several references to the same document.

Referencing issues

Second-hand references

Occasionally you make a reference to an item which you yourself have not read directly, but which is referred to in another document which you have read. This can be called a *second-hand* reference. It is misleading, somewhat unethical, and risky, to give a full reference to the original if you have not read it directly yourself. The reference should be given to the second-hand source, *not* to the original. For example:

> Kerlinger characterises research as 'systematic, controlled, empirical, and critical investigation of hypothetical propositions about the presumed relations among natural phenomena' (quoted in Iso-Ahola, 1980, p. 48).

In this instance the writer has not read Kerlinger in the original but is relying on Iso-Ahola's quotation from Kerlinger. The Kerlinger item is not listed in the references; only the Iso-Ahola reference is listed. It is ethical to treat the second-hand reference this way and it is also safe, since any inaccuracy in the quotation then rests with the second-hand source.

In academic research reports – journal articles and theses – second-hand references should be avoided and every effort made to access and refer to the original source.

Excessive referencing

A certain amount of judgement must be used when a large number of references is being made to a single source. It becomes very tiresome when repeated reference is made to the same source on every other line of a report! One way to avoid this is to be very 'up-front' about the fact that a large section of your literature review is based on a single source. For example, if you are summarising MacCannell's work on tourism, rather than have large numbers of formal references to MacCannell cluttering up the text, it may be preferable to have a separate section of the report and announce it as follows:

> The Work of MacCannell
> This section of the review summarises MacCannell's (1976) seminal work, *The Tourist: A New Theory of the Leisure Class*. . . .

Subsequently, formal references need only be given when using specific quotations.

Latin abbreviations

A number of Latin abbreviations is used in referencing:

et al.   If there are more than two authors of a work, the first author's name and *et al.* may be used in text references, but all authors should be listed in the bibliography: *et al.* stands for the Latin *et alia*, meaning 'and the others', and is generally presented in italic.

op. cit.   stands for the Latin *opere citato*, meaning 'in the work cited'.

ibid.   In the footnote system, if reference is made to the same work in consecutive footnotes, the abbreviation *ibid.* is sometimes used, short for *ibidem*, meaning 'the same'.

Summary

This chapter provides an overview of the process of reviewing the literature, as a research tool in its own right and as an essential element of any research project. It is noted that a literature review can have a number of purposes and can take a number of forms, ranging from being the entire basis of a research project to being the source of ideas and methods for conducting a research project. The mechanics of searching for relevant literature is examined, including library catalogues, published bibliographies and indexes and electronic sources. The process of reviewing the literature is examined, addressing the sorts of questions which should be asked when conducting such a review for research purposes. Finally, the chapter reviews the process of referencing the literature, examining the characteristics and advantages and disadvantages of the author/date or Harvard system and the footnote or endnote system.

Test questions

1. What are the potential uses of the literature review in research?

2. Name three different sources of bibliographical information and their advantages and limitations.

3. What is the difference between conducting a literature review for the purpose of writing an essay compared with providing the context for a research project?

4. What are the advantages and disadvantages of the author/date referencing system compared with the footnote/endnote system?

5. What is a 'second-hand' reference?

Exercises

1. Compile an *inclusive* bibliography on a topic of your choice, using the sources outlined in this chapter.

2. Choose a research topic and:
   a. investigate the literature using a library computerised catalogue and any other electronic database available to you;
   b. explore the literature via literary sources, such as reference lists and indexes in general textbooks, journal contents and lists of references in articles;
   c. compare the nature and extent of the bibliography arising from the two sources.

Resources

Websites

- CABI Leisure Tourism site: www.leisuretoursim.com

- Sport Discus: www.ebscohost.com/academic/sportdiscus-with-full-text

- UTS bibliographies: www.business.uts.edu.au/lst/research/publications/bibliographies/

- World Tourism Organisation: www.unwto.org/pub/index.htm

Examples of bibliographies:

- an early example on the sociology of leisure: Meyersohn (1958);
- on tourism generally: Baretje (1964), Goeldner, 1994;
- on tourism and travel research: Goeldner and Dicke (1980);
- on recreational use of beaches: Veal (1997);
- on the Olympic Games: Veal and Toohey (2009);
- on leisure, sport and ethnicity: Geary *et al.* (1996);
- on disability and tourism: Darcy (1998);
- on urban parks: Veal (2004);
- on education, training and professional development in leisure: Veal (2003).

Evaluative literature reviews:

- on the concept of lifestyle: Veal (1993, 2000);
- on tourism forecasting: Calantone *et al.* (1987).

Meta-analysis:

- generally: Glass *et al.* (1981);
- on international tourism demand: Crouch and Shaw (1991);
- on contingent valuation (willingness-to-pay) and the arts: Noonan (2003);
- on contingent valuation (willingness-to-pay) and outdoor recreation economic values: Shrestha and Loomis (2003).

Style manuals:

- American Psychological Association (APA) (1983) and www.apastyle.org; AGPS style manual: Snooks and Co. (2002);
- electronic style manual: Walker and Taylor (1998); APA guidelines at: www.apastyle.org/elecref.html.

Part

II

Data collection

This part of the book is concerned with six forms of data collection and the process of sampling, which is relevant to all empirical methods. The chapters are:

Chapter 7   *Secondary data sources* – existing data collected by other organisations for research or administrative purposes.

Chapter 8   *Observation* – quantitative and qualitative: looking with the naked eye or using technology.

Chapter 9   *Qualitative methods: data collection* – the range of approaches.

Chapter 10 *Questionnaire surveys: typology, design and coding*.

Chapter 11 *Experimental methods* – classic model and quasi-experimental models in leisure and tourism research.

Chapter 12 *The case study method* – the study of one or more cases, typically using multiple data sources.

Chapter 13 *Sampling: quantitative and qualitative* – achieving representativeness, random and non-random sampling and issues of sample size.

Specific chapters on data analysis are provided in Part III.

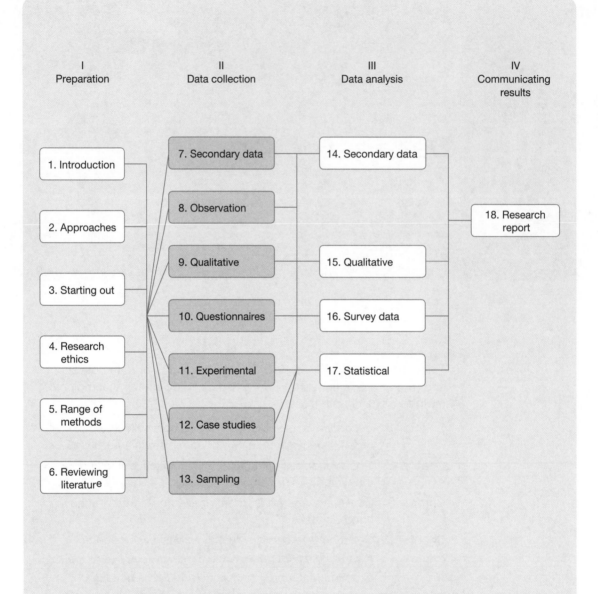

I Preparation	II Data collection	III Data analysis	IV Communicating results
1. Introduction	7. Secondary data	14. Secondary data	18. Research report
2. Approaches	8. Observation		
3. Starting out	9. Qualitative	15. Qualitative	
4. Research ethics	10. Questionnaires	16. Survey data	
5. Range of methods	11. Experimental	17. Statistical	
6. Reviewing literature	12. Case studies		
	13. Sampling		

7 Secondary data sources

Introduction – measurement

Before giving specific consideration to secondary data sources, we address the issue of measurement in leisure and tourism. This relates not only to secondary sources, but also to any form of quantitative method, including quantitative forms of observation, as discussed in Chapter 8, the design of questionnaires, as discussed in Chapter 10, and aspects of experimental methods and case study research, as discussed in Chapters 11 and 12 respectively. Therefore this initial section of the chapter can be seen as an introduction to the quantitative parts of Part II of the book. We consider the issue of measurement of leisure and tourism in general, then addresses the topic of counting heads, as raised in Chapter 5.

Measuring leisure and tourism activity

Figure 7.1 presents a five-fold typology of ways in which leisure and tourism activity can be measured and the relationships between them:

● The percentage *participation rate* is the most commonly used measure in leisure policy and planning research: it indicates the proportion of the

Measure	Definition	Relationships	Leisure example	Tourism example
A Participation rate	The proportion of a defined population which engages in an activity in a given period of time		6 per cent of the adult population of community X go swimming at least once a week	5 per cent of the adult population of country X make an overseas trip each year
B Number of participants	Number of people in a defined community who engage in an activity in a given period of time.	A × pop'n. or C ÷ frequency of visit	20,000 people in community X swim at least once a week	700,000 residents of country X visit country Y in a year
C Volume of activity (visits)	The number of visits made or games played in an activity by members of a defined community or to a defined geographical area for an activity in a specified time-period	B × visits/games per time-period*	There are 1.2 million visits to swimming pools in community X (one million by local residents) in a year	850,000 trips are made to country Y by residents of country X in a year
D Time	The amount of leisure time available to the individual in a defined community, over a specified period – or time spent on specific activity.	C × time per visit	The average retired person has 5 hours leisure time per day/or spends an average of 3 hours watching television per day	The average tourist visiting region Z spends 5.5 nights in the region
E Expenditure	The amount of money spent per individual or by a defined community on leisure or particular leisure goods or services over a specified time-period.	C × spend per visit	Consumer expenditure on leisure in Britain is over £50 billion a year	Tourists visiting region Z spend £25 million in the region per annum

Figure 7.1   Measuring leisure and tourism activity

* In tourism a further distinction is made between 'trips' (e.g. a complete holiday) and visits (i.e. places visited during the holiday).

** In tourism the measure 'bed-nights' is often used.

population participating or the proportions of particular social groups participating. This is particularly salient because of the public policy emphasis on equity and access. By contrast, in tourism research the emphasis tends to be on the other four measures. In fact, the participation rate for tourism – the proportion of the population who go on holiday in the course of a year – is a rarely compiled statistic.

- The *number of participants* is equal to the participation rate multiplied by the population, so if the latter is rising, the number of participants can be rising even as the participation rate is falling.

- The *volume of activity* is equal to the numbers of participants multiplied by frequency of participation and is one of the measures of greatest interest to facility managers because it indicates the number of tickets sold. In the case of tourism, this measure arises in three forms:
  - trips (the traveller's full, possibly multi-destination, itinerary);
  - visits (to a single destination);
  - visitor-nights (overnight stay in a destination).

- *Time* spent on an activity is relevant in some sectors, such as electronic media and is of key importance in a number of policy contexts: for example, the amount of time people spend taking exercise versus the amount of time they spend in sedentary activities.

- *Expenditure* per visit and in total is, of course, the key measure for the private sector, and increasingly in the public sector. It is the prime measure for tourism since, from the point of view of the host country or region, net economic benefits are its main justification.

Counting heads

As noted in Chapter 5, a key aspect of leisure/tourism policy-making, planning and facility management is the identification of levels of use – 'counting heads' or, in the case of audiences and spectators, counting 'bums on seats'. Figure 7.2 shows a variety of sources of information on leisure participant/visitor numbers in three sections: administrative, or secondary, sources; questionnaire-based surveys; and direct counts. Because counting tourists involves people entering a country or region from elsewhere, typically for multiple trips and activities, it presents particular challenges and these are summarised in Figure 7.3.

Figures 7.2 and 7.3 clearly involve more than just secondary data but the full range of sources/methods is included here to make the point that none of these methods should be considered in isolation; indeed, for many estimation purposes data from different sources must be combined. Observation and survey methods are discussed in Chapters 8 and 10 where further reference is made to Figures 7.2 and 7.3.

Depending on how much information is gathered in the process, counting heads generally enables much more than presentation of numbers. It can

Method	Data available	Additional data required to estimate numbers
Administrative – facility-based		
1. Individual ticket sales	Ticket sales per time-period	–
2. Bookings data	Facility bookings per time-period	Group size (by sample observation)
3. Season ticket/annual pass sales	Annual/season ticket sales	No. of trips per time-period per ticket (by survey)
4. Membership records/surveys	a. If member visits are automatically recorded: visits/time-period b. If not: visits/time-period from member survey	Number of members
5. Parking ticket sales data	Parking ticket sales per time-period	Vehicle occupancy (by sample observation)
Questionnaire-based surveys (see Chapter 10)		
6. Resident survey	% participating in activity and/or visiting particular facilities or facility types Avge frequency per time-period	Population (from census)
7. Tourist survey	% visiting facility/facility type No. of visits during stay, length of stay	No. of tourists (from national/regional tourist body or local research)
8. On-site visitor interview surveys	% commuters, neighbours ** (Tourists could be included here)	–
On-site visitor counts (see Chapter 8)		
Automatic counters		
9. Automatic vehicle counters	Number of vehicles per time-period	Vehicle occupancy (by sample observations)
10. Automatic pedestrian counters	Number of persons per time-period	–
11. Video/time-lapse cameras/aerial photography	Number of persons/vehicles/craft present – sampled times, gives person/vehicle/craft-hours	For vehicles/craft: vehicle occupancy For all: average length of stay (by survey)
Visual/manual counts		
12. Entrance or exit flows	Number of visitors per time-period	–
13. Spot counts of numbers present	Number of persons present – sampled times, gives person-hours	– Average length of stay (by survey)

Figure 7.2 Counting heads: sources and methods – leisure*

* For more detailed discussion see Veal (2010a, Chapter 10)
** Commuters and neighbours live in other council areas and use local facilities: commuters work in the study area and use facilities from workplace; neighbours use local facilities from home.

Method	Nature
Administrative	
1. Ports of entry short-term arrival/departure data	All incoming passengers complete arrival cards, number of non-residents recorded
2. Public transport data	In situations where all visitors arrive by one or more public transport modes (e.g. island destinations by boat); visits = ticket sales (may need calibration for number of locals)
Questionnaire-based surveys (see Chapter 10)	
3. Road cordon survey: interview	• On major entry roads: total vehicle numbers noted by camera/traffic counter. • Sample of vehicles stopped: vehicle occupancy noted. • driver interviewed re origin/destination, proportion tourists noted.
4. Road cordon survey: questionnaire	As above with additional self-completion mail-in questionnaire.
5. International visitors survey	Interviews with sample of departing tourists at airports: provides characteristics, itinerary, etc., but dependent on method 1 for actual numbers.
6. Domestic tourism survey	Survey of sample of residents on domestic tourism travel (e.g. ≥ 1 overnight stay and ≥ 40 km) over specified period: indicates proportion who have travelled in period.
7. On-site tourist survey	Interview a sample of tourists at known tourist gathering places. Filter tourists only. Dependent on other sources for actual numbers.
8. On-site facility visitor survey	Appropriate when one facility dominates the destination – e.g. a major national park. Interview a sample of all visitors to a leisure/tourist attraction: identify tourist proportion. Total visits to site available from other source.
9. Accommodation survey	Survey of accommodation operators to ascertain number of guests over a particular period (may need calibration for VFR (visiting friends and relatives)).
Direct counts/observation (see Chapter 8)	
10. Road cordon survey: automatic	Camera technology used to count all vehicles and record origin state/county/country of vehicle registration: proportion of non-local vehicles noted.

Figure 7.3 Counting heads: sources and methods – tourism*

* For more detailed discussion see Veal (2010a, Chapter 10).

facilitate examination of, explanation of and extrapolation of: trends in usage; performance levels (e.g. costs or income per visit); market reach; and social/ economic impact. The process of analysing these various forms of data and using them to estimate visitor numbers is addressed in Chapter 14.

Introduction to secondary sources

In this chapter we consider the use of existing sources of data, as opposed to the collection of new data which is the subject of most of the rest of the book. The chapter examines mainly published statistical sources, such as the census and national leisure and tourism participation surveys, but other sources, such as archives and management data are also included.

In undertaking research it is clearly wise to use existing information where possible, rather than embarking on expensive and time-consuming new data collection exercises. One aspect of this has already been touched on in Chapter 6 in relation to the use of the literature. In searching the literature the researcher may come across references to statistical or other data which are open to alternative analyses and interpretations or which may not have been fully analysed or exploited by the original collectors of the data, because of their particular interests or limitations on time or money. In other cases information may exist which was not originally collected for research purposes – for example, the administrative records of a leisure or tourism organisation – but which can provide the basis for research:

- *Primary* data are new data specifically collected in the current research project – the researcher is the *primary user* of such data.

- *Secondary data* already exist and were collected for some other (primary) purpose but can be used a second time in the current project – the researcher is the *secondary user*. Further analysis of such data is referred to as *secondary analysis*.

As with the literature, secondary data can play a variety of roles in a research project, from being the whole basis of the research to being a vital or incidental point of comparison. But to be seen as a research method in its own right in a project, the use of secondary data should contribute significantly to answering its research questions or testing hypotheses.

Some secondary data are available in a very 'raw' form – for example, organisational membership data – in such cases the dividing line between primary and secondary data becomes blurred. In other cases the data are highly processed: for example, the results of national leisure or tourism surveys. However, in such cases the data may still require considerable additional processing to be useful for the purpose in hand, and data from different sources may need to be combined in various ways. In other cases, the data available in published form are not adequate for the purpose in hand and fresh analysis of the raw data is required – for example, involving accessing computer files of survey data for re-analysis. In this chapter we address just the sources of data: data analysis is addressed in Chapter 14.

Advantages and disadvantages of using secondary data

Some advantages and disadvantages of using secondary data are listed in Figure 7.4.

A considerable amount of leisure and tourism data are collected on a regular basis at considerable cost, particularly by government agencies. Often the immediate policy requirements of the data are quite limited – for example, to announce a global figure on tourism numbers or numbers of participants in sport. In a sector where research funds are limited, it would seem unwise for the research community to waste such resources by failing to extract all possible research potential from them. This requires careful consideration of ways in which available data might be used, and often calls for a quasi-inductive approach to research, posing the question: what can these data tell us?

Types of secondary data

Six main sources of secondary data are listed in Figure 7.5. The inclusion of national leisure and tourism surveys might seem incongruous, since they are questionnaire-based surveys and so it might be thought that they should be discussed in Chapter 10. But the class of surveys discussed here are large-scale and typically conducted on an annual basis so they take on the characteristics of 'official statistics'. The government agencies which commission them can be seen as the primary users, but they are also used by a variety of other

---

Advantages
- Timing – data may be instantly available.
- Cost – cost of collecting new data avoided.
- Experience – the 'trial and error' experience of those who collected the original data can be exploited.
- Scale – secondary data may be based on larger samples than would otherwise be possible.
- Serendipity – inductive process of data analysis may yield serendipitous findings, which may not have arisen with primary, purpose-designed data collection.

Disadvantages
- Design – secondary data have been designed for another purpose, so may not be ideal for current project.
- Analysis limitations – if access to the raw data for re-analysis is not possible, opportunities for analysis/manipulation of the data for the current project may be limited.

Figure 7.4 Advantages and disadvantages of using secondary data

---

Administrative/management data
National leisure participation surveys
Tourism surveys
Economic surveys
The census of population
Documentary sources
Opportunism

Figure 7.5   Types of secondary data

organisations and individuals, including industry bodies and firms, other levels of government, consultants and academics. The categories listed in Figure 7.5 are examined in turn in this chapter. Where appropriate, reference is made to examples in Britain and Australia.

Administrative/management data

Tourist arrivals and departures

At airports and international borders governments collect data on individuals arriving and departing from the country via the familiar landing and departure cards. While the data are gathered for 'border protection' reasons, a by-product is information on tourist and resident arrivals and departures. For the most part tourism agencies rely on their own surveys of international tourists because they provide more detailed information, but the arrivals/departure data provide data which are internationally more complete and comparable, hence their use by organisations such as the World Tourism Organization (WTO) and the Organisation for Economic Cooperation and Development (OECD) (see the Resources section).

Management data

Most leisure and tourism organisations generate routine data which can be of use for research purposes and many have *management information systems* specifically designed to produce data upon which assessments of the performance of the organisation are based. Examples of such data, which may be available on an hourly, daily, weekly, monthly, seasonal or annual basis, are listed in Figure 7.6. It is usually advisable to explore fully the nature, extent and availability of such data, and their potential utilisation, before embarking on fresh data collection. For example, in Case study 3.1, the manager of a facility is concerned about declining levels of visits. Before initiating expensive

Visitor numbers (in various categories)
Visitor expenditure/income (in various categories)
Bookings and facility utilisation
Customer enquiries
Membership numbers and details
Customer complaints
Results of visitor/customer surveys
Expenditure of the organisation (under various headings)
Staff turnover/absenteeism, etc.

Figure 7.6 Management data

procedures, such as surveys, to investigate the causes it would be advisable to study the *available visitor data* to see whether the decline was across all services, and whether it was taking place at all times or only at certain times of the day, week, season or year.

Numerous agencies are involved in collection of management data for their own administrative purposes, and in most cases the information is available in the annual reports of those organisations, and sometimes on their websites. But generally the data made public is only presented in summary form and the detail remains unpublished. Collation of such information, for example as input to a local plan, therefore becomes a research project in its own right. And if information is required at national level, even in summary form, that also often requires considerable effort. There are some limited examples of such national collations, and examples are listed in the Resources section.

National leisure participation surveys

The national leisure survey phenomenon

In most developed countries surveys of leisure participation are conducted by government departments or agencies on a regular basis. In the USA such surveys have been conducted since the early 1960s, particularly on outdoor recreation (Cordell *et al.*, 2005). Other countries began collecting leisure participation data in the 1970s and 1980s: the volume edited by Cushman *et al.* (2005a) includes data from 15 countries. Each country has tended to adopt different design principles, particularly in the way 'participation' is defined, as discussed below, so that the findings between different countries are generally not comparable.

In Britain the General Household Survey (GHS), commissioned by government agencies and conducted by the Office for National Statistics and its predecessors, has provided leisure participation information every 3–5 years since 1973 (Gratton and Veal, 2005). The last set of published results from the GHS including data on sport and some arts/cultural activities relates to 2002 (Fox and Richards, 2004).

Since 2007 the Active People Survey, with a massive sample of 190,000, has been conducted annually by Sport England and, on behalf of the government, covers cultural activities as well as sport. The large sample size is necessary so that data can be made available for every local council with a minimum sample size of 500 to be used in annual monitoring of performance. Figure 7.7 indicates the range of data available from the survey. The data are available online on the Sport England website (see the Resources section).

The existence of this data-base demonstrates both the merits and drawbacks of secondary data. It is most unlikely that the £3–4 million a year which the Active People Survey costs to conduct would be available for purely research purposes: it is conducted to meet the policy requirements of Sport England, the Department of Communities and Local Government (DCLG) and the Department of Culture Media and Sport (DCMS) in regard to its 'broad Departmental Strategic Objective to encourage more widespread enjoyment of culture and sport, and support talent and excellence' (DCMS, 2009). This has implications for the design of the survey and the ways in which the data are analysed and published and these features are discussed further in Chapter 14.

In addition to the Active People Survey, the British government also conducts the annual Taking Part Survey, details of which can be found on the DCMS website. This survey seems to cover much the same ground as the Active People Survey, but with a much smaller, but still large, sample (27,000) which provides data down to the regional level but not to individual council level. The survey also covers children's participation.

In Australia the national government statistics agency, the Australian Bureau of Statistics (ABS), was responsible for the main sports and physical recreation participation surveys during the 1990s and continues to conduct such surveys from time to time. In addition it conducts periodic surveys on participation in the arts, on children's leisure participation and on sport spectating. Since 2001, however, the main source of national and state-level sport and physical recreation participation data has been the annual Exercise Recreation and Sport Survey (ERASS) conducted by the Standing Committee on Recreation and Sport (SCORS), which represents the Australian Sports Commission and the state governments' ministries of sport and recreation. Details are shown in Figure 7.7.

National leisure participation surveys are the main source of information available to researchers on overall participation levels in a range of leisure activities. How they fit into the spectrum of methods for 'counting heads' is discussed at the end of the chapter. A number of issues arise in the use of these important data bases, including questions of validity and reliability, sample size, the participation reference period used, the age range of the population covered, the range of activities included, and availability of information on the social characteristics of respondents. These topics are discussed in turn below.

Britain: Active People Survey

Conducted by: Sport England
Sample size: 190,000

Dates: Annual since 2007
Age-range: persons aged 16 and over

Participation data items
Sport and recreational physical activity

Walking – at least 30 mins (freq. in last four weeks, pace)

Cycling – as for walking

Other sport/recreation/physical activity – as for walking

Sports club membership

Competitive sports participation

Instruction/coaching in sport

Overall satisfaction with sports provision

Likelihood to do more sport: name one activity

Change in participation in last year: reason

Socio-demographic data items
Gender

Age

Ethnic group

Age completed full-time education

Highest qualification

Accommodation type

No. of children in household

Car/van availability

Disability

Current work status

Cultural

Museum/gallery attendance in last year

Public library use in last year

Attendance at creative, artistic, theatrical or musical events in last year: number attended

Actually doing creative, artistic, theatrical or musical activities in last year: frequency

Socio-economic status (ten questions)

Main income-earner occupation

Postcode

Australia: Exercise, Recreation and Sport Survey (ERASS)

Conducted by: Standing Committee on Recreation and Sport (SCORS)
Sample size: 13,000

Dates: Annual since 2001

Age-range: persons aged 15 and over

Participation data items
Individual sport/physical activities participated in at least once in previous year

For the above activities: number of times; whether organised by club etc. or informal

Of the above activities: Those participated in during previous two weeks: frequency, time spent

Socio-demographic data items
Gender, Age, Marital status
Parental status, No. of children

Highest education qualification
Employment status, hours worked

Aboriginal
Language spoken at home
Postcode

Figure 7.7   National leisure participation survey details

Source: Britain: DCMS website: www.culture.gov.uk/images/research/Active_People_Survey_questionnaire.pdf
Australia: Standing Committee on Recreation and Sport (SCORS): Exercise, Recreation and Sport Survey: www.ausport/information/scors). For further information, see the Resources section.

Validity and reliability

National leisure surveys suffer from the limitation of all interview surveys in that they are dependent on respondents' own reports of their patterns of leisure participation. How sure can we be, therefore, that the resultant data are accurate? We cannot be absolutely sure, as discussed in Chapter 10; however, a number of features of national surveys lend credence to their reliability and value as sources of data:

- national government statistical organisations have an enviable reputation for quality and professionalism in their work;
- the surveys are often based on large sample sizes;
- the fact that there has been little dramatic variation in the findings of the various surveys over the years is reassuring (Cushman and Veal, 1993; Gratton and Tice, 1994; Gratton and Veal, 2005) – erratic and unexplainable fluctuations in reported levels of participation would have led to suspicions that the surveys were unreliable, but this has not happened.

Some commentators have questioned the validity of participation surveys, conducting experiments which show that there is a tendency for respondents to exaggerate levels of participation substantially, at least in relation to some activities (Chase and Godbey, 1983; Chase and Harada, 1984). However, as Boothby (1987) suggests, for some groups, some activities and some surveys there may also be under-reporting of levels of activity. While national survey data, especially when sponsored by governments, have the imprimatur of being 'official statistics', they are subject to all the limitations of questionnaire-based surveys as discussed in Chapter 10.

Sample size

It is generally the case that the larger the sample size the more reliable and precise are the survey findings. The Australian survey discussed above is based on a sample of around 13,000 interviews and is therefore subject to only minimal 'statistical error' – a term explained in Chapter 13. The British survey, at 190,000 is much larger; in fact it would be unnecessarily large if its only purpose was to provide national-level data. But it is designed to provide data for each of the 350 local councils in England, giving most a sample of only 500, which is subject to considerable margins of statistical error, as can be seen in Chapter 13 (Figure 13.1).

For many activities covered in the surveys the proportion of the population participating is less than 1 per cent. However, even 1 per cent of the adult population of Britain is almost half a million people, so small percentages can represent large numbers of people. While this issue is discussed in more detail in Chapter 13, the constraints of a small sample size compared with a large sample size can be imagined from the following:

- Exercise, Recreation and Sport Survey: national sample size 13,000: 1% = 130;

- Active People Survey: national sample size 190,000: 1% = 1900;

- Active People Survey sub-sample for one council area: 500: 1% = 5.

Main question – participation reference period and duration

The level of participation depends substantially on the 'reference period' used, that is, the period of time to which the participation relates. Thus, for example, the proportion of the population who have been swimming in the last 24 hours would be quite small, the proportion who have done so in the last month would be higher, while the proportion who have ever been swimming would be almost 100 per cent. Furthermore, in the case of physical activity, the *duration* of participation is important when considering the question of health benefits. Thus for some activities measuring only the proportion of participants who have participated for at least a minimum prescribed time, such as 30 minutes a week, would reduce the reported participation rate considerably. This is illustrated in Table 7.1 which shows, for a number of sports activities:

Table 7.1   Participation rates in sports, England, 2002, 2008–09

Sports*	2002		2008-9	
	Participated at least once in last year	Participated at least once in last 4 weeks	Participated at least once in last month	Participated for at least 30 mins in last week
	% of persons aged 16 and over		% of persons aged 16 and over[†]	
Walking	45.9	34.9	na	na
Swimming	34.8	13.8	13.2	7.6
Cycling	19.1	9.0	9.3	4.5
Football	9.1	4.9	7.4	5.1
Athletics**	1.0	0.3	6.4	4.2
Golf	12.1	4.8	3.5	2.1
Badminton	6.4	1.8	2.4	1.3
Tennis	7.0	1.9	2.4	1.3
Squash	3.8	1.3	1.2	0.7
Cricket	2.4	0.6	1.0	0.5
Equestrian	3.5	1.9	1.0	0.8
Bowls	3.8	1.3	1.0	0.6

Sources: 2002: Office for National Statistics General Household Survey: www.statistics.gov.uk/lib2002/tables/#sport. 2008–9: Sport England: Active People Survey www.sportengland.org/research/active_people_survey/active_people_ survey_3.aspx

* Activities with at least 1% participation in last month in 2008–9 included.
** 2002 definition is 'track and field' – 2008–9 includes all jogging, marathons, etc.
[†] National participation rates estimated from aggregated county figures.

- the proportion of the population participating at least once in the last year compared with the proportion in the last four weeks (2002);

- the proportion participating in the last month and, of those who have participated for at least 30 minutes in the last week (2008–9).

It can be seen that the second measure in each case reduces the participation rate by at least half, and in some cases by two thirds.

The published results from the Australian ERASS do not include the one-week measure for individual activities, but the proportion taking part in any form of exercise, recreation or sport activity in 2007–08 was 83.4 per cent while the proportion who participated at least three times a week was just 49.3 per cent.

The one-year reference period is becoming the international norm (Cushman *et al.*, 2005b: 284). This practice has the advantage of covering participation in all seasons of the year in one survey and including most infrequent participants. However, it has the disadvantage of introducing possible errors in respondents' recall of their activities over such a long time-period. Furthermore, for sport and physical exercise activity policy-makers are interested in minimum frequency and duration which produce health benefits, so a one-week or two-week measure is becoming an additional norm for that sector. Use of the shorter reference period has the advantage of increased accuracy of recall, but the disadvantage that seasonal variation must be covered by interviewing at different times of the year.

Age range

Participation surveys are restricted in terms of age range covered. Some include respondents as young as 12 years old, while some cover only those aged 18 and over. And some have upper age limits. The British and Australian surveys presented here cover people aged 16 and over. The reasons for not interviewing young children are three-fold:

1. It may be difficult to obtain accurate information from very young children.

2. It may be considered ethically unacceptable to subject children to the sort of questioning which adults can freely choose to face or not (see Chapter 4).

3. There is a question as to when children are considered to engage in their own independent leisure activities as opposed to being under the control of parents.

Some surveys present data on children from 'proxy' interviews, in which questions about children's activities are answered by parents: an example is the Australian Bureau of Statistics (2000a) survey of children's participation in culture and leisure activities. By contrast, the DCMS Taking Part Survey includes, for a sub-sample, direct interviews with children, but this is limited to children aged 11–15.

An age limit in the mid-teens has effects on the results, in that for some activities – for example swimming or cycling – young teenagers may be a significant proportion of total participants. For other activities – for example gardening or going to the opera – the age limit may be inconsequential because young people are not among the most frequent participants. When using data from leisure participation surveys, particularly when seeking to compare results from different surveys, it is therefore important to bear in mind the age-range covered.

Social characteristics

In addition to the basic information on participation, national leisure surveys generally include a wide range of background information on the people inter- viewed, including such variables as gender, occupation, age, education level reached, size of family or household unit and ethnicity or country of birth. This information can be used to examine levels of participation by different social groups from either an equity or a marketing point of view, and can also be used to predict demand, as future changes in the underlying social structure of the community affect patterns of demand; this is explored in Chapter 14.

The importance of participation surveys

Leisure participation surveys, despite their limitations, are the main source of information, not only on overall levels of participation but also on differences in participation between different groups in the community, such as the young and the old, men and women, and different occupational and income groups. Any leisure researcher or professional should therefore be familiar with such key data sources.

National time-use surveys

Time-use, or time-budget, research became a significant focus of international social research with the conduct of the UNESCO-funded *Multinational Com- parative Time-Budget Research Project* in the 1960s (Szalai, 1972). In Britain such surveys were conducted as long ago as the 1930s when the BBC used them to explore the public's patterns of use of broadcast media, while in Australia they date back to the 1970s. In recent years, time-use surveys have been of par- ticular interest because of the belief that people are becoming increasingly time-pressured. The most recent UK time-use surveys which permit analysis of trends in time-use were conducted in 2001 and 2005. UK time-use surveys are conducted in association with 14 other European countries under the auspices of the Harmonised European Time Use Survey which makes data available online (see the Resources section). The most recent in Australia were the 1997 and 2006 surveys conducted by the Australian Bureau of Statistics.

Time-use surveys ask respondents to keep a diary of their activities for one or two days, so they cover all aspects of time-use, including leisure, and are a key source of information for leisure studies. Compared with the participation surveys discussed above, the 'reference period' for a time-use survey is effectively one or two days. This overcomes the problem of recall accuracy involved in surveys which use longer recall periods, resulting in more reliable data, but drastically reduces the proportion of respondents engaging in any one activity. Apart from activities which large numbers of people engage in on most days, notably watching television and listening to the radio, time-use surveys are not ideal for studying individual leisure activities but are used to examine broad categories of time-use, as shown in Table 7.2.

While time-use surveys may give an adequate representation of day trips from home, they tend not to include holiday activity because of the obvious practical difficulties of sampling in the context of a domestic survey. There is, however, a parallel process of studying the time-budgets of holiday-makers at their destination. Douglas Pearce (1988) discussed the idea over two decades ago, drawing attention to a number of existing examples.

Table 7.2   Time use: Britain and Australia

	Britain, 2005	Australia, 2006
	Hours per week, persons aged 15+*	
Sleep	57.3	59.6
TV/video/radio/music	18.3	16.3
Other leisure	23.4	18.2
Paid work	19.8	24.1
Personal care	14.7	17.1
Domestic work/childcare	22.3	22.7
Travel and other	12.3	10.0
Total	168.0	168.0

Sources: Britain: data from Office for National Statistics: Time Use Survey, 2005, available at: www.ons.gov.uk
Australia: data from Australian Bureau of Statistics *How Australians Use Their Time, 2006*, online resource at: www.abs.gov.au/ausstats/abs@.nsf/mf/4153.0

* NB. Some differences between Britain and Australia may due to differences in definitions and some due to differing age structure.

Tourism surveys

International and domestic tourism surveys

The information on each traveller gathered by the landing and departure cards discussed above is typically limited to under ten items, including country of origin, transport mode, length of stay, purpose of visit (holiday, business, visiting friends or relatives, etc.), gender, age and occupation and the area/destination where the traveller will be spending most time. For data on such matters as tourist expenditure, destinations and satisfaction questionnaire-based surveys are used. Typically one survey is conducted of international visits to a country and another of domestic tourism trips within a country. The international survey tends to be conducted by face-to-face interviews of passengers at ports of entry/departure. For domestic tourism the survey is conducted either as a face-to-face household survey or by telephone. Questions on overseas trips by residents are sometimes added to the domestic tourism survey and sometimes covered by including residents as a sub-sample of the international arrivals/departure survey.

Details of such surveys conducted in Britain and Australia are provided in Figure 7.8. Quarterly or annual summaries of the results of the surveys are available online (see the Resources section).

Sample size

It will be noted, in Figure 7.8, that the samples are substantial. This is because information is required:

- on a quarterly as well as annual basis;
- for regional or country sub-samples (including breakdowns of demographics, expenditure, etc. for the sub-samples);
- to provide a basis or grossing up to provide estimates of actual numbers of visits and visitor-nights (see Chapter 13, Confidence intervals applied to population estimates, for discussion of the sample size implications of grossing up).

Definitions

As with leisure surveys, the data on tourist trips is influenced by the definition of 'tourist' and the reference time-periods used. Most definitions of tourism require a person to stay away from their normal place of residence for at least one night and travel a certain minimum distance to qualify as a tourist. This means that people who take a trip from London to Southend or Brighton, but

UK: International Passenger Survey

Conducted by	Office for National Statistics
Frequency	Annual, continuous
Included	UK residents and international visitors to UK
Sample size	250,000
Method	Face-to-face interviews at major air/sea/Channel Tunnel port custom points

UK: UK Tourist Survey

Conducted by	Tourism commissions: Britain, England, Scotland, Wales
Frequency	Annual, continuous
Included	Residents aged 16+
Sample size	100,000
Trips included	Trips in last four weeks involving at least one night away from home.
Method	Face-to-face home-based interviews

Australia: International Visitor Survey

Conducted by	Tourism Research Australia
Frequency	Annual, continuous (quarterly and annual reports)
Included	Visitors to Australia
Sample size	40,000
Method	Face-to-face interviews in departure lounges of eight airports

Australia: National Visitor Survey

Conducted by	Tourism Research Australia
Frequency	Annual, continuous (quarterly and annual reports)
Included	Australian residents, 15+
Sample size	120,000
Trips included	Overnight stays $\geq$40km from home in last four weeks Daytrips $\geq$50km, $\geq$4 hours, in last week Overseas trips in last 3 months
Method	Telephone survey

Typical data collected	International destination: country Domestic destination: region Length of stay, nights Purpose of trip (holiday, business, VFR, etc.) Expenditure Transport mode used Accommodation type used Information sources used Leisure activities Demographics (age, gender, etc.)

Figure 7.8 National tourism survey details

do not stay overnight, are not classified as tourists, but as day trippers. But many tourism surveys include day trips, usually defined by a minimum distance travelled (e.g. at least 40km) and a minimum time away from home (e.g. 4 hours), because catering to day trippers is a significant component of the tourism industry in many destinations.

Comprehensive data on border crossings are no longer collected in Europe because of the sheer volume of such crossings and the increasing liberalisation of travel regulations. Thus, while arrivals and departure data are collected by governments and their agencies for official purposes, the 'hard' data on tourism flows can, in reality, be every bit as 'soft' as the data on leisure participation (Edwards, 1991).

Economic data

Household expenditure

In most developed countries surveys of *household expenditure* are conducted on a regular basis. In Britain the survey is an annual one and is called the *Expenditure and Food Survey*, while the Australian equivalent, the *Household Expenditure Survey*, is conducted every five years (see the Resources section). These surveys collect information from a cross-section of families throughout their respective countries on their weekly expenditure on scores of items, many of which relate to leisure and tourism. Figure 7.9 indicates the range of leisure-related items included in such surveys.

These economic data sources provide the basis for the regular leisure expenditure forecasting and market trend analysis reports produced by such organisations as the Sport Industries Research Centre at Sheffield Hallam University for the UK, and Richard K. Miller and Associates for the USA (details are in the Resources section).

Typical leisure expenditure items included in natonal household expenditure surveys

Alcoholic drink	Cinema, theatre, museums etc. admissions
Tobacco	Restaurant meals
Audio-visual, photographic, computer equipment	TV, video, Internet costs
Games, toys, hobbies	Photographic
Computer software and games	Gambling (net losses)
Sporting, camping, outdoor recreation equipment	Newspapers, magazines, books, stationery
Gardening equipment, plants	Holidays – domestic and abroad
Pets, pet food	Transport (leisure about 30% of total)
Sports admissions, subscriptions, fees	

Figure 7.9 Household expenditure survey leisure items

Satellite accounts

Leisure and tourism industries – tourism, sport, gambling, etc. – are multi-sectoral, including direct service components, hospitality, transport, local government and so on. In national accounting systems which establish the economic scale and impact of industry sectors, leisure industries do not feature in their own right; their economic activity is spread across a range of the major industry sectors. Yet, were these components to be identified and information on them drawn together, they would be seen to be substantial industry sectors. Special projects have therefore been established in a number of countries, at the behest of interested government departments and agencies and industry groups, to establish satellite accounts to extract relevant data from across the national accounts and assemble it in an accessible form. The aim is to provide economic data on the leisure industries on an annual basis. It is not proposed to examine the results of these projects here, but sources are indicated in the Resources section. In Australia a tourism satellite account has been in existence since 1999–2000, while in the UK sport and tourism satellite accounts appear to be only at the planning stage.

The population census

And it came to pass in those days, that there went out a decree from Caesar Augustus, that all the world should be taxed. . . And all went to be taxed, every one into his own city. *(Luke, 2: 1–3)*

While the accuracy of the details in this quotation from the Bible referring to the time of the birth of Christ is disputed by scholars, it indicates that the taking of a census of the whole population, for taxation and other purposes, is a long-standing practice of governments. Another well-known historical example is the Domesday Book, compiled by William the Conqueror for the whole of England in the eleventh century.

The modern population census

The *population census* is an important source of information and any aspiring leisure/tourism manager or researcher should be fully aware of its content and its potential. A complete census of the population is taken in Britain by the Office for National Statistics every ten years; the latest was 2001, and before that 1991, 1981 and so on. In Australia, because the population is growing relatively rapidly, the Australian Bureau of Statistics undertakes a census every five years. As in most countries, it is a statutory requirement for householders (and hoteliers, hospital managers, boarding school principals and prison governors) to fill out a census form on 'census night', indicating the number of people, including

Britain	Australia
National	National
Regions	State
Counties	Postal codes
Local government areas	Local government areas
Parliamentary constituencies	State and federal Parliament electorates
Enumeration districts (EDs)	Collection districts (CDs)

Figure 7.10 Census data: levels of availability

visitors, in the building, and their age, gender, occupation and so on. Some people escape the net, for instance some people sleeping rough or illegal immigrants, but generally the information is believed to be reliable and comprehensive.

Data from the census are available at a number of levels, from national down to the level of Enumeration Districts (EDs) (Collection Districts, CDs, in Australia), as indicated in Figure 7.10. CDs are small areas, with populations of around 250 to 500, which a single census collection officer deals with on census night. By adding together data from a few CDs, a leisure facility manager can obtain data on the demographic characteristics of the population of the catchment area of the facility. An enormous amount of information is available on each of these areas, as listed in Figure 7.11.

Resident population
Number of males/females
Number/proportion in five-year age-groups (and single years for under-20s)
Numbers of people:
- with different religions
- by country of birth
- speaking different languages
- by country of birth of parents

Numbers of families/households:
- of different sizes
- with different numbers of dependent children
- which are single-parent families
- with various numbers of vehicles

Numbers of people:
- who left school at various ages
- with different educational/technical qualifications
- in different occupational groups
- by working hours
- unemployed
- living in different types of dwelling

Figure 7.11 Census data available

Uses of census data

It can be seen that none of the census information, with the possible exception of working hours, is concerned directly with leisure or tourism, so why should the census be of interest to the leisure or tourism researcher? Among the uses, which are explored further in Chapter 14, are:

● planning facilities and conducting feasibility studies,

● area management/marketing,

● facility performance evaluation,

● market segmentation.

Documentary sources

Documentary sources lie somewhere between literature and management data as an information source for research. Typical examples are listed in Figure 7.12. Many of such sources are important for historical research, either for a primarily historical research project, or as background for a project with a contemporary focus. In some cases the documents are a focus of research in their own right – for example, some research on women and sport has examined the coverage of women's sport in the media (e.g. Rowe and Brown, 1994). As the links between cultural and media studies and leisure and tourism studies increase, so analysis of media content, including television, is likely to increase (Critcher, 1992; Tomlinson, 1990). Approaches to analysing such data are addressed in Chapter 15.

● Minutes of committee/council/board meetings

● Correspondence of an organisation or an individual

● Archives (may include both of the above and other papers)

● Popular literature, such as novels, magazines

● Newspapers, particularly coverage of specific topics and/or particular aspects, such as editorials, advertising or correspondence columns

● Brochures and advertising material

● Diaries

Figure 7.12   Documentary sources

Opportunism

Secondary data often give rise to what might be called opportunistic research, as discussed in Chapter 3. This applies to many of the government-sponsored surveys discussed above: data exist and have been used by the collecting agency only for limited purposes, or in internal policy-making processes which are not in the public domain. Examples include:

● the use of routinely collected playground accident data to study the effects of introducing new playground equipment (see Case study 11.6);

● the use of official data on sport participation to examine the validity of the claimed 'trickle down' effect of hosting major sporting events (Veal and Frawley, 2009).

Summary

This chapter is concerned with sources of secondary data, that is, data which have been collected by others for other purposes but might be utilised for current research purposes. There are potential cost and time-saving advantages to such a strategy and even an ethical dimension, which suggests that scarce resources should not be expended on new data collection if adequate data already exist. The chapter reviews a number of sources of secondary data commonly used in leisure and tourism research, namely: national leisure participation surveys; tourism surveys; economic data on consumer expenditure; the census of population; management data; and documentary sources. Analysis of such data is discussed in Chapter 14.

Test questions

1. What are the advantages and disadvantages of secondary data analysis?

2. What are some of the issues to be considered when using data from leisure participation surveys?

3. What are the names of the main surveys conducted in your country related to the following:
   (a) leisure participation
   (b) domestic tourism
   (c) international tourism
   (d) household expenditure?

4. The chapter lists nine sources of 'management data'. What are they?

5. The chapter lists seven types of 'documentary' source. What are they?

NB. No exercises are offered for this chapter, but exercises using secondary data are presented in Chapter 14.

Resources

Websites

Tourist arrivals/departures:

- Australia: www.abs.gov.au/ausstats/abs@.nsf/mf/3401.0

National collation of facility use data:

- Museums and galleries, UK: www.culture.gov.uk/what_we_do/research_ and_statistics/ 3375.aspx

- Museums and galleries, Australia: www.abs.gove.au, select Topics @ a Glance, then Culture and Recreation.

UK national leisure/tourism surveys:

- Sport/culture participation: Department for Culture, Media and Sport (DCMS) Taking Part Survey: www.culture.gov.uk/what_we_do/research_and_ statistics/4828.aspx

- Active People Survey: www.sportengland.org/research/active_people_ survey.aspx

- UK Tourist Survey (domestic): www.visitbritain.org/insightsandstatistics/ index.aspx

- International Passenger Survey: www.statistics.gov.uk/ssd/surveys/ international_ passenger_survey.asp

- Living Costs and Food Survey: www.statistics.gov.uk, search on 'Living costs'.

- Population census: www.ons.gov.uk/census/index.html

Australia national surveys:

- Exercise, Recreation and Sport Survey: www.ausport.gov.au/information/ scors/ERASS

- Australian Bureau of Statistics data: www.abs.gov.au. select 'Topics @ a Glance' and then 'Culture and Recreation'.

- International Visitor Survey and National Visitor Survey: Tourism Research Australia: www.ret.gov.au/tourism/tra/Pages/default.aspx.

- Arts participation: Australia Council for the Arts: www.australiacouncil. gov.au/research.

- Household Expenditure Survey: www.abs.gov.au/ausstats/abs@nsf/mf/ 6530.0

- Population census: www.abs.gov.au, click on 'Census'.

International data:

- Harmonised European Time Use Survey: https://www.h2.scb.se/tus/tus/

- Organisation for Economic Cooperation and Development (OECD): www.oecd.org, search for 'Tourism' and 'Society at a glance' then locate Chapter 2 'Measuring Leisure in OECD Countries'

- World Tourism Organization: www.unwto.org.

Annual industry/consumer expenditure surveys:

- UK annual leisure/sport industry reviews: Sport Industry Research Centre, Sheffield Hallam University: www.shu.ac.uk/research/sirc/publications.html

- USA annual leisure industry review: Richard K. Miller and Associates: www.rkma.com.

Sport tourism satellite accounts:

- Australia: www.abs.gov.au/AUSSTATS/abs@.nsf/MF/5249.0

- UK: for details of planning studies for sport and tourism accounts: see Department of Culture, Media and Sport website: www.dcms.gov.uk.

Publications

- National collation of local authority facility use data, UK: Chartered Institute of Public Finance and Accountancy (CIPFA) (annual) – data for individual councils on open space, golf courses, playing fields, swimming pools, cultural facilities: costs, income, use levels (some gaps for some data items).

- Leisure surveys: international: Cushman *et al.* (2005a) includes data from leisure, time-use and some tourism surveys for 15 countries: Australia; Canada; Finland; France; Germany; Great Britain; Hong Kong; Israel; Japan; The Netherlands; New Zealand; Poland; Russia; Spain; and the USA.

- Leisure surveys, Australia: Veal (2003, 2005).

- Tourism data sources: Burkart and Medlik (1981, Part III); Edwards, 1991; Goeldner, 1994.

- Time-use surveys: Pentland *et al.* (1999), Gershuny (2000).

- Tourism satellite accounts: ABS (2009), Frechtling (2010).

- Documentary sources: Kellehear (1993).

8 Observation

Introduction

The aim of this chapter is to draw attention to the importance of *looking* in research and to introduce some of the specific approaches of observational methods. It examines situations in which observation is particularly appropriate and outlines the main steps to be taken in designing and conducting an observation-based project. Observation is a neglected technique in leisure and tourism research; nevertheless, while it is rarely possible to base a whole project on observation, the technique has a vital role to play, formally or informally, in most research strategies. Typically, observation is one of a number of techniques that may be used in a study, especially when 'head counting' is concerned, as indicated in Figures 7.2 and 7.3.

The chapter is located in Part II of the book which is concerned with data collection, but there is no corresponding separate data analysis chapter in Part III. This is because, in the case of quantitative observation, data can readily be analysed using simple spreadsheet collation, calculation and graphics. In the case of qualitative observation, the field notes to be analysed are similar to any other field-notes or interview transcripts, so are covered by the discussion of qualitative data analysis in Chapter 15. Some case studies are, however, included to demonstrate the outcomes of observational research.

Sometimes observational research is referred to as *unobtrusive* methods, since often there is generally no involvement with the observed, who are generally not even aware that they are being observed. But the term 'unobtrusive methods' is also used in relation to documentary sources, such as the media, organisational records and diaries (see Kellehear, 1993); in this book these sources are dealt

Structured or systematic observation	Observation process subject to formal rules about what should be observed, how often, etc. – results typically recorded on a form and analysed quantitatively. Equivalent to the formal questionnaire survey in survey research.
Unstructured/naturalistic/ qualitative observation	No formal rules established; relatively informal recording or analysis procedures. Observer seeks to describe the phenomenon of interest and develop explanations and understandings in the process. Observational equivalent of the informal, in-depth interview.
Quasi-experimental observation	Researcher intervenes to change the environment and observes what happens – for example, changing the design of a children's playground. May be structured or unstructured.
Participant observation	The researcher is a participant in the milieu being studied – for example, the guided tour or the youth gang – rather than a separate, 'objective' researcher. May involve any of the above forms of observation. Discussed in Chapter 9.

Figure 8.1 Types of observational research

with in the chapters on secondary data and qualitative methods – in this chapter we concentrate on direct visual engagement with leisure or tourism sites.

The chapter comprises three main sections:

- an overview of possible situations where observational methods might be used;
- a step-by-step examination of the typical observational research process;
- the use of technology.

Types of observational research: quantitative and qualitative

Observation involves *looking*. It can take a number of forms, as indicated in Figure 8.1. Of importance here, is that observational research can be quantitative, qualitative or a combination of both. There is also overlap with experimental methods and with participant observation, as discussed in Chapter 9.

Possibilities

A number of types of situation where observation is appropriate or necessary can be identified, as listed in Figure 8.2. These situations are discussed in turn below.

Children's play

There is some research which can only be tackled by means of observation. One example is children's play. Such research is concerned with such issues as:

- Children's play
- Level and type of use of informal leisure/tourism sites – counting heads
- Spatial patterns of use of sites
- Visitor profile
- Deviant behaviour
- Mystery shopping
- Complementary research
- Everyday life
- Social behaviour

Figure 8.2 Situations for observational research

- patterns of play in different environments;

- the types of equipment children of different ages prefer;

- whether boys have a different pattern of play from that of girls;

- whether there are differences in play patterns between children from different cultural backgrounds.

It is unlikely that such questions could be fully answered by interviewing children, particularly very young children. The obvious approach is to *observe* children at play and record their behaviour.

Informal recreation/tourism areas visit numbers: counting heads

Structured observation methods can be used to estimate the level of use of informal recreation areas, such as beaches, urban parks or tourist sites, where there is no admission charge and therefore no ticket sales data to inform managers and planners of levels of use. Further, in such situations, there are often few formal constraints on capacity or spatial usage patterns, such as fixed seating.

An indication of the level of use of sites may be required for a variety of reasons. For example:

- A public agency might decide that it would be useful, for political or public relations reasons, to be able to state the total number of visitors which a facility serves in a week or a year – in order to justify the level of taxpayers' money being spent on maintaining it.

- In management terms it is often useful to be able to relate the costs of maintaining a site to the number of visits which it attracts, as one of a number of inputs into decisions on how much money should be spent on different sites.

- A single site manager might wish to compare levels of use over time to assess the impact of various marketing and other management measures.

- In a multi-purpose agency, such as a local council, performance is often measured by levels of use and costs across different types of facility. For those facilities without ticket sales data it becomes necessary to obtain an estimate by *observing* and *counting* the number of users.

Where the bulk of users arrive at a facility by private car and a charge is made for parking, indications of use levels may be provided by parking income, but this does not account for non-vehicular use and in some cases parking charges do not apply outside of certain hours, or there may be season permit holders who are not recorded every time they enter. To account for all vehicular use it may be possible to install automatic vehicle counters to count the number of vehicles entering and leaving the site, as discussed later in the chapter. Vehicle counts, however, provide information on the number of *vehicles* using a site but not the number of *people*. To obtain estimates of the numbers of people it is necessary to supplement the vehicle counts by direct observation for a period of the time to ascertain the average number of persons in vehicles and, at some sites, to estimate the numbers arriving by foot or bicycle, who may not be recorded by the mechanical counting device.

Manual methods of counting usage levels are discussed in the section on 'main elements of observational research' below.

Informal recreation/tourism areas: spatial/functional patterns of use

Observation is useful not only for gathering data on the number of users of a site but also for studying the way people make use of a site. This is particularly important in relation to the design and layout of leisure spaces, and their capacity. For instance, if people tend to crowd close to entrances and parking areas (which they often do in outdoor sites) then where those entrances and parking areas are positioned will affect the pattern of use of the site. This can be used as a management/design tool to influence the pattern of use of a site.

Similarly if, as has been found, people tend to locate themselves along 'edges' – such as walls, fences, banks, areas of trees and shrubs – then this tendency can be used to influence the pattern of use of a site, by determining the nature and location of such 'edges' (Ruddell and Hammitt, 1987). While this applies particularly to outdoor natural areas, it can also have some relevance in built-up areas, such as shopping malls, and in buildings, such as museums.

Buildings and open spaces for public use are often designed with either little or no consideration as to how people will actually use them, or on the basis of untested assumptions about how they will be used. In reality it is often found that people do not actually behave as anticipated by the designers and some spaces are under-used while others are over-crowded, or spaces are not actually used for the activities for which they were designed or equipped. The pattern of movement of people around exhibitions can affect the information absorbed, depending on the relative prominence and attraction of exhibits, as demonstrated in Case study 8.1. Observation is the means by which these aspects of space utilisation can be discovered.

Case study 8.1   Observation of museum visitor behaviour

In a book chapter reviewing a number of issues related to visitors to museums and visitor centres, Philip Pearce (1988: 90–113) at one point discusses the implications of visitors' decision to turn to the right on entering a museum and proceeding in an anti-clockwise direction, as opposed to turning left and proceeding in a clockwise direction. Research in the Telecom Museum in Victoria, Australia, as shown in Figure 8.3, shows that the two groups of visitors do indeed have different patterns of attention paid to the exhibits, as measured by the proportion of visitors who stop to view each exhibit.

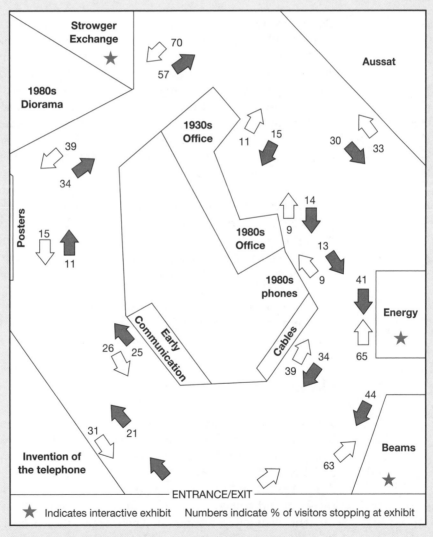

Figure 8.3 Visitor movement patterns in a museum

Further, those who turn right and proceed anti-clockwise have a higher level of attention throughout the exhibition – but this, it is argued, is likely to be due to the fact that they immediately encounter interactive exhibits, whereas those who turn to the left first encounter static, audio-visual exhibits. The methodology used is clearly simple, but possibly time-consuming, depending on how long visitors stay and the extent to which more than one group can be studied at the same time. But it clearly produces data which are likely to be of interest to and readily understood and interpreted by managers.

Visitor profiles

Questionnaire-based site surveys are the typical means for researching demo-graphic and group composition data which combine to provide a *visitor* or *user profile*. However, depending on the design of the questionnaire, and given that questionnaires in such situations are invariably quite brief, the information collected can miss vital features of the characteristics of the users of a site which can be identified by observation. For example, two music venues could have identical user age/gender/group size profiles, but, because of the different types of music offered, could attract very different crowds, in terms of fashion, lifestyle and behaviour. Even at a single venue an overall profile based on aver-ages and percentages may hide the fact that it is used by a number of distinct user-groups. Questionnaire-based profiles may also miss distinctive usage pat-terns. For example, a park survey may indicate that there are x per cent mothers with young children, or single elderly users, but fail to pick up the fact that these groups attend at particular times and meet together and socialise. Of course a questionnaire survey could pick up these features if the questionnaire included appropriate questions and if the sample was large enough and the analysis sophisticated enough, but this is not always the case. In addition to being a research approach in its own right, observational research can be used as a preliminary process to identify features of the user profile so that appropriate questions can be included in a questionnaire.

Deviant behaviour

The notion of *deviant* behaviour is a contested one, with one person's 'deviance' being another person's 'acceptable behaviour'. One term which has been used to cover this area is 'leisure on the margins of conventional morality' (Lynch and Veal, 2006: 317–38), covering such activities as the use of recreational drugs, graffiti and vandalism, various types of sexual activity, gambling and rowdy crowd behaviour or other forms of 'rule-breaking' in leisure settings. Deviant behaviour is a situation where observation is likely to be more fruitful than interviews. People are unlikely to tell an interviewer about their litter-dropping habits, their lack of adherence to the rules in a park, or their beer can throwing habits at a football match. Finding out about such things requires observation – usually of a covert nature! This of course raises ethical issues, such as people's rights to privacy, as discussed in Chapter 4. Case study 8.2 shows parts of the results from a study of riots between police and bikie gangs at a motor-sport event in New South Wales in the 1980s, indicating that the safety of the researchers can be at stake in observational research in some environments.

Case study 8.2   Observing riots

In their book, *The Dynamics of Collective Conflict*, Cunneen *et al.* (1989) present the results of their study of a series of violent conflicts, including pitched battles, which took place between police and fans at the annual Bathurst Motorcycle Grand Prix meetings in New South Wales, Australia, in the

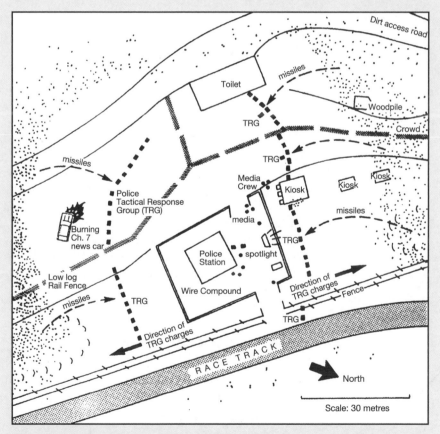

Figure 8.4 Pattern of conflict at the Bathurst Bike Races, Easter Saturday, 1985

mid-1980s. They use a variety of research methods, including observation, interviews, historical research and analysis of press and television reports, in an attempt to understand the origins and nature of the conflicts between the two groups and the role of the media, which reported the events and created images and interpretations for the consumption of the public and politicians. While media reports portrayed the fans as 'mindless hooligans' on the rampage, detailed research revealed a history of suspicion between police and 'bikies' and a picture of excessive and escalatory police response to the carnivalesque behaviour of the crowd. There was no single explanation of the riots – the meaning and interpretation of the events depended on who was doing the interpretation – the police, the fans, the press or politicians. Figure 8.4 presents the results of detailed observation of the layout of the site and the parties involved in one of the pitched battles. Clearly it would be difficult to describe the scene entirely verbally – visual presentation of the results of the observational exercise is the obvious approach to adopt.

Mystery shopping

Mystery shopping is another potentially fruitful but under-exploited use of observation. It involves a researcher playing the role of user/visitor/customer as a method of obtaining information on the quality of the experience enjoyed by users of a leisure or tourism facility or product. The mystery shopper is required to make use of the facilities or services on offer on an *incognito basis*. The researcher has a checklist of features to observe – such as cleanliness, information availability and clarity, staff performance – and makes a report after using the facilities or services. Such an approach draws on the expertise of the observer to assess quality of service and to record details, for example related to safety, which might not be noticed by routine users. Again, ethical and industrial relations issues may arise in such a study because of the element of deception involved in a researcher playing the part of a customer, typically on behalf of management.

Complementary research

Observation can provide essential quantitative or qualitative complements to other research methods.

Quantitative

Observation involving counts of users can be a necessary complement to interview surveys to correct for variation in sampling rates. For instance in a typical tourist attraction, park or beach, two interviewers, working at a steady rate, may be able to interview virtually all (100 per cent) users in the less busy periods in the early morning but only manage to interview a small proportion of the users (say 5 per cent) during the busy lunch hour and afternoon periods. The final sample would therefore, in this case, over-represent early morning users and under-represent mid-day and afternoon users. If these two groups have different characteristics, the differential rate of sampling would be likely to have a biasing effect on, for example, the overall balance of views expressed by the users. Observational counts of the hourly levels of use can provide data to give an appropriate *weight* to the mid-day and afternoon users at the analysis stage. The process of *weighting* is described in more detail in Chapter 16.

Qualitative

Informal observation may provide complementary material for any study which is focused on a particular location or a type of location in order to set the research in context and provide some 'local colour'. More specifically, Seaton (1997) describes a project where interviewers involved in conducting interview surveys at various sites at an arts festival realised, from their own experience and observations, that the survey method had significant limitations. For example, obtaining an adequate sample of evaluative responses at the end of a performance was often impossible because audience members were in a hurry to depart from the venue; a short standardised questionnaire designed in advance and used for a number of disparate performance-type events failed to capture the variety of experiences; and widespread resentment at the treatment of VIPs was not captured by the questionnaire. An observational schedule was implemented which supplemented survey data by providing observers' own assessments of: audience profile based on type of cars in the car park, type of dress and age; satisfactions and resentments from audience responses; quality of catering by observation of refreshments and customer numbers; significance of friends and relatives of performers in the audience; and equipment and organisational issues. This had some of the features of the 'mystery shopping' technique discussed above.

Everyday life

The idea of simply observing *everyday life* as an approach to studying a society is associated with Britain's Mass Observation anthropological study of the British way of life in the 1930s and 1940s and with the work of Irving Goffman (1959). An anthology of mass observation sketches, published in 1984 (Calder and Sheridan, 1984) includes descriptions of everyday events in pubs, on the Blackpool seafront promenade and in the period of the wartime blitz in London. Goffman's work was more theoretical and concerned the ways individuals use space and interact in public and private places. An anthology of work in the Goffman style (Birenbaum and Sagarin, 1973) includes observational studies of such leisure activities as pinball, bars, card games and restaurants.

Social behaviour

Observation has been used in sociological research to develop ideas and theories about social behaviour in specific milieux and generally. The research of Fiske (1983) and Grant (1984) on the use of beaches and Marsh and his colleagues (1978) on football fans are examples of this approach. These researchers use an interactive, inductive process to build explanations of social behaviour from what they observe. Very often a key feature of such studies is the way the researchers seek to contrast what they have observed with what has apparently been observed – or assumed to be taking place – by others, particularly those with influence or authority, such as officials, police and the media. Observational research can challenge existing stereotypical interpretations of events.

Main elements of observational research

Observation seems to be essentially a simple research method with little 'technique' to consider. However, as with any research method, careful thought must go into the design, conduct and analysis stages of a project. In structured observation what is mainly required from the researcher is precision, painstaking attention to detail, and patience. In unstructured observation the same skills and attributes are required but, in addition, there is a need for a creative 'eye' which can perceive the significance and potential meanings of what is being observed and relate this to the research question. The main tasks in planning and conducting an observational project are as set out in Figure 8.5.

As with the 'elements of the research process' outlined in Chapter 3, it is difficult to produce a list of steps which will cover all eventualities. In particular, if the approach is unstructured rather than structured, then a number of the steps discussed here, particularly those concerning counting, may be redundant.

---

1. Choice of site(s)
2. Choice of observation point(s)
3. Choice of observation time-period(s)
4. Continuous observation or sampling?
5. Number and length of sampling periods
6. Deciding what to observe
7. Division of site into zones
8. Determination of information recording method
9. Conducting the observation
10. Analysing/interpreting data

Figure 8.5 Steps in an observation project

Step 1: Choice of site(s)

In the case of a provider-organisation's in-house or consultancy research the sites to be studied may be fixed; but where there is an element of choice some time should be devoted to inspecting and choosing sites which will not only offer the appropriate leisure/tourism behaviour but also provide suitable conditions for observation and/or will be representative of the ranges of types of site to be studied.

Step 2: Choice of observation point(s)

Choice of observation points within a site is clearly important and needs to be done with care. Some sites can be observed in their entirety from one spot. In other cases a circuit of viewing spots must be devised. For structured observation – for example involving counting the number of people present or passing a point over a period of time – it may be vital to conduct the observation from the same point(s) in various study periods, but for unstructured observation this may not be a consideration, indeed, exploring and observing from different locations within a site may be desirable.

When unstructured, but intensive observation of people's behaviour is involved, it may be necessary to choose observation points which are unobtrusive to avoid attracting attention, particularly in a confined space with relatively few people. This is related to the issue of the method of recording observations, as discussed in Step 8 below, since some forms of formal recording are more obvious than others.

Step 3: Choice of observation time-period(s)

The choice of time-period is important because of variations in use of a site, by time of the year, day of the week, time of day or weather conditions, according to external social factors such as public holidays, or internal factors, such as the type of music – and hence of patron – offered on particular nights in a club. Observation to cover all time-periods may be very demanding in terms of resources, so some form of sampling of time-periods will usually be necessary.

Step 4: Continuous observation or sampling?

The question of whether to undertake continuous observation or to sample different time-periods is related to the resources available and the nature of the site and the overall design of the project. The issue is particularly important if one of the aims of the research is to obtain an accurate estimate of the number of visitors to the site, when the terminology used to refer to the two approaches is *continuous counts* versus *spot counts*. It could, for example, be very expensive to place observers at the numerous gates of a large urban park for as much as

100 hours in a week to count the number of users during all the time the park is open. Even if that were possible, it is unlikely that resources would be available to cover a whole year – except using automatic mechanical devices. A sampling approach must be adopted in most observation projects. Having decided to sample, it is of course necessary to decide how often to do this. This is discussed further under Step 5.

If counting is being undertaken, there is also a decision to be made as to whether to count the number of people *entering* or *leaving* the site during specified time-periods or the number of people *present* at particular points in time. Counting the number of people present is, of course, a form of spot count. Counting the number of people entering or leaving over a period of time generally constitutes continuous counting, but if the time-periods are relatively short – for example half and hour or an hour – then the results can be seen as a form of spot count. Counting the number of people present at particular points in time is generally less resource-intensive since it can be done by one person regardless of the number of entrances to the site, and can provide information on the spatial use of the site at the same time. Thus one person, at specified times, makes a circuit of the site and records the numbers of people present in designated zones (see Step 7).

When unstructured observation is being undertaken, it is more likely that continuous observation will be adopted since the aim will generally be to observe the dynamics of events and behaviour at the site. However, the question of when to undertake such observation in order to cover all aspects of the use of the site still needs careful consideration.

Step 5: Count frequency

When the study involves counts of users, how often should the counts be undertaken? This will depend to a large extent on the rate of change in the level of use of the site. For example, the four counts in Figure 8.6 are clearly insufficient since, if the broken line is the pattern of use observed in a research project, but the unbroken line is the true pattern, the research would have inaccurately represented the true situation. There is little advice that can be given to overcome this problem, except to sample frequently at the beginning of a project until the basic patterns of peaks and troughs in usage have been established; subsequently it may be possible to sample less often.

Step 6: What to observe

One approach to observing the spatial behaviour of visitors within a site is to record people's positions directly as indicated in Figure 8.7. In addition to observing numbers of people and their positions, it is possible to observe and record different types of activity. It is also possible, to a limited extent, to record visitor characteristics. For instance, men and women could be separately identified and it is possible to distinguish between children and adults and to

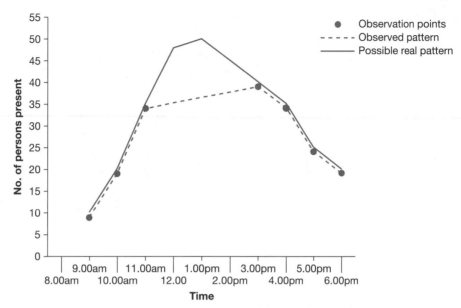

Figure 8.6 Counts of site use

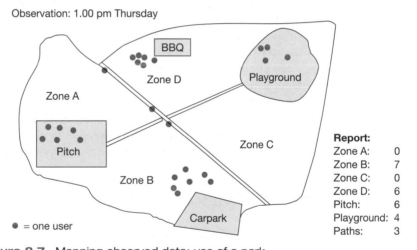

Figure 8.7 Mapping observed data: use of a park

distinguish senior citizens, although, if a number of people are involved as counters, care will need to be taken over the dividing line between such categories as child, teenager, young adult, adult and elderly person. It is also possible, again with care, to observe the size of parties using a site, especially if they are observed arriving or leaving at a car park.

These additional items of information would of course complicate the recording sheet, and symbols would be necessary to record the different types of person on a map. Care needs to be taken not to make the data collection so complicated that it becomes too difficult for the observers to observe and

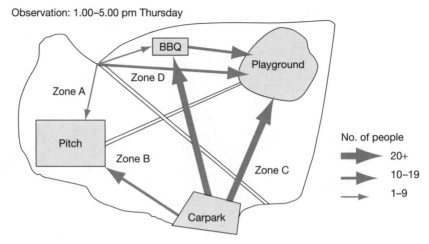

Figure 8.8 Flows within a site

collect and leads to inaccuracies. This is one of those situations where it is necessary to consider carefully *why* the data are being collected and not to get carried away with data collection for its own sake.

In addition to observing people statically, or as they arrive at an entrance, it is also possible to observe visitors' movements through a site, and illustrate the results graphically, A simple example is shown in Figures 8.7 and 8.8. Of course care must be taken not to give offence by letting visitors become aware that they are being 'followed', but routes taken by visitors can be revealing for management.

Car registration numbers can be a useful source of information. Firstly they can provide information on where people have travelled from. Secondly number plates can be used to trace the movement of vehicles within an area – for instance within a National Park with a number of stopping points.

Step 7: Division of site into zones

In large sites it is advisable to divide the site into areas or zones and record the number of people and their activities within those zones, as indicated in Figures 8.7 and 8.8. The zones should be determined primarily by management concerns – for example, in a park: the children's playground, the sports areas, the rose garden. But they should also be designed for ease of counting; ideally zones should be such that they can be observed from one spot and should be clearly demarcated by natural or other features.

Step 8: Recording information

Figure 8.9a provides an example of a counting sheet used in a structured observation project requiring counts of use in a study area with six zones and the

a. Structured

Site	Observer	Date	Start time	Finish time

	Zone:						
Activity	**A**	**B**	**C**	**D**	**E**	**F**	**G**
Walking							
Sitting							
Playing sport							
Children playing							
Eating							
Total							

b. Unstructured

Site	Observer	Date	Start time	Finish time
Zone A				
Zone B				
Zone C				
Zone D				

Figure 8.9 Examples of observation recording sheets

possibility of a variety of activities. The data collected using such a form are ideal for storage, manipulation and presentation in graphic form using a spreadsheet computer program as discussed in Step 10 below. An alternative to this sort of form is to record data on copies of maps of the site, using numerals or dots, as in Figure 8.7 (with symbols for different types of activity).

Figure 8.9b is an example of a recording sheet for an unstructured observation exercise. There are less zones since the observation is likely to be more intensive and time-consuming. In each zone, space is provided for free-form notes. The amount of space to reserve on the sheet depends on the length of time spent and the detail of the observation; it is possible that a whole page, or even more, may be required per zone per time-period, or that additional sheets could be used for different time-periods.

Step 9: Conducting the observation

In the case of a structured observational project, if the project has been well planned then the actual conduct should be straightforward. The main danger in a major project involving a lot of counting can be boredom, leading to inaccuracies in observing and recording data. It is therefore advisable to vary the work of those involved with, where appropriate, data collectors being involved in alternate spells of behavioural observation and counting and, where possible, being switched between sites. Counting can be done manually or using a hand-held mechanical counter.

In the case of unstructured observational projects, more demands are placed on the observer. Such a project is, in effect, a visual form of the qualitative type of research discussed in the next chapter. The observer is required to observe and describe what is going on at the site, but must also engage directly with the research questions of the project in order to determine what to observe and what aspects of the observed scene should be described and recorded and at least begin the process of explanation.

Step 10: Analysing data

In some cases of structured observation, the visual presentations of the sort presented in Figures 8.7 and 8.8 constitute the analysis. In other cases data must be analysed and processed to present useable results. Four examples are presented here: presentation of usage patterns over the course of a day; estimating usage numbers from spot count data; weighting; and analysis of unstructured data.

Usage patterns

Consider the set of counts shown in Table 8.1, which relate to the numbers of people present in a park, which opens at 8 am and closes at 7 pm. This pattern is illustrated graphically in Figure 8.10. Again, this presentation may be sufficient for the project in hand, but it can be taken further, including converting the sample counts into an estimate of overall use numbers.

Estimating usage numbers

Table 8.2 sets out a process to estimate usage numbers from spot count data. It is estimated in the example that there is an average of 95.1 people in the park, over a 12-hour period, giving a total of 1141 *visitor-hours*. The number of visitor-hours is a valid measure of use in its own right and could be used to compare different sites or to compare the performance of the same site over time. But, for example, 12 visitor-hours could result from:

Table 8.1   Observed use of a park

	Walking	Sitting	Playing sport	Kids playing	Total
	No. of people observed				
8 am	5	1	0	2	8
9 am	52	6	5	5	68
10 am	44	19	10	7	80
11 am	28	25	12	11	76
12 am	31	40	25	13	109
1 pm	32	56	32	17	137
2 pm	37	46	23	22	128
3 pm	38	45	12	22	117
4 pm	39	40	33	32	144
5 pm	40	33	27	15	115
6 pm	42	20	12	12	86
7 pm	45	15	4	9	73
Total	433	346	195	167	1141
Average	36.1	28.8	16.3	13.9	95.1

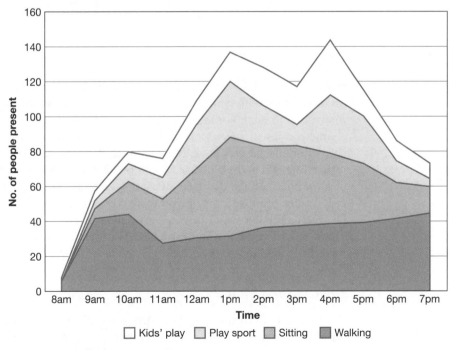

Figure 8.10   Park usage pattern

Table 8.2 Estimating visit numbers from count data

Data	Source	Result
A Average no. of users present	Counts (Table 8.1)	95.1
B No. of hours open	Table 7.1	12 hours
C No. of user-hours	A × B	1141*
D Average length of stay	User survey	0.5 hours
E No. of visits	C/D	2282

* Same as total number of people observed (Table 8.1), but would be different if counts were not made hourly.

- one person visiting the park and staying all day;
- two people staying six hours each;
- 12 people staying one hour each; or
- 24 people staying half an hour each.

So if an estimate is required of the number of different *persons* visiting the park over the course of the day, additional information, on the *length of stay*, is necessary – this would usually be obtained from a questionnaire-based user survey, although it might possibly be obtained from detailed observation of a sample of groups. In the example in Table 8.2, the length of stay is 0.5 hour, so every user-hour represents two users, giving a total of 2281 visits for the day. Thus the number of visits is equal to the number of visitor-hours divided by the average length of stay.

Weighting

Details of user characteristics obtained from observation can be used as a check on the accuracy of sampling in interview surveys and may be used to *weight* the results of such surveys so that the final result is a better reflection of the characteristics of the users of the facility. This is similar to the time-of-day correction discussed above, but relates to the personal characteristics of users, rather than their time of use of the facility. For instance, if it was found by observation that half the users of a site were women but in an interview survey only a third of those interviewed were women, the women in the sample could be given a greater weighting at the analysis stage so that their views and attitudes would receive due emphasis. The details of weighting are described more fully in Chapter 16.

Qualitative analysis

The raw form of the data from unstructured observation is likely to comprise a set of notes, possibly with some numbers, and probably with some diagrams. The immediate task for the researcher is therefore to ensure that these notes are in a readable form for future reference; this may involve writing or typing them out to provide a narrative. In the course of doing this a start may be made on the analysis process. For example, the absence of a particular group of users on one occasion and their presence on another may be linked to the absence or presence of another group or some other change in the environment. The result is therefore likely to be an extended set of notes which can be seen as comparable with sets of notes or transcripts from other forms of qualitative research, as discussed in Chapter 9. Similar approaches to analysis are therefore appropriate, including identification of themes and patterns. The inductive interaction between data collection, data analysis and theory development which apply to qualitative research generally also apply to unstructured observational research. The *NVivo* software described in Chapter 15 for analysing informal interview transcripts might also be used to analyse notes from observational research.

Use of technology

Automatic counters

Automatic counters are available for vehicles and pedestrians. Vehicle counters are based on one of four technologies:

- induction loop buried under the roadway: creates a magnetic field which detects vehicles passing through it – this option is relatively permanent, and expensive due to installation costs;

- pressure pad or tube: vehicles passing over the pad or tube complete an electrical circuit – this is cheaper than induction loop, but has limited life due to wear and tear;

- infra-red beam: vehicle is recorded when it breaks the beam – the cheapest option;

- CCTV (closed circuit television): software can be used to analyse the images and count vehicles passing in view of the camera.

In each case, the device is attached to computerised equipment which can produce a variety of reports for users, for example, hourly, daily, weekly, monthly or annual counts and trend analysis. The technologies can generally detect vehicles of different types/sizes, for example, motorcycles, passenger vehicles, heavy vehicles.

Infra-red beams and CCTV can also be used to count pedestrian movements. But because pedestrians do not necessarily cross the beam one at a time, the counters may have to be *calibrated* using some direct observational data collected for a sample period. For example, direct visual counts may reveal that, in a certain location, a count of 100 on the automatic counter may represent, say, 120 individuals.

Cyclists sometimes use roadways, where they may be picked up by traffic counters, or they may use exclusive cycleways, where infra-red devices can be used. Where they share paths with pedestrians the mix of pedestrians and cyclists would need to be determined by calibration based on direct observation as discussed above.

One of the disadvantages of these devices is their fixed nature; one device can only monitor one route or pathway. Locating a device at every point or entrance of interest may be expensive and moving them around on a roster may be costly. Again, calibration using a period of direct visual counts may be the solution. For example, if direct counts revealed that the main entrance to a site typically accounted for half of all visits, the counts from an automatic counter located at that entrance would need to be doubled to provide an estimate of total visits.

GPS

Tracking visitors through a site or tourists around a destination is discussed above. Various satellite and land-based radio and telephonic geographic positioning systems (GPS) devices may be used to assist in this task. Case study 11.3B provides a short summary of a research project by Shoval and Isaacson (2007) which evaluated a number of such devices.

Aerial photography

The use of aerial photography is well developed in geography and geology, where a whole sub-discipline of *remote sensing* has developed using a variety of techniques. It can also be effective in leisure and tourism research. Where large areas are concerned, such as coastlines and estuaries, and where access is difficult and recreational use of the site is very scattered, aerial photography may be the only way of obtaining estimates of levels and patterns of use. In harbours and estuaries it is probably the best means of obtaining estimates of numbers of craft using the area since, as they are generally moving about in random patterns, it can be difficult to count manually on a crowded waterway. Needless to say a good quality camera is needed for such work.

Still photography

The value of ordinary, land-based, photography as an adjunct to direct observation should not be overlooked. Digital photography and editing software have made the incorporation of photographs into research increasingly easy. The level of crowding of a site, its nature and atmosphere can be conveyed to the reader of a report with the aid of photographs. Particular problems, for instance of erosion, or design faults, can be conveyed better visually than verbally – a picture speaks a thousand words. A 'photo-essay' can be composed around a number of themes or messages to convey simple research findings.

Video

Video can be used to record patterns of use of a site. As noted in relation to automatic counters and CCTV, software now exists to perform some types of analysis of digital images. The medium can provide a useful illustration of 'before' and 'after' situations, to illustrate the nature of problems on a site and the effect of measures to ameliorate the problems – for example congestion, erosion or littering.

Time-lapse photography

Time-lapse photography lies somewhere between still photography and video. A time-lapse camera can be set up to take pictures of a scene automatically, say, every ten seconds or every minute. The resultant sequence of pictures can then be projected as a film or video to show the speeded-up pattern of use of the area viewed. This is the technique used in wildlife documentaries which show a plant apparently growing before your eyes, but it can also be used to show the changing pattern of use of a leisure or tourism site.

Just looking

Finally we should not forget just how important it is to use our eyes in research, even if the research project does not involve systematic observational data collection. Familiarity with a leisure activity or a leisure or tourism site helps in the design of a good research project and aids in interpreting data. Many studies have been based just on informal, but careful, observation. All useful information is not in the form of numbers. Careful observation of what is happening in a particular leisure or tourism situation, at a particular facility or type of facility or among a particular group of people can be a more appropriate research approach in some circumstances than the use of questionnaires or even informal interviews. The good researcher is all eyes.

Summary

This chapter is concerned with the neglected technique of observation – *looking* – as a tool for research in leisure and tourism. It is noted that observation can be formalised or structured, involving counting of leisure and tourism site users and strict time and space sampling methods, or it can be informal or unstructured. In general observation is non-intrusive in the study site, but 'contrived observation', as in the experimental method, is also possible. Participant observation is a further type of observational research, but is dealt with in Chapter 9. Observational research spans the quantitative/qualitative methodological spectrum and can therefore involve both quantitative and qualitative analysis methods. A number of leisure and tourism situations is described in which observation methods might be used, including: children's play; the usage of informal leisure/tourism areas where no entrance fee is required and capacity and use patterns are not constrained by factors such as formal seating or booking systems; spatial and functional patterns of use of sites; user profiles; studying deviant behaviour; mystery shopping; research which is complementary to research conducted using other methods; everyday life; and social behaviour. The chapter outlines the observational research process in ten steps: 1. choice of study site(s); 2. choice of observation point(s); 3. choice of observation time-period(s); 4. deciding on continuous observation or sampling; 5. deciding on the number and length of sampling periods; 6. deciding what to observe; 7. division of the study site(s) into zones; 8. recording observational information; 9. conducting the observation; and 10. analysing data. Finally brief consideration is given to various technological aids, including: automatic counters; GPS devices; and still, video and time-lapse cameras.

Test questions

1. Four types of observational research are identified at the beginning of the chapter. What are they?

2. A total of eight leisure or tourism situations is described where observation is a suitable, and sometimes the *most* suitable form of research. Name three of these situations and explain in each case why observation is a suitable research method.

3. What is the difference between spot counting and continuous counting?

4. What forms can data from observational research be presented?

5. How can observational research findings assist in regard to weighting of survey data?

Exercises

1. Select an informal leisure or tourism site, position yourself in an unobtrusive location, but where you can see what is going on. Over a period of two hours, record what happens. Write a report on: how the site is used; who it is used by; how many people use it; what conflicts there are, if any, between different groups of users; and how the design aids or hinders the activity which people engage in on the site.

2. Establish a counting system to record the number of people present in a leisure or tourism site at hourly intervals during the course of a day. Estimate the number of visitor-hours at the site for the day.

3. In relation to exercise 2: conduct interviews with three or four visitors each hour, and ask them how long they have stayed, or expect to stay, at the site. Establish the average length of stay and, using this information and the data from exercise 2, estimate the number of persons visiting the site in the course of the day.

4. Use photographs to record examples of neglect or damage to leisure or tourism sites known to you.

Resources

- General/methodological: Burch (1981), Ely (1981), Tyre and Siderelis (1978), Kellehear (1993), Adler and Adler (1994);

- Distinction between structured and unstructured observation: Bryman and Bell (2003);

- Counting heads: Gartner and Hunt (1988);

- Automated counters: Green Space (1998);

- GPS: Edwards *et al.* (2010); Shoval and Isaacson (2007) – see Case study 11.3B;

- Use of video: Arnberger and Eder (2008), Wuellner (1981);

- Use of photography: Garrod (2008);

- Mystery shopping: General: Dawson and Hillier (1995); Travel agents: Hudson *et al.* (2001);

- En route surveys: Gartner and Hunt (1988);

- Examples of leisure/tourism studies using observation:
  - General: Birenbaum and Sagarin (1973);
  - Children's play: Child (1983);
  - Events: Seaton (1997);
  - Sporting crowds/riots: Cuneen *et al.* (1989); football: Marsh *et al.* (1978);
  - Beach use: Fiske (1983), Grant (1984), Douglas *et al.* (1977);
  - Countryside recreation: Glyptis (1981a, 1981b), Van der Zande (1985), Keirle and Walsh (1999);
  - Urban parks: Floyd *et al.* (2008); counting methods: Green Space (1998);
  - Museums: Bitgood *et al.* (1988); Pearce (1988); and see Case study 8.1.

9 Qualitative methods: introduction and data collection

Introduction

This chapter addresses methods of research which involve the collection and analysis of *qualitative* information using the media of words, images or sounds, as distinct from numbers as used in quantitative methods. The chapter discusses the nature, history and advantages of qualitative methods, their role in research and the range of specific methods available, including in-depth interviews, group interviews/focus groups, participant observation, biographical methods and ethnographic approaches. The qualitative analysis of *texts* is also discussed.

For most qualitative research methods data collection, analysis and interpretation are intermingled, rather than being functionally and temporally separated as is generally the case in quantitative methods. Nevertheless, distinct data collection and analysis processes can be identified and analysis procedures tend to have common characteristics across the range of qualitative data collection methods, so qualitative data *analysis* is discussed in Part III of the book, in Chapter 15.

The nature of qualitative methods

The term *qualitative* is used to describe research methods and techniques which use and give rise to, qualitative rather than quantitative information, that is information in the form of words, images and sounds rather than numbers. In general the qualitative approach tends to collect a great deal of detailed (sometimes referred to as 'rich' or 'thick') information about relatively few cases or subjects rather than the more limited information about a large number of cases or subjects which is typical of quantitative research. It is, however, possible to envisage qualitative research which actually deals with large numbers of cases. For example, a research project on sports spectators, involving observation and participation in spectator activity could involve information relating, collectively, to tens of thousands of people.

Qualitative methods can be used for pragmatic reasons, in situations where formal, quantified research is not necessary or is not possible, but there are also theoretical grounds for using such methods. Qualitative research is generally based on the belief that the people personally involved in a particular (leisure or tourism) situation are best placed to describe and explain their experiences, feelings and world-view in their own words, and that they should be allowed to speak without the intermediary of the researcher and without being overly constrained by the framework imposed by the researcher.

History and development

The history of the use of qualitative methods in leisure studies is different for North America, where the bulk of English-language leisure research activity has taken place, and Britain and Australasia, which came later to the scene and have smaller research communities. The history in tourism studies, however, follows a similar trajectory worldwide.

The difference in regard to leisure is illustrated by the earliest large-scale empirical studies of leisure in the two countries. The 1934 American study *Leisure: a Suburban Study* by George Lundberg *et al.* (1934) was based primarily on time-budget diaries completed by almost 2500 respondents and this was just one of 18 different survey formats used. The main results were presented in tables, although there are no statistical tests and the discussion is presented in a narrative style. By contrast, the earliest large-scale British study, Rowntree and Lavers' 1951 *English Life and Leisure,* while based on a substantial sample, used primarily qualitative methods, as indicated in Case study 9.1.

The divide between qualitative and quantitative methods continued to be stronger in North America than in the UK; indeed, it has been argued that qualitative methods played a significant role in British leisure research as it entered its first major growth phase in the 1970s (Veal, 1994).

The difference in traditions is also reflected in research methods textbooks. For example, in the earliest English-language research methods textbook in the field, published in the United States in 1987, Richard Kraus and Lawrence Allen presented only the classical scientific model of research using quantitative methods. They recognised the existence of qualitative methods, but cautiously stated:

> Both forms of research represent important and valid approaches. However, there is a widely held view that the most significant kinds of research studies are those that

Case study 9.1   Early qualitative research: *English Life and Leisure*

In the earliest large-scale British study of leisure, *English Life and Leisure*, published in 1951, the authors describe their research method as follows:

> In making our study of contemporary life in England and Wales, we concluded that, besides the usual and obvious methods of approaching the subject, we needed some means of letting a substantial number of men and women, of all ages and social classes, speak for themselves, in the hope that, as they told their individual stories, we should build up a living picture of English life and leisure. For such a purpose as we had in mind, formal interviewing, or the use of questionnaires, would have been useless, for many of the matters about which we desired information are intensely personal, and in any case we were interested more in behaviour than in such opinions as could be elicited by answers to short, set questions. We therefore decided to build up our picture of what people are like by a system of indirect interviewing. This method consists of making an acquaintance of an individual – the excuses for doing so are immaterial – and developing the acquaintance until his or her confidence is gained and information required can be obtained in ordinary conversation, without the person concerned ever knowing that there has been an interview or that any specific information was being sought. Such a method is laborious but effective. *(Rowntree and Lavers, 1951: xii)*

Apart from likely ethics committee concerns about 'informed consent' on the part of interviewees, such an explanation would not look out of place in a twenty-first century account of the rationale for use of qualitative methods. The first 121 pages of *English Life and Leisure* consist of individual 'case histories' of 220 (103 female, 117 male) of the almost 1000 people interviewed in 11 cities. These vary from just a few lines to almost a page in length and, although anonymous, are often remarkably candid. The scope of the interviews and case histories is indicated by the titles of the following twelve summary chapters which are:

- Commercialised gambling
- Drink
- Smoking
- Sexual promiscuity
- How honest is Britain?
- The cinema
- The stage
- Broadcasting [radio]
- Dancing
- Reading habits
- Adult education
- Religion.

Half of the chapters include one or two small tables based on the survey respondents, but most of the discussion is qualitative in nature, including frequent short quotations from interviews.

Also of note is that the report includes perhaps the earliest example, in a leisure study, of the analysis of 'texts', in this case films. In a distinctive indicator of the times, the authors say:

When we started our investigations early in 1946 neither of us knew much about the cinema. We were not in any way hostile to it, but it so happened that preoccupation with other matters had prevented both of us from paying other than very infrequent visits to cinemas. We decided, however, that we must be in a position to write from first-hand knowledge, and one of us . . . has accordingly during the course of our investigations visited 125 cinemas of all types in London [and 10 other cities]. After every visit a careful analysis was made of the principal film shown, and our remarks in this section are based on these analyses. *(Rowntree and Lavers, 1951: 232–3)*

The section includes summary details of seven of the films, the researcher's own assessment of the 'desirability' of the 125 films viewed and a discussion of the censorship system. Desirability is assessed in a way which is unlikely to be seen in a contemporary study, using a five-category scale, as follows:

- broadly of cultural or educational value;
- reasonable entertainment but nothing more;
- harmless but inane;
- glorifying false values;
- really objectionable.

are based on quantitative analysis, and that science must rely on actual measurement of scientific data. As a result, researchers tend to use quantitative measures wherever possible. . . . in such an individualistic and diversified field as recreation and leisure, there ought to be a place for research of a more intuitive or descriptive nature. *(Kraus and Allen, 1987: 24–5)*

They further stated that qualitative research methodology was 'less easily described', so there was no guidance on qualitative methods in their text. By contrast, the first British research methods textbook in the field, the first edition of this book, published in 1992, included a chapter on qualitative methods.

A shift in attitudes towards qualitative methods in leisure studies took place across the anglophone world during the 1980s, and this was reflected in the publication of Karla Henderson's *Dimensions of Choice: A Qualitative Approach to Recreation, Parks and Leisure Research* (Henderson, 1991). The shift was also reflected in the second edition of Kraus and Allen's textbook, published in 1998, in which they devoted a whole chapter to qualitative methods and one to documentary methods. The 'naturalistic perspective' was discussed alongside the scientific model and the first edition observations noted above were cautiously modified to state:

Quantitative research has tended to be more highly regarded than qualitative methods in varied scholarly disciplines, in part because this has been the approved method of investigation in the physical and natural sciences. However, a strong case can be made that, in such an individualistic and diversified field as recreation and leisure, there ought to be a place for research of a more deeply probing, intuitive, or philosophical nature. *(Kraus and Allen, 1998: 36)*

The shift from an almost exclusively quantitative approach to a mix of quantitative and qualitative methods also took place in tourism studies. Ritchie and Goeldner's (1994) *Travel, Tourism and Hospitality Research* and Ryan's (1995) *Researching Tourist Satisfaction* both included chapters on qualitative methods, although the overall emphasis of the texts was quantitative. In 2004, a book of readings on *Qualitative Research in Tourism* (Phillimore and Goodson, 2004a) was published, with various contributions arguing strongly for the use of qualitative approaches, generally associating them with a critical/interpretive approach to tourism research. In that book the editors provide a view of the evolutionary story (Phillimore and Goodson, 2004b) and Hollinshead (2004: 66) concludes that, in the early 2000s, tourism researchers were still not 'consummately skilful' in exploring ontology and selecting appropriate research methods.

Thus, in recent decades qualitative methods have become widely accepted and are no longer seen as exceptional and in need of special justification. In leisure studies qualitative studies are now at least as common in the literature as quantitative studies (see Case study 2.1) and in tourism studies they are commonplace.

Merits, functions, limitations

Kelly (1980), in making a plea for more qualitative leisure research 30 years ago, suggested that qualitative research has the following advantages over quantitative research in the leisure context:

● The method corresponds with the nature of the phenomenon being studied – that is, leisure is a qualitative experience for the individual.

● The method 'brings people back in' to leisure research. By contrast, quantitative methods tend to be very impersonal – *real* people with names and unique personalities do not generally feature.

● The results of qualitative research are more understandable to people who are not statistically trained.

● The method is better able to encompass personal change over time – by contrast much quantitative research tends to look only at current behaviour as related to current social, economic and environmental circumstances, ignoring the fact that most people's behaviour is heavily influenced by their life history and experience.

- Reflecting his first point, Kelly argues that leisure, including tourism, involves a great deal of face-to-face interaction between people – involving symbols, gestures, etc. – and qualitative research is well suited to investigating this.

- Kelly argues that qualitative techniques are better at providing an understanding of people's needs and aspirations, although some researchers in the psychological field in particular might disagree with him.

In this book it has been argued that different methods are not inherently good or bad, but just more or less appropriate for the task in hand. Thus Kelly's comments relate to particular types of research with particular purposes. Qualitative methods would clearly be most appropriate if the focus of interest, following Kelly, is: the qualitative experience of leisure or tourism; personal leisure or tourism histories; the use of symbols, gestures, etc. in leisure/ tourism contexts; people's leisure/tourism needs and aspirations; and/or communicating with an audience without statistical training.

Peterson (1994), speaking from a market researcher's perspective, lists the potential uses of qualitative research as:

- to develop hypotheses concerning relevant behaviour and attitudes;

- to identify the full range of issues, views and attitudes which should be pursued in larger-scale research;

- to suggest methods for quantitative enquiry – for example in terms of deciding who should be included in interview surveys;

- to identify language used to address relevant issues (thus avoiding the use of jargon in questionnaires);

- to understand how a buying decision is made – questionnaire surveys are not very good at exploring *processes*;

- to develop new product, service or marketing strategy ideas – the free play of attitudes and opinions can be a rich source of ideas for the marketer;

- to provide an initial screening of new product, service or strategy ideas;

- to learn how communications are received – what is understood and how – particularly related to advertising.

In the leisure and tourism research literature there is an apparent on-going debate between proponents of quantitative and qualitative methods. It is, however, a debate which has often been somewhat one-sided. Proponents of qualitative methods, in seeking to defend the approach in the face of assumed opposition, often ascribe views about the merits or limitations of quantitative and qualitative methods to unnamed proponents of quantitative methods, sometimes bracketed with positivists. But it is difficult to locate references to original sources for such critiques. Thus, for example, the first quotation from Kraus and Allen above is a rare example of an explicit statement of the view that quantitative methods are innately superior to qualitative methods, but even here the authors distance themselves from the comment by referring to it as a 'widely held view', leaving open the possibility that they themselves might not subscribe to it. Jenny Phillimore and Lisa Goodson (2004b: 3–4) refer to qualitative research as being 'prone to criticisms that it is a 'soft', 'non-scientific' and inferior approach', but this is referenced to a paper by Guba and Lincoln (1998) which itself refers to just a single critical source (Sechrest, 1992).

While partisan proponents of qualitative methods are vigorous in promoting their virtues, like all methods, they also have their limitations. For example, Matthew Miles and Michael Huberman, in their book on *Qualitative Data Analysis*, note the substantial increase in the prevalence of qualitative research in the social sciences but caution:

> . . . in the flurry of this activity, we should be mindful of some pervasive issues that have not gone away. These issues include the labour-intensiveness (and extensiveness over months or years) of [qualitative] data collection, frequent data overload, the distinct possibility of researcher bias, the time demands of processing and coding data, the adequacy of sampling when only a few cases can be managed, the generalizability of findings, the credibility and quality of conclusions, and their utility in the world of policy and action. *(Miles and Huberman, 1994: 2)*

In practice, Keith Hollinshead (2004: 67–8) observes in regard to tourism research: 'many qualitative approaches to research turn out to be poorly handled' and 'all too often qualitative researchers unquestioningly adopt a pre-formulated, generalised or etic orientation to their subject of study'. Similar comments are expressed by Sherry Dupuis (1999) in relation to qualitative leisure research.

The qualitative research process

Qualitative methods generally require, and enable, a more flexible, although no less rigorous, approach to overall research design and conduct than other approaches. Most quantitative research tends to be *sequential* in nature; the components of research as set out in Chapter 3 tend to be distinct and follow in a pre-planned sequence. This is inevitable because of the nature of the typical quantitative core data collection task. Much qualitative research involves a more fluid relationship between the various elements of the research – an approach which might be called *recursive*. In this approach hypothesis formation evolves as the research progresses, data analysis and collection take place concurrently and writing is also often evolutionary and on-going, rather than a separate process which takes place at the end of the project. The two approaches are represented diagrammatically in Figure 9.1.

Although the sequential and recursive models are presented here in the context of a contrast between quantitative and qualitative methods, in fact both quantitative and qualitative methods can involve sequential and recursive approaches. Thus, it is possible for an essentially quantitative study to involve

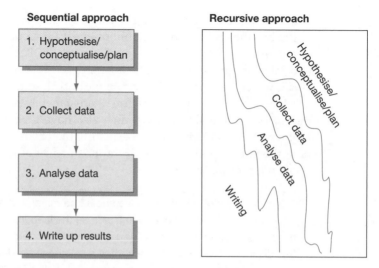

Figure 9.1 Sequential and recursive approaches to research

a variety of data sources and a number of small-scale studies, which build on one another in an iterative way. On the other hand, it is also possible for an essentially qualitative study to be conducted on a large scale, with a single data source – for example, a nation-wide study of council leaders, involving fairly standardised in-depth interviews.

An important philosophical perspective in the analysis of qualitative data is the concept of *grounded theory* developed by two sociologists, Barney Glaser and Anselm Strauss (1967). Grounded theory is concerned with the generation of theory from research, as opposed to research that tests *a priori* theory. It is therefore, in the terms discussed in Chapter 2, inductive rather than deductive. In this paradigm, theories and models should be *grounded* in real empirical observations rather than being governed by traditional methodologies and theories. In the generation of theory the researcher approaches the data with no pre-formed notions in mind, instead seeking to uncover patterns and contradictions through close examination of the data. To achieve this the researcher needs to be very familiar with the data, the subjects and the cultural context of the research. The process is a complex and personal one.

One way in which qualitative research has been characterised is by referring to the *researcher* as 'research instrument', in contrast to, for example, the survey method where the research instrument is a questionnaire.

The range of qualitative methods – introduction

Qualitative techniques commonly used in leisure and tourism research and which are discussed in more detail in this chapter include: in-depth interviews; group interviews or focus groups; participant observation; textual analysis;

In-depth interviews	• Usually conducted with a relatively small number of subjects. • Interview guided by a checklist of topics rather than formal questionnaire. • Interviews often tape-recorded and notes or verbatim transcript prepared. • Interviews typically take at least half an hour and may extend over several hours. • Repeat/follow-up interviews possible.
Group interviews/ focus groups	• Interviews/discussions conducted with a group, typically from 6 to 12. • Process is managed by a *facilitator* who guides the discussion. • Interaction between subjects takes place as well as between facilitator and subjects. • Proceedings generally tape-recorded and notes or verbatim transcript prepared.
Participant observation	• Researcher gathers information by being an actual participant with the subjects being studied. • Researcher may be known by the subjects as a researcher or may be *incognito*.
Biographical research	• Focusses on individual full or partial life histories. • May involve in-depth interviews but also documentary evidence and subjects' own written accounts.
Textual analysis	• Analysis of the content of 'texts', including print and audio-visual media.
Ethnography	• Utilises a number of the above techniques rather than being a single technique – borrowed from anthropology.

Figure 9.2 Qualitative methods: summary

biographical methods; and ethnography. The basic characteristics of these approaches are summarised in Figure 9.2.

As indicated above, while data collection and data analysis are, in practice, often difficult to separate in qualitative research, the discussions of individual methods below concentrate on data collection.

In-depth interviews

Nature

An in-depth interview, sometimes referred to as semi-structured, is characterised by its length, depth and structure.

● *Length*: In-depth interviews tend to be much longer than questionnaire-based interviews, typically taking at least half an hour and sometimes several hours. The method may involve interviewing people more than once.

Interview type	Question format	Responses	Interviewer/interviewee interaction
Structured A	Prescribed by questionnaire	Pre-coded	Formal, consistent
Structured B	Prescribed by questionnaire	Open-ended	Formal, consistent
Structured + semi-structured elements	Prescribed by questionnaire + supplementary	Open-ended	Mostly formal, consistent
Semi-structured	Checklist: question format not prescribed	Open-ended	Conversational, variable
Unstructured	Only the broad topic area is prescribed	Open-ended	Free-flowing conversational, variable

Figure 9.3   Questions, responses and interview types

- *Depth*: As the name implies, the in-depth interview seeks to probe more deeply than is possible with a questionnaire-based interview. Rather than just asking a question, recording a simple answer, and moving on, the in-depth interviewer typically encourages respondents to talk, asks supplementary questions and asks respondents to explain their answers.

- *Structure*: The in-depth interview is therefore less structured than a questionnaire-based interview. While questionnaire-based interviews may be seen as *structured*, in-depth interviews are seen as *semi-structured* or *unstructured*, as discussed further below. As a result, every interview in a qualitative study, although dealing with the same issues, will be different.

Arguably, interviews in general can be said to span part of a spectrum related to the extent to which the questions and their wording are fully pre-scribed in advance or not prescribed at all and the extent to which responses are pre-coded or open-ended. This is shown in Figure 9.3, which shows that questionnaire-based and in-depth interviews overlap in the middle of the spectrum.

Purposes and situations

In-depth interviews tend to be used in three situations.

1. The subjects of the research may be relatively few in number so a questionnaire-based, quantitative style of research would be inappropriate.

2. The information likely to be obtained from each subject is expected to vary considerably, and in complex ways. An example would be interviews with the management staff of a recreation or tourism organisation, or interviews with the coaches of different national sports teams. Each of these interviews would be different and would be a 'story' in its own right. In reporting the

research it would be the unique nature and structure of each of these accounts which would be of interest – data on 'what percentage of respondents said what' would not be relevant.

3. A topic is to be explored as a preliminary stage in planning a larger study, possibly a quantitative study, such as a questionnaire-based survey.

Checklist

Rather than a formal questionnaire the 'instrument' used for semi-structured in-depth interviews is often a *checklist* of topics to be raised, although a few key pre-determined, prescribed questions may be included. For example, a formal questionnaire might ask a question: 'Which of the following countries have you ever visited on holiday?' The informal interview checklist might simply include the words 'Countries visited'. The interviewer would shape the question according to the circumstances of a particular interview. If the interviewer is interested, for example, in the influence of childhood holiday experiences on adult visit patterns, in some interviews it may be necessary to ask a specific question such as: 'What overseas holiday trips did you take as a child?' In other interviews, in response to the interviewer's initial question, the interviewee might talk at length and volunteer detailed information on childhood trips unprompted. It is then not necessary to ask the separate question about childhood trips. Thus in-depth interviews vary from interview to interview; they take on a life of their own.

The skill on the part of the interviewer is to ensure that all relevant topics are covered – even though they may be covered in different orders and in different ways in different interviews. This, however, assumes that the list of relevant topics is known from the beginning and is already covered by the checklist. In practice the qualitative research allows the range of topics – and hence the content of the checklist – to evolve during the research process. New topics may emerge from interviewees themselves.

The design of the checklist should nevertheless be as methodical as the design of a formal questionnaire – in particular, the items to be included on the checklist should be based on the conceptual framework for the study and the resultant list of data needs, whether this be detailed or general in nature, as discussed in Chapter 3. An example of a checklist is included as Figure 9.4. The example given is in the form of a fairly terse list of topics. An alternative would be to include fully worded questions to initiate discussion of various topics, as would appear in a questionnaire; this may be advisable when a number of interviewers is involved. The problem with fully worded questions is that actually turning to the clipboard and reading out lengthy questions can interrupt the flow and informality of the interview. The more detailed the checklist, the more the interview would be described as *semi-structured*. If only a very brief checklist is used, or even none at all, the interview would be described as unstructured.

It should be noted that this typology and terminology would not be universally accepted among writers in the field: for example, Gayle Jennings

This is part of a checklist devised in connection with a study of people's use of leisure time and attitudes towards leisure.

Current activities	How often?
	Why?
Explore each one – compare	Where? – home/away from home
	Who with?
	Meaning/importance
	Type of involvement
Activities would like to do	Why not?
Meaning of 'leisure' to you	
Constraints:	Home
	Work – time/energy/colleagues
	Family roles
	Being a woman/man
	Being a parent
	Money/costs
	Car/transport
Past activities	At school
Why changes?	At college/univ.
	With family
Facilities	Locally: favourite
	City: use/non-use – why?
Clubs/associations	
Personality	Skills
Dislikes	Aspirations

Figure 9.4 Example of a checklist for in-depth interviewing

(2005: 101) describes the questionnaire used in a structured interview as a 'checklist' and her corresponding entry for semi-structured and unstructured interviews is 'Field notes. Transcription and recording', although this seems to confuse information elicitation with information recording.

The interviewing process

Conducting a good in-depth interview could be said to require the skills of a good investigative journalist. As Dean and his colleagues put it:

Many people feel that a newspaper reporter is a far cry from a social scientist. Yet many of the data of social science today are gathered by interviewing and observation techniques that resemble those of a skilled newspaper [reporter] . . . at work on the study of, say, a union strike or a political convention. It makes little sense for us to belittle these less rigorous methods as 'unscientific'. We will do better to study them and the techniques they involve so that we can make better use of them in producing scientific information. *(Dean et al., quoted in McCall and Simmons, 1969: 1)*

There are two approaches to conducting an in-depth interview: standardised and informal or unstructured.

The standardised approach

A standardised approach is one in which the emphasis in 'semi-structured' is on the 'structured' and where elements of the traditional scientific approach are replicated. The interaction between researcher and subject is, as far as possible, similar for all subjects. So prescribed questions are used, although the interviewer also improvises, depending on the flow of the interview. In this case, an important skill in interviewing is to avoid becoming so taken up in the conversational style of the interview that the interviewee is 'led' by the interviewer. The interviewer avoids agreeing – or disagreeing – with the interviewee or suggesting answers. This is more difficult than it sounds because in normal conversation we tend to make friendly noises and contribute to the discussion. In this situation the interviewer is torn between the need to maintain a friendly conversational atmosphere and the desire *not* to influence the interviewee's responses. Some of the carefully planned sequencing of questions which would be built into formal questionnaires must be achieved by the interviewer being very sensitive and quick thinking. For example, having discovered that the respondent does not go to the theatre, the interviewer should not lead the respondent by saying: 'Is this because it is too expensive?' Rather, the interviewee should be asked a more open question, such as: 'Why is that?' If the interviewee does not mention cost, but cost is of particular interest in the study, then the respondent might be asked a question such as: 'What about seat prices?' But this would be only *after* the interviewee has given his or her own unprompted reasons for not attending the theatre.

An important skill in interviewing of this sort is not to be afraid of silence. Some questions puzzle respondents and they need time to think. The interviewer does not have to fill the space with noise under the guise of 'helping' the interviewee. The interviewee is allowed time to ponder. The initiative can be left with the respondent to ask for an explanation if a question is unclear. While it is pleasant to engender a conversational atmosphere in these situations, the semi-structured interview is in fact different from a conversation. The interviewer is meant to listen and encourage the respondent to talk – not to engage in debate.

The informal or unstructured approach

A more informal or unstructured approach is favoured by some researchers. Sherry Dupuis, for example, sees the semi-structured approach as inappropriately seeking to reflect the positivist paradigm in qualitative research. She argues that using qualitative methods involves full interaction with research informants, so interviewers should be free to engage in a relatively free-flowing two-way conversation with interviewees. But she also makes the further point that, if this is to happen, then much more detail about this aspect of the research process should be reported in research accounts than is usually the case. Thus, for example, information gained by means of a full two-way conversation and exchange of views with an outgoing interviewee is arguably different in nature from information gained from interviews where the interviewee is more reserved.

The distinctions

Chris Ryan (2000: 125) argues that the distinction between the standardised and non-standardised interview corresponds to the phenomenographic and phenomenological approach to research. In the former, researchers adopt a minimalist approach to intervention in the interview and subsequently analyse and interpret the output – typically in the form of a transcript – in the same way that any text would be analysed. In the latter, researchers/interviewers are more active in eliciting responses to assist them to achieving an understanding of the interviewee's world-view during the course of the interview.

Whyte (1982) provides a sort of hierarchy in interviewer responses which vary in their degree of *intervention* in the interview. He also sees this as the interviewer exercising varying degrees of *control* over the interview. Beginning with the least intrusive style of intervention, Whyte's list is as shown in Figure 9.5. It should be noted that, except for the sixth of these responses, the interviewer is essentially drawing on what the subject has already said and is inviting her or him to expand on it.

1. 'Uh-huh'	A non-verbal response which merely indicates that the interviewer is still listening and interested.
2. 'That's interesting'	Encourages the subject to keep talking or expand on the current topic.
3. Reflection	Repeating the last statement as a question: e.g. 'So you don't like sport?'
4. Probe	Inviting explanations of statements: e.g. 'Why don't you like sport?'
5. Back tracking	Remembering something the subject said earlier and inviting further information: e.g. 'Let's go back to what you were saying about your school days'.
6. New topic	Initiating a new topic: e.g. 'Can we talk about other leisure activities – what about entertainment?'

Figure 9.5 Interviewing interventions – Whyte

Recording

Sound or video recording of in-depth interviews is common, although in some cases it might be felt that such a procedure could inhibit respondents. If recording is not possible then notes must be taken during the interview or immediately afterwards. There can be great value in producing complete *verbatim* (word for word) transcripts of interviews from recordings, although online services now exist which use voice-recognition technology to transcribe digitised recordings automatically. This is a laborious process – one hour of interview taking as much as six hours to transcribe. Such transcripts can, however, be used to analyse the results of interviews in a more methodical and complete manner than is possible with notes.

Focus groups

Nature

The idea of interviewing groups of people together rather than individually is becoming increasingly popular in market and community research. In this technique the interviewer becomes the *facilitator, convenor* or *discussion leader* rather than an interviewer as such. The aim of the process is much the same as in an in-depth interview, but in this case the participants interact with each other as well as with the researcher/facilitator.

Purposes

The technique can be used:

- when a particular group is important in a study but is so small in number that members of the group would not be adequately represented in a general community questionnaire-based survey – for example, members of minority ethnic groups or people with disabilities;
- when the interaction/discussion process itself is of interest – for example, in testing reactions to a proposed new product, or when investigating how people form political opinions;
- as an alternative to the in-depth interview, when it may not be practical to arrange for individual in-depth interviews but people are willing to be interviewed as a group – for example, some youth groups or members of some ethnic communities.

Methods

A group will usually comprise between 6 and 12 participants. They may be chosen from a 'panel' of people who make themselves available to market researchers for this sort of exercise, or they may be chosen because they are members of a particular group of interest to the research – for instance local residents in a particular area, members of a sports club, or a group of people on a holiday package. The members of the group may or may not be known to one another.

The usual procedure is to record the discussion and for the researcher to produce a written summary from the recording.

Many of the same considerations apply here as in the in-depth interview situation: the process is informal but the facilitator still has a role in guiding the discussion and ensuring that all the aspects of the topic are covered. In addition, in the group interview, the facilitator has the task of ensuring that everyone in the group has their say and that the discussion is not dominated by one or two vociferous members of the group.

Participant observation

Nature

In participant observation the researcher becomes a participant in the social process being studied. The classic study of this type is Whyte's *Street Corner Society* (1955), in which the researcher spent several years living with an inner-city US Italian community. Smith's (1985) study of pubs in England is a direct leisure example as is Wynne's (1986) study of community involvement with recreation facilities.

Purposes

In leisure and tourism, elements of participant observation are common in many types of research. For instance, a researcher involved in studying the use of a park or resort can easily spend periods as a user of the facility. Many studies of individual sports and sports clubs are by participants in the sport and/or members of the club. Researchers of tourist destinations are invariably themselves visitors to those destinations. Traditionally the process has involved considerable interaction of the researcher with the people being researched. In many cases some sort of participant observation is the only way of researching particular phenomena – for instance it would be difficult to study what really goes on in a drug sub-culture or in some youth sub-cultures using a questionnaire and clip-board. Becoming part of the group and immersion in its activities is the obvious way of studying the group.

Methods

Participant observation raises a number of practical/tactical, and sometimes ethical, challenges. For example, in some cases actually gaining admittance to the social setting of interest may be difficult, especially where close-knit groups are involved. Having gained admittance to the setting, the question arises as to whether to pose as a typical member of the group, whether to adopt a plausible disguise or persona (e.g. a 'journalist' or 'writer') or whether to admit to being a researcher.

Selection of informants is an issue to be addressed by the participant observer in the same way that sampling must be considered by the survey researcher. The members of the study group who are most friendly and talkative may be the easiest to communicate with, but may give a biased picture of the views and behaviour of the group.

In addition, there are practical problems to be faced over how to record information. When the researcher's identity as a researcher has not been revealed, the taking of notes in real time or the use of a recorder may be impossible. Even when the researcher has identified her- or himself as such, or has assumed a plausible identity, the use of such devices may interfere with the sort of natural relationship which the researcher is trying to establish. The taking of regular and detailed notes is, however, the basic data recording method. This may be supplemented by photographs and even video- and sound recordings in some instances. The ethical questions raised by the researcher's relationship with informants are discussed in Chapter 4 (see Case Study 4.1).

Analysing texts

Nature

The analysis of texts, such as plays and novels, is the very basis of some disciplines in the humanities, such as literature, media studies and cultural studies. As researchers from these disciplines have turned their attention to leisure and tourism issues, and as the relationships between leisure, tourism and 'cultural products' have become recognised, the approach is playing an increasingly important role in leisure and tourism research. The term *text* is now used to embrace not just printed material, but also pictures, posters, recorded music, film and television. Indeed, virtually any cultural product can, in the jargon, be *read* as *text*. The trend is reflected in the increasing use of the term *gaze* to describe the activity of both leisure and tourism researchers and the subjects of their research. John Urry, in his book *The Tourist Gaze* states the following:

> Tourism research should involve the examination of texts, not only written texts but also maps, landscapes, paintings, films, townscapes, TV programmes, brochures, and so on ... Thus, social research significantly consists of interpreting texts, through various mainly qualitative techniques, to identify the discursive structures which give rise to and sustain, albeit temporarily, a given tourist site. *(Urry, 1994: 238–9)*

It is not proposed to outline analysis techniques in detail in this book, since approaches are very varied, including the qualitative, literary 'reading' of texts, the *interpretation* of texts sometimes referred to as *hermeneutics*, and the highly quantified form of analysis known as *content analysis*. The approach here is, rather, to introduce some examples of work in this area.

Novels and other literature

- Sönmez *et al.* (1993) examine the concept of leisure as portrayed in the novels of Kenyan author Ngugi wa Thiong'o. The analysis provides a perspective on a non-Western view of leisure and its place in a culture faced with the upheaval of the colonial and post-colonial experience.

- In two papers, Hultsman and Harper (1992, Harper and Hultsman, 1992) analyse a collection of 1930s essays on life in the 'Old South' of the USA to reveal new insights into leisure and class at that time.

- One chapter in Paul Barry's (2006: 414–4) biography of media business-man Kerry Packer, provides a fascinating insight into one, very rich, man's approach to 'serious leisure' (Stebbins, 1992) – in this case polo – illustrating the value of biographies as a source of material on leisure.

Mass media coverage

Media coverage of selected topics can be studied quantitatively by measuring the column centimetres devoted to the topic in newspapers or the time devoted to the topic on television. Examples are the studies by:

- Brown (1995) and Rowe and Brown (1994), of press coverage of women's sport in Australian newspapers;

- Toohey's (1990) analysis of the television coverage of the Barcelona Olympic Games;

- the study by Cuneen *et al.* (1989) involving an analysis of the verbal and pictorial press coverage of a sporting event.

Film

- MacCannell (1993) provides an extensive analysis of the tourist film *Cannibal Tours*, upon which he builds a detailed theoretical interpretation of the role of tourism in the modern world; Burns and Lester (2005) also examine this film.

- Rojek (1993) provides an analysis of Disney films and their role in contemporary culture, in his paper 'Disney culture'.

Material culture

● Hodder (1994), in his paper on 'The interpretation of documents and material culture', devotes relatively little space to documents, but concentrates on the idea of studying 'material culture' or artifacts. Among the latter he includes dress fashions, national flags and the archaeological study of garbage.

● Examples of the direct study of leisure and toursm-related cultural products in the research literature are studies of:
  ● the theme parks of the Disney Corporation (Rojek, 1993; Klugman *et al.*, 1995);
  ● postcards (Cohen, 1993);
  ● American musicals (Dyer, 1993);
  ● heavy metal rock music (Straw, 1993).

Biographical research

Nature

Biographical research covers a range of techniques which involve researching all or a substantial part of individuals' or groups of individuals' lives. The most common example of such research is the conventional biography or autobiography, but the biographical approach includes a number of other research approaches and outputs, including: oral history; memory work; and personal domain histories. Detailed guidance on the conduct of biographical research is not given in this book, but a brief overview of the field is given here and sources of further information in the Resource section.

Biography/autobiography

There are many published accounts of lives of business leaders which, while often read for entertainment, also provide insight into how business and business leaders operate. Perhaps the most well-known is the autobiography of Lee Iacocca (1984), the CEO of Chrysler during a turbulent period. In the case of Walt Disney, there is an enormous literature in which the biography of Disney himself and the story of the corporation are intertwined (e.g. Bryman, 1995; Foglesong, 2001; Project on Disney, 1995). In Australia, *The Rise and Fall of Alan Bond* (owner of breweries and television stations among other things) and the *Rise and Rise of Kerry Packer* (owner of television stations, magazines and casinos), both by Paul Barry (1990, 2006), are notable examples of leisure business biographies.

Oral history

Oral history involves recording eye-witness accounts of events and typically storing the recordings and/or a transcription of them in an archive as a source for research. While such accounts range more widely than the interviewees' own lives, they are nevertheless personal accounts. An example is Parker's (1988) study of a British mining community during the miners' strikes of the 1980s – the book includes accounts by miners, Coal Board employees, police and community members.

Memory work

Memory work is a structured way of eliciting subjects' memories of events; it can be seen as a focus group aided by individual writing. Participants are asked to write a short account of an experience related to the research topic – for example bullying at the workplace or successful selling. The written accounts are read aloud in focus group settings and discussed, and may be followed up with further writing and/or interviewing (see Small, 2004).

Personal domain histories

In the 1980s, a technique termed 'personal leisure histories' was developed by Hedges (1986) to study the ways in which significant changes in life circumstances (marriage, birth of a child, change of job, health issues, etc.) impacted on patterns of leisure participation. While no known example exists, it seems clear that such a technique might be used to focus on other domains of life – hence the use of the term personal *domain* histories.

Ethnography

The ethnographic style of research is not one technique but an approach drawing on a variety of techniques. Generally, as applied to leisure and tourism research, it seeks to see the world through the eyes of those being researched, allowing them to speak for themselves, often revealed through extensive direct quotations in the research report. Often also, the aim is to debunk conventional, establishment, 'common sense' views of 'social problems', 'deviants', sexual and ethnic stereotypes, and so on. In leisure studies the approach has become particularly associated with 'cultural studies', for example of youth sub-cultures and ethnic groups.

Validity and reliability, trustworthiness

The issues of validity – the extent to which research accurately represents what it is intended to represent – and reliability – the extent to which research is replicable – were discussed in Chapter 2, and it was noted there that some researchers prefer to use the term *trustworthiness* when discussing qualitative methods. Internal validity is concerned with the processes by which information is gathered from the subjects of the study. A case could be made that information collected by qualitative methods has a greater chance of being internally valid than information gathered by means of, for example, a short questionnaire, since in the qualitative data collection situation more time and effort is generally taken to collect any one piece of information: thus the exchange between interviewer and interviewee in an in-depth interview or the discussion in a focus group should increase the likelihood of interviewer/ facilitator and interviewee/participants understanding one another.

External validity is concerned with the applicability of the findings beyond the subjects of the research. Typically, no formal claim of generalisability is made on the basis of qualitative study but, as noted in Chapter 2, this strict rule is often implicitly ignored. It is noted in Chapter 13, that efforts are often made to select samples of subjects for qualitative research which have some semblance of representativeness, at least in terms of the qualitative diversity of the population being studied. It would be strange if researchers conducting qualitative research projects did not believe that there were *some* implications beyond the limited sample of subjects studied. Thus the belief is that what has been found is true of *some people* among the population from which the study subjects were drawn, but the extent cannot be quantified. In theoretical terms, if the findings of qualitative research are inconsistent with existing theory it at least establishes that the theory is not *universally* valid. Furthermore, theoretical propositions arising from qualitative research *may* be more widely applicable.

Unlike the physical sciences, exact replicability of qualitative social research findings is clearly unlikely. However, accumulation of similar, or logically consistent, findings from a wide range of studies lends strength to the findings, not in a statistical sense, but in terms of the robustness of the findings in different settings. There is a parallel in quantitative meta-analyses, where it can be argued that similar, but statistically insignificant, findings from a number of studies may be given some cumulative support if the level of significance of individual studies was affected by sample sizes.

Thus, while qualitative research cannot offer the rigorous tests of validity and reliability of quantitative research, the issues can be discussed, and some form of assessment of *trustworthiness* arrived at.

Summary

This chapter introduces the role of qualitative approaches in leisure and tourism research. One of the basic assumptions of qualitative research is that reality is socially and subjectively constructed rather than objectively determined. In this perspective researchers are seen as part of the research process seeking to uncover meanings and understanding of the issues they are researching. In general, qualitative research involves the collection of a large amount of 'rich' information concerning relatively few people or organisations rather than more limited information from a large number of people or organisations.

Qualitative methods generally require a more flexible, recursive, approach to overall research design and conduct in contrast with the more linear, sequential approach used in most quantitative research. Hypothesis formation evolves as the research progresses; data collection and analysis take place concurrently and writing is also often an evolutionary process, rather than a separate process which happens at the end of the project.

There is a range of qualitative methods available to the researcher, including in-depth interviews, group interviews, focus groups, participant observation, textual analysis, biographical methods and ethnographic methods. The chapter outlines the nature and techniques involved in using each of these methods.

Validity and reliability of qualitative methods cannot be assessed using the rigorous, quantified tests of quantitative methods, but the issues can be addressed and assessed to give an assessment of what some have termed *trustworthiness*.

Test questions

1. Outline some of the merits of qualitative data.

2. Explain the difference between sequential and recursive approaches to research.

3. Outline Whyte's levels of interviewer intervention in an in-depth/informal interview.

4. In-depth interviews involve an interviewer: what is the equivalent in a focus group?

5. Name three types of biographical research.

Exercises

For exercises in qualitative methods, see Chapter 15.

Resources

- Qualitative methods in social science: Lofland and Lofland (1984), Burgess (1982), Denzin and Lincoln (1994, 2006), Silverman (1993).

- In leisure studies: Henderson (1990, 2006), Godbey and Scott (1990), Kelly (1980), Kamphorst *et al.* (1984).

- In tourism studies: Cohen (1988), Davies (2003), Peterson (1994), Riley and Love (2000), Walle (1997), Phillimore and Goodson (2004b).

- In sport studies: Andrews *et al.* (2005).

- Examples in leisure studies: Cuneen *et al.* (1989), Griffin *et al.* (1982), Hollands (1985), Marsh *et al.* (1978), Walker (1988), Wynne (1986).

- Examples in tourism studies: Palmer and Dunford (2002), Jordan and Gibson (2004).

- Informal/in-depth interviews: Dunne (1995), Moeller *et al.* (1980a, b), Jennings (2005); example: Rapoport and Rapoport (1975).

- Participant observation: Campbell (1970), Glancy (1986).

- Focus groups: Calder (1977), Greenbaum (1998, 2000), Krueger (1988), Reynolds and Johnson (1978), Stewart and Shamdasani (1990), Morgan (1993).

- Textual/visual: travel photography: Albers and James (1988).

- Biographical methods: Atkinson (1998), Bertaux (1981), Roberts (2002), Project on Disney (1995); in tourism: Ladkin (2004); personal domain histories: Hedges (1986); memory work in tourism: Small (2004).

- Grounded theory: in general: Glaser and Strauss (1967), Strauss (1987), Strauss and Corbin (1994); in tourism: Connell and Lowe (1977).

- Ethnography: in tourism: Sandiford and Ap (1998), Davies (1997).

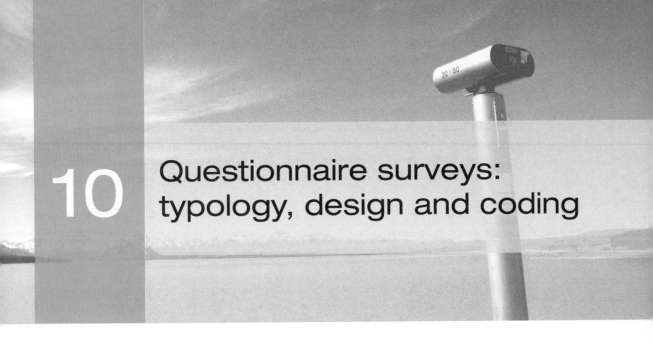

10 Questionnaire surveys: typology, design and coding

Introduction

This chapter presents an overview of the range of types of questionnaire survey and questionnaire design. Questionnaire surveys involve the gathering of information from individuals using a formally designed *questionnaire* or *interview schedule* and is arguably the most commonly used technique in leisure and tourism research.

The first part of the chapter discusses the merits of questionnaire methods and the distinction between interviewer-completion and respondent-completion questionnaire surveys, followed by an overview of the characteristics of: the household questionnaire survey; the street survey; the telephone survey; the postal or mail survey; on-site or user surveys; and captive group surveys.

The second half of the chapter considers the factors which must be taken into account in designing questionnaires for leisure and tourism studies. First, the relationship between research problems and information requirements are examined. This is followed by consideration of the types of information typically included in leisure and tourism questionnaires, the wording of questions, coding of questionnaires for computer analysis, the ordering and layout of questions and the problem of validity. Finally some consideration is given to the special requirements of time-budget studies.

Definitions and terminology

A questionnaire can be defined as a 'a written/printed or computer-based schedule of questions and a *pro forma* for recording answers to the questions'.

It is therefore both a means of eliciting information from respondents and a medium for recording answers.

The term *questionnaire survey* or *questionnaire-based survey* is used deliberately in this chapter to emphasise that the words *survey* and *questionnaire* mean two different things. There is a tendency in common parlance – and unfortunately in some research literature – to use the terms survey and questionnaire synonymously. For example, researchers have been known to make statements such as: '1000 surveys were distributed'. This is inappropriate; only *one* survey was involved – 1000 *questionnaires* were distributed. To distinguish the two terms:

- a questionnaire is a written/printed or computer-based schedule of questions;

- a survey is the *process* of designing and conducting a study involving the gathering of information from a number of subjects.

A 'survey' does not always include a questionnaire; thus, for example, a study could involve a visual survey of beach crowding or a documentary survey of the contents of organisations' annual reports.

Alternative terms for the word questionnaire are 'research instrument' or 'survey instrument', which reference the science laboratory context. In addition 'survey form' or 'question schedule' are sometimes used.

Roles

Questionnaire surveys are used when a specified range of information is required from an individual or organisation. The most common form of questionnaire-based survey is based on a representative sample of a defined population of individuals or organisations (as discussed in Chapter 13), although in some cases the whole population is included, as in a national census of the population (see Chapter 7): in both cases the aim is to make statements about the characteristics of the population, typically in the form of percentages, averages, relationships and trends.

Typically, questionnaire-based surveys are used to collect responses to questions which have a limited number of possible answers, for example, a person's gender or educational level, but some questions can be open-ended, with an unspecified range of answers – for example an open question on a visitor's complaints or suggestions regarding the management of a leisure or tourism facility.

Questionnaire-based surveys can play a role in the task of estimating the number of visits to leisure facilities and tourism destinations where visit numbers are not automatically gathered by administrative means, such as the sale of tickets. Examples include urban parks and tourism destinations car-borne access. This phenomenon is discussed in Chapter 7, where it is noted that information on visitor numbers may be gathered administratively (ticket sales, landing cards), by direct counts/observation or wholly or in part by questionnaire-based survey – see Figures 7.2 and 7.3.

Merits

Compared with the qualitative techniques discussed in Chapter 9, questionnaire surveys usually involve quantification – the presentation of results in numerical terms. This has implications for the way the data are collected, analysed and interpreted. In Chapter 9 a list of merits of qualitative methods, as put forward by Kelly, is presented. The merits of questionnaire surveys can be similarly examined. Some of the qualities of questionnaire surveys which make them useful in leisure and tourism research are set out below.

- Contemporary leisure and tourism are often mass phenomena, requiring major involvement from governmental, non-profit and/or commercial organisations, which rely on quantified information for significant aspects of their decision-making. Questionnaire surveys are an ideal means of providing some of this information.

- While absolute objectivity is impossible, questionnaire methods provide a transparent set of research procedures such that the way information was collected and how it was analysed or interpreted is clear for all to see, although, it must be said, journal articles vary in the amount of detail provided. Questionnaire survey data, which are invariably available in digital form, can often be re-analysed by others if they wish to extend the research or provide an alternative interpretation.

- Quantification can provide relatively complex information in a succinct, easily understandable, form, including graphics.

- Methods such as longitudinal surveys and annually repeated surveys provide the opportunity to study change over time, using comparable methodology.

- Leisure and tourism encompass a wide range of activities, with a range of characteristics, such as frequency, duration and type of participation, expenditure, location, level of enjoyment and aspirations. Questionnaires are a good means of ensuring that a complete picture of a person's patterns of participation is obtained.

- While qualitative methods are ideal for exploring attitudes, meanings and perceptions on an individual basis, questionnaire methods provide the means to gather and record simple information on the incidence of attitudes, meanings and perceptions among the population as a whole, thus indicating not only that certain attitudes exist but also how widespread they are.

Comparison of this list and the one referring to qualitative methods at the beginning of Chapter 9 reinforces the view that each method has its merits and appropriate uses – the 'horses for courses' idea. Questionnaire surveys have a role to play when the research questions indicate the need for fairly structured data and generally when data are required from samples which are explicitly representative of a defined wider population. Examples of the role of questionnaire surveys versus other methods are shown in Figure 10.1.

Organisation	Topic	Questionnaire survey	Qualitative methods	Other methods
Leisure facility	How to increase number of visitors	• User/visitor survey on what types of people use which services and when. • Community survey on socio-demographic characteristics of users vs non-users and perceptions of facility.	• Observation and/or focus groups on experience of visiting the facility – quality, atmosphere, service.	• Secondary analysis of ticket sales and utilisation data re. relative popularity of different activities/ services.
Tourism Commission	Data for tourism strategic plan	• Intercept survey of visitors on accommodation used, sites visited, expenditure patterns and socio-demographic characteristics of visitors from different places.	• In-depth interviews or focus groups with visitors on quality of visitor experience • Focus groups with residents on attitudes towards tourists and tourist development.	• Arrival and departure data (if national study).
Individual researcher	The role of the holiday in leisure	• Household survey on socio-demographic characteristics and numbers of those who do and do not take holidays – measures of income, health and attitudes.	• In-depth interviews on meanings and importance of holidays and local leisure in individuals' lifestyles.	• Secondary analysis of official data on holiday entitlements and leave-taking.

Figure 10.1 The use of questionnaire surveys compared with other methods – examples

Limitations

Questionnaire-based surveys have a number of limitations, related to the fact that they are often based on samples and self-reported data.

Samples

Questionnaire surveys usually, but not always, involve only a proportion, or *sample*, of the population in which the researcher is interested. For example, the national surveys discussed in Chapter 7 are based on samples of only a few thousand to represent tens of millions of people. How such samples are chosen, how the size of the sample is decided and the implications of relying on a sample to represent a population are discussed in Chapter 13.

Self-reported data

As discussed in Chapter 2, questionnaire surveys rely on information from respondents. The accuracy of what respondents say depends on their own powers of recall, on their honesty and, fundamentally, on the format of the questions included in the questionnaire. There has been relatively little research on the validity or accuracy of questionnaire data in leisure and tourism studies, but some examples are indicated in the problems of validity and accuracy which arise from a number of sources, including exaggeration and under-reporting; accuracy of recall; and sensitivity:

- *Exaggeration/under-reporting*: Some research (see the Resources section) has suggested that respondents exaggerate levels of participation in some activities and under-report others. This may be conscious or unconscious and may be for reasons of prestige or lack of it – what Oppenheim (2000: 138) calls 'social desirability bias' – or a desire to be positive and friendly towards the interviewer, at least in a face-to-face situation. For example, if the interview is about sport or the arts, respondents may tend to exaggerate their interest in and involvement with sport or the arts, just to be helpful and positive.

- *Accuracy of recall*: Mistakes can be made in recalling events at all or in estimating frequency of involvement: for example, if someone claims to take part in an activity twice a week, is that equivalent to 104 times a year? Apart from seasonality, which could be addressed in the questionnaire, such factors as weather conditions, illness, public holidays and family and work emergencies may all reduce the actual level of participation. Even if the question attempts to avoid this problem by asking respondents about the actual number of occasions on which they have participated in a given time period, respondents may be working from the 'once a week' notion and still over-estimate. Where alternative sources of information, such as club records, are available it is possible to check the accuracy of questionnaire-based information. Studies of this phenomenon suggest substantial over-estimation in sporting/physical activity – examples are listed in the Resources section.

- *Sensitivity*: Sensitive topics can also give rise to under-estimation or over-estimation, and some leisure-related activities fall into this category: for example, Nora Schaeffer (2000) provides information on responses regarding sexual activity and recreational drug use.

This suggests the need for careful questionnaire design and cross-checking/triangulation where possible, but also that the researcher and the user of research results should always bear in mind the nature and source of the data and not fall into the trap of believing that, because information is presented in numerical form and is based on large numbers, it represents immutable 'truth'.

Interviewer-completion or respondent-completion?

Questionnaire surveys can take one of two forms:

- *Interviewer-completed*: the questionnaire provides the *script* for an interview; an interviewer reads the questions out to the respondent and records the respondent's answers on the questionnaire – the classic 'clipboard' situation, where the method may also be referred to as *face-to-face* interviewing. When telephone surveys are involved the interviewer may record answers on a computer.

- Respondent-completed, often referred to as *self-completion*: respondents read and fill out the questionnaire for themselves, on paper or online.

Each approach has its particular advantages and disadvantages, as summarised in Figure 10.2. Interviewer-completion is more expensive in terms of interviewers' time (which usually has to be paid for) but the use of an interviewer usually ensures a more accurate and complete response. Respondent-completion can be cheaper and quicker but often results in low response rates, which can introduce bias into the results because those who choose not to respond or are unable to respond, perhaps because of language or literacy difficulties, may differ from those who do respond. When designing a questionnaire for respondent-completion, greater care must be taken with layout and presentation since it must be read and completed by 'untrained' people. In terms of design, respondent-completion questionnaires should ideally consist primarily of *closed* questions – that is, questions which can be answered by ticking boxes. *Open-ended questions* – where respondents have to write out their answers – should generally be avoided in such a situation, since they invariably achieve only a low response. For example, in an interview, respondents will often give expansive answers to questions such as 'Do you have any comments

	Interviewer-completion	Respondent-completion
Advantages	More accuracy	Cheaper
	Higher response rates	Quicker
	Fuller and more complete answers	Relatively anonymous
	Design can be less 'user-friendly'	
Disadvantages	Higher cost	Patchy response
	Less anonymity	Incomplete response
		Risk of frivolous responses
		More care needed in design

Figure 10.2 Interviewer-completion compared with respondent-completion

to make on the overall management of this facility?' But they will not as readily write down such answers in a respondent-completion questionnaire.

There may, however, be cases when respondent-completion is to be preferred, or is the only practicable approach. For example, people to be surveyed may be widely scattered geographically, making face-to-face interviews impossibly expensive, so a mail or postal survey, which intrinsically involves respondent-completion is an obvious choice. Furthermore, when a questionnaire deals with sensitive matters, respondents might prefer the anonymity of the respondent-completed questionnaire. Some of the issues connected with respondent-completion questionnaires are discussed more fully in the section on mail surveys.

It should be noted that some commentators, in discussions of research methods, draw a distinction between 'interview methods' and 'questionnaire methods'; this is clearly misleading because the interviewer-completed questionnaire-based survey clearly involves an interview, so the 'questionnaire method' may involve an interview, so is not distinct from the 'interview method'. What such comments are invariably referring to is a distinction between questionnaire-based methods and in-depth or semi-structured interviews, as discussed in Chapter 9.

Types of questionnaire survey

Questionnaire surveys in the leisure and tourism field can be divided into seven types: household surveys; street surveys; telephone surveys; mail surveys; e-surveys; user/on-site/visitor surveys; and captive group surveys. Each of these is discussed in more detail below and some of their basic characteristics are summarised in Figure 10.3.

Type	Interviewer or respondent completion	Cost	Sample	Possible length of questionnaire	Response rate
Household					
Standard	Either	Expensive	Whole population	Long	High
Time-use	Respondent	Expensive	Whole population	Long	High
Omnibus	Either	Medium per client	Whole population	Long	High
Street	Interviewer	Medium	Most of population	Short	Medium
Telephone	Interviewer	Medium	People with land-line telephone	Short	High but falling
Mail	Respondent	Cheap	General or special	Varies	Low
E-survey	Respondent	Cheap	People accessible via email/internet	Medium	Medium
On-site	Either	Medium	Site users only	Medium	High
Captive	Respondent	Cheap	Captive group only	Medium	High

Figure 10.3 Types of questionnaire survey – characteristics

The household questionnaire survey

Nature

Much of the quantified data in the field of leisure and tourism derive from household questionnaire surveys. While academics draw on the data extensively, the majority of such surveys are commissioned by government and commercial leisure and tourism organisations for policy or marketing purposes. The advantage of household surveys is that they are generally representative of the community – the samples drawn tend to include all age-groups, above a certain minimum, and all occupational groups. They also generally represent a complete geographical area – a whole country, a state or region, a local government area or a neighbourhood. Household surveys are therefore designed to provide information on the reported leisure or tourism behaviour of the community as a whole or a particular group drawn from the whole community – for example, the older population aged 65 and over, or young people aged 15–24.

While some household leisure/tourism surveys are specialised, many are broad-ranging in their coverage. That is, they tend to ask, among other things, about participation in a wide range of leisure activities, holiday-taking patterns or buying habits. This facilitates exploration of a wide range of issues which other types of survey cannot so readily tackle.

Conduct

Normally household questionnaire surveys are interviewer-completed by face-to-face interview. However, it is possible for a questionnaire to be left at a respondent's home for respondent-completion and later collection, in which case the field-worker then has the responsibility of checking that questionnaires have been fully completed and perhaps conducting an interview in those situations where respondents have been unable to fill in the questionnaire, either because they have been too busy, have forgotten, or have lost the questionnaire, or because of literacy or language problems or infirmity.

Being home-based this sort of survey can involve quite lengthy questionnaires and interviews. By contrast, in the street, at a leisure or tourism facility, or over the telephone, it can be difficult to conduct a lengthy interview. General leisure participation surveys in particular, with their wide range of possible activities, often involve a very complex questionnaire which is difficult to administer 'on the run'. With the home-based interview it is usually possible to pursue issues at greater length than is possible in other settings. An interview of three-quarters of an hour in duration is not out of the question and 20–30 minutes is quite common.

A variation on the standard household questionnaire interview survey is to combine interviewer-completed and respondent-completed elements. This often happens with leisure surveys: the interviewer conducts an interview with one member of the household about the household – how many people live there, whether the dwelling is owned or rented, perhaps information on recreational equipment, or anything to do with the household as a whole. Then an individual questionnaire is left for each member of the household to complete, concerning their own leisure behaviour. The interviewer calls back later to collect these individual questionnaires.

The potential length of interviews, the problems of contacting representative samples and, on occasions, the wide geographical spread of the study area, mean that household surveys are usually the most expensive to conduct, per interview. Costs of the order of £25 or £30 per interview are typical, depending on the amount of analysis included in the price. When samples of several thousands are involved, the costs can therefore be substantial.

Omnibus surveys

While considering household surveys mention should be made of the *omnibus* survey. These are surveys conducted by a market research or survey organisation with various questions included in the questionnaire on behalf of different clients. The main costs of conducting the survey, which lie in sampling and contacting respondents, are therefore shared by a number of clients. The cost of collecting fairly standard demographic and socio-economic information – such as age, gender, family structure, occupation and income – is also shared among the clients. With regular omnibus surveys many of the procedures, such as sampling and data processing, have become routinised, and interviewers are in place throughout the country already trained and familiar with the type of questionnaire and the requirements of the market research company – these factors can reduce costs significantly.

The British *General Lifestyle Survey* (GLF) (formerly *General Household Survey* (GHS)) is an omnibus survey of 20,000 people run by the Office for National Statistics, the clients being government departments and agencies. In the years when leisure questions were included, the clients for those questions were the various national leisure/recreation agencies, such as the Sports Council and the Countryside Commission.

Although discussed here as a sub-category of household surveys, omnibus surveys amy also be conducted using other formats, notably telephone and e-surveys.

Time-use surveys

Time-use, or time-budget, surveys are designed to collect information about people's use of time. Such information is generally collected as the main or subsidiary part of a household survey, but, in addition to a answering a questionnaire, respondents are asked to complete a diary, typically covering a period of between one and two days. Respondents are asked to record their waking hours activities in a time-use diary, including starting and stopping times, together with information on where the activity was done, with whom, and possibly whether the respondent considered it to be paid work, domestic work or leisure. Secondary activities are also generally gathered, for example, listening to music while doing the housework. Radio and television viewing audience data were traditionally collected using time-use diaries, but the trend now is towards automated/electronic recording. Home-based time-use surveys can clearly not be used in relation to tourism, but the technique has been suggested for use with tourists to study their temporal and spatial behaviour at a destination (Pearce, 1988).

Coding and analysis of time-use data presents a considerable challenge, since hundreds of leisure and non-leisure activities must be given a code and information processed for, say, 60 or 70 quarter-hour periods each day. Space does not permit a detailed treatment of this specialised topic here, but it can be followed up in the literature indicated in the Resources section.

National surveys

Chapter 7 discusses national leisure and tourism participation surveys, typically conducted by government statistical agencies, as a source of secondary data. These surveys are typically large-scale household or telephone surveys. Often their main secondary use is comparison with locally conducted surveys: the aim being to establish whether, on some participation measure, the local community is above or below the national average. If such comparisons are to be made, it follows that the local survey must be conducted in a similar way and the comparison questions in the questionnaire must be similarly worded. This clearly places a constraint on design, but, apart from the ability to make comparisons, it also has the advantage that the question format has been thoroughly tested.

The street survey

Nature

The street survey involves a relatively short questionnaire and is conducted, as the name implies, on the street – usually a shopping street or business area – or in squares or shopping malls, where a cross-section of the community might be expected to be found. The method can also be used to interview tourists to an area, in which case surveys are conducted at locations where tourist are known to congregate, such as the environs of major attractions, restaurant or tourist accommodation areas, or transport locations, such as airports or bus-stations. In the tourism case the survey could be seen as having some of the characteristics of the on-site, user or visitor survey, as discussed below.

Conduct

Stopping people in the street or similar environments for an interview places certain limitations on the interview process. First, an interview conducted in the street cannot generally be as long as one conducted at someone's home – especially when the interviewee is in a hurry. Of course there are some household interviews which are very short because the interviewee is in a hurry or is a reluctant respondent and there are street interviews which are lengthy because the respondent has plenty of time. As a general rule, however, the street interview must be shorter. Both in the home and street interview situation, before committing themselves to an interview, potential respondents often ask 'How long will it take?' In the home-based situation a reply of '15–20 minutes' is generally acceptable but in the street situation anything more than '5 minutes' would generally lead to a marked reduction in the proportion of people prepared to cooperate. The range of topics/issues/activities which can be covered in a street interview is therefore restricted and this must be taken into account in designing the questionnaire.

The second limitation of the street survey is the problem of contacting a representative sample of the population. Certain types of people might not frequent shopping areas at all, or only infrequently – for instance, people who are housebound for various reasons or people who have other people to do their shopping. Some types of tourist – for example, business tourists or those visiting friends or relatives – may not be found in the popular tourist areas. Such individuals might be of particular importance in some studies, so their omission can significantly compromise the results. There is little that can be done to overcome this problem; it has to be accepted as a limitation of the method. The other side of this coin is that certain groups will be over-represented in shopping streets – notably full-time home/child carers, the retired and the unemployed in suburban shopping areas, or office workers in business areas. It might also be the case that certain areas are frequented more by, for example, young people than old people or by men rather than women, so any sample would be representative of the users of the area, but not of the local population or visitor population as a whole.

Quota sampling

The means used to attempt to overcome the problem of unrepresentative samples is the technique of *quota sampling*, in which the interviewer is given a pre-determined quota of different types of people – for example, by age, sex, occupation – to interview. The proportions in each category in the target population must be known in advance – for example, by reference to the Population Census (see Chapter 7) or, in the case of international tourists, by reference to the official short-term arrivals and departure data (see Chapter 7). When the survey is complete, if the sample is still not representative with regard to the key characteristics, further adjustments can be achieved through the process of *weighting*, as discussed in Chapter 13.

The telephone survey

Nature

The telephone survey is particularly popular with political pollsters because of its speed and the ease with which a widespread sample of the community can be contacted. It is also used extensively in market and academic research for the same reasons.

An obvious limitation of the technique is that it excludes non-telephone subscribers – generally low-income groups and some mobile sections of the population. With telephones in virtually all homes in developed countries, this is not now as serious a problem as it was in the past. In the case of relatively simple surveys like political opinion polls, where the researcher has access to previous results from both telephone and face-to-face interviews, this problem may be overcome by the use of a correction factor – for instance, it might be known that inclusion of non-telephone subscribers always adds x per cent to the Labour vote. In certain kinds of market research the absence of the poorer parts of the community from the survey may be unimportant because they do not form a significant part of the market, but for much public policy and academic research, however, this can be a significant limitation.

An emerging problem is the case of households which do not have land-line telephones, relying only on mobile phones, which are not listed. This is likely to involve mainly young people, who are an important target of much survey work. Again, it may be possible to correct for this statistically if the characteristics of this group are known.

Conduct

Length of interview can be a limitation of telephone surveys – but not as serious as in the case of street interviews; telephone interviews of 10 or 15 minutes are acceptable.

The technique has its own unique set of problems in relation to sampling. Generally the numbers to be called are selected at random from the telephone directory. Market research companies generally use Computer Assisted Telephone Interviewing (CATI), involving equipment and software which automatically dials random telephone numbers from a digital database. CATI systems also enable the interviewer to key answers directly into a computer, so dispensing with the printed questionnaire. This speeds up the analysis process considerably and cuts down the possibility of error in transcribing results from printed questionnaire to computer. It explains how the results of overnight political opinion polls can be published in the newspapers the next morning.

If a representative cross-section of the community is to be included, then it is necessary for telephone surveys to be conducted in the evenings and/or at weekends if those who have paid jobs are to be included.

A limitation of the telephone interview is that respondents cannot be shown such things as lists or images. This is particularly relevant to leisure and tourism surveys. In leisure participation surveys, respondents are frequently shown lists of activities and asked if they have participated in them. Such lists can include 20 or 30 items, which can be tedious to read out over the telephone. Similarly in tourism studies respondents may be shown a list of places and asked which they have visited. Surveys which involve long checklists – for example attitude dimensions – are also not easily conducted by telephone.

It can be argued that telephones have an advantage over face-to-face interviews in that respondents may feel that they are more anonymous and may therefore be more forthcoming in their opinions. But it could also be argued that the face-to-face interview has other advantages in terms of eye-contact and body language which enable the skilled interviewer to conduct a better interview than is possible over the telephone.

The main advantage of the telephone survey is that it is quick and relatively cheap to conduct. However, in some countries there is growing reluctance on the part of the public to cooperate with telephone surveys, resulting in the need to make a number of calls to contact cooperative respondents, thus raising the costs and raising questions about representativeness.

Representativeness and response levels

An increasing number of problems arise in the conduct of telephone surveys, including consumer, technological, legal and social factors.

Reference has already been made to problems caused by the consumer shift to mobile or cell phone technology: unlike land-line telephones, mobile phone numbers are not publicly listed and geographically identifiable and people who rely entirely on mobile phones are not a cross-section of the whole community, so continued reliance on land-line telephones for surveys can result in biased samples. In developing countries the history is unfolding differently since the mobile phone has arrived in advance of universal access to land-line telephones.

Technological devices used to control and manage telephone access also present difficulties in contacting survey respondents, including user ID and answer machines/voice mail. Added to this, privacy legislation enables telephone subscribers to deny access for tele-marketing, although bona-fide social research calls are generally exempt.

In addition to consumer and technological change, surveyors note an increasing tendency for members of the public to refuse to cooperate with telephone surveys. Thus, one American organisation reports that, once contact is made, using standard survey techniques, while 58 per cent agreed to an interview in 1997, this had fallen to 38 per cent by 2003, although these figures increased to 74 per cent and 59 per cent when more rigorous techniques, including call-backs, were used (Pew Research Center, 2004).

The result of these changes is leading to increased costs for telephone surveys as well as increased concerns about representativeness. The result is a trend towards e-surveys which, as discussed below, face their own challenges.

National surveys

The comments about national surveys, made in relation to household surveys above, also apply to telephone surveys.

The mail survey

Nature

There are certain situations where the mail or postal method is the only practical survey technique to use. The commonest example is where members or customers of some national organisation are to be surveyed. The costs of conducting face-to-face interviews with even a sample of the members or customers would be substantial – a mail survey is the obvious answer. The mail survey has the advantage that a large sample can be included. In the case of a membership organisation, there may be advantages in surveying the whole membership, even though this may not be necessary in statistical terms. It can, however, be very helpful in terms of the internal politics of the organisation for all members to be given the opportunity to participate in the survey and to 'have their say'.

The problem of low response rates

The most notorious problem of postal surveys is low response rates. In many cases as few as 25 or 30 per cent of those sent a questionnaire bother to reply, and when surveys are poorly conceived and designed the response rate can fall to 3 or 4 per cent. Surveys with only 30 per cent response rates are regularly reported in the research literature, but questions must be raised as to their validity when 70 per cent of the target sample is not represented.

What affects the response rate? Seven different factors can be identified, as listed in Figure 10.4. The various factors and measures listed are discussed in turn below.

---

1. The interest of the respondent in the survey topic
2. The length of the questionnaire
3. Questionnaire design/presentation/complexity
4. Style, content and authorship of the accompanying letter
5. Provision of a postage-paid reply envelope
6. Rewards for responding
7. Number and timing of reminders/follow-ups

Figure 10.4 Factors affecting mail survey response

1. Interest of the respondent in the survey topic

A survey of a local community about a proposal to route a six-lane highway through the neighbourhood would probably result in a high response rate, but a survey of the same community on general patterns of leisure behaviour would probably result in a low response rate. Variation among the population in the level of interest in the topic can result in a biased (that is, unrepresentative) response. For example, a survey on sports facility provision might evoke a high response rate among those interested in sport and a low response rate among those not interested – giving a false impression of overall community enthusiasm for sports facility provision. To some extent this can be corrected by weighting if the bias corresponds with certain known characteristics of the population (see Chapter 13). For example, if there was a high response rate from young people and a low response rate from older people, information from the Census on the actual proportions of different age-groups in the community could be used to weight the results.

2. Length of the questionnaire

It might be expected that a long questionnaire would discourage potential respondents. It can, however, be argued that other factors, such as the topic and the presentation of the questionnaire, are more important than the length of the questionnaire – that is, if the topic is interesting to the respondent and is well presented, then length of questionnaire and the time taken to complete it may be less of an issue.

3. Questionnaire design/presentation/complexity

More care must be taken in design and physical presentation with any respondent-completed questionnaire. Typesetting, colour coding of pages, graphics and so on may be necessary. Leisure and tourism surveys often present awesome lists of activities which can make a questionnaire look very complicated and demanding to complete.

4. The accompanying letter

The letter from the sponsor or researcher which accompanies the questionnaire may have an influence on people's willingness to respond. Does it give a good reason for the survey? Is it from someone or the type of organisation whom the potential respondent trusts or respects?

5. Postage-paid reply envelope

It is usual to include a postage-paid envelope for the return of the questionnaire. Some believe that an envelope with a real stamp on it will produce a better response rate than a business-reply-paid envelope. Providing reply envelopes with real stamps is more expensive because, apart from the time spent in sticking stamps on envelopes, stamps are provided for both respondents and non-respondents.

6. Rewards

The question of rewards for taking part in a survey can arise in relation to any sort of survey but it is a device used most often in postal surveys. One approach is to send every respondent some small reward, such as a voucher for a firm's or agency's product or service, or even money. A more common approach is to enter all respondents in a draw for a prize. Even a fairly costly prize may be money well spent if it results in a substantial increase in the response rate, and when considered in relation to the cost of the alternative methods, such as a household survey involving face-to-face interviews. It could, however, be argued that the introduction of rewards causes certain people to respond for the wrong reasons and that it introduces a potential source of bias in responses. It might also be considered that the inclusion of a prize or reward 'lowers the tone' of the survey and places it in the same category as other, commercial, junk mail that comes through people's letter boxes every day.

7. Reminders/follow-ups

Sensible reminder and follow-up procedures are perhaps the most significant tool available to the researcher. They can include postcard/email/phone reminders, supplying a second copy of the questionnaire and offering a telephone interview, indicated in the sequence suggested in Figure 10.5. Dillman *et al.* (2009) have conducted experiments with the offer of a telephone interview and note that this clearly increases the response rate but may provide different responses from the standard mail survey – this may be seen as a strength (a sort of triangulation) or a weakness.

An example of the effects of follow-ups can be seen in Figure 10.6, which relates to a mail survey of residents' recreational use of a river estuary. It can be

Day	Reminder	Attachments	Comment
1	Initial mail-out	Questionnaire	–
8	Postcard reminder	–	Email or telephone might be used if available and resources permit.
15	Letter reminder	Copy of questionnaire	Copy of questionnaire is enclosed 'in case the original has been mislaid'). Email might be used. Offer of telephone interview.
22	Final postcard reminder	–	As above, email or phone might be used and offer of telephone interview.

Figure 10.5 Mail survey follow-ups

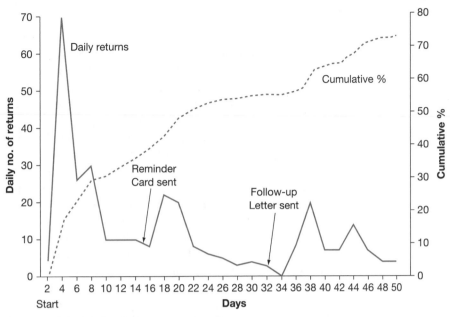

Figure 10.6 Mail survey response pattern

seen that the level of responses peaked after only 3 days and looked likely to cease after about 16 days, which would have given a potential response rate of just 40 per cent. The surges in responses following the sending of the post-card and the second copy of the questionnaire can be seen and the net result was a 75 per cent response rate, which is very good for this type of survey. The need for follow-ups must be considered when budgeting for a postal survey, since postage and printing costs are often the most significant item in such budgets.

The sending out of reminders means that it must be possible to identify returned questionnaires, so that reminders are not sent to those who have already replied. This means that questionnaires or envelopes must have an identifying number which can be matched with the mailing list. Some respondents resent this potential breach of confidentiality but it cannot be avoided if only non-respondents are to be followed up. The confidentiality issue may be overcome if the identifier is placed on the reply envelope rather than the questionnaire. A further possibility is for the replies to be sent to a 'neutral' party, such as a solicitor or accountant. There is often a further advantage to being able to identify responses; they can be used to check the representativeness of the response. For instance, the questionnaire may not include respondents' addresses, but the geographical spread of the response can be examined if the identity of the responses is known, and any necessary weighting can then be carried out.

Richard Gitelson and Ellen Drogin (1992) showed that sending final reminders with a personalised letter and sending it via certified/registered mail significantly increased the response rate compared with non-personalised letters and ordinary mail (see the summary in Case study 11.3).

How much is enough?

What level of response is acceptable? One answer would be to say that an adequate response has been achieved if the characteristics of non-respondents and the responses they would have given are not significantly different from those of respondents. But how do you know the characteristics and responses of non-respondents? In some cases the researcher has access to some limited information on non-respondents – for example, their geographical location and other information which might be held on the database from which addresses were drawn. This can be used to make comparisons.

One approach which covers both characteristics and question responses is to compare early respondents with later respondents – if there is no difference, this may indicate that further pursuit of non-respondents is not necessary. It would of course be helpful to the research community if results of such examinations were publicly available so that conclusions could be drawn as to whether there is a general response rate at which further response patterns stabilise, whether there is no such rate or whether it is variable. Just a few researchers have conducted experiments on this question and some examples are summarised in Chapter 11 in Case study 11.3 (Gitelson and Drogin, 1992; Hammitt and McDonald, 1982).

The Gitelson and Drogin (1992) study was a user/site/visitor and mail survey combo (described below). Since the mail survey sample respondents and non-respondents had all been interviewed on-site, it was possible to compare the characteristics of the two groups in terms of the information from the on-site survey questionnaires.

Mail and user/site/visitor survey combos

A common practice is to conduct a brief face-to-face interview at a leisure or tourism site or event and ask respondents to complete a mail survey (or e-survey) questionnaire on their return home. This shortens the time taken to conduct the on-site interview but also means that respondents can give views about the facility or event when their visit has been completed in its entirety. In some cases the mail-back questionnaire may be provided after the on-site interview: in other cases addresses (or email addresses) may be obtained and the questionnaire mailed to them. Of course the mail or email survey will be subject to the problems of non-response discussed under mail surveys.

E-surveys

Nature and conduct

E-surveys, or electronic or online surveys, are conducted via the Internet. Standard 'hard copy' mail has been the traditional medium for mail surveys

Type	Request	Questionnaire	Completion	Return
Hybrid email/mail	Email	Attached text file	Manual on hard-copy	Mail
Hybrid email	Email	Attached text file	Word-processor/ spreadsheet	Email + attached text file
Fully electronic: *ad hoc*	Email	Online, interactive	Online	Online submission
Fully electronic – panel	Panel member email	Online, interactive	Online	Online submission

Figure 10.7   Types of e-survey

and is still popular, but costs, speed and response rates, as discussed above, are increasingly seen as drawbacks of the method. Similarly, the growing problems of traditional telephone surveys have been outlined above. The result has been increasing uses of the electronic or e-survey. A number of formats exist, ranging from simply using an email to transmit a traditional questionnaire, to a fully electronic, online format, as summarised in Figure 10.7.

The first version simply uses email to replace the sending out process. The second version uses email to send out and return, and uses a word-processor and/or spreadsheet rather than hard-copy, but the questionnaire is still in traditional format. In the electronic versions the whole process takes place online and the questionnaire has become interactive. The questionnaire simplifies completion for the respondent so that, when 'filter' questions are involved, which require the respondent to skip certain questions and jump to a particular section of the questionnaire, this take place automatically.

Commercial survey organisations offer e-survey services in which the customer/researcher specifies the questions to be included, then asks survey participants to access the survey organisation's website to complete the survey. The customer/researcher can download the results on demand.

Many corporate organisations, such as banks, from time to time invite their online customers to complete online questionnaire surveys to obtain customer feedback on service quality. Similarly, while hotels still invite guests to complete a hard-copy feedback questionnaire on completion of their stay, it is now common for guests to receive an invitation to participate in an online survey via email some time after their return home.

An e-survey may be combined with a user/site/visitor in a similar way to the 'mail and user/site visitor survey combo' discussed above.

Advantages and disadvantages

The advantages of e-surveys to the researcher are the low cost and the speed with which they may be conducted. The fully electronic versions are designed to be very user-friendly, as noted above.

The disadvantage of the e-survey is that it is confined to those with access to the Internet and, while the sending of reminders is cheap, the problem of low response may still be a problem for some surveys because they may be seen as part of the increasing volume of 'junk mail' received via email.

User/on-site/visitor surveys

Nature

The terms *on-site*, *site*, *user* or *visitor* survey are used to refer to this type of survey. *On-site* and *site survey* tend to be used in the context of outdoor recreation studies, *user survey* in the context of indoor recreation facilities, and *visitor survey* when tourists or day trippers are involved or types of facility where visits are relatively infrequent, such as museums or zoos. A fourth term, *audience survey*, is used in the arts environment, for example for surveys of theatre audiences. Researchers with a background in transport tend to use the tem *intercept* survey. The term *user survey* is utilised in this section to cover all these situations.

The user survey is the most common type of survey used by managers in leisure and tourism. Surveys of local users and tourists are carried out at recreation or leisure facilities and surveys of tourists are carried out at hotels and *en route* on various types of transport, particularly international air trips. As noted above, general surveys of visitors to a tourist area often take the form of street surveys. Visitors are interviewed in the street, in squares/plazas or in seafront areas – anywhere where tourists are known to congregate. In this case the 'facility' is the tourist town or area, so the 'street survey' and the 'site survey' overlap and consideration must be given to the features of both types of survey. In general the site survey is more controlled than the street survey; interviewers are seen by respondents to be part of the management of the facility and usually it is possible to interview users at a convenient time when they are not in a rush, as they may be in the street or shopping mall.

Conduct

User surveys can be conducted by interviewer- or by respondent-completion. Unless carefully supervised, respondent-completion methods can lead to a poor standard in the completion of questionnaires and a low response level. And as with all low response levels, this can be a source of serious bias in that those who reply may be unrepresentative of the users or visitors as a whole.

The usual respondent-completion survey involves handing users a questionnaire on their arrival at the site and collecting them on their departure, or conducting the whole procedure upon departure. Where respondent-completion is thought to be desirable or necessary, then sufficient staff should be employed to check all users leaving the site, to ask for the completed questionnaires, to provide replacements for questionnaires which have been mislaid, and to assist in completing questionnaires, including completion by interview if necessary. Leaving a pile of questionnaires with a busy receptionist to hand out and collect rarely works well.

Conducting user surveys by interview is generally preferable to respondent-completion for the reasons discussed earlier in this chapter. The use of interviewers obviously has a cost disadvantage but, depending on the length of the interview, costs per interview are usually comparatively low. Typically a user-survey interview will take about five minutes, but in some longer-stay facilities, such as a park or beach, significantly longer interviews are possible. Given the need to check through completed questionnaires, the gaps in user traffic and the need for interviewers to take breaks, it is reasonable to expect interviewers in such situations to complete about six interviews in an hour. Such estimates are of course necessary when considering project budgets and timetables.

The survey methods considered so far have been fairly multi-purpose – they could be used for market research for a range of products or services, by public agencies for a variety of policy-oriented purposes, or for academic research, which may or may not be policy or management oriented. User surveys are more specific. The most common use of such surveys is for policy, planning or management purposes. They are the type of survey which readers of this book are most likely to be involved with; they are the most convenient for students to 'cut their teeth' on, and they are the most common surveys for individual managers to become involved in. For these reasons the roles of user surveys are considered in some detail below.

The uses of user surveys

What can user surveys be used for? Four topics are discussed briefly below: catchment area; user socio-demographic profile; user opinions and non-users.

Catchment area

What is the *catchment* or *market* area of the facility or service? That is, what geographical area do most of the users come from? This can be important in terms of advertising policy. Management can concentrate on its existing catchment area and focus its advertising and marketing accordingly or it can take conscious decisions to use marketing to attempt to extend its catchment area. But in order to take either of these approaches, it is first necessary to establish the current catchment area. In some cases this information is already available from membership records, but this does not always reflect the pattern of actual use, so in most cases it can only be discovered by means of a survey.

User socio-demographic profile

What is the socio-economic/demographic profile of the facility users? It might be thought that a management capable of observation would be able to make this assessment without the need for a survey. This depends on the type of facility, the extent to which management is in continuous contact with users and the variability of the user profile. For example, a restaurant, hotel or resort manager might be very well informed on this because of the prices charged, but managers of beaches, urban parks, national/state parks or theatres might, for various reasons, be less well informed, or even mis-informed.

Profile information can be used in a number of ways. As with data on catchment area, it can be used to consolidate or extend the market. Very often the commercial operator will opt to consolidate – to focus on a particular client group and maximise the market share of that group, by appropriate advertising, pricing and product development. In the case of a public sector facility the remit is usually to attract as wide a cross-section of the community as possible, so the data would be used to highlight those sections of the community not being catered for and therefore requiring marketing, pricing or product development attention. More broadly, a public agency responsible for a range of facilities could use the data to check whether the community is being appropriately provided for by all its facilities taken together.

User opinions

What are the opinions of users about the design, accessibility and service quality of the facility? Such opinion data are invariably collected in user surveys and are usually of great interest to managers, but the interpretation of the data it is not without its difficulties. If management is looking for pertinent criticisms, current users may be the wrong group to consult. Those who are most critical are likely no longer to be using the facility. Those using the facility may be reluctant to be very critical because it undermines their own situation – if the place is so poor why are they there? Those who are prepared to be critical may not be the sorts of clients for whom the facility is designed.

In some situations people have little choice between facilities so criticisms are perhaps more easily interpreted. For example, parents' comments about the suitability of a local park for children's play can be particularly pertinent when it is the only play area available in the neighbourhood.

When opinion data have been collected, it is often difficult to know precisely what to do with the results. Very often the largest group of users has no complaint or suggestion to make – either because they cannot be bothered to think of anything in the interview situation or because of the respondent selection process referred to above. Often the most common complaint is only raised by as few as 10 per cent of users. If this is the most common complaint, then logically something ought to be done about it by the management – but it could also be said that 90 per cent of the users are not concerned about that issue, so perhaps there is no need to do anything about it! Very often, therefore, management can use survey results to suit their own preferenes. If they want to do something about X, they can say that X was complained about by more users than anything else: if they do not want to do anything about X they can say that 90 per cent of users are satisfied with X the way it is.

Managers mostly want to enhance and maximise the quality of the experience enjoyed by their visitors: it may not be criticism of specific features that is important but users' overall evaluation of the experience. Thus users can be asked to rate a facility or area using a scale such as: very good/good/fair/poor/very poor or very satisfied/satisfied/dissatisfied/very dissatisfied. The results of such an evaluation can be used to compare users' evaluation of one facility with another – for example in a system of parks. Or they could be used to examine the same facility at different times to see if satisfaction has increased or declined. This is of course related to evaluation research, as discussed in Chapters 1 and 2.

Non-users

User surveys by definition involve only current users of a facility or current visitors to an area. This is often cited as a limitation of such surveys, the implication being that non-users may be of more interest than users if the aim of management is to increase the number of users or visitors. Caution should, however, be exercised in moving to consider conducting research on non-users. For a start the number of non-users is usually very large. For example, in a city of a million population, a facility which has 5000 users has 995,000 non-users! In a country with a population of 50 million, a tourist area which attracts a million visitors a year has 49 million non-visitors, and if management is interested in international visitors, they have around six billion non-visitors! The idea that all non-users are potential users, and should therefore be researched, is therefore somewhat naive.

At least, therefore, the user survey can help in focusing any research which is to be conducted on non-users. For example, in the case of a local recreation facility the user survey defines the catchment area and, unless there is some reason for believing that the catchment area can or should be extended, the non-users to be studied are those who live within that area. Similarly the user profile indicates the type of person currently using the facility and, again, unless there is a conscious decision to attempt to change that profile, the non-users to be studied are the ones with that profile living within the defined catchment area. Importantly, comparison between the user profile and the profile of the population of the catchment area, as revealed by population census data (see Chapter 7), can be used to estimate the numbers and characteristics of non-users in the area. Thus user surveys can reveal something about non-users!

User/site/visitor and mail/e-survey combo

In the discussion of mail surveys above, the idea of a 'mail and user/site/visitor survey combo' is discussed, in which a short face-to-face on-site interview is followed by a request to the respondent to complete a mail survey or e-survey questionnaire on their return home.

Captive group surveys

Nature

The *captive group* survey is not referred to in other research methods texts. It refers to the situation where the people to be included in the survey comprise the membership of some group where access can be negotiated *en bloc*. Such groups include school children, adult education groups, clubs of various kinds and groups of employees – although all have their various unique characteristics. The ethics of groups being 'volunteered' for research in this way are discussed in Chapter 4.

Conduct

A roomful of cooperative people can provide a number of respondent-completed questionnaires very quickly. Respondent-completion is less problematic in captive situations than in less controlled situations because it is possible to take the group through the questionnaire question by question and therefore ensure good standards of completion.

The most common example of a captive group is schoolchildren, since the easiest way to contact children under school-leaving age is via schools. The method may, however, appear simpler than it is in practice. Research on children for education purposes has become so common that education authorities are cautious about permitting access to children for surveys. Very often permission for any survey work must be obtained from the central education authority – the permission of the class teacher or head teacher is not sufficient.

While the most economical use of this technique involves using a respondent-completed questionnaire, interview methods can also be used. The essential feature is that access to members of the group is facilitated by their membership of that group and the fact that they are gathered together in one place at one time. It is important to be aware of the criteria for membership of the group and to compare that with the needs of the research. In some cases an apparent match can be misleading. For example, attendees at a retired people's club meetings do not include all retired people – it excludes 'non-joiners' and the house-bound. While schools include all young people, care must be taken over their catchment areas, compared with the study area of the research, and with the mix of public-sector and private schools.

Questionnaire design

Introduction – research problems and information requirements

The important principle in designing questionnaires is to take it slowly and carefully and to remember why the research is being done. Very often researchers move too quickly into 'questionnaire design mode' and begin listing all the things 'it would be interesting to ask'. In many organisations a draft questionnaire is circulated for comment and everyone in the organisation joins in. The process begins to resemble Christmas tree decorating – nobody must be left out and everybody must be allowed to contribute their favourite bauble. This is not the best way to proceed!

The decision to conduct a questionnaire survey should itself be the culmination of a careful process of thought and discussion, involving, as discussed in Chapter 3, consideration of all possible methods, not just surveys. The concepts and variables involved, and the relationships to be investigated, possibly in the form of hypotheses, theories, models or evaluative frameworks, should be clear and should guide the questionnaire design process, as illustrated in Figure 10.8. It is not advisable to *begin* with a list of questions to be included in the questionnaire. The starting point should ideally be an examination of the management, planning, policy or theoretical questions to be addressed, followed by the drawing up of a list of information required to address the problems. This is outlined in Chapter 3 as elements 1–5 of the research process. Element 6, deciding the research strategy, involves determining which of the listed information requirements should be met by means of a questionnaire survey and which should be met by other methods. Questions should be included in the questionnaire only if they relate to requirements listed in element 5. This means that every question included must be linked back to the *research questions*.

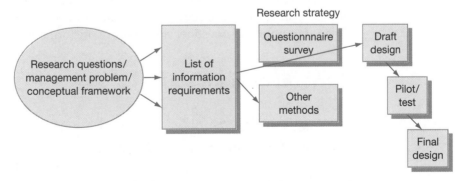

Figure 10.8 Questionnaire design process

In designing a questionnaire, the researcher should of course have sought out as much previous research on the topic or related topics as possible. This can have an effect on the overall design of a project as discussed in Chapter 3. More specifically, if it is decided that the study in hand should have points of comparison with earlier studies, then data will need to be collected on a similar basis to that in the earlier studies. Questionnaires from previous studies therefore become part of the input into the questionnaire design process.

Example questionnaires

Before considering questionnaire design in more detail, some examples of short questionnaires are presented in Case study 10.1, including typical questions used in household and site surveys, with interviewer-completed and respondent-completed examples:

● *Example A: site/street survey* is a questionnaire used to assess students' attitudes to campus social life – it is labelled as a site/street survey since, as it would be administered to students on-campus, it partly resembles a site or user survey, but since not all students may make use of the services being examined, it resembles a survey conducted in a street or shopping centre. It is presented as respondent-completed, but completion would probably best be conducted 'under supervision' – that is, completed and handed back to a survey worker at the time, rather than being handed out for later return, which would inevitably produce a low response rate. If the cooperation of the university authorities was obtained so that the questionnaire could be handed out and completed in class time, it would become a 'captive group' survey.

● *Example B: household survey* is an interviewer-completed questionnaire for a household survey on short-stay holidays.

● *Example C: site survey* is an interviewer-completed questionnaire for a site survey of park users.

Annotations in the left-hand margin of these example questionnaires indicate the type of question involved, as discussed later in the chapter. These example questionnaires cannot, of course, cover all situations, but they give a wide range of examples of questions and appropriate formats.

General design issues

Wording of questions

In wording the questions for a questionnaire the researcher should:

● avoid jargon;

● simplify wherever possible;

Case study 10.1   Example questionnaires

A: Site/street survey respondent-completed

Campus Life Survey 2003

Office use
#____
qno

Standard
pre-coded

1. Which of the following best describes your current situation?

Full-time student with no regular paid work ☐1
Full-time student with some regular paid work ☐2
Part-time student with full-time job ☐3
Part-time student – other ☐4

__ status

Pre-coded
Multiple response
– dichotomous

2. Which of the following university services have you used in the last 4 weeks?

Used campus cafe/bar ☐1
Attended university club/association meeting ☐1
Attended a live music performance on campus ☐1
Watched a movie on campus ☐1

__ cafebar
__ club
__ music
__ movie

Ranking

3. In thinking about the social and entertainment services provided on campus, what are the most important considerations for you? Please rank the items below in terms of their importance to you. Rank them from 1 for the most important to 5 for the least important.

Rank

Free or cheap access ____
Day time attractions ____
Acts, films, etc. not available elsewhere ____
Opportunities to socialise/meet people ____
Cost ____

__ cheap
__ daytime
__ unusual
__ meet
__ cost

Numerical –
uncoded

4. Approximately how much do you spend in an average week on entertainment and social activities on and off campus?

£_____

____
spend

Likert scales

5. Please indicate the importance of the following to you in relation to campus life

	Very important	Important	Not at all important	
Relaxation	☐3	☐2	☐1	__ relax
Social interaction	☐3	☐2	☐1	__ social
Mental stimulation	☐3	☐2	☐1	__ mental

Open-ended
Multiple
response –
categories

6. What suggestions would you make for improving campus social life?
_____
_____

__ sug1
__ sug2
__ sug3

Standard
pre-coded

7. You are: Male ☐1   Female ☐2

__ gend

Numerical –
uncoded

8. Your age last birthday was: ____ years

__ age

B: Household survey – interviewer-completed

Respondent No.	**Short Stay Holiday Survey** ___#
	Introductory remarks: Hallo. We are from St. Anthony's College and we are conducting a survey on people's short-stay holidays. Would you mind answering a few questions? It will take just a few minutes and the results will be kept confidential.

Pre-coded, factual

1. In the last six months, have you been on a short holiday trip of one, two or three nights away from home?   Yes 1 – go to Q. 2

No 2 – go to Q.5   _____

Open-ended, factual, numerical

2. How many times did you go on such trips in the six months?

Number of times: ___ go to q. 2   _____

Open-ended, factual

3. On your last trip, where did you go? _____   _____

4. What were the main activities you engaged in on your visit?

Multiple response

a. Sightseeing	1	
b. Eating and drinking	1	
c. Sporting activities	1	
d. Walking	1	

e. Arts activities/events	1	
f. Visit friends/relatives	1	
g. Just doing nothing	1	
h. Other	1	

_____
_____
_____
_____

Simple pre-coded, factual

5. To what extent do you agree with the following statements?

	Agree strongly	Agree	Neither	Disagree	Disagree strongly
A short break is as valuable as long holiday	1	2	3	4	5
Holidays make life worth living	1	2	3	4	5

_____
_____

Pre-coded with showcard factual

6. Can you tell me which of the following age-groups you fall into?

Under 15	A
15–19	B
20–29	C
30–59	D
60+	E

_____

Pre-coded with showcard factual

7. Which of the following best describes your current situation?

In full-time paid work	A
In part-time paid work	B
In full-time education	C
Full-time home/child care	D
Retired	E
Looking for work	F
Other	G

_____

Pre-coded, factual, observed

THANK YOU FOR YOUR HELP

Observe gender:	Male	1
	Female	2

_____

C: Site survey – interviewer-completed

The survey is being carried out for the local council to find out what users of the park think of the park, and what changes they would like to see. A total of 100 users of the park are interviewed at the only entrance, in batches of 10, at different days of the week, at different times of the day, and in different weather conditions.

Ramsey Street Park Survey
Excuse me: we are carrying out a survey for the council to find out what people think about the park. Could you spare a few minutes to answer a few questions?

Simple pre-coded

1. How often do you visit this park?

Every day	1
Several times a week	2
Once a week	3
Every 2 or 3 weeks	4
Once a month	5
Less often	6
First visit	7

Simple pre-coded, factual

2. Where have you travelled from today?

Home	1
Work	2
School/college/univ.	3
Other	4

Open-ended, factual

3. What suburb is that in?

_____

Simple pre-coded, factual

4. How long did it take you to get here?

5 minutes or less	1
6–15 minutes	2
16–30 minutes	3
31 minutes or more	4

Simple pre-coded, factual

5. How did you travel here?

Walk	1
Car	2
Motorbike	3
Bicycle	4
Bus/tram	5
Other	6

Open-ended, opinion

6. What do you like most about the park?

_____

Open-ended, opinion

7. What do you like least about the park?

_____

Attitude statement with show-card

8. Looking at the card, where would you place this park, in relation to others you know?

A. Way below average	1
B. Below average	2
C. Average	3
D. Above average	4
E. Well above average	5

Pre-coded, factual with showcard

9. Can you tell me which of these age-groups you fall into?

Under 15	A
15–19	B
20–29	C
30–59	D
60+	E

Pre-coded, factual

10. How many people are there in your group here today, including yourself?

Alone	1
Two	2
3–4	3
5 or more	4

Open-ended, factual, numerical

11. How many vehicles did your group arrive in? ___

Observe, factual

THANK YOU FOR YOUR HELP

Observe: Male   1
          Female 2

Principle	Bad example	Improved version
Use simple language	What is your frequency of utilisation of retail travel outlets?	How often do you use travel agents?
Avoid ambiguity	Do you play sport very often?	Have you played any of the following sports within the last four weeks? (show list)
Avoid leading questions	Are you against the extension of the airport?	What is your opinion on the extension of the airport? Are you for it, against it or not concerned?
Ask just one question at a time	Do you use the local arts centre, and if so what do you think of its facilities?	1. Do you use the local arts centre? Yes/No 2. What do you think of the facilities in the local arts centre?

Figure 10.9 Question-wording: examples of good and bad practice

- avoid ambiguity;

- avoid leading questions;

- ask only one question at a time (i.e. avoid multi-purpose questions).

Examples of good and bad practice in question wording are given in Figure 10.9.

Pre-coded vs open-ended questions

As illustrated in Figure 10.10, an *open-ended* question is one where the interviewer asks a question without any prompting of the range of answers to be expected, and writes down the respondent's reply verbatim. In a respondent-completed questionnaire a line or space is left for respondents to write their answers. A closed or pre-coded question is one where the respondent is offered a range of answers to choose from, either verbally or from a show card or, in the case of a self-completed questionnaire, having the range of answers set out in the questionnaire and (usually) being asked to tick boxes.

In the open-ended case there is no prior list. In the closed/pre-coded case there is a list which is shown to the respondent. A third possibility, in an interviewer-administered survey, is a combination of the two, where the question is asked in an open-ended manner, no card is shown to the respondent, but the answer is recorded by the interviewer ticking the appropriate box on a pre-coded list. If the answer does not fit any of the items on the list it is written in an 'other' category and may be given a code at the analysis stage.

The advantage of the open-ended question is that the respondent's answer is not unduly influenced by the interviewer or by the questionnaire wording and the verbatim replies from respondents can provide a rich source of varied material which might have been hidden by categories on a pre-coded list.

Open-ended

What is the main constraint on your ability to study?

_____

Pre-coded/closed

Which of the following/items listed on the card is the main constraint on your ability to study? (show card – if interviewer-completed)

A. My job $\Box_1$
B. Timetabling $\Box_2$
C. Child care $\Box_3$
D. Spouse/partner $\Box_4$
E. Money $\Box_5$
F. Energy $\Box_6$
G. Other _____ $\Box_7$

Card shown to respondent:

A. My job
B. Timetabling of the course
C. Child care
D. Spouse/partner
E. Money
F. Energy
G. Other _____

Figure 10.10   Open-ended vs pre-coded questions – example

Figure 10.11 gives an example of the range of responses which can result from a single open-ended question.

While pre-coded groups are often used when asking respondents about quantified information, such as age, income, expenditure, because of convenience and saving any embarrassment respondents may have about divulging precise figures, there is an advantage in using the open-ended approach for such data, that is in obtaining actual figures rather than group codes. Recording the actual number permits the flexible option of grouping categories in alternative ways when carrying out the analysis. It also enables _averages_ and other measures to be calculated and facilitates a range of statistical analysis which is not possible with groups. The actual figure is therefore often more useful for analysis purposes.

Open-ended questions have two major disadvantages. First, the analysis of verbatim answers to qualitative questions for computer analysis is laborious and may result in a final set of categories which are of no more value than a well-constructed pre-coded list. In the case of the answers in Figure 10.11, for example, for detailed analysis it may be necessary to group the answers into, say, six groups – this would be time-consuming and would involve a certain amount of judgement in grouping individual answers, which can be a source of

Question: Do you have any complaints about this (beach/picnic) area?
(Site survey in a beachside National Park with boating and camping. Number of responses in brackets)

Sand bars (22)
Parking (5)
Wild car driving (1)
Lack of beach area (1)
Too few shops (1)
Too few picnic tables (4)
No timber for barbecue (2)
Need more picnic space (3)
Need boat hire facilities (1)
Need active recn facilities (1)
Litter/pollution (74)
Urban sprawl (1)
Need wharf fishing access (1)
Lack of info. on walking trails (1)
Not enough facilities (3)
Slow barbecues (2)
Uncontrolled camping (1)
Lack/poor toilets (9)
Amenities too far from camp site (1)
Too much development (4)
(Speed) boats (44)
Need more trees for shade (1)
Yobbos drinking beer on beach (1)
Spear fishermen (1)
Water skiers (2)
Against nudism (3)
Loud music (1)
Dumped cars (1)
Traffic (1)
Poor roads (1)
Sand flies (1)
More barbecues (1)
Shells/oysters (1)
Need outdoor cafes (1)
Need more food places (1)
Water too shallow (1)

Uncontrolled boats (23)
Jet skis (39)
Surveys (1)
Should be kept for locals (1)
Seaweed (3)
Need showers (1)
Administration of National Park (1)
Maintenance & policing of Park (1)
Trucks on beach (2)
Anglers (1)
Crowds/tourists (26)
Having to pay entry fee (6)
Houses along waterfront (2)
Unpleasant smell (drain) (2)
Sales people (1)
Need electric barbecues (1)
Dogs (21)
No access to coast (1)
Park rangers not operating in interest of the public (1)
Behaviour of others (20)
Access – long indirect road (1)
Need more shops (2)
Navigation marks unclear (1)
Need more taps (1)
Need more swings (1)
No first-aid facilities (1)
Need powered caravan sites (1)
Allow dogs (1)
Private beach areas (1)
Lack of restaurant (1)
Need rain shelters (1)
Can't spear fish (1)
No road shoulders for cyclists (1)
Remove rocks from swim areas (1)
Dangerous boat ramp pollutant activities (1)

Figure 10.11 Example of range of replies resulting from an open-ended question

Source: Robertson and Veal, 1987

errors. This process is discussed in more detail under coding below. Often, therefore, an open-ended question is used in a pilot survey, the results from which are then used to devise a coded list of categories for the main survey.

The second disadvantage of the open-ended approach is that, in the case of respondent-completed questionnaires, response rates to such questions can be very low: people are often too lazy or too busy to write out free-form answers and may have literacy or language problems. When to use open-ended or closed questions is therefore a matter of judgement.

Types of information

Generally the information to be gathered from questionnaire surveys can be divided into three groups:

1. Activities/events/places   What?
2. Respondent characteristics   Who?
3. Attitudes/motivations   Why?

Figure 10.12 lists some of the more common types of information collected under these three headings. The items covered are of course necessarily general in nature and do not cover all the specialised types of information which can be collected by questionnaire surveys. Some of these items of information require more intrusive questions than others – for example, income. And some can be difficult to ascertain accurately – for example, occupation or details of expenditure while on a tourist trip. They are not therefore all equally suitable for all survey situations.

Activity/events/places questions

Leisure and tourism activity is at the core of leisure and tourism research and the procedure for measuring it is far from simple. A variety of possible measures of leisure and tourism activity is indicated earlier in Figure 7.1, including the participation rate, the number of participants, the volume of activity or visits, the time spent and money spent. In any study consideration should be given as to which types of measure are necessary. The issues are discussed in turn below: in relation to leisure and tourism participation and frequency separately.

In addition to *activity*, the terms *events* and *places* are used to reflect the scope of the phenomena being studied. For some research purposes it is only necessary to know that a person has engaged in a generic activity – for example, 'visited a park'. In yet other cases it is necessary to know the geographical location, or 'place', of the activity – for example, 'visited a park within/outside the local government area'; or the precise facility – for example, 'visited X park'. Geographical location is obviously important for most tourism research. In other cases, it is not just the generic activity or the place that is of interest but also the specific organised event – for example, 'summer concert in the park'.

Activities and events/places

Site/visitor surveys
- Activities while on site or in the area
- Use of site attractions/facilities
- Frequency of visit
- Time spent on site
- Expenditure per head – amounts/purposes
- Travel-related information
  - Trip origin (where travelled from)
  - Trip purpose
  - Home address
  - Travel mode
  - Travel time
- Accommodation type used

Household/telephone/postal surveys
- Leisure activities (including holidays) – what, where, how often, time spent, when, who with?
- Use of particular facilities/sites
- Travel mode to out-of-home leisure
- Expenditure patterns
- Past activities (personal leisure histories)
- Planned future activities

Respondent characteristics – all survey types
- Gender
- Age
- Economic status (paid work, retired, etc.)
- Occupation/social class (own or 'head of household')
- Previous employment history
- Income (own or household)
- Education/qualifications

- Marital/family status
- Household type/family size
- Life-cycle
- Ethnic group/country of birth
- Residential location/trip origin
- Mobility – driving licence, access to private transport
- Party/group size/type (site/visitor surveys)

Attitude/motivation information – examples

Site/visitor surveys
- Reasons for choice of site/area
- Meaning/importance/values
- Satisfaction/evaluation of experience/services
- Comments on facility
- Future intentions/hopes

Household/telephone/postal surveys
- Leisure/travel aspirations/needs
- Evaluation of services/facilities available
- Psychological meaning of activities/satisfactions
- Reactions to development/provision proposals
- Values – re environment, etc.

Figure 10.12 Range of information in leisure/tourism questionnaires

The problem of devising questions to gather information on leisure activities in leisure participation surveys is a difficult one. The difficulties centre on two main issues:

- whether to use an open-ended or pre-coded format;
- the reference period for participation.

An open-ended format question simply asks respondents to list the activities they have engaged in during their leisure time or free time over a specified period.

Without any prompting of the range of activities intended to be included, respondents might have difficulty in recalling all their activities, and in any case may not understand the full scope of the word 'leisure' or 'free time'. The word 'leisure' in particular has different connotations for different people. Without explanation, some people might assume that having a cup of coffee and chatting with a friend is not leisure, or that knitting or gardening is not leisure. Using the word 'free time' might help a little, but it is still open to variation in interpretation.

Although providing people with checklists of activities to choose from may be unwieldy, it at least ensures that all respondents consider the same range of options. The disadvantage of the checklist is that the length of the list may be daunting to some respondents, particularly the less literate, and activities later in the list may be under-represented. In the case of an interviewer-completed questionnaire the main problem may be the time it takes to read out the list and the problem of patience and tedium which it may entail, so a show-card may be used; but of course, this is not possible with telephone interviews. The British General Household Survey compromised by offering a checklist of about a dozen 'types' of leisure activity, such as home-based activities, outdoor recreation, arts and entertainment, as an *aide-mémoire* for the respondent. The complexity is partly avoided by the tendency for separate surveys to be used for different categories of activity, such as sport and physical activity or arts and culture. This means, however, that a person's leisure activity cannot be seen as a whole and some activities, notably home-based activities and social activities like going to the pub or a restaurant, are omitted because they are not of interest to the policy agencies which fund most publicly available leisure participation surveys.

The reference period for recalling activities is crucial to the nature of the findings. Table 10.1 shows the results from a 2001 survey in which respondents were asked about attendance at arts events in the previous four weeks, but if they had not participated in the previous four weeks they were asked if they had participated in the last year. The results are plain to see. The time-period used to measure participation affects the absolute levels of participation recorded and also the apparent relative popularity of activities (see also Table 7.1). The shorter the time-period used the more accurate the recall of respondents is likely to be, but shorter time-periods exclude large proportions of participants in those activities which are engaged in relatively infrequently. Furthermore, a time-period shorter than a year necessitates conducting the survey at a different time of the year in order to take account of seasonal variation in types and levels of participation.

In addition to asking whether they have participated in an activity, respondents can also be asked *how often* they have participated and *how much time* was spent on the activity. This can lead to very lengthy interviews for people who have engaged in a wide range of activities. To avoid this, in some surveys a particular leisure occasion, say, the last trip to the countryside, is explored in more detail – where the respondent went, who with, what day of the week and what time of day, what specific activities were engaged in, and so on.

In local surveys or surveys focused on specific policy areas, it may be of interest to explore the use of specific, named, leisure facilities or tourist attractions – for example, visits to particular National Parks or to sports centres – using a variety of approaches to measuring use.

Table 10.1 Attendance at arts events, England, 2003

	% of persons aged 16+ attending in last:	
	12 months	**4 weeks**
Film at a cinema or other venue	59	22
Play or drama	25	4
Carnival, street arts or circus	26	4
Art, photography or sculpture exhibition	22	6
Craft exhibition	19	4
Pantomime	14	–
Cultural festival	8	2
Event connected with books or writing	8	2
Event including video or electronic art	7	2
A musical	26	4
Pop or rock concert	20	4
Classical music concert	10	2
Opera or operetta	6	1
Jazz concert	6	1
Folk or country and western concert	2	–
Other music	7	–
All types of live dance performance	12	–
Contemporary dance	4	–
Ballet	2	–
Other dance	7	–
Sample	6,025	6,025

Source: Fenn *et al.*, (2004).

– data not collected

In the case of site/user surveys there is usually little problem in asking about activities, since the range of possible activities is limited. It is usual to ask people what activities they plan to engage in or have engaged in during their visit. Use of specific amenities at the site – such as refreshment facilities – are also generally explored.

Tourism activities/events/places

In the case of household questionnaire surveys concerned with tourism, the activity question concerns trips taken away from the home area over a specified time-period. As with local leisure activities, a major consideration is the recall time-period. For major holidays a one-year recall period is not out of the question; but for short breaks, asking about trips during that length of time may lead to inaccuracies in recall, so a shorter time-period of, say, three months is often adopted. This means that a survey must be conducted at different times of the year to capture seasonal variation.

A second time-period issue concerns the definition of tourist 'trip'. The definition used in a survey may follow an accepted definition of tourism: for example, a trip involving a stay away from home of one night or more. However, in some local tourism studies *day trips* may also be of interest.

In addition to indicating trips taken, household tourism questionnaires also generally include questions on where the respondent has been on the trip, length of stay, travel mode and type of accommodation used. Tourism surveys are usually much more concerned with economic matters than leisure surveys, so questions on the cost of the trip and of expenditure in various categories are often included.

For site surveys in a tourism context, including *en route* surveys, the activity questions asked of tourists may be similar to those asked of locals, but the reference period will of course be the period of their stay in the destination.

Media use

Questionnaires often include questions on media use, sometimes because it is considered a leisure activity, but also because such information can be useful when considering advertising policy. To obtain accurate information in this area would require a considerable number of questions on frequency of reading/viewing/listening and, in the case of electronic media, the type of programmes favoured. When the research is concerned with small-scale local facilities or services, television advertising is generally out of the question because of cost, so information on television watching need not be gathered. Similar considerations may apply to magazine and national newspaper reading. For many surveys therefore, two questions are involved (show cards with lists of publications would usually be used):

- What (local) newspapers do you read regularly, that is at least weekly?

- What (local) radio stations do you listen to regularly, that is at least twice a week?

Respondent characteristics

Age

Any examination of leisure participation and tourism data will show the importance of age in differentiating patterns of behaviour and attitudes; it is therefore one of the data items most commonly included in questionnaires. The main decision to be made is whether to use pre-coded groups or ask for respondents' actual age. The advantages and disadvantages of the two approaches are discussed above, under pre-coded vs open-ended questions. If using pre-coded groups, ensure that there are no overlapping age categories. For example, in the following it would not be clear into which group a 14-year-old respondent would fall.

A   0–14
B   14–19

Note that, to ensure comparability with census data, age-groups should be specified as: 15–19, 20–24, 25–29, etc., *not* 16–20, 21–25, 26–30, etc.

Economic status/occupation/socio-economic group/class

A person's economic and occupational situation clearly impinges on leisure and tourism behaviour. Information on such matters is important for marketing and planning and also in relation to public policy concerns with equity. Economic status is a person's situation vis-à-vis the formal economy, as listed in Figure 10.13. In contemporary developed economies, only about half the population is engaged in the paid workforce.

Economic status
- In full-time paid work
- In part-time paid work
- Full-time home or child care
- In full-time education
- Retired
- Unemployed/looking for paid employment
- Other

Market research occupation/SEG classification
AB   Managerial, administrative, professional (at senior or intermediate level)
C1   Supervisory or clerical (i.e. white collar) and junior managerial, administrative or professional
C2   Skilled manual
DE   Semi-skilled, unskilled and casual workers and those entirely dependent on state pensions

Census occupation/SEG classification
- Professional
- Employers, managers
- Other self-employed
- Skilled workers and foremen
- Non-manual
- Service, semi-skilled and agricultural
- Armed forces
- Unskilled

Figure 10.13 Economic status, occupational and socio-economic groupings

Occupation is generally used to denote a person's type of paid work, so it is generally asked only of those identified from the economic status question as being in paid work. Others are sometimes asked what their last paid job was or what the occupation of the 'main bread-winner' of the household is. Such questions can, however become complex because of full-time students living with parents or independently, single parents living on social security and so on. In a household survey it may be possible to pursue these matters, but in other situations, such as site surveys, it may not be appropriate because it would seem too intrusive. For those in paid work the sorts of question asked are:

- What is your occupation?
- What sort of work do you do?
- Which of the groups on this card best describes your occupation?

Sufficient information should be obtained to enable respondents to be classified into an appropriate occupational category. Market researchers and official bodies, such as Office of National Statistics, tend to use slightly different classifications, as shown in Figure 10.13. Such groupings, along with economic status, are often referred to as a person's *socio-economic group* or SEG. This is closely related to the idea of *class* or social class. Space does not permit a discussion of this complex concept here, but sources are given in the Resources at the end of this chapter.

Because people can be vague in response to an open-ended question on occupation, it is wise to include a supplementary question to draw out a full description. For example 'office worker', 'engineer' or 'self-employed' are not adequate answers because they can cover such a wide variety of grades of occupation. A supplementary question could be: 'What sort of work is that?' In a household survey it may be possible to ask additional questions to be absolutely sure of the respondent's occupation. Such questions would check on the industry involved and the number of staff supervised by the respondent.

Income

A typical wording of a question on income would be:

- What is your own personal gross income from all sources before taxes? or
- Which of the groups on the card does your own personal gross income from all sources fall into?

Gross income is normally asked for, since it can be too complicated to gather information on income net of taxes and other deductions. Since there is often a major difference between gross and net income, this makes the variable a somewhat imprecise one. A further problem with income as a variable is that personal income is not a particularly useful variable for those who are not income recipients or who are not the main income recipients of the household. This can be overcome if all members of the household are being interviewed or if the respondent is asked about the 'main income earner' in the household.

However, many teenage children, for example, do not know their parents' income and it might be seen as improper to ask them. Income is a sensitive issue and, in view of the limitations discussed above, is often excluded in site or visitor surveys.

Marital status

Since legal marital status fails to indicate the domestic situation of increasing numbers of people, the usefulness of this variable is declining. In terms of leisure and tourism behaviour, whether or not a person has responsibility for children is likely to be a more important variable. Usual categories for marital status are:

- married
- single – never married
- widowed/divorced/separated.

Respondents who are not formally married but living in a *de facto* relationship can then decide for themselves how they want to be classified, or a separate category can be created.

Household type and group type and size

Household type is a useful variable for many leisure and tourism studies but, except in the household interview situation, the data may be difficult to collect, because a number of items of information are required. In a household interview it is possible to ask 'Who lives here?' A simplified version would be to ask about the number of children of various ages in the household. Classifying the information into 'household type' must be done subsequently. Typical categories are as set out in Figure 10.14a.

In the case of user/site surveys it is more usual to ask about the size of the party or group and its composition – for example, how many children and adults of various ages are present. Clearly such information is important for planning, marketing, managing and programming facilities. A typical categorisation of groups is as shown in Figure 10.14b.

It should be noted, however, that 'size of group' is not the same as 'vehicle occupancy', since some larger groups may arrive in several vehicles. So if the latter information is required for traffic management purposes, it must be asked separately.

Life-cycle

Some researchers have argued that individual variables, such as age and marital status, are not good predictors of leisure and tourism behaviour; rather, we should examine the composite variable *life-cycle* (Rapoport and Rapoport, 1975). As with household type, a person's stage in the life-cycle is not based on a single question but built up from a number of items of information, including

a. Household type – Household survey

Question format:

Can you please tell me who lives here?

Person	Relationship to respondent	Gender M/F	Age	Occupation
1	Respondent			
2				
3				
4				
5				

Household type classification:
A. Single parent and 1 dependent child
B. Single parent and 2 or more dependent children
C. Couple and 1 dependent child
D. Couple and 2 or more dependent children
E. Couple, no children
F. Related adults only
G. Unrelated adults only
H. Single person
I. Other.

b. Visitor groups – Site survey

Question format:
a. How many people are there in this group, including yourself? ___
b. How many children aged under 5 are there in the group? ___
c. How many children aged between 5 and 15 are there? ___
d. How many people aged 60 or over are there? ___

Group classification:
A. Youngest member aged 0–4
B. Youngest member aged 5–15
C. Lone adult
D. Two adults (under 60)
E. Older couple (60 and over)
F. 3–5 adults
G. 6+ adults.

Figure 10.14 Household type and visitor group type

A. Child/young single – dependent (on parents)
B. Young single – independent
C. Young married/partnered – no children
D. Parent – dependent children
E. Parent – children now independent
F. Retired – up to 70
G. Retired – over 70

Figure 10.15   Life-cycle stages

age, economic status and marital/family status. A possible classification is as set out in Figure 10.15. Life*style*, as discussed in Chapter 2, is a further development of this idea, but generally involves collection of a considerable amount of additional data.

Ethnic group

Ethnic group is included in leisure and tourism surveys because ethnically based cultures influence leisure and tourism behaviour and also because of policy concerns for equity between social groups. Everyone belongs to an ethnic group – that is, a social group that shares religious, language and other cultural values and practices and experiences – including leisure and tourism. Ethnicity therefore becomes important in leisure and tourism policy, planning and management, particularly as regards minority groups whose needs may not be met by mainstream facilities and services. A common approach to ethnicity in the past was to ask the respondent's country of birth, since most ethnic minority groups were migrant groups. But this of course does not identify members of ethnic minority groups not born overseas. Parents' place of birth identifies the second generation of migrant groups but not third and subsequent generations. Country of birth has therefore become less and less useful as an indicator of ethnic group membership. Observation is an obvious solution but is not reliable for many groups. The solution is to ask people what ethnic group they consider they belong to. While this may cause offence to some, it is the most satisfactory approach overall.

Residential location/trip origin

Where a person lives can be a significant determinant of access to leisure facilities and is a reflection of socio-economic position and related patterns of consumption. And residential location and trip origin are the basis of catchment area analysis for individual facilities. The situation varies depending on the survey type:

● Household survey: the residential location is already known by the interviewer and some sort of code – for street, suburb, local government area, county, as appropriate – can be recorded on the questionnaire.

- Street survey: home location is not always required, but if it is, a broad category, such as suburb, is usually adequate.

- Site/visitor surveys: in order to study the catchment area of the facility, it is necessary to ask people where they live or where they have travelled from. How much detail is required? This depends on the nature of the facility. For local facilities with small catchment areas, it may be necessary to know the street (but not the number of the dwelling). For less local urban facilities the suburb is sufficient. For countryside/tourist facilities the town/city will be required. For overseas visitors the country is usually adequate information, although there may be interest in where they are staying.

In Case study 14.5 an example is given of the use of home-location data to show the catchment area of a facility. In that example the information came from membership records, but it could equally well arise from a questionnaire survey of users.

Market research firms often record full addresses and/or telephone numbers of survey respondents in order to undertake subsequent quality checks on interviewers, to ensure that the respondents have in fact been interviewed.

Housing information

Information on the type of dwelling in which respondents live is usually collected in household surveys because it can easily be gathered by observation. The information is clearly relevant in leisure research because of the implications of dwelling type for access to private recreational space – a phenomenon often referred to in policy documents but rarely researched. Whether or not people own their own home is an important socio-economic variable. Typical categories for these items of information are shown in Figure 10.16.

Type of dwelling
A. Separate house
B. Semi-detached house
C. Terrace house
D. Flat/maisonette
E. Caravan, houseboat
F. Other

Tenure
A. Owned outright
B. Being purchased
C. Rented
D. Other

Figure 10.16 Housing information

Transport

Because mobility is such an important factor in leisure and tourism behaviour, questionnaires often include questions on ownership of and access to vehicles. People are sometimes asked if they possess a current driver's licence. In the case of site surveys, the mode of transport used to travel to the site, and vehicle occupancy as discussed under household/groups above, is often asked. If people claim to have used two or more modes of transport to reach a site, the various modes can all be recorded or respondents can be asked to indicate the one on which they travelled the furthest.

Attitude/opinion questions

Attitudes and opinions are more complex aspects of questionnaire design. A range of techniques exists to explore people's opinions and attitudes, as listed in Figure 10.17. The first three formats, direct, open-ended questions, checklists and ranking, are straightforward, but the other formats presented merit some comment.

Likert scales

Scaling techniques are sometimes known as 'Likert scales' after the psychologist who developed their use and analysis. In this technique respondents are asked to indicate their agreement or disagreement with a proposition or the importance they attach to a factor, using a standard set of responses. One of the advantages of this approach is that the responses can be quantified, as discussed below under coding.

Ranking

Asking respondents to rank items in order of importance is a relatively straightforward process, provided the list is not too long: more than five or six items could test respondents' patience. Again, the responses can be quantified – for example, in the form of average ranks.

Attitude statements

Attitude statements are a means of exploring respondents' attitudes towards a wide range of issues, including questions of a philosophical or political nature. Respondents are shown a series of statements and asked to indicate, using a scale, the extent to which they agree or disagree with them.

Responses to both Likert scale questions and attitude statements can be scored, as indicated by the numerals beside the boxes in Figure 10.17. For example, 'agree strongly' could be given a score of 5, 'agree' a score of 4, and so on to 'disagree strongly' with a score of 1. Scores can then be averaged across a number of respondents. So, for example, a group of people who mostly either 'agreed' or 'agreed strongly' with a statement would produce an average score

a. Open-ended/direct: What attracted you to apply for this course?

_____

b. Checklist: Of the items on the card, which was the most important to you in applying for this course?

> A. Good reputation
> B. Easy access
> C. Curriculum
> D. Level of fees
> E. Easy parking

c. Ranking: Please rank the items on the card in terms of their importance to you in choosing a course. Please rank them 1 for the most important to 5 for the least important.

	Rank
A. Good reputation	___
B. Easy access	___
C. Curriculum	___
D. Level of fees	___
E. Easy parking	___

d. Likert scales: Looking at the items on the card, please say how important each was to you in deciding to visit this area; was it: Very important, Quite important, Not very important or Not at all important?

	Very important	Quite important	Not very important	Not at all important
Good reputation	$\square_1$	$\square_2$	$\square_3$	$\square_4$
Easy access	$\square_1$	$\square_2$	$\square_3$	$\square_4$
Curriculum	$\square_1$	$\square_2$	$\square_3$	$\square_4$
Level of fees	$\square_1$	$\square_2$	$\square_3$	$\square_4$
Easy parking	$\square_1$	$\square_2$	$\square_3$	$\square_4$

e. Attitude statements: Please read the statements below and indicate your level of agreement or disagreement with them by ticking the appropriate box.

	Agree Strongly	Agree	No opinion	Disagree	Disagree strongly
The learning experience is more important than the qualification in education	$\square_1$	$\square_2$	$\square_3$	$\square_4$	$\square_5$
Graduate course fees are too high	$\square_1$	$\square_2$	$\square_3$	$\square_4$	$\square_5$

f. Semantic differential: Please look at the list below and tick the line to indicate where you think this course falls in relation to each factor listed.

Difficult	|___|___|___|___|___|	Easy
Irrelevant	|___|___|___|___|___|	Relevant
Professional	|___|___|___|___|___|	Unprofessional
Dull	|___|___|___|___|___|	Interesting

Figure 10.17   Opinion or attitude question formats

between 4 and 5, whereas a group who 'disagreed' or 'disagreed strongly' would produce a low score, between 1 and 2. Such scores enable the strength of agreement with different statements to be compared, and the opinions of different groups of people to be compared.

Semantic differential

The semantic differential method involves offering respondents *pairs* of contrasting descriptors and asking them to indicate how the facility, place or service being studied relates to the descriptors. This technique is suitable for a respondent-completion questionnaire, since the respondent is required to place a tick on each line. It would be difficult to replicate this exactly in an interview situation with no visual prompts, such as in a telephone survey; the effect would be to reduce the possible answers to three: close to one end or the other and 'in the middle'. The choice of pairs of words used in a semantic differential list should arise from the research context and theory.

Repertory grid

A further development of this approach is the *repertory grid* technique, as discussed in Chapter 5. Here the pairs of words – called *personal constructs* – are developed by the respondent. This technique is not explored further here, but references to examples of its use in leisure and tourism are given in the Resources section.

Market segments

The idea of market segmentation or lifestyle studies is introduced in Chapter 1. This involves classifying survey respondents according to a mix of activity, socio-demographic and attitude variables. All the necessary data items for this have therefore been discussed above. Actually determining market segments or lifestyle groupings is then an analytical task and this is discussed in Part III of the book, notably in Chapter 17 under factor and cluster analysis.

Ordering of questions and layout of questionnaires

Survey introductory remarks

Should a questionnaire include introductory remarks: for example, explaining the purpose of the survey and asking for the respondent's assistance? In the case of a mail survey such material is generally included in the covering letter. In the case of other forms of respondent-completion questionnaire a short note at the beginning of the questionnaire is advisable, although field-workers handing out questionnaires will usually provide the necessary introduction and explanation. In the case of interviewer-administered questionnaires, the remarks can be printed on the top of each questionnaire or can be included in the interviewers' written instructions.

In practice, interviewers are unlikely to approach potential interviewees and actually read from a script. When seeking cooperation of a potential interviewee it is usually necessary to maintain eye contact, so interviewers must know in advance what they want to say. In the case of household surveys, potential interviewees may require a considerable amount of information and proof of identity from the interviewer before agreeing to be interviewed. But in the case of site interviews, respondents are generally more interested in knowing how long the interview will take and what sort of questions they will be asked – so only minimal opening remarks are necessary. For example, for a site survey the introduction could be as brief as: 'Excuse me, we are conducting a survey of visitors to the area; would you mind answering a few questions?'

It is usually necessary for an interviewer to indicate what organisation they represent, and this can be reinforced by an identity badge. Market research or consultancy companies often instruct interviewers to indicate only that they represent the company and not the client. This can ensure that unbiased opinions are obtained, although in some cases it can raise ethical considerations if it is felt that respondents have a right to know what organisation will be using the information gathered.

One function of opening remarks can be to ensure the respondent of confidentiality. In the case of site surveys, where names and addresses are not generally collected, confidentiality is easy to maintain. In the case of household and some postal surveys respondents can be identified, so assurances are generally necessary. The issue of confidentiality, including practical means of ensuring it, is an ethical issue and is discussed in Chapter 4.

Question order

It is important that an interview based on a questionnaire flow in a logical and comfortable manner. A number of principles should be borne in mind:

1. Start with easy questions.

2. Start with 'relevant' questions – for example, if the respondent has been told that the survey is about holidays, begin with some questions about holidays.

3. Personal questions, dealing with such things as age or income, are generally best left to near the end: while they do not generally cause problems, and respondents need not answer those personal questions if they object, they are less likely to cause offence if asked later in the interview when a rapport has been established between interviewer and respondent. Similar principles apply in relation to respondent-completion questionnaires. It is sometimes suggested that this is an unethical practice, in that people might not agree to cooperate if they knew in advance that personal questions would be asked. But since in leisure and tourism surveys the personal information is rarely deeply personal, and respondents can and do decline to answer such questions, the practice is widely seen as acceptable.

Layout

- *General*: A questionnaire should be laid out and printed in such a way that the person who must read it – whether interviewer or interviewee – can follow all the instructions easily and answer all the questions that they are meant to answer. In the case of respondent-completion questionnaires extra care must be taken with layout because it can be very difficult to rectify faults once the survey process is underway. Clarity of layout, and the over-all impression given by the questionnaire can be all-important in obtaining a good response. Mail surveys, where the researcher does not have direct contact with the respondent, are the most demanding. A professionally laid out, typeset and printed questionnaire will pay dividends in terms of response rate and accuracy and completeness of responses.

- *Filtering*: Layout becomes particularly important when a questionnaire contains filters – that is, when answers to certain questions determine which subsequent questions must be answered. An example, with alternative ways of dealing with layout, is shown in Figure 10.18.

- *Length*: A typeset format can reduce the number of pages considerably, which may increase the response rate if the perceived length of the ques-tionnaire is a factor. Even where interviewers are used, there are advantages in keeping the questionnaire as compact as possible for ease of handling. A two-column format, as used in Case study 10.1, example C, is worth exploring and can be easily achieved with word-processing packages.

- *Tick boxes and codes*: The questionnaire shown in Case study 10.1-A is designed for respondent-completion and the layout therefore involves boxes for the respondent to tick. Boxes can, however, be laborious to type and lay out, so where an interviewer is being used, as in examples B and C, the interviewer can circle codes.

Layout 1

1. a. Have you studied at this university before?

    Yes $\square_1$
    No $\square_2$

  b. If YES: How long ago did you study here? ___ years

Layout 2

1. Have you studied at this university before?

    Yes $\square_1$ Go to question 2
    No $\square_2$ Go to question 3

2. How long ago did you study here? ___ years

Figure 10.18 Filtering: examples

- *Office use column*: The 'office use' column is not always necessary in such interviewer-administered questionnaires, but is included in examples A and B for exposition purposes. This type of layout can be used for respondent-completion in some situations – for example in certain 'captive group' situations or where respondents are known to be highly literate and are unlikely to be deterred by the apparent technicalities of the layout.

Coding

Most questionnaire survey data are now analysed by computer. This means that the information in the questionnaire must be coded – that is, converted into generally numerical codes and organised in a systematic, 'machine-readable', manner. Different procedures apply to pre-coded and open-ended questions and these are discussed in turn below.

Pre-coded questions

The principle for coding of pre-coded questions is illustrated in many of the questions in the example questionnaires in Case study 10.1. For example, for question 1 in example A, the codes are as shown beside the boxes. Only one answer is possible, so only one *code* is recorded as the answer to this question.

Where the answer is already numerical, there is no need to code the answer because the numerical answer can be handled by the computer. For example, in question 4 of example A actual expenditure is asked for, which is a number and does not require coding.

Scaled answers, as in Likert scales and attitude statements, readily lend themselves to coding, as shown by the numerals in the examples given in Figure 10.17. In the case of the semantic differential each of the sections of the response line can be numbered, say 1–4, so that answers can be given a numerical code, depending on where the respondent marks the line.

Open-ended questions

In the case of completely open-ended questions quite an elaborate procedure must be followed to devise a coding system. As already suggested, the answers to open-ended questions can be copied from the questionnaires and presented in a report 'raw', as in Figure 10.11. If this is all that is required from the open-ended questions, then there is no point in spending the considerable labour necessary to code the information for computer analysis: the computer will merely reproduce what can be more easily achieved manually.

Computer analysis comes into its own if it is intended to analyse the results in more detail – for example, comparing the opinions of two or more groups.

Answers from 25 respondents to the question: 'What suggestions would you make for improving campus life?'

More live music ///	Better food ///
Upgrade facilities ///	Keep out non-students //
More weekday events //	Something with a theme, like a film festival //
More lunch-time events /	Better acoustics in main hall //
More evening events //	Events for socialising, e.g. barbecues //
Better PA system /	Events should start and finish on time ///
Cheaper drinks ///	More unusual acts, films, etc. . . . not just
Free transport from city /	what can be seen in town ///
More free events //	More participatory events – e.g. debates //
Less hard rock acts //	Free entry to all events //

Suggested coding system	
Comments on programme content	1
Comments on timing	2
Comments on facilities	3
Comments on costs	4
Comments on organisation	5
Other	6

Figure 10.19 Coding open-ended questions – example

If such comparisons are to be made it will usually be difficult to do so with, say, 50 or 60 different response groups to compare, especially if many of the responses are only given by one or two respondents. The aim then is to devise a coding system which groups the responses into a manageable number of categories.

If a large sample is involved, it is advisable that the coding system be devised using a pilot survey, so that open-ended questions become pre-coded, but if this is not considered desirable then a representative sub-sample of the main survey responses, say 50 or 100, might be used for the purpose. All responses are written down, noting the number of occurrences of each answer as in Figure 10.19. Then individual codes are given for the most frequent responses and the others are grouped into meaningful categories, as indicated. This is a matter of judgement. The aim is not to leave too many responses in the 'Other' category.

Recording coded information

Computer analysis is conducted using the coded information from a questionnaire. This is best illustrated by an example – a completed questionnaire from Case study 10.1-A is set out in Figure 10.20.

In the 'office use' column, *spaces* are provided into which the codes from the answers can be written. The 'variable names' in the office column – qno, crse, lib, etc. – are explained in more detail in Chapter 16. Note the following:

Campus Life Survey 2008

	Office use
	#_1_
	qno

1. Which of the following best describes your current situation?

Full-time student with no regular paid work	☐₁	
Full-time student with some regular paid work	☑₂	_2_ status
Part-time student with full-time job	☐₃	
Part-time student – other	☐₄	

2. Which of the following university services have you used in the last 4 weeks?

Used campus cafe/bar	☑₁	_1_ cafebar
Attended a live music performance on campus	☑₁	_1_ music
Used campus sport facilities	☐₁	_0_ sport
Used campus travel service	☐₁	_0_ travel

3. In thinking about the social and entertainment services provided on campus, what are the most important considerations for you? Please rank the items below in terms of their importance to you. Rank them from 1 for the most important to 5 for the least important.

	Rank	
Free or cheap access	_1_	_1_ cheap
Daytime attractions	_4_	_4_ daytime
Acts, films, etc. not available elsewhere	_2_	_2_ unusual
Opportunities to socialise/meet people	_3_	_3_ meet
Quality of presentation	_5_	_5_ quality

4. Approximately how much do you spend in an average week on entertainment and social activities on and off campus?

£ _100_

_100_
spend

5. Please indicate the importance of the following to you in relation to campus life

	Very important	Important	Not at all important	
Relaxation opportunities	☑₃	☐₂	☐₁	_3_ relax
Social interaction	☑₃	☐₂	☐₁	_3_ social
Mental stimulation	☐₃	☐₂	☑₁	_1_ mental

6. What suggestions would you make for improving campus social life?

Provide more for minority tastes – less rock bands

_1_ sug1
__ sug2
__ sug3

7. You are: Male ☑₁   Female   ☐₂

_1_ gend

8. Your age last birthday was: _22_ years

_22_ age

Figure 10.20 Completed questionnaire

- Questionnaire number, in the 'office use' column, is an identifier so that a link can be made between data in the computer and actual questionnaires – the example questionnaire is number 1.
- Question 1 – only one answer/code can be given.
- Question 2 – respondents can tick up to four boxes.

- Question 3 – five ranks must be recorded.

- Question 4 – asks for an actual number and this will be transferred into the computer without coding.

- Question 5 – consists of three Likert-scale items.

- Question 6 – an open-ended question. It is envisaged that some respondents might give more than one answer, so spaces have been reserved for three answers (although, in the example, only one has been given). The answers have a coding system (devised as discussed above) as follows:

Comments on programme content	1
Comments on timing	2
Comments on facilities	3
Comments on costs	4
Comments on organisation	5
Other	6

The data from this particular completed questionnaire therefore become a single row of numbers, as shown in the first row of Figure 10.21, which shows how data from 15 completed questionnaires would look. How such a set of data may be analysed by computer is discussed in Chapter 16.

Validity of questionnaire-based data

Threats to validity

Questionnaires are designed to gather information from individuals about their characteristics, behaviour and attitudes. Whether or not they actually achieve this depends on a number of possible threats to validity. Some of these are summarised in Figure 10.22.

The principles of questionnaire design discussed above, and the principles of sampling outlined in Chapter 13 are designed to minimise threats to validity. To some extent the researcher must simply live with the limitations of the survey method and hope that inaccuracies are not significant and that some of them cancel each other out. There are, however, some measures which can be taken to check on the presence of this type of problem.

Checking validity

Some aspects of validity can be checked. The possibility of random or systematic error in responses may be checked by: the use of dummy questions or answer categories; semi-disguised duplication of questions; comparing time-periods;

qno	status	cafebar	music	sport	travel	cheap	daytime	unusual	meet	quality	spend	relax	social	mental	sug1	sug2	sug3	gend	age
1	2	1	1	0	0	1	4	2	3	5	100	3	3	1	1			1	18
2	2	1	1	1	0	1	4	2	3	5	50	2	3	1	2	1		1	19
3	3	1	0	0	0	2	5	1	3	4	250	2	2	2	3	4		2	19
4	4	0	0	0	0	2	3	1	4	5	25	3	2	2	1	2	4	1	22
5	3	1	0	0	0	1	4	3	2	5	55	3	3	1				2	24
6	3	1	1	1	1	2	4	1	3	5	40	2	3	1	2			2	20
7	2	1	0	0	0	3	2	1	4	5	150	2	3	2	3			2	20
8	2	1	0	1	0	3	4	2	1	5	250	1	2	2	4	5		1	21
9	4	0	1	0	0	1	5	2	3	4	300	2	3	2				1	21
10	3	1	1	0	0	2	3	1	5	4	100	1	2	1	1	1		2	21
11	3	1	1	0	1	2	3	1	4	5	75	2	2	1	2	3		2	19
12	2	1	0	1	0	1	4	3	2	5	50	2	3	1				1	22
13	1	1	0	1	0	1	5	2	3	4	55	2	3	2	1	2		2	21
14	3	1	1	0	0	2	4	1	3	5	75	3	3	2	4			2	20
15	1	1	1	0	0	3	2	1	5	4	150	3	3	1	1	2	5	1	20

Figure 10.21 Data from 15 questionnaires

Threat	Nature
Non-response	Non-respondents may be significantly different from respondents, thus resulting in a biased sample.
Questionnaire design: lack of clarity	Leading questions, ambiguity, etc. results in inaccurate data.
Accuracy of recall	Respondents vary in their ability to recall activity or its timing/nature, especially over long time-periods.
Desire to impress	People have a natural desire to impress others, to give a good report of themselves, resulting in exaggeration of good points and down-playing of bad points.
Privacy concerns/ sensitivity	People may be reluctant to provide information at all on private/sensitive matters, or may provide incomplete or inaccurate information.
Language/accent	Respondent may have difficulty with the language of the interview and respondent or interviewer may have difficulty in understanding the other's accent.
Interviewee patience/ fatigue	Interviews perceived to be excessively long or uninteresting may lead to incomplete responses.
Physical context	If interview or questionnaire completion takes place in a distracting environment, inaccuracies or incompleteness may result.
Interviewer-administered	
Interviewer-respondent rapport	Particularly good or poor interviewer–respondent rapport may affect the accuracy and completeness of responses.
Interviewer consistency	If interviewer does not consistently follow instructions, or different interviewers interpret instructions differently, inaccuracies may result.
Respondent-completed	
Literacy	Respondents have difficulty in understanding questions or, in case of open-ended questions, in writing answers.
Non-completion	For a variety of reasons, some questions are not answered.

Figure 10.22 Questionnaire surveys: threats to validity

and by referring to an alternative data source, where one exists. These possibilities are discussed in turn below.

Dummy questions or answer categories

In a survey of recreation managers in Britain in the early 1980s, respondents were asked to indicate, from a list, what books and reports they had heard of and had read. Included in the list was one plausible, but non-existent title. A significant proportion of respondents indicated that they had heard of the report and a small proportion claimed to have read it! Such a response does not necessarily mean that respondents were lying – they may simply have been confused about the titles of particular publications. But it does provide cautionary information to the researcher on the degree of error in responses to such questions, since it suggests that responses to the genuine titles may also include a certain amount of inaccuracy. For example, if 2 per cent of respondents claim to have heard of the non-existent report, this could suggest that all answers are subject to an error of plus or minus 2 per cent.

Semi-disguised duplication of questions

A similar approach is to include two or more questions in different parts of the questionnaire, which essentially ask the same thing. For example, an early question could ask respondents to rank a list of activities or holiday areas in order of preference. Later in the questionnaire, in the context of asking some detailed questions, respondents could be asked to indicate their favourite activity or holiday area. In the analysis, the responses could be tested for consistency.

Rather than detecting error, it is possible that this approach can discover that the interview or questionnaire completion experience itself has caused respondents to change their opinion, because it causes them to think through in detail something which they might previously have only considered superficially. In an Australian survey of gambling behaviour and attitudes towards a proposed casino development, Grichting and Caltabiano (1986) asked, at the beginning of the interview: 'What do you think about the casino coming to Townsville? Are you for it or against it?' At the end of the interview they asked: 'Taking everything you have said into consideration, what do you think now about the casino coming to Townsville? Are you for it or against it?' It was found that about 'one in six respondents changed their attitude toward the casino during the course of the interview'.

Comparing time-periods

Bachman and O'Malley (1981) used data from a survey of marijuana and alcohol use among senior high school students to explore apparent inconsistencies in reported use levels in the last month and in the last year. Except for seasonal activities, it might be expected that use levels in the last month would be about one-twelfth of use levels for the whole year. It was found that use levels reported for the last month were very much higher than this, suggesting that either the one-month figures were exaggerated or the one-year figures were under-reported.

Ideally, such findings should be followed up with additional research to confirm the patterns in the case of alcohol and drug use, investigate its prevalence in relation to other types of leisure or tourism activity and suggest ways in which it might be taken into account in future survey work. There is little evidence of this being done. One study related to tourism has been conducted by Beaman et al. (2001), not only exploring the phenomenon of inaccurate recall but also suggesting how data might be corrected to take it into account. Two studies which investigate the problem using a different methodology are noted under 'Use of an alternative data source' below.

Use of an alternative data source

One area where alternatives to survey data are available is consumer expenditure on items subject to licensing and excise taxation, such as alcohol and tobacco consumption and gambling. No formal analysis of this type of data has been identified in the literature, but one source for Australia suggests that estimated expenditure on gambling (total net losses by gamblers) based on a household expenditure survey was A$2.1 billion in 2003–4, whereas the estimate based on gambling taxes collected by state governments was A$15.0 billion (Lynch and Veal, 2006: 149, 158). While the latter figure includes expenditure by international tourists, this is partly offset by Australians' gambling expenditure overseas, and it is inconceivable that tourists accounted for more than a small proportion of the A$13 billion discrepancy. It is far more likely that when members of the household complete the Household Expenditure Survey questionnaire for the Australian Bureau of Statistics, gambling losses are grossly understated, both to the ABS and fellow household members!

Two studies conducted at the University of Pennsylvania by David Chase and colleagues compared questionnaire survey results on estimated numbers of visits to swimming and tennis over two seasons with club sign-in records. In the first study (Chase and Godbey, 1983) it was found that over 75 per cent of respondents in both swimming and tennis clubs overestimated their visits and in over 40 per cent of cases the error was greater than 100 per cent. The second larger-scale study of a swimming club (Chase and Harada, 1984) confirmed the general picture, with survey respondents' estimate of previous season visits averaging 30, while the club records indicated that the actual frequency was 17.

Taking account of validity problems

There is no indication in the research and policy literature that those organisations and researchers conducting and using questionnaire survey results in the leisure and tourism area take the above findings on validity problems into account. The above discussions refer only to recall of factual information, but questions may also arise in regard to the validity of responses to questions on attitudes and aspirations. There does not seem to be much interest in exploring these problems among the leisure and tourism research community. Some of the issues have, however, been addressed by researchers in the medical sector, as the volume of papers edited by Stone *et al.* (2000) demonstrates.

Conducting questionnaire surveys

Planning fieldwork arrangements

The scale and complexity of the data collection, or fieldwork, process in survey research can obviously vary enormously. At one extreme the process is largely

a. Seek permissions – to visit sites, obtain records, etc.

b. Obtain lists for sampling – e.g. voters lists

c. Arrange printing – of questionnaires etc.

d. Check insurance issues

e. Prepare written instructions for interviewers

f. Prepare identity badges/letters for interviewers

g. Recruit interviewers and supervisors

h. Train interviewers and supervisors

i. Obtain quotations for any fieldwork to be conducted by other organisations

j. Appoint and train data coders/processors

Figure 10.23 Fieldwork planning tasks

a matter of personal organisation on the part of the researcher; at the other extreme a staff of hundreds may need to be recruited, trained and supervised. Fieldwork must be organised in any type of empirical study involving primary data collection, but because of the popularity of the survey method and the likelihood that it will involve organisation of individuals other than the single researcher, some attention is given to the task in this chapter.

Some of the items which need consideration are listed in Figure 10.23. Brief notes on these tasks are presented below.

a. Seek permissions

It is important to remember that permission is often needed to interview in public places, such as streets and beaches, because of local by-laws. Many areas which are thought of as 'public' are in fact the responsibility of some public or private organisation – for example, shopping centres and parks. Permission must be sought from these organisations to conduct fieldwork. It is also good practice to inform the local police if interviewing is being conducted in public places, in case of complaints or queries from the public.

b. Obtain lists

Obtaining lists, such as voters or membership lists, for sampling may seem routine, but often apparently straightforward tasks can involve delays, or the material may not be quite in the form anticipated and it takes time to process. Often research projects are conducted on very tight schedules and delays of a few days can be crucial. Therefore the earlier these routine tasks are tackled the better.

c. Arrange printing

Printing sounds straightforward, but the in-house print-shop has busy periods when it may not be possible to obtain a quick job turnround. Checking on printing procedures and turnround times at an early stage is therefore advisable.

d. Check insurance

When conducting fieldwork away from a normal place of work, insurance issues may arise, including public liability and workers' compensation for interviewers. In the case of educational institutions, staff and students are normally covered as long as they are engaged in legitimate university/college activities, but these matters should be checked with a competent legal authority in the organisation.

e. Prepare written instructions for interviewers

Provision of written instructions for interviewers is advisable and may cover:

- detailed comments on questionnaires and/or other instruments;
- instructions in relation to checking of completed questionnaires etc. for legibility and completeness;
- instructions on returning questionnaires, etc.;
- dress and behaviour codes;
- roster details;
- 'wet weather' instructions, if relevant;
- instructions on what to do in the case of 'difficult' interviewees, etc.;
- details of time-sheets, payment, etc.;
- contact telephone numbers.

A note on questionnaire-based interviewing is appropriate here. The general approach to interviewing when using a questionnaire is that the interviewer should be instructed to adhere precisely to the wording on the questionnaire. If the respondent does not understand the question, the question should simply be repeated exactly as before; if the respondent still does not understand then the interviewer should move on to the next question. If this procedure is to be adhered to then the importance of question wording and the testing of such wording in one or more pilot surveys is clear.

The above procedure is clearly important in relation to attitude questions. Any word of explanation or elaboration from the interviewer could influence, and therefore bias, the response. In relation to factual questions, however, it may be less important – a word of explanation from the interviewer may be acceptable if it results in obtaining accurate information.

f. Prepare identity badges/letters

If working in a public or semi-public place, fieldworkers should be clearly identified. A badge with the institutional logo and the fieldworker's given name is advisable. A letter from the research supervisor indicating that the fieldworker is engaged in legitimate research activity for the organisation may also be helpful.

g. Recruit interviewers and supervisors

Where paid interviewers, supervisors or other fieldworkers are to be used it will be necessary to go through the normal procedures for employing part-time staff. Advice from the organisation's Human Resources Unit, or someone familiar with their procedures, will need to be sought.

h. Training

The length of training will vary with the complexity of the fieldwork and the experience of the fieldwork staff. Paid fieldworkers should be paid for the training session(s) (and this should be budgeted for). A two- or three-hour session is usually sufficient, but more may be necessary for a complex project. It is advisable for interviewers to practise interviews on each other and report back on difficulties encountered.

i. Obtain quotations

In some cases certain aspects of the project are to be undertaken by other organisations – for example, data processing. Obtaining detailed quotations on price as early as possible is clearly advisable.

j. Appoint and train data processors

In some cases the coding, editing and processing of data for computer analysis is a significant task in its own right, requiring staff to be recruited. Recruitment and training procedures will need to be followed as for fieldworkers.

Conducting a pilot survey

Pilot surveys are small-scale 'trial runs' of a larger survey. Pilot surveys relate particularly to questionnaire surveys, but can in fact relate to trying out any type of research procedure. It is always advisable to carry out one or more pilot surveys before embarking on the main data collection exercise. The purposes of pilot surveys are summarised in Figure 10.24. Clearly the pilot can be used to test all aspects of the survey, not just question wording. Item e., 'familiarity with respondents', refers to the role of the pilot in alerting the researcher to any characteristics, idiosyncrasies or sensitivities of the respondent group with which he or she may not have been previously familiar. Such matters can affect the design and conduct of the main survey. Items h and i, concerned with the response rate and length of interview, can be most important in providing

a. Test questionnaire wording
b. Test question sequencing
c. Test questionnaire layout
d. Code open-ended questions
e. Gain familiarity with respondents
f. Test fieldwork arrangements
g. Train and test fieldworkers
h. Estimate response rate
i. Estimate interview etc. time
j. Test analysis procedures

Figure 10.24   Pilot survey purposes

information to 'fine tune' the survey process. For example, it may be necessary to shorten the questionnaire and/or vary the number of field staff so that the project keeps on schedule and within budget.

In principle, at least some of the pilot interviews should be carried out by the researcher in charge, or at least by some experienced interviewers, since the interviewers will be required to report back on the pilot survey experience and contribute to discussions on any revisions to the questionnaire or fieldwork arrangements which might subsequently be made. The de-briefing session following the pilot survey is very important and should take place as soon as possible after the completion of the exercise, so that the details are fresh in the interviewers' minds.

Summary

This chapter provides an introduction to questionnaire surveys, arguably the most commonly used data collection vehicle in leisure and tourism research. The merits of questionnaire surveys are discussed, including the ability to quantify, transparency, succinctness in data presentation, the ability to study change over time, comprehensive coverage of complex phenomena and generalisability to the whole population. The second part of the chapter is devoted to discussing the features of seven different forms of the questionnaire survey: the household survey, the street survey, the telephone survey, the mail survey, the e-survey, the user/on-site/visitor survey and the captive group survey. The third part of the chapter considers questionnaire design and coding. Finally the chapter considers fieldwork arrangements for questionnaire surveys, including the conduct of pilot surveys.

Test questions

1. What are the merits of questionnaire surveys?

2. Seven types of questionnaire survey are discussed in the chapter; what are they?

3. List three of these questionnaire survey types and outline their characteristics in terms of: self- or interviewer-completion, cost, nature of the sample, possible length of questionnaire, and likely response rate.

4. What type of survey would you conduct for a sample of 500 of the following:
   a. Tourists visiting a seaside resort
   b. Members of 'Greenpeace'
   c. The users of a theatre
   d. The users of a large urban park
   e. Overseas visitors to Great Britain
   f. People who do not play sport
   g. People who play sport
   h. People who rent videos
   i. People aged 14 and over living in the local council area
   j. Young people aged 11–13 living in the local council area.

5. What is quota sampling?

6. What measures might be used to increase response rates in mail surveys?

7. What principles should be followed in wording questions in questionnaires?

8. What is the difference between pre-coded and open-ended questions and what are the advantages and disadvantages of the two formats?

Exercises

1. Design a questionnaire in relation to one of the studies discussed in Case studies 3.1 or 3.4, limiting the questionnaire to ten questions only.

2. Design a question on people's attitudes towards legalisation of drugs, using three alternative question formats.

3. If you are a member of a leisure/tourism class, invite members of the class to complete the questionnaire in Case study 10.1A and devise a coding system for the answers to open-ended question based on the answers obtained.

4. Locate a published research report or thesis which includes a questionnaire survey and contains a copy of the questionnaire used (usually in an appendix) and provide a critique of the questionnaire design.

Resources

Websites

Time-budget diaries/time-use surveys:

- Australian Bureau of Statistics: 2006 time-use survey: www.abs.gov.au/ausstats/abs @.nsf/mf/4153.0

- UK Office for National Statistics: 2005 time use survey: www.statistics.gov.uk/cci/article.asp?ID=1600

- Harmonised European Time Use Survey: www.h2.scb.se/tus/tus/default.htm

- Centre for Time Use Research, University of Oxford: www.timeuse.org/

Publications

- Attitude measurement: McDougal and Munro (1994), Oppenheim (2000), Chapter 11.

- E-surveys: Dillman *et al.* (2009).

- Large-scale, national household surveys: see the Resources section in Chapter 7.

- Mail surveys: Dillman *et al.* (2009).

- Questionnaire design generally: Oppenheim (2000); life-cycle: Rapoport and Rapoport (1975), Zuzanek and Veal (1998); class: Giddens (1993: 211–250; lifestyle: O'Brien and Ford (1988).

- Repertory grid technique: Kelly (1955), Botteril (1989), Stockdale (1984).

- Surveys generally: Hudson (1988), Cushman and Veal (1993), Ryan (1995).

- Telephone surveys: Lavrakas (1993), Lepkowski *et al.* (2008).

- Time-budget diaries/time-use surveys: Burton (1971), Szalai (1972), Australian Bureau of Statistics (1998), Gershuny (2000), Pentland *et al.* (1999); and tourists: Pearce (1988).

- Validity: exaggerated/unreliable, etc. responses to questionnaires: Chase and Godbey (1983), Chase and Harada (1984), Bachman and O'Malley (1981), Schaeffer (2000), Beaman *et al.* (2001), Oppenheim (2000: 138–9).

- Visitor (user) surveys vs conversion (coupon) surveys in tourism: Perdue and Botkin (1988).

Experimental research

Introduction

The essence of the experiment is that the researcher aims to control all the relevant variables in the research environment. Selected variables related to the subjects or objects of the research are manipulated while others are held constant and the effects on subjects/objects are measured. As discussed in Chapter 2, the experimental approach is closely associated with the positivist paradigm and is consistent with the classic scientific model of testing hypotheses and seeking to establish cause-and-effect relationships. The first part of this chapter explores in turn: the principles of experimental research; the issue of validity; and quasi-experimental designs.

Use of the experimental method is generally believed to be rare in the leisure and tourism context but when consideration is given to the full range of experimental and quasi-experimental methods used and the diversity of disciplinary contributions to the field, the body of experimental research in leisure and tourism research is found to be quite substantial. The second part of the chapter examines the use of experimental methods in a range of leisure and tourism research contexts.

This chapter is located in Part II of the book which is concerned with data collection, while data analysis is addressed in Part III. In the case of experimental methods, however, there is no corresponding separate analysis chapter in Part III. This is because, in the leisure and tourism context, context experimental data are invariably collected via questionnaire: thus the questionnaire survey method is embedded in the experimental method, or vice versa. Furthermore, as noted in Chapter 8, in cases where data are gathered by means of observation, the analysis of observations from subjects/cases is analogous to analysis of answers to questions, so the data file from an experimental study can be analysed in the same way as the data file from a questionnaire survey.

Principles of experimental research

Components

The essence of the experiment is that, ideally, the researcher controls all the relevant variables in the research environment. Selected variables are manipulated while others are held constant and the effects on subjects are measured. In the terminology of experimental study the researcher is concerned with a *dependent variable*, an *independent* or *treatment variable*, a *treatment group* and a *control group*. There may be one or more of each of these variables in any one study:

- *Dependent variable*: The dependent variable is a measurable outcome of the experiment. Participation in a leisure/tourism activity, level of satisfaction with a service and level of fitness or health could all be dependent variables.

- *Independent variable*: The independent variable or *treatment variable* represents a quality or characteristic that is varied or manipulated during the experiment. Some examples of independent variables are: provision of information/training or incentives and variation in the level and/or quality of service received. The independent or treatment variable is manipulated during the experiment to examine its effect on the dependent variable.

- *Treatment* or *experimental group*: The group of participants or subjects receiving the treatment is referred to as the *treatment* or *experimental group*.

- *Control group*: In order to take account of the possible effects of other variables on the outcome of the experiment, the researcher often uses a control group that is not subject to the treatment. The attributes of the control group may be matched with the attributes of the experimental or treatment group so that the two groups are as similar as possible or subjects may be randomly assigned to the two groups.

The classic experimental design

The classic or true design for experimental research, the pre-test–post-test control group design, is summarised in Figure 11.1 and involves five steps:

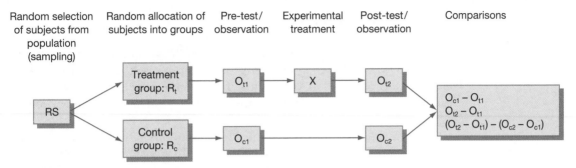

Figure 11.1 Classic experimental design

1. Subjects are randomly allocated to two groups: A, the treatment group, and B, the control group.

2. In the pre-test observation, subjects in both groups are measured with respect to the dependent variable.

3. The experimental treatment, X, is applied to the treatment group, A, but not to control group, B.

4. In the post-test observation, subjects in both groups are measured again with respect to the dependent variable.

5. For the experimental treatment to be judged positive:

   - there should be no significant difference between O_{t1} and O_{c1}

   - there should be a significant difference between $(O_{t2} - O_{t1})$ and $(O_{c2} - O_{c1})$.

Typically in step 5 the calculations will be based on mean scores for each measurement for each group. The concept of *significant* difference is discussed in Chapter 18.

Validity

The aim of the classic design is to ensure, as far as possible, the *validity* of the research findings. As noted in Chapter 2, validity refers to the extent to which the information collected in a research study truly reflects the phenomenon being studied. There is generally a trade-off to be made between research validity and practicality and cost. While perfection is impossible, researchers should be aware of *threats to validity* and take these into account in the design of the experiment.

Threats to validity

Threats to the validity of experimental research fall into two main groups: *internal*, in which design components are compromised, and *external*, which relate to the application of the findings to the population to which the results are intended to apply. Some of these threats are summarised in Figure 11.2.

In the figure, reference is made to the 'Hawthorne effect', in which being part of a study affects people's behaviour. This was demonstrated many years ago in a study in the Hawthorne Plant of the Western Electric Company in the USA, which investigated the relationship between productivity and the brightness of lighting in the factory. As expected, productivity increased as illumination was increased. However, as brightness was decreased productivity also rose. It was concluded that it was the attention the workers were receiving as a result of the study, rather than lighting, that was affecting production.

Internal validity	Aspects of the experimental design which raise doubts as to whether change in dependent variable can be attributed entirely to the independent variable/treatment.
Maturation	Change occurs in study subject during the study period – e.g. fatigue.
History	Change in the external environment affects the study – e.g. weather conditions.
Testing	The test/observation process itself may affect subjects – e.g. asking questions raises awareness of, and therefore changes, behaviour.
Instrumentation	Inconsistency or unreliability in the measuring instruments or observation procedures during a study – e.g. change in the way a questionnaire is designed.
Selection bias	Treatment group and control group have significantly different characteristics – e.g. one group markedly older than the other.
Mortality	Attrition of subjects from a study – likely to happen if treatment process is spread over a long period of time.
External validity	Extent to which results may be generalised beyond the study subjects and setting.
Reactive effects of testing	Tests/observation may sensitise subjects and affect behaviour responses, which would not happen in 'real life' – e.g. subjects wish to impress the researchers.
Effects of selection	Subjects may not be representative of wider population – e.g. when experiments conducted with tertiary students or city-centre dwellers. The very fact of involvement with a study may cause subjects to behave differently from people generally – the 'Hawthorne effect'.

Figure 11.2 Threats to validity of experiments

Field experiments versus laboratory experiments

There is a trade-off between field experiments, or experiments in naturalistic settings, and laboratory experiments in relation to external and internal validity. In the case of leisure and tourism research, the equivalent of 'laboratory' is often an office, meeting room or classroom where data are elicited from subjects. In general, field experiments undertaken in natural leisure or tourism settings have greater external validity than laboratory-based experiments. On the other hand, laboratory-based experiments tend to have greater internal reliability than field experiments. There is more control of extraneous variables in a laboratory. The decision should only be made after careful consideration of the threats to internal and external validity described above, and consideration of the objectives of the research. The 'obvious' approach may not in fact be ideal. For example, it might be thought obvious that it would be appropriate to gather data from tourists at a holiday destination or from sports participants at a sports facility, but if the interest is in general patterns of tourist or sporting behaviour, it might be best to avoid the possibility of subjects being over-influenced by any particular holiday/destination or sport/facility experience.

Quasi-experimental designs

Types of quasi-experimental design

In a natural science experiment, the subjects will be identical specimens or samples of organic or inorganic matter, or laboratory animals that are as near as possible identical, and are treated identically except for the experimental treatment. This is not possible in the sorts of social or organisational contexts with which leisure and tourism are involved. In such contexts, therefore, compromises must be made with the classic model and *quasi-experimental* designs must be devised.

Four common quasi-experimental designs are shown in Figure 11.3. Some designs simplify the classic model, for example by dispensing with a control group or the pre-test stage, while others complicate it, for example by adding additional treatments. They are often used where time, cost and practicality are important considerations, but there is often a loss of validity associated with each design. They are: the one-shot design; the one group pre-test–post-test design, the static group design and the Latin square. It can be seen that some designs dispense with the control group, while others dispense with the pre-treatment test.

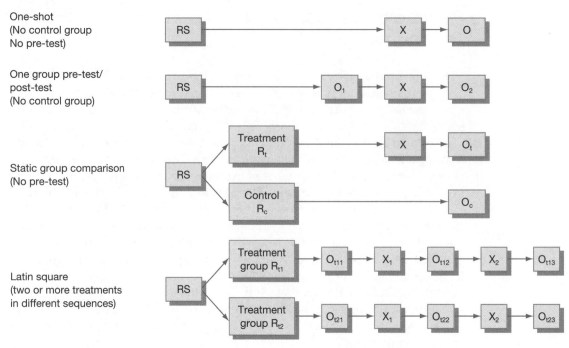

Figure 11.3 Quasi-experimental designs

Experiments and projects

There is a tendency in some references to the experimental method to equate 'experiment' with 'research project'. But typically a research project will comprise a series of experiments. In order to conduct an individual experiment it is necessary to define the relevant dependent and independent/treatment variables. But a project can comprise a number of experiments and the programme of experiments may evolve during the course of the project. Imagine a medical scientist searching for a drug to treat a virus: a number of possibilities may be explored before a successful treatment is discovered. This may take a number of experiments, even a number of projects. Thus an experimental project, or sequence of projects, may be much more exploratory, even inductive, than the formal hypothetical-deductive model of the single experiment.

Experimental methods in leisure and tourism research

Experiments involve research in a controlled environment in which the researcher is able to vary the conditions of the environment for research purposes. Opportunities to do this in leisure and tourism contexts, when

Discrete choice experiments (DCE)	Consumption or activity choice processes are studied by presenting subjects with hypothetical product descriptions with differing combinations of features and asking them to express their preferences.
Policy/management pilot/trial projects	Innovations in policy or management practice are tested out by experimental or pilot projects and evaluated using a variety of methods and with varying degrees of rigour.
Experimenting with research methods	Testing of innovative or alternative research methods or techniques, usually in the same setting, with the same subjects or split samples.
Psychological/ perceptual	Samples of subjects exposed to hypothetical situations/questions or images.
Sport-related	Studies of exercise effects, sport motivation, etc. using a variety of experimental methods.
Children's play	Observational studies of children with different play equipment/environments.
Other examples	Action research; Q methodology; qualitative methods; training of tourism professionals; mental mapping; and physical models.

Figure 11.4 Types and contexts of experiments in leisure and tourism research

people – customers, employees or the general public – are involved are limited, which explains the preference for non-experimental methods, notably questionnaire-based surveys. Experimental or quasi-experimental methods are nevertheless used in a variety of leisure and tourism contexts, as indicated in Figure 11.4, and these are discussed in turn below.

It is often assumed that the use of experimental methods is rare in leisure and tourism, but this is true only in relative terms. In an examination of six leisure studies journals over a six-year period, Mark Havitz and Jane Sell (1991) found that only 5 per cent used experimental methods, but this nevertheless amounted to 46 papers. However, in a 2001 review of the first category mentioned in Figure 11.4, the consumer choice technique or discrete choice experiment, Geoffrey Crouch and Jordan Louviere (2001) identified over 40 published studies in the tourism, hospitality and leisure area, although less than half were in leisure/tourism journals. In the case of the second category, policy/management experimental projects, the number of studies would be much greater, although only a small proportion are reported in the peer-reviewed literature, and many tend to be criticised for lack of methodological rigour. Then if we move into the areas of psychology and sport/exercise-related physiological research, which have considerable overlaps with leisure and tourism, the experimental method is dominant.

Discrete choice experiments (DCEs)

In Chapter 5, reference is made to *conjoint analysis*, which is the analytical basis for discrete choice experiments (DCEs) which seek to explore people's decision-making processes in regard to choice of products or activities, including such phenomena as holiday types or destinations and leisure activities, services or facilities. The 'experimental' feature of this approach is that, rather than researching people's actual decision-making, it involves asking subjects to make choices among hypothetical alternative products defined in terms of various combinations of features. In some cases the information is presented via a questionnaire and subjects record their choices on the questionnaire, so the approach could be seen as a particular form of questionnaire-based survey. In other cases subjects are presented with information on cards containing information on products with different combinations of features and are asked to sort them in order of preference.

Some examples of DCEs in the leisure/tourism field are summarised in Case study 11.1. Conjoint analysis, the mathematical procedure which underpins DCE, is discussed briefly in Chapter 18, as is multidimensional scaling, which is a similar process.

Case study 11.1   Discrete choice experiments: examples

In their review of the discrete choice experiment (DCE) literature, Geoffrey Crouch and Jordan Louviere (2001: 76)* state that 'preference data elicitation procedures supported by careful experimental design and analysis can be used to tackle many of the questions facing managers and researchers who desire to understand tourism, hospitality and leisure choice processes with greater insight'. They identified over 40 discrete choice experiment studies using the approach. Two examples are summarised here.

A. Cultural events

In an early example not only of discrete choice experiments but also of events research, Ronald Cosper and Brian Kinsley (1984) present an analysis of preferences of Canadians for different types of cultural festival, for which the fieldwork, involving a nationwide survey of 6000 people aged 15 years and above, was conducted in 1978. Their paper does not use the DCE terminology but refers to *conjoint analysis*, the basic analytical method used in DCE. Respondents were asked to rank in order of preference eight cards containing descriptions of cultural events described in terms of four attributes – content, medium, quality and price – each with four possible values/categories, as shown in Figure 11.5. The cards contained eight of the possible 256 (4 × 4 × 4 × 4)

---

* In their 2001 paper Crouch and Louviere use the term 'choice modelling research' to describe the technique, while in other publications Louviere and collaborating authors have used the term 'simulated consumer choice or allocation experiments' (Louviere and Woodworth, 1983) and 'stated choice methods' (Louviere *et al.* 2000). The term 'discrete choice experiment' has been adopted here from Kelly *et al.* (2007).

Attributes							
Content		**Medium**		**Quality**		**Price**	
A	**B**	**A**	**B**	**A**	**B**	**A**	**B**
Sports	0.20	Shown on TV	0.34	International/ prof.	0.14	Free	0.03
Drama	0.19	Live	0.20	National/prof.	0.06	$3	−0.23
Classical music	−0.47	Recorded, audio	−0.25	Provincial/ amateur	−0.14	$7	0.13
Popular music	0.08	On radio	−0.28	Local/amateur	−0.58	$5	0.06

Figure 11.5 Cultural events: attributes, values and preferences

Source: summarised from Cosper and Kinsley (1984: 229)

A = Values/categories   B = Preference weights derived from the research.

combinations of the attributes and values/categories. The analysis produced weights reflecting the respondents' mean preferences for the various attributes/ values/categories, as shown in the columns B in Figure 11.5. These weights are additive and can be used to assess the preference for an event with any combinations of attribute and value/category. Thus, for example, a sporting event, shown on TV, with international/professional performers and free of charge would have a score of 0.71. (The authors note and discuss the implausibility of the price weights, where the free option is not the most popular.)

B. Eco-tourism

Joe Kelly and colleagues (2007) conducted a DCE with visitors to the Whistler, British Columbia, ski resort to assess their preferences for 'eco-efficient' resorts. A sample of 1825 visitors were interviewed and asked for an email address to which an online questionnaire was sent for them to respond to after their visit. Of these, 876 submitted completed questionnaires. A list of 14 resort attributes was drawn up which would distinguish between an eco-efficient resort planning model, a 'business-as-usual' (i.e. current) model and a resource-intensive model. Thus, for example, looking at three attributes: 1. *form of development*: an eco-efficient resort would have a compact rather than a dispersed form; 2. *recreation activities*: an eco-efficient resort would exclude motorised sports; and 3. *energy needs*: in an eco-efficient resort a high proportion would be met from renewable resources. Respondents each received a questionnaire presenting one of 18 possible pairs of resorts, labelled A and B, with differing combinations of attributes and were asked to express their preference. Using a different form of statistical analysis from the Cosper and

Kinsley study, a similar set of preference weights for each attribute/value/category was produced, for day-visitors and overnight stayers. In general, it was found that a 'business-as-usual' model was the most preferred, an eco-efficient model was second and a more resource-intensive model least popular. It should be noted that, having recruited respondents at a single site, the study of course had a built-in bias towards a resort of that type.

Other examples of studies using DCEs are listed in the Resources section of the chapter.

Policy/management experimental projects

Conducting experiments, often called *pilot projects*, *pilot programmes* or *trials*, is popular in the government sector, partly for the overt reason that it is wise to test effectiveness of policies on a small scale before implementing them on a wide scale, but also because, to be somewhat cynical, they are much cheaper than a full-scale policy roll-out and can delay having to make a decision on the roll-out. Invariably such projects include an evaluation component, although this is not always adequately resourced or rigorously conducted. One of the earliest examples in the leisure sector in Britain took place in the late 1970s when a combination of government departments in Britain sponsored the 'Leisure and the Quality of Life' study which comprised 'four local experiments' designed to 'develop and increase a full range of leisure activities – cultural, recreational and sporting – and to record and learn as much as possible from the experience' (Dept of the Environment, 1977: ix).

In some cases the declared policy-related experimentation is to increase levels of participation, often in sport and physical exercise, but also in culture and leisure activities generally, as the above quotation exemplifies. However, invariably the rationale behind the policy to boost participation is related to other policy areas, notably health and crime reduction in the case of sport and, more recently in Britain, 'social inclusion': the notion that all groups should enjoy the rights of citizenship, including engagement with social and cultural activity. In these cases, the criterion for the success of a project is not just participation itself, but also the resultant hoped-for improvements in health, crime reduction or social inclusion. The experimental model is therefore as shown in Figure 11.6. Two lots of measurements/observations are made, relating to participation and the social policy criterion, and the 'control' is often, in effect, the community at large: for example, the general level of sports participation or crime rates, related to the whole population or, in some cases, youth.

Projects involving sport are particularly notable because, given its association with health, it involves not just social scientists but also medical, sport and human movement scientists. Thus both policy-makers and researchers involved are familiar with the experimental method and it is often accepted in this environment that evidence-based policy should be based on rigorously conducted experiments. In order to provide such a basis for policy development,

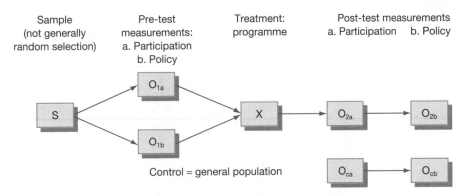

Figure 11.6 Experimental model of policy projects

therefore, a number of reviews of available research has been carried out to establish what evidence exists on the effectiveness, or otherwise, of various types of experimental intervention. One of these is summarised in Case study 11.2, which also includes summaries of examples of individual studies.

Case study 11.2	Policy/management-related experimental studies

A. Sport participation: review

Naomi Priest and her colleagues conducted a review of available literature on experiments/projects conducted by sporting organisations and designed to increase sport participation, involving the scanning of databases containing some 15,000 research publications. They note that interventions to boost sports participation can take a variety of forms, including:

- mass media campaigns;
- information or education sessions;
- management or organisational change strategies;
- policy changes, for example to improve the socio-cultural environment to encourage people of specific age, gender or ethnicity to participate;
- changes to traditional or existing programmes, for example club- or association-initiated rule modification programmes;
- provision of activities beyond traditional or existing programmes, for example 'Come and Try' initiatives (teaser or taster programmes), skill improvement programmes, and volunteer encouragement programmes (Priest, *et al.*, 2008: no pagination).

The aim of the review was to identify suitable studies, to evaluate them methodologically and to draw conclusions about the effectiveness of various forms of intervention in promoting sport participation. Their conclusions were:

We found no controlled studies that met the inclusion criteria. We identified no uncontrolled studies, with pre- and post-test data, suitable to be included in . . . this review . . . and therefore assessed no studies for methodological quality. Despite using the most comprehensive search methods to date, no studies were identified that employed a controlled evaluation design. *(Priest et al., 2008: no pagination)*

This extraordinary finding indicates that, despite the involvement of health and sport scientists, along with social scientists, as discussed above, none of the studies identified conformed to the classic scientific model, with control groups and pre-intervention and post-intervention data. Even when relaxing the requirement for a control group (uncontrolled studies), no studies were found with pre-test and post-test data.

This is an extreme example of a problem recognised by others in attempting to review this field of study. Blamey and Mutrie (2004: 748) note one study which identified 253 publications for review but excluded 159 due to limitations in study design, and another where only 12 out of 254 papers satisfied the review criteria. Fred Coalter (2007: 27–9) notes that this situation is not unique to sport and refers to discussion in the policy literature which suggests that the rigorous experimental criteria used in the natural sciences may not be appropriate in social policy areas and that, in any case, there is an absence of theoretical understanding of the causes of sport participation and non-participation to inform the design and evaluation or programmes/projects/experiments (pp. 171–4).

B. Sport and crime reduction

Geoff Nichols (2007), in his book on *Sport and Crime Reduction*, presents eight case studies of projects designed to prevent young people from engaging in crime through participation in a sport-related programme. Just one project is described here. During a three-year period, 194 probationers volunteered to take part in a 12-week 'sports counselling' service which introduced them to a range of local council sporting facilities and courses such as lifesaving. No follow-up was undertaken in relation to sport participation, but the social outcome was measured by reconviction rates over the following two years. The reconviction rate for participants who completed the 12-week programmes was significantly lower than for those who completed less than eight weeks and matched control groups who had not taken part in the programme at all. Programme participants' self-esteem was also measured, at the beginning and end of the programme, and participation in the full course was found to make a significant positive difference.

C. Count me in: social inclusion through sport, culture

Count ME IN: the Dimensions of Social Inclusion through Culture and Sport is the title of a report prepared by the Centre for Leisure and Sport Research (2002) at Leeds Metropolitan University for the UK Department for Culture, Media and Sport. It presents the results of a study of 14 publicly funded short-term social projects which had the common aim of 'enhancing the quality of life in areas of disadvantage'. The 14 were made up of:

- *Sport*: three projects 'providing sporting opportunities as a constructive socially acceptable focus for the energies of young people'.
- *Arts and media*: six projects: two using the arts to 'stimulate public aware-ness of health issues', three 'directed to skills development among disaffected/ vulnerable young people with a view to improving employment prospects'; and one 'orientated to educational development'.
- *Heritage and libraries*: three projects: one 'designed to attract disadvantaged groups into the museum'; one 'an arts in education project using heritage to stimulate imagination'; and one 'a library service to develop communica-tion in rural areas'.
- *Outdoor adventure*: two projects providing 'adventure education as a means of personal development and the fostering of self-confidence and self-esteem'.

The report notes that project managers generally report on progress to funding agencies using 'milestones' in the development of the project and 'outputs' in the form of such things as events staged and numbers of people attending. More challenging was assessing policy-related social inclusion-related 'out-comes', such as improved health, access to employment, improved educa-tional performance or crime reduction. Project-by-project evaluations are not presented but chapters on a number of themes: education employment; crime prevention; health; personal development; and social cohesion. The report concludes by noting the practical and conceptual difficulties involved in evaluating outcomes of projects of this nature.

Experimenting with research methods

The practice of conducting experimental research to test the efficacy of dif-ferent research methods has a long history in the leisure sector: for example, the report of one of the earliest research projects funded by the Sports Council in England, in the late 1960s, was entitled *Experiments in Recreation Research* (Burton, 1971). While the basic methods being examined in this type of study are not themselves experimental, the experimental quality of the studies lies in the practice of going beyond what would be normal practice, namely using multiple methods or variations on methods, in order to discover the effects of different research practices. Examples are presented in Case study 11.3. All examples are quasi-experimental although none conforms precisely to the designs indicated in Figure 11.3.

Case study 11.3   Experiments with research methods: examples

Experimental methods have been used in leisure and tourism contexts to compare the efficacy of different data collection techniques. Some examples are presented here.

A. Attitude measurement techniques

Angie Driscoll, Rob Lawson and Brian Niven (1994) conducted an experiment to collect the same data in two different ways. The data comprised respondents' assessment of 12 holiday destinations on the basis of 18 attributes. Using a postal survey method, one sample of 571 respondents was presented with 12 semantic differential (see Chapter 10) tables, one for each destination and each with 18 destination attributes. A second sample of 528 respondents was presented with a single grid with destinations across the top and the 18 attributes down the side and asked to score each country on each attribute. The two samples were found to have similar socio-demographic profiles. Whereas in theory the two techniques were measuring the same thing, in practice it was found that the results obtained from the two methods differed significantly.

B. Tourist tracking method

Noam Shoval and Michaal Isaacson (2007) examined the use of a number of devices to track tourist movements in a destination. Three experiments were conducted involving devices using combinations of three electronic technologies: satellite-based global positioning system (GPS), land-based time difference of arrival (TDOA) and cell sector identification (based on cell/mobile telephone systems). Single subjects, wearing one or more of these devices conducted round trips in three different tourist destinations (Heidelberg, Germany, Jerusalem, Israel, and Nazareth/Akko, Israel). Graphical output of the subjects' routes are reproduced in the article and comments offered on the convenience of use by the subjects. While these procedures are described as experiments in the article, there is no comparison with traditional non-technological methods and the evaluation is minimal, so they should perhaps be more appropriately described as 'demonstrations'.

	Data available from:			Total
	On-site qu're	15-page mail qu're	2-page mail qu're	
A. 15-page mail survey respondents	A_1	A_2		A_t
B. 2-page mail survey respondents	B_1		B_2	B_t
C. On-site survey only	C_1			C_t

Figure 11.7 Survey respondent groups – Hammitt and McDonald

Source: Hammitt and McDonald (1982)

C. Response rate, follow-up and bias

William Hammitt and Cary McDonald (1982) conducted an on-site survey of users at two river recreation sites followed up with a 15-page mail questionnaire to all who participated in the on-site survey. A response rate of 52 per cent was achieved with two follow-ups. Remaining non-respondents were sent a two-page reduced version of the mail questionnaire, resulting in an overall response rate of 75 per cent. They therefore had data from three different groups, as depicted in Figure 11.7. Because of the on-site interview they had data even on members of group C, who did not respond to either mail questionnaire.

By comparing the results on the common data items between the three groups it was possible to determine whether the additional follow-ups made any difference to the pattern of responses. On one comparison using 17 data items, only four showed a significant difference and on another, only one item out of 19 showed a significant difference. It was therefore concluded that there was no major benefit, in terms of representativeness, in pursuing a high response rate. Subsequent correspondence in the *Journal of Leisure Research* concerning this and similar studies cautioned that the findings were not necessarily universal, since they were contingent on the population being relatively homogenous, which may not apply in all cases (Christensen, 1982).

D. Mail survey follow-ups

Richard Gitelson and Ellen Drogin (1992) conducted an experiment on the effectiveness of different forms of follow-up letter in a mail-back survey. Spectators at a Pennsylvania agricultural show were interviewed on-site to obtain basic socio-demographic information and addresses and were subsequently sent a questionnaire by mail. After sending a post-card reminder and a duplicate questionnaire, a response rate of 67 per cent had been achieved. The remaining 33 per cent were divided into three groups: all were sent a replacement questionnaire, but in addition, they received the following treatments with the following results:

- Group 1: non-personalised letter via ordinary mail: response rate: 13 per cent
- Group 2: personalised letter via ordinary mail: response rate: 17 per cent
- Group 3: personalised letter via certified/registered mail: response rate: 43 per cent.

The use of certified/registered mail was clearly effective in increasing the response rate, although at additional cost. However, comparison of early and late respondents' survey results indicated that, in regard to the great majority of the data items in the questionnaire, the additional response had not made a significant difference, but the authors make no reference to the earlier Hammitt and McDonald study and subsequent correspondence which had discussed this issue in the same journal a decade earlier.

E. Photographs versus written descriptions versus observation – ecological impacts

If managers/designers wish to gauge users' reactions to various levels and types of human impacts on ecological values at tourism/recreation sites, the use of written or photographic representation of the impacts would be a more convenient and cheaper method than gathering data on-site. But how accurately do they reflect on-site evaluations? This study, by Bo Shelby and Richard Harris (1985) used all three methods at 20 different campsites in five study areas. In each study area, for each of the methods, 30 visitors assessed the three or four sites within the area – so over 400 visitors were involved in the assessment. Participants assessed the acceptability of various types of impact and the overall desirability of the site on a five-point scale. In 90 per cent of cases, photograph-based assessments were not significantly different from on-site assessments, but written assessments differed more often.

Psychological/perceptual studies

The study of some psychological and perceptual aspects of leisure and tourism lends itself to experimental research, where subjects can be exposed to visual stimuli and their reactions or opinions recorded. Some examples are summarised in Case study 11.4.

Sport-related experiments

Experiments are the main methodology used in the disciplines associated with sport and human movement, such as bio-mechanics, sport psychology. Some examples of such experiments are summarised in Case study 11.5.

Case study 11.4   Psychological/perceptual experiments

A. Landscape images

Landscape preservation and planning of scenic roads and trails within natural areas are guided in part by aesthetics. Planners and designers need to check their aesthetic judgements against those of the general public. Arranging for members of the public to provide assessments on-site is time-consuming and expensive, so photographs have been used. But just how this should be done and how to interpret the results has become a research area in its own right. In one such study by Glenn Wade (1982) 100 students and academic and support staff at two Virginia universities viewed a sequence of ten scenic colour slides. Individuals viewed the slides alone and had control of the slide projector (today this would be done with computer images). At the end they were asked to rank the views in order of preference. In another study using photography Gabriel Cherem and Bev Driver (1983) used a different approach, this time involving on-site visits as well. A sample of users using a natural trail were presented with a relatively cheap camera and asked to take ten photographs of views which they liked: the most popular views photographed were classified as 'consensus photographs'. In terms of quasi-experimental models depicted in Figure 11.3, these were 'one-shot' studies.

B. Independence and psychological well-being

Most conceptualisations of leisure involve a personal sense of independence of action, of individuals feeling in control of their lives. As a result of economic, social and physical factors, this sense of independence is often at risk among older people, resulting in reduced participation in engaging leisure activity which in turn can have negative impacts on physical and psychological well-being. One way in which public agencies might intervene to counter this tendency is to provide courses which provide information about leisure opportunities and encourage and enable participation. Searle *et al.* (1995) report on an experiment designed to evaluate such an intervention. A treatment group and a control group each of 15 persons aged 65 and over were recruited and both groups completed pre-test and post-test questionnaires, 16 weeks apart, designed to assess general independence and psychological well-being. This was done using five scales: the Perceived Leisure Control Scale; Perceived Leisure Competence Scale; Life Satisfaction Index; Locus of Control Scale; and Leisure Boredom Scale (the use of scales in general is discussed in Chapter 5 and sources for these specific scales are given in the Resources section of that chapter). The treatment group attended a 16-week course and showed significant improvements in the post-test, compared with the control group, on four out of the five scales.

▶

C. Leisure and stress/tension relief

One of the qualities often attributed to leisure activity is relaxation and relief of stress and tension. A study by Lloyd Heywood (1978) was designed to test whether recognised leisure activities were better at relieving stress and tension than non-leisure activities, such as studying. The subjects were 60 psychology students, who were required, in part A of the experiment, to undertake about 20 minutes of mental arithmetic, while their physiological state (heart rate, skin resistance, respiration and forehead and upper back tension) was electronically monitored. This was followed by a contrived 'short break' of 15 minutes when subjects were provided with either a 'recreative' (e.g. listening to music or watching television) or 'non-recreative' (e.g. reading a professional journal) distraction to pass the time, as indicated above, but their physiological state continued to be monitored. In fact, the 'break' was part B of the experiment. Statistical tests showed that the leisure, or 'recreative', experiences were more effective in reducing stress levels than 'non-recreative' experiences. This study followed the 'Latin square' pattern of quasi-experiment as indicated in Figure 11.3 and used a formal set of three null hypotheses to be tested, as discussed in Chapter 17.

Case study 11.5   Sport-related experiments

A. Mood and physical activity

One of the reasons why participation in sport and other forms of physical activity is encouraged is because of the health benefits it brings. This can be physical or mental. One aspect of poor mental health is depression. Martina Kanning and Wolfgang Schlicht (2010) conducted a study to examine the effect of physical activity on mood. A sample of 13 subjects kept diaries over a ten-week period, in which, on a daily basis, they recorded three randomly chosen distinct activities and how they felt before and after the activity. They found a positive relationship between physical activity and mood level, with the greatest effect being when people started the activity in a depressed mood. In this quasi-experimental method the 'treatment' is selected and the pre-test and post-test observations are under the control of the subjects. The method has some similarities with experience sampling method (ESM), as discussed in Chapter 5, but without the real-time prompts and recording.

B. Players and sporting equipment

Noting that elite tennis players are very particular about the tension at which their rackets are strung, Rob Bower and Rod Cross (2008) conducted experiments to examine the ability of elite players to detect differences in string tension and the efficiency of different string tensions in play. Participants in the study were 18 elite tennis players (i.e. nationally ranked or in the world top 1500, and aiming for a professional career) taking part in a tournament. Each participant compared two rackets with a string tension difference of 11 pounds, by using each racket to hit four balls projected by a machine. The test was conducted twice. If the player successfully detected a difference, the test was repeated with two rackets with a string tension difference of 6 pounds; if they were unsuccessful, the repeat involved rackets with a string tension difference of 17 pounds. Only 5 (28 per cent) players detected the 11 pound difference; but of these, only 2 could detect the 6 pound difference. Of the 13 (72 per cent) players who could not detect the 11 pound difference, 11 could not detect even the 17 pound difference. These findings were clearly at variance with the players' typical concern about string tension in their rackets. Other experiments, not summarised here, were conducted to test the rebound efficiency of rackets with different tensions.

Children's play

The study of children's play can be pursued by experimental methods because young children in particular spend much of their time in play environments controlled to a greater or lesser degree by adults. The play environment can be modified and changes in the children's behaviour observed without children being aware that a controlled experiment is being conducted. Some examples are presented in Case study 11.6.

Case study 11.6	Children's play experiments

A. Play equipment safety

Safety is of course a key consideration in children's play equipment design, and safety standards have developed over time. Howard *et al.* (2005) report on a project which assessed the effectiveness of the implementation of new standards promulgated in Canada in 1998. In Toronto, all school playgrounds were assessed against the new standards in 2000 and 136 were found to require replacement of dangerous equipment, while 225 were deemed satisfactory. By December 2001 the dangerous equipment had been removed from all 136 playgrounds and 86 of these had received replacement equipment. This offered the opportunity to conduct a study with an experimental format

▶

– this might be termed an opportunistic experiment. The 86 playgrounds with replaced equipment were seen as the 'intervention' or treatment group and 225 which required no replacement were the 'non-intervention' group. Data on injuries per 1000 students were collated for all playgrounds for the ten months before and after the replacement of equipment. Injury rates declined between the two periods at the intervention schools while actually increasing at the non-intervention schools. This clearly supported the adoption of the new equipment safety standards.

B. Play equipment design

A study by Gramza *et al.* (1972) examined 4–5-year-old children's preferences for play equipment of differing complexity. Four groups of children were involved in the project, each experiencing two 12–15 minute sessions in a playroom. The project involved three A-frame climbing trestles: A. a plain trestle; B. a trestle modified by the addition of plain boards with a number of hand-foot holes; and C. a trestle with more additions, including irregular-shaped boards with hand–foot holes, a platform and a climbing rope. In Phase I the playroom contained trestles A and B and the number of children on each was recorded every five seconds for a 500-second period. This was repeated four weeks later. In Phase II the procedure was repeated with trestles A and C. It was found that the children were attracted to the more complex equipment and that their use of the equipment, in conjunction with other toys in the room, was creative and developed over time.

C. Adult inhibition and peer disinhibition

Children are socialised partly by adult guidance, rule-setting and enforcement (adult inhibition) and partly by peer influence, which may run counter to the adult rules (peer disinhibition). An experiment by Lance Wuellner (1981) was designed to investigate the influence of these two factors. The experiment took place in a supervised playroom and involved a control group of preschool children and two treatment groups playing for about 1.5 hours, with their behaviour video-recorded. One of the control groups was monitored for one day and the other for two days. The control group played without any intervention. For the treatment groups an area of the room, including some of the play equipment, was marked off by yellow tape on the floor and the experimenter, in the absence of the supervisor, indicated to the children that they should not play in that area because it was not fully set up (adult inhibition), and then departed and did not reappear. On the second day, a photograph of children playing in the 'no-go' area was displayed in the room (peer disinhibition). It was found that the adult inhibition effect was much more marked than the peer disinhibition, although the latter became more influential on the second day for the second treatment group.

Other examples

Action research

Action research is discussed in Chapter 5 and it is noted there that it has some features of an experimental design. The approach is depicted in Figure 5.5 as comprising four steps and it can be seen that:

- steps 1 and 2, which identify and assess a social problem, can be seen as the pre-test observation, with selection of a treatment group implied;
- step 3, the campaign for and achievement of action, is the treatment;
- step 4, researching the results of the action, is the post-test observation.

One of the features of the experimental method is that the researcher controls the experimental process. In action research the researchers do not necessarily *control* the process but the philosophy of action research is that they are involved with and therefore seek to have an *influence* on the process.

Q methodology

Q methodology, in which research participants arrange cards containing statements into a predetermined distribution, is also described in Chapter 5. While the approach can be seen as merely an elaboration of a questionnaire-based survey, the design and manipulation of the card-sorting process indicates a level of control which reflects features of the experimental approach.

Qualitative methods

Paradoxically, much qualitative research which is presented as distinct from the classic, positivist scientific experimental method, notably those methodologies in which the researcher engages actively with the subjects – such as some participant observation and non-standardised interviewing – have features of the experimental method. The researcher's involvement can be seen as parallelling the 'treatment' in an experiment, although, of course, it is not in a controlled environment.

Training

Gianna Moscardo (1997) conducted experiments to assess the effectiveness of different exercises to train tourism professionals in *mindfulness*, defined as 'the active processing of information to create new categories, new definitions of situations, new routines for behaviour, and flexible and effective solutions to problems'. The study involved experimental and control groups. The experimental groups were exposed to a training exercise relating to the travel needs of seniors, followed by completion of a questionnaire on a possible holiday itinerary for seniors and also people with disabilities. The control group completed the same questionnaire but without the training exercise. The experimental and control group questionnaire responses were then compared to determine the effects of the training.

Mental mapping

Jim Walmsley and John Jenkins (1991) used a mental mapping medium (discussed as 'perceptual mapping' in Chapter 5) to explore tourists' knowledge of a tourist destination. Two groups of visitors carried out the same exercise, to draw a map of the Coffs Harbour resort, but subsequently completed different questionnaires related to 'locus of control' and active/inactive personality characteristics. The maps of the two groups were compared in terms of their identification of landmarks, districts and paths.

Physical models

In a study concerned with public reactions to reuse of heritage buildings, Neil Black (1990) arranged for 1:25 models to be made of four heritage buildings and photographed them in three situations: 'as is now', with a 'small change' and 'large change', the changes indicating adaptation for commercial use as cafes/restaurants. A group of study participants were asked to scale the photographs on a range of features and the results were compared with a theoretical classification based on a limited number of physical characteristics. Arguably this type of research might now be conducted using computer graphics.

Summary

Experimental methods are closely associated with the *positivist paradigm* and are consistent with the classic 'scientific' model of testing hypotheses and establishing cause-and-effect relationships. The essence of the experiment is that the researcher ideally controls all the relevant variables in the experiment. Selected variables are manipulated, while others are held constant and the effects on subjects are measured. Components of the experiment are: the treatment or experimental group; the control group; dependent variable; and the independent or treatment variable. The independent or treatment variable is manipulated during the experiment to examine its effect on the dependent variable. Typically, variables are measured before the treatment (pre-test) and after the treatment (post-test). Quasi-experimental designs vary this model by, for example, omitting a control group, omitting the pre-test or including more than one treatment group or treatment. Although *experimental methods* are usually associated with natural science and laboratories, it is possible to conduct some experiments in leisure and tourism contexts. Among these contexts are: discrete choice experiments (DCE); policy/management pilot or trial projects; experiments with research methods; pychological/perceptual studies, sport-related experiments and children's play.

Test questions

1. What are the defining characteristics of the experimental method?

2. Outline two examples of quasi-experimental models and indicate how they deviate from the classic experimental model.

3. Give three examples of contexts where experimental methods have been used in leisure or tourism research.

Exercises

1. Outline a true experimental research design to test the hypothesis that regular walking is a more effective way of achieving physical fitness than playing organised sport.

2. How could a leisure or tourism organisation set up an experiment to test the effectiveness of two forms of advertising? What elements of the 'classic' experimental design would need to be sacrificed? What type of quasi-experiment would this be?

Resources

- The classic work on experimental design for research is Campbell and Stanley (1972).

- Leisure: Havitz and Sell (1991).

- Discrete choice experiments/stated choice method: Cosper and Kinsley (1984), Kelly *et al.* (2007), Crouch and Louviere (2001), Louviere and Woodworth (1983), Louviere *et al.* (2000).

- Policy-related experiments: Batty (1977), Department of the Environment (1977).

- For a discussion of experimenter effects in research, see Rosenthal (1966).

- Research on alternative research methods: Burton (1971), Gitelson and Drogin (1992), Hammitt and McDonald (1982), Perdue and Botkin (1988).

12 Case study method

Introduction

A case study involves the study of an individual example – a case – of the phenomenon being researched. The aim is to seek to understand the phenomenon by studying one or more single examples. To some extent all social research is a case study at some level, since all research is geographically and temporally unique. Thus, for example, a survey of 500 visitors to a particular leisure or tourism site can be seen as a case study of the use of that site, and even a nation-wide survey of the leisure or tourism activities of thousands of people in a Western country carried out in 2010, could be viewed, in one sense, as a case study of the activities of the population of one affluent country in the early twenty-first century.

The case study *research method* should be distinguished from other uses of the concept of cases, including in the law, where it refers to an individual crime, arrest and trial and may be important in setting precedents, and in medicine, where cases refer to individual patients. In both these examples, the case – either live or as a written record – becomes a vehicle for teaching and in the business sector this is its exclusive use, the most well-known example being the Harvard Business School cases (Harvard Business School, nd).

This chapter considers in turn: the definition of the case study method; the merits of the case study method; types of case study; data collection and data analysis. A number of examples of case study research in leisure and tourism contexts are then presented.

Definitions

What is the case study method?

John Gerring (2007: 19–20) defines a *case* as 'a spatially delimited phenomenon (a unit) observed at a single point in time or over some period of time' and a *case study* as 'the intensive study of a single case'. He goes on to observe:

> Case study research may incorporate several cases, that is, multiple case studies. However, at a certain point it will no longer be possible to investigate those cases so intensively. At the point where the emphasis of a study shifts from the individual case to a sample of cases, we shall say that a study is *cross-case*. Evidently the distinction between case study and cross-case study is a matter of degree. The fewer cases there are, and the more intensively they are studied, the more the work merits the appellation 'case study'. . . . All empirical work may be classified as either case study (comprising one or a few cases) or cross-case study (involving many cases). *(Gerring, 2007: 20)*

Thus, there is a continuum between the case study method and cross-case research rather than a sharp line of separation. Gerring hopes that his book

> will contribute to breaking down the rather artificial boundaries that have separated these genres within the social science. Properly constituted, there is no reason that case study results cannot be synthesized with results gained from cross-case analysis, and vice versa. *(Gerring, 2007: 13)*

What the case study method is not

The fact that research projects using the case study method typically involve only one or a few cases suggests some similarity with qualitative research methods and in some texts the case study method is subsumed under 'qualitative methods' (e.g. Finn *et al.*, 2000: 81) but, as leading authority Robert Yin states,

> the case study method is not just a form of 'qualitative research', even though it may be recognised among the array of qualitative research choices. . . . Some case study research goes beyond being a type of qualitative research, by using a mix of quantitative and qualitative evidence. In addition, case studies need not always include the direct and detailed observational evidence marked by other forms of 'qualitative research'. *(Yin, 2009: 19)*

In fact, the use of a variety of types of data and types of analysis can be said to be a key feature of the case study method.

Some commentators (for example, Zikmund, 1997: 108) have implied that the case study method is used only for 'exploratory' purposes but this is not the only possible purpose: as Yin (2009: 6) asserts, 'case studies are far from being only an exploratory strategy'. They can be the basis of substantive research projects in their own right, as the case studies listed later in the chapter demonstrate.

Scale

Cases can consist of individuals, communities (villages, islands, cities), whole countries, organisations and companies, places and projects or events. These demographic and geographic dimensions are illustrated in Figure 12.1.

If a study involves just an individual or small group, such as a family, the methodological options are generally limited and are likely to be mostly qualitative (although studying an individual or small group over time could involve quantitative data). As we move up in scale the range of methods increases, both in terms of primary and secondary sources, including, for example, the use of information on a site and its environment and history and the social and demographic characteristics of the population of a community or country. Thus the sheer variety of types of data and types of data analysis would offer a 'rich' description of the *case* – the site or the country and its people. Furthermore, a case study at one level (for example, of a community or an organisation) could involve a variety of quantitative and qualitative methods and data sources involving components at lower levels (for example, questionnaire surveys of residents or employees, or financial and membership data).

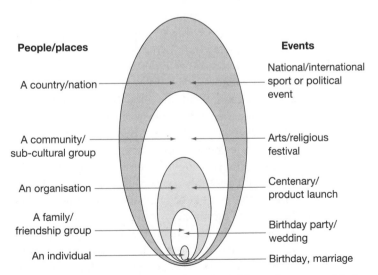

Figure 12.1 The case study method: demographic and geographic levels

Validity and reliability

Arguably, the multiple methodologies and data sources used by the typical case study method offer the possibility of achieving as high a level of internal validity as any single method discussed elsewhere in this book, since the limitations of one method or data source, as discussed in each of the previous five chapters, may be overcome by drawing on the qualities of another.

External validity – the extent to which findings apply beyond the specific case study – may also be aided by the use of multiple data sources, such as the use of secondary data from the wider population for comparative purposes and to establish the extent to which the case study is typical or unique – drawing on cross-case research as suggested by John Gerring above. Because, in case study research, only one or a few cases are examined, the method does not seek to produce findings which are generally or universally representative. Thus a case study of an organisation does not include statements of the kind: 'this explains the behaviour of organisation X, therefore it will explain or predict the behaviour of the 50,000 similar organisations in similar situations or a significant proportion of them'. However, if research has *no* implications beyond the particular case at a particular time and place, there would be little point in conducting it. Referring again to Gerring:

> To conduct a case study implies that one has also conducted cross-case analysis, or at least thought about the broader set of cases. Otherwise, it is impossible for an author to answer the defining question of all case study research: what is this a case *of*? *(Gerring, 2007: 13)*

The relationship between case study research and the world beyond the case itself can be mediated by theory and policy issues, so conclusions might be in the form: 'this explains the behaviour of organisation X, which is inconsistent with theoretically based expectations, suggesting the possible need for some modification to the theory', or: 'this explains the behaviour of organisation X, suggesting that other types of organisation might be examined to see whether the explanation applies more widely'. Thus, while case study research may not result in generalisations about a population, it can have valid things to say in relation to theory in the case of explanatory research and in relation to policy in the case of evaluative research. Thus a number of scenarios can be envisaged in regard to theory and policy, as shown in Figure 12.2.

Using the typology discussed in the first chapter of this book, in the case of *explanatory* research a case study can be used to *test the applicability of an existing theory*. This might occur in situations where a theoretical proposition has never been tested empirically or where it has not been tested in a particular environment. Thus in leisure studies many propositions have in fact been developed using empirical evidence from sport, so a case study of non-sporting leisure activity could be used to test the universality of such propositions. Similarly,

Type of research	Research purpose	Case study outcomes
Explanatory research	Testing a single existing theory	Case study *confirms* applicability of theory in at least one setting or, alternatively, *raises doubts* as to applicability of theory and suggests modification or alternatives.
	Testing alternative/ competing theories	Case study demonstrates that one theory works better than the other in a particular situation, or that neither works universally.
	Developing theory where none exists	The task of the case study is to suggest *possible* theory.
Evaluative research	Testing effectiveness of a single policy	Case study *confirms* effectiveness of the policy in at least one setting or, alternatively, *raises doubts* as to effectiveness of the policy and possibly suggests modification or alternatives.
	Testing alternative/ competing policies	Case study demonstrates that one policy is more effective than the other in a particular situation, or that neither works universally.
	Establishing need for policy measures	The case study outlines the current problems and their likely causes and suggests the need for policy action.

Figure 12.2 Case study research: theory and policy

much tourism research is concerned with travel to varied places of interest in search of 'authenticity', so such ideas could be tested in the context of different types of holiday – for example, a case study of a caravan site visited by the same families at the same time every year. If the theory is found to be non-applicable in a case study situation, this does not necessarily 'disprove' it, but can raise doubts as to its universality.

In the case of policy-related *evaluative* research the corresponding research task would be to test the effectiveness of a policy or type of management practice. For example, while the impact of promotional/advertising policy could be examined by use of aggregate national statistics on customer/participant numbers, it could also be examined by means of a case study of the experience in one or two communities or neighbourhoods, particularly if the results of the national statistical analysis were unclear or indicated an apparent lack of impact.

Reliability, in the sense of exact replication of research, is, of course, impossible in case study research, but the accumulation of evidence from a number of case studies may build a consensus around the findings of a programme of case study research and other evidence.

Merits of the case study approach

The particular merits of the case study method can be summarised as follows.

- the ability to place people, organisations, events and experiences in their social and historical context;

- the ability to treat the subject of study as a whole, rather than abstracting a limited set of pre-selected features;

- multiple methods – triangulation – are implicit and seen as a strength;

- the single, or limited number of, cases offers a manageable data collection task when resources are limited;

- flexibility in data collection strategy allows researchers to adapt their research strategy as the research proceeds;

- there is no necessity to generalise to a defined wider population.

Design of case studies

While the case study method offers flexibility, it does not absolve the researcher from undertaking the usual initial preparatory steps – specifying research questions, reviewing the literature, establishing a theoretical framework and determining data needs and sources – as discussed in Chapter 3. As in any research, it is important to plan to avoid the problem of having collected a lot of data and not knowing what to do with it. The amount of flexibility offered is rarely unlimited – for example, in some circumstances it may be possible to interview people, or ask them for data, a number of times as new issues emerge in the course of the research, but in other circumstances this may not be possible.

In addition to the general guidance on the planning of research projects set out in Chapter 3, three specific issues are discussed here: defining the unit of analysis; selection of cases and data gathering.

Defining the unit of analysis

While it might be a somewhat obvious point to make, it is necessary to be clear about the *unit of analysis* in case study research. For example, if the unit of analysis – the case – is a single leisure or tourism facility owned by a large organisation, it is important to keep the analysis at the facility level. Thus, for example, the policies and practices of the parent organisation are inevitably relevant, but they are 'given' influences on the facility management, so the research is not *about* the parent organisation. Conversely, data on the staff of the facility will form part of the research, but only in so far as they contribute to an understanding of the operation of the facility as a unit.

Selecting the case(s)

Of key importance in the case study method is the selection of the case or cases. This is, of course, comparable to sampling in a quantitative study. Four types of case selection can be considered.

- *Purposive:* Where multiple cases are involved, the selection of cases is likely to be purposive – for example, in selecting a range of firms of similar or different sizes, in the same or different industries, in comparable or contrasting geographical locations or of similar or contrasting levels of profitability.

- *Illustrative:* Often the case(s) will be deliberately chosen to increase the likelihood of illustrating a particular proposition – for example, if the research is concerned with leadership success, then *successful* organisations with high-profile leaders may be deliberately chosen.

- *Typical/atypical:* The case may be chosen because it is believed to be typical of the phenomenon being studied, or it may be deliberately chosen as an extreme or atypical case. Thus, a study examining the secrets of success in a particular industry might well select the *most* successful company for study.

- *Pragmatic/opportunistic:* In some cases the selection of cases may be pragmatic – for example, when the researcher has ready access to a company, possibly because he or she is an employee of it.

Whatever the rationale for the selection of a case or cases, it should be clearly articulated in the research report, and the implications of the selection discussed.

Data gathering

A case study project generally uses a number of data sources and data gathering techniques, including: the use of documentary evidence; secondary data analysis; in-depth interviews; questionnaire surveys; observation; and participant observation. The process of selecting data sources and collection techniques is the same as in any other research process, as discussed in Chapter 3. In that chapter, the idea that different data sources might be used in the same project to address different research questions or aspects of research questions is discussed. It is noted that all data collection should be linked to the research questions – even in cases where the research questions are being modified as the research progresses.

When a number of disparate data types and sources are involved, two other issues should be born in mind:

- *consistency of the unit of analysis* – if, for example, participation data are involved, it is important that the data relate to the same geographical unit;
- *temporal consistency* – ideally all data should relate to the same time-period – this is related to the issue of the unit of analysis, since reorganisation – of, for example, a corporate body or administrative boundaries – can result in changes in the size, composition and functions of organisations over time.

Analysis

To the extent that the design of the case study, or parts of it, resembles that of more formalised research projects, with fixed research questions and corresponding data collection and analysis procedures, the analysis process will tend to be deductive in nature; the data analysis will be designed to address the questions posed in advance. But a case study can involve qualitative methods with a recursive, more inductive format, as discussed in Chapter 15. Indeed, the flexibility of the whole case study approach suggests a more inductive approach. Thus the discovery, in the course of the research, of a previously unknown source of information might lead the researcher to ask the question: can this data add something to the research? While the new data source might help in addressing the existing research questions in unanticipated ways, it could also suggest whole new research questions.

Three main methods of analysis are outlined by both Burns (1994: 324–5) and Yin (2009: 106–18):

- *pattern matching* – relating the features of the case to what might be expected from some existing theory;
- *explanation building* – often an iterative process whereby a logical/causal explanation of what is discovered is developed by to-and-fro referencing between theory/explanation and data;
- *time-series analysis* – explanations are developed on the basis of observing change over time.

In fact, all forms of analysis are possible within the context of a case study. It is the pulling together of the results of analyses of different sorts to form coherent conclusions which presents the challenge.

Case studies in practice

Four case studies of case studies conclude the chapter. The case studies provide brief details on each study, but further details can followed up in the references provided.

Case study 12.1 revisits the Rowntree and Lavers's *English Life and Leisure* study previously examined for its qualitative content (Case study 9.1), but here noting the use of individual interview-based *case histories* of the leisure lives of individuals and a secondary/documentary source-based case study of a small town and its leisure infrastructure.

Case study 12.1   *English Life and Leisure*

Case study 9.1 refers to Seebohm Rowntree and G. R. Lavers' (1951) study of *English Life and Leisure*, the earliest large-scale study of leisure in Britain, which began in 1947 during the post-World War II period of austerity. The study used a primarily qualitative approach which involved the case study method in two ways.

First, the bulk of the study involved interviews with almost 1000 individuals in 11 cities and 220 of these are reported in a remarkable 121-page chapter of 'case histories', as described in Case study 9.1. Information from these and the rest of the interviews are then drawn on for the subsequent chapters on specific leisure activities.

Second, the report also includes a single chapter which is a case study of one small town, High Wycombe in Buckinghamshire, located between London and Oxford and with a population of 40,000. It is a purely descriptive account of the 30 or so social and special-interest clubs, cinema, library, dancing, music and drama facilities, outdoor recreation/sporting facilities and clubs, and a range of religious-based leisure facilities and organisations. Reports of the activities of the nine coach operators in the town offer an insight into day trips and holidays at this time:

> One of the largest companies sends on the average 20 coaches a week to London from October to the end of April. In 8 weeks they sent 100 coaches to London filled with people going to see 'Skating Varieties'. They took 32 coach-loads of people to see a fight for the heavy-weight world championship. . . . During June 1949, one of the largest companies sent 367 coach-loads of people to the coast and to attractions in various towns. *(Rowntree and Lavers, 1951: 403)*

Case study 12.2 presents a history of events over a ten-year period, in which the Euro Disney theme park and resort, north of Paris, was conceived, planned, developed and opened, up to its third year of operation, when it made its first profit, following a series of losses. Based on participant observation, interviews and secondary sources, it covers a wide range of development, design, marketing and financial issues.

Case study 12.2   Euro Disneyland

Andrew Lainsbury's (2000) book, *Once Upon an American Dream*, is based on his experiences in a year spent working as a general hand (and a period playing Prince Charming) in the Euro Disneyland theme park and resort, north of Paris. Opened in 1992 amid much publicity and controversy over its appropriateness and viability in a European context, the development had a chequered history in its early years. The book has five main chapters, dealing with: 1. the development of the idea of a European Disneyland and the political activity of selecting and securing a site; 2. the design, or 'imagineering', of the project; 3. marketing of the project; 4. the financial struggles of the early years; and 5. the global Disney operation.

The book is written in a popular, narrative style, but is underpinned by extensive endnotes and references. The historical accounts draw mostly on press coverage which, given the high profile of the Walt Disney Company, was extensive. Use is also made of the considerable body of literature on Disney, which comprises a mixture of popular and academic books, and papers in journals in such fields as cultural, media and American studies.

Numerous themes emerge in each of the chapters. Thus Chapter 1 provides an insight into the common phenomenon of countries and communities competing to attract industry and jobs, the financial and other 'deals' that are struck to attract enterprises, and the 'Not in My Back Yard' (NIMBY) politics of communities living in the immediate neighbourhood of proposed projects – in France the Disney project led to the establishment of the 'Association for the Protection of People Concerned by the Euro Disney Development'. Chapter 1 also discusses the clash of cultures between 'old Europe' and 'new America', an increasingly salient issue in an era of globalisation.

Much of Chapter 2 is design-oriented rather than business-oriented, but the 'vertical integration' practice of Walt Disney Company in developing not only the theme park but also the ancillary hotels and golf courses – which it failed to do in the original Disneyland in California – is outlined. Chapter 3 outlines the complex strategy for marketing the project, both before and after its opening.

The development made substantial losses in its early years and Chapter 4 documents the various measures taken to 'rescue' the project by improving income and attendance, cutting costs and reorganising its finances. This resulted in the achievement of the first profits in 1995. The final chapter examines briefly the international development of Disney theme parks and the growth of competitors.

While the book does not present 'hard' research data, it uses a variety of perspectives, issues and data sources to explore the saga of Euro Disneyland and therefore presents a valid case study of a major transnational leisure/tourism investment project.

Case study 12.3 summarises research by Victoria Carty (1997) on a single aspect of the behaviour of a single organisation, the sports apparel multi-national Nike. She uses a number of data sources but in particular illustrates the use of content analysis of print, poster and television advertising. The study focuses on the issue of whether Nike's rhetoric about treating women as respected customers is followed through in their advertising. We have discussed above, the proposition that, while conclusions from case studies can, strictly speaking, apply only to the 'case' involved in the study, they would be of limited use if they did not at least raise the possibility of wider implications. Here the implication is that Nike may not be unique among multinational companies in its exploitative approach to women.

Case study 12.3   Nike, advertising and women

Victoria Carty's (1997) study of the Nike sportswear company draws on a number of information sources and theoretical perspectives to explore and critique the *modus operandi* of the company, particularly in regard to its treatment of women. The main information sources are existing accounts of the development of Nike from the academic and popular literature and examples of Nike advertising on television and in print. Theoretical perspectives include theories of globalisation and postmodernism and the concept of 'global commodity chains', which geographically trace manufactured products from the point of consumption to the point of manufacture.

The thesis of the study is that Nike's advertising aimed at Western women consumers projects an image of the independent woman, while its manufacturing practices exploit Third World women who make up the majority of its manufacturing labour employed at low wages and working in poor conditions in its own factories and those of its sub-contractors. The research seeks to demonstrate the validity of well-established theoretical frameworks which are critical of the role of multinational global corporations, particularly in the production of fashion products where the costs of manufacturing are heavily outweighed by the costs of marketing and the retail mark-up. Thus, using a case study of a single firm, the study seeks to 'illustrate the interdependencies between production and consumption, or economics and culture, as organized in the global economy'.

Derek Wynne's (1998) *Leisure, Lifestyle and the New Middle Class* is a study of some 250 residents of a new middle-class housing estate using a questionnaire survey, in-depth interviews and ethnographic/participant observation methods, focusing on class situation and lifestyle groups and their distinctive pattern of use of the estate's leisure centre/club.

Case study 12.4   *Leisure, Lifestyle and the New Middle Class*

Derek Wynne's (1998) *Leisure, Lifestyle and the New Middle Class: a Case Study* demonstrates clearly the use of multiple methods in a case study. It is a study of the residents of 'The Heath', a new middle-class southern England development of some 250 dwellings with its own leisure centre/club. The author lived in the development for three years and based his research on a questionnaire survey of all residents, in-depth interviews with selected residents and participant observation/ethnography. He uses the theoretical frameworks developed by Pierre Bourdieu in his book *Distinction* (1984) to explore the social class situation and lifestyles of the 500 or so adult residents of The Heath. While the current occupational and educationally shaped social class positions of the residents were similar, their origins (working-class or middle-class parents) differed and were reflected in differing leisure patterns and cultural states. And these differences were further reflected in the differences between two distinct user groups of the leisure centre/club: the 'drinkers' and the 'sporters'. Summaries of aspects of the case study can be found in Wynne (1986, 1990).

Summary

This chapter considers the case study method which involves the study of a single case, or a small number of cases, on the phenomenon of interest, which contrasts with other methods discussed in the book which generally involve *cross-case* methods. But cross-case research may be embedded in a case study – for example, a study of a single community or tourist destination may involve a questionnaire-based survey of residents or visitors respectively. Thus case studies often use multiple methods, including any or all of the other methods discussed in the book. The chapter examines tasks in the design and conduct of case studies, including definition of the unit of analysis and selection of cases. Four case studies of contrasting leisure and tourism case studies complete the chapter.

Test questions

1. Define case study research and cross-case research.

2. Discuss the external validity challenges involved in case study research.

3. What are the five approaches to selecting cases discussed in the chapter?

4. Three approaches to case study analysis have been suggested in the literature: name and describe these approaches.

Exercises

1. Consider a leisure or tourism facility/attraction known to you and outline the elements which might be involved in setting up a case study to explore the reasons for its success.

2. Read one of the example studies listed in the Resources section below and identify the range of data sources used, methods of analysis and how the various types of information are drawn together to draw conclusions.

Resources

- General texts: Yin (2009), Bromley (1986), Burns (1994: 312–31), Rose (2000), Stake (1995).

- In leisure studies: Henderson (1991: 88–90).

- In tourism studies: Xiao and Smith (2005).

- Examples:
  - individuals: Saunders and Turner (1987), Rapoport and Rapoport (1975)
  - communities: Rowntree and Lavers (1951, ch. 14) – see Case Studies 9.1, 12.1 and 12.4
  - whole countries: Williams and Shaw (1988), Bramham *et al.* (1993)
  - organisations and companies: Harris and Leiper (1995)
  - places and projects: Murphy (1991), Hayllar *et al.* (2008)
  - events: Mules (2004)
  - a sporting/social club in a residential community: Wynne (1986, 1998)
  - sport and social exclusion: four case studies: Collins (2003)
  - city governance and sport: Henry and Paramio Salcines (1998)
  - city governance and tourism: Long (2000)
  - tourism planning: Murphy (1991).

13 Sampling: quantitative and qualitative

Introduction

This chapter is an introduction to the principles of sampling and addresses the idea of sampling; samples and populations; representativeness and random sampling; sample sizes and their consequences in terms of 'confidence intervals; weighting; and sampling for qualitative research.

The idea of sampling

In most survey research and in some observational research it is necessary to *sample*. Mainly because of costs, it is not usually possible to gather data from *all* the people, organisations or other entities which are the focus of the research. For example, if the aim of a research project is to study the leisure patterns or holiday-making behaviour of the adult population of a country, no one has the resources to conduct interviews with the millions of individuals who make up the adult population. The only time when the whole population is interviewed is every five or ten years, when the government statistical agency conducts the official Census of Population – and the cost of collecting and analysing the data runs into tens of millions of pounds or dollars.

At a more modest level, it would be virtually impossible to conduct face-to-face interviews with all the users of an urban park or a busy tourist area since, in busy periods, many hundreds might enter the site and leave in a short space of time. It might be possible to hand respondent-completion questionnaires to all users but, as discussed in Chapter 10, this approach has disadvantages in terms of quality and level of response. The usual procedure is to interview a sample – a proportion – of the users.

In Chapter 8, on observational methods, the problems of continuous counting of numbers of users of leisure and tourism sites were discussed and it was noted that often available resources demand that sample counts be undertaken – that is, the numbers entering the site or present at the site are counted on a sample of occasions.

Sampling has implications for the way data are collected, analysed and interpreted.

Samples and populations

One item of terminology should be clarified initially. The total category of subjects which is the focus of attention in a particular research project is known as the *population*. A *sample* is selected from the population. The use of the term 'population' makes obvious sense when dealing with communities of people – for instance when referring to the population of Britain or the population of London. But in social research the term also applies in other instances; for example, the visitors to a resort over the course of a year constitute the *population of resort visitors*; and the users of a sports facility are the *population of users*.

The term 'population' can also be applied to non-human phenomena – for example, if a study of the physical characteristics of Australia's beaches found that there were 10,000 beaches in all, from which 100 were to be selected for study, then the 10,000 beaches can be referred to as the *population of beaches* and the 100 selected for study would be the sample. In some texts the word *universe* is used instead of population.

If a sample is to be selected for study then two questions arise:

1. What procedures must be followed to ensure that the sample is representative of the population?

2. How large should the sample be?

These two questions are related, since, other things being equal, the larger the sample, the more chance it has of being representative.

Representativeness

A sample which is not representative of the population is described as *biased*. The whole process of sample selection must be aimed at *minimising* bias in the sample. The researcher seeks to achieve representativeness and to minimise bias by adopting the principles of *random sampling*. This is not the most helpful term since it implies that the process is not methodical. This is far from the case – random does not mean haphazard! The meaning of random sampling is as follows:

> In random sampling all members of the population have an equal chance of inclusion in the sample.

For example, if a sample of 1000 people is to be selected from a population of 10,000 then every member of the population must have a 1 in 10 chance of being selected. In practice most sampling methods involving human beings can only approximate this rule. The problems of achieving random sampling vary with the type of survey and are discussed below in relation to: household surveys; telephone surveys; site/user/visitor surveys; street surveys and quota sampling; mail surveys; and complex events/destinations.

Sampling for household surveys

The problem of achieving randomness can be examined in the case of a household survey of the adult residents of a country. If the adult population of the country is, say, 40 million and we wish to interview a sample of 1000, then every member of the adult population should have a 1 in 40,000 chance of being included in the sample. How would this be achieved? Ideally there should be a complete list of all 40 million of the country's adults – their names should be written on slips of paper and placed in a revolving drum, physically or electronically, as in a lottery draw, and 1000 names should be drawn out. Each time a choice is made everyone has a 1 in 40 million chance of selection – since this happens 1000 times, each person has a total of 1000 in 40 million or 1 in 40,000 chance of selection.

This would be a very labourious process. Surely a close approximation would be to forget the slips of paper and the drum and choose every 40,000th name on the list. But where should the starting point be? It should be some random point between 1 and 40,000. There are published 'tables of random numbers', which can also be produced from computers, which can be used for this purpose. Strictly speaking the whole sample should be chosen using random numbers, since this would approximate most closely to the 'names in a drum' procedure.

In practice, however, such a list of the population being studied rarely exists. The nearest thing to it would be the electoral registers of all the constituencies in the country. Electoral registers are fairly comprehensive because adults are required by law to register, but they are not perfect. Highly mobile/homeless people are often not included; many who live in multi-occupied premises are omitted. The physical task of selecting the names from such a list would be immense, but there is another disadvantage with this approach. If every 40,000th voter on the registers were selected the sample would be scattered throughout the country. The cost of visiting every one of those selected for a face-to-face interview would be very high.

In practice therefore, organisations conducting national surveys compromise by employing 'multi-stage' sampling and 'clustered' sampling. Multi-stage means that sampling is not done directly but by stages. For example, if the country had, say, four states or regions the proposed sample of 1000 would be sub-divided in the same proportions as the populations of the regions. Within each region local government areas would then be divided into rural and urban and, say, four urban and two rural areas would be selected at random – with the intention of selecting appropriate sub-samples, of perhaps 25, 40 or 50 from each area. These sub-samples could be selected from electoral registers, or streets could be selected and individuals contacted by calling on, say, every fifth house in the street. In any one street interviewers may be instructed to interview, say, 10 or 15 people. By interviewing 'clusters' of people in this way costs are minimised. But care must be taken not to reduce the number of clusters too much since then the full range of population and area types would not be included.

Once a house has been selected for interview a procedure must be devised for selecting a respondent from the household members; this is discussed in relation to telephone surveys below.

Sampling for telephone surveys

The traditional process for sampling for telephone surveys from the public residential telephone directories and the move to computer aided telephone interviewing (CATI) methods is described in Chapter 9. Some of the emerging difficulties with this method, given the rise of mobile telephones, are also discussed in Chapter 9, threaten the representativeness of samples. Insofar as the resultant bias is age-related, this can be corrected by weighting, but if it reflects lifestyle differences, not much can be done about it. The printed or electronic directory is close to the list of people on the electoral register, as discussed above, except that, since there is typically only one land-line telephone per house, the list effectively refers to households rather than individuals. As with household surveys, it is therefore necessary to use some procedure for selecting a respondent from among household members.

If, in face-to-face household surveys or telephone surveys, the interviewer were to interview the person who happened to answer the door or the telephone this could result in bias, depending on local customs as to who in the household is more likely to answer the door or the phone. There is of course invariably a lower age limit, so persons under the prescribed age will not be selected. A typical procedure to 'randomise' the process of choosing among eligible household members is to ask to interview the person whose birthday is nearest to the interview date.

Sampling for site/user/visitor surveys

Conditions at leisure/tourism sites or facilities vary enormously, depending on the type and size of facility, the season, day of the week, time of day or the weather. This discussion can only therefore be in general terms. To ensure randomness, and therefore representativeness, it is necessary for interviewers to adhere to strict rules. Site interviewers operate in two ways. First, the interviewer can be stationary and the users mobile – for instance when the interviewer is located near the entrance and visitors are interviewed as they enter or leave. Second, the user may be stationary and the interviewer mobile – for instance when interviewing beach users or users of a picnic site.

In the case of stationary interviewers, the instructions they should follow should be something like:

> When one interview is complete, check through the questionnaire for completeness and legibility. When you are ready with a new questionnaire stop the next person to enter the gate. Stick strictly to this rule and do not select interviewees on any other basis.

The important thing is that interviewers should not avoid certain types of user by picking and choosing whom to interview. Ideally there should be some rule such as interviewing every fifth person to come through the door/gate but, since users will enter at a varying rate and interviews vary in length, this is rarely possible.

In the case of stationary users and a mobile interviewer, the interviewer should be given a certain route to follow on the site and be instructed to interview, say, every fifth group they pass.

Where interviewers are employed, the success of the process will depend on the training given to the interviewers and this could involve observation of them at work to ensure that they are following the rules.

As indicated in Chapter 10, sampling in site/visitor surveys leads inevitably to variation in the proportion of users interviewed at different times of the day. Where users tend to stay for long periods – as in the case of beaches – this may not matter, but where people stay for shorter periods and where the type of user may vary during the course of the day or week, the sample will probably be unrepresentative – that is, biased. This should be corrected by weighting as indicated at the end of the chapter.

When surveys involve the handing out of questionnaires for respondent-completion – as, for example, in a number of tourist en route/hotel surveys – unless field staff are available to encourage their completion and return, respondents will be self-selected. Busy hotel or leisure facility receptionists can rarely be relied upon to do a thorough job in handing out and collecting in questionnaires, unless the survey is a priority of the management and therefore closely supervised. Normally a significant proportion of the population will fail to return the questionnaire – but it is unlikely that this self-selection process will be random. For example, people with difficulties in reading or writing English, or people who are in a hurry, may fail to return their questionnaires. Those with 'something to say', whether positive or negative, are more likely to return their questionnaires than people who are apathetic or just content with the service, thus giving a misleading impression of the proportion of users who have strong opinions. Thus it can be seen that this type of 'uncontrolled' survey is at risk of introducing serious bias into the sample and should therefore be avoided if at all possible.

Sampling for street surveys and quota sampling

Although the technique of quota sampling can be used in other situations, it is most common in street surveys. The street survey is usually seen as a means of contacting a representative sample of the community but in fact it can also be seen as a sort of 'site survey', the site being the shopping area. As such, a street survey which involved a random sample of the users of the street would be representative of the users of the shopping area rather than of the community as a whole – in a suburban shopping centre it would, for instance, have a high proportion of retired people or full-time home/child carers.

If the aim is in fact to obtain a representative sample of the whole community, then to achieve this interviewers are given 'quotas' of people of different types to contact, the quotas being based on information about the community which is available from the census. For example, if the census indicates that 12 per cent of the population is retired, then interviewers would be required to include 12 retired people in every 100 interviewed. Once interviewers have filled their quota in certain age/gender groups, they are required to become more selective in whom they approach in order to fill the gaps in their quotas.

The quota method can only be used when background information on the target population is known – as with community surveys. In most user surveys this information is not known so the strict following of random sampling procedures must be relied upon.

Sampling for mail surveys

The initial list of people to whom the questionnaire is sent in a mail survey may be the whole population (in the statistical sense) or a sample. If a sample is selected, it can usually be done completely randomly because the mailing list for the whole population is usually available.

The respondents to a mail survey form a sample; it is not randomly selected but self-selected. This introduces sources of bias similar to those in the uncontrolled self-completion site surveys discussed above. There is little that can be done about this except to make every effort to achieve a high response rate. In some cases information may be available on the population which can be used to weight the sample to correct for certain sources of bias – for example, in the case of a national survey the sample could be weighted to correct for any geographical bias in response because the geographical distribution of the population would be known. If, for example, the survey is of an occupational association and the proportion of members in various grades is known from records, then this can be used for weighting purposes. But ultimately, mail surveys suffer from an unknown and uncorrectable element of bias caused by non-response. All surveys experience non-response of course, but the problem is greater with mail surveys because the level of non-response is usually greater.

Sampling for complex events and destination studies

As indicated in Chapter 5, events with multiple ticketed and non-ticketed sites and studies of tourist destinations present particular challenges for the researcher, not least in the task of sampling. Typically research is required to provide information on a number of matters, including: the number of visitors to the destination/host community; number of visitors and locals attending individual sites and individual events; and socio-demographic profile, expenditure patterns and satisfactions/evaluation of visitors and local participants. This information will be gathered by one or more of the methods discussed above. The sampling task, then, involves considering the relevant protocols discussed above. In addition, secondary data sources, such as ticket sales records, will be drawn upon. The unique challenge, therefore, is not the sampling and data collection *per se* but combining data from different sources to provide estimates for the whole event, particularly when an event involves large non-ticketed components and where a destination attracts significant numbers of day trippers in addition to staying visitors.

Sample size

There is a popular misconception that the size of a sample should be decided on the basis of its relationship to the size of the population – for example that a sample should be, say, 5 per cent or 10 per cent of the population. *This is not so.* What is important is the absolute size of the sample, regardless of the size of the population. For example, a sample size of 1000 is equally valid, provided proper sampling procedures have been followed, whether it is a sample of the British adults (population 50 million), the residents of London (population 7 million), the residents of Brighton (population 100,000) or the students of a University (population, say, 10,000).

It is worth repeating that it is the *absolute size of the sample* which is important, not its size relative to the population. This rule applies in all cases, except when the population itself is small – this exception and its implications are discussed later in the chapter.

On what criteria therefore should a sample size be determined? The criteria are basically threefold: the required level of precision in the results; the level of detail in the proposed analysis; and the available budget. These issues are discussed in turn below. In addition, some comments are offered on application of confidence intervals to population estimates and sample size for small populations.

Level of precision – confidence intervals

The idea of the level of precision can be explained as follows. The question to be posed is: to what extent do the findings from a sample precisely reflect the population from which it is drawn? For example, if a survey was designed to investigate holiday-making and it was found that 50 per cent of a sample of 500 people took a holiday in the previous year, how sure can we be that this finding – this *statistic* – is true of the population as a whole? How sure can we be, despite all efforts taken to choose a representative sample, that the sample is not in fact unrepresentative, and that the real percentage of holiday-taking in the population is in fact, say, 70 per cent or 30 per cent?

This question is answered in terms of probabilities. How sure can we be, having taken all appropriate measures to choose a representative sample, that the sample is indeed representative and that the percentage of holiday-taking in the population is not infact, say, 70 per cent or 30 per cent? On the other hand, the *probability* of coming up with, say, 48 or 49 per cent or 51 or 52 per cent would, one would think, be fairly high. The probability of coming up with 70 or 30 per cent would be somewhere in between.

Statisticians have examined the likely pattern of distribution of all possible samples of various sizes drawn from populations of various sizes and established that, when a sample is randomly drawn, the sample value of a statistic has a certain probability of being within a certain range either side of the real value of the statistic. That range is plus or minus twice the 'standard error' of the statistic. The size of the standard error depends on the size of the sample and is unrelated to the size of the population. A properly drawn sample has a 95 per cent chance of producing a statistic with a value which is within two standard errors of the true population value so, conversely, there is a 95 per cent chance that the true population value lies within two standard errors of the sample statistic. This means that, if a hundred samples of the same size were drawn, in 95 cases we would expect the value of the statistic to be within two standard errors of the population value; in five cases we would expect it to be outside the range. Since we do not generally actually know the population value, we have to rely on this theoretical statement of probability about the likely accuracy of our finding: we have a 95 per cent chance of being approximately right and a 5 per cent chance of being wrong.

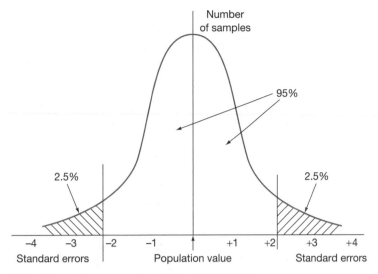

Figure 13.1 Normal curve and confidence intervals

This 'two standard errors' range is referred to as the '95 per cent confidence interval' of a statistic. The relationships between standard errors and level of probability is a property of the 'normal curve' – a bell-shaped curve with certain mathematical properties, which we are not able to pursue here. The idea of a normal curve and 95 per cent confidence intervals is illustrated in Figure 13.1. The general idea of probabilities related to the properties of certain types of 'distribution' is pursued in more detail in Chapter 17.

Tables have been drawn up by statisticians which give the confidence intervals for various statistics for various sample sizes, as shown in Table 13.1. Down the side of the table are various sample sizes, ranging from 50 to 10,000. Across the top of the table are statistics which one might find from a survey – for example 20 per cent play tennis. The table shows 20 per cent together with 80 per cent because if it is found that 20 per cent of the sample play tennis, then clearly 80 per cent *do not* play tennis. Any conclusion about the accuracy of the statistic 20 per cent also applies to the corresponding statistic 80 per cent. In the body of the table are the *confidence intervals*.

An example of how the table is interpreted is as follows: suppose we have a sample size of 500 and we have a finding that 30 per cent of the sample have a certain characteristic – say, have been away on holiday in the previous summer (so 70 per cent have *not* been away on holiday). Reading off the table, for a sample size of 500, we find that a finding of 30 per cent (and 70 per cent) is subject to a confidence interval of plus or minus 4.0. So we can be fairly certain that the population value lies in the range 26.0 per cent to 34.0 per cent.

An important point should be noted about these confidence intervals: to halve the confidence interval it is necessary to quadruple the sample size. In the example above, a sample of 2000 people (four times the original sample) would give a confidence interval of plus or minus 2.0 per cent (half the original confidence interval). The cost of increasing the precision of surveys by increasing the sample is therefore very high.

Table 13.1   Confidence intervals related to sample size

Sample size	Percentages found from sample ('results')							
	50%	40 or 60%	30 or 70%	20 or 80%	10 or 90%	5 or 95%	2 or 98%	1 or 99%
	Confidence intervals (± %)							
50	±13.9	±13.6	±12.7	±11.1	±8.3	*	*	*
80	±11.0	±10.7	±10.0	±8.8	±6.6	*	*	*
100	±9.8	±9.6	±9.0	±7.8	±5.9	±4.3	*	*
150	±8.0	±7.8	±7.3	±6.4	±4.8	±3.5	*	*
200	±6.9	±6.8	±6.3	±5.5	±4.2	±3.0	±1.9	*
250	±6.2	±6.1	±5.7	±5.0	±3.7	±2.7	±1.7	*
300	±5.7	±5.5	±5.2	±4.5	±3.4	±2.5	±1.6	*
400	±4.9	±4.8	±4.5	±3.9	±2.9	±2.1	±1.4	±1.0
500	±4.4	±4.3	±4.0	±3.5	±2.6	±1.9	±1.2	±0.9
750	±3.6	±3.5	±3.3	±2.9	±2.1	±1.6	±1.0	±0.7
1000	±3.1	±3.0	±2.8	±2.5	±1.9	±1.3	±0.9	±0.6
2000	±2.2	±2.1	±2.0	±1.7	±1.3	±1.0	±0.6	±0.4
4000	±1.5	±1.5	±1.4	±1.2	±0.9	±0.7	±0.4	±0.3
10,000	±1.0	±1.0	±0.9	±0.8	±0.6	±0.4	±0.3	±0.2

* confidence interval greater than the percentage.

Interpretation of table: for example, for a sample size of 400 a finding of 30% is subject to a confidence interval of ±4.5 (that is to say, we can be 95% certain that the population value lies in the range 25.5% to 34.5%). For formula to calculate confidence intervals see Appendix 13.1.

Note that for smaller samples the confidence intervals become very large – for instance, for a sample of 50 the interval is plus or minus 13.9 per cent, meaning that a finding of 50 per cent can only be estimated to be within the range 36.1 to 63.9 per cent. For some statistics, for the smaller sample sizes, the confidence intervals are not calculable because the total margin of error is larger than the original statistic.

It should be noted that these confidence intervals apply only for samples which have been drawn using random sampling methods; other methods, such as multi-stage sampling, tend to produce larger confidence intervals, but the difference is often small, so the matter is not pursued here.

The implications of the precision criterion for deciding sample size now become clear. A sample size of, say, 1000 would give a confidence interval for a finding of 50 per cent of plus or minus 3.1 per cent. If that margin of error was not considered acceptable then a larger sample size would be necessary. Whether or not it is considered acceptable depends on the uses to which the data will be put and is related to the type of analysis to be done, as discussed below. An alternative way of considering these relationships between sample size and confidence interval is presented in Table 13.2. This presents, in the body of the table, the necessary sample size to achieve a given confidence interval.

Table 13.2 Necessary sample sizes to achieve given confidence intervals

Conf. interval	Percentages found from sample ('results')						
	50%	40 or 60%	30 or 70%	20 or 80%	10 or 90%	5 or 95%	1 or 99%
	Minimum necessary sample size						
±1%	9,600	9,216	8,064	6,144	3,456	1,824	380
±2%	2,400	2,304	2,016	1,536	864	456	*
±3%	1,067	1,024	896	683	384	203	*
±4%	600	576	504	384	216	114	*
±5%	384	369	323	246	138	73	*
±6%	267	256	224	171	96	*	*
±7%	196	188	165	125	71	*	*
±8%	150	144	126	96	54	*	*
±9%	119	114	100	76	43	*	*
±10%	96	92	81	61	35	*	*

Detail of proposed analysis

The confidence intervals in Table 13.1 illustrate further the second criterion concerning the choice of sample size – the type of analysis to be undertaken. If many detailed comparisons are to be made, especially concerning small proportions of the population, then the sample size may preclude very meaningful analysis. For instance, suppose a survey is conducted with a sample of 200 and it is found that 20 per cent of respondents went bowling and 30 per cent played tennis. The 20 per cent is subject to a margin of error of plus or minus 5.5 per cent and the 30 per cent is subject to a margin of plus or minus 6.3 per cent. Thus it is estimated that the proportions playing the two activities are as follows:

Bowling: between 14.5 and 25.5 per cent   Tennis: between 23.7 and 36.3 per cent

The confidence intervals overlap, so we cannot conclude that there is any 'significant' difference in the popularity of the two activities, despite a 10 per cent difference given by the survey. This is likely to be very limiting in any analysis. If the sample were 500 the confidence intervals would be 3.5 per cent and 4.0 per cent respectively, giving estimates as follows:

Bowling: between 16.5 and 23.5 per cent   Tennis: between 26.0 and 34.0 per cent

In this case the confidence intervals do *not* overlap and we can be fairly certain that tennis *is* more popular than bowling.

The detail of the analysis, the extent of subdivision of the sample into sub-samples, and the acceptable level of precision will therefore determine the necessary size of the sample. By and large this has nothing to do with the overall size of the original population, although there is a likelihood that the larger the population the greater its diversity and therefore the greater the need for subdivision into sub-samples.

Budget

A further point to be noted is that it could be positively wasteful to expend resources on a large sample when it can be shown to be unnecessary. For example, a sample of 10,000 gives estimates of statistics with a maximum confidence interval of ±1 per cent. Such a survey could cost, say, £200,000 to conduct. To halve that confidence interval to ±0.5 per cent would mean quadrupling the sample size to 40,000 at an additional cost of £800,000. There can be very few situations where such expenditure would be justified for such a small return.

Ultimately then, the limiting factor in determining sample size will be the third criterion, the resources available. Even if the budget available limits the sample size severely, it may be decided to go ahead and risk the possibility of an unrepresentative sample. If the sample is small, however, the detail of the analysis will need to be limited. If resources are so limited that the validity of quantitative research is questionable, it may be sensible to consider qualitative research which may be more feasible. Alternatively the proposed research can be seen as a 'pilot' exercise, with the emphasis on methodology, preparatory to a more adequately resourced full-scale study in future.

How should the issue of sample size and confidence intervals be referred to in the report on the research? In some scientific research, complex statistical tests are considered necessary in reporting statistical results from surveys. In much social science research, and leisure and tourism research in particular, requirements are less rigorous. This is true to some extent in academic research, but is markedly so in the reporting of applied research. While it is necessary to be aware of the limitations imposed by the sample size and not to make comparisons which the data cannot support, explicit reference to such matters in the text of a consultancy report is rare. A great deal of statistical jargon is not generally required: the lay reader expects the researcher to do a good job and expert readers should be given enough information to check the analysis in the report for themselves. It is recommended that an appendix be included in reports indicating the size of the sampling errors. Appendix 13.1 gives a possible format.

In academic journals the rules are somewhat different and there is an expectation that statistical tests be 'up front'. The variety of tests available is pursued in Chapter 17.

Confidence intervals applied to population estimates

The above comments are focused on confidence intervals applied to percentages of samples. Caution should be used when discussing population estimates based on sample surveys. But in many cases the sample statistics are applied to the population as a whole to obtain estimates of, for example, total visits to a destination or type of facility. For example, it could be found, from a sample of 1000 residents, that 12 per cent have visited a certain national park in the last year, on an average of 2.5 occasions. Given the sample size, the 12 per cent would be subject to a confidence interval of ±2.0 per cent. Suppose the population from which the sample had been drawn was 500,000 and an estimate of total visits was required. The estimate of the number of people visiting national parks in the last year would be 60,000 and, with an average number of visits of 2.5, this would give a total 150,000 visits a year. What is the confidence interval for this figure? The temptation is to say ±2.0 per cent of the 150,000, that is ±3000. But this is incorrect. In the ±2.0 per cent the percentage relates to the whole sample, so in grossing up it should be applied to the whole population, not to the number of visits, which is based on only 12 per cent of the population. The confidence interval for the number of *persons* is ±2.0 per cent of the population of 500,000, that is ±10,000. So the estimate of the number of persons is 60,000 ±10,000 and the estimate of the number of *visits* is 150,000 ±25,000. The interval of 25,000 is ±16.7 per cent of the number of visits. To obtain a confidence interval of ±2.0 per cent of the number of visits (i.e. ±3000), a sample size of 75,000 would be required.

The formula to obtain the confidence interval for the number of visits is: $f \times (PCI \times P)/100$, where f is the average frequency of visit per year (2.5 in the above example), PCI is the percentage confidence interval from the survey (2) and P is the population (500,000).

Sample size and small populations

The above discussion of sample size assumes that the population is large – in fact the statistical formulae used to calculate the confidence intervals are based on the assumption that the population is, in effect, infinite. The relationship between the size of confidence intervals and the size of the population becomes noticeable when the population size falls below about 50,000, as shown in Table 13.3. The table presents sample sizes necessary to produce 95 per cent confidence intervals of ±5 per cent and ±1 per cent for a sample finding of 50 per cent for different population sizes. Only the sample sizes for a 50 per cent finding are presented since, as shown in Figure 13.1, the 50 per cent finding is the most demanding in terms of sample size: for a given sample size, the confidence intervals for other findings – for example 30/70 per cent – is always smaller. The table first indicates the sample sizes for an infinite population and it can be seen that these are the same as indicated for a ±5 per cent or ±1 per cent confidence interval in the first column of Table 13.3. The details of the formula relating confidence intervals to population size can be found in Krejcie and Morgan (1970).

Table 13.3 Sample size and population size: small populations

Population size	Minimum sample sizes for confidence interval of ±5% and ±1% on a sample finding of 50%:	
	±5%	±1%
Infinite*	384	9,602
10,000,000	384	9,593
5,000,000	384	9,584
1,000,000	384	9,511
500,000	384	9,422
100,000	383	8,761
50,000	381	8,056
25,000	378	6,938
20,000	377	6,488
10,000	370	4,899
5000	357	3,288
2000	322	1,655
1000	278	906
500	217	475
200	132	196
100	80	99
50	44	50

* as in Tables 13.1 and 13.2.

Weighting

Situations where weighting of survey or count data may be required have been referred to at various points in this chapter. In Chapter 16 the procedures for implementing weighting using the SPSS computer package are outlined. Here we discuss the principles involved. Take the example of the data shown in Table 13.4. In the sample of 45 interviews the number of interviews is spread fairly equally through the day, whereas more than half the actual users visit around the middle of the day (this information probably having been obtained by observation/counts). This can be a source of bias in the sample, since the mid-day users may differ from the others in their characteristics or opinions and they will be under-represented in the sample. The aim of weighting is to produce a weighted sample with a distribution similar to that of the actual users.

One approach is to 'gross up' the sample numbers to reflect the actual numbers: for example, the 9–11 am group is weighted by $25 \div 10 = 2.5$, the 11–1 pm group is weighted by $240 \div 12 = 20$, and so on, as shown in Table 13.5.

The weighting factors can be fed into the computer for the weighting to be done automatically, as discussed in Chapter 16. The initial weighting factors are

Table 13.4 Interview/usage data from a site/visitor survey

Time	# of interviews	%	Actual # of users (counts)	%
9–11 am	10	22.2	25	5.7
11.01–1 pm	12	26.7	240	55.2
1.01–3 pm	11	24.4	110	25.3
3.01–5 pm	12	26.7	60	2.7
Total	45	100.0	435	100.0

Table 13.5 Weighting

	A	B	C	D
Time	No. of interviews	No. of users	Weighting factors	Weighted sample no.
Source:	Survey	Counts	B/A	CxA
9–11 am	10	25	2.5	25
11.01–1 pm	12	240	20.0	240
1.01–3 pm	11	110	10.0	110
3.01–5 pm	12	60	5.0	60
Total	45	435		435

equal to the user number divided by the sample number for that time period. The weighted sample therefore is made to resemble the overall user numbers. It should be noted, however, that the sample size is still 45, not 435! If statistical tests are to be carried out, then it would be advisable to multiply the weighting factors by 0.103 (= 45/435) to bring the weighted sample total back to 45.

In this example the basis of the weighting relates to the pattern of visits over the course of the day, which happened to be information which was available in relation to this particular type of survey. Any other data available on the population could be used – for example, if age structure is available from the census, then age-groups rather than time-periods might be used.

Sampling for qualitative research

As discussed in Chapter 9, qualitative research generally makes no claim to quantitative representativeness and, by definition, does not involve statistical calculation demanding prescribed levels of precision. Generally, therefore, the quantitative considerations outlined above are not relevant to qualitative research. This is not to say that representativeness is ignored entirely. As Karla Henderson (1991: 132) puts it: '. . . the researcher using the qualitative approach

Method	Characteristics
Convenience	Use of conveniently located persons or organisations – e.g. friends. colleagues, students, organisations in the neighbourhood, tourists visiting a local popular attraction.
Criterion	Individuals selected on the basis of a key criterion – e.g. age-group, membership of an organisation, purchasers of souvenirs
Homogeneous	Deliberately selecting a relatively homogeneous sub-set of the population – e.g. university-educated male cyclists aged 20–30.
Opportunistic	Similar to 'convenience' but involves taking advantages of opportunities as they arise – e.g. studying major sporting event taking place locally, or a holiday resort the researcher is holidaying at.
Maximum variation	Deliberately studying contrasting cases. Opposite of 'homogeneous'.
Purposeful	Similar to 'criterion' but may involve other considerations, such as 'maximum variation', typicality.
Snowball	Interviewees used as source of suggestions for additional contacts.
Stratified purposeful	Selection of a range of cases based on set criteria, e.g. representatives of a range of age-groups or nationalities.

Figure 13.2   Selected qualitative sampling methods

is not concerned about adequate numbers or random selection, but in trying to present a working picture of the broader social structure from which the observations are drawn'. Thus if the population being studied includes young and old people, then both young and old people will be included in the sample, unless an explicit decision has been made to concentrate on one age-group only. But the sample will not necessarily reflect the *proportions* of young and old in the study population. Miles and Huberman (1994: 28) list 16 'strategies' for qualitative sampling. Some of these are presented in Figure 13.2. In the research report, the qualitative sampling methods used should be adequately described. In all cases, just how individuals are selected and contacted should be described. For example, if the 'criterion' sampling method was used, what was the criterion used and how were the people who met the criterion contacted? If a 'snowball' method was used, how was it started? If 'convenience' sampling was used, what was the convenience factor – friendship, family, colleagues, students, neighbours?

Summary

This chapter covers the topic of sampling, which is the process of selecting a proportion of the 'population' of subjects for study. It also examines the implications of sampling for data analysis. Two key issues are considered: *representativeness* of samples, and sample *size*. The researcher seeks representativeness by following the principles of *random sampling*, which means that, as near as possible, every member of the population has an equal chance of being selected. Different types of survey involve different practical procedures for achieving random sampling. If a sample has been randomly selected, the question still arises as to the extent to which the statistical findings from the sample truly reflect the population. Statistical procedures have been developed to assess the level of probability that a sample finding lies within a certain margin of the true population value. This margin is known as a *confidence interval* and its size is related to the size of the sample, regardless of the size of the population – the larger the sample the smaller the confidence interval or margin of statistical error. The necessary sample size for a study therefore depends on the precision required in the results, the detail of the analysis to be undertaken and the available budget. Finally, the chapter considers the practice of *weighting* to correct a sample for known bias and sampling for qualitative research.

Test questions

1. Define random sampling.

2. What is the opposite of a random/representative sample?

3. What is multi-stage sampling and why is it used?

4. What is a confidence interval?

5. What determines the size of the sample to be used in a study?

6. What is weighting?

7. Name three mathods which exist for sampling in qualitative research.

Exercises

1. Examine either a published research report or a journal article related to an empirical study and identify the procedures used to ensure a random sample.

2. Using the report in exercise 1, produce confidence intervals for a range of percentage statistics occurring in the report.

3. In the example comparing bowling and tennis on page 365 above, what would the confidence intervals be if the sample size was 4000?

4. Examine the results from a national recreation participation survey or a domestic or international tourism survey and produce confidence intervals for a number of the key findings.

5. Select two qualitative research reports/articles (See Resources, Chapter 9) and contrast the information provided on sampling methods used and assess their suitability.

Resources

Sampling and the statistical implications of sampling are addressed in numerous statistics textbooks; Kidder (1981) Ch. 4; Spatz and Johnston (1989), Ch. 6; Sampling for telephone interviews: Lepkowski *et al.* (2008).

Appendix 13.1: Suggested appendix on sample size and confidence intervals

This is a suggested wording for an appendix or note to be included in research reports based on sample data. Suppose the survey has a sample size of 500.

Statistical note

All sample surveys are subject to a margin of statistical error. The margins of error, or 'confidence intervals' for this survey, with a sample of 500, are as follows:

Finding from the survey	95 per cent confidence interval
50 per cent	± 4.4 per cent
40 per cent or 60 per cent	± 4.3 per cent
30 per cent or 70 per cent	± 4.0 per cent
20 per cent or 80 per cent	± 3.5 per cent
10 per cent or 90 per cent	± 2.6 per cent
5 per cent or 95 per cent	± 1.9 per cent
1 per cent or 99 per cent	± 0.9 per cent

This means, for example, that if 20 per cent of the sample are found to have a particular characteristic, there is an estimated 95 per cent chance that the true population percentage lies in the range 20 ± 3.5, i.e. between 16.5 and 23.5 per cent.

These margins of error have been taken into account in the analyses in this report.

Part

III

Data analysis

This part of the book considers analysis of data in various forms and from various sources so each of the four chapters has particular links with specific chapters in Part II. Some Part II chapters, namely, on observation (Chapter 8), experimental methods (Chapter 11), the case study method (Chapter 12) and sampling, are linked to all four of the Part III chapters in various ways.

● Chapter 14, Secondary data analysis, provides examples of the use of some of the types of data source discussed in Chapter 7.

● Chapter 15, Qualitative data analysis, considers both manual and computer-aided analysis of the type of data discussed in Chapter 9.

● Chapter 16, Survey analysis, continues where Chapter 10 left off, examining the use of both spreadsheet programs and a statistical computer package for the analysis of questionnaire-based survey data.

● Chapter 17, Statistical analysis, relates particularly to the questionnaire-based data discussed in Chapters 10 and 16, but is also particularly related to Chapter 11, Experimental methods.

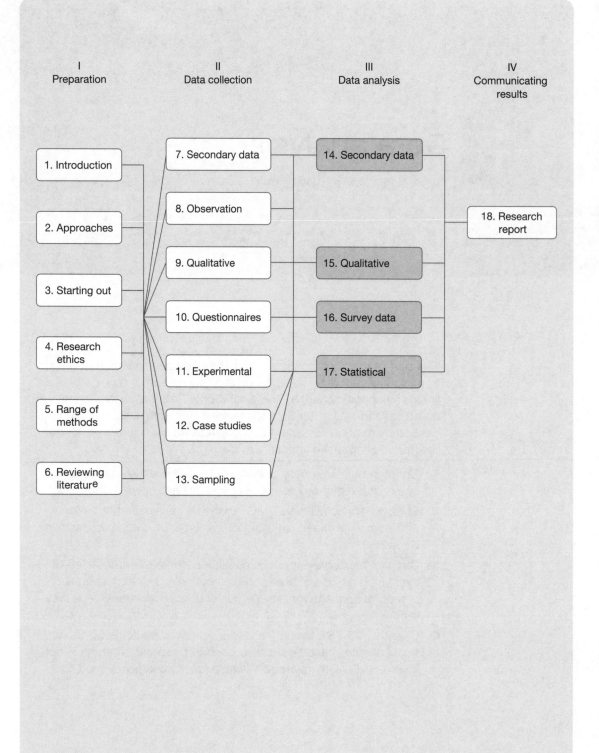

I Preparation	II Data collection	III Data analysis	IV Communicating results
1. Introduction	7. Secondary data	14. Secondary data	18. Research report
2. Approaches	8. Observation		
3. Starting out	9. Qualitative	15. Qualitative	
4. Research ethics	10. Questionnaires	16. Survey data	
5. Range of methods	11. Experimental	17. Statistical	
6. Reviewing literature	12. Case studies		
	13. Sampling		

14 Analysing secondary data

Introduction

The secondary data phenomenon and its various forms and sources is described in Chapter 7. There are no specific analytical techniques or computer packages associated with such data, given its diversity. Most of the quantitative data is susceptible to relatively simple spreadsheet analysis. Where re-analysis of survey data is involved, the procedures outlined in Chapter 16 and 17 for the analysis stage of the primary project in which the data were gathered will apply. Similarly, for qualitative data, the procedures in Chapter 15 will apply. In this chapter, therefore, the aim is not to address the detail of analytical techniques, but to provide summaries of examples of practical and imaginative uses of secondary data for leisure and tourism research purposes.

Case studies of secondary data analysis

Children's play safety

Case study 11.6A, presented in Chapter 11, is an example of a quasi-experiment involving children's playground safety, but it can also be seen as an example of use of secondary data. The 'experiment' involved before and after data on accident numbers in school playgrounds at the time of installation of new play equipment with higher safety standards. The accident statistics were collected routinely for legal, administrative and insurance purposes, but the researchers took the opportunity of using them for research purposes.

International data on inequality, leisure and tourism

Case study 14.1 relates to a recently published book, *The Spirit Level*, which is addressed to a popular/political audience and is based on analysis of secondary data from the United Nations and other sources. It makes the case that countries with a high degree of income equality perform better than countries with a low degree of income equality in relation to a range of quality of life measures. The book does not consider leisure, so this case study introduces some leisure-related data to the analysis.

Estimating demand for a leisure facility

Case study 14.2 demonstrates an approach to estimating demand for a possible new facility based on national leisure participation data and the population census. This is the type of exercise which might be used in a feasibility study.

Tourism trend analysis

Case study 14.3 is concerned with establishing trends from quarterly tourism arrivals data. Typically, such data have a seasonal pattern which must be 'smoothed out' to see the long-term trend and one approach to this is to calculate a 'moving average'.

Facility utilisation

Facilities with a number of components, such as a leisure centre with different halls and specialist facilities or a convention centre with a variety of rooms and auditoria, usually routinely record booking data for each component, in terms of booking/no booking or an event in terms of numbers of users/ticket sales. Case study 14.4 demonstrates how such data might be used to assess utilisation as a basis for management action on programming, promotion or pricing.

Facility catchment area

While information of visitors' residential location may be collected by means of on-site questionnaire-based surveys, in some cases that information is already available to management via membership or reservation data. Case study 14.5 shows an example of the use of such data to plot the catchment or market area of a facility. While the example assumes a leisure facility drawing visitors from an urban area, the method could be applied to a hotel or tourist attraction with a regional, national, and even international catchment.

Case study 14.1   *The Spirit Level* and leisure and tourism

The Spirit Level

In *The Spirit Level: Why More Equal Societies Almost Always do Better*, Richard Wilkinson and Kate Pickett (2009) use cross-national secondary data from the United Nations and other sources to make the case that the more equal the distribution of income in a country the more favourable are the outcomes on a range of indicators of human well-being, including life expectancy, infant mortality, physical and mental health, educational performance and the level of crime.

The book concentrates mainly on the 21 countries with the highest per capita national incomes (NI), with Portugal, Greece and Israel at the lower end (NI per capita ≤ $20K) and Norway and the USA at the upper end (NI per capita ≥ $35K). For each country, inequality is measured by the ratio of the average share of income of the top 20 per cent of households to that of the bottom 20 per cent, income being net of income tax and benefits and adjusted for size of household. This measure identifies the USA, Portugal, the UK, New Zealand and Australia as the most unequal countries and Japan and the Scandinavian countries, Norway, Finland, Sweden and Denmark, as the most equal.

Leisure and sport

The book does not, however, include leisure-related indicators, except for some data on working hours for a few of the countries, where the authors rely on a previously published paper relating to the period before 1998. It is possible to remedy this deficiency with more up-to-date secondary data on working hours, and with data on time use and holidays, which is the purpose of this case study.

Country-specific data on working hours, leisure time, sport and holiday time were obtained from a variety of sources as shown in Table 14.1. Using a presentation format similar to that used by Wilkinson and Pickett, their inequality measure was plotted against weekly working hours and weekly leisure time, which showed quite weak relationships, but a closer relationship was found between inequality and the ratio of working time to leisure time – that is, the number of employee working hours it takes to gain an hour of

▶

Table 14.1   Inequality and leisure and tourism data

	a. Index of inequality	b. Average weekly working hrs	c. Average weekly leisure hrs	d. Ratio of b to c	e. Sport participation (Europe)
Australia	19	32.6	4.2	7.8	–
Belgium	6	29.8	5.5	5.4	64
Canada	12	32.8	5.5	6.0	–
Finland	2	32.3	5.6	5.8	96
France	11	29.4	4.4	6.7	65
Germany	8	26.8	5.5	4.9	64
Italy	16	34.4	4.6	7.5	42
Japan	1	33.1	5.1	6.5	–
New Zealand	18	32.5	4.6	7.1	–
Norway	3	27.5	5.8	4.7	–
Spain	10	31.3	4.9	6.4	53
Sweden	4	30.8	5.1	6.0	93
UK	20	31.5	5.1	6.2	69
USA	22	33.5	5.2	6.4	–

Sources:

a. *The Spirit Level*, Wilkinson and Pickett (2009: Fig. 2.1, p. 17). Ratio of income of top 20% to income of bottom 20%
b. Groningen Growth and Development Centre, Groningen University: www.ggdc.net/ Averaged across the labour force
c. Harmonised European Time Use Study: https://www.h2.scb.se/tus/tus/ OECD Society at a Glance, Chapter 2: search at: www.oecd.org/ Leisure time data averaged across adult population
e. Participation in vigorous physical activity in last 7 days. Source: Eurobarometer (EU, 2004).

leisure time for the adult population. The results are shown in Figure 14.1. This was produced with the graphics facility of the Excel spreadsheet program and includes a plot of the data and a trend (regression) line and a measure of goodness of fit (R^2), concepts discussed in Chapter 17.

Turning to sport-related data, participation data from a survey conducted by the European Commission in 2004 is shown in Table 14.1 (column e) and represented graphically in Figure 14.1b. This indicates quite strongly ($R^2 = 0.6$) that countries with more unequal incomes are less involved in active sport and physical recreation.

Comment

The data for different countries relate to different years and often use different methodologies, and some data relate to workers, some to all adults. This illustrates one of the drawbacks of using secondary sources, that the data were not collected for the current purpose so are rarely ideal. But conducting international data collection exercises would of course be very expensive so there is,

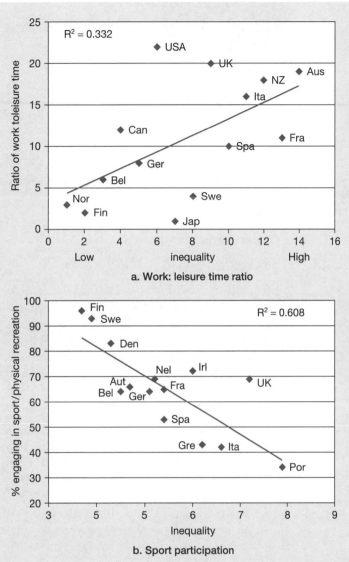

Figure 14.1 Inequality and leisure and tourism

Data source: see Table 14.1

in effect, no alternative but to use secondary data. The Harmonised European Time Use Study is one example of attempts to reconcile different countries' data-sets and to improve comparability in the future. Given the limitations of the data, it is perhaps not surprising that the relationships between the indicators used are not particularly strong, but on visual inspection they appear to be as strong as some of the relationships presented in *The Spirit Level*. The sport survey is, however, based on a single cross-national survey, albeit confined to Europe.

Case study 14.2   Estimating likely demand for a leisure facility

The problem

A developer or local council is considering whether to build a cinema on a particular site in a town centre, as part of a multi-purpose leisure complex. A cinema is used as an example, but the methodology could be applied equally to other types of facility. The town has a population of 100,000 and already has two 400-seat cinemas. The developer wants to know what demand exists in the area for such a facility. A range of approaches could be considered to investigate this question.

Possibilities

1. Existing facilities

Existing cinemas in the area could be examined to see whether they are overused or underused, that is whether demand is already being adequately met by existing facilities. This, however, may not give the full answer, since it might be found that a well-managed, well-located cinema is well used while another, perhaps poorly managed and poorly located, is poorly used. It might also be difficult to obtain commercially sensitive data from potential competitors.

2. Resident survey

An interview survey of local residents could be conducted to ask whether they would like to go to the cinema but do not do so at present because of lack of suitable facilities. Even if the time and money were available to conduct such a survey, the results could not be relied on as the main piece of information on which to base the decision because, while people's honesty and accuracy in recalling activities might be relied on in relation to activities which they have actually taken part in, asking them to predict their behaviour in hypothetical future situations is very risky.

3. Similar communities

Communities of similar population size and type could be examined to see what levels of cinema provision they have and how well they are used. Again this may be a time-consuming process and somewhat 'hit-and-miss' because it is not easy to find comparable communities and because some of the data required, being commercially 'sensitive', may not be readily available.

4. Use of secondary data

Secondary data – an appropriate national survey (NS) and the Population Census – could be used to provide an approximate estimate of likely demand for cinema seats in the area. The aim is to provide an estimate of the level of

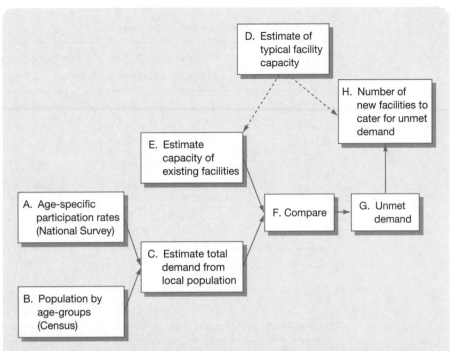

Figure 14.2 Estimating likely demand for a leisure facility

demand which a community of the size of that in the study area is likely to generate and compare that with the level of demand already likely to be catered for by existing cinemas, to see whether or not there is a surplus of demand over supply.

The approach

The general approach is represented diagrammatically in Figure 14.2. The steps A to G shown in the diagram are discussed in turn below.

A. Age-specific participation rates

One of the features of cinema attendance is that it varies considerably by age. Cinema is attended more by young people than by older people. If, for example, the study town contains a higher than average proportion of young people, it would be expected that it would produce a higher than average demand for cinema, and vice versa. The NS gives information on the percentage of people of different ages who go to the cinema, as shown in Table 14.2. It can be seen that teenagers are almost six times as likely to attend the cinema as the over-60s. The particular NS deals only with people aged 16 and over. Obviously children under that age do go to the cinema; but it may be that there is sufficient demand for an additional cinema even without taking account of the under-16s; so the under-16s can be ignored for the moment, only returning to them if necessary.

Table 14.2 Cinema attendance by age

Age group	% of age-group who go to the cinema in an average week (from national survey)
15–19 years	14.9
20–24	11.5
25–29	7.4
30–39	5.2
40–49	4.8
50–59	3.5
60+	2.5
Total/average	6.6

Source: Hypothetical data

Table 14.3 Study town and national age structure compared

Age groups	National population: census data %	Study town population: census data %
15–19	12.5	19.5
20–24	11.9	19.0
25–29	10.6	14.2
30–39	20.1	21.1
40–49	14.2	9.0
50–59	11.8	7.7
60+	18.9	9.5
Total	100.0	100.0

Source: Hypothetical data

B. Population by age-groups

Suppose the census gives the population of the town as 100,000, and the population aged 15 and over as 80,000. In Table 14.3 the age structure of the national population aged 15 and over is compared with that of the study town. Clearly the town has a much younger age profile than the national average with only just over half the proportion of over-55s and correspondingly larger proportions in the young age-groups. So it is clearly advisable to give consideration to the question of age structure.

Table 14.4 Estimating demand for cinema attendance

	% of age-group participating per week (X)	Town population (Y)	Estimated demand (visits per week)
Data source:	National survey	Census	XY/100
15–19 years	14.9	15,600	2324
20–24	11.5	15,200	1748
25–29	7.4	11,360	841
30–39	5.2	16,880	878
40–49	4.8	7,200	346
50–59	3.5	6,160	216
60+	2.5	7,600	190
Total/average	8.2	80,000	6543

C. Estimate total demand from local population

Table 14.4 indicates how demand for cinema attendance would be estimated: attendances are estimated for each age-group and summed to give a total of 6543 attendances per week.

D. Estimate of typical facility capacity

For this exercise it is assumed that a typical 400-seat cinema auditorium requires 1500 ticket sales a week to be viable.

E. Estimate capacity of existing facilities

Two cinemas already exist in the town. If they have a seating capacity of 400 each, then they would accommodate some 3000 visits a week.

F. Compare

The total estimated demand is 6500 visits per week, and the existing cinemas have a capacity of 3000 per week.

G. Unmet demand

Unmet demand can therefore be estimated as about 3500 visits per week.

H. Number of new facilities to cater for unmet demand

It would take two typical 400-seat cinemas to cater for the unmet demand – that is, it is estimated that the town could support four cinemas.

Comment

The above approach does not predict demand precisely – it merely indicates a 'ball park' demand figure. A well managed and programmed cinema might draw far more demand than is estimated. The national survey attendance rates relate to average attendances across the country, so clearly there are places where higher attendance rates occur as well as places where lower rates occur. What the exercise indicates is that, on the basis of data to hand, 6500 cinema attendances a week seems likely. This seems a very simple and crude calculation, but quite often investors – in the public and private sector – fail to carry out even this sort of simple calculation to check on 'ball park' demand figures; investments are made on the basis of personal hunch, and then surprise is expressed when demand fails to materialise.

Forecasting note: to provide a simple forecast of future demand, for, say, the year 2020 it would be necessary merely to insert population forecasts for the year 2020 into column B of Table 14.4 and rework the calculations.

Economic note: while the exercise here has been outlined in terms of 'number of users or customers', use of household expenditure data, such as that discussed in Chapter 7, can convert the unit of analysis into expenditure.

Case-study 14.3   Tourism trend analysis

Typically tourism statistics are produced on a monthly or quarterly basis, as in Table 14.5 (column A). Each quarterly figure of tourist arrivals reflects two factors: seasonal variation and longer-term trends. One way of examining the longer-term trend without the distraction of the seasonal variation is to produce a 'smoothed' series by calculating a 'moving average' (column B). The moving average consists of the average of the previous four quarters' figures.

Table 14.5 Tourist arrivals 2004–9

Year	Quarter	A. No. of arrivals, '000s	B. Moving average, '000s
2004	Jan–Mar	1307	
	Apr–Jun	1111	
	Jul–Sept	1273	
	Oct–Dec	1523	1304
2005	Jan–Mar	1469	1344
	Apr–Jun	1143	1352
	Jul–Sept	1349	1371
	Oct–Dec	1539	1375
2006	Jan–Mar	1431	1365
	Apr–Jun	1166	1371
	Jul–Sept	1323	1365
	Oct–Dec	1612	1383
2007	Jan–Mar	1497	1400
	Apr–Jun	1209	1410
	Jul–Sept	1359	1419
	Oct–Dec	1580	1411
2008	Jan–Mar	1503	1413
	Apr–Jun	1188	1407
	Jul–Sept	1354	1406
	Oct–Dec	1541	1396
2009	Jan–Mar	1451	1383
	Apr–Jun	1195	1385
	Jul–Sept	1319	1376
	Oct–Dec	1619	1396

Source: Australian Bureau of Statistics: 3401.0.55.001 – Short-term Visitor Arrival Estimates, Australia, at: www.abs.gov.au/ausstats/abs@.nsf/mf/3401.0.55.001/1

For example: the moving average figure for Oct–Dec, 2004, is the average of the four figures for 2004: 1,304,000.

The calculations can be done very easily with a spreadsheet program. The effect is to present a 'smoothed' trend series, as shown graphically in Figure 14.3.

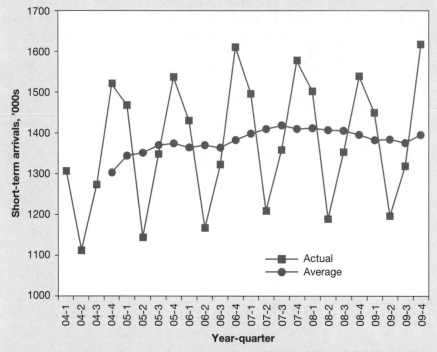

Figure 14.3   Tourism trends – quarterly arrivals and moving average

Data source: see Table 14.5

Case study 14.4   Facility utilisation

Managers typically have information available on the use of facilities, but this is also often neglected as a source of data for research. As indicated in Case study 14.2, the level of utilisation of existing facilities is an important issue for managers and planners: this case study illustrates how existing data can be used to address this question.

Table 14.6 presents data which might be routinely collected on the level of use of particular areas of a leisure facility (e.g. various rooms or halls in an indoor leisure centre or various rides in a leisure park). The daily usage levels might be averaged over a number of weeks. For each of the areas it is

Table 14.6   Facility utilisation data

	Area A		Area B		Area C	
	Number	**% utilisation**	**Number**	**% utilisation**	**Number**	**% utilisation**
Capacity	300	100.0	120	100.0	500	100.0
Mon. usage	120	40.0	60	50.0	310	62.0
Tues. usage	150	50.0	40	33.3	210	42.0
Wed. usage	180	60.0	30	25.0	180	36.0
Thurs. usage	120	40.0	80	66.7	375	75.0
Fri. usage	100	33.3	95	79.2	430	86.0
Sat. usage	210	70.0	110	91.7	420	84.0
Sun. usage	250	83.3	40	33.3	310	62.0
Total for week	1130	53.8	455	54.2	2235	63.9

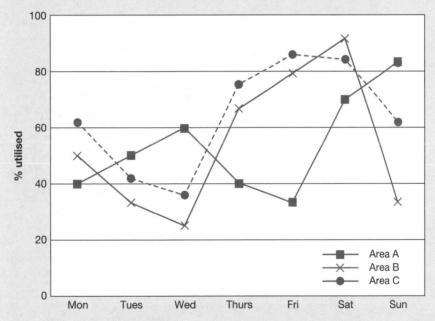

Figure 14.4   Facility utilisation

necessary to estimate the daily capacity: this is a reasonable assessment of the number of users which would equate to the facility being deemed 'fully used' (see Veal, 2010a: Ch. 10). The numbers of users are related to the capacity in the form of percentages, and these are graphed in Figure 14.4.

The graph shows a different pattern of use for Area A, compared with the other two areas. Area A is underused on Monday, Thursday and Friday, while areas B and C are underused between Sunday and Wednesday. This suggests the need for different programming and marketing policies for the various areas.

Case study 14.5   Facility catchment or market area

Leisure and tourism facilities often have available information on users' addresses which can be used to study the *catchment area* or *market area* – an important aspect of planning and management. Many leisure facilities, for example, have membership or subscriber lists. Hotels and resorts have details of home addresses of patrons.

Figure 14.5 shows how such data can be plotted on a map to produce a visual representation of the catchment or market area of the facility. Such information can be used either to concentrate marketing to increase sales in the existing area, or to focus marketing outside the identified area in order to extend the catchment or market area.

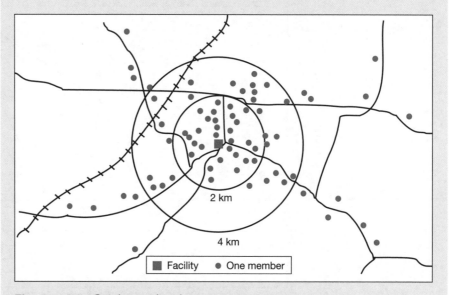

Figure 14.5 Catchment/market area

Source: Membership/patron address records (hypothetical)

When very large numbers are involved, it may be necessary to sample membership or customer lists – for example, selecting every fifth or tenth member or patron on the list.

While this case study is used to illustrate the use of secondary data, catchment areas can also be based on survey data, which will be necessary if existing information on client addresses is not available (see Chapter 10, particularly the discussion of user/site surveys).

Summary

The chapter presents five case studies demonstrating potential uses of secondary data in planning and management situations, including: cross-national examination of inequality, leisure and sport, demand for new facilities, analysis of trends in seasonal tourism data, assessment of levels of resource utilisation and analysis of a facility catchment area.

Exercises

1. Take a leisure activity of your own choice, and a community of your own choice and, using data from a national leisure participation survey (see Chapter 7) and data from the census, provide an estimate of the likely demand for the activity in the selected community, using the methodology outlined in Case study 14.2.

2. In relation to exercise 1, what would be the implications of a predicted increase of 15 per cent in the number of people aged 60 and over and a 15 per cent decrease in the number of people aged 25 and under, over the next five years?

3. Undertake an exercise similar to Case study 14.4 for a leisure facility for which you can obtain usage data.

4. Undertake an exercise similar to Case study 14.5 for a leisure facility for which you can obtain user/member address data.

5. Select an activity from a national leisure participation survey and provide a *profile* of the activity, indicating the overall level of participation and how participation is related to age, gender, occupation and education.

Resources

See the Resources section in chapter 7 for details of secondary data sources.

15   Analysing qualitative data

Introduction

Data collection and analysis

This chapter addresses the task of analysing qualitative data. As indicated in Chapter 9, it is sometimes difficult to separate the collection and analysis processes for qualitative data, at least in a temporal sense; but there is nevertheless a clear difference between certain data collection activities, such as interviewing someone with a sound recorder, and certain analysis activities, such as poring over typed interview transcripts. While, as discussed in Chapter 2, quantitative research can be inductive and qualitative research can be deductive, the qualitative approach lends itself to a more inductive process, especially when conducted on a small scale. This difference is illustrated in Figure 15.1, which presents variations on the circular process of research depicted in Figure 2.5.

Traditionally qualitative data were analysed by manual means, and this continues, but in recent years computer software has become available to aid the process. Computers replicate and speed up some of the more mechanical aspects of the manual processes but, of course, the task of interpretation remains with the researcher. The chapter first discusses the question of data storage and confidentiality and then considers manual analysis methods and computer-based methods in turn. Since the most common form of qualitative data is interview or focus group transcripts or notes, the following discussions are based on this form of data. Most of the procedures nevertheless apply, in adapted form, to other forms of data, such as printed materials from organisational archives or the media.

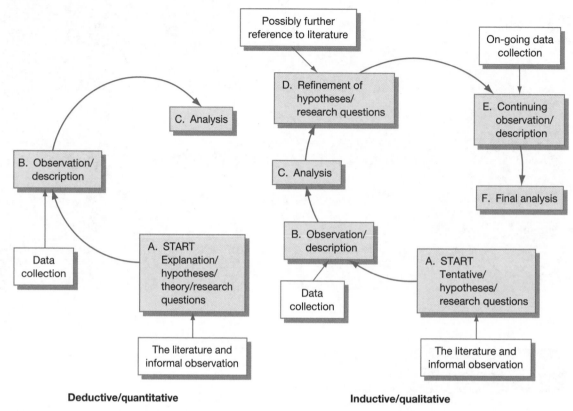

Figure 15.1   Circular model of the research process in quantitative and qualitative contexts

Data storage and confidentiality

Regardless of whether qualitative data are analysed manually or by computer, consideration should be given to the security and confidentiality of transcripts and digital files, particularly if sensitive material is involved. This raises ethical issues, as discussed in Chapter 4.

As a precaution, research material should ideally not be labelled with real names of organisations or people. Fictitious names or codes should be created. If it is felt that it will be necessary to relate recordings and transcripts back to original respondents at some later date, for example for second interviews, the list relating fictitious identities to real identities should be kept in a separate, secure place. Of course actual names mentioned by respondents on tapes cannot easily be erased, and it is a matter of judgement as to whether it is necessary to disguise such names in transcripts, although in most cases they should be disguised in any quotations of the material in the research report. In some cases, however, it is necessary to create transcripts which are, in a way, less anonymous than the original. For example, an interviewee might say: 'I find it difficult to get on with John' – the transcript might change 'John' to 'David', but may need to identify John/David's position – for example: 'I find it difficult to get on with David [Supervisor]'.

Digitised research material stored on computer hard drives and other storage media is subject to the security risks of any digitised information. Some software, including NVivo discussed in this chapter, offers password protection which may be a useful precaution.

Case study example

A case study of some in-depth interview data is used to illustrate qualitative data analysis – both manual and by computer, as shown in Case study 15.1.

Case study 15.1   Activity choice qualitative study

Figure 15.2 presents a very simple conceptual framework for studying leisure activity choice. It is based on a model presented by Brandenburg *et al.* (1982) and further developed in Veal (1995) and suggests that individuals' choice of leisure activity is influenced by background characteristics and experiences, present constraints and personal factors, but also by key events which trigger participation.

While this example is expressed in terms of leisure as a whole, the framework would be suitable for analysis of a sector of leisure, such as sport, or holiday-taking, or the arts. Thus the activity choices, X, Y, Z, could relate to the whole range of leisure activities or a restricted sector. The model could be explored quantitatively, for example, by means of a questionnaire, but that would be likely to require prior definition of the three sets of influences and a set of key events. Further, since any one of the three groups could involve a substantial list of items (e.g. background/experience, parental influence, school experience, higher education experience, geography/climate, activities experienced), the analysis task would be daunting. A qualitative approach would enable the various factors and influences to be identified and analysed in a

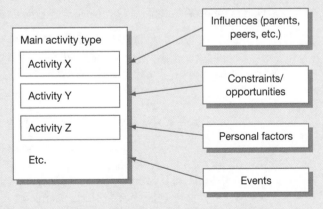

Figure 15.2 Outline conceptual framework for qualitative study of activity choice

more exploratory manner. Interviews could be conducted using a checklist of the sort presented in Figure 9.4.

Figure 15.3 contains short extracts from three interviews with individuals about their leisure choices. The comments in the first column are explained

---

Mark (Age 22, Male, Student, Income £8K)

Act.: Sport – football
Constraint:
Commitments,
Need to keep fit,
Time, Money

> Q. What would you say is your most time-consuming leisure activity outside of the home at present?

Well, I would say it's playing football, at least during the season. While the football's on, because of training twice a week and needing to be fairly serious about keeping fit I don't do much else: I probably only go to a pub once – or at most twice – a week. I don't have the time or the money to do much more.

> Q. How were you introduced to football?

Influence:
Parent+

Teacher ++

Event:
Coaching clinic

Oh, I've always played . . . since I could run around I suppose. My dad says he spotted my talent – so-called – when I was a toddler, but it was one of the teachers at primary school that really encouraged me. He persuaded my mum to take me to a coaching clinic when I was about 8 or 9, then I got into the local under-11s.

> Q. Why do you think you are attracted to football?

Personal:
Competitive, Team
oriented, Active

Well, I'm pretty competitive – so I like sport generally. I like the team-spirit thing with football – I don't think I could do an individual sport where you didn't have a team around you. You make good friends. And it's fast and you're involved the whole time . . . I get bored playing cricket where you're standing around half the time.

Donna (Age 27, Female, FT Employed, Income £19K)

> Q. What would you say is your most time-consuming leisure activity outside of the home at present?

Act.: Socialising

Just socialising I would say . . . you know, going out for a meal or a drink with friends . . . I go to the gym once or twice a week . . . and I like to swim a bit in the summer, but they don't take up much time overall.

> Q. When did you first start going out socially on a regular basis?

Event: Earning
money

Influence: Peers

I was about 16, I guess: the parents were a bit restrictive, but once I started earning a bit of money at weekends I managed to go out at least twice a week – to parties and to the cinema and stuff . . . my mum and dad didn't have any money to give me, so it wasn't until I started to work part-time that I could go out, sort of regularly. I've always had a fairly close-knit group of friends, girlfriends, about the same age as me, who've always gone out together . . . even with boyfriends – and one husband – arriving on the scene and disappearing from time to time!

Q. What limits the number of times you go out socialising in a week?

Constraint:
Time, Money

Time and money! But mostly it's time these days – cos we don't always spend a lot.

Q. What are the essential ingredients for a good night out?

Personal:
Social – informal

Constraint: Time

It's all about people . . . people you know and people you might meet! Things like good food – and drink – or good music are important, but the enjoyment comes from doing it with your friends and knowing they have the same sorts of tastes and the same sense of fun. I am serious enough at work, I couldn't imagine myself spending a lot of time with some team sport with serious training and all that: I just don't have the time – or the inclination!

Lee (Age 23, Male, FT Employed, Income £22K)

Q. What would you say is your most time-consuming leisure activity outside of the home at present?

Event: Girlfriend
Personal:
Anti-routine

It varies. I don't have any set pattern. Up until a couple of weeks ago I was going out with this girl and, apart from going round each other's house, we spent a lot of time going out, one way or another – to the pub, cinema, walking, shopping – it varied. Now that's stopped, it's still a bit of a mixture, but with various friends. I hate routine, so I don't get involved with anything regular.

Q. So what single thing – from among the mixture of things you do – would you say you spent most time doing in the last week?

Act.: Cinema

In the last week? Well, I haven't been out that much: it would have to be the movies: I went twice and one of them was one of those late-night double billers – about four hours.

Q. Are you a movie buff?

Event:
Good review

I wouldn't go that far, but I like movies. I read reviews and that. The movie I saw on Tuesday had a lot of hype and I saw two or three good reviews. For once, the hype was justified: it was really good. Really good: better than the reviews – and that doesn't happen often.

Figure 15.3   Interview transcript extracts

below. These transcripts are used to illustrate manual and computer analysis of texts. The aim is to illustrate the mechanics of analysis in a way which could be readily replicated by the student. The length of the transcript extracts and their number has therefore been limited. The substantive outcomes are therefore incidental and not particularly meaningful taken in isolation. In a complete research exercise, full transcripts running to many pages would be involved and, although we are dealing with qualitative research, the number of interviews/transcripts in a study of this type would normally be more than three.

Manual methods of analysis

Introduction

There are various ways of analysing interview transcripts or notes. The essence of any analysis procedure must be to return to the terms of reference, the conceptual framework and the research questions or hypotheses of the research, as discussed in Chapter 3. The information gathered should be sorted through and evaluated in relation to the concepts identified in the conceptual framework, the research questions posed or the hypotheses put forward. In qualitative research, those original ideas may be tentative and fluid. Questions and/or hypotheses and definitions and operationalisation of concepts may be detailed or general; the more detailed and specific they are, the more likely it is that they will influence the initial stages of the analysis. Conversely, the more general and tentative they are, the more likely it is that the data analysis process will influence their development and refinement. Data gathering, hypothesis formulation and the identification of concepts is a two-way, evolving process. Ideas are refined and revised in the light of the information gathered, as described in relation to the *grounded theory* approach and the *recursive* approach discussed in Chapter 9 and summarised in Figure 9.1. In Chapter 3 it is noted that the development of a conceptual framework and of research questions or hypotheses is the most difficult and challenging part of a research project.

In addition to the problem of ordering and summarising the data conceptually, the researcher is faced with the very practical problem of just how to approach the pile of interview notes or transcripts.

Reading

The basic activity in qualitative analysis is *reading* of notes, transcripts, documents or *listening* or *viewing* audio and video materials. In what follows, it is assumed that the material being analysed is text – while practical adaptations are necessary for audio and video material, the principles are the same. The reading is done initially in light of initial research questions and/or hypotheses and/or those which have evolved during the data collection process.

Emergent themes

A typical approach to qualitative analysis is to search for *emergent themes* – the equivalent of *variables* in quantitative research. Indeed, it has been argued, for example by Sherry Dupuis (1999), that the practice mimics too closely the positivistic approach to research which many proponents of qualitative methods deprecate. There is certainly the temptation to begin adopting a quasi-quantitative approach to the process, identifying as themes only those which arise from the transcripts of a number of subjects. Clearly this would be inconsistent with the qualitative approach: a theme which emerges from just one subject is as valid as one which emerges from ten subjects. The criterion for identification should be the extent to which the theme appears to be salient to the interviewee.

The themes may arise from the conceptual framework and research questions, and therefore be consciously searched for in a deductive way, or they may emerge unprompted in a more inductive way. Typically, both processes will be at work.

Themes which emerge from the transcripts are 'flagged' in the left-hand margin of the transcripts in Figure 15.3. The researcher's judgement of the strength with which the views are expressed is indicated here with one or more plus or minus signs. It is clear that other themes might be identified and alternative terms might be used for the items which are identified, illustrating the personal and subjective nature of qualitative analysis.

The 'developed' conceptual framework presented in Figure 15.4 shows how some of the themes/concepts/factors and relationships emerging from the interviews might begin to be incorporated into the conceptual framework. On the basis of information from short abstracts from three interviews, the conceptual framework is *developed* but not *fully* developed; it represents work in progress. The 'levels' referred to relate to discussion of computer-aided analysis discussed later in the chapter.

Mechanics

The initial steps in qualitative analysis involve fairly methodical procedures to classify and organise the information collected.

Analysis can be done by hand on hard-copy transcripts, which should have a wide margin on one side to accommodate the 'flagging' of themes as discussed above. Colour coding can be used in the flagging process and 'Post-it' notes may also be used to mark key sections.

Standard word-processor packages can be of considerable assistance in the analysis process. The space for flagging can then be secured using the

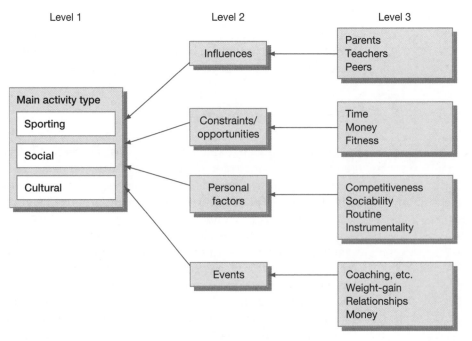

Figure 15.4 Developed conceptual framework for qualitative study of activity choice

'columns' or tables facility in the word-processor. Word-processing packages also have facilities for:

- adding 'Comments' (e.g. in the Tracking facility in Word);
- blocking text with colour, underlining or bold;
- 'searching' to locate key words and phrases;
- paragraph and/or line numbering;
- coding and cross-referencing using indexing or cross-referencing procedures.

A *cataloguing* process can be used to group together subjects who appear to be associated with particular themes:

Constraint – time:	Mark: p. 2, para. 3
	Anna: p. 7, para. 4
Constraint – money:	Mark: p. 2, para. 3

This is often necessary to keep track of topics across a number of interviews, but also because topics are typically covered several times in the same interview. A particular focus of the analysis may be related not only to particular substantive topics raised by the interviewer, and therefore related to particular questions, but also to, for example, underlying attitudes expressed by interviewees, which might arise at any time in an interview.

The catalogue becomes the basis for further analysis and writing up the results of the analysis: being able to locate points in the transcripts where themes are expressed enables the researcher to check the wording used by respondents and explore context and related sentiments and facilitates the location of suitable quotations to illustrate the write-up of the results.

Analysis

In qualitative data analysis it is possible to use techniques and presentation methods that are similar to those used in quantitative analysis. For example, in Figure 15.5 an analysis similar to a crosstabulation is shown, with twelve hypothetical interviewees 'plotted' on a two-dimensional space based on two variables derived from the interviews referred to above. The placing of the respondents depends on a qualitative assessment based on the interview transcripts. It can be seen that, in the example, the respondents fall into four groups. Given that this is a qualitative survey and the sample of interviewees is unlikely to be statistically representative, the *numbers* in each group are not important, but simply the identification of the existence of four groups. Such a grouping would provide the basis for further analysis of the transcripts (see Huberman and Miles, 1994: 437).

Thus analysis of qualitative data has certain parallels with quantitative analysis, with themes corresponding to variables and relationships explored in ways which parallel crosstabulation and correlation. But they are parallels only, not equivalents. Whereas quantitative analysis generally seeks to establish whether certain observations and relationships are generally true in the wider population on the basis of statistical probability, qualitative analysis seeks to establish the existence of relationships on the basis of what individual people say and do. If only one person or organisation in the study is shown to

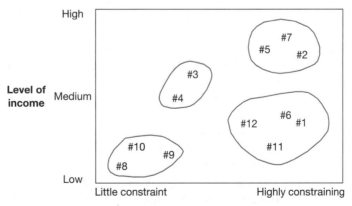

Figure 15.5 'Crosstabulation' of qualitative data

Numbers refer to individual interviewees.

behave in a certain way as a result of certain forces, this is a valid finding for qualitative research – the question of just how widespread such behaviour is in the wider society becomes a matter for other types of research.

Detailed analysis may be less important when the purpose of in-depth or informal interviews is to provide input into the design of a formal question-naire. In that case the interviewer will generally make a series of notes arising from the interview which are likely to be of relevance to the questionnaire design process, and can also provide input to the design process from memory, as long as the questionnaire design work is undertaken fairly soon after the interviews.

Qualitative analysis using computer software – introduction

When the researcher is faced with a substantial number of lengthy documents to analyse, the decision may be made to ease the laborious process of coding and analysing by making use of one of the computer-aided qualitative data analysis software (CAQDAS) packages now available. As with statistical pack-ages, it takes time to learn how to use qualitative analysis packages and to set up a system for an individual project, so a decision has to be made, on the basis of the size and complexity of the documentary material to be analysed, as to whether that investment of time will result in a net time saving, compared with manual analysis. Consideration should, however, be given to the fact that, once an analysis system has been set up, more analysis can be relatively quickly undertaken, possibly resulting in better quality of output than may have been possible using manual methods. Further, looking to the future, a computerised analysis system can more easily be returned to at future dates for additional interrogation. Finally, even if the amount of data in a given project does not justify setting up a computerised analysis system, a smaller project may be an easier vehicle for learning to use and gain experience with a pack-age. Familiarity and experience with a computer package merits an entry on a *curriculum vitae*.

It has been noted above that standard word-processing packages such as Microsoft Word offer facilities which can aid in sorting and locating mater-ial in transcripts. The standard word-processing package is, however, limited in its capabilities for this purpose. A number of purpose-designed CAQDAS packages are now on the market. One of the most commonly used, and which is demonstrated here, is NVivo, part of a stable of packages from QSR (Qualitative Solutions and Research Pty Ltd), which includes N6, an updated version of the well-known NUD*IST, and XSight designed for market researchers. Details of these and other packages can be found on the QSR website, the address for which is given at the end of the chapter.

Interview transcripts

As with the manual analysis discussed above, the extracts of interview transcripts from the Activity Choice project as outlined in Case study 15.1 (Figure 15.3) are used to demonstrate the operation of NVivo here. An ideal way for readers to engage with this section is to replicate the processes outlined on a computer. In what follows it is assumed that the reader has access to a computer with NVivo installed.

Readers who wish to replicate the procedures should first either type the text of the transcripts into three files or download them from the book's website. They should be in files named: Mark.doc; Donna.doc; and Lee.doc (a small font and wide margins are advised for ease of viewing on the NVivo screen). The suffix .doc (or .docx) indicates Word format, but NVivo will also accept text format (suffix .txt), rich text format (.rtf) or portable document format (.pdf). The files are introduced in the procedure 'Importing documents' below.

NVivo

Introduction

NVivo is one of the most widely used CAQDAS packages. The software enables the researcher to index and coordinate the analysis of text stored as computer files. This includes primary material, such as interview transcripts and field notes, and other material such as newspaper clippings, reports and video clips. In addition it assists in shaping and understanding data and in developing and testing theoretical assumptions about the data.

It is not possible in a short summary such as this to present all the features of the package – this is done in the on-line tutorials and 'Help' built into the package and in other specialist texts, such as that by Patricia Bazeley (2007). Details of support materials are provided on the QSR website (see the Resources section). Just a few NVivo procedures, considered to be sufficient to get started with the package, are outlined here, as shown in Figure 15.6.

Starting up

The Nvivo opening window displays a list of 'My recent projects', including an already loaded demonstration project on volunteering.

Creating a project

To demonstrate the system, we start with Create Project. This involves creating a named location for a research project, into which the documents to be analysed,

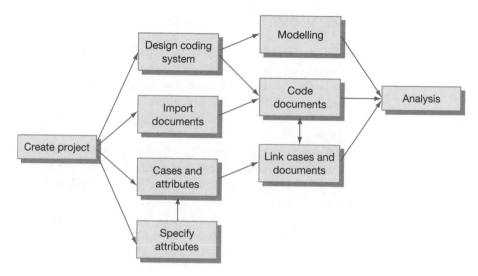

Figure 15.6   NVivo procedures covered

such as interview transcripts, will be added. The NVivo procedures to create a project for the Activity Choice project are shown in Figure 15.7.

Saving

During an NVivo session, the program will periodically remind the user to save the current version of the project. Back-up copies should also be created at the end of a session.

---

1. Click on *Create Project*
2. In the Title box enter: ActivityChoice
3. A file name *ActivityChoice.nvp* automatically appears in the *File Name* box – it will have a default 'My documents' location on your computer but this can be altered by clicking on *Browse* and specifying a location of choice.
4. Click on *OK*.
5. The screen appears, as shown below.
6. At the top of the screen a number of 'Toolbars' may appear. In addition to the standard Windows 'File, Edit, View, etc.' toolbar, the important one to have available is the 'Main' toolbar as shown below. Others can be viewed or deleted using: View> Toolbars.
7. The rest of the screen is divided into three areas:
   - Left-hand side: *Navigation View* – clicking on one of the items in the bottom half brings up a menu in the top half

- Right-hand-centre: *List View* – contents of folders
- Right-hand-lower: *Detail View* – contents of files: not shown below, but see Figure 15.8.

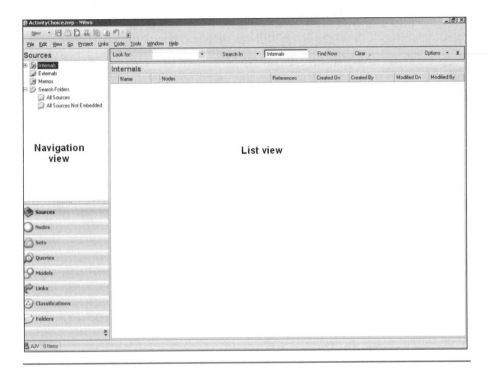

Figure 15.7   Create NVivo project – procedure

Attributes

Attributes of subjects/cases involved in a study can be recorded as for variables in a quantitative study. At the top of the transcripts we have four items of information for each respondent: age; gender; employment status; and income (see Figure 15.3) and these can be recorded as a set of attributes in the NVivo system, as shown in Figure 15.8.

Cases and their attributes

We can now introduce our three interviewees, as *cases* and record their individual socio-demographic attributes. Procedures are shown in Figure 15.9.

Importing documents

Information on the interviewees and their attributes have been imported into the Activity Choice project system and the three transcript files must also be

1. Click on *Classifications* on the bottom left of the screen: the *Attributes* screen appears.
2. Right click in the blank *Attributes* List View area of the screen and select *New Attribute*.
3. In the *New Attribute* dialog box enter the name *Gender*.
4. Click on the *Values* tab:
   - 'Unassigned' and 'Not applicable' default values are already in place:
   - click on *Add* and type in the value *Male*
   - click on *Add* again and type in *Female*, then click on *OK*
   - the attribute *Gender* should now be listed under *Attributes.*
5. Repeat steps 2–4 for attribute *Empstat* (employment status), with values *FT Employed* and *Student*.
6. Repeat step 2 and 3 for attribute *Age* and *Income*, changing the *Type* from *String* to *Number*. Step 4 is not necessary because these are uncoded numerical variables.
7. The four attributes, *Age, Empstat, Gender, Income*, should now be listed under *Attributes*.

Figure 15.8   Attributes – procedure

1. Click on *Nodes* in the bottom left-hand corner of the screen, then under the *Nodes* menu click on *Cases*.
2. Right click in the *Cases* List View area of the screen and select *New Case*.
3. In the New Case dialog box enter the name *Mark*.
4. Still in the New Case dialog box, click on the *Attribute Values* tab.
5. In the *Attribute Values* dialog box the four attributes are listed:
   - for *Age* and *Income:* key in Mark's age in years (22) and income in £000s (8)
   - from the drop-down lists of values for *Gender* and *Empstat*, select *Male* and *Student* respectively. Then click on *OK*.
6. Repeat steps 2–5 for Donna and Lee.
7. Save the project to disk using *File> Save Project* on the Windows toolbar.
8. Right click in the *Cases* List View area and select *Open Casebook*: the three cases and their attributes appear in a spreadsheet-style table as below.
9. The Case/Attributes data can be presented in spreadsheet format, so if the information is already held in spreadsheet format, the spreadsheet can be imported into NVivo, replacing the above procedure. This is achieved via, in the Windows menu : *Tools > Casebook > Import Casebook* where the location of the spreadsheet file is requested.
10. Conversely, the Casebook can be exported to a spreadsheet file via, in the Windows menu : *Tools > Casebook > Export Casebook*.

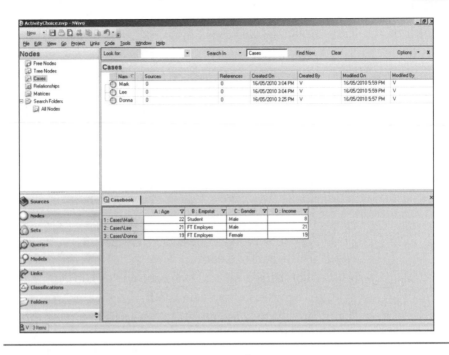

Figure 15.9 Cases and attributes – procedure

imported, as shown in Figure 15.10. It will be seen that other types of material can be incorporated, including sound and video material and external material such as links to websites. This demonstration is confined to dealing with text documents generated internally as part of the research project.

Linking cases and documents

The interview transcript files must now be linked with the three interviewees/ cases, Mark, Donna and Lee, already identified in the system, as shown in Figure 15.11.

Setting up a coding system

As with questionnaires, documents such as interview transcripts must be *coded* in order to be analysed by computer. This involves setting up a *coding system*. A coding system can develop and evolve as the research progresses, but it has to start somewhere. In the section on manual coding above, the 'flagging' process is similar to the coding process involved here. On the basis of an initial conceptual framework (Figure 15.2) and reading short extracts from three interview transcripts, it was possible to develop a coding system which is displayed in the notes in Figure 15.3 and reflected in the more developed conceptual framework in Figure 15.4. In a fully fledged project the researcher would go on to

1. In the Navigation View area, click on *Sources*.
2. In the menu which now appears above, click on *Internals*.
3. In the Main toolbar click on *New* and select *Subfolder in This Folder*.
4. In the *New Folder* dialog box enter the Name *Interviews* and click *OK*.
5. *Interviews* now appears as a sub-folder to the *Internals* folder in the *Sources* menu to the left.
6. Click on *Interviews*, then in the Windows toolbar click on *Project*, then select *Import Internals*.
7. In the *Import Internals* dialog box: click on *Browse* to locate Mark.doc and click on *OK*.
8. The *Document Properties* dialog box appears: click on *OK*.
9. The file name Mark.doc should now be listed in the *Internals* List View area, with its date of creation.
10. Repeat steps 7–9 for Donna.doc and Lee.doc.
11. All three files will now be listed.
12. Save the modified project to disk using *File> Save Project* on the Windows toolbar.

Figure 15.10   Importing internal documents – procedure

1. In the Navigation View area, click on *Sources*, then *Internals> Interviews* on the menu, so that the three files appear in List View, under the heading *Internals*.
2. Click on the file icon on the left of the *Mark* file to highlight it.
3. In the Windows toolbar, select *Code,* then *Code Sources*, then *At Existing Nodes*.
4. The *Select Project Items* dialog box appears: select *Cases* and the list of three files will appear.
5. Check *Mark* and click on *OK*.
6. Repeat steps 2–5 for Donna and Lee.
7. The three cases/interviewees, with their attributes, are now linked with their respective interview transcripts – if you go to *Nodes> Cases* and click on one of the files, you will see in the Display View area that the link is noted on the top of the transcript.

Figure 15.11   Linking documents and cases – procedure

read and code the full interview transcripts of the three example interviewees and other interviewees as well, and would apply the flagging/coding system to the other text read and would further develop the system in an inductive way. Coding systems using NVivo are developed in the same way. In the example below, the codes developed in the manual process are entered into the Activity Choice project to demonstrate the beginnings of a coding system.

The grouping of related concepts, as shown in Figure 15.4, are referred to in NVivo as *Tree Nodes*. Free-floating concepts, which have not been linked to any tree structure are referred to as *Free Nodes*. The procedures in Figure 15.12 describe the process for entering information presented in Figure 15.4 into the NVivo project file. The relevance of the three *levels* mentioned in Figure 15.4 should become apparent in this process.

Modelling

The coding system can be depicted diagrammatically as a *model*. The procedures and output are shown in Figure 15.13. Here the model is depicted generically. Later it is shown how the way the model works for an individual case can be depicted.

Coding text

Once a coding system has been set up documents, such as interview transcripts, can be coded. This process is outlined in Figure 15.14.

This illustration uses the coding system developed above, which arose from the manual analysis and theoretical framework outlined earlier in chapter, but the coder is not restricted to this framework: additional codes/nodes can be added as you go along. This reflects the qualitative methodology and is of course very likely to arise with longer interview transcripts. The procedure involves selecting 'At new node' at step 5b in Figure 15.14.

Project summary

The Activity Choice project information is now assembled and coded, as summarised in Figure 15.15. Analysis involves exploring the content of the coded interview transcripts and the cases and their attributes.

Analysis

Software packages invariably include a wide range of procedures which it is impossible to cover in a short summary such as this. Here we cover two very basic analysis procedures/issues which will be sufficient to get the researcher started. In reality, these procedures do not encompass data analysis as such, which is concerned with identifying relationships and meanings, discussed in a limited way in the manual analysis section above. The procedures covered here are related to data processing so that the analysis can begin. Two procedures are described below: *Coding Query* and *Matrix Coding Query*.

1. In the Navigation View area, click on *Nodes*
2. In the *Nodes* menu click on *Tree Nodes*
3. Right click in the List View area (or, in the main toolbar, click on *New*): from the drop-down menu select *New Tree Node*, type in the name *Main Activity* and click on *OK*. Main Activity is now listed under *Tree Nodes*.
4. Highlight *Main Activity* and, holding the pointer on *Main Activity*, right click and, in the drop-down menu, select *New Tree Node*, then in the *New Tree Node* dialog box type in the name *Activity type* and click on *OK*. *Activity type* should now be listed under *Main Activity*.
5. Repeat step 4 for: Influences, Constraints, Personal and Events.
6. Highlight *Activity type* and, holding the pointer on *Activity type*, right click, select *New Tree Node*, type in the name *Sporting* and click on *OK*.
7. Repeat step 5, adding *Social* and *Cultural* – Sporting, Social, Cultural should now be listed under *Activity type*.
8. Repeat steps 6–7 for:
   - *Influences*: *Parents, Teachers, Peers*
   - *Constraints*: *Time, Money, Fitness*
   - *Personal*: *Competitive, Social-non-social, Anti-routine, Instrumental*
   - *Events*: *Parents, Teachers, Peers*.

   The screen should then appear as follows.

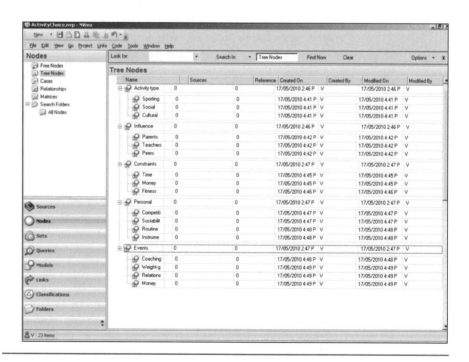

Figure 15.12 Setting up a coding system – procedure

The following NVivo procedures show how the coding system can be presented diagrammatically as a *model*.

1. In the Navigation View area select *Nodes* and then *Tree Nodes* from the menu: the *Main Activity* node specified in Figure 15.12 will appear in the List View area.

2. In the Navigation View area, select *Models*, which will now replace *Tree Nodes* in the List View area.

3. Right click in the List View area and from the menu, select *New Model*.

4. In the *New Model* dialog box enter a name for the model e.g. *Model 1*, and click on *OK*.

5. A workspace for *Model 1* appears below in the Detail View area, with a selection of *Shapes* down the lefthand side. NB. The workspace can be expanded to half or full screen by clicking on *Window* in the Windows menu and clicking on *Docked* (and on Undock All to reverse).

6. Right click in the work space and, from the drop-down menu, select *Add Project Items*.

7. In the *Add Project Items* dialog box, click on the actual name *Tree Nodes* (not the adjacent tick-box for this exercise)

8. *Main Activity* appears in the space to the right: check the tick-box and click on *OK*.

9. The first part of the graphic, a circle containing *Main Activity*, should appear in the work space. Drag it to the centre, top of the work space.

10. Right click on the circle and in the drop-down menu select *Add Associate Data*.

11. The five factors (Personal, Activity type, Events, Events, Influence and Constraints) appear, as shown below.

12. Click on *Influence* and repeat step 10: the three influences, teachers, peers, parents, appear as below.

13. Click on *Events* and repeat step 10.

14. This can be repeated for all factors, but it will be necessary to click and drag the shapes around to fit them appropriately into the work space. The sizes of the shapes and the font can be increased or reduced.

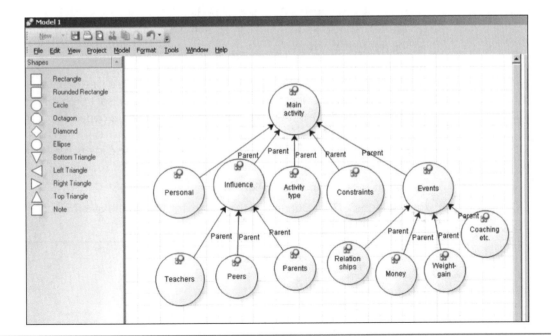

Figure 15.13 Modelling – procedure

1. In the Navigation View area, select *Sources* then *Internals> Interviews* in the menu. The three interview transcript files should appear in th List View area.

2. Double click on *Mark* and the transcript should appear below in the Display View area.

3. A section of text is coded by highlighting: to have this highlighting indicated visually on the text after it has been coded: on the Windows menu, select *View > Highlight > Coding for selected items*.

4. The coding can also be indicated visually with *Coding stripes* which appear in the space to the right of the text. To activate this: on the Windows menu select: *View > Coding Stripes > Nodes Most Coding*. (It will be noted that two coding stripes are already in place: one indicates that the Mark transcript as a whole is coded to the *Case* Mark and the other is a 'coding density' stripe which relates to the amount of coding.)

5. To code the activity 'playing football' in Mark's transcript:
   a. Highlight *playing football*.
   b. In the Windows menu, select *Code> Code Selection > At Existing Nodes* – the *Select Project Items* dialog box should appear.
   c. In the *Select Project Items* dialog box: select *Tree Nodes – Main Activity* should appear.
   d. Click on the + on the left of the *Main Activity* listing and factors, *Personal, Influence, Activity type*, etc. will be listed below.
   e. Click on the + on the left of *Activity type* and *Sporting, Social, Cultural* will be listed below.
   f. Select *Sporting* using the tick-box and click *OK*.
   g. The text should appear highlighted and a *Sporting* stripe should appear in the right-hand space.

6. Repeat step 5 for:
   - text 'While the football's on, because of training twice a week and needing to be fairly serious about keeping fit I don't do much else: I probably only go to a pub once – or at most twice – a week', which is coded as *Constraints* > Time;
   - text: 'I'm pretty competitive – so I like sport generally' coded: *Personal > Competitive*

7. The result should appear as below.

8. Repeat steps 2–7 for Donna and the statement 'I go to the gym once or twice a week' (result not shown below).

Figure 15.14 Coding text – procedure

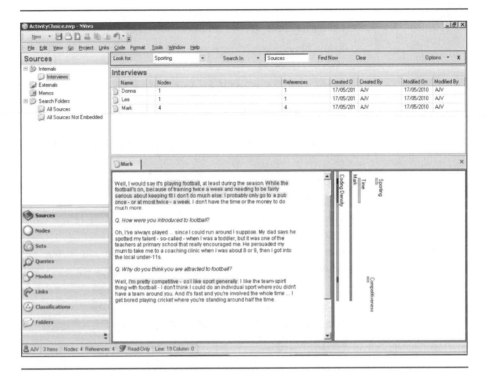

Figure 15.14 (*continued*)

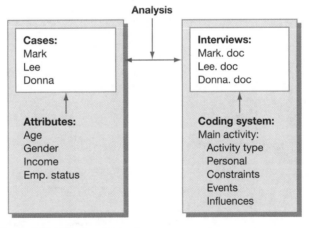

Figure 15.15 Activity Choice project summary

Coding query

One of the simplest forms of analysis is simply to obtain a listing of all the sections of text coded in a certain way. Thus a listing of all passages in the transcripts coded with Sporting as the Main Activity is obtained as shown in Figure 15.16.

Rather than searching for text coded as a node in the coding system it is possible to search for any item of specified text. This would involve selecting *Text Search* instead of *Coding* at step 2 in Figure 15.16.

To select the text which has been coded *Sporting* as *Main Activity*:

1. In the Navigation View area, select *Queries*: the List View area will now be headed *Queries.*

2. Right click in the List View area and select *New Query > Coding.*

3. A *Coding Query* dialog box appears offering selection by *Node* or by *Any case where* (which refers to attributes).

4. To select by the *Node* 'Sporting': click on *Select* and select *Tree Node > Main Activity > Activity Type > Sporting.*

5. Click on *Run* and a listing will appear in the Detail View area with the names of the cases, Mark and Donna, and a printout of the relevant text, as shown below.

6. The results of this query can be saved for future reference: right click in the result area and from the drop-down menu select *Story Query Results* and type in a name, e.g. Query_Sporting. This material can subsequently be accessed when required via the Navigation View area: *Queries > Results.*

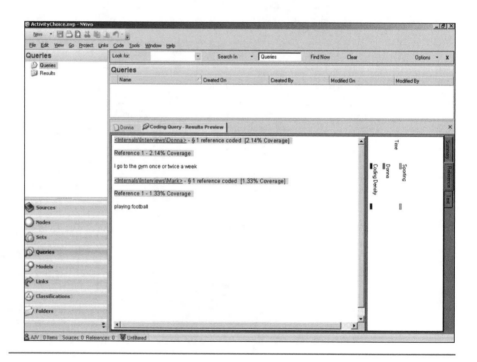

Figure 15.16   Queries – procedure

To divide interviewees engaging in sporting activities into males and females:

1. In the Navigation View area, select *Queries*: the List View area will now be headed *Queries*.
2. Right click in the List View area and select *New Query > Matrix Coding*.
3. In the *Matrix Coding Query* dialog box, under *Matrix Coding Criteria* and *Rows* and *Define More Rows*: *Selected Items* will be displayed.
4. Click on the *Select* button on the right. The *Select Project Items* dialog box will be displayed.
5. In the *Select Project Items* dialog box click on *Tree Nodes* to bring up *Main Activity*, then go down to *Sporting* (as in Figure 15.14 steps 5d–f) and click on *OK*.
6. On returning to the *Matrix Coding Query* dialog box, click on *Add to List* and *Tree Nodes/Main Activity/Activity Type/Sporting* will appear under *Name*.
7. Click the Columns tab and then Select.
8. In the *Select Project Items* dialog box select *Attributes* and then *Gender* then OK.
9. On returning to the *Matrix Coding Query* dialog box, click on *Add to List* and *Tree Nodes/Main Activity/Activity Type/Sporting* will appear under *Name*.
10. Click on *Run* and the results will be displayed in a table as follows (it may be necessary to widen the columns to display the labels in full):

	A Gender = Unassigned	B Gender = Not Applicable	C Gender = Male	D Gender = Female
Sporting	0	0	1	1

11. This shows one male and one female coded as taking part in sport as their main activity: double clicking in the cells containing a number will bring up the relevant coded text.

Figure 15.17 Matrix coding query – procedure

Matrix coding query

The *Coding query* can be seen as the equivalent of a frequency count in questionnaire survey analysis; the equivalent of a crosstabulation is a *Matrix coding query*. Figure 15.17 shows the procedure for conducting such an analysis in the Activity Choice project to separate sports participants by gender.

Summary

The chapter is divided into two sections dealing respectively with manual and computer-aided qualitative data analysis methods.

Manual methods of data analysis involve 'flagging' issues or themes which emerge in texts such as interview transcripts. Such issues or themes may relate to an existing draft conceptual framework, to research questions and/or hypotheses; or, in a 'grounded theory', inductive approach, they may be used to build up a conceptual framework from the data. Since texts are invariably available as word-processed files, it is noted that certain features of word-processor packages, such as 'search' and 'list' or 'index' can be used to assist in the 'flagging' process. This provides a link to the custom-made Computer Aided Qualitative Data Analysis Software (CAQDAS) packages.

The second part of the chapter introduces the NVivo CAGDAS package, covering the setting up of a project file and a coding system, coding of data and some elementary analysis procedures. While the package has a large range of capabilities – including the handling of data other than interview transcripts – just a limited range of analysis procedures is presented in this short outline; but it is believed this is adequate for the qualitative researcher to make a start with computer-aided data analysis.

Test questions

1. What are the two major activities involved in manual analysis of qualitative data?

2. What word-processor procedures might be used in 'manual' analysis of qualitative data?

3. What is the difference between a 'Node' and a 'Document' in NVivo?

4. What is the difference between a 'Tree Node' and a 'Free Node' in NVivo?

Exercises

1. Download from the book's website the three transcript files for the 'Leisure choice' project used above – or type them out from Figure 15.3 – and replicate the coding and analyses presented above. This can be done manually or by using NVivo.

2. Run the NVivo tutorials included with the package, particularly exploring features of NVivo not presented in this chapter.

3. Select an example of a quantitative and a qualitative research report from a recent edition of one of the leisure or tourism journals and consider whether the qualitative research project could have been approached using quantitative methods and whether the quantitative project could have been approached using qualitative methods.

4. Use the checklist in Figure 9.4 to interview a willing friend or colleague. Assess your performance as an interviewer.

5. If you are studying with others, organise yourselves into groups of 5 or 6 and organise a focus-group interview, with one person as facilitator, choosing a topic of mutual interest, such as 'the role of education and qualifications in the leisure/tourism industries' or 'holiday choice processes', or 'fitness versus the enjoyment of sport'. Take turns in acting as convenor and assess each others' skills as convenor.

6. Using the issues of a newspaper for one week, provide a qualitative and quantitative analysis of the coverage of a topic of interest, such as: the environment, ethnic minorities, women and sport or overseas locations.

7. Arrange to view a copy of *Cannibal Tours* and discuss the film in the light of MacCannell's (1993) essay on the film. Or view any Disney cartoon film and discuss it in relation to Rojek's (1993) paper.

Resources

Websites

- NVivo website: www.qsrinternational.com/ – includes a downloadable bibliography on qualitative data analysis sources.

- CATPAC – text analysis package – see Ryan (2000).

- *Qualitative Research* journal: http://qrj.sagepub.com/.

- The Qualitative Report (portal): www.nova.edu/ssss/QR/.

Publications

- *Analysis of qualitative data generally*: Miles and Huberman (1994).

- *Use of computer software packages* in qualitative data analysis: Miles and Weitzman (1994), Richards and Richards (1994).

- *Use of NVivo software*: Bazeley (2007), Gibbs (2002 – does not include latest version of NVivo).

16 Analysing survey data

Introduction

In this chapter the analysis of questionnaire survey data is addressed using two types of computer package:

- *Spreadsheets*: are the most widespread computer application used for general data analysis and Microsoft Excel is used to demonstrate certain analysis procedures.

- *Statistical packages*: are used to analyse statistical data in a research context and one of the most widely used packages is the Statistical Package for the Social Sciences (SPSS) and is used here for demonstration purposes. Other packages include *Minitab*, *BMD* (Biomedical Data analysis), *SAS* (Statistical Analysis System) and *Turbostats*.

Figure 10.20, in Chapter 10, contains a copy of a simple questionnaire which is used to demonstrate analysis processes in this chapter. Chapter 10 dealt with the procedure for coding the data from this questionnaire in a form suitable for computer analysis, as shown in Figure 10.21.

Before addressing the mechanics of data analysis, however, the typology of research discussed in Chapter 1 is discussed in relation to the analysis process.

Survey data analysis and types of research

In Chapter 1 it was noted that research might be of three kinds: descriptive, explanatory and evaluative. Before considering the process of analysing questionnaire survey data, these types of research and their relationship to survey analysis are discussed in turn below and summarised in Figure 16.1.

Descriptive research

Descriptive research usually involves the presentation of information in a fairly simple form. Of the analytical procedures described in this chapter, the two most appropriate for descriptive research are:

- *frequencies* which present counts and percentages of responses for single variables;

- *means* which present averages for numerical variables.

Explanatory research

Descriptive data do not, of themselves, *explain* anything. To explain the patterns in data or relationships between phenomena represented by the data, it is necessary to consider the question of *causality* – how to determine whether A is caused by B. In Chapter 2 it was noted that to establish causality it is necessary to fulfil four criteria: association, time priority, non-spurious relation and rationale:

- *Associations* between variables can be explored using such procedures as *crosstabulations* (described in this chapter) and *regression* (described in Chapter 17).

- *Time priority* – involves establishing that, for A to be the *cause* of B, then A must take place *before* B – this is sometimes testable in social science research

Research type	Analytical procedures
Descriptive	Frequencies, Means
Explanatory	Crosstabulation, Comparison of means, regression
Evaluative	Frequencies – compared with targets or benchmarks
	Crosstabulations – comparing user/customer-groups
	Means – compared with some benchmark or target

Figure 16.1 Research types and analytical procedures

and is sometimes obvious, but is generally more appropriate for the conditions of the natural science laboratory.

● *Non-spurious* relationships are those which 'make sense' theoretically (that is, the relationship between A and B is not mediated by a third, extraneous variable C), and are not just a 'fluke' of the data. This can be approached using survey analysis techniques. For example, suppose it is found that leisure and tourism expenditure is inversely related to age for the whole sample. If this relationship is also found for, say, men and women separately, and for other sub-groups – even random sub-samples – this suggests a non-spurious relationship.

● *Rationale*, or *theory*, is of course not produced by computer analysis but should be integral to the research design. As indicated in Chapter 2, the research may be *deductive* in nature, with pre-established hypotheses which are tested by the data analysis, or it may be *inductive*, in which development of theory and explanation building take place to a greater or lesser extent as part of the data analysis process. Either way, *explanation*, or the establishment of causality, is not complete without some sort of rational, conceptual explanation of the relationships found.

The example questionnaire from Chapter 10 offers only limited scope for *explanatory* research. For example, differences in attitudes between the various student groups – full-time and part-time or different age-groups for, example – may indicate that varying expectations from campus life may be a function of student group characteristics.

The particular procedures which are appropriate for explanatory analysis and which are covered in this chapter are the production of *crosstabulations*, which facilitates examination of the relationship between two or more variables based on frequencies, and the examination of the *means* of two or more variables. These procedures can establish whether or not statistical relationships exist between variables, but whether or not they are spurious and/or supported by theory involves reference to the theoretical or conceptual framework.

Evaluative research

Evaluative research basically involves comparisons between survey findings and some benchmark derived from expectations, past figures, other similar facilities or programmes or target performance standards. The analysis called for, therefore, is relatively simple, generally involving comparisons between findings from the survey and some benchmark value.

The example questionnaire could be used for evaluative purposes – for example, a low level of use of any of the services listed in question 2 could imply that the existing service is not performing well in meeting the demands of students and low levels of use by particular groups could indicate a failure to meet the needs of all groups.

Overlaps

Analysis does not always fall exclusively into one of the above three modes. For example, in presenting a descriptive account of the example Campus Life survey results, it would be natural to provide a breakdown of the participation patterns and preferences of the four student groups included. While this could be descriptive in form, it would begin at least to hint at explanation, in that any differences in the groups' patterns of behaviour or opinions would seem to call for explanation; the analysis would be saying 'these groups are different' and would be implicitly posing the question 'why?' In so far as the providers of campus services aimed to serve all sections of the student community, the data could be used in evaluating management.

Reliability

In Chapter 2 reference was made to questions of *validity* and *reliability*. It has been noted that some attempt at testing validity – whether the data are measuring what they are intended to measure – can be achieved in the design of questionnaires. Reliability – whether similar results would be obtained if the research were replicated – is a difficult issue in the social sciences, but an approach can be made at the analysis stage. While statistical procedures are well suited to establishing the magnitude and strength of associations, the question of the reliability of such associations is more complex. Unlike the natural sciences, it is not always possible, for practical or resource reasons, to replicate research in the social sciences to establish reliability. While reference to previous research reported in the literature can be relevant and helpful in this respect, in fact, the changing nature of human nature over time and space means that consistency with previous research findings is by no means a guarantee of reliability – indeed, it is the tracking of *change* which is often the aim of social research.

If the sample is large enough, one approach to reliability is to split the sample into two or more sub-samples on a random basis, or on the basis of a selected variable, and see whether the results for the sub-samples are the same as for the sample as a whole. In the *SPSS* package this can be achieved using the procedure *split file*: the procedure is not covered here but is relatively straightforward to operate.

Spreadsheet analysis

Since most users of this book will be familiar with spreadsheet use, this section does not provide a guide to elementary spreadsheet procedures, but only to procedures specific to analysis of the type of data produced from questionnaire surveys.

The shaded part of Figure 16.2, reproduces in spreadsheet format the data for 15 completed questionnaires from Figure 10.21. There is one change: the

	A	B	C	D	E	F	G	H	I	J	K	L	M	N	O	P	Q	R	S	T	U	V
1	qno	status	cafebar	music	sport	travel	cheap	daytime	unusual	meet	quality	relax	social	mental	sug1	sug2	sug3	gend		age		spend
2	1	2	1	1	0	0	1	4	2	3	5	3	3	1	1			1		18		100
3	2	2	1	1	1	0	1	4	2	3	5	2	3	1	2	1		1		19		50
4	3	3	1	0	0	0	2	5	1	3	4	2	2	2	3	4		2		19		250
5	4	4	0	0	0	0	2	3	1	4	5	3	2	2	1	2	4	1		22		25
6	5	3	1	0	0	1	1	4	3	2	5	3	3	1				2		24		55
7	6	3	1	1	1	0	2	4	1	3	5	2	3	1	2			2		20		40
8	7	2	1	0	0	0	3	2	1	4	5	2	3	2	3			2		20		150
9	8	2	1	0	1	0	3	4	2	1	5	1	2	2	4	5		1		21		250
10	9	4	0	1	0	0	1	5	2	3	4	2	3	2						21		300
11	10	3	1	1	0	0	2	3	1	5	4	1	2	1	1	1		2		21		100
12	11	3	1	1	0	1	2	3	1	4	5	2	2	1	2	3		2		19		75
13	12	2	1	0	1	0	1	4	3	2	5	2	3	1				1		22		50
14	13	1	1	0	1	0	1	5	2	3	4	2	3	2	1	2		2		21		55
15	14	3	1	1	0	0	2	4	1	3	5	3	3	2	4			2		20		75
16	15	1	1	1	0	0	3	2	1	5	4	3	3	1	1	2	5	1		20		150
17																						
18	Code	Freq	Freq	Freq	Freq	Freq	Freq	Freq	Freq	Freq	Freq	Freq	Freq	Freq	Freq	Freq	Freq	Freq	Cat.	Freq	Cat.	Freq
19	0	0	2	7	10	13	0	0	0	0	0	0	0	0	0	0	0	0	19	4	74	6
20	1	2	13	8	5	2	6	0	8	1	0	2	0	8	5	2	0	7	21	8	100	4
21	2	5	0	0	0	0	6	2	5	2	0	8	5	7	3	3	0	8	23	2	200	2
22	3	6	0	0	0	0	3	3	2	7	0	5	10	0	2	1	0	0	25	1		3
23	4	2	0	0	0	0	0	7	0	3	5	0	0	0	2	1	1	0				
24	5	0	0	0	0	0	0	3	0	2	10	0	0	0	0	1	1	0				
25	Total	15	15	15	15	15	15	15	15	15	15	15	15	15	12	8	2	15		15		15
26	Averages																			20.5		115

Figure 16.2 Survey data: spreadsheet analysis

expenditure variable (*spend*) has been shifted to the end to sit alongside *age*, since both are uncoded numerical variables which are treated individually below. The unshaded part is produced by the FREQUENCY procedure provided in Excel. This procedure is described in Figure 16.3.

Spreadsheet analysis is suitable for a small data-set when simple frequency tables are required. In Chapter 18 certain statistical procedures, such as correlation and regression, are outlined using a spreadsheet. But for larger data-sets, particularly longer questionnaires, and more complex analyses, a statistical software package, as outlined below, is advisable.

Statistical Package for the Social Sciences (SPSS)

The main part of the chapter is organised as a step-by-step introductory manual for operating the Statistical Package for the Social Sciences (SPSS).[1] It is envisaged that the reader will have access to a computer with SPSS available on it, so that the procedures described here can be tried out in practice.

The question arises as to what point it is worthwhile to invest time and energy in mastering a computer package for survey analysis, rather than relying on a spreadsheet program, with which many people are already familiar. This of course depends on the scale and complexity of the task in hand and the likely future career path of the researcher. It is clear that a specialist survey package has far more capabilities than a spreadsheet, as this chapter and the next demonstrate. It should be noted that basic coding and data preparation is identical for both approaches and the basic data file is interchangeable between a spreadsheet and a survey analysis package such as SPSS. As noted in Chapter 15, it is also the case that familiarity and experience with a computer package merits an entry on a *curriculum vitae*.

SPSS for Windows is the version of the package which is available for IBM-compatible personal computers using the Microsoft *Windows* system. Version 18 of the package is referred to here. Most universities provide access to the software and further details and information on specialist guides can be found on the SPSS Inc. website (see the Resources section).

---

[1]SPSS Inc. was acquired by IBM in 2008; but remains in operation as an IBM company. Initially, under IBM, the SPSS software was renamed Predictive Analytics Software (PASW). This change took place with the launch of SPSS Version 17, which became PASW 17. However, with version 19, the name has reverted to SPSS. Readers with access to versions 17 and 18 of the package will therefore see that the package is called PASW. As noted in the Preface, SPSS is used in this book, not as a result of a consumer test of available packages, but simply because it is the package with which I am familiar, which I have used in my teaching and reserach, partly because of its availability in the institutions in which I have taught, and which has generally satisfied my requirements.

1. Type: **Code** in cell A18.
2. Type **Freq** in cell B18.
3. Type the codes **0, 1, 2, 3, 4, 5** in cells A19 to A24 respectively (0–5 covers all the codes used by variables *status* to *gend*.
4. Select cells B19 to B24 (the cells in which the results of the frequency counts will be placed, referred to in Excel as the 'bin array').
5. Type the following 'array formula' in the 'formula bar' (not shown in Figure 16.2):
   a. =FREQUENCY(B2:B16,$A19:$A24) and then press Ctrl+Shift+Enter together.
   b. The results will appear as shown in cells B19 to B24 in Figure 16.2.
   c. Note:
      - When you have typed =FR Excel will offer you a pop-up FREQUENCY which you can select with a double click.
      - You can select the cells B2:B16 rather than typing the cell references manually.
      - The $A format is used in $A19:$A24 because the codes in cells A19:A24 will be utilised for all 17 coded variables, so in spreadsheet parlance, an absolute rather than a relative column location must be specified.
      - General instructions on the use of the FREQUENCY formula are provide by the Excel Help facility.
6. The heading in cell B18 and the formulae in cells B19:B24 can now be copied to produce the frequencies for the other 16 variables: copy cells B18:B24 as one array and paste into cells C18:R24 in one 'copy and paste' operation.
7. Create totals in row 25 using normal spreadsheet procedures.
8. Example results, for *status*, are as follows:

Category	No.
Full-time student with no regular paid work	2
Full-time student with some regular paid work	5
Part-time student with full-time job	6
Part-time student – other	2
Total	15

8. For each variable percentages can be created from the frequencies, and graphics can be created from the frequencies or the percentages using normal spreadsheet procedures.
9. Type category groupings for the non-coded variables, *age* and *spend*, in cells S18:S22 and U18:U20 respectively:
   - cell S19: 19 indicates a group aged 19 and under
   - cell S20: 21 indicates a group aged 20–21
   - cell S21: 23 indicates a group aged 22–23
   - cell S22: 25 indicates a group aged 24–25 (if blank, indicates '24 and over').
10. Select cells T19:T22, then type the following 'array formula' in the 'formula bar' (not shown in Figure 16.2):
    - =FREQUENCY (T2:T16, S19:S22) (note: $S is not required, because the information is only being used for one variable) and then press Ctrl+Shift+Enter together.
    - The results will appear as shown in cells T21 to T22 in Figure 16.2.
11. Results for *age* are therefore:

Age	No.
18–19	4
20–21	8
22–23	2
24–25	1

12. A similar process can be followed for the variable *spend*.
13. Totals, percentages and graphics can be produced as for the other variables. In addition, for the two non-coded variables, averages may be calculated.

Figure 16.3 Questionnaire survey data: steps in spreadsheet analysis

A full list of SPSS procedures can be found in the online *SPSS* manual which is included in the software package. In this chapter five analysis procedures only are described:

- *descriptives* – key descriptive statistics for specified variables;
- *frequencies* – counts and percentages of individual variables;
- *crosstabs* – the crosstabulation of two or more variables;
- *means* – obtaining means/averages of appropriate variables;
- *graphs* – the production of charts and graphs.

The areas covered in this chapter and the statistical procedures covered in Chapter 18 are summarised in Figure 16.4.

The chapter deals with the analysis of data from questionnaire surveys. But SPSS can be used to analyse data from other sources also. And although the package is ideally suited to dealing with numerical data it can also handle non-numerical data. Any data organised on the basis of *cases* and a common range of *variables* for each case can be analysed using the package (*cases* and *variables* are defined below).

The chapter does not deal with procedures for logging into a computer, file handling or the installation of the SPSS software onto the computer; it is assumed that SPSS for Windows is already installed on a computer available to the reader. The information in the chapter provides an introduction to the basics only.

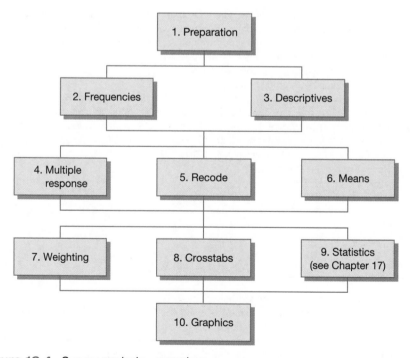

Figure 16.4 Survey analysis – overview

Preparation

Cases and variables

Statistical analysis packages deal with data which are organised in terms of *cases* and *variables*.

- A *case* is a single example of the phenomenon being studied and for which data have been collected – for example, an individual member of a community who has been interviewed, a participant in a leisure activity, an employee of a company, a visitor to a country, a leisure or tourism organisation or a country for which data are available. So a *sample* is made up of a number of *cases*.

- A *variable* is an item of information which is available for all or some of the cases, which can take on different values or categories – for example, the *gender* of an individual, which can take on the category 'male' or 'female'; the salary of an employee, which can be any monetary value; the *number of employees* of a company; the *population* of a country.

The use of *variables* is further discussed here, while *cases* arise when entering data, as discussed later in the chapter.

Specifying variables

In order to communicate with the program it is necessary to identify each item of data in the questionnaire by a *variable name*. The questionnaire (Figure 10.20) is *annotated with variable names* in the 'Office Use' column. The question numbers and corresponding variable names are listed in Figure 16.5, together with an additional nine items of information for each variable, which are required by the software. These items are discussed in turn below.

Name

- In addition to variables related to the eight questions in the questionnaire, there is a variable *qno* to record a reference number for each case or questionnaire.

- Every item of information on the questionnaire is given a *unique* name (no two variables with the same name).

- The length of variable names is limited to 8 letters/numbers (no spaces), beginning with a letter. It is not permitted to use any of the following for variable names, because the SPSS program already uses these names for other purposes and would get confused!

  ALL   AND   BY   EQ   GE   GT   LE   LT   NE   NOT   OR   TO   WITH

Question No.*	Name*	Type	Width**	Decimal places	Label	Values/Value labels	Missing values	Columns	Alignment	Measure/Data type
–	qno	Numeric	4	0	Questionnaire number	None	None	4	Right	Scale
1.	status	Numeric	1	0	Student status	1 F/T student – no work 2 F/T student – working 3 P/T student – F/T job 4 P/T student – other	None	4	Right	Nominal
2.	cafebar	Numeric	1	0	Campus cafe/bar in last 4 wks	1 Yes 0 No	None	4	Right	Nominal
	music	Numeric	1	0	Live campus music in last 4 wks	as for cafebar	None	4	Right	Nominal
	sport	Numeric	1	0	Sport facilities in last 4 wks	as for cafebar	None	4	Right	Nominal
	travel	Numeric	1	0	Travel service in last 4 wks	as for cafebar	None	4	Right	Nominal
3.	cheap	Numeric	1	0	Free/cheap (rank)	None	None	4	Right	Ordinal
	daytime	Numeric	1	0	Daytime events (rank)	None	None	4	Right	Ordinal
	unusual	Numeric	1	0	Not available elsewhere (rank)	None	None	4	Right	Ordinal
	meet	Numeric	1	0	Socialising (rank)	None	None	4	Right	Ordinal
	quality	Numeric	1	0	Quality of presentation (rank)	None	None	4	Right	Ordinal
4.	spend	Numeric	4	0	Expenditure on entertainment/month	None	None	4		Scale
5.	relax	Numeric	1	0	Relaxation opportunities – importance	3 Very important 2 Important 1 Not at all important	None	4	Right	Scale
	social	Numeric	1	0	Social interaction – importance	as for relax	None	4	Right	Scale
	mental	Numeric	1	0	Mental stimulation – importance	as for relax	None	4	Right	Scale
6.	sug1	Numeric	2	0	Improvement suggestion – 1	1 Programme content§ 2 Timing 3 Facilities 4 Costs 5 Organisation	None	4	Right	Nominal
	sug2	Numeric	2	0	Improvement suggestion – 2	as for sug1	None	4	Right	Nominal
	sug3	Numeric	2	0	Improvement suggestion – 3	as for sug1	None	4	Right	Nominal
7.	gender	Numeric	1	0	Gender	1 Male 2 Female	None	4	Right	Nominal
8.	age	Numeric	2	0	Age	None	None	4	Right	Scale

Figure 16.5   Variable names, labels and values

* From Figure 10.20.
** max. no. of characters.
§ See Figure 10.19 for derivation of coding system.

Three possible systems for naming variables are:

- practice adopted here, which is to use variables names which are full or shortened versions of how the item might be described – for example *status* for student status, and *sug1* for improvement suggestion 1;

- use a generalised name such as *var* for variable; so a questionnaire with 5 variables would have variable names: *var1, var2, var3, var4, var5* – in fact *SPSS* has a system of 'default' variable names already set up in this form, which can be used instead of the customised names used here;

- use of question numbers – for example, *Q1, Q2a, Q2b*, and so on.

Question 6 should be noted. It is an open-ended question and respondents might wish to give any number of answers. In this case the designer of the questionnaire has assigned three variables to record up to three answers (*sug1, sug2* and *sug3*), on the assumption that a maximum of three answers would be given by any one respondent. Not all respondents will necessarily give three answers – this is no problem, because *sug2* and/or *sug3* can be left blank. Some may, however, give *more* than three answers, in which case it would not be possible to record the fourth and subsequent answers and that information would be lost. If more than a handful of respondents give more than three answers then a fourth variable (*sug4*) could be added. The decision on how many answers to allow for must depend on a preliminary scanning of the questionnaires. As an open-ended question, the coding system for question 6 applies to all three variables and was devised from the range of free-form answers as discussed in Chapter 10.

Type

All the variables in the Campus Life survey questionnaire are *numeric* – that is, they can only be numbers. A number of other possibilities exist, including *date* and *string*, the latter meaning text comprising any combination of letters and numbers, but these options are not pursued here.

Width

Width specifies the maximum number of digits for the value of a variable. In the Campus Life survey questionnaire, all variables are single-digit except three:

- *qno*: width will depend on the size of the sample – here a width of four digits is indicated, indicating a maximum possible sample size of 9999;

- *cost*: width has been put at four, suggesting maximum possible individual weekly expenditure on entertainment of £9999 – which should accommodate all respondents!

- *sug1, sug2, sug3*: two digits allowing for ten or more codes.

Decimal places

None of the variables in the Campus Life questionnaire includes *decimal places*, so the number of decimal places is set to zero for all of them. Many variables could, however, include decimals or dollars/cents, pounds/pence – for example, a person's height, or a tourist's expenditure per day.

Label

The variable *label* is fuller and more descriptive than the variable *name*, and there is no restriction on content or length. It can be included in output tables, making them more readily understandable by the reader. This is often necessary with long questionnaires with many variables, and particularly when the short variable *names* are not immediately recognisable.

Value labels

Value labels identify the codes used for each variable: e.g. for *gend*, 1 = male and 2 = female. In the case of the Campus Life questionnaire:

- The questionnaire number is just a reference number so it has no value labels.
- Variables based on questions 1, 2 and 5 have specific codes or values (1, 2, 3, etc.) with value labels as specified in the questionnaire.
- Variables based on question 3 are ranks from 1 to 5 – they have therefore been specified in Figure 16.5 as having no value labels. In fact, the values for these variables *could* be given value labels as follows: 1 = 'First', 2 = 'Second', 3 = 'Third', 4 = 'Fourth', 5 = 'Fifth'.
- The variable *cost* is an uncoded numerical sum of money and *age* is a number of years – they therefore have no value labels.
- The values/labels for the open-ended question, 6, were derived as shown in Figure 10.19.

Missing

If a respondent does not answer a question in a questionnaire, the data entry may be left blank, or a 'No answer' or 'Not applicable' code may be provided. The software will automatically treat a blank in the data as a 'missing value', but 'No answer' and 'Not applicable' codes can be provided and specified as *missing values*. The implications are that missing values are excluded when means and percentages are being calculated. In the Campus Life data-set, the phenomenon of missing values becomes apparent in the case of variables *sug1*, *sug2* and *sug3*, since some respondents offer no suggestions at all, many offer only one and very few offer three – so there are usually numerous blanks in the data, particularly for *sug2* and *sug3*. In the case of the four variables associated with question 2, it would be possible for non-use of services to be left as a blank, giving rise to missing values, but in this case non-use has been coded as a zero. The *missing value* phenomenon is not pursued in detail in this chapter but is apparent in a number of the outputs from *SPSS*.

Columns

The number of columns or digits per variable is a presentational matter concerning the layout of the 'Data view' screen discussed below. A variable can be *displayed* with any number of columns regardless of the specified *width* of the underlying variable. In the Campus Life example, the specification is four columns for all variables enabling all the data to be seen on the 'Data view' screen at once, without scrolling on most computer screens.

Alignment

Alignment is also presentational. As in a spreadsheet, or table, numerical data are easier to read if aligned to the right, while text is often more suitably aligned to the left.

Measure

Data can be divided into *nominal, ordinal* and *scale* types.

- *Nominal data* are made up of non-numerical *categories*, such as the status categories in question 1 and 'Yes/No' in question 2 of the example questionnaire. In this situation, while numerical codes are used in computer analysis, they have no numerical meaning – for example, code 2 is not 'half' of code 4 – the 1/0 codes could equally well be 6 and 7, A and B, or X and Y. It does not make sense, therefore, to calculate, for example, an average or mean of *nominal data* codes.

- *Ordinal data* reflect a *ranking*, as in question 3 of the example questionnaire; the 1, 2, 3 in this question represent the *order of importance*, but rank 3 cannot be interpreted as being '3 times as high as' rank 1. It is, however, possible to take an average or mean rank – for example, to speak of an 'average ranking'.

- *Scale data* are fully numerical – as in questions 4 (*spend*) and 8 (*age*) of the example questionnaire. Numerical information, such as a person's age, travel expenditure or frequency of participation in an activity, are *scale data*. In this case an answer of 4 *is* twice as high as an answer of 2 and averages or means are clearly appropriate.

The data type, or type of measure, of a variable affects the range of statistical analysis which can be performed and the appropriate formats for graphical presentation, and these are discussed later, particularly in Chapter 17.

In Figure 16.5 each variable is identified as nominal, ordinal or scale, as follows:

- *qno* is identified as a *scale* variable, although it will not be used in analysis;
- variables from questions 1, 2, 6 and 7 are *nominal*;

- variables from question 3 are *ordinal*;
- the question 4 variable, *spend* and question 8 variable, *age* are *scale* variables;
- question 5 variables are 'Likert-style' variables, specified as *scale* variables for the reasons discussed below.

Attitude/Likert variables

Variables arising from *Attitude/Likert variables* (see Chapter 10) have been used extensively in psychological and market research and have come to be seen almost as *scale* variables when, in reality, they are just ordinal. Means are therefore accepted as an appropriate form of analysis when using such variables. The scores of 1 to 3 in question 5 in the Campus Life questionnaire can be treated as numerical indicators of the level of importance respondents attach to the items listed. The means can be interpreted as average 'scores' on importance. It is possible to add scores in some circumstances.

Role

The default setting for all variables is *input*. This need not concern us here. The idea of an *output* variable will be apparent when the *Recode* procedure is discussed below.

Starting up

To start a *SPSS Statistics* session on a computer, activate the program as indicated in Figure 16.6. Switch to the *Variable View* screen to start the process outlined below.

Entering information about variables – Variable View window

The information about the variables arising from a questionnaire, as shown in Figure 16.5 above, must be typed into the *Variable View* window. The result of

---

1. Start *SPSS Statistics* on your computer using the appropriate screen icon or *Start* and *All Programs*.
2. The dialog box headed *SPSS Statistics*, with the question *What do you want to do?* is presented.
3. Click on *Type in data* then *OK*.
4. The *Data View* window, which will receive the data, and *Variable View* window, which will receive information about the variables, should now be available, as in Figure 16.7, and you can switch between them using the tab at the bottom of the screen.

Figure 16.6 Starting a *SPSS Statistics* session

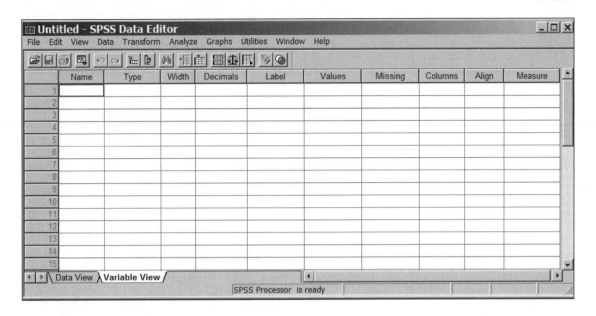

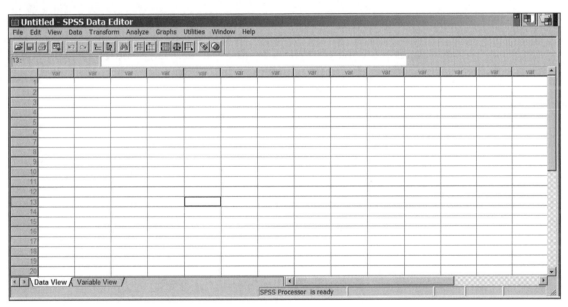

Figure 16.7   Blank Variable View and Data View windows

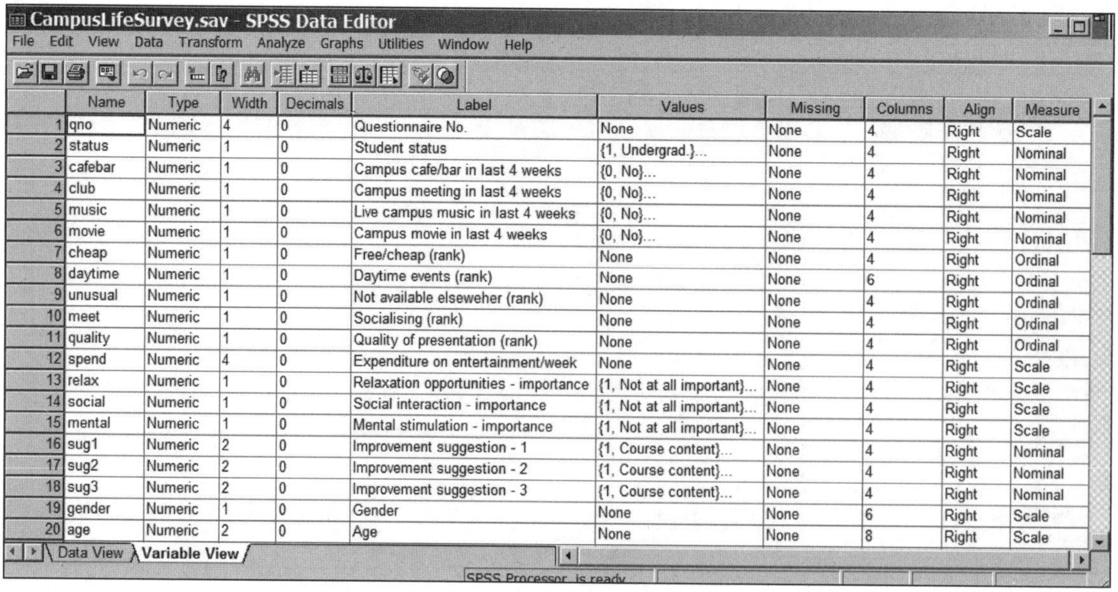
CampusLifeSurvey.sav - SPSS Data Editor

File Edit View Data Transform Analyze Graphs Utilities Window Help

	Name	Type	Width	Decimals	Label	Values	Missing	Columns	Align	Measure
1	qno	Numeric	4	0	Questionnaire No.	None	None	4	Right	Scale
2	status	Numeric	1	0	Student status	{1, Undergrad.}...	None	4	Right	Nominal
3	cafebar	Numeric	1	0	Campus cafe/bar in last 4 weeks	{0, No}...	None	4	Right	Nominal
4	club	Numeric	1	0	Campus meeting in last 4 weeks	{0, No}...	None	4	Right	Nominal
5	music	Numeric	1	0	Live campus music in last 4 weeks	{0, No}...	None	4	Right	Nominal
6	movie	Numeric	1	0	Campus movie in last 4 weeks	{0, No}...	None	4	Right	Nominal
7	cheap	Numeric	1	0	Free/cheap (rank)	None	None	4	Right	Ordinal
8	daytime	Numeric	1	0	Daytime events (rank)	None	None	6	Right	Ordinal
9	unusual	Numeric	1	0	Not available elseweher (rank)	None	None	4	Right	Ordinal
10	meet	Numeric	1	0	Socialising (rank)	None	None	4	Right	Ordinal
11	quality	Numeric	1	0	Quality of presentation (rank)	None	None	4	Right	Ordinal
12	spend	Numeric	4	0	Expenditure on entertainment/week	None	None	4	Right	Scale
13	relax	Numeric	1	0	Relaxation opportunities - importance	{1, Not at all important}...	None	4	Right	Scale
14	social	Numeric	1	0	Social interaction - importance	{1, Not at all important}...	None	4	Right	Scale
15	mental	Numeric	1	0	Mental stimulation - importance	{1, Not at all important}...	None	4	Right	Scale
16	sug1	Numeric	2	0	Improvement suggestion - 1	{1, Course content}...	None	4	Right	Nominal
17	sug2	Numeric	2	0	Improvement suggestion - 2	{1, Course content}...	None	4	Right	Nominal
18	sug3	Numeric	2	0	Improvement suggestion - 3	{1, Course content}...	None	4	Right	Nominal
19	gender	Numeric	1	0	Gender	None	None	6	Right	Scale
20	age	Numeric	2	0	Age	None	None	8	Right	Scale

Data View / Variable View

SPSS Processor is ready

Figure 16.8 Variable View window with variable names, labels, etc.

this exercise for the Campus Life questionnaire is as shown in Figure 16.8. It should be noted that for variables with identical value labels, the value labels can be copied and pasted.

Saving work

As with any computer work, the file should be saved to hard disk or a memory stick from time to time during the course of preparation and when completed, and a back-up copy should be made also. The suffix for an *SPSS* datafile is .sav, so the example file could be called CampusLifeSurvey.sav. Once the file is *saved* the title 'CampusLifeSurvey' appears at the top of the screen.

Entering data – Data View window

Switching to the *Data View* window reveals that the variable names entered via the *Variable View* window have automatically been put in place, and the system is ready to receive data. Data from the questionnaires can now be keyed in: one row on the screen per questionnaire, or *case*. Figure 16.9 shows the *Data View* window with data from the 15 cases/questionnaires shown in Figure 10.21. While a sample of 15 would generally be seen as too small for a typical leisure/tourism survey, it is used here for demonstration purposes.

It can be seen that this is similar to the spreadsheet data file as shown in Figure 16.2. Indeed, if the data have already been typed into a spreadsheet and saved in a file, this file can be uploaded directly by *SPSS*. Go to File > Open >

	qno	status	cafebar	club	music	movie	cheap	daytime	unusual	meet	quality	spend	relax	social	mental	sug1	sug2	sug3	gender	age
1	1	2	1	1	0	0	1	4	2	3	5	100	3	3	1	1	.	.	2	18
2	2	2	1	1	1	0	1	4	2	3	5	50	2	3	1	2	1	.	2	19
3	3	3	1	0	0	0	2	5	1	3	4	250	2	2	2	3	4	.	3	19
4	4	4	0	0	0	0	2	3	1	4	5	25	3	2	2	1	2	4	3	22
5	5	3	1	0	0	1	1	4	3	2	5	55	3	3	1	.	.	.	3	24
6	6	3	1	1	1	0	2	4	1	3	5	40	2	3	1	2	.	.	3	20
7	7	2	1	0	0	0	3	2	1	4	5	150	2	3	2	3	.	.	2	20
8	8	2	1	0	1	0	3	4	2	1	5	250	1	2	2	4	5	.	2	21
9	9	4	0	1	0	0	1	5	2	3	4	300	2	3	2	.	.	.	3	21
10	10	3	1	1	0	0	2	3	1	5	4	100	1	2	1	1	1	.	3	21
11	11	3	1	1	0	1	2	3	1	4	5	75	2	2	1	2	3	.	3	19
12	12	2	1	0	1	0	1	4	3	2	5	50	2	3	1	.	.	.	2	22
13	13	1	1	0	1	0	1	5	2	3	4	55	2	3	2	1	2	.	1	21
14	14	3	1	1	0	0	2	4	1	3	5	75	3	3	2	4	.	.	3	20
15	15	1	1	1	0	0	3	2	1	5	4	150	3	3	1	1	2	5	1	20

Figure 16.9   Data View window with data from 15 questionnaires

Data and, in the 'Open Data' dialog box, locate the file and change the 'Files of type' to the appropriate type – e.g. Excel.

Once the Data View and Variable View windows have been completed and the file saved, you are ready to begin analysis.

SPSS Statistics procedures

Starting an analysis session

The data-file with which you are dealing may already be on-screen (as in Figure 16.5) if you have just completed typing in data. If not, and in subsequent sessions, you will need to open the file, as shown in Figure 16.10.

Descriptives

The *Descriptives* procedure produces a range of statistics for specified variables. It is a useful initial procedure to run as a check on certain minimal information for all variables. The details for running the procedure and an example of the resultant output are shown in Figure 16.11. In the example used, five statistics are produced for each variable (except *qno*).

---

1. Start *SPSS Statistics* on your computer using the appropriate screen icon or *Start* and *All Programs.*
2. The dialog box headed *SPSS Statistics*, with the question *What do you want to do?* is presented.
3. If this is the computer on which you set up your *SPSS* file it may be listed in the *Open an existing data source* window – e.g. CampusLifeSurvey.sav – and you can select by clicking on it. If your file is not displayed, select *More files . . .* and locate your file in the appropriate location.
4. The completed *Data View* and *Variable View* windows should now be displayed.

Figure 16.10 Starting a *SPSS* analysis session

Procedures

1. Select *Analyze* then *Descriptive Statistics* then *Descriptives.*
2. Select all variables except *qno* and transfer them to the *Variable(s)* box.
3. Select Options and ensure that the following are ticked: *Mean, St. Deviation, Minimum, Maximum* then click on *Continue.*
4. Click on *OK* to produce the following output.

PASW Output

Descriptive Statistics

	N	Minimum	Maximum	Mean	Std. Deviation
Student status	15	1	4	2.53	.915
Campus cafe/bar in last 4 wks	15	0	1	.87	.352
Live campus music in last 4 wks	15	0	1	.53	.516
Sport facilities in last 4 wks	15	0	1	.33	.488
Travel service in last 4 wks	15	0	1	.13	.352
Free/cheap (rank)	15	1	3	1.80	.775
Daytime events (rank)	15	2	5	3.73	.961
Not available elsewhere (rank)	15	1	3	1.60	.737
Socialising (rank)	15	1	5	3.20	1.082
Quality of presentation (rank)	15	4	5	4.67	.488
Expenditure on entertainment/month	15	25	300	115.00	87.076
Relaxation opportunities – importance	15	1	3	2.20	.676
Social interaction – importance	15	2	3	2.67	.488
Mental stimulation – importance	15	1	2	1.47	.516
First suggestion	12	1	4	2.08	1.165
Second suggestion	8	1	5	2.50	1.414
Third suggestion	2	4	5	4.50	.707
Gender	15	1	2	1.47	.516
Age	15	18	24	20.47	1.506

Figure 16.11 Descriptives

N – total count

The total count is 15 for all variables except the second and third suggestion since only 12 respondents offered a second suggestion and only 8 offered a third; for the others these variables were blank.

Minimum and Maximum

For coded variables, this is a check that nothing has been miscoded outside the coding range, e.g. 1–3. For the non-coded numerical variables, the maximum and minimum provided may be a useful finding.

Mean

The mean, or average is the sum of all the values for that variable divided by the number of responses (N) for that variable. It is one measure of the idea of the 'middle' – or 'central tendency' of the values for a variable for this sample; other *measures of central tendency* are discussed under the *Frequencies* procedure below.

The mean is generally a useful statistic for:

● numerical variables – in this case, mean Expenditure is £115 and the mean Age of the sample members is 20.47 years;

● ordinal variables – for example, the average rank for the Free/cheap variable is 1.8.

In general, this is not a useful statistic for nominal/coded variables, but there are exceptions:

● Likert scales – Relaxation, Social interaction, Mental stimulation – as discussed in Chapter 10, the score can be seen as an index of importance, so the mean is an indicator of the average level of importance for the sample: thus in this example, Social interaction (mean 2.67) is the most important and mental stimulation (mean 1.47) is the least important.

● 1–0 variables (Campus cafe/bar to travel service): since non-users score zero, the mean effectively is the number of users divided by the total, which is the proportion of users: thus, for example, the proportion of users of the cafe/bar is 0.87 or 87 per cent.

Standard deviation

The standard deviation is a measure of the spread of values around the mean. In this example, among the variables which respondents were asked to rank, for the Quality of presentation, the standard deviation is 0.467, while that for Socialising is 1.082: this makes sense when we see from the maximum/minimum that for the former all responses were either 4 or 5, whereas for the latter they ranged from 1 to 5. The standard deviation is discussed further in Chapter 17.

Frequencies

The *Frequencies* procedure is the simplest form of descriptive analysis: it merely produces counts and percentages for individual variables – for example, the numbers and percentages of respondents registered in each student status group. The procedure can be run for one variable at a time or for a number of variables. It is advisable to begin the analysis of a data-set by running *Frequencies* for one variable – so that the computer can read through the data and establish that the data file is in working order.

Frequencies for one variable

The steps to obtain a table for the variable *status* are set out in Figure 16.12, together with the resultant output. The *Output* window presents two tables. The first, *Statistics*, indicates the number of 'valid cases' on which the analysis is based – in this case 15. The second table, headed *Student status*, shows:

● *Frequency* – count of the numbers of students is each status group;

● *Percent* converts frequency numbers into percentages;

● *Valid Percent* is explained under 'missing values'; and

● *Cumulative Percent* adds percentages cumulatively – which may be useful for a variable like *spend* or *age*, but is not particularly useful for the variable *status*.

Procedure

1. Select *Analyze* from the menu bar at the top of the screen, then *Descriptive Statistics*, then *Frequencies*. This opens the *Frequencies* dialog box.
2. In the *Frequencies* dialog box:
   a. select the variable *status* by highlighting it. Then click on the right arrow to transfer it to the *Variable(s)* box for analysis.
   b. make sure that *Display frequency tables* is ticked.
   c. select *OK* and the results will appear in a new *Output* window as shown below.

PASW Output

Frequencies

Statistics

Student status

N	Valid	15
	Missing	0

Student status

		Frequency	Percent	Valid Percent	Cumulative Percent
Valid	F/T student/no paid work	2	13.3	13.3	13.3
	F/T student/paid work	5	33.3	33.3	46.7
	P/T studen – F/T job	6	40.0	40.0	86.7
	P/T student/Other	2	13.3	13.3	100.0
	Total	15	100.0	100.0	

Figure 16.12 Frequencies for one variable

Frequencies for a number of variables

If the single variable table has worked satisfactorily, frequency tables for all the variables can be obtained by transferring all the variables (except *qno*) into the *Variable(s)* box in Step 2 in Figure 16.12. Running frequency tables for all variables is a common initial instruction in survey analysis: it is a good way of obtaining an overview of the results, and checking that all is well with the data. The results of this exercise for the example questionnaire are in the Appendix 16.1.

It should be noted that the list of variables in the *Frequencies* dialogue box can appear in the form of variable *names* or the longer variable *labels* and can be arranged in the order they appear in the Variable View window or alphabetically. To change these settings, go to *Edit > Options > General > Variable Lists*. Changes to the format of output tables can also be made here. The changes will not be implemented until the file has been saved and closed and then re-started.

Checking for errors

After obtaining the *Frequencies* printout for all variables check through the results to see if there are any errors. This could be, for example, in the form of an invalid code or an unexpected missing value. The error must be traced in the data file and corrected, perhaps by reference back to the original questionnaire. The data must then be corrected on the data window and the *Frequencies* table for that variable run again. *The corrected, 'clean' data file should then be saved to disk, CD or USB memory device.*

Multiple response

Questions 2 and 6 in the example questionnaire are *multiple response* questions. They are single questions with a number of possible responses and must be analysed using a number of variables. Particular 'multiple response' analysis procedures are available in *SPSS* to handle their particular characteristics. There are two types of multiple response question:

- *Multiple response – dichotomous*: question 2 on use of campus services is a dichotomous variable, because each answer category is essentially a yes/no (two values) variable; any one respondent could tick one, two, three or all four boxes, so each is a separate variable.

- *Multiple response – categories*: question 6 on suggestions for improvements, has three variables, *sug1, sug2, sug3*, each coded with the same five category values, as discussed earlier.

It can be seen from Appendix 16.1 that the normal *Frequencies* procedure produces output for these questions in a rather inconvenient format – four tables for question 2 and three tables for question 6. The *Multiple Response* procedure combines multiple responses into a single table for each question. The procedure is operated as shown in Figure 16.13, together with the results – one table each for questions 2 and 6. It should be noted that percentages are

Procedure

1. Select *Analyze*, then *Multiple Response* then *Define Variable Sets*

Multiple response – dichotomous

2. Transfer *cafebar, music, sport* and *travel* into the *Variables in Set* box
3. Under the *Variables are coded as . . .* box, select *Dichotomies*
4. Enter *1* in the *Counted value* box
5. Give the 'set' a *Name* – e.g. *services*
6. Add a *Label* – e.g. *Services used*
7. Select *Add*
8. A new variable, *$services*, is listed automatically
9. Select *Close*

Multiple response – categories

2. Put *sug1, sug2, sug3* into the *Variables in Set* box
3. Under *Variables are coded as . . .*, select *Categories*
4. Enter *Range 1* through *5*
5. Add *Name*, e.g. *sugs*
6. Add *Label*, e.g. *Suggestions for improvement*
7. Select *Add*
8. A new variable *$sugs* is listed automatically
9. Select *Close*

To produce a table:
10. Select *Analyze*
11. Select *Multiple Response*
12. Select *Frequencies* and use the new variables

SPSS Output

Multiple Response

Group: $Service – Services used (Value tabulated = 1)

Dichotomy label	Name	Count	Pct of Responses	Pct of Cases
Campus cafe/bar in last 4 wks	cafebar	13	46.4	92.9
Live campus music in last 4 wks	music	8	28.6	57.1
Sport facilities in last 4 wks	sport	5	17.9	35.7
Travel service in last 4 wks	travel	2	7.1	14.3
Total responses		28	100.0	200.0

1 missing case; 14 valid cases

Group: $Sug – Suggestions for improvement

Category label	Code	Count	Pct of Responses	Pct of Cases
Programme content	1	7	31.8	58.3
Timing	2	6	27.3	50.0
Facilities	3	3	13.6	25.0
Costs	4	4	18.2	33.3
Organisation	5	2	9.1	16.7
Total responses		22	100.0	183.3

3 missing cases; 12 valid cases

Figure 16.13   Multiple response – procedure

given related to the number of respondents and to the number of responses – which of these to use depends on the aims of the research.

Recode

As the name implies, *Recode* is a procedure which can be used to change the codes of variable values. The procedure can be applied to scale, ordinal or nominal variables. This might be done for a number of reasons:

- presentational purposes, when there is a large number of categories and several contain small numbers of responses especially with scale uncoded scale varaiables;
- theoretical purposes, when different parts of the analysis call for different groupings of response categories;
- for comparative reasons, when comparisons with previous research require different groupings;
- for statistical reasons, as discussed in Chapter 17.

Recode with scale and ordinal variables

Scale and ordinal variables are not pre-coded – the actual value given by respondents is recorded in the data file. In the case of scale variables in particular, this means that the *Frequencies* procedure outlined above produces a table with one line for every value in the data-set – as can be seen in Appendix 16.1 for variables *spend* and *age*. With large samples this can produce impractically large tables with possibly hundreds of lines, which would be unreadable and unmanageable, particularly for crosstabulation (discussed below). A *Recoded*, grouped, version of such variables can be produced using the method demonstrated in the first part of Figure 16.14.

Ordinal variables, such as those in question 3, can be recoded – for example, ranks first and second could be grouped together, and third and fourth, and so on. Similarly Likert-type variables, as in question 5, can be recoded – for example, grouping 'very important and 'important' together.

It might be asked: if the variable is to be grouped anyway, why not present groupings in the questionnaire, where respondents can tick a box? This is often done, but the advantage of not having the variable pre-coded is that it is possible to be flexible about what groupings are required and it is also possible to use such procedures as *Means* and *Regression*, which is not generally possible with pre-coded or nominal variables.

Recode with nominal/pre-coded variables

It is also possible to change the groupings of nominal or pre-coded variables using *Recode*. For instance, analysis could be conducted comparing all full-time students and all part-time students – that is, two groups rather than four. This is illustrated in the second part of Figure 16.14.

Part 1 For a scale or ordinal variable

Example: recode the variable *spend* as follows:

Proposed groupings	New code	Value labels
0–50	1	£0–50
51–100	2	£51–100
101–200	3	£101–200
201+	4	£201 and over

Procedure

1. From the top of the screen, select *Transform*, then *Recode into Different Variables*.
2. Select the variable to be recoded, *spend*, and transfer to the *Numeric variable -> Output variable* box
3. In the *Output Variable* box, add a *Name* (e.g. *spendr*) and *Label* (e.g. *Spend on entertainment – recoded*).
4. Select *Old and New Values*.
5. In the *Old Value* box select *Range*. In the first box enter *1* and in the second box, enter *50*.
6. In the *Value* box, enter *1*, then click on *Add*. The *Old–New* box should now contain '1 thru 50 --> 1'.
7. Repeat steps 5 and 6 for: *51* through *100 – Value 2*; and 101 through 200 – *Value 3*
8. Select *Range through Highest*: enter *201*. In the *Value* box enter *4*, then click on *Add*.
   The *Old–New* box should now contain: 1 thru 50-->1, 51 thru 100 --> 2, 101 thru 200 --> 3, 201 thru Highest --> 4.
9. Select *Continue*
10. Select *Change*, then *OK*. The new variable now appears on the Data View and Variable View screens.
11. Add *Value Labels*, as above, via the *Variable View* window, as for any variable.
12. *Save* the data file with the new variable, if you will want to use it again.
13. Produce a *Frequencies* table for the recoded variable *spendr* in the usual way, to produce the output below.

SPSS Output Spend Recoded

	Frequency	Percent	Valid Percent	Cumulative Percent
£ 0–50	4	26.7	26.7	26.7
£ 51–100	6	40.0	40.0	66.7
£ 101–200	2	13.3	13.3	80.0
£ 201+	3	20.0	20.0	100.0
Total	15	100.0	100.0	

Part 2. For a string (pre-coded) variable

Example: recode the variable *status* as follows:

Current coding	New code	Value labels
1. F/T student – no work	1	Full-time student
2. F/T student – working		
3. P/T student – F/T job	2	Part-time student
4. P/T student – other		

Procedure

1–4. Repeat steps 1–3 above, using variable *status*, recoded variable name *statusr* and label *Status – recoded*.
5. In the *Old Value* box select *Range*. In the first box enter *1* and in the second box, enter *2*.
6. In the *Value* box, enter *1*, then click on *Add*. The *Old–New* box should now contain '1 thru 2--> 1.
7. Repeat steps 5 and 6 for: 3 through *4 – Value 2*. The *Old–New* box also now contains '3 thru 4--> 2.
8. Select *Continue*
9. Select *Change*, then *OK*. The new variable now appears on the Data View and Variable View screens.
10. Add *Value Labels*, as above, via the *Variable View* window, as for any variable.
11. *Save* the data file with the new variable, if you will want to use it again.
12. Produce a *Frequencies* table for the recoded variable *statusr* in the usual way, to produce the output below.

SPSS Output: Status recoded

	Frequency	Percent	Valid Percent	Cumulative Percent
Full-time student	7	46.7	46.7	46.7
Part-time student	8	53.3	53.3	100.0
Total	15	100.0	100.0	

Figure 16.14 Recode procedures and output

Mean, median and mode – measures of central tendency

We have already considered the idea of measures of central tendency and the mean in the discussion of *Descriptives* above. As noted there, a *mean* is the same as an *average* and is only appropriate for scale or ordinal data, not for nominal variables with codes which represent qualitative categories, except for the exceptions discussed above.

Here we also consider two other measures of central tendency:

- the *median*, which is the value for which there are as many members of the sample above as there are below;
- the *mode*, which is the value which contains the largest number of sample members.

Two procedures are available in *SPSS* for producing means, as shown in Figure 16.15.

Method 1 uses a feature of the *Frequencies* procedure:

- Example 1a shows that:
  - mean expenditure on entertainment among the sample is £115;
  - the median value is £75, which is lower than the mean because there are more people in the lower expenditure categories than in the higher categories;
  - the mode is £50, £75, £100, £200 and £250, since all have two responses.
- Example 1b demonstrates the use of the procedure for producing mean scores for Likert-type scales – the median does not have a lot of meaning, but the mode, which is the most popular value for each variable, may be meaningful and useful in some situations.

Method 2 uses the *Means* procedure which produces means for sub-groups as well as for the whole sample. For example, in Figure 16.15, mean expenditures on entertainment are shown for students of different statuses. Note that this moves beyond description into the area of possible *explanation*, since it reveals that a student's full-time/part-time and employment status may lead to different levels of expenditure.

Presenting the results: statistical summary

The layout of the frequency tables produced by the software contains more detail than is necessary for most reports. It is recommended that a *Statistical Summary* be prepared for inclusion in any report, rather than include a copy of the computer printout. The summary must be prepared with a word-processor, either typing it out afresh or editing the saved *SPSS Output* file. For example, the output from the *Frequencies, Recodes, Multiple response* and *Means* analysis covered so far, could be summarised as in Figure 16.16.

Method 1. Using *Frequencies* procedure

a. Scale variable

1. Select *Analyze*, then *Descriptive Statistics* then *Frequencies*.
2. Select *spend* and transfer to the *Variable(s)* box.
3. Select *Statistics* and click on *Mean*, *Median* and *Mode*.
4. Select *Continue*.
5. Select *OK* to run the *Frequencies* in the normal way.

SPSS Output (Frequency table not reproduced)

Statistics: Expenditure on entertainment/month

N Valid	15
Missing	0
Mean	115.00
Median	75.00
Mode	50*

a. Multiple modes exist. The smallest value is shown

b. Attitude statements/Likert scales
Using the procedure as in *a.*, above, to produce means for the three variables: *relax*, *social* and *mental*, results in output is as follows.

SPSS Output (Frequency table not reproduced)

	Relaxation opportunities – importance	Social interaction – importance	Mental stimulation – importance
N Valid	15	15	15
Missing	0	0	0
Mean	2.20	2.67	1.47
Median	2.0	3.0	1.0
Mode	2	3	1

Method 2. Using *Means* procedure

a. Scale variable
1. Select *Analyze*, then *Compare Means*, then *Means*.
2. Select *status* and put it into the *Independent list** box.
3. Select *spend* and put it into the *Dependent list** box.
4. Select *OK*. Means and standard deviations for each course group are produced, as below, showing different values for different groups.

(* Dependent and independent variables and standard deviations are discussed in Ch. 17.)

SPSS Output – Report

Expenditure on entertainment/week

Student status	Mean	N	Std. Deviation*
F/T student/no paid work	102.50	2	67.175
F/T student/paid work	120.00	5	83.666
P/T student – F/T job	99.17	6	76.643
P/T student/Other	162.50	2	194.454
Total	115.00	15	87.076

Figure 16.15 *Means* procedures and output

Sample size	15
Student status	%
F/T student/no paid work	13.3
F/T student/paid work	33.3
P/T student – F/T job	40.0
P/T student/Other	13.3
Total	100.0

Campus services used in the last 4 weeks	%
Cafe/bar	86.7
Live campus music	53.3
Sport facilities	33.3
Travel service	13.3

Importance of factors in campus services (avge rank)	
Free/cheap access	1.8
Daytime events	3.7
Not available elsewhere	1.6
Opportunities for socialising	3.2
Quality of presentation	4.7

Expenditure on entertainment/month	%
£0–50	26.7
£51–100	40.0
£101–200	13.3
Over £200	20.0
Average expenditure/month	£115.00

Suggestions for improving the course	% of cases
Comments on programme content	58.3
Comments on timing	50.0
Comments on facilities	25.0
Comments on costs	33.3
Comments on organisation	16.7

Gender	%
Male	53.3
Female	46.3

Age	%
18–19	26.7
20–21	53.4
22 and over	20.0

Importance of factors in campus services

	Very important %	Important %	Not Important %	Mean score*
Relaxation opportunities	33.3	53.3	13.3	2.2
Social interaction	66.7	33.3	0.0	2.7
Mental stimulation	0.0	46.7	53.3	1.5

Figure 16.16 Campus Life Survey 2010: statistical summary

(* 3 = very important 2 = important 1 = not important.)

The following should be noted about the summary:

- The results from *Multiple Response* variables are presented in single tables.
- Recoded versions of *spend* and *age* are included.
- The mean *spend* and *age* and the mean scores for the attitude/Likert-type variables come from the *Means* procedure discussed above.
- It is generally not necessary to include raw frequency counts as well as percentages in reports, since the sample size is indicated: readers of the summary can work out the raw numbers for themselves if required.

Crosstabulation

Introduction

After calculation of frequencies and means, the most commonly used procedure used in survey analysis is probably crosstabulation. This relates two or more variables to produce tables of the sort commonly encountered in social research. In analysing the relationships between variables, crosstabulation marks the move from purely descriptive to explanatory analysis. The *SPSS Crosstabs* procedure and output are demonstrated in Part 1 of Figure 16.17.

Part 1 Crosstabs – Counts only

Procedure

1. Select *Analyze*, then *Descriptive Statistics*, then *Crosstabs*.
2. Transfer *music* to the *Columns* box.
3. Transfer *status* to the *Rows* box.
4. Select *OK*. Output is as below.

SPSS Output

Student status * Live campus music in last 4 wks Crosstabulation

		Live campus music in last 4 wks		Total
		No	Yes	
Student status	F/T student/no paid work	1	1	2
	F/T student/paid work	3	2	5
	P/T student – F/T job	2	4	6
	P/T student/Other	1	1	2
Total		7	8	15

Part 2 Crosstabs with percentages

Procedure

1–3. Repeat steps 1–3 above.
4. In the *Crosstabs* dialog box select *Cells*. The *Crosstabs: Cell Display* dialog box is presented.
5. In the *Counts* box click on the tick in the Observed box to make it disappear (NB. omit this step if you wish to retain counts as well as percentages).
6. In the *Percentages*, select *Row*.
7. Select *Continue*, then *OK*. Output appears as follows.

SPSS Output

Student status * Live campus music in last 4 wks Crosstabulation

		Live campus music in last 4 wks		Total
		No	Yes	
Student status	F/T student/no paid work	50.0%	50.0%	100.0%
	F/T student/paid work	60.0%	40.0%	100.0%
	P/T student – F/T job	33.3%	66.7%	100.0%
	P/T student/Other	50.0%	50.0%	100.0%
Total		46.7%	53.3%	100.0%

Part 3 Three-way crosstabulation

Procedure

1. Repeat steps 1–3 in Part 1 above.
4. In the *Crosstabs* dialog box: transfer *gender* into the *Layer* box.
5. Select *OK* to produce output as follows.

SPSS Output

Student status * Live campus music in last 4 wks *Gender Crosstabulation

Gender			Live campus music in last 4 wks		Total
			No	Yes	
Male	Student status	F/T student/no paid work	1	1	2
		P/T student – F/T job	2	3	5
		P/T student/Other	0	1	1
	Total		3	5	8
Female	Student status	F/T student/paid work	3	2	5
		P/T student – F/T job	0	1	1
		P/T student/Other	1	0	1
	Total		4	3	7

Figure 16.17 Crosstabs – procedure

Rows and columns

Having been specified as the *row* variable in Figure 16.17 Part 1, *status* appears down the side of the table, while the *column* variable, *music*, appears across the top. Specifying the two variables the other way round would produce a table with *status* across the top and *music* down the side.

Percentages

In most cases percentages are required in tables rather than just the raw figures. The Figure 16.17 Part 1 procedure includes percentages only for the row and column totals (which are the same as the percentages in the *Frequencies* tables for the individual variables). The cells in the body of the table contain only counts of the raw data, not percentages. To produce percentages in the body of the table it is necessary to specify the 'cell contents'. There are four relevant options for individual cell contents:

- counts
- row percentages – where percentages add to 100 going across a row
- column percentages – where percentages add to 100 going down the column
- total percentages – where all cell percentages add to 100.

The choice of which percentages to use depends on the context and the purpose of the analysis – it generally becomes apparent in the course of discussing the contents of a table; often 'trial and error' is involved in testing out the use of particular percentages in particular situations. The procedures for producing percentages in *Crosstabs* are as shown in Part 2 of Figure 16.17.

Three-way crosstabulations

Often three-way crosstabulations are required. For example, the above table could be further subdivided by gender. This is demonstrated in Part 3 of Figure 16.17. Further subdivision is possible, although often sample size places limits on how far this can go.

Weighting

The weighting of data to correct for biased samples is discussed in Chapter 13, where the procedure for calculating a weighting factor is discussed. The simplest way of introducing a weighting factor to the *SPSS* process is to add the weights as an additional variable. For example, the 'weighting' variable might be called *wt* and the weights typed into the data-file like any other item of data.

To weight data, select *Data* and use the *Weight Cases* feature, specifying the appropriate variable (e.g. *wt*) as weighting variable. To save having to type in the weights for every respondent, *SPSS* provides a logical procedure. For example, if all Master's course students are to be given a weight of 1.3, it is possible to indicate this in the *Weight cases* procedure. It is not intended to explain the detail of this procedure here – the reader is referred to the Help facility in the *Weight Cases* dialog box.

Graphics

Graphical presentation of data is an aid to communication in most situations: for example, most people can see trends and patterns in data more easily in graphic form. Computer packages generally offer the following graphic formats for data presentation:

- bar graph,
- stacked bar graph,
- pie chart,
- line graph,
- scatter plot.

Computers can produce all five formats from any one set of data. But all formats are not equally appropriate for all data types: the appropriate type of graphic depends on the type of data or level of measurement involved. The three data types therefore lend themselves to different graphical treatment. The relationships between these types of data and permitted graphical types are summarised in Figure 16.18:

- The *bar graph* or *histogram* is perhaps the most commonly used graphic in leisure and tourism research. Because it deals with *categories* for each bar, any scale variable must first be divided into groups – using the *Recode* procedure. The 'stacked' bar graph includes information on two variables – the graphical equivalent of the crosstabulation.
- The *pie chart* is just that: it divides something into sections like a pie. The segments making up the pie chart must therefore add up to some sort of meaningful total – often the total sample.
- The *line graph* is the most constrained and is used more generally in research in more quantified fields such as economics and the natural sciences. Strictly speaking they should only be used with *scale* variables.

	Data type		
	Nominal	**Ordinal**	**Scale**
Data characteristics	Qualitative categories	Ranks	Numerical
Example questions in Fig.10.20	1, 2, 6, 7	3, 5	4, 8
Mean/average possible	No	Yes	Yes
Types of graphic			
Bar graph	Yes	Yes	Yes*
Pie chart	Yes	Yes	Yes*
Line graph	No	No	Yes
Scatter plot	No	No	Yes

Figure 16.18   Data types and graphics

* Grouped.

- A line graph with a single *scale* variable indicates the distribution of a variable although, for the type of data in the example survey, this is probably best done by means of a bar chart.
- A line graph can be used to show the relationship between two *scale* variables – with one variable on each axis. However, a fitted *regression* line, as discussed in Chapter 17, is generally more meaningful than a line traced through all observation points, as would happen with a line graph.

- A *scatter plot* is based on two *scale* variables, but involves just plots of the observation points, rather than drawing a line through them. This may be overcome by use of a 'best fit' line based on *regression*, as discussed in Chapter 17.

Graphics are easily produced in *SPSS* using an optional feature of the *Frequencies* command, but this is not very flexible. A better option is the *Graphs* facility. Examples of graphics output from this facility are shown in Figure 16.19. It is not proposed to consider graphics procedures in detail here; details can be found in the *SPSS* Graphs Help facility.

a. Bar chart
1. Select *Graphs* at the top of the screen, then *Legacy Dialogs*.
2. Select *Bar* and then *Simple* then *Define* to produce the dialog box: *Define Simple Bar: Summaries for Groups of Cases*.
3. Transfer *status* to the *Category Axis* box.
4. Select *N of cases* or *% of cases*. In example here, *% of cases* has been selected.
5. Select *OK* to produce the bar chart.

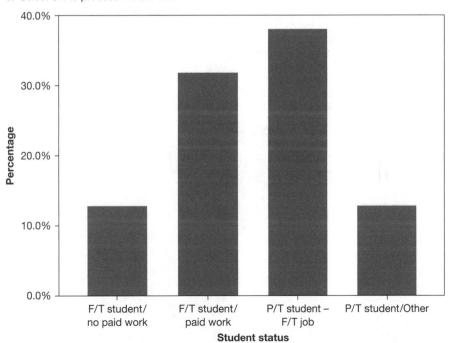

Figure 16.19 Graphics procedure and output

b. Stacked bar chart

1. Select *Graphs* at the top of the screen, then *Legacy Dialogs*.
2. Select *Bar* and then *Stacked* then *Define* to produce the dialog box: *Define Stack Bar: Summaries for Groups of Cases*.
3. Transfer *status* to the *Category axis* box and *gender* to the *Define Stacks by* box.
4. Select *N of cases* or *% of cases*. In the example here, *N of cases* has been selected.
5. Select *OK* to produce the stacked bar chart.

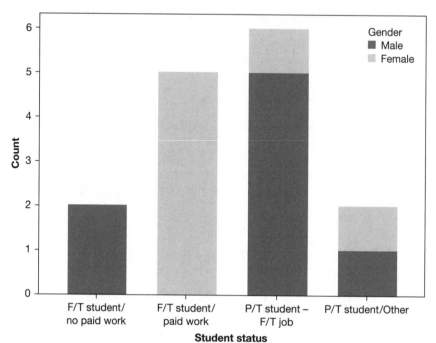

c. Pie chart

1. Select *Graphs* at the top of the screen, then *Legacy Dialogs*.
2. Select *Pie* and then *Summary for Groups of Cases* then *Define* to produce the dialog box: *Define Pie: Summaries for Groups of Cases*.
3. Transfer *status* to the *Define slices by* box.
4. Select *N of cases* or *% of cases*. In the example here, *N of cases* has been selected.
5. Select *OK* to produce the pie chart.

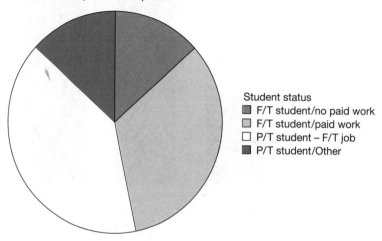

Figure 16.19 (*continued*)

d. Line graph
1. Select *Graphs* at the top of the screen, then *Legacy Dialogs*.
2. Select *Line* and then *Simple* then *Define* to produce the dialog box: *Define Simple Line: Summaries for Groups of Cases.*
3. Transfer *age* to the *Category axis* box.
4. Select *N of cases* or *% of cases*. In the example here, *N of cases* has been selected.
5. Select *OK* to produce the graphic.

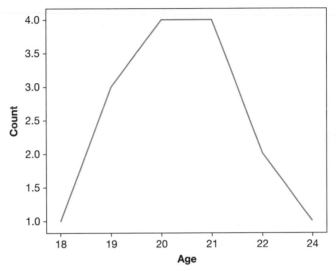

e. Scattergram
1. Select *Graphs* at the top of the screen, then *Legacy Dialogs*.
2. Select *Scatter/Dot* and then *Simple Scatter,* then *Define* to produce the dialog box: *Simple Scatterplot.*
3. Transfer *spend* to the *Y-axis* box and *age* to the *X-axis* box.
4. Select *OK* to produce graphic e.

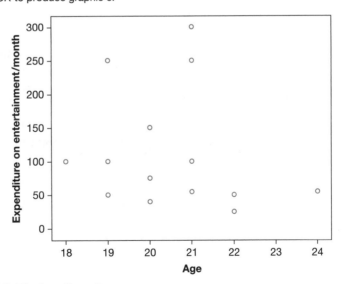

Figure 16.19 (*continued*)

The analysis process

The above is only a brief introduction to the mechanics of survey data analysis. While *SPSS* is capable of much more sophisticated analyses, mastery of the procedures presented here can provide a sound basis for a viable programme of analysis.

Summary

This chapter provides an introduction to the use of the *SPSS* software package for analysis of data from a questionnaire survey. Based on the introduction to coding in Chapter 10, the process of introducing survey data and information on variables into the *SPSS* package is demonstrated. This includes a discussion of levels of measurement and three corresponding variable types: nominal, ordinal and scale. Following a discussion of the relationship between types of research and types of data analysis, the chapter covers six *SPSS* analysis procedures, as follows:

- *Frequencies* provides counts and percentages for individual and multiple variables.

- *Multiple response* creates single tables for the two or more variables arising from questions with multiple responses.

- *Recode* is used to create groups for scale variables and regroup pre-coded variables.

- *Means* calculates the means, or averages of variables and compares means medians and modal values for sub-samples.

- *Crosstabs* creates crosstabulations or frequency tables showing the relationships between two or more variables.

- *Weight* is used to weight data according to some criterion variable, as discussed in Chapter 13.

- *Graphs* produces graphical representations of data in various forms, including bar charts, pie charts, line graphs and scatter plots.

Test questions

1. Explain the difference between nominal, ordinal and scale variables and give examples.

2. What is the advantage of using an uncoded format for a scale variable in a questionnaire, rather than coding it into groups?

3. Outline the characteristics of the two types of multiple response question.

4. Why might an analyst wish to recode variables?

5. What are the two methods for obtaining means in *SPSS*?

Exercises

1. The major exercise for this chapter is to replicate the analyses presented in the chapter. This can be done by typing the data and variable definition data in Figures 16.8 and 16.9 or downloading it from the book website, and carrying out the instructions for the various procedures in the chapter.

2. Repeat each of the procedures in exercise 1 using at least one different variable in each procedure.

3. Conduct a survey of students using the questionnaire in Figure 10.20; and analyse the data using SPSS, following the analysis procedures outlined in this chapter.

Resources

Regarding SPSS

- Access and guidance: It is envisaged that most readers will have access to a teacher/tutor to assist as problems arise. The *SPSS* package itself includes a tutorial for beginners and there are numerous books available on the use of *SPSS*, as indicated below. In higher education institutions *SPSS*, as with other computer packages, is generally made available in computer laboratories on licence. Further training is available in *SPSS*, and other survey packages, through universities, commercial computer training organisations and the *SPSS* company itself in major centres around the world.

- The *SPSS* website is at: www.SPSS.com.

- A number of guides to the use of *SPSS* exist, some using the previous name, SPSS: Carver and Nash (2005); Coakes and Steed (1999); George and Mallery (2005); Pallant (2007).

Regarding questionnaire survey analysis generally

- It is difficult to locate published research reports which give full details of questionnaire surveys and their analysis. While many journal articles are based on survey research, they typically do not provide a copy of the questionnaire and provide only a brief summary of the analysis process – often only part of the analysis arising from the data.

- Few commercially published books are based primarily on questionnaire survey data, and, even when they are, full details are not always provided: one exception is Bennett *et al.* (1999), which not only provides a listing of the questions in the questionnaire, but also provides a detailed discussion of the relationship between existing theory (by Bourdieu) and the empirical research described in the book.

- Government-sponsored survey reports, by the government statistical agency or other agencies, often contain these details – although inevitably they are generally either purely descriptive or related in a fairly straightforward manner to policy issues. Such reports are inconsistently available in libraries, but are sometimes available on the Internet, as indicated in the Resources section of Chapter 10.

- For an international review of survey evidence on leisure, time-use and tourism surveys in 15 countries, see Cushman *et al.* (2005a).

Appendix 16.1: *SPSS* frequencies output file

Statistics (only scale and ordinal variables included here)

	Free/cheap	Daytime events	Not available elsewhere	Socialising	Quality of presentation	Expenditure on entertainment/ month	Relaxation: importance	Social interaction: importance	Mental stimulation: importance
N Valid	15	15	15	15	15	15	15	15	15
Missing	0	0	0	0	0	0	0	0	0
Mean	1.8	3.73	1.6	3.2	4.67	115	2.2	1.67	1.47

Student status

		Frequency	Percent	Valid Percent	Cumulative Percent
Valid	F/T student/no paid work	2	13.3	13.3	13.3
	F/T student/paid work	5	33.3	33.3	46.7
	P/T student – F/T job	6	40.0	40.0	86.7
	P/T student/Other	2	13.3	13.3	100.0
	Total	15	100.0	100.0	

Campus cafe/bar in last 4 wks

		Frequency	Percent	Valid Percent	Cumulative Percent
Valid	No	2	13.3	13.3	13.3
	Yes	13	86.7	86.7	100.0
	Total	15	100.0	100.0	

Live campus music in last 4 wks

		Frequency	Percent	Valid Percent	Cumulative Percent
Valid	No	7	46.7	46.7	46.7
	Yes	8	53.3	53.3	100.0
	Total	15	100.0	100.0	

Sports facilities in last 4 wks

		Frequency	Percent	Valid Percent	Cumulative Percent
Valid	No	10	66.7	66.7	66.7
	Yes	5	33.3	33.3	100.0
	Total	15	100.0	100.0	

Travel service in last 4 wks

		Frequency	Percent	Valid Percent	Cumulative Percent
Valid	No	13	86.7	86.7	86.7
	Yes	2	13.3	13.3	100.0
	Total	15	100.0	100.0	

Free/cheap (rank)

		Frequency	Percent	Valid Percent	Cumulative Percent
Valid	1	6	40.0	40.0	40.0
	2	6	40.0	40.0	80
	3	3	20.0	20.0	100.0
	Total	15	100.0	100.0	

Daytime events (rank)

		Frequency	Percent	Valid Percent	Cumulative Percent
Valid	2	2	13.3	13.3	13.3
	3	3	20.0	20.0	33.3
	4	7	46.7	46.7	80.0
	5	3	20.0	20.0	100.0
	Total	15	100.0	100.0	

Not available elsewhere (rank)

		Frequency	Percent	Valid Percent	Cumulative Percent
Valid	1	8	53.3	53.3	53.3
	2	5	33.3	33.3	86.7
	3	2	13.3	13.3	100.0
	Total	15	100.0	100.0	

Socialising (rank)

		Frequency	Percent	Valid Percent	Cumulative Percent
Valid	1	1	6.7	6.7	6.7
	2	2	13.3	13.3	20.0
	3	7	46.7	46.7	66.7
	4	3	20.0	20.0	86.7
	5	2	13.3	13.3	100.0
	Total	15	100.0	100.0	

Quality of presentation (rank)

		Frequency	Percent	Valid Percent	Cumulative Percent
Valid	4	5	33.3	33.3	33.3
	5	10	66.7	66.7	100.0
	Total	15	100.0	100.0	

Expenditure on entertainment/month

		Frequency	Percent	Valid Percent	Cumulative Percent
Valid	25	1	6.7	6.7	6.7
	40	1	6.7	6.7	13.3
	50	2	13.3	13.3	26.7
	55	2	13.3	13.3	40.0
	75	2	13.3	13.3	53.3
	100	2	13.3	13.3	66.7
	150	2	13.3	13.3	80.0
	250	2	13.3	13.3	93.3
	300	1	6.7	6.7	100.0
	Total	15	100.0	100.0	

Relaxation opportunities – importance

		Frequency	Percent	Valid Percent	Cumulative Percent
Valid	Very important	2	13.3	13.3	13.3
	Important	8	53.3	53.3	66.7
	Not at all important	5	33.3	33.3	100.0
	Total	15	100	100	

Social interaction – importance

		Frequency	Percent	Valid Percent	Cumulative Percent
Valid	Important	5	33.3	33.3	33.3
	Not at all important	10	66.7	66.7	100.0
	Total	15	100.0	100.0	

Mental stimulation – importance

		Frequency	Percent	Valid Percent	Cumulative Percent
Valid	Very important	8	53.3	53.3	53.3
	Important	7	46.7	46.7	100.0
	Total	15	100.0	100.0	

Improvement suggestion – 1

		Frequency	Percent	Valid Percent	Cumulative Percent
Valid	Programme content	5	33.3	41.7	41.7
	Timing	3	20.0	25.0	66.7
	Facilities	2	13.3	16.7	83.3
	Costs	2	13.3	16.7	100.0
	Total	12	80		
Missing	System	3	20		
Total		15	100.0		

Improvement suggestion – 2

		Frequency	Percent	Valid Percent	Cumulative Percent
Valid	Programme content	2	13.3	25.0	25
	Timing	3	20.0	37.5	62.5
	Facilities	1	6.7	12.5	75
	Costs	1	6.7	12.5	87.5
	Organisation	1	6.7	12.5	100.0
	Total	8	53.3	100.0	
Missing	System	7	46.7		
Total		15	100.0		

Improvement suggestion – 3

		Frequency	Percent	Valid Percent	Cumulative Percent
Valid	Costs	1	6.7	50.0	50
	Organisation	1	6.7	50.0	100.0
	Total	2	13.3	100.0	
Missing	System	13	86.7		
Total		15	100.0		

Gender

		Frequency	Percent	Valid Percent	Cumulative Percent
Valid	Male	8	53.3	53.3	53.3
	Female	7	46.7	46.7	100.0
	Total	15	100.0	100.0	

Age

		Frequency	Percent	Valid Percent	Cumulative Percent
Valid	18	1	6.7	6.7	6.7
	19	3	20.0	20.0	26.7
	20	4	26.7	26.7	53.3
	21	4	26.7	26.7	80
	22	2	13.3	13.3	93.3
	24	1	6.7	6.7	100.0
	Total	15	100.0	100.0	

17 Statistical analysis

Introduction

This chapter provides an introduction to statistics, building on the outline of sampling theory presented in Chapter 13 and the introduction to the PASW/SPSS package outlined in Chapter 16. It *is* only an introduction: it is not intended to be a complete course in statistics. There are many textbooks covering approximately the same ground as covered here, but in more detail and more depth, and reference to some of these texts is given in the Resources section. The outline of survey analysis in Chapter 16 deals with quantification and the generation and analysis of statistical information, but this chapter is concerned with more than just quantification. Given that, as discussed in Chapter 13, data based on samples are subject to a margin of error when generalising to the population from which they were drawn, this chapter examines how the accuracy of sample-based statistical data can be assessed and in particular how relationships between variables might be analysed and their statistical significance determined.

After dealing with some general concepts related to the statistical method, the chapter covers a number of statistical tests which are appropriate for different types of data. These tests are: the Chi-square test, the t-test, analysis of variance, correlation, linear and multiple regression and multi-variate analysis. In each case the PASW/SPSS procedures for carrying out the tests are described. At the end of the chapter some analysis procedures which are not covered by *PASW/SPSS* but are used in some leisure/tourism research are discussed in general terms, including: odds ratios, multidimensional scaling and structural equation modelling.

The statistics approach

Before examining particular statistical tests, some preliminary statistical concepts and ideas should be discussed, namely: the idea of probabilistic statements; the normal distribution; probabilistic statement formats; statistical significance; the null hypothesis; and dependent and independent variables.

Probabilistic statements

In general, the science of 'inferential statistics' seeks to make *probabilistic* statements about a *population* on the basis of information available from a *sample* drawn from that population. The statements are *probabilistic* because, as discussed in Chapter 13, it is not possible to be absolutely sure that any randomly drawn sample is truly representative of the population from which it has been drawn, so we can only estimate the *probability* that results obtained from a sample are true of the population. The 'statements' which might be made on the basis of sample survey findings can be descriptive, comparative or relational:

● descriptive: for example, 10 per cent of adults play tennis;

● comparative: for example, 10 per cent play tennis but 12 per cent play golf;

● relational: for example, 15 per cent of people with high incomes play tennis but only 7 per cent of people with low incomes do so: there is a positive relationship between tennis-playing and income.

If they are based on data from samples, such statements cannot be made without qualification. The *sample* may indicate these findings, but it is not certain that they apply precisely to the population from which the sample is drawn, because there is always an element of doubt about any sample. Inferential statistics modifies the above example statements to be of the form:

● We can be 95 per cent confident that the proportion of adults that plays tennis is between 9 per cent and 11 per cent.

● The proportion of golf players is *significantly* higher than the proportion of tennis players (at the 95 per cent level of probability).

● There is a positive relationship between level of income and level of tennis playing (at the 95 per cent level).

The normal distribution

Descriptive statements and 'confidence intervals' are discussed in general terms in Chapter 13 in relation to the issue of sample size. The probability or confidence interval statement is based on the *theoretical* idea of drawing repeated samples of the same size from the same population. The sample drawn in any one piece of research is only one of a large number of *possible* samples which *might* have been drawn. If a large number of samples *could* be drawn, such an exercise would produce a variety of results, some very unrepresentative of the population but most, assuming random sampling procedures are used, tending to produce results close to the true population values. Statistical theory – which we are unable to explore in detail here – is able to quantify this tendency, so that we can say that, in 95 or 99 out of a hundred of such samples, the values found from the sample will fall within a certain range either side of the true population value – hence the idea of 'confidence intervals' as discussed in Chapter 13.

The theory relates to the bell-shaped 'normal distribution' which would result if repeated samples were drawn and the values of a statistic (for example the proportion who play tennis) plotted, as shown in Figure 17.1. The 'normal curve' which would result if a very large number of samples was drawn was shown in Figure 13.1. The population value of a statistic (such as a percentage or the average of a variable) lies at the centre of the distribution and the value of the statistic found from a sample in a particular research project is just one among the many sample possibilities. The probabilistic statement is made on the basis of this distribution, which has theoretically known properties for different samples and measures, such as percentages and means.

This idea of levels of probability about the accuracy of sample findings based on the theoretical possibility of drawing many samples is common to most of the statistical procedures examined in this chapter.

Probabilistic statement formats

It is customary in social research to use probability levels of 95 per cent or 99 per cent – and occasionally 90 per cent or 99.9 per cent. As probability estimates these can be interpreted exactly as in everyday language – for example, when we say '90 per cent certain', '50:50' or '9 times out of ten', we are making probabilistic statements. So, if a survey finding is *significant* (a concept discussed further below) at the '99 per cent level', we are saying that we believe that there is a 99 per cent chance that what we have found is true of the population – there is therefore, conversely, a 1 per cent chance that what we have found is *not* true. If we can only say that something is significant at the lower 95 per cent level, we are less confident – there is a 5 per cent chance that what we have found is not true. Thus the terminology *highly significant* is sometimes used in relation to findings at the 99 per cent level and *significant* for the 95 per cent level.

In some cases, instead of the computer-generated results of statistical tests using these conventional cut-off points, they present the exact probability – for example, it might be found that a result is significant at the 96.5 per cent level or the 82.5 per cent level. It is then left up to the researcher to judge whether such levels are acceptable.

Note also, that sometimes the result is expressed as 1 per cent and sometimes as 99 per cent, or as 5 per cent rather than 95 per cent. A further variation is to express the probability as a proportion rather than a percentage – for example, 0.05 rather than 5 per cent, or 0.01 rather than 1 per cent. Similarly the

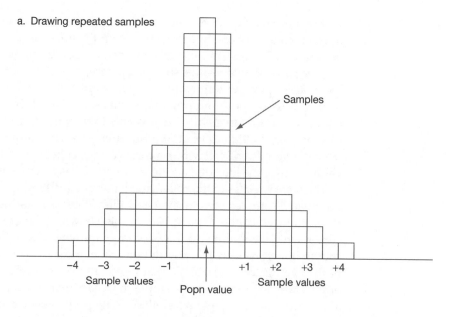

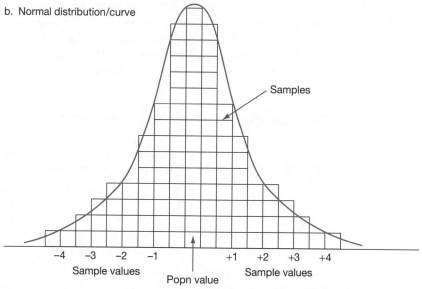

Figure 17.1 Drawing repeated samples and the normal distribution

exact calculations may be expressed as proportions, for example 0.035 rather than 3.5 per cent or 96.5 per cent.

In the following, therefore, in each row the three forms are equivalent.

5%	95%	0.05
1%	99%	0.01
0.1%	99.9%	0.001
3.5%	96.5%	0.035
7.5%	92.5%	0.075

In computer printouts from PASW, if the probability is below .0005 it sometimes comes out as .000 because it is printed only to three decimal places. In some research reports and computer printouts, results which are significant at the 5 per cent level are indicated by * and those significant at the 1 per cent level are indicated by **.

In the examples and discussions in this chapter the 5 per cent/95 per cent value is used as the criterion levels of tests of significance.

Significance

The second common feature of statistical tests and procedures is that they deal with the idea of *significance*. A *significant* difference or relationship is one which is *unlikely to have happened by chance*. So, for example, the bigger the difference between two sample percentages, the more likely it is that the difference is *real* and not just a statistical chance happening.

For example, if it was found from a sample that 10 per cent of women played tennis and 11 per cent of men played tennis we would be inclined, even from a common-sense point of view, to say that the difference is not significant. If another sample were selected, we would not be surprised to find a larger difference between the two figures, for them to be exactly the same or even the opposite way around: it is 'too close to call'. However, whether or not such a small difference is *statistically* significant depends on the sample size. If the findings were based on a small sample, say around 100 people, 50 men and 50 women, the difference would not be significant – the chances of getting a different result from a different sample of 100 people from the same population would be high – one person more or less in each group would change the percentage by two. But if the sample were large – say 1000 men and 1000 women – then a small difference of even one percentage point might be found to be statistically significant since in this case the difference would represent not just one or two persons, but ten persons. So if the result is based on such a large sample, we can be much more confident that it is 'real' and would be reproduced if another sample of similar size were drawn.

Statistical theory enables us to quantify and assess 'significance' – that is, to say what sizes of differences are significant for what sizes of sample.

Statistical significance should not, however, be confused with *social, theoretical* or *managerial* significance. For example, if the above finding about men's and women's tennis playing was based on a sample of, say, 10,000 people, it would be *statistically* significant, but this does not make the difference significant in any social sense. For all practical purposes, on the basis of such findings, we would say that men's and women's tennis playing rates are the same or very similar. This is a very important point to bear in mind when reading research results based on statistics; large samples can produce many 'statistically significant' findings; but that does not necessarily make them 'significant' in any other way.

The null hypothesis

A common feature of the statistical method is the concept of the *null hypothesis*, referred to by the symbol H_0. It is based on the idea of setting up two mutually incompatible hypotheses, so that only one can be true. If one proposition is true then the other is untrue. The null hypothesis usually proposes that there is *no difference* between two observed values or that there is *no relationship* between variables. There are therefore two possibilities:

H_0 – Null hypothesis: there is *no* significant difference or relationship.
H_1 – Alternative hypothesis: there *is* a significant difference or relationship.

Usually it is the *alternative* hypothesis, H_1, that the researcher is interested in, but statistical theory explores the implications of the *null* hypothesis.

In terms of the types of research approach discussed in Chapter 2, this is very much a *deductive* approach: the hypothesis is set up in advance of the analysis. However, as noted in Chapter 2, this may be set in the context of an exploratory or even inductive project in which a number of relationships is explored, but the testing of each relationship is set up as a deductive process.

The use of the null hypothesis idea can be illustrated by example. Suppose, in a study of leisure participation patterns, using a sample of 1000 adults, part of the study focuses on the relative popularity of golf and tennis. The null hypothesis would be that the participation levels are the same.

H_0 – tennis and golf participation levels are the same;
H_1 – tennis and golf participation levels are significantly different.

Suppose it is found that 120 (12 per cent) play tennis and 120 (12 per cent) play golf. Clearly there is no difference between the two figures; they are consistent with the null hypothesis. The null hypothesis is accepted and the alternative hypothesis is rejected.

But suppose the numbers playing tennis were found to be 121 (12.1 per cent) and the number playing golf was 120 (12.0 per cent). Would we reject the null hypothesis and accept the alternative, that tennis and golf participation levels are different? From what we know of samples, clearly not: this would be too close to call. Such a small difference between the two figures would still be consistent with the null hypothesis. So how big would the difference have to be before we reject the null hypothesis and accept that there is significant difference? A difference of 5, 10, 15? This is where statistical theory comes in, to provide a test of what is and is not a significant difference. And this is basically what the rest of this chapter is all about: providing tests of the relationship between sample findings and the null hypothesis for different situations. The null hypothesis is used in each of the tests examined.

Dependent and independent variables

The terminology *dependent variable* and *independent variable* is discussed in Chapter 1 and is frequently used in statistical analysis. If there is a significant

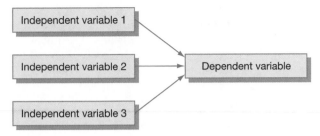

Figure 17.2 Dependent and independent variables

relationship between a dependent and an independent variable, the *implication* is that changes in the former are caused by changes in the latter: the independent variable *influences* the dependent variable.

For example, if it is suggested that the level of holiday-taking is influenced by a person's income level, then the level of holiday-taking is the *dependent* variable and income is the *independent* variable. Even though a certain level of income does not *cause* people to go on holiday, it makes more sense to suggest that level of income facilitates or constrains the level of holiday-taking, than to suggest the opposite. So it makes some sense to talk of holiday-taking being *dependent* on income. One variable can be dependent on a number of independent variables, as illustrated in Figure 17.2 – for example, it may be hypothesised that holiday-taking is dependent on income *and* occupation *and* age.

Statistical tests

Types of data and appropriate tests

The idea of levels of measurement, or types of data, was introduced in Chapter 16, when nominal, ordinal and scale data were discussed. The higher the level of measurement the greater the range of analysis that can be carried out on the data. For example, it is possible to calculate means averages of ordinal and scale measures, but not of nominal data. Consequently, different statistical tests are associated with different levels of measurement. The rest of the chapter sets out different statistical tests to be used in different situations, as summarised in Figure 17.3. The tests all relate to comparisons between variables and relationships between variables. The appropriate type of test to be used depends on the format of the data, the level of measurement and the number of variables involved.

In what follows:

● Data from a questionnaire survey similar to that used in Chapter 16 are used to illustrate the various tests, but with a larger sample and additional leisure and tourism participation variables added.

Task	Format of data	No. of variables	Types of variable	Test
Relationship between two variables	Crosstabulation of frequencies	2	Nominal	Chi-square
Difference between two means – paired	Means: for a whole sample	2	Two scale/ordinal	t-test – paired
Difference between two means – independent samples	Means: for two sub-groups	2	1. Scale/ordinal (means) 2. Nominal (2 groups only)	t-test – independent samples
Relationship between two variables	Means – for 3+ sub-groups	2	1. Scale/ordinal (means) 2. Nominal (3+ groups)	One-way analysis of variance
Relationship between three or more variables	Means: crosstabulated	3+	1. Scale/ordinal (means) 2. Two or more nominal	Factorial analysis of variance
Relationship between two variables	Individual measures	2	Two scale/ordinal	Correlation
Linear relationship between two variables	Individual measures	2	Two scale/ordinal	Linear regression
Linear relationship between three or more variables	Individual measures	3+	Three or more scale/ordinal	Multiple regression
Relationships between large numbers of variables	Individual measures	Many	Large numbers of scale/ordinal	Factor analysis Cluster analysis

Figure 17.3 Types of data and statistical test

- Listings of the variables and data used are included as Appendix 17.1.

- The variable *statusr* in the data-set is produced as shown in Figure 16.13.

- As in Chapter 16, the examples have been created using PASW for Windows, Version 18.

- For readers who are mathematically inclined, formulae for various of the test statistics are shown in Appendix 17.2.

Chi-square

Introduction

The Chi-square test (symbol: χ^2, pronounced ky, to rhyme with sky) can be used in a number of situations, but its use is demonstrated here in relation to crosstabulations of two *nominal* variables – the familiar tables produced *from* such packages as PASW. When examining crosstabulations it is possible to use 'common-sense' and an underlying knowledge of the size of confidence intervals, as discussed in Chapter 13, to make an approximate judgement as to whether there is any sort of relationship between the two variables involved in the table. However, unless the pattern is very clear, it can be difficult to judge whether the overall differences are *significant*. The chi-square test is designed to achieve this.

Null hypothesis

The null hypothesis is that *there is no difference in student full-time/part-time status between male and female respondents*: that is:

H_0 – there is *no* relationship between student status and gender in the population of students.
H_1 – there *is* a relationship between status and gender in the population of students.

Note that the proposition being tested can therefore be expressed in three ways, as shown in Figure 17.4.

Procedures

Figure 17.5 shows the PASW procedures to obtain a crosstabulation with a chi-square test, and the resultant output. The example chosen relates student full-time/part-time status (*statusr*) to gender (*gender*). The interpretation of this output is discussed below.

Expected frequencies

The cells of the table include counts and column percentages, as discussed in relation to crosstabulations in Chapter 16. But they also include *expected counts*. These are the counts which *would be expected* if the null hypothesis were true –

Option 1	Option 2	Option 3
Null hypothesis (H_0): there is *no* relationship between full-time/part-time status and gender in the population of students.	Male and female full-time/part-time status in the population of students is the same.	Observed and expected values are not significantly different.
Alternative hypothesis (H_1) there *is* a relationship between full-time/part-time status and gender in the population of students.	Male and female full-time/part-time status in the population of students is different.	Observed and expected values are significantly different.

Figure 17.4   Alternative expressions of hypotheses

Procedure

1. Select *Analyze*, then *Descriptive Statistics*, then *Crosstabs*.
2. Transfer the variable *statusr* to the *Row(s)* box and *gender* to the *Column(s)* box.
3. Select *Statistics*, then, in the *Crosstabs: Statistics* dialog box, select *Chi-square* then *Continue*.
4. Select *Cells*, then, in the *Crosstabs: Cells Display* dialog box:
   - in *Counts*: select *Observed* and *Expected*
   - in *Percentages*: select *Column*, then *Continue*.
5. Select *OK* to produce the output below (*Case Processing Summary* table omitted).

PASW Output

Student status recoded * Gender Crosstabulation

			Gender		Total
			Male	Female	
Student status recoded	Full-time	Count	18	9	27
		Expected Count	13.5	13.5	27.0
		% within Gender	72.0%	36.0%	54.0%
	Part-time	Count	7	16	23
		Expected Count	11.5	11.5	23.0
		% within Gender	28.0%	64.0%	46.0%
Total		Count	25	25	50
		Expected Count	25.0	25.0	50.0
		% within Student status recoded	50.0%	50.0%	100.0%

Chi-Square Tests **(key items highlighted)**

	Value	df	Asymp. Sig. (2-sided)	Exact Sig. (2-sided)	Exact Sig. (1-sided)
Pearson Chi-Square	**6.522**[a]	**1**	**.011**		
Continuity Correction[b]	5.153	1	.023		
Likelihood Ratio	6.676	1	.010		
Fisher's Exact Test				.022	.011
Linear-by-Linear Association	6.391	1	.011		
N of Valid Cases	50				

a. 0 cells (.0%) have expected count less than 5. The minimum expected count is 11.50.
b. Computed only for a 2 × 2 table.

Figure 17.5 Procedure for the Chi-square test

that is, if there was no difference between males and females in their full-time/part-time status. In this case we have an equal number of men and women in the sample, so the expected values show a 50:50 split for each status.

The value of Chi-square

Chi-square is a statistic based on the sum of the differences between the counts and the expected counts: the greater this sum the greater the value of Chi-square. However, if the differences between the observed and expected counts in the table are simply added, it will be found that the positives cancel out the negatives, giving zero. Chi-square is therefore based on the sum of the *squared* values of the differences. The PASW package calculates the value of Chi-square, so it is not necessary to know the details of the formula. It is sufficient to understand that Chi-square is a statistical measure of the difference between the observed and expected counts in the table.

In the example in Figure 17.5, the value of Chi-square is 6.522. We are using the 'Pearson' value, devised by the statistician Karl Pearson – the other values (Continuity Correction, Likelihood Ratio, Fisher's Exact Test and Linear-by-Linear Association) do not concern us here.

Interpretation

How should this value of Chi-square be interpreted? We have noted that the greater the difference between the observed and expected values the greater the value of Chi-square. Our null hypothesis is that there is *no* difference between the two sets of values. But clearly, we would accept some *minor* differences between two sets of values and still accept the null hypothesis. But just how big would the differences have to be before we would reject the null hypothesis and conclude that there *is* a difference between male and female full-time/part-time status?

For a given size of table (in this case two cells by two), statisticians have been able to calculate the likelihood of obtaining various values of Chi-square when the null hypothesis is true. As with the normal distribution discussed in Chapter 16, this is based on the theoretical possibility of drawing lots of samples of the same size. This is shown in Figure 17.6. It shows that, for a particular table size, if the null hypothesis is true, some differences in observed and expected counts can be expected from most samples drawn from a given population, so a *range of values* of Chi-square can be expected. Most values of Chi-square would be expected to be fairly small; some larger values would occur, but only rarely – they are unlikely.

Therefore, any value of Chi-square in the range to the right of the 5 per cent point in the diagram is considered unlikely and *inconsistent* with the null

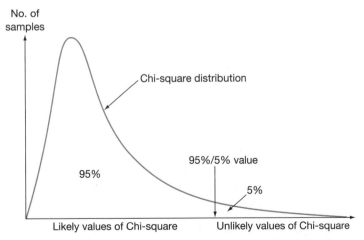

Figure 17.6 Distribution of Chi-square assuming the null hypothesis is true

hypothesis: we *reject* the null hypothesis. If it is in the range to the left of the 5 per cent point we *accept* the null hypothesis.

In Figure 17.5, the output tells us the value of Chi-square for the table: 6.522. It also indicates the likelihood, or probability, of this value: 0.011, or 1.1 per cent. Our value of Chi-square is therefore an unlikely one (it has a likelihood less than 5 per cent), so we reject the null hypothesis and conclude that there *is* a significant difference between the proportion of full-time/part-time status for male and female students.

Degrees of freedom

The values of Chi-square depend of the table size, which is indirectly measured by the *degrees of freedom*. Degrees of freedom are calculated by: *the number of rows minus one* multiplied by *the number of columns minus one*. So, for the table in Figure 17.5, the degrees of freedom are: $(2-1) \times (2-1) = 1 \times 1 = 1$. This is shown in the output table under *df*.

Expected counts rule

One rule for the application of Chi-square is that there should not be more than one-fifth of the cells of the table with expected counts of less than five, and none with an expected count of less than one. The output indicates whether such cells exist. Note a at the bottom of the table indicates that no cells have an expected count of less than 5 and the minimum expected count is 11.5, so there is no problem. Grouping of some of the values by recoding can be used to reduce the number of cells and thus increase the expected frequencies. In fact this was done in the example with the recoded variable – if the analysis is run with the original *status* variable, the test infringes the expected counts rule and is invalid.

Reporting

How should the results of statistical tests such as Chi-square be reported? Four solutions can be considered, as follows.

1. Include the results of the test in the table in the research report, as in Figure 17.7. The commentary might then merely say: 'The relationship between full-time/part-time status and gender was significant at the 5 per cent level.'

2. Include the test results in the text, for example: 'The relationship between full-time/part-time status and gender was significant at the 5 per cent level $(\chi^2 = 6.5, 1 \text{ DF})$.'

3. Make the statistics less intrusive by including a note in the report or paper indicating that all tests were conducted at the 5 per cent level and that test values are included in the tables, or are listed in an appendix, or even excluded altogether for non-technical audiences.

4. Use the * and ** approach to indicate significant and highly significant results in tables, as discussed above.

Table 1   Full-time/part-time status by gender

Status	Male	Female	Total
			%
Full-time student	72.0	36.0	54.0
Part-time student	28.0	64.0	46.0
Total	100.0	100.0	100.0
Sample size:	25	25	50

$\chi^2 = 6.52$, DF 1, significant at the 5% level

Figure 17.7   Presentation of Chi-square test results

Comparing two means: the t-test

Introduction

So far we have dealt only with proportions or percentages, either singly or in crosstabulations; but many research results are in the form of averages – for example, the average age of a group of participants in an activity, the average holiday expenditure of visitors from different countries, or the average score of a group on a Likert scale. In statistical parlance an average is referred to as a *mean*. Means can only be calculated for *ordinal* and *scale* variables, not nominal variables.

The simplest form of analysis is to compare two means to see whether they are significantly different. For example, we might want to test whether the average age of golf players in a sample is significantly different from that of the tennis players, or whether the average amount spent on holidays by a group of people is greater or less than the amount spent on the arts and entertainment. In this situation the null hypothesis is expressed as follows:

H_0 – Null hypothesis: there is *no* difference between the means.
H_1 – Alternative hypothesis: there *is* a difference between the means.

For this situation, rather than Chi-square, a statistic referred to as 't' is calculated – but the interpretation is similar. This is based on a formula involving the sample size and the two means to be compared. If there is *no difference* between two means in the population (H_0) then, for a given sample size, t has a known 'distribution' of likely values, as illustrated in Figure 17.8 in comparison with the Chi-square distribution. High values are rare, so if the value from a sample is high – in the top 5 per cent of values for that sample size – then we reject H_0 and accept H_1; that is, we conclude that there *is* a significant difference at the 5 per cent level of probability respectively. Note that, because 't' can take on negative or positive values there are two 'tails' to its distribution – hence the reference to 'two-tailed test' in some of the output discussed below.

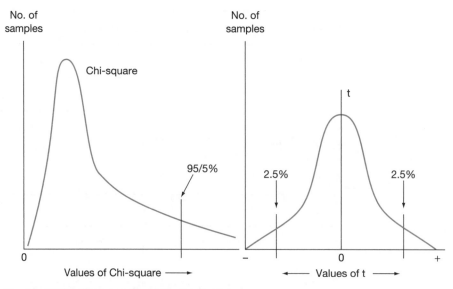

Figure 17.8 Chi-square and t distributions

There are two situations where we might want to compare means:

A. To compare the means of two variables which apply to the whole sample – for example, comparing the average amount spent on holidays with the average amount spent on the arts and entertainment (for everybody in the sample). This is known as a *paired samples test.*

B. To compare the means of one variable for two sub-groups – for example, comparing the average age of men in the sample with that of women. The sample is divided into two sub-groups, men and women; this is known as a *group* or *independent samples* test.

A. Paired samples test

Figure 17.9 presents two examples of the paired samples test. The *PASW* output provides a range of statistics with which we are not concerned here – including a correlation, which is discussed later in the chapter. The items we are interested in are depicted in bold in Figure 17.9.

Example 1 compares the frequency of playing sport/fitness with the frequency of visiting national parks.

● The people in the sample play sport/fitness on average 12.2 times in three months and visit national parks on average 9.8 times, a difference of 2.4 – the question is whether this difference is significant.

● The value of t is 1.245 and its (2-tail) significance is 0.219 or 21.9 per cent.

● The result is consistent with the null hypothesis (0.219 is much higher than 0.05).

● so we accept the null hypothesis, that the difference between the level of sport playing and the level of visits to national parks is *not* significant.

Procedure
1. Select *Analyze*, then *Compare Means*.
2. Select *Paired Samples T-Test*.
3. Highlight the first variable to be compared and transfer to the *Paired variables* box, then transfer the second variable.
4. Select *OK* to obtain t-test output.

PASW Output

Example 1: Playing sport vs Visiting national parks

Paired Samples Statistics

		Mean	N	Std. Deviation	Std. Error Mean
Pair 1	**Play sport/fitness**	**12.20**	50	13.095	1.852
	Visit national park	**9.80**	50	8.804	1.245

Paired Samples Correlations (IGNORE)

		N	Correlation	Sig.
Pair 1	Play sport/fitness & Visit national park	50	.274	.054

Paired Samples Test

		Paired Differences					t	df	Sig. (2-tailed)
		Mean	Std. Deviation	Std. Error Mean	95% Confidence Interval of the Difference				
					Lower	Upper			
Pair 1	**Play sport/fitness – Visit national park**	**2.400**	13.631	1.928	–1.474	6.274	**1.245**	49	**.219**

Example 2: Visit national parks vs Going out for a meal

Paired Samples Statistics

		Mean	N	Std. Deviation	Std. Error Mean
Pair 1	**Visit national park**	**9.80**	50	8.804	1.245
	Go out for meal	**6.54**	50	3.157	0.446

Paired Samples Correlations – IGNORE

		N	Correlation	Sig.
Pair 1	Visit national park & Go out for meal	50	–.044	.759

Paired Samples Test

		Paired Differences					t	df	Sig. (2-tailed)
		Mean	Std. Deviation	Std. Error Mean	95% Confidence Interval of the Difference				
					Lower	Upper			
Pair 1	**Visit national park – Go out for meal**	**3.26**	9.484	1.341	0.565	5.955	**2.431**	49	**.019**

Figure 17.9   Comparing means: t-test: paired samples – procedure

Example 2 compares the frequency of visiting national parks and going out for a meal. In this case:

● the difference in the mean frequencies is 3.26;

● the value of t is 2.431;

● its significance level is 0.019, which is below 0.05;

● so we reject the null hypothesis and conclude that there *is* a significant difference between the frequency of visiting national parks and going out for meals.

B. Independent samples test

Figure 17.10 compares levels of expenditure on entertainment by male and female students.

● For males expenditure is £110 and for females it is £138.60, a difference of £28.60;

Procedure
1. Select *Analyze* and then *Compare Means*.
2. Select *Independent Samples T-Test*.
3. Select the variable for which the mean is required (*spend*) and transfer to *Test variables* box.
4. Select variable to be used to divide the sample into two groups (*gender*) and transfer to *Grouping variable* box.
5. Select *Define groups* and enter the values used to divide the sample into two groups (in the example: 1 for Male and 2 for Female). Select *Continue* and the two values appear in brackets following the name of the grouping variable: *gender*(1, 2).
6. Select *OK* to obtain t-test.

PASW Output

Group Statistics

	Gender	N	Mean	Std. Deviation	Std. Error Mean
Course costs, $ p.a.	**Male**	25	**110.00**	77.607	15.521
	Female	25	**138.60**	84.613	16.923

Independent Samples Test

	Levene's Test for Equality of Variances		t-test for Equality of Means						
	F	Sig.	t	df	Sig. (2-tailed)	Mean Difference	Std. Error Difference	95% Confidence Interval of the Difference	
								Lower	Upper
Equal variances assumed	.431	.514	**−1.245**	48	**.219**	−28.600	22.963	−74.770	17.570
Equal variances not assumed			−1.245	47.646	.219	−28.600	22.963	−74.779	17.579

Figure 17.10 Comparing means: t-test: independent samples – procedure

- t has a value of –1.25 and a significance level of 0.219;

- since 0.219 is above 0.05, this is consistent with the null hypothesis, so we accept that there is no significant difference between the two expenditure figures.

A number of means: one-way analysis of variance (ANOVA)

Introduction

The t-test was used to examine differences between means two at a time. *Analysis of variance* (ANOVA) is used to examine *more than two* means at a time. This begins to resemble the crosstabulation process, but with *means* appearing in the cells of the table instead of counts. An example is shown in Figure 17.11, which compares mean leisure participation levels and holiday expenditure for the various student status groups. Here the question which we seek to answer with ANOVA is whether, for each activity/expenditure item, the mean for the different groups of students are different from the overall mean – that is, whether participation/expenditure is related to student status.

Procedure

To obtain a table showing the means to be compared:

1. Select *Analyze* and then *Compare Means*.
2. Select *Means*.
3. Select the variable for which the mean is required (*sportfit, theatre, npark, meal, hols*) and transfer to the *Dependent list* box.
4. Select variable for grouping (*status*) and transfer to the *Independent list* box.
5. In *Options* ensure that *Mean* and *Number of cases* are in the *Cell statistics* box.
6. Select *OK* to produce the output.

PASW Output

Student status		Play sport/fitness	Visit theatre	Visit national park	Go out for meal	Holiday expenditure
F/T student/no paid work	Mean	9.69	2.62	9.77	6.46	328.46
	N	13	13	13	13	13
F/T student/paid work	Mean	9.64	2.93	8.64	4.00	342.50
	N	14	14	14	14	14
P/T student – F/T job	Mean	19.06	2.25	8.63	8.19	425.63
	N	16	16	16	16	16
P/T student/Other	Mean	6.29	3.29	14.86	8.00	752.86
	N	7	7	7	7	7
Total	Mean	12.20	2.68	9.80	6.54	422.90
	N	50	50	50	50	50

Figure 17.11 Comparing ranges of means – procedure

Null hypothesis

The null hypothesis is therefore: that all the means are equal to the overall mean. How different must the group means be from the overall mean before we reject this hypothesis?

Variance

Whether or not the means are in effect from *one* population (with *one* mean) or from *different* sub-populations (with *different* means) depends not only on the differences between the means but also on the 'spread', or *variance*, of the cases upon which they are based. Figure 17.12 shows four examples of three means, with the associated spread of cases around them.

- A: the means are well spaced and there is very little overlap in the cases – there *is* a significant difference between the means.

- B: the means are closer together and there is considerable overlap, suggesting that they may be from the same population.

- C: the means are spaced as in A, but the spread around the means is greater and so overlap is considerable, suggesting uncertainty as to whether or not the means are significantly different.

- D: the worst case of overlap – so we can be fairly certain that the three sets of data are from the same population.

A visual presentation of this type of information, although in a different format, can be obtained using the *Boxplot* feature within the *Graphics* procedure of PASW.

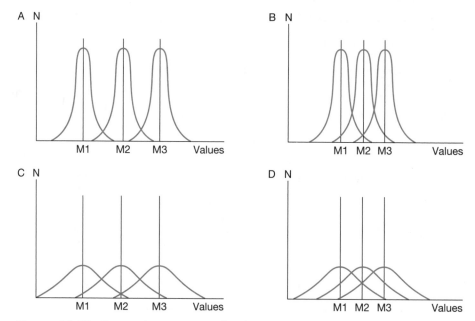

Figure 17.12 Comparing means and variances

The 'spread' of sample values is referred to as the *variance* and can be measured by adding up the differences between the scores of individual cases and the mean score.

Analysis of variance

Whether or not the means are significantly different from the overall mean depends on:

- the spread of the separate sub-group means around the overall mean – the *between-groups* variance – the greater the between groups variance the *greater* the likelihood of significant difference; and

- the spread of each of sub-group cases around the sub-group mean – the *within-groups* variance – the greater the within groups variance the *less* the likelihood of significant difference.

Analysis of variance is based on the ratio of these two measures, which produces a statistic referred to as F. As with the other statistics examined, values of F for a given number of degrees of freedom (based on sample sizes and number of groups) have a known probability distribution in the null hypothesis situation. High values are unlikely and result in the rejection of the null hypothesis.

Procedures for analysis of variance

The PASW procedures for analysis of variance and examples of output are shown in Figure 17.13.

In Figure 17.13, it can be seen that:

- For the first three activities significance is above 0.05, so the null hypothesis is accepted and it is concluded that participation in these activities is not related to student status.

- For the last two activities, going out for a meal and holiday expenditure, significance is below 0.05 so the null hypothesis is rejected and we conclude that there is a relationship between these activities and student status.

A table of means: factorial analysis of variance (ANOVA)

Introduction

As with one-way analysis of variance, factorial analysis of variance deals with *means*. But while the former deals with means of groups determined on the basis of *one* variable, the latter is designed for sets of means grouped by more than one classifying variable, or 'factor'. An example is shown in

Procedure

1. Select *Analyze* and then *Compare Means*.
2. Select *One-way ANOVA*.
4. Select variables for which means are required (*sportfit, theatre, npark, meal, hols*) and put in the *Dependent list* box.
5. Select variable for grouping (*status*) and put in the *Independent list* box.
6. Select *OK* to produce the output.

PASW Output

ANOVA

		Sum of Squares	df	Mean Square	F	Sig.
Play sport/fitness	Between Groups	1171.650	3	390.550	2.485	.072
	Within Groups	7230.350	46	157.182		
	Total	8402.000	49			
Visit theatre	Between Groups	6.446	3	2.149	.411	.746
	Within Groups	240.434	46	5.227		
	Total	246.880	49			
Visit national park	Between Groups	219.871	3	73.290	.942	.428
	Within Groups	3578.129	46	77.785		
	Total	3798.000	49			
Go out for meal	Between Groups	148.752	3	49.584	6.715	.001
	Within Groups	339.668	46	7.384		
	Total	488.420	49			
Holiday expenditure	Between Groups	968661.162	3	322887.054	6.644	.001
	Within Groups	2235593.338	46	48599.855		
	Total	3204254.500	49			

Figure 17.13   One-way analysis of variance – procedure

Figure 17.14, which presents a table of mean frequency of theatre-going by status and gender, with no statistical test at this stage. It can be seen that:

- there is little difference in frequency of attendance by status, with the lowest mean frequency 2.6 and the highest 3.3;

- there is little difference in frequency of attendance by gender (male 2.2, female 3.1);

- but when the two variables are put together, considerable differences emerge, with the lowest mean frequency at 1.4 and the highest at 5.4.

Analysis of variance examines this 'crosstabulation of means' and determines whether the differences revealed are significant. As with the one-way analysis of variance, the procedure examines the differences *between* group means and the spread of values *within* groups.

Null hypothesis

The null hypothesis is that there is no interaction between the variables – that the level of theatre-going of the students in the various categories is not affected by gender. A table of 'expected counts' consistent with the null hypothesis

Procedure
1. Select *Analyze* then *Compare Means* then *Means*.
2. Select *theatre* and transfer to the *Dependent list* box.
3. Select *status* and transfer to the *Independent list* box.
4. Click on *Next* to get *Layer 2 of 2*, then *gender* and transfer to the *Independent list* box
5. Select *OK* to obtain the output.

PASW Output

Visit theatre

Student status	Gender	Mean	N	Std. Deviation
F/T student/no paid work	Male	3.11	9	1.833
	Female	1.50	4	2.380
	Total	2.62	13	2.063
F/T student/paid work	Male	1.56	9	1.130
	Female	5.40	5	2.191
	Total	2.93	14	2.433
F/T student – F/T job	Male	1.40	5	2.074
	Female	2.64	11	2.730
	Total	2.25	16	2.543
P/T student/Other	Male	3.50	2	2.121
	Female	3.20	5	1.643
	Total	3.29	7	1.604
Total	Male	2.24	25	1.786
	Female	3.12	25	2.587
	Total	2.68	50	2.245

How the above might be presented in a report

Table 1   Frequency of visiting theatre, by status and gender

Course	Mean number of visits in three months		
	Male	Female	Total
F/T student/no paid work	3.1	1.5	2.6
F/T student/paid work	1.6	5.4	2.9
P/T student – F/T job	1.4	2.6	2.3
P/T student/Other	3.5	3.2	3.3
Total	2.2	3.1	2.7

Figure 17.14   A table of means – procedure

could be produced as for the Chi-square example, but the values would be means rather than numbers of cases.

Procedures for factorial analysis of variance

Figure 17.15 shows the results of a factorial analysis of variance on the above data. The underlined F probabilities indicate the relationship between:

Procedure

1. Select *Analyze* then *General Linear Model*.
2. Select *Univariate*.
3. Select the *Dependent* variable – the one for which the means are to be calculated (*theatre*).
4. Select the *Fixed Factors* – the two variables affecting the dependent variable (*status* and *gender*).
5. Click on the *Post Hoc* box and in the dialog box transfer *status* and *gender* to the *Post Hoc tests for*: box, then select *LSD*, then click *Continue*.
6. Select *OK* to obtain the output.

PASW Output

Tests of Between-Subjects Effects

Dependent Variable: Visit theatre (**key items in bold**)

Source	Type III Sum of Squares	df	Mean Square	F	Sig.
Corrected Model	66.523(a)	7	9.503	2.213	.052
Intercept	299.090	1	299.090	69.650	.000
status	18.308	3	6.103	**1.421**	.250
gender	6.041	1	6.041	**1.407**	.242
status * gender	47.424	3	15.808	**3.681**	.019
Error	180.357	42	4.294		
Total	606.000	50			
Corrected Total	246.880	49			

a R Squared = .269 (Adjusted R Squared = .148)

Figure 17.15 Factorial analysis of variance – procedure

Relating to data in Figure 17.14.

- theatre-going and status alone is not significant (Sig. = 0.250);
- theatre-going and gender is not significant (Sig. = 0.242);
- theatre-going and course and gender together is significant at the 5 per cent level (Sig. = 0.019) – so the null hypothesis is rejected: the interaction between gender and status with regard to theatre-going is significant at the 5 per cent level.

Correlation

Introduction

Correlation can be used to examine the relationships between two or more *ordinal or scale* variables. If two variable are related in a systematic way they are said to be *correlated*. They can be:

- *positively* correlated (as one variable increases so does the other);
- *negatively* correlated (as one variable increases the other decreases); or
- *un-correlated* (there is no relationship between the variables).

It is often helpful to think of correlation in visual terms. Relationships between income and the four variables are shown in Figure 17.16, illustrating a

a. **Theatre-going increases with income – a weak positive correlation (r = 0.46)**

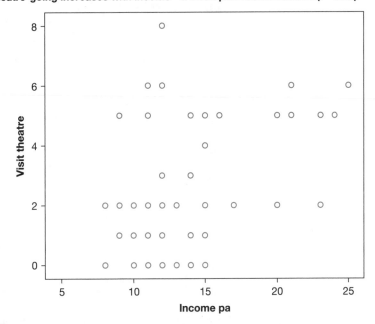

b. **Sport/fitness participation declines with income – a moderate negative correlation (r = −0.44)**

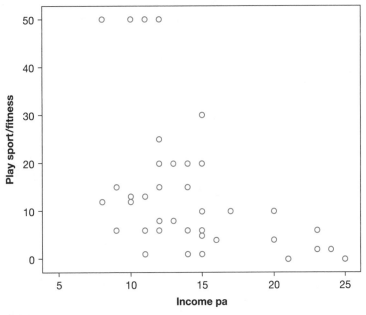

Figure 17.16 Relationships between variables

c. **No apparent relationship between national park visiting and income –
    almost zero correlation (r = 0.024)**

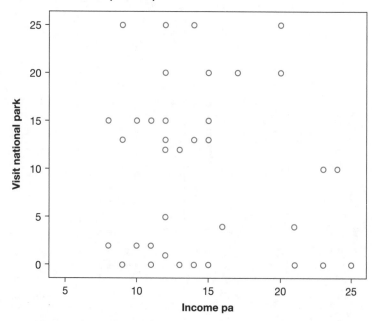

d. **Holiday expenditure clearly increases with income – very strong positive
    correlation (r = 0.91)**

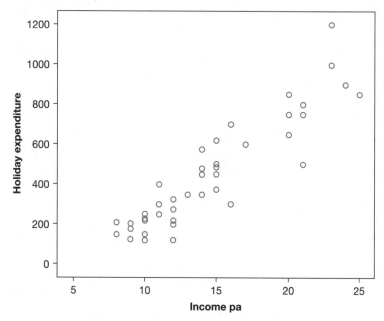

Figure 17.16   (*continued*)

variety of types of correlation. The graphics were produced using the *PASW* graphics *Scatterplot* procedure discussed in Chapter 16. Each dot represents one person (or case or observation). The correlation coefficients, r, are explained below.

Correlation coefficient (r)

Correlation can be measured by means of the *correlation coefficient*, usually represented by the letter r. The coefficient has the following characteristics:

- zero if there is no relationship between two variables;
- +1.0 if there is perfect positive correlation between two variables;
- −1.0 if there is perfect negative correlation between two variables;
- between 0 and +1.0 if there is *some* positive correlation;
- between 0 and −1.0 if there is *some* negative correlation;
- the closer the coefficient is to 1.0, the higher the correlation, for example:
  - 0.9 is a *high positive* correlation;
  - 0.2 is a *low positive* correlation;
  - −0.8 is a *high negative* correlation.

The correlation coefficient is calculated by measuring how far each data point is from the mean of each of the two variables and multiplying the two differences. In Figure 17.17 it can be seen that the result will be a positive number for data points in the top right-hand and bottom left-hand quadrants (B and C) and negative for data points in the other two quadrants (A and D). The calculations are shown for two of the data points by way of illustration. If most of the data points are in quadrants B and C a positive correlation will

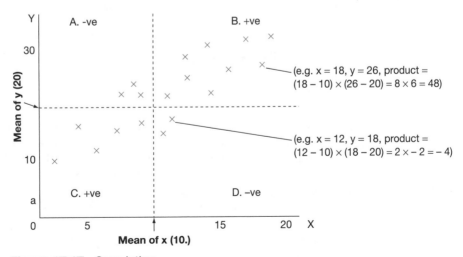

Figure 17.17 Correlation

result, while if most of the data points are in A and D a negative correlation will result. If the data points are widely scattered in all four quadrants, then the negatives cancel out the positives, resulting in a low value for the correlation. This explains in very broad terms the basis of the positive and negative correlations, and high and low correlations. It is beyond the scope of this book to explain how the 'perfect' correlation is made to equal one, but, for those with the requisite mathematics, this can be deduced from the formula for r, which is given in Appendix 17.2.

Significance of r

The *significance* of a correlation coefficient depends on its size, as discussed above, and also the sample size, and is assessed by a t-test.

Null hypothesis

The null hypothesis is that the correlation is zero. The t-test therefore indicates only whether the correlation coefficient is *significantly different from zero*. Quite low coefficients can emerge as 'significant' if the sample is large enough.

Procedures for correlation

The PASW procedures for producing correlation coefficients between pairs of variables are shown in Figure 17.18. The output is in the form of a symmetrical matrix, so that, for example, the correlation between sport and income is the same as between income and sport. For each pair of variables, the output includes the correlation coefficient, the sample size (the number in brackets) and P, the probability related to the t-test. The starring system discussed above is used to indicate significance at the 5 per cent and 1 per cent levels. As with other tests, if the probability is below the 0.05 or 0.01 levels we reject the null hypothesis and conclude that the correlation is significantly different from zero, at the 5 per cent or 1 per cent level respectively.

Linear regression

Introduction

Linear regression takes us one step further in this type of quantitative analysis – in the direction of 'prediction'. If the correlation between two variables is consistent enough, one variable can be used to predict or estimate the other. In particular, easily measured variables (such as age or income) can be used to predict variables which are more difficult or costly to measure (such as participation in leisure or tourism activities). For example:

- Knowledge of the relationship between age and leisure participation can be used in planning leisure facilities for a community: the future age structure

Procedure

1. Select *Analyze*.
2. Select *Correlate*.
3. Select *Bivariate*.
4. Select variables to be included (*inc, sportfit, theatre, npark, meal, hols*) and transfer to the *Variables* box.
5. Select *OK* to produce output.

PASW Output

Correlations

		Income pa	Play sport	Visit theatre	Visit national park	Go out for meal	Holiday expenditure
Income pa	Pearson Correlation	1.000	−.439**	.460**	.024	.076	.915**
	Sig. (2-tailed)	.	.001	.001	.866	.598	.000
	N	50	50	50	50	50	50
Play sport	Pearson Correlation	−.439**	1.000	−.679**	.274	.454**	−.368**
	Sig. (2-tailed)	.001	.	.000	.540	.001	.008
	N	50	50	50	50	50	50
Visit theatre	Pearson Correlation	.460**	−.679**	1.000	−.292*	−.286*	.379**
	Sig. (2-tailed)	.001	.000	.	.039	.044	.007
	N	50	50	50	50	50	50
Visit national park	Pearson Correlation	.024	.274	−.292*	1.000	−.044	.058
	Sig. (2-tailed)	.866	.054	.039	.	.759	.688
	N	50	50	50	50	50	50
Go out for meal	Pearson Correlation	.076	.454**	−.286*	−.044	1.000	.119
	Sig. (2-tailed)	.598	.001	.044	.759	.	.410
	N	50	50	50	50	50	50
Holiday expenditure	Pearson Correlation	.915**	−.368**	.379	.058	.119	1.000
	Sig. (2-tailed)	.000	.008	.007	.688	.410	.
	N	50	50	50	50	50	50

Figure 17.18 Correlation matrix – procedure

** Correlation is significant at the 0.01 level (2-tailed).
* Correlation is significant at the 0.05 level (2-tailed).

of the community can be relatively easily estimated and with this information future demand for leisure activities can be estimated.

- Relationships between income per head and amount of overseas air travel per head in different countries or over various time-periods can be used to predict growth of air travel as incomes rise, or fall.

The procedures described here are just one format in which the relationships between variables of interest can be examined. If the variables can be quantified, then the techniques enable the strength and nature of the relationship to be quantified also.

Regression model

To predict one variable on the basis of another a *model* or equation is needed of the type:

Example 1: Leisure participation = *some number* multiplied by AGE
Example 2: Demand for overseas travel = *some number* multiplied by INCOME.

Suppose leisure participation is measured in terms of the number of visits or days participation for some activity over the course of a year, and demand for overseas travel is measured by the number of overseas trips in a year. Regression analysis produces an equation of the form:

Example 1: Days participation = a + b * AGE
Example 2: Trips = a + b * INCOME.

The *coefficients* or *parameters*, a and b, are determined from examination of existing data, using regression analysis. The process of finding out the values of the parameters or coefficients is referred to as *calibration* of the model.

In general terms this is represented by the equation: y = a + bx, where y stands for participation or travel demand and x stands for age or income. Note that here *Participation* and *Travel demand* are the *dependent* variables and AGE and INCOME are the *independent* variables.

In visual terms this describes a 'regression line' fitted through the data, with 'intercept' or 'constant' of *a* and 'slope' of *b*, as shown in Figure 17.19. The regression procedure finds the 'line of best fit' by finding the line which minimises the sum of the (squared) differences between it and the data points, and specifies this line by giving values for a and b.

Procedures for regression

Examples of regression output from PASW are shown in Figure 17.20. The program produces a large amount of output with which we are not concerned here – only the items in bold are discussed. However, the output illustrates the point that regression is an involved process and only the broad outlines are dealt

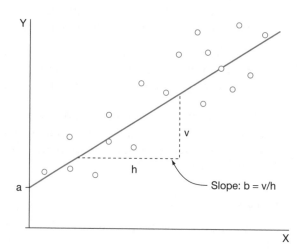

Figure 17.19 Regression line

Procedure
1. Select *Analyze* then *Regression.*
2. Select *Linear.*
3. Select *dependent* and **independent** variables.
4. Select *OK* to produce the output.

PASW Output (key items in bold)

Example 1: Income (independent) by holiday expenditure (dependent)

Model Summary

Model	R	R Square	Adjusted R Square	Std. Error of the Estimate
1	**.915**	**.836**	.833	104.51

a   Predictors: (Constant), Income pa

ANOVA

Model		Sum of Squares	df	Mean Square	F	Sig.
1	Regression	2679971.336	1	2679971.336	**245.361**	**.000**
	Residual	524283.164	48	10922.566		
	Total	3204254.500	49			

a   Predictors: (Constant), Income pa   b   Dependent Variable: Holiday expenditure

Coefficients

		Unstandardized Coefficients		Standardized Coeffs	t	Sig.
Model		B	Std. Error	Beta		
1	**(Constant)**	**–323.493**	49.890	.950	–6.484	.000
	Income pa	**52.563**	3.356		15.664	.000

a   Dependent Variable: Holiday expenditure

Example 2: Income (independent) by theatre-going (dependent)

Model Summary

Model	R	R Square	Adjusted R Square	Std. Error of the Estimate
1	**.460**	**.212**	.195	2.01

a   Predictors: (Constant), Income pa

ANOVA

Model		Sum of Squares	df	Mean Square	F	Sig.
1	Regression	52.284	1	52.284	**12.896**	**.001**
	Residual	194.596	48	4.054		
	Total	246.880	49			

a   Predictors: (Constant), Income pa   b Dependent Variable: Visit theatre

Coefficients

		Unstandardized Coefficients		Standardized Coeffs	t	Sig.
Model		B	Std. Error	Beta		
1	**(Constant)**	**–.617**	.961		–.642	.524
	Income pa	**.232**	.065	.460	3.591	.001

a   Dependent Variable: Visit theatre

Figure 17.20   Regression analysis – procedure

with in this book. The output relates to *multiple* regression, which involves more than one independent variable, as discussed in the next section – but here we have only one independent variable, income.

The items we are interested in are the value of the regression coefficient, R (similar to the correlation coefficient, r), the value of R^2, which is an indicator of how well the data fit the regression line, its test of significance, and the coefficients listed under B. For Example 1 in Figure 17.20, the relationship between income and holiday expenditure:

- the value of R is 0.915;
- R^2 is 0.836;
- probability (as measured by an F test) is 0.000 which makes it highly significant;
- the *constant* (a) is –323.493 and the *coefficient* of *slope* (b) for income is 52.563.

The regression equation is therefore:

Holiday expenditure ($ pa) = –323.493 + 52.563 * income (in $000s pa)

This regression line can be plotted onto a graph, as shown in Figure 17.21, using the *PASW Curve estimation* procedure.

Procedure
1. Select *Analyze* then *Regression* then *Curve Estimation*.
2. Select *hols* and transfer to *Dependents* box and *inc* and transfer to Independent box.
3. Select *OK* to produce output.

PASW Output

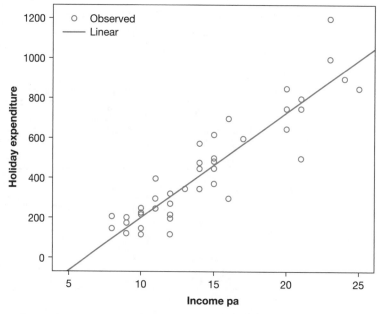

Figure 17.21 Regression line: curve fit – procedure

With this equation, if we knew a student's income we could estimate their level of holiday expenditure, either by reading it off the graph or calculating it. For example, for a student with an income of £10,000 a year:

Holiday expenditure $= -323.49 + 52.56 * 10 = -323.49 + 525.60 = \$202.11$

So we would estimate that such a student would spend $202 on holidays in a year. Of course we are not saying that *every* student with that income will spend this sum: the regression line/equation is a sort of average; it is not precise.

Example 2 in Figure 17.20 produces similar output for the relationship between theatre-going and income. In this case the resultant regression equation would be:

Theatre-going (frequency in 3 months) $= -0.62 + 0.23 *$ income

Non-linear regression

In Figure 17.22 the relationship between the two variables is *non-linear* – that is, the relationship indicated is curved, rather than being a straight line. The *PASW Curve fit* procedure offers a number of models which may produce lines/ curves which fit the data better than a simple straight line. Theory or trial and error may lead to a suitable model. In Figure 17.22 a 'cubic' model is presented, in which the independent variable is raised to the power of three – this results in the curved line indicated and a small increase in the value of R^2 to 0.843.

This emphasises the importance of examining the data *visually*, as done here, and not relying just on correlation coefficients.

Multiple regression

Multiple regression is linear regression involving more than one independent variable. For example, we might hypothesise that sports participation is dependent not just on income but also on age, or that overseas travel is dependent not just on income but also on the price of airfares. Thus our models, or regression equations, would be:

Example 1: Sports participation $= a + b *$ income $+ c *$ age
Example 2: Travel $= a + b *$ income $+ c *$ fares

In *linear* regression, as discussed above, the procedure fits a straight line to the data – the line of *best fit*. In *multiple* regression the procedure fits a *surface* to the data – the surface of best fit. It is possible to visualise this in three dimensions (one dependent and two independent variables), with the axes forming a three-dimensional box, the observations suspended in space and the regression surface being a flat plane somewhere within the box (*PASW* offers a 3-D graphical option to represent this in the *Scattergram* procedure). When additional variables are included then four, five or 'n' dimensions are involved and it is not possible to visualise the process, but the mathematical principles used to establish the regression equation are the same.

Procedure

1. Select *Analyze* then *Regression* then *Curve Fit*.
2. Select *dependent* and *independent* variables (*hols* and *inc*).
3. Under *Models* select *Cubic*.
4. Select *OK* to produce output.

PASW Output

Independent: inc

Dependent	Mth	Rsq	d.f.	F	Sigf	b0	b1	b2	b3
hols	CUB	.843	46	82.43	.000	494.351	−113.10	10.5471	−.2118

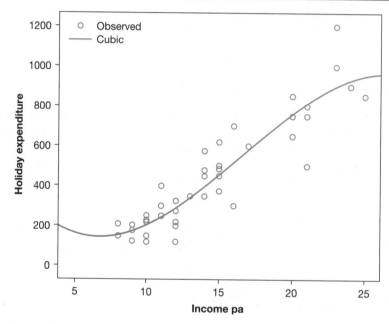

Figure 17.22 Regression: curve fit, non-linear – procedure

An example, in which theatre-going is related to income and age, is shown in Figure 17.23. It will be noticed that the value of R has risen from 0.46 in the single variable case (Figure 17.20, Example 2) to 0.58, indicating an improvement in the 'fit' of the data to the model. The model equation is now:

$$\text{Theatre-going (per 3 months)} = -0.349 + 0.056 * \text{income} + 0.0227 * \text{age}$$

It is possible, in theory, to continue to add variables to the equation. This should, however, be done with caution, since it frequently involves *multicollinearity*, where the independent variables are themselves inter-correlated. The 'independent' variables should be, as far as possible, just that: independent. Various tests exist to check for this phenomenon. Often, in leisure and tourism, a large number of variables is involved, many intercorrelated, but each contributing something to the leisure or tourist phenomenon under

Procedure
1. Select *Analyze* then *Regression* then *Linear*.
4. Transfer *theatre* to *dependent* box and *age, income* to *independents* box.
5. At *Method*, select *Enter* for all the selected variables to be included immediately, or *Stepwise* for the program to select and include variables in order of influence.
6. Select *OK* to produce the output.

PASW Output (key items in bold)

Variables Entered/Removed[b]

Model	Variables Entered	Variables Removed	Method
1	**Age, Income pa**[a]	.	Enter

a All requested variables entered.   b Dependent Variable: Visit theatre

Model Summary

Model	R	R Square	Adjusted R Square	Std. Error of the Estimate
1	**.580**[a]	**.336**	.308	1.87

a Predictors: (Constant), Age, Income pa

ANOVA[b]

Model		Sum of Squares	df	Mean Square	F	Sig.
1	Regression	83.023	2	41.512	**11.907**	**.000**[a]
	Residual	163.857	47	3.486		
	Total	246.880	49			

a Predictors: (Constant), Age, Income pa   b Dependent Variable: Visit theatre

Coefficients[a]

		Unstandardized Coefficients		Standardized coefficients	t	Sig.
Model		B	Std. Error	Beta		
1	(Constant)	**-3.493**	1.316		-2.654	.011
	Income pa	**.056**	.084	.111	.662	.511
	Age	**.227**	.076	.497	2.969	.005

a Dependent Variable: Visit theatre

Figure 17.23 Multiple regression – procedure

investigation. Multi-variate analysis procedures, such as cluster and factor analysis, discussed below, are designed partly to overcome these problems.

A technique often used in leisure research is *structural equation modelling (SEM)*, or *path analysis* in which a network of equations is established to model a particular social process. An example is shown in Figure 17.24, relating to health and fitness. This suggests that a person's exercise regime affects a person's fitness which in turn affects the person's health. But engaging in exercise might also affect health directly because it produces a sense of well-being. There are direct and indirect influences among the variables and SEM seeks to identify and quantify them using regression equations. Special computer packages are available to do this, as indicated in the Resources section.

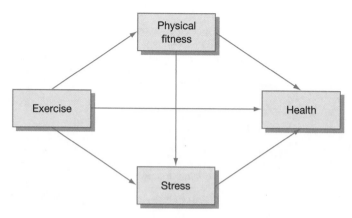

Figure 17.24   Structural equation modelling

Source: Adapted from Kline (2005: 67)

Cluster and factor analysis

Introduction

Cluster and factor analysis techniques are used when the number of independent variables is large and there is a desire to group them in some way. The theoretical counterpart to this is that there are some complex phenomena which cannot be measured by one or two variables, but require a 'battery' of variables, each contributing some aspect to the make-up of the phenomenon. Examples are:

- a person's 'lifestyle' or 'psychographic' group (made up of variables such as leisure and work patterns, income and expenditure patterns, values, age, and family/household situation);

- a person's characteristics as a tourist – a 'tourist type' (made up of variables such as travel experience, expenditure patterns, products desired and satisfactions sought).

Each of these is often researched using a large number of data items – for example, lifestyles/psychographics have been measured by asking people as many as 300 questions about their attitudes to work, politics, morals, leisure, religion and so on.

Both factor and cluster analysis may be:

- *exploratory* – the analytical process is used to discover any factors/clusters which may exist in the data; or

- *confirmatory* – the analytical process is used to test the existence of one or more hypothesised clusters or factors.

Factor analysis

Factor analysis is based on the idea that certain variables 'go together', in that people with a high score on one variable also tend to have a high score on

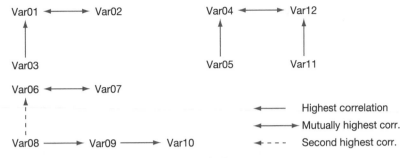

Figure 17.25 Simple manual factor analysis

certain others, which might then form a group – for example, people who go to the theatre might also visit galleries; people with strong pro-environment views might be found to favour certain types of holiday. Analysis of this type of phenomenon can be approached using a simple, manual technique involving a correlation matrix of the variables (as outlined above), as illustrated in Figure 17.25. Groupings of variables can be produced by indicating which variables have their highest and second highest correlations with each other. In Figure 17.25 three groupings of variables is shown.

This procedure only takes account of the highest and second highest correlation, as indicated. But variables will have a range of lower order relationships with each other which are difficult to take account of using this manual method. A number of lower order correlations may, cumulatively, be more significant than a single highest correlation. Factor analysis is a mathematical procedure which groups the variables taking account of *all* the correlations. The details of the method are, however, beyond the scope of this book.

Cluster analysis

Cluster analysis is another 'grouping' procedure, but it focuses on the individuals directly rather than the variables. Imagine a situation with two variables, age and some behavioural variable, and data points plotted in the usual way, as shown in Figure 17.26. It can be seen that there are three broad 'clusters' of respondents – two young clusters and one older cluster. Each of these clusters might form, for example, particular market segments. With just two variables and a few observations it is relatively simple to identify clusters visually. But with more variables and hundreds of cases this would be more difficult.

Cluster analysis involves giving the computer a set of rules for building clusters. It first calculates the 'distances' between data points, in terms of a range of specified variables. Those points which are closest together are put into a first round 'cluster' and a new 'point' halfway between the two is put in their place. The process is repeated to form a second round of clustering, and a third and fourth and so on, until there are only two 'points' left. The result is usually illustrated by a 'dendrogram', of the sort shown in Figure 17.27.

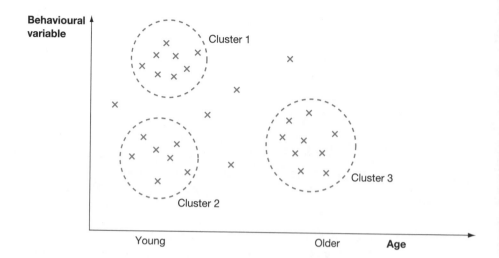

Figure 17.26 Plots of 'clusters'

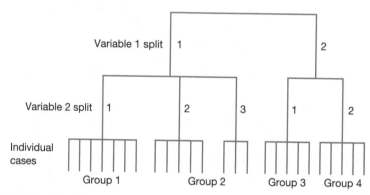

Figure 17.27 Dendrogram

In conclusion

Much leisure and tourism research, even of a quantitative nature, is conducted without the use of the techniques covered in this chapter. This is a reflection of the descriptive nature of much of the research in the field, as discussed in Chapter 1, the nature of the data involved and the needs of the audience or client for the research. Often in leisure and tourism the need is for 'broad brush' research findings: accuracy is required but a high level of precision is not. Contrast this with medical research, where precision can be a matter of life or death. To some extent the level of use of statistical techniques is related to disciplinary traditions. Thus, for example, the use of statistical techniques in the American *Journal of Leisure Research* is quite common as a result of the heavy involvement of psychologists in American leisure research, whereas in the British journal *Leisure Studies* statistical techniques are less often deployed, reflecting the British tradition of qualitative sociology. In the case of tourism journals, statistical techniques such as regression and correlation tend to arise quite often because of the strong economic dimension of some tourism research.

Many leisure or tourism researchers could therefore find that they rarely make use of the techniques presented in this chapter, but they should be able to interpret research reports which do make use of them, and they should be able to utilise them if called upon.

As has been stressed throughout this book, data collection and analysis should be determined by a theoretical, conceptual or evaluative framework. At the analysis stage the researcher should, ideally, not be wondering what to relate to what, and choosing variables and analyses in an *ad hoc* manner. While a certain amount of inductive exploration and even serendipity is inevitable, ideally there should be a basic analysis plan from the beginning. Key variables and the question of relationships between them should have been thought about in advance, for example as a result of an early 'concept mapping' exercise. Thus, while the examples given in this chapter may appear *ad hoc* and 'data driven', in a real research project the procedures used should be theory driven or problem or hypothesis driven.

Summary

This chapter builds on Chapter 13, which introduces the idea of sampling and its effects, and on Chapter 16, which deals with the analysis of questionnaire survey data using the package *PASW*. Here, the principles and processes involved in statistical analysis are introduced. The phenomenon of statistics, in this context, does not refer just to quantification, but to the processes required to generalise findings from samples to the wider population. Statistical concepts are initially introduced, including: the idea of probabilistic statements; the normal distribution; significance; the null hypothesis; and dependent and independent variables. The chapter then outlines *PASW* procedures and presents outputs for a number of statistical tests, as follows.

- Chi-square – for examining the relationship between two variables in frequency table;
- the t test – for comparing the significance of the difference between two means;
- one-way analysis of variance (ANOVA) – for examining the relationship between two variables as expressed by a set of means;
- factorial analysis of variance (ANOVA) – for examining the relationship between one dependent variable and two independent variables based on means;
- correlation – the relationship between two scale variables;

- linear regression – which establishes the 'line of best fit' between two variables;

- multiple regression – which examines the relationship between one dependent variable and two or more independent variables;

- cluster and factor analysis – which deal with summarising the relationships among large numbers of variables.

Test questions and exercises

It is suggested that the reader replicate the various analyses set out in this chapter, first using the data in Appendix 17.1 and then using their own data-set. This can be based on data which may have been collected for Chapter 16, but will involve adding a range of scale variables to the questionnaire, similar to those listed in Appendix 17.1.

Resources

Websites

- SPSS/PASW software: www.spss.com
- Structural equation modelling (SEM):
  - Semnet discussion group: www2.gsu.edu/~mkteer/semnet.html
  - Amos software: www.spss.com/amos/
  - Lisrel software: www.ssicentral.com/lisrel/index.html

Publications

- There are many excellent statistics textbooks available which cover the range of techniques included in this chapter, and, of course, much more. Texts vary in terms of the degree of familiarity with algebra that they assume on the part of the reader, so readers with limited mathematical knowledge should 'shop around' to find a text which deals with the topic in conceptual terms rather than in detailed mathematical terms. However, a certain amount of mathematical aptitude is, of course, essential. Examples of general research methods texts which include statistics are Ryan (1995) and Burns (1994); and a specialist text: Spatz and Johnston (1989).

- For examples of the use of the techniques covered here, the reader should browse through *Journal of Leisure Research* and, to a lesser extent, *Leisure Sciences*.

- For structural equation modelling (SEM): Kline (2005).

Appendix 17.1: Details of example data file used – variable details and data

Name	Type	Width	Decimals	Lab	Values	Missing	Columns	Align	Measure
qno	Numeric	5	0	Questionnaire number	None	None	8	Right	Scale
status	Numeric	5	0	Student status	1 Undergrad. 2 Grad. Dip. 3 Masters 4 Other	None	8	Right	Nominal
cafebar	Numeric	5	0	Campus cafe/bar in last 4 wks	0 No 1 Yes	None	8	Right	Nominal
music	Numeric	5	0	Live campus music in last 4 wks	0 No 1 Yes	None	8	Right	Nominal
sport	Numeric	5	0	Sport facilities in last 4 sks	0 No 1 Yes	None	8	Right	Nominal
travel	Numeric	5	0	Travel service in last 4 wks	0 No 1 Yes	None	8	Right	Nominal
cheap	Numeric	5	0	Free/cheap (rank)	None	None	8	Right	Ordinal
daytime	Numeric	5	0	Day-time events (rank)	None	None	8	Right	Ordinal
unusual	Numeric	5	0	Not available elsewhere (rank)	None	None	8	Right	Ordinal
meet	Numeric	5	0	Socialising (rank)	None	None	8	Right	Ordinal
quality	Numeric	5	0	Quality of presentation (rank)	None	None	8	Right	Ordinal
spend	Numeric	5	0	Expenditure on entertainment/month	None	None	8	Right	Scale
relax	Numeric	5	0	Relaxation opportunities – importance	1 Not Important 2 Important 3 Very Important	None	8	Right	Scale
social	Numeric	5	0	Social interaction – importance	As above	None	8	Right	Scale
mental	Numeric	5	0	Mental stimulation – importance	As above	None	8	Right	Scale
sug1	Numeric	5	0	First suggestion	1 Programme connect 2 Timing 3 Facilities 4 Costs 5 Organisation	None	8	Right	Nominal
sug2	Numeric	5	0	Second suggestion	As above	None	8	Right	Nominal

Name	Type	Width	Decimals	Lab	Values	Missing	Columns	Align	Measure
sug3	Numeric	5	0	Third suggestion	As above	None	8	Right	Nominal
age	Numeric	5	0	Age	None	None	8	Right	Scale
gender	Numeric	5	0	Gender	1 Male 2 Female	None	8	Right	Nominal
inc	Numeric	5	0	Income pa, $'000s	None	None	8	Right	Scale
sport	Numeric	5	0	Played sport – times in last 3 months	None	None	8	Right	Scale
theatre	Numeric	5	0	Visit theatre – times in last 3 months	None	None	8	Right	Scale
npark	Numeric	5	0	Visit national park – times in last 3 months	None	None	8	Right	Scale
hols	Numeric	5	0	Holiday expenditure	None	None	8	Right	Scale
statusr	Numeric	5	0	Student status – recoded	1 Full-time 2 Part-time	None	8	Right	Nominal

Data

Qno	status	cafebar	music	sport	travel	cheap	daytime	unusual	meet	quality	spend	relax	social	mental	sug1	sug2	sug3	age	gender	inc	sportit	theatre	npark	meal	hols
1	2	1	1	0	0	1	4	2	3	5	100	3	3	1	1	.	.	18	1	12	25	1	5	8	220
2	2	1	1	1	0	1	4	2	3	5	50	2	3	1	2	1	.	23	1	15	30	0	15	10	485
3	3	1	0	0	0	2	5	1	3	4	250	2	2	2	3	4	.	28	2	15	5	4	20	2	450
4	4	0	0	0	0	2	3	1	4	5	25	3	2	2	1	2	4	35	2	21	0	5	4	12	750
5	3	1	0	0	1	1	4	3	2	5	55	3	3	1	.	.	.	29	2	20	4	5	25	4	650
6	3	1	1	1	0	2	4	1	3	5	40	2	3	1	2	.	.	29	1	14	20	0	0	8	480
7	2	1	0	0	0	3	2	1	4	5	150	2	3	2	3	.	.	23	2	11	6	6	0	3	250
8	2	1	0	1	0	3	4	2	1	5	250	1	2	2	4	5	.	22	1	12	8	0	12	1	120
9	4	0	1	0	0	1	5	2	3	4	300	2	3	2	.	.	.	22	2	15	10	2	20	6	450
10	3	1	1	0	0	2	3	1	5	4	100	1	2	1	1	1	.	19	2	12	50	0	15	10	220
11	3	1	1	0	1	2	3	1	4	5	75	2	2	1	2	3	.	20	1	11	13	1	2	9	300
12	2	1	0	1	0	1	4	3	2	5	50	2	3	1	.	.	.	19	1	14	6	3	13	5	575
13	1	1	0	1	0	1	5	2	3	4	55	2	3	2	1	2	.	21	2	11	1	5	0	7	300
14	3	1	1	0	0	2	4	1	3	5	75	3	3	2	4	.	.	35	2	25	0	6	0	9	850
15	1	1	1	0	0	3	2	1	5	4	150	3	3	1	1	2	5	22	1	9	15	1	25	6	200
16	2	1	0	1	0	3	4	1	2	5	200	1	2	2	4	5	.	28	2	12	6	8	1	2	220
17	1	0	0	0	0	1	5	2	3	4	175	2	3	2	.	.	.	20	2	12	20	0	20	11	275
18	1	1	1	1	0	2	3	1	5	4	100	1	2	1	1	2	.	21	1	8	12	2	2	8	150
19	4	1	1	0	1	2	3	1	4	5	105	2	3	1	1	3	4	32	2	23	2	5	10	10	1200
20	1	1	0	1	0	1	4	3	2	5	50	2	2	1	2	.	.	23	1	16	4	5	4	0	300
21	1	1	0	0	0	3	2	1	4	5	150	2	3	2	3	.	.	18	1	11	6	2	0	3	250

hols	325	600	400	230	125	350	500	200	850	350	1000	275	750	150	250	450	500
meal	1	6	12	9	5	7	9	6	4	8	3	4	6	10	9	5	7
npark	12	20	15	2	13	0	0	25	25	0	0	12	20	15	2	13	0
theatre	2	2	0	1	5	5	6	1	5	0	2	6	2	0	1	1	5
sportfit	8	10	50	13	6	1	0	15	4	20	6	8	10	50	13	6	1
inc	12	17	11	10	9	14	21	12	20	13	23	12	20	10	10	15	15
gender	1	2	2	1	2	1	2	1	1	1	1	2	1	2	2	1	1
age	25	22	29	23	19	21	35	22	29	20	23	25	22	19	20	19	21
sug3	.	.	.	.	.	.	.	5	.	.	.	.	.	.	.	.	.
sug2	5	.	1	3	.	2	.	2	.	.	.	5	.	1	3	.	2
sug1	4	.	1	2	.	1	4	1	.	2	3	4	.	1	2	.	1
mental	2	1	1	1	1	2	2	1	1	1	2	2	2	1	1	1	2
social	2	3	2	2	3	3	3	3	3	3	3	2	3	2	2	3	3
relax	1	2	1	2	2	2	3	3	3	2	2	1	2	1	2	2	2
spend	250	300	100	75	50	55	75	150	55	40	150	250	300	100	75	50	55
quality	5	5	4	5	5	4	5	4	5	5	5	5	4	4	5	5	4
meet	1	3	5	4	2	3	3	5	2	3	4	1	3	5	4	2	3
unusual	2	2	1	1	3	2	1	1	3	1	1	2	2	1	1	3	2
daytime	4	5	3	3	4	5	4	2	4	4	2	4	5	3	3	4	5
cheap	3	1	2	2	1	1	2	3	1	2	3	3	1	2	2	1	1
travel	0	0	0	1	0	0	0	0	1	0	0	0	0	0	1	0	0
sport	1	0	0	0	1	1	0	0	0	1	0	1	0	0	0	1	1
music	0	1	1	1	0	0	1	1	0	1	0	0	1	1	1	0	0
cafebar	1	0	1	1	1	1	1	1	1	1	1	1	0	1	1	1	1
status	2	4	3	3	2	1	3	1	3	3	2	2	4	3	3	2	1
Qno	22	23	24	25	26	27	28	29	30	31	32	33	34	35	36	37	38

800	9	0	6	0	21	2	35	.	.	4	2	3	3	75	5	3	1	4	2	0	0	1	1	3	39
450	6	25	1	15	14	2	22	5	2	1	1	3	3	150	4	5	1	2	3	0	0	1	1	1	40
375	11	20	0	20	15	2	20	.	.	.	2	3	2	175	4	3	2	5	1	0	0	0	0	1	41
220	8	2	2	12	10	1	21	.	2	1	1	2	1	100	4	5	1	3	2	0	1	1	1	1	42
900	10	10	5	2	24	1	32	4	3	1	1	3	2	105	5	4	1	3	2	1	0	1	1	4	43
700	4	4	5	4	16	1	28	.	.	2	1	2	2	50	5	2	3	4	1	0	1	0	1	1	44
180	3	0	2	6	9	2	23	.	.	3	2	3	2	150	5	4	1	2	3	0	0	0	1	2	45
350	1	12	2	8	13	1	25	.	5	4	2	2	1	250	5	1	2	4	3	0	1	0	1	2	46
620	6	20	2	10	15	2	22	.	.	.	2	3	2	300	4	3	2	5	1	0	0	1	0	4	47
210	10	15	0	50	8	2	19	.	1	1	1	2	1	100	4	5	1	3	2	0	0	1	1	3	48
120	9	2	1	13	10	2	20	.	3	2	1	2	2	75	5	4	1	3	2	1	0	1	1	3	49
220	5	13	3	6	12	1	19	.	.	.	1	3	2	50	5	2	3	4	1	0	1	0	1	2	50

Appendix 17.2: Statistical formulae

- **95 per cent Confidence interval for normal distribution for percentage p**

$$C.I. = 1.96 \sqrt{\frac{p\,(100 - p)}{n - 1}}$$

Where n = sample size

- **Chi-square**

$$\chi^2 = \sqrt{\Sigma((O - E)/E)^2}$$

- **t for difference between means**

$$t = \sqrt{\frac{(\bar{x}_1 - \bar{x}_2)}{(s_1^2/n_1 + s_2^2/n_1)}}$$

- **Standard Deviation**

$$SD = \sqrt{\frac{\Sigma(x - \bar{x})^2}{n}}$$

- **Correlation Coefficient**

$$r = \sqrt{\frac{\Sigma((x - \bar{x})(y - \hat{y}))^2}{(s_1^2/n_1 + s_2^2/n_2)}}$$

- **Value of t for Correlation Coefficient**

$$t = r\sqrt{(N - 2)/(1 - r)^2}$$

Part

IV Communicating results

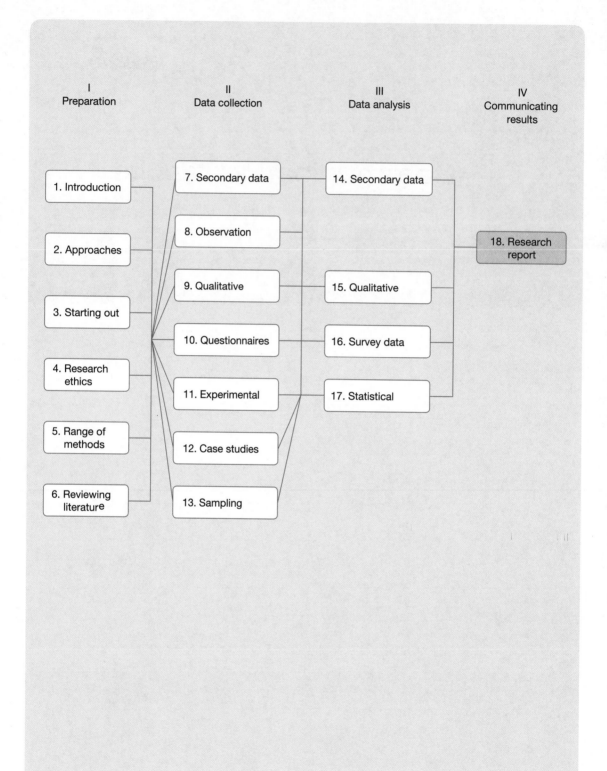

I Preparation	II Data collection	III Data analysis	IV Communicating results
1. Introduction	7. Secondary data	14. Secondary data	18. Research report
2. Approaches	8. Observation		
3. Starting out	9. Qualitative	15. Qualitative	
4. Research ethics	10. Questionnaires	16. Survey data	
5. Range of methods	11. Experimental	17. Statistical	
6. Reviewing literature	12. Case studies		
	13. Sampling		

18 Preparing a research report

Introduction

This chapter outlines key aspects of the reporting of research results. It concentrates primarily on the preparation and presentation of written research reports, including discussion of content, structure and layout, and considers the varying requirements and conventions of different reporting formats, including academic articles, consultancy reports, books and theses. It concludes with a brief consideration of non-written formats, particularly the oral presentation.

Written research reports

Written reports of research are a key element of the world of management and planning. Applied studies of the sort discussed in Chapter 1, namely feasibility studies, marketing plans, recreation needs studies, tourism development plans, market research studies and performance appraisals, all tend to be presented in the form of written reports. The results of academic studies are produced in article, report, book, or thesis format. In this chapter we deal with three report formats: management/planning/project reports, academic articles and theses. The first of these may arise in a management/planning context or may arise from a funded academic project when the researcher reports to the funding body; this style of report is referred to as a *project report* in the discussion below. Project reports prepared for a policy or practitioner readership are referred to as *management reports*. In North America the word 'dissertation' is generally used rather than 'thesis'. The main distinguishing characteristics of the three styles of report are summarised in Figure 18.1.

The medium is the message and in this case the medium is the written report. The ability to prepare a report and to recognise good quality and poor quality reports should be seen as a key element in the skills of the manager. While form is no substitute for good content, a report which is poorly presented can undermine or even negate good content. While most of the researcher's attention should of course be focused on achieving high quality substantive content, the general aspects raised in this chapter also merit serious attention.

Getting started

In discussing research proposals in Chapter 3 it was noted that researchers invariably leave too little time for report writing. Even when adequate time has been allocated in the timetable this is often whittled away and the writing of the report is delayed, leaving too little time. There is a tendency to put off report writing because it is difficult and it is often felt that, with just a little more data analysis or a little more reading of the literature, the process of writing the report will become easier. This is rarely the case – it is invariably difficult!

A regrettably common practice is for writers of research reports to spend a great deal of their depleted time, with the deadline looming, writing and preparing material which could have been attended to much earlier in the process. There are often large parts of any report which can be written before data analysis is complete, or even started. Such parts include the introduction, statement of objectives, outline of theoretical or evaluative framework, literature review and description of the methodology. In addition, time-consuming activities such as arranging for maps, illustrations and cover designs to be produced need not be left until the last minute!

Report components

Reports generally include certain standard components, although some are unique to certain report styles, as shown in Figure 18.2. The components listed are discussed in turn below.

Cover

For a project report the cover should include minimal information, such as title, author(s) and publisher or sponsor. The lavishness and design content will vary with the context and the resources available.

Characteristic	Management/planning/ project report	Academic article	Thesis
Authors	In-house staff, external consultants or funded academics.	Academics.	Honours, Master's or doctoral students.
Content	Report of commissioned or grant-funded project.	Report of academic research.	Report of academic research.
Brief	Provided by commissioning organisation or outlined in grant application.	Generally self-generated (although may arise from commissioned work).	Generally self-generated (although may arise in part from grant-funded project).
Quality assurance	In-house: internal consultants/academics: reputation of consultants/ researchers.	Anonymous refereeing process (see Chapter 1).	Supervision + examination by external examiners.
Readership	Professional managers/ planners and possibly elected or appointed board/council/committee members.	Primarily academics.	Primarily academics.
Published status	May or may not be publicly available.	Publicly available (often online) in published academic journals.	Publicly available in libraries and, recently, online; findings generally published in summary form in one or more academic articles.
Length	Varies.	In the social/ management sciences, including leisure/tourism studies, generally 5000–7000 words.	In the social/management sciences, including leisure/tourism studies: Honours: c. 20,000 words Master's: c. 40,000 words PhD: c. 70,000 words +.
Emphasis	Emphasis on findings rather than links with the literature/theory and methodology (although the latter must be described).	Methodology, theory, literature as important as the findings.	Methodology, theory, literature as important as the findings.

Figure 18.1 Types of research report

Component	Content	Management/Planning/Research report	Academic article	Thesis
Cover	• Title of report • Author(s) • Institution/publisher • ISBN (if published), back cover.	All items listed left.	Not applicable.	Prescribed by university regulations.
Title page	• Title of report • Author(s) • Institution/publisher, including address, phone, fax numbers, email, website* • Sponsoring body (e.g. 'Report to the Tourism Commission') • Date of publication* • If the report is for sale: ISBN*. (* sometimes on reverse of title page)	All items listed left.	Submitted article includes cover page containing: • Title of article • Author(s) • Institutional affiliation • Contact details (Page omitted by editors when article is sent for anonymous refereeing).	Prescribed by university regulations.
Contents page(s)	See Figure 18.3 for example.	As in Figure 18.3.	Not applicable.	As in Figure 18.2 but less detailed section numbering.
Summary	Summary of *whole* report, including background, aims, methods, main findings, conclusions and (where applicable) recommendations.	Executive Summary: Length: 20 pp report: ½–1 page 21–50 pp report: 3–4 pp 50–100 pp report: 5–6 pp.	Abstract: Length: typically about 300 words.	Synopsis: Length: typically 3–5 pages.
Preface/Foreword	Optional. Contains background information, sometimes an explanation of authors' involvement with the project. Or may be by a significant individual not directly involved in the project. Not applicable in academic article, where such information may be included in an endnote.			
Acknowledgements	• Funding organisations • Liaison officers of funding organisations • Members of steering committees • Organisations/individuals providing access to information etc. • Staff employed (e.g. including interviewers, coders, computer programmers, secretaries, word processors) • Individuals (including academic supervisors) who have given advice, commented on report drafts, etc. • (Collectively) Individuals who responded to questionnaires, etc.			
Main body of report	Discussed separately.			
Appendices	Text/statistical material included for the record but which, because of its size, would interrupt the flow if included in the main body of the report.			

Figure 18.2　Report style and components

If the report is available for sale it should include an International Standard Book Number (ISBN) on the back cover. The ISBN is a 13-digit (10 before 2007) product identifier for books and other published materials used by publishers, booksellers and libraries. The ISBN system is overseen by the London-based International ISBN Agency and registered with the International Organization for Standardization (ISO) in Geneva. ISBNs are allocated by National ISBN Agencies, which are often national libraries which, under national legislation, generally receive free deposit copies of all publications in their country. The ISBN makes it easy to order publications through bookshops and ensures that the publication is catalogued in library systems around the world.

Title page

The title page is the first page inside the cover of a project report. It may include much the same information as the cover or considerably more detail, as indicated in Figure 18.2. In some cases, as in commercially published books, some of the detail is provided on the reverse of the title page.

List of contents

Lists of contents are required in project reports and theses and may include just chapter titles, but usually also include full details of sub-sections. An example of a contents list is shown in Figure 18.3. Word-processor packages include procedures for compiling tables of contents and lists, such as tables and diagrams.

Summary – executive summary/abstract/synopsis

A summary is required for all three styles of report except for very short project reports. The summary is called, *executive summary*, *abstract* or *synopsis*, depending on the context. The typical length also varies, depending on the context.

An executive summary is sometimes thought of as the summary for the 'busy executive' who does not have time to read the whole report, but really refers to the idea that it should contain information necessary to take *executive action* on the basis of the report.

A summary should contain a summary of the *whole* report, article or thesis, as indicated in Figure 18.2; it is *not* the introduction. The summary should, of course, be written *last*.

Preface/foreword

Prefaces or forewords are used for a variety of purposes. Usually they explain the origins of the study and outline any qualifications or limitations. Acknowledgements of assistance may be included if there is no separate 'acknowledgements' section. Sometimes a significant individual is asked to write a Foreword, such as the director of an institution, a government minister or an eminent academic.

CONTENTS

Page

Executive summary .... (i)

Preface .... (iii)

Acknowledgements .... (iv)

1. INTRODUCTION 1
   1.1 Background to the study 1
   1.2 The nature of the problem 3
   1.3 Aims of the study 4
   1.4 Outline of the report 4

2. LITERATURE REVIEW 5
   2.1 Research on youth and leisure generally 5
   2.2 Research on student leisure 8
   2.3 Conclusions: the state of knowledge on students and leisure 10
   2.4 Questions still to be answered 12

3. METHODOLOGY 13
   3.1 Data requirements 13
   3.2 Selection of methods 15
   3.3 Secondary data: sources and proposed analysis 16
   3.4 In-depth interviews 18
   3.5 Questionnaire survey 19
   3.6 Pilot survey 21

4. STUDENT LEISURE IN THE 21st CENTURY 22
   4.1 Data sources 22
   4.2 Students at school 22
   4.4 Students at college/university 25
   4.5 Conclusions 27

5. STUDENT WORK AND LEISURE
   5.1 Sample characteristics 29
   5.2 Attitudes towards academic work 30
   5.3 Attitudes towards paid work 32
   5.4 Attitudes towards leisure 34
   5.5 Work and leisure: a synthesis 37

6. SUMMARY AND CONCLUSIONS
   6.1 Summary 40
   6.2 Conclusions 42

REFERENCES 44

APPENDICES
1. Copy of questionnaire 49
2. In-depth interview checklist 51
3. Census data on student population 53
4. Survey statistical summary 56

LIST OF TABLES
1.1 Title xx
1.2 Title xx
Etc.

LIST OF DIAGRAMS/ILLUSTRATIONS
1.1 Title .... yy
1.2 Title .... yy
Etc.

Figure 18.3 Example report contents page

Acknowledgements

It is clearly a matter of courtesy to acknowledge any assistance received during the course of a research project. People and institutions who might be acknowledged are listed in Figure 18.2.

Main body of the report – technical aspects

Clearly the main body of the report is its most important component. The substantive content is discussed in the next section; here we consider a number of technical aspects of organisation and presentation, as listed in Figure 18.4.

Section numbering

In project reports it is usual to number not only the major sections/chapters, but also sub-sections within chapters, as shown in the example in Figure 18.3. Once a numbering system is established it should be carried through consistently throughout the report. Word-processor packages often provide 'style' templates to facilitate this process.

In project reports, section numbers may extend to several levels, for example, within section 4.2, there could be sub-sections: 4.2.1, 4.2.2, etc. Further levels can become cumbersome and are generally not required throughout the report, so if there is an occasional need for further sub-sections it is often advisable to use a simple a., b., c. or (i), (ii), (iii), etc.

Journal articles rarely include section numbering; when it is included it is typically one level only.

In theses chapters are numbered, and possibly one level of section within chapters, but sub-section numbering is not generally used.

Section numbering

Paragraph numbering

'Dot point' lists

Page numbering

Headers/footers

Heading hierarchy

Typing layout/spacing

Tables and graphics

Referencing

Which person?

Figure 18.4 Main body of report: technical aspects

Paragraph numbering

In some reports, notably government reports, paragraphs are individually numbered, although this is rare. This can be useful for reference purposes when a report is being discussed in committees, etc. Paragraphs can be numbered in a single series for the whole report or chapter by chapter: in chapter 1: paragraphs 1.1, 1.2, 1.3, etc.; in chapter 2: paragraphs 2.1, 2.2, 2.3 etc., and so on.

'Dot point' lists

'Dot point' lists are very common in project reports, and quite common in the other reporting formats. This device assists the reader to understand the structure of the material and assists in visual scanning of a document. Project reports are often discussed in committee or written comments are offered in various consultation exercises, and this process is eased by dot-point lists, although numbered lists may be even more helpful: it is easier to refer to and to locate 'item 5' than 'the fifth dot point'.

Where possible, grammatical rules should be followed in dot-point lists. For example, in Figure 18.5, the list is, in effect, all one sentence. There are therefore, semi-colons at the end of each list item, a full stop at the end and no capital letters at the beginning of each item. This principle is difficult to follow when the individual dot points are lengthy, perhaps themselves involving more than one sentence: in this case each dot point in a sequence should be treated as one or more complete sentences with capital letters and full stops.

Page numbering

One problem in putting together long reports, especially when different authors are responsible for different sections, is to organise page numbering so that it follows on from chapter to chapter. This can be eased by numbering each chapter separately, for example: Chapter 1: pages 1.1, 1.2, 1.3, etc.; Chapter 2: pages 2.1, 2.2, 2.3, etc. and so on. Such a numbering system can also aid readers in finding their way around a report. Word processors can be made to produce page numbers in this form by using the header and/or page-numbering facilities.

It is general practice for the title page, contents page(s), acknowledgements, and the executive summary pages to be numbered as a group using roman numerals (as in this book) and for the main body of the report to start at page 1 with normal numbers. Most word processors will facilitate this.

In preparing a research report, the author should take account of:

- the likely readership;
- the requirements of the funding agency, as indicated in the study brief;
- printing or other distribution format;
- likely costs; and
- delivery of a clear message.

Figure 18.5   Dot-point list example

Headers/footers

Word-processing packages provide the facility to include a running header or footer across the top or bottom of each page. This can be used to indicate sections or chapters, as in this book, or, in the case of a consultancy report, can be used to indicate title and authorship of the report, perhaps even displaying the consultancy logo on each page.

Heading hierarchy

In the main body of the report a hierarchy of heading styles should be used, with the major chapter/section headings being in the most prominent style and with decreasing emphasis for sub-section headings. For example:

1. Chapter Titles
1.1 Section Headings
1.1.1 Sub-section Headings

Such a convention helps readers to know where they are in a document. When a team is involved in writing a report it is clearly sensible to agree these heading styles in advance. Modern word-processor systems provide a large hierarchy and report 'styles' which standardise heading formats and section numbering systems, linked to assembly of tables of contents. Word-processing packages offer style templates to facilitate this.

Typing layout/spacing

Essays and books tend to use the convention of starting new paragraphs by indenting the first line. Report style is to separate paragraphs by a blank line and not to indent the first line. Report style also tends to have more headings. For a document in report style it is usual to leave wide margins, which raises the question as to whether it is necessary to print documents in 1.5 or double space format or whether single spacing is adequate (and more environmentally friendly!). Different journals have different format specifications for submission of articles, usually indicated in the journal itself and/or on the journal website. Universities provide their own guidelines for the layout of theses.

Tables and graphics

Balance: When presenting the results of quantitative research, an appropriate balance must be struck between the use of tables, graphics and text. In most cases, very large or complex tables are consigned to appendices and simplified and/or graphical versions included in the body of the report. It may be appropriate to place *all* tables in appendices and provide only 'reader-friendly' graphics in the body of the report. The decision on which approach to use depends partly on the complexity of the data to be presented, but mainly on the type of audience.

Tables/graphics vs text: Tables, graphics and text each have a distinctive role to play in the presentation of the study findings:

- tables provide information;
- graphics illustrate that information so that patterns can be seen in a visual way; while
- the text should be telling a story or developing an argument and 'orchestrating' tables and graphics to support that task.

There seems to be little point in the text of a report simply repeating what is in a table or graphics. The text should at least highlight the main features of the data; ideally it should develop an argument or draw conclusions based on the data. In the example in Figure 18.6, Commentary A does little more than

---

Table X. Participation in top 5 sports/physical activities, persons aged 16+, Great Britain, 1986

Activity	% Participating in four weeks prior to interview (most popular quarter)	
	Males	Females
Walking	21	18
Football	6	*
Snooker/billiards	17	3
Swimming – indoor	9	10
Darts	9	3
Keep-fit/yoga	1	5

Source: General Household Survey, OPCS

* less than 0.05%.

Commentary A
The table indicates that the top five sports and physical recreation activities for men are walking, with 21% participation, snooker/billiards (17%), indoor swimming (9%), darts (9%) and football (6%), whereas for women the five most popular activities are walking (18%), indoor swimming (10%), keep-fit/yoga (5%), snooker/billiards (3%) and darts (3%).

Commentary B
Men and women may have more in common in their patterns of leisure activity than is popularly imagined. The table indicates that four activities – walking, swimming, snooker/billiards and darts – are included in the top five most popular sport and physical recreation activities for both men and women. While in general men's participation levels are higher than those of women, the table shows that women's participation rate exceeds that of men for two of the activities, namely keep-fit/yoga and swimming.

Figure 18.6   Table and commentaries

repeat what is in the table: it says nothing to the reader about the difference between men's and women's participation patterns, which is presumably the purpose of the exercise. Commentary B, on the other hand, is more informative, pointing out particular features of the data in the table.

Statistical tests: In the more quantitative disciplines there is a convention that, in academic reports such as journal articles and theses, the results of statistical tests should be mentioned in the text, even if the information is also available in a table. Thus, for example, a sentence in the text might read: 'Mean weekly frequency of participation by men (2.1) is significantly higher than for women (1.7, $t = 5.6$, $p < 0.001$, see Table 2). Clearly the information in brackets 'clutters' the text and makes it less 'reader-friendly' if there are a number of such insertions; it seems unnecessary to include it in the text if it can be seen in the table; and the information on the t-test may be meaningless to readers without statistical knowledge. In less quantitative fields it is not necessary to include the information in brackets, particularly the t-test result, in the text if it is available in a table. In management reports, results of statistical tests are often not included at all, although they may have been carried out, and such terms as 'significantly different' or 'not significantly different' may be used.

Presentation: Diagrams and tables should, as far as possible, be complete in themselves. That is, the title should be informative and the columns, rows or axes should be fully labelled so that the reader can understand them without necessarily referring to the text. The table in Figure 18.6 follows these principles. Thus tables or graphics presenting data from leisure and tourism surveys or other data sources should include information on:

- the geographical area to which the data refer;

- the year to which the data refer or the year collected;

- gender and age-range of the sample or population to which the data relate;

- sample size, where relevant; and

- units of measurement.

Reproductions of secondary data should indicate the source of data, but tables or graphics presenting results from the primarily data collection of the study, such as a survey, do not need to indicate this on every table and diagram – however, some consultants tend to do this for intellectual property reasons so that if a user copies just one table or diagram, then its source is still indicated.

Referencing

References to the literature and other sources in academic reports should follow the referencing conventions as set out in Chapter 6. This may, however, be inappropriate for the non-academic readerships of management reports. While sources should be acknowledged in such reports, it is generally appropriate to do so in an unobtrusive manner – for example by use of the end note rather than author/date reference style. In some management reports the 'review of the literature' is relegated to an appendix with just the conclusions being presented in the body of the report.

Which person?

In academic reports, it is conventional to report the conduct and findings of research in an 'impersonal style' – for example to say: 'A survey was conducted' rather than 'I/we conducted a survey'; and 'It was found that . . .' rather than 'I/we found that . . .'. Some believe that this attempt to appear 'scientific' is inappropriate in the social sciences, particularly in qualitative research where the researcher personally engages with the research subjects (see Dupuis, 1999). First person accounts are therefore sometimes, but not commonly, used in some leisure and tourism reports. The first person plural is also quite commonly used by consultants in management reports, especially when the consultants wish to convey the impression that they are bringing particular personal skills and experience to bear on a project.

The impersonal style can appear odd or pretentious when authors refer to their own work. Thus for me to say: 'Veal (2002) has argued that leisure is pluralistic' seems odd, and for me to say: 'The author has argued that leisure is pluralistic (Veal, 2002)' seems pretentious. The solution in such a situation is either to use the first person – 'I have argued that leisure is pluralistic (Veal, 2002)' – or to 'de-centre' the author – 'It has been argued that leisure is pluralistic (Veal, 2002)'.

Main body of the report – structure and content

Structure

It could be said that the three most important aspects of a research report are: 1. structure, 2. structure, and 3. structure! The *structure* of a report is of fundamental importance and needs to be thoroughly considered and discussed, particularly when a team is involved. While all reports have certain structural features in common, the important aspects of any one report concern the underlying argument and how that relates to the objectives of the study and any data collection and analysis involved. This is linked fundamentally to the *research objectives*, the *theoretical or evaluative framework* and the *overall research strategy*, as discussed in Chapter 3.

Before writing starts it can be useful to agree not only the report structure and format, but also target word lengths for each chapter or section. While an agreed structure is a necessary starting point, it is also necessary to be flexible. As drafting gets going it may be found that what was originally conceived as one chapter needs to be divided into two or three chapters, or what was thought of as a separate chapter can be incorporated into another chapter or into an appendix. Throughout, consideration needs to be given to the overall length of the report, in terms of words or pages.

When a questionnaire survey is involved, there is a tendency for some to structure the presentation according to the sequence of questions in the questionnaire and, correspondingly, the sequence of tables as they are produced by the computer. This is not an appropriate way to proceed! Questionnaires are structured for ease of interview, for the convenience of interviewer and/or respondent: they do *not* provide a suitable sequence and structure for a report. The report should be structured around the substance of the research problem.

The table of contents, as shown in Figure 18.3, indicates the formal broad structure of the report to the reader. The example relates to project reports and theses, which tend to be lengthy and to be divided into chapters and to have tables of contents. Journal articles are shorter and do not have tables of contents, but structure is, of course, still important. There is a conventional overall structure for journal articles involving about seven sections, as shown in Figure 18.7. This structure is not hard and fast: in particular, not all articles are empirical, so 'methods' and 'results' sections are not universal.

In the case of a project report, the contents page indicates the general organisation of the report and should make the reader aware of the structure, but it is only a broad indication. This, however, is rarely enough: it must be *explained* – often more than once. Being clear in your own mind about structure is one thing; conveying it to the reader can be quite another. Thus it is good practice, particularly in the case of a lengthy report/thesis, to provide an outline of the structure of the whole report in the introductory chapter, and outlines of each chapter in the introduction to each chapter. Summaries are useful at the end of each chapter and these can be revisited and summarised at the end of the report when drawing conclusions together. It is advisable to provide numerous references backwards and forwards, as reminders to the reader as to where you are in the overall 'story' of the report. When a list of 'factors', 'issues' or 'topics' is about to be discussed, one by one, it is useful to list the factors or issues to be discussed, and then summarise at the end of the section to indicate what the review of factors or issues has achieved.

Articles are, of course, shorter, so organising the structure is less of a challenge. There is no table of contents as such, although the abstract – typically just

---

- Background/introduction/justification for the research/nature of the problem/issue
- Review of the literature
- Specific outline of problem/issue/hypotheses
- Methods
- Results
- Conclusions
- References

Figure 18.7 Conventional academic article structure

a paragraph – is usually printed at the beginning of an article and can give some impression. But the logic and structure should also be explained within the article proper.

Between methods and results

All empirical research reports, regardless of format, should include a clear summary of the methods used to gather data. In journal articles the description is often quite short, because of the limitation of word length. In management reports the description may be short in the body of the report because of the type of readership, but there is scope to provide more detail in appendices. In a thesis an extensive and explicit description of methods used is essential.

In all formats, but particularly in a thesis, the *choice* of methods should also be discussed. Why was a particular method selected? What alternatives were considered and why were they rejected? Such a discussion should be related to the nature of the research questions/hypotheses. It is not sufficient merely to list the characteristics and merits of the methods chosen, but to indicate why those *particular* characteristics were appropriate in *this particular project*. Factors to consider in selecting a research method are discussed at the end of Chapter 5 and these should be referred to in justifying the choice of method.

Part of the reporting of results of empirical research involves provision of some very basic information on the success of the chosen method in achieving a suitable sample of subjects for study. Since this is technical in nature and not concerned directly with the substantive findings, it can be reported in the 'methods' section, although it is often reported as the first part of the 'results' sections. This component of the report should provide information on:

- the size of the sample achieved;

- response rates and an indication as to whether they are deemed to be acceptable or likely to have caused bias;

- characteristics of the sample, particularly in so far as they can indicate the representativeness of the sample – thus a sample from a household or community survey might be compared with the known age/gender structure of the local population from the population census data for the area, while the age structure of a site-survey sample might be compared with junior/adult ticket sales ratios or information from other similar surveys;

- any measures taken to correct sample bias by means of weighting, and a description of that process.

Audiences and style

The style, format and length of a report is largely influenced by the type of audience at which it is aimed. The amount of technical jargon used and the detail with which data are presented will be affected by this question of audience. Audiences may be of three kinds:

- *Popular audience*: consisting of members of the general public who might read a report of research in a newspaper or magazine – full research reports are therefore not generally written for a popular readership.

- *Decision-makers*: groups, such as elected members of councils, government ministers, members of boards of companies, or senior executives, who may not have a detailed knowledge of a particular field, or may have a particular knowledge, which might be technical, managerial or political.

- *Experts*: professionals or academics who are familiar with the broad subject matter of the research.

Report functions: record and narrative

A research report can be thought of in two ways: first the report as *narrative* and, second, the report as *record*. Balancing these demands as the report is being put together can be a major challenge.

Report as narrative: Narrative means that a report has to tell a *story* to the reader. The writer of the report therefore needs to think of the flow of the argument – the 'story' – in the same way that the writer of a novel has to consider the plot. The report as narrative may call for presentation of only simplified factual information or key features of the data, possibly in graphical form, to demonstrate and illustrate the argument. The narrative of a research report usually develops as indicated in Figure 18.8. The items listed may emerge in a

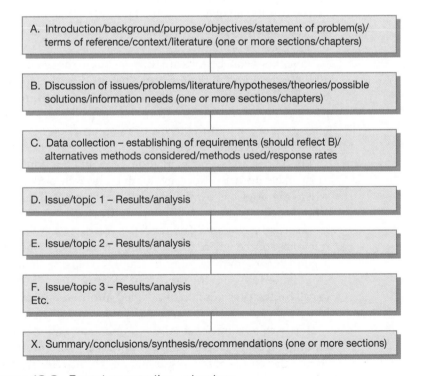

Figure 18.8   Report as narrative – structure

variety of chapter-section configurations. For example, sections A and B could be one chapter/section or three or four, depending on the complexity of the project.

The introductory section(s), A, should reflect the considerations which emerged in the initial steps in the planning stages of a project (components 1, 2 and 6 in Figure 3.1). The term 'context' is used to include the environment in which the research is situated, including any initial literature review which may be involved. Section(s) B should reflect components 3–5 and 7–8 in the research planning process and may include further reference to the literature.

In sections B and C it is important that the relation between data require-ments and the research questions and theoretical or evaluative framework be explained, as discussed in Chapter 3. It should be clear from the discussion why the data are being collected – and how this relates to the planning/management/theoretical issues raised; how it was anticipated that the infor-mation collected would solve or shed light on the problems/issues raised, or aid decision-making.

In section C methodology should be described in detail; it should be clear why particular techniques were chosen, how samples or subjects were selected, and what data collection instruments were used. Where sample surveys are involved, full information should be given on response rates and sample sizes obtained and some indication given of the consequences in terms of confidence intervals, as discussed in Chapter 13. These technical aspects of the results of any survey work can be included in the methodology section of the report or in the first of the results sections.

The results/analysis sections (D, E, F, etc.) should ideally be structured by the earlier conceptual or theoretical discussion (B) around issues and elements of the research problem.

Sometimes conclusions are fully set out in the results/analysis section(s) and all that is required in the final conclusions section is to reiterate and draw them together. In other cases the final section includes the final stage of analysis and the drawing of conclusions from that analysis. In writing the final section it is vital to refer back to the terms of reference/objectives of the study to ensure that all objectives have been met.

Not all research reports include 'recommendations'. Recommendations are most likely to arise from evaluative research and in management research where the brief has explicitly asked for them. It should, of course, be clear to whom such recommendations are addressed.

The report as 'record': The report as *record* means that a report is often also a reference source where future readers may wish to look for information. Being a good record may involve including extensive detailed information which would interfere with the process of 'story telling'. The report as record is likely to call for the presentation of detailed information – even data which were col-lected but did not prove particularly relevant for the overall study conclusions.

It is wise to think beyond the immediate readership and use of a research report, and think of it also as the definitive record of the research conducted. It should therefore contain a summary of all the relevant data collected in a form which would be useful for any future user of the report. This means that, while data may be presented in the main body of the report in a highly condensed and summarised form in order to produce a readable narrative, it should *also* be presented in as much detail as possible 'for the record'. To avoid interfering with the narrative, data included for record purposes can be placed in appendices or, when large amounts of data are involved, in a separate statistical volume.

In the case of questionnaire survey data it can be a good idea to provide a statistical appendix which includes tables from all the questions in the order they appear in the questionnaire, as discussed in Chapter 16. Any reader interested in a specific aspect of the data is then able to locate and use it. The main body of the report can then be structured around issues and need not be constrained by the structure of the questionnaire.

In conclusion

Ultimately the writing of a good research report is an art and a skill which develops with practice. Reports can be improved enormously as a result of comments from others – often because the writer has been 'too close' to the report for too long to be able to see glaring faults or omissions. The researcher/ writer can also usually spot opportunities for improvement if he or she takes a short break and returns to the draft report with 'fresh eyes'.

Finally, *checking and double checking the report for typing, spelling and typographical errors is well worth the laborious effort*!

Other media

While the written report is still the most common medium for the communication of research results, this is likely to change in future. In particular, the researcher is often required to present final or interim results of research in person and some sort of audio-visual aids are usually advisable, including: handouts, posters, computers and video devices. The most common medium is the oral presentation aided by computer-based visuals using such packages as Microsoft 'PowerPoint'.

Oral presentations

An important point to bear in mind is the obvious fact that the audio-visual presentation is *not* the same as a written report. The presentation must be designed as a medium/message in its own right. The information to be presented must fit into the time allotted and must be suitable for the medium. Therefore a conscious selection of material must be made. This will normally be explained at the beginning of the presentation, but constant references to what is *not* being covered in the presentation because of lack of time are an indication of an unprofessional approach. For example, if there are six 'key findings' from a study, rather than rushing to cover all six, it is in most cases better to say to an audience: 'There are six findings from the study and in this presentation I am going to concentrate on the three most important.'

It goes without saying that the presenter should *practise* presenting the material to ensure that it fits into the time allotted. Such practice sessions can be seen as the equivalent of various drafts of the written report. Typically it is necessary to be selective in making such a presentation. Judgement must be used in deciding what to include and what to leave out. As with the writing of abstracts and synopses, this can be a considerable challenge. Practice runs help in this process since programs such as PowerPoint include a 'rehearse timings' procedure which helps in deciding how long to spend on particular parts of the presentation and what to leave out on grounds of time.

Reading from a prepared script is rarely as successful as talking directly to an audience. However, if a prepared script *is* being used, then practising the presentation so that the presenter is very familiar with the script is even more advisable; then frequent eye contact can be made with the audience.

Arranging and reviewing video-recordings of practice runs of a presentation can pay dividends.

Use of PowerPoint-type software

Most of the readers of this book are students, who sit through hundreds of PowerPoint-type presentations during the course of their studies. Students are therefore experienced judges of what is and is not a good presentation. These notes distil just a few of the 'do's and don'ts'.

- Don't stand in front of the screen!

- Don't overcrowd slides. The standard slide templates available in programs such as PowerPoint provide a default font size and a default number of 'dot points' on a slide. This is for a good reason. Viewing an image when preparing it on a personal computer screen from less than a metre is different from viewing the same image projected on a screen in a lecture hall or meeting room. Thus, while a table or graphic with 30 lines of data may be readable in a printed report and on a personal computer screen, it may not be readable to someone 20 metres from a projection screen. In such a situation the most important, say, ten lines of the table or items in the graphic must be selected, or the table or graphic must be divided into two or more sequential slides. As an example, the PowerPoint slides available for this book include eight slides for Figure 18.3: one containing the main chapter/section headings only (the headings in capital letters) and one each for the detail of each chapter/section and the references, appendices, etc. One of the worst things to hear from a presenter is: 'You probably won't be able to read this from the back of the room but. . . .' A practice run-through with a full-size screen viewed from the back of a room is advisable.

- Use graphics. The PowerPoint-type presentation is a visual medium. Ideally, therefore, graphical images should be mixed with verbal material. Photographs, and even video material, from the research process and/or relating to the research subject can make a presentation 'come alive'. On the other hand, excessive use of such material can be a distraction and may limit time available for presentation of key material. A balance must be struck.

- Be careful about colour. Maximum contrast aids viewing. Yellow lettering on an orange background may look effective in close-up on a computer screen but could be unreadable when projected. Lighting conditions in rooms vary and projector colour definition can also vary: it's better to play it safe. Similarly, photographs which look good on a small screen may not impress when projected.

- Use the dynamic features of the program. PowerPoint-type programs include 'animation'. While items flying into view from all directions may be a distraction, the sequential appearance of, for example, items in a dot-point list, at least concentrate the viewer/listener on the item which the presenter is talking about. This works even more effectively with graphics. Again, using an example from the PowerPoint slides made available with this book: in the case of Figure 3.1, which summarises the ten components of the research process, the ten boxes appear sequentially, so that the presenter can talk about each component in turn as it appears.

Summary

This chapter considers the preparation of what is generally the final outcome of a research project, namely a written report. It considers the varying demands of three types of report: the management/planning/research project report, the academic journal article and the thesis, each with different audiences, different constraints and different conventions. The chapter reviews the various ancillary components of a report, including the cover, cover page, title page, list of contents, synopsis/abstract/executive summary, preface/foreword and acknowledgements. It then considers the main body of the report in terms of technical aspects, largely to do with format, and structure and content. Structure is emphasised as the key feature of a research report, particularly in their longer formats.

A final comment

Research is a creative process which, in the words of Norbert Elias with which we began this text, aims to 'make known something previously unknown to human beings . . . to advance human knowledge, to make it more certain or better fitting . . . the aim is . . . discovery'. It is hoped that this book will provide some assistance in that process of discovery and that the reader will enjoy some of the satisfactions and rewards which can come from worthwhile research.

Test questions/exercises

No specific exercises are offered here. By now the reader should be capable of venturing into the world of research by carrying out a research project from beginning to end.

Resources

The best reading relevant to this chapter is the critical reading of research reports. As regards non-print media, most readers of this book have ample opportunity in the course of their academic and/or professional lives to see good and bad examples of audio-visual presentations from which they can discern good and bad practice!

References

ABS – see Australian Bureau of Statistics.

Adler, P. A. and Adler, P. (1994) Observational techniques. In N. K. Denzin and Y. S. Lincoln (eds) *Handbook of Qualitative Research*. Thousand Oaks, CA: Sage, 377–92.

Albers, P. C., and James, W. R. (1988) Travel photography a methodological approach. *Annals of Tourism Research*, 15(1), 134–58.

Allen, L. R. (1982) The relationship between Murray's personality needs and leisure interests. *Journal of Leisure Research*, 14(1), 63–76.

American Psychological Association (APA) (2001) *Publication Manual of the American Psychological Association, Fifth Edition*. Washington, DC: APA.

Andrews, D. L., Mason, D. S. and Silk M. L. (eds) (2005) *Qualitative Methods in Sports Studies*. Oxford: Berg.

Annear, M. J., Gidlow, B. and Cushman, G. (2009) Neighbourhood deprivation and older adults' preferences for and perceptions of active leisure participation. *Annals of Leisure Research*, 12(2), 96–128.

Archer, B. H. (1994) Demand forecasting and estimation. In J. R. B. Ritchie and C. R. Goeldner (eds) *Travel, Tourism and Hospitality Research, Second edn*. New York: John Wiley, 105–14.

Arensberg, C. M. (1954) The community-study method. *American Journal of Sociology*, 60(2), 109–24.

Arnberger, A. and and Eder, R. (2008) Assessing user interactions on shared recreational trails by long-term video monitoring. *Managing Leisure*, 13(1), 36–51.

Atkinson, R. (1998) *The Life Story Interview*. London: Sage.

Australian Bureau of Statistics (ABS) (1998) *How Australians Use their Time, 1997*. (Cat. No. 4153.0), Canberra: ABS.

Australian Bureau of Statistics (ABS) (2000a) *Children's Participation in Cultural and Leisure Activities*. (Cat. No. 4901.0), Canberra: ABS.

Australian Bureau of Statistics (ABS) (2000b) *1998–99 Household Expenditure Survey, Detailed Expenditure Items*. (Cat. No. 6535.0), Canberra: ABS.

Bachman, J. G. and O'Malley, P. M. (1981) When four months equal a year: inconsistencies in student reports of drug use. *Public Opinion Quarterly*, 45(4), 536–48.

Baretje, R. (1964) *Bibliographie Touristique*. Aix-en-Provence: Centre d'Etudes du Tourisme.

Barry, P. (1999) *The Rise and Fall of Alan Bond*. Sydney: Bantam/ABC.

Barry, P. (2006) *The Rise and Rise of Kerry Packer – Uncut*. Sydney: Bantam/ABC.

Batty, A. (1977) The action research background to the leisure experiments. In Department of the Environment *Leisure and the Quality of Life: a Report on Four Local Experiments* (2 Volumes). London: HMSO, 3–16.

Bazeley, P. (2007) *Qualitative Data Analysis with NVivo.* Thousand Oaks, CA.: Sage.

Beard, J. G. and Ragheb, M. (1980) Measuring leisure satisfaction. *Journal of Leisure Research*, 12(1), 20–33.

Beaman, J., Beaman, J., O'Leary, J. T. and Smith, S. (2001) The impact of seemingly minor methodological changes on estimates of travel and correcting bias. In A. G., Woodside, G. I., Crouch, J. A., Mazanec, M. Oppermann and M. Y. Sakai (eds) *Consumer Psychology of Tourism, Hospitality and Leisure.* Wallingford, UK: CABI Publishing, 49–65.

Bennett, T. and Frow, J. (1991) *Art Galleries: Who Goes?* Redfern, NSW: Australia Council.

Bennett, T., Emmison, M. and Frow, J. (1999) *Accounting for Tastes: Australian Everyday Cultures.* Cambridge: Cambridge University Press.

Bertaux, D. (ed.) (1981) *Biography and Society.* London: Sage.

Bialeschki, M. D. and Henderson, K. (1986) Leisure in the common world of women. *Leisure Studies*, 5(3), 299–308.

Billings, A. C. and Tyler Eastman, S. (2002) Selective representation of gender, ethnicity and nationality in American television coverage of the 2000 Summer Olympics. *International Review for the Sociology of Sport*, 37(3/4), 351–70.

Birenbaum, A. and Sagarin, E. (eds) (1973) *People in Places: The Sociology of the Familiar.* London: Nelson.

Bitgood, S., Patterson, D. and Benefield, A. (1988) Exhibit design and visitor behaviour. *Environment and Behaviour*, 20(4), 474–91.

Black, N. (1990) A model and methodology to assess changes to heritage buildings. *Journal of Tourism Studies* 1(1), 15–23.

Blackshaw, T. and Crawford, G. (2006) *The Sage Dictionary of Leisure Studies.* London: Sage.

Blamey, A. and Mutrie, N. (2004) Changing the individual to promote health-enhancing physical activity: the difficulties of producing evidence and translating it into practice. *Journal of Sports Sciences*, 22(8), 741–54.

Boothby, J. (1987) Self-reported participation rates: further comment. *Leisure Studies*, 6(1), 99–104.

Borman, K. M., LeCompte, M. D. and Goetz, J. P. (1986) Ethnographic and qualitative research design and why it doesn't work. *American Behavioral Scientist*, 30(1), 42–57.

Botterill, T. D. (1989) Humanistic tourism? Personal constructions of a tourist: Sam visits Japan. *Leisure Studies*, 8(3), 281–94.

Bourdieu, P. (1984) *Distinction: a Social Critique of the Judgement of Taste.* London: Routledge.

Bower, R. and Cross, R. (2008) Elite tennis player sensitivity to changes in string tension and the effect on resulting ball dynamics. *Sports Engineering*, 11(1), 31–6.

Bramham, R., Henry, I., Mommaas, H. and Van Der Poel, H. (eds) (1993) *Leisure Policies in Europe.* Wallingford, UK: CAB International.

Brandenburg, J., Greiner, W., Hamilton-Smith, E., Scholten, H., Senior, R. and Webb, J. (1982) A conceptual model of how people adopt recreation activities. *Leisure Studies*, 1(3), 263–76.

Bromley, D. B. (1986) *The Case-Study Method in Psychology and Related Disciplines.* New York: John Wiley and Sons.

Brown, P. (1995) Women, sport and the media: an historical perspective on sports coverage in the *Sydney Morning Herald*, 1890–1990. In C. Simpson and B. Gidlow (eds)

Australian and New Zealand Association for Leisure Studies, Second Conference – Leisure Connexions. Canterbury, New Zealand: Lincoln University, 44–50.

Brown, P. R., Brown, W. J. and Powers, J. R. (2001) Time pressure, satisfaction with leisure and health among Australian women. *Annals of Leisure Research*, 4, 1–16.

Brown, W. J., Heesch, K. and Miller, Y. (2009) Life events and changing physical activity patterns in women at different life stages. *Annals of Behavioral Medicine*, 37(3): 294–305.

Brownson, R. C., Kelly, C. M. *et al.* (2008) Environmental and policy approaches for promoting physical activity in the United States: a research agenda. *Journal of Physical Activity and Health*, 5(4), 488–503.

Brukner, P., Khan, K. and John Kron, J. (eds) (2003) *Encyclopedia of Exercise, Sport and Health*. Crows Nest, NSW: Allen and Unwin.

Bruner, G. C. and Hensel, P. J. (1992) *Marketing Scales Handbook: A Compilation of Multi-Item Measures*. Chicago, IL: American Marketing Assoc.

Bruner, G. C., James, K. E. and Hensel, P. J. (2001) *Marketing Scales Handbook: a compilation of Multi-item Measures*, vol. III. Chicago, IL: American Marketing Assoc.

Bryman, A. (1995) *Disney and his Worlds*. London: Routledge.

Bryman, A. and Bell, E. (2003) Breaking down the quantitative/qualitative divide, and Combining quantitative and qualitative research. Chapters 21–2 of: *Business Research Methods*. Oxford: Oxford University Press, 465–94.

Bryman, A. and Bell, E. (2003) *Business Research Methods*. Oxford: Oxford University Press.

Burch, W. R. (1981) The ecology of metaphor: spacing regularities for humans and other primates in urban and wild habitats. *Leisure Sciences*, 4(3), 213–30.

Burdge, R. (1989) The evolution of leisure and recreation research from multidisciplinary to interdisciplinary. In E. L. Jackson and T. L. Burton (eds) *Understanding Leisure and Recreation: Mapping the Past and Charting the Future*, State College, PA: Venture, 29–48.

Burgess, R. G. (ed.) (1982) *Field Research: A Sourcebook and Field Manual*. London: Allen and Unwin.

Burkart, A. J. and Medlik, S. (1981) *Tourism: Past, Present and Future*, Second edition. London: Heinemann.

Burns, P. and Lester, J. (2005) Using visual evidence: the case of *Cannibal Tours*. In B. W. Ritchie, P. Burns and C. Palmer (eds) *Tourism Research Methods: Integrating Theory with Practice*. Wallingford, UK: CABI Publishing, 49–62.

Burns, R. B. (1994) *Introduction to Research Methods, Second edn*. Melbourne: Longman Cheshire.

Burton, T. L. (1971) *Experiments in Recreation Research*. London: Allen and Unwin.

CACI Ltd (2006) *ACORN User Guide*. London: CACI Ltd., available at: www.caci.co.uk/financialacorn.aspx.

Calantone, R. J., Di Benedetto, C. A. and Bojanic, D. (1987) A comprehensive review of the tourism forecasting literature. *Journal of Travel Research*, 26(2), 28–39.

Calder, A. and Sheridan, D. (1984) *Speak for Yourself: A Mass Observation Anthology, 1937–49*. London: Jonathan Cape.

Calder, B. (1977) Focus groups and the nature of qualitative marketing research. *Journal of Marketing Research*, 14, Aug., 353–64.

Campbell, D. T. and Stanley, J. C. (1972) *Experimental and Quasi-Experimental Designs for Research*. Chicago: Rand McNally.

Campbell, F. L. (1970) Participant observation in outdoor recreation. *Journal of Leisure Research*, 2(4), 226–36.

Carlsen, J., Ali-Knight, J. and Robertson, M. (2008) Access – a research agenda for Edinburgh festivals. *Event Management*, 11(1–2), 3–11.

Carty, V. (1997) Ideologies and forms of domination in the organization of the global production and consumption of goods in the emerging postmodern era: a case study of Nike Corporation and the implications for gender. *Gender, Work and Organization*, 4(4), 189–201.

Carver, R. H. and Nash, J. G. (2005) *Doing Data Analysis with SPSS Version 12.0*. Belmont, CA: Thomson/Brooks/Cole.

Cashman, R. (1999) Legacy. In R. Cashman and A. Hughes (eds) *Staging the Olympics: the Event and its Impact*. Sydney: University of New South Wales Press: 183–94.

Centre for Leisure & Sports Research (2002) *Count me in: the Dimensions of Social Inclusion through Culture & Sport, a Report for the Department for Culture, Media & Sport*. Centre for Leisure & Sport Research, Leeds Metropolitan University.

Chadwick, R. A. (1994) Concepts, definitions, and measures used in travel and tourism research. In J. R. B. Ritchie and C. R. Goeldner (eds) *Travel, Tourism and Hospitality Research, Second edn*. New York: John Wiley, 65–80.

Chase, D. and Harada, M. (1984) Response error in self-reported recreation participation. *Journal of Leisure Research*, 16(4), 322–29.

Chase, D. R. and Godbey, G. C. (1983) The accuracy of self-reported participation rates. *Leisure Studies*, 2(2), 231–36.

Cherem, G. J. and Driver, B. L. (1983) Visitor employed photography: a technique to measure common perceptions of natural environments. *Journal of Leisure Research*, 15(1), 65–83.

Child, E. (1983) Play and culture: a study of English and Asian children. *Leisure Studies*, 2(2), 169–86.

Chisnall, P. M. (1991) Market segmentation analysis. Chapter 6 of *The Essence of Marketing Research*, New York: Prentice-Hall, 76–91.

Christensen, J. E. (1980) A second look at the informal interview. *Journal of Leisure Research*, 12(2), 183–6.

Christensen, J. E. (1982) On generalizing about the need for follow-up efforts in mail response surveys. *Journal of Leisure Research*. 14(3), 263–5.

Clarke, J. and Critcher, C. (1985) *The Devil Makes Work: Leisure in Capitalist Britain*. London: Macmillan.

Claxton, J. D. (1994) Conjoint analysis in travel research: a manager's guide. In J. R. B. Ritchie and C. R. Goeldner (eds) *Travel, Tourism and Hospitality Research*, Second edn. New York: John Wiley, 513–252.

Coakes, S. J. and Steed, L.G. (1999) *SPSS Analysis Without Anguish: (Version 11.0 for Windows)*. Brisbane: John Wiley and Sons.

Coalter, F. (2007) *A Wider Social Role for Sport*. London: Routledge.

Cohen, E. (1988) Traditions in the qualitative sociology of tourism. *Annals of Tourism Research*, 15(1), 29–46.

Cohen, E. (1993) The study of touristic images of native people: mitigating the stereotype of a stereotype. In D. G. Pearce and R. W. Butler (eds) *Tourism Research: Critiques and Challenges*. London: Routledge, 36–69.

Collins, M. F. (2003) *Sport and Social Exclusion*. London: Routledge.

Connell, J. and Lowe, A. (1997) Generating grounded theory from qualitative data: the application of inductive methods in tourism and hospitality management research. *Progress in Tourism and Hospitality Research*, 3, 165–73.

Conner, T. S., Tennen, H., Fleeson, W. and Barrett, L. F. (2009) Experience sampling methods: a modern idiographic approach to personality research. *Social and Personality Psychology*, 3(3), 292–313.

Cordell, H. K., Green, G. T., Leeworthy, V. R., Stephens, R., Fly, M. J. and Betz, C. J. (2005) United States of America: outdoor recreation. In G. Cushman, A. J. Veal and J. Zuzanek (eds) *Free Time and Leisure Participation: International Perspectives*. Wallingford, UK: CABI Publishing, 245–64.

Cosper, R. and Kinsley, B. L. (1984) An application of conjoint analysis to leisure research: cultural preferences in Canada. *Journal of Leisure Research*, 16(3), 224–33.

Critcher, C. (1992) Is there anything on the box? Leisure studies and media studies. *Leisure Studies*, 11(2), 97–122.

Crouch, G. I. and Louviere, J. J. (2001) A review of choice modelling research in tourism, hospitality and leisure. In J. A. Mazanec, G. I. Crouch, J. R. B Ritchie and A. G. Woodside (eds) *Consumer Psychology of Tourism, Hospitality and Leisure, Volume 2*. Wallingford, UK: CABI Publishing, 67–86.

Crouch, G. I. and Shaw, R. N. (1991) *International Tourism Demand: A Meta-Analytical Integration of Research Findings*. Management Paper No. 36, Melbourne: Graduate School of Management, Monash University.

Csikszentmihalyi, M. (1990) *Flow: the Psychology of Optimal Experience*. New York: Harper and Row.

Csikszentmihalyi, M. and Larson, R. (1977) The ecology of adolescent activity and experience. *Journal of Youth and Adolescence*, 6(3), 281–94.

Cuneen, C., Findlay, M., Lynch, R. and Tupper, V. (1989) *Dynamics of Collective Conflict: Riots at the Bathurst 'Bike Races*. North Ryde, NSW: Law Book Co.

Cushman, G. and Veal, A. J. (1993) The new generation of leisure surveys – implications for research on everyday life. *Leisure and Society*, 16(1), 211–20.

Cushman, G., Veal, A. J. and Zuzanek, J. (eds) (2005a) *Free Time and Leisure Participation: International Perspectives*. Wallingford, UK: CABI Publishing.

Cushman, G., Veal, A. J. and Zuzanek, J. (2005b) National leisure participation and time-use surveys: a future. In G. Cushman, A. J. Veal and J. Zuzanek, J. *Free Time and Leisure Participation: International Perspectives*. Wallingford, UK: CABI Publishing, 283–92.

Dann, G., Nash, D. and Pearce, P. (1988) Special issue: methodological issues in tourism research. *Annals of Tourism Research*, 15(1).

Darcy, S. (1998) *People with a Disability and Tourism: A Bibliography*. School of Leisure and Tourism Studies, University of Technology, Sydney, On-line Bibliography 7, available at: www.business.uts.edu.au/lst/research/publications/bibliographies/index.html (Accessed March 2005).

Davies, B. (2003) The role of quantitative and qualitative research in industrial studies of tourism. *Journal of Travel Research*, 30(1), 59–63.

Davies, C. (1997) *Reflexive Ethnography: a Guide to Researching Selves and Others*. London: Routledge.

Dawson, J. and Hillier, J. (1995) Competitor mystery shopping: methodological considerations and implications for the MRS Code of Conduct. *Journal of the Market Research Society*, 37(4), 417–43.

Dayton, T. (2005) *The Living Stage: a Step-by-step Guide to Psychodrama, Sociometry and Experiential Group Therapy*. Deerfield Beach, FL: Health Communication Books.

DeCrop, A. (2004) Trustworthiness in qualitative tourism research. In J. Phillimore and L. Goodson (eds) *Qualitative Research in Tourism: Ontologies, Epistemologies and Methodologies*. London: Routledge, 156–69.

De Moragas, M., Kennett, C. and Puig, N. (eds) (2003) *The Legacy of the Olympic Games, 1984–2000: International Symposium*. Lausanne, 14–16 November, 2002. International Olympic Committee, Lausanne.

Denzin, N. K. and Lincoln, Y. S. (eds) (1994) *Handbook of Qualitative Research*. Thousand Oaks, CA: Sage.

Denzin, N. K. and Lincoln, Y. S. (eds) (2006) *Handbook of Qualitative Research, Third Edition*. Thousand Oaks, CA: Sage.

Department for Culture, Media and Sport (DCMS) (2009) *National Indicators 8, 9, 10 and 11: Interim Progress Statistical Release 17 December 2009*. London: DCMS, available at: www.culture.gov.uk/images/research/NI_Cultural_sport_indicators_stat_release.pdf

Department of the Environment (1977) *Leisure and the Quality of Life: a Report on Four Local Experiments* (2 Volumes). London: HMSO.

Dillman, D. A., Smyth, J. D. and Christian, L. M. (2009) *Internet, Mail, and Mixed-Mode Surveys: the Tailored Design Method, Third Edition*. New York: Wiley.

Donne, K. (2006) From outsider to quasi-insider at Wodin Watersports: a reflexive account of participant observation in a leisure context. In S. Fleming and F. Jordan (eds) *Ethical Issues in Leisure Research*. LSA Publication 90, Eastbourne, UK: Leisure Studies Association, 63–82.

Donohue, H. M. and Needham, R. D. (2009) Moving best practice forward: Delphi characteristics, advantages, potential problems, and solutions. *International Journal of Tourism Research*, 11(3), 415–37.

Douglas, J. D., Rasmussen, P. K. and Flanagan, C. A. (1977) *The Nude Beach*. Beverley Hills, CA: Sage.

Driscoll, A., Lawson, R. and Niven, B. (1994) Measuring tourists' destination perceptions. *Annals of Tourism Research*, 21(3), 499–511.

Driver, B. L., Tinsley, H. E. A. and Manfredo, M. J. (1991) The 'Paragraphs About Leisure' and 'Recreation Experience Preference' scales: results from two inventories designed to assess the breadth of perceived psychological benefits of leisure. In B. L. Driver, P. J. Brown and G. L. Peterson (eds) *Benefits of Leisure*. State College, PA: Venture, 263–301.

Duffy, M. E. (1987) Methodological triangulation: a vehicle for merging qualitative and quantitative research methods. *IMAGE: Journal of Nursing Scholarship*, 19(1), 130–3.

Dunne, S. (1995) *Interviewing Techniques for Writers and Researchers*. London: A. and C. Black.

Dupuis, S. (1999) Naked truths: towards a reflexive methodology in leisure research. *Leisure Sciences*, 21(1), 43–64.

Dyer, R. (1993) Entertainment and utopia. In S. During (ed.) *The Cultural Studies Reader*. London: Routledge, 271–83.

Echtner, C. M. and Ritchie, J. R. B. (1993) The measurement of destination image: an empirical assessment. *Journal of Travel Research*, 21(1), 3–13.

Edwards, A. (1991) The reliability of tourism statistics. *Economist Intelligence Unit: Travel and Tourism Analyst*, (1), 62–75.

Edwards, D., Dickson, T., Griffin, T. and Hayllar, B. (2010) Tracking the urban visitor: methods for examining tourists' spatial behaviour and visual representations, in G. Richards and W. Munsters (eds.) *Cultural Tourism Research Methods*. Wallingford, UK: CABI, 104–14.

Elias, N. (1986) Introduction. In Elias, N. and Dunning, E. *Quest for Excitement: Sport and Leisure in the Civilizing Process*. Oxford: Basil Blackwell, 19–62.

Ely, M. (1981) Systematic observation as a recreation research tool. In D. Mercer (ed.) *Outdoor Recreation: Australian Perspectives*. Malvern, Vic.: Sorrett, 57–67.

EU – see European Commission

European Commission (2004) *Eurobarometer: 2004*. Brussels: EU, available at: http://ec.europa.eu/sport/pub/doc892_en.htm

Faulkner, B., Pearce, P., Shaw, R. and Weiler, B. (2003) Tourism research in Australia: confronting the challenges of the 1990s and beyond. In L. Fredline, L. Jago and C. Cooper (eds) *Progressing Tourism Research – Bill Faulkner*. Clevedon, UK: Channel View Publications, 303–40.

Fenn, C., Bridgwood, A., Dust, K., Hutton, L., Jobson, M. and Skinner, M. (2004) *Arts in England 2003: Attendance, Participation and Attitudes: Findings of a Study Carried out by the Social Survey Division of the Office for National Statistics*. London: Arts Council England.

Finn, M., Elliott-White, M. and Walton, M. (2000) *Tourism and Leisure Research Methods*. Harlow, UK: Longman.

Fiske, J. (1983) Surfalism and sandiotics: the beach in Oz popular culture. *Australian Journal of Cultural Studies*, 1(2), 120–49.

Fleming, S., and Jordan, F. (eds) (2006) *Ethical Issues in Leisure Research*. LSA Publication 90, Eastbourne, UK: Leisure Studies Association.

Floyd. M. F., Spengler, J. O., Maddock, J. E., Gobster, P. E. and Suau, L. (2008) Environmental and social correlates of physical activity in neighbourhood parks: an observational study in Tampa and Chicago. *Leisure Sciences*, 30(4), 360–75.

Fogleson, R. E. (2001) *Married to the Mouse: Walt Disney World and Orlando*. New Haven, CN: Yale University Press.

Fox, K., and Rickards, L. (2004) *Sport and Leisure: Results from the Sport and Leisure Module of the 2002 General Household Survey*. London: HMSO, available at: www.statistics.gov.uk/downloads/theme_compendia/Sport&Leisure.pdf (accessed Nov. 2010).

Frawley, S., Veal, A. J., Cashman, R. and Toohey, K. (2009) *'Sport For All' and Major Sporting Events: Introduction to the Project*. School of Leisure, Sport and Tourism Working Paper 5, Sydney: University of Technology, Sydney (available at www.business.uts.edu.au/lst/research/research_papers.html).

Frechtling, D. C. (1996) *Practical Tourism Forecasting*. Oxford: Butterworth-Heinemann.

Frechtling, D. C. (2010) The tourism satellite account: a primer. *Annals of Tourism Research*, 37(1), 136–63.

Garrod, B. (2008) Exploring place perception: a photo-based analysis. *Annals of Tourism Research*, 35(2), 381–401.

Gartner, W. and Hunt, J. D. (1988) A method to collect detailed tourist flow information. *Annals of Tourism Research*, 15(1), 159–72.

Geary, C., Taylor, T., Toohey, K. and Lynch, R. (1996) *Leisure, Sport and Ethnicity: A Bibliography*. School of Leisure and Tourism Studies, University of Technology, Sydney, On-line Bibliography 6, available at: www.business.uts.edu.au/lst/research/publications/bibliographies/index.html (Accessed March, 2005).

George, D. and Mallery, P. (2005) *SPSS for Windows Step by Step: A Simple Guide and Reference, 12.0 Update*. Boston, MA: Pearson Education.

Gerring, J. (2007) *Case Study Research: Principles and Practices*. New York: Cambridge University Press.

Gershuny, J. (2000) *Changing Times: Work and Leisure in Postindustrial Society*. Oxford: Oxford University Press.

Getz, D. (1993) Impacts of tourism on residents' leisure: concepts and a longitudinal case study of Spey Valley, Scotland. *Journal of Tourism Studies*, 4(2), 33–44.

Gibbs, G. R. (2002) *Qualitative Data Analysis: Explorations with NVivo*. Maidenhead, UK: Open University Press.

Giddens, A. (ed.) (1974) *Positivism and Sociology*. London: Heinemann.

Giddens, A. (1993) *Sociology*. Cambridge: Polity Press.

Gitelson, R. J. and Drogin, E. B. (1992) An experiment on the efficacy of a certified final mailing. *Journal of Leisure Research*, 24(1), 72–8.

Glancy, M. (1986) Participant observation in the recreation setting. *Journal of Leisure Research*, 18(2), 59–80.

Glancy, M. (1993) Achieving intersubjectivity: the process of becoming the subject in leisure research. *Leisure Studies*, 12(1), 45–60.

Glaser, B. and Strauss, A. L. (1967) *The Discovery of Grounded Theory: Strategies for Qualitative Research*. Chicago, IL: Aldine.

Glass, G. V., McGaw, B. and Smith, M. L. (1981) *Meta-Analysis in Social Research*. Beverly Hills, CA: Sage.

Glyptis, S. A. (1981a) People at play in the countryside. *Geography*, 66, 277–85.

Glyptis, S. A. (1981b) Room to relax in the countryside. *The Planner*, 67(5), 120–22.

Godbey, G. and Scott, D. (1990) Reorienting leisure research – the case for qualitative methods. *Society and Leisure*, 13(1), 189–206.

Goeldner, C. R. (1994) Travel and tourism information sources. In J. R. B. Ritchie and C. R. Goeldner (eds) *Travel, Tourism and Hospitality Research*, Second edn. New York: John Wiley, 81–90.

Goeldner, C. R. and Dicke, K. (1980) *Bibliography of Tourism and Travel Research*. (9 vols), Boulder, CO: University of Colorado.

Goffman, I. (1959) *The Presentation of Self in Everyday Life*. Garden City, NY: Doubleday/ Anchor.

Gramza, A. F., Corush, J. and Ellis, M. J. (1972) Children's play on trestles differing in complexity: a study of play equipment design. *Journal of Leisure Research*, 4(3), 303–11.

Grant, D. (1984) Another look at the beach. *Australian Journal of Cultural Studies*, 2(2), 131–8.

Gratton, C. and Jones, I. (2004) *Research Methods for Sport Studies*. London: Routledge.

Gratton, C. and Tice, A. (1994) Trends in sports participation in Britain 1977–1987. *Leisure Studies*, 13(1), 49–66.

Gratton, C. and Veal, A. J. (2005) Great Britain. In G. Cushman, A. J. Veal and J. Zuzanek (eds) *Free Time and Leisure Participation: International Perspectives*. Wallingford, UK: CABI Publishing, 109–26.

Green, H., Hunter, C. and Moore, B. (1990) Application of the Delphi technique in tourism. *Annals of Tourism Research*, 17(2), 270–9.

Green Space (1998) *A Guide to Automated Methods for Counting Visitors to Parks and Green Spaces*. Reading, UK: Green Space (available at: www.green-space.org.uk).

Greenbaum, T. L. (1998) *The Handbook for Focus Group Research*. Second edition. Thousand Oaks, CA: Sage.

Greenbaum, T. L. (2000) *Moderating Focus Groups: A Practical Guide for Group Facilitation.* Thousand Oaks, CA: Sage.

Greenwood, D. J. and Levin, M. (2007) *Introduction to Action Research.* Thousand Oaks, CA: Sage.

Grichting, W. L. and Caltabiano, M. L. (1986) Amount and direction of bias in survey interviewing. *Australian Psychologist,* 21(1), 69–78.

Griffin, C., Hobson, D., MacIntosh, S. and McCabe, T. (1982) Women and leisure. In J. Hargreaves (ed.) *Sport, Culture and Ideology.* London: Routledge, 99–116.

Guba, E. G. and Lincoln, Y. S. (1998) Competing paradigms in qualitative research. In N. K. Denzin and Y. S. Lincoln (eds) *The Landscape of Qualitative Research: Theories and Issues.* Thousand Oaks, CA: Sage, 195–220.

Guba, E. G. and Lincoln, Y. S. (2006) Paradigmatic controversies, contradictions and emerging confluences. In N. K. Denzin and Y. S. Lincoln (eds) *Handbook of Qualitative Research,* Third edn. Thousand Oaks, CA: Sage, 191–216.

Guy, B. S., Curtis, W. W. and Crotts, J. C. (1990) Environmental learning of first-time travellers. *Annals of Leisure Research,* 17(2), 419–31.

Hammitt, W. E. and McDonald, C. D. (1982) Response bias and the need for extensive mail questionnaire follow-ups among selected recreation samples. *Journal of Leisure Research,* 14(3), 207–16.

Hanley, N., Shaw, W. D. and Wright, R. E. (eds) (2003) *The New Economics of Outdoor Recreation.* Cheltenham, UK: Edward Elgar.

Harper, J. A. and Balmer, K. R. (1989) The perceived benefits of public leisure services: an exploratory investigation. *Society and Leisure,* 12(1), 171–88.

Harper, W. and Hultsman, J. (1992) Interpreting leisure as text: the whole. *Leisure Studies,* 11(3), 233–42.

Harris, R. and Leiper, N. (eds) (1995) *Sustainable Tourism: an Australian Perspective.* Melbourne: Butterworth-Heinemann.

Hartmann, R. (1988) Combining field methods in tourism research. *Annals of Tourism Research,* 15(1), 88–105.

Harvard Business School (nd) *Harvard Business School Case Studies.* Cambridge, MA: Harvard University, available at: www.hbsp.harvard.edu (Accessed Oct. 2004).

Hatry, H. P. and Dunn, D. R. (1971) *Measuring the Effectiveness of Local Government Services: Recreation.* Washington, DC: The Urban Institute.

Havitz, M. E. and Sell, J. A. (1991) The experimental method and leisure/recreation research: promoting a more active role. *Society and Leisure,* 14(1), 47–68.

Hayllar, B., Griffin, T. and Edwards, D. (eds) (2008) *City Spaces, Tourist Places: Urban Tourism Precincts.* Oxford: Butterworth-Heinemann.

Hedges, B. (1986) *Personal Leisure Histories.* London: Sports Council/Economic and Social Research Council.

Hektner, J. M., Schmidt, J. A. and Csikszentmihayli, M. (eds) (2006) *Experience Sampling Method: Measuring the Quality of Everyday Life.* Thousand Oaks, CA: Sage.

Henderson, K. A. (1990) Reality comes through a prism: method choices in leisure research. *Society and Leisure,* 13(1), 169–88.

Henderson, K. A. (1991) *Dimensions of Choice: A Qualitative Approach to Recreation, Parks and Leisure Research.* State College, PA: Venture.

Henderson, K. A. (2006) *Dimensions of Choice: A Qualitative Approach to Recreation, Parks and Leisure Research,* Second Edition. State College, PA: Venture.

Henderson, K. A. (2009) *Just* research and physical activity: diversity is more than an independent variable. *Leisure Sciences*, 31(2), 100–5.

Henderson, K. A. and Bialeschki, D. (2002) *Evaluating Leisure Services: Making Enlightened Decisions*, Second edition. State College, PA: Venture.

Henry, I. and Paramio Salcines, J. L. (1998) Sport, culture and urban regimes: the case of Bilbao. In M. F. Collins and I. S. Cooper (eds) *Leisure Management: Issues and Applications*. Wallingford, UK: CAB International, 97–112.

Heywood, L. A. (1978) Perceived recreative experience and the relief of tension. *Journal of Leisure Research*, 10(2), 86–97.

Hindson, A., Gidlow, B. and Peebles, C. (1994) The 'trickle-down' effect of top-level sport: myth or reality? A case-study of the Olympics. *Australian Journal of Leisure and Recreation*, 4(1), 16–24, 31.

Hodder, I. (1994) The interpretation of documents and material culture. In N. K. Denzin and Y. S. Lincoln (eds) *Handbook of Qualitative Research*. Thousand Oaks, CA: Sage, 393–402.

Hogan, K. and Norton, K. (2000) The 'price' of Olympic gold. *Journal of Science and Medicine in Sports*, 3(2), 203–18.

Hollands, R. G. (1985) Working class youth, leisure and the search for work. In S. R. Parker and A. J. Veal (eds) *Work, Non-work and Leisure*. London: Leisure Studies Association, 3–29.

Hollinshead, K. (2004) A primer in ontological craft: the creative capture of people and places through qualitative research. In J. Phillimore and L. Goodson (eds) *Qualitative Research in Tourism: Ontologies, Epistemologies and Methodologies*. London: Routledge, 63–82.

Howard, A. W., MacArthur, C., Willan, A., Rothman, L., Moses-McKeag, A. and MacPherson, A. K. (2005) The effect of safer play equipment on playground injury rates among school children. *Canadian Medical Association Journal*, 172(11), 1443–6.

Howard, K. and Sharp, J. A. (1983) *The Management of a Student Research Project*. Aldershot, UK: Gower.

Howat, G., Crilley, G., Absher, J. and Milne, I. (1996) Measuring customer service quality in sports and leisure centres. *Managing Leisure*, 1(2), 77–90.

Howat, G., Crilley, G., Mikilewicz, S., Edgecombe, S., March, H., Murray, D. and Bell, B. (2003) Service quality, customer satisfaction and behavioural intentions of Australian aquatic centre customers, 1999–2001. *Annals of Leisure Research*, 5, 52–65.

Howe, D. (2009) Reflexive ethnography, impairment and the pub. *Leisure Studies*, 28(4), 489–96.

Huberman, A. M. and Miles, M. B. (1994) Data management and analysis methods. In N. K. Denzin and Y. S. Lincoln (eds) *Handbook of Qualitative Research*. Thousand Oaks, CA: Sage, 428–44.

Hudson, S. (1988) *How to Conduct Community Needs Assessment Surveys in Public Parks and Recreation*. Columbus, OH: Publishing Horizons.

Hudson, S., Snaith, T., Miller, G. and Hudson, P. (2001) Distribution channels in the travel industry: using mystery shoppers to understand the influence of travel agency recommendations. *Journal of Travel Research*, 40(2), 148–54.

Huh, C. and Vogt, C. A. (2008) Change in residents' attitudes toward tourism over time: a cohort analytical approach. *Journal of Travel Research*, 46(3), 446–55.

Hultsman, J. and Harper, W. (1992) Interpreting leisure as text: the part. *Leisure Studies*, 11(2), 135–46.

Humberstone, B. (2004) Standpoint research: multiple versions of reality in tourism theorising and research. In J. Phillimore and L. Goodson (eds) *Qualitative Research in Tourism: Ontologies, Epistemologies and Methodologies*. London: Routledge, 119–36.

Hung, P. and Petrick, J. F. (2010) Developing a measurement scale for constraints to cruising. *Annals of Tourism Research*, 37(1), 206–28.

Hurst, F. (1994) En route surveys. In J. R. B. Ritchie and C. R. Goeldner (eds) *Travel, Tourism and Hospitality Research*, Second edition. New York: John Wiley, 453–72.

Iacocca, L. A. (1984) *Iacocca: an Autobiography*. Toronto: Bantam Books.

Iso-Ahola, S. E. and Weissinger, E. (1990) Perception of boredom in leisure: conceptualisation, reliability and validity of the leisure boredom scale. *Journal of Leisure Research*, 22(1), 1–17.

Israel, M. and Hay, I. (2006) *Research Ethics for Social Scientists*. Los Angeles, CA: Sage.

Jackson, E. L. (ed.) (2006) *Leisure and the Quality of Life: Impacts on Social, Economic and Cultural Development: Hangzhou Consensus*. Hangzhou, China: Zhejiang University Press/World Leisure Organisation.

Jafari, J. (ed.) (2000) *Encyclopedia of Tourism*. London: Routledge.

Jenkins, J. and Pigram, J. (eds) (2003) *Encyclopedia of Leisure and Outdoor Recreation*. London: Routledge.

Jennings, G. (2010) *Tourism Research*. Milton, Qld: John Wiley.

Jennings, G. R. (2005) Interviewing: a focus on qualitative techniques. In B. W. Ritchie, P. Burns and C. Palmer (eds) *Tourism Research Methods: Integrating Theory with Practice*. Wallingford, UK: CABI Publishing, 99–117.

Jones, R. A. (1991) Enhancing marketing decisions using conjoint analysis: an application in public leisure services. *Society and Leisure*, 14(1), 69–84.

Jones, R. L., Potrac, P., Haleem, H. and Cushion, C. (2006) Exposure by association: anonymity and integrity in autobiographical research. In S. Fleming and F. Jordan (eds) *Ethical Issues in Leisure Research*. LSA Publication 90, Eastbourne, UK: Leisure Studies Association, 45–62.

Jordan, F. and Gibson, H. (2004) Let your data do the talking: researching the solo travel experiences of British and American women. In J. Phillimore and L. Godson (eds) *Qualitative Research in Tourism: Ontologies, Epistemologies and Methodologies*. London: Routledge, 215–35.

Kamphorst, T. J., Tibori, T. T. and Giliam, M. J. (1984) Quantitative and qualitative research: shall the twain ever meet? *World Leisure and Recreation*, 26 Dec., 25–27.

Kanning, M. and Schlicht, W. (2010) Be active and become happy: an ecological momentary assessment of physical activity and mood. *Journal of Sport & Exercise Psychology*, 32(2), 253–61.

Kasprzyk, D., Duncan, G., Kalton, G. and Singh, M. P. (1989) *Panel Surveys*. New York: John Wiley and Sons.

Keirle, I. and Walsh, S. (1999) Objective assessment of countryside recreation by observation. *Journal of Environmental Planning and Management*, 42(6), 875–87.

Kellehear, A. (1993) *The Unobtrusive Researcher: A Guide to Methods*. Sydney: Allen and Unwin.

Kelly, G. A. (1955) *The Psychology of Personal Constructs*. New York: Norton.

Kelly, J., Haider, W., Williams, P. W. and Englund, K. (2007) Stated preferences of tourists for eco-efficient destination planning options. *Tourism Management*, 28(3), 377–90.

Kelly, J. R. (1980) Leisure and quality: beyond the quantitative barrier in research. In T. L. Goodale and P. A. Witt (eds) *Recreation and Leisure: Issues in an Era of Change.* State College, PA: Venture, 300–14.

Kelly, J. R. (1987) *Recreation Trends – Toward the Year 2000.* Champaign, IL: Management Learning Laboratories.

Kelsey, C. and Gray, H. (1986) *The Feasibility Study Process for Parks and Recreation.* Reston, VA: American Alliance for Health, P. E., Recreation and Dance.

Kidder, L. (1981) *Selltiz, Wrightsman and Cook's Research Methods in Social Relations.* New York: Holt, Rinehart and Winston.

Kline, R. B. (2005) *Principles and Practice of Structural Equation Modelling,* Second edition. New York: Guilford Press.

Klugman, K., Kuenz, J., Waldrop, S. and Willis, S. (1995) *Inside the Mouse: The Project on Disney.* Durham, NC: Duke University Press.

Kraus, R. and Allen, L. (1998) *Research and Evaluation in Recreation, Parks, and Leisure Studies,* Second edition. Boston, MA: Allyn and Bacon.

Krejcie, R. V. and Morgan, D. W. (1970) Determining sample size for research activities. *Educational and Psychological Measurement,* 30(4), 607–10.

Krenz, C. and Sax, G. (1986) What quantitative research is and why it doesn't work. *American Behavioral Scientist,* 30(1), 58–69.

Krueger, R. A. (1988) *Focus Groups: A Practical Guide for Applied Research.* Newbury Park, CA: Sage.

Labovitz, S. and Hagedorn, R. (1971) *Introduction to Social Research.* New York: McGraw-Hill.

Ladkin, A. (2004) The life and work history methodology: a discussion of its potential use for tourism and hospitality research. In J. Phillimore and L. Godson (eds) *Qualitative Research in Tourism: Ontologies, Epistemologies and Methodologies.* London: Routledge, 236–54.

Lainsbury, A. (2000) *Once Upon an American Dream: The Story of Euro Disneyland.* Lawrence, KS: University of Kansas Press.

LaPage, W. F. (1981) A further look at the informal interview. *Journal of Leisure Research,* 13(2), 174–6.

LaPage, W. F. (1994) Using panels for tourism and travel research. In J. R. B. Ritchie and C. R. Goeldner (eds) *Travel, Tourism and Hospitality Research,* Second edn. New York: John Wiley, 481–6.

Lavrakas, P. K. (1993) *Telephone Survey Methods: Sampling, Selection and Supervision,* Second edn. Newbury Park, CA: Sage.

Lee, A. S. (1989) Case studies as natural experiments. *Human Relations,* 42(2), 117–37.

Leiper, N. (2000) An emerging discipline. *Annals of Tourism Research,* 27(3), 805–9.

Lepkowski, J. M., Tucker, C., Brick, J. M., de Leeuw, E., Japec, L., Lavrakas, P. J., Link, M. W. and Sangster, R. L. (eds) (2008) *Advances in Telephone Survey Methodology.* New York: John Wiley.

Levenson, H. (1974) Activism and powerful others: distinction within the concept of internal–external control. *Journal of Psychology and Aging,* 1(1), 117–26.

Levinson, D. and Christensen, K. (eds) (1996) *Encyclopedia of World Sport: From Ancient Times to the Present.* Santa Barbara, CA: ABC-CLIO.

Lincoln, Y. (2005) Institutional review boards and methodological conservatism: the challenge to and from phenomenological paradigms. In N. K. Denzin and Y. S.

Lincoln (eds) *Handbook of Qualitative Research.* Third edition. Thousand Oaks, CA: Sage, 165–90.

Lincoln, Y. S. and Guba, E. G. (1985) *Naturalistic Inquiry.* Beverly Hills, CA: Sage.

Litvin, S. W. and Mouri, N. (2009) A comparative study of the use of 'iconic' versus 'generic' advertising images for destination marketing. *Journal of Travel Research,* 48(2), 152–61.

Lofland, J. and Lofland, L. H. (1984) *Analyzing Social Settings: A Guide to Qualitative Observation and Analysis,* Second edition. Belmont, CA: Wadsworth.

Long, J. (2007) *Researching Leisure, Sport and Tourism: the Essential Guide.* London: Sage.

Long, P. (2000) Tourism development regimes in the inner city fringe: the case of Discover Islington, London. In B. Bramwell and B. Lane (eds) *Tourism Collaboration and Partnerships: Politics, Practice and Sustainability.* Clevedon, UK: Channel View Publications, 183–99.

Loue, S. (2002) *Textbook of Research Ethics: Theory and Practice.* New York: Kluwer.

Louviere, J. J. and Woodworth, G. (1983) Design and analysis of simulated consumer choice or allocation experiments: an approach based on aggregate data. *Journal of Marketing Research,* 20(3), 350–67.

Louviere, J. J., Hensher, D. A. and Swait, J. D. (2000) *Stated Choice Methods: Analysis and Applications.* Cambridge: Cambridge University Press

Lundberg, G. A., Komarovsky, M. and McInerny, M. A. (1934) *Leisure: A Suburban Study.* New York: Columbia University Press.

Lynch, R. and Brown, P. (1995) *An Australian Leisure Research Agenda.* Canberra: AGPS.

Lynch, R. and Brown, P. (1999) Utility of large-scale leisure research agendas. *Managing Leisure,* 4(2), 63–77.

Lynch, R. and Veal, A. J. (2006) *Australian Leisure.* Third edition. Melbourne: Longman Australia.

MacCannell, D. (1976) *The Tourist: A New Theory of the Leisure Class.* London: Macmillan.

MacCannell, D. (1993) *The Empty Meeting Grounds.* London: Routledge.

Maller, C., Townsend, M., Brown, P. and St. Leger, L. (2002) *Healthy Parks Healthy People: the Benefits of Contact with Nature in a Park Context: A Review of Current Literature.* Report to Parks Victoria and International Park Strategic Partners Group, Melbourne: Faculty of Health and Behavioural Sciences, Deakin University, available at: www.parkweb.vic.gov.au/resources/mhphp/pv1.pdf.

Mannell, R. C. and Kleiber, D. A. (1997) *A Social Psychology of Leisure.* State College, PA: Venture.

Marans, R. W. and Mohai, P. (1991) Leisure resources, recreation activity, and the quality of life. In B. L. Driver, P. J. Brown and G. L. Peterson (eds) *Benefits of Leisure.* State College, PA: Venture, 351–64.

Markula, P. and Denison, J. (2005) Sport and personal narrative. In D. L. Andrews, D. S. Mason and M. L. Silk (eds) *Qualitative Methods in Sports Studies.* Oxford: Berg, 165–84.

Marsh, P., Rosser, E. and Harré, R. (1978) *The Rules of Disorder.* London: Routledge.

Martilla, J. A. and James, J. C. (1977) Importance-performance analysis. *Journal of Marketing,* 41(1), 77–9.

Mazanec, J. A., Crouch, G. I., Brent Ritchie, J. R. and Woodside, A. G. (eds) (2001) *Consumer Psychology of Tourism, Hospitality and Leisure, Volume 2.* Wallingford, UK: CABI Publishing.

McCall, G. J. and Simmons, J. L. (eds) (1969) *Issues in Participant Observation.* Reading, MA: Addison-Wesley.

McDougall, G. H. G. and Munro, H. (1994) Scaling and attitude measurement in travel and tourism research. In J. R. B. Ritchie and C. R. Goeldner (eds) *Travel, Tourism and Hospitality Research*, Second edn. New York: John Wiley, 115–29.

McGuiggan, R. L. (2000) The Myers–Briggs Type Indicator and leisure attribute preference. In A. G., Woodside, G. I., Crouch, J. A., Mazanec, M. Oppermann and M. Y. Sakai (eds) *Consumer Psychology of Tourism, Hospitality and Leisure*. Wallingford, UK: CABI Publishing, 245–67.

McGuiggan, R. L. (2001) What determines our leisure preferences: demographics or personality? In J. A. Mazanec, G. I. Crouch, J. R. B. Ritchie and A. G. Woodside (eds) *Consumer Psychology of Tourism, Hospitality and Leisure, Volume 2*. Wallingford, UK: CABI Publishing, 195–214.

McKeown, B. and Thomas, D. (1988) *Q Methodology*. Newbury Park, CA: Sage.

McNiff, J. and Whitehead, J. (2002) *Action Research: Principles and Practice*. London: Routledge/Falmer.

Mehl, M. R., Pennebaker, J. W., Crow, D. M., Dabbs, J. and Price, J. H. (2001) The Electronically Activated Recorder (EAR): a device for sampling naturalistic daily activities and conversations. *Behavior Research Methods, Instruments, and Computers*, 33(4), 517–23.

Meyersohn, R. (1958) A comprehensive bibliography on leisure. In E. Larrabee and R. Meyersohn (eds) *Mass Leisure*. Glencoe, IL: Free Press, 389–420.

Middleton, V. T. C., Fyall, A. and Morgan, M. (2009) *Marketing in Travel and Tourism*, Fourth edn. Oxford: Butterworth-Heinemann.

Miles, M. and Weitzman, E. (1994) *Computer Programs for Qualitative Data Analysis*. Thousand Oaks, CA: Sage.

Miles, M. B. and Huberman, A. M. (1994) *Qualitative Data Analysis*, Second edn. Thousand Oaks, CA: Sage.

Mitra, A. and Lankford, S. (1999) *Research Methods in Park, Recreation, and Leisure Services*. Champaign, IL: Sagamore.

Moeller, G. H., Mescher, M. A. *et al.* (1980a) The informal interview as a technique for recreation research. *Journal of Leisure Research*, 12(2), 174–82.

Moeller, G. H., Mescher, M. A. *et al.* (1980b) A response to 'A second look at the informal interview'. *Journal of Leisure Research*, 12(2), 187–8.

Moeller, G. H. and Shafer, E. L. (1994) The Delphi technique: a tool for long-range tourism and travel planning. In J. R. B. Ritchie and C. R. Goeldner (eds) *Travel, Tourism and Hospitality Research*, Second edn. New York: John Wiley, 473–80.

Montford, A. W. (2010) *The Hockey Stick Illusion: Climategate and the Corruption of Science*. London: Stacey International.

Morgan, D. L. (ed.) (1993) *Successful Focus Groups: Advancing the State of the Art*. Newbury Park, CA: Sage.

Moscardo, G. (1997) Making mindful managers: evaluating methods for teaching problem solving skills for tourism management. *Journal of Tourism Studies*, 8(1), 16–24.

Mules, T. (2004) Case study evolution in event management: the Gold Coast's Wintersun festival. *Event Management*, 9(1–2), 95–101.

Murphy, P. (1991) Data gathering for community-oriented tourism planning: a case study of Vancouver Island, British Columbia. *Leisure Studies*, 10(1), 65–80.

National Council on Public Polls (1995) *Push Polls*. Press release, 25 May, Clifton, NJ: NCPP, available at: www.ncpp.org/?q=node/41 (Accessed March 2010).

National Health and Medical Research Council (NHMRC) (nd) *National Ethics Application Form*. Canberra: NHMRC, available at: www.neaf.gov.au/default.aspx, (accessed March 2010).

National Health and Medical Research Council (NHMRC)/Australian Research Council (ARC) and Universities Australia (2007) *Australian Code for the Responsible Conduct of Research*. Canberra: Australian Government, available at: www.nhmrc.gov.au/filesnhmrc/file/publications/synopses/r39.pdf

Neugarten, P. L., Havighurst, R. J. and Tobin, S. S. (1961) The measurement of life satisfaction. *Journal of Gerontology*, 16(1), 134–43.

Nichols, G. (2007) *Sport and Crime Reduction: the Role of Sports in Tackling Youth Crime*. London: Routledge.

Noonan, D. S. (2003) Contingent valuation and cultural resources: a meta-analytic review of the literature. *Journal of Cultural Economics*, 27(3/4), 159–70.

O'Brien, S. and Ford, R. (1988) Can we at last say goodbye to social class? An examination of the usefulness and stability of some alternative methods of measurement. *Journal of the Market Research Society*, 30(3), 289–332.

Oppenheim, A. N. (2000) *Questionnaire Design, Interviewing and Attitude Measurement: New edition*. London: Pinter.

Oppermann, M. (2000) Triangulation: a methodological discussion. *International Journal of Tourism Research*, 2(2), 141–6.

Pallant, J. F. (2007) *SPSS Survival Manual: a Step by Step Guide to Data Analysis Using SPSS*, 3rd edition. Sydney: Allen and Unwin.

Palmer, I. and Dunford, R. (2002) Managing discursive tension: the co-existence of individualist and collaborative discourses in Flight Centre. *Journal of Management Studies*. 39(8), 1045–70.

Parasuraman, A., Zeithaml, V. A. and Berry, L. L. (1985) A conceptual model of service quality and implications for future research. *Journal of Marketing*, 49(4), 41–50.

Parker, T. (1988) *Red Hill; a Mining Community*. London: Coronet.

Parsons, W. (1995) *Public Policy*. Cheltenham, Glos., UK: Edward Elgar.

Pawson, R. (2006) *Evidence-based Policy: a Realist Perspective*. London: Sage.

Pearce, D. (1988) Tourist time budgets. *Annals of Tourism Research*, 15(1), 106–21.

Pearce, D. G. and Butler, R. W. (eds) (1993) *Tourism Research: Critiques and Challenges*. London: Routledge.

Pearce, P. L. (1988) *The Ulysses Factor: Evaluating Visitors in Tourist Settings*. New York: Springer-Verlag.

Pearce, P. L. (2005) *Tourist Behaviour: Themes and Conceptual Schemes*. Clevedon, UK: Channel View.

Pendergast, T. and Pendergast, S. (eds) (1999) *St. James Encyclopedia of Popular Culture*. Detroit, MI: St. James Press.

Pentland, W. E., Harvey, A. S., Powell Lawton, M. and McColl, M. A. (eds) (1999) *Time Use Research in the Social Sciences*. New York: Kluwer/Plenum.

Perdue, R. R. and Botkin, M. R. (1988) Visitor survey versus conversion study. *Annals of Tourism Research*, 15(1), 76–87.

Peterson, K. I. (1994) Qualitative research methods for the travel and tourism industry. In J. R. B. Ritchie and C. R. Goeldner (eds) *Travel, Tourism and Hospitality Research, Second edn*. New York: John Wiley, 487–92.

Pew Research Center for the People and the Press (2004) *Polls Face Growing Resistance, But Still Representative, Survey Experiment Shows.* Washington, DC: Pew Research Center, available at: http://people-press.org/report/211/.

Philips, D. (2004) Stately pleasure domes – nationhood, monarchy and industry: the celebration exhibition in Britain. *Leisure Studies*, 23(2), 95–108.

Phillimore, J. and Goodson, L. (eds) (2004a) *Qualitative Research in Tourism: Ontologies, Epistemologies and Methodologies.* London: Routledge.

Phillimore, J. and Goodson, L. (2004b) Progress in qualitative research in tourism. In J. Phillimore and L. Goodson (eds) *Qualitative Research in Tourism: Ontologies, Epistemologies and Methodologies.* London: Routledge, 3–29.

Pieper, J. (1999) *Leisure, the Basis of Culture.* Indianapolis, IN: Libert Fund (originally published 1952).

Pizam, A. (1994) Planning a tourism research investigation. In J. R. B. Ritchie and C. R. Goeldner (eds) *Travel, Tourism and Hospitality Research*, Second edn. New York: John Wiley, 91–104.

Pollard, W. E. (1987) Decision making and the use of evaluation research. *American Behavioral Scientist*, 30(6), 661–76.

Potter, R. B. and Coshall, J. (1988) Sociopsychological methods for tourism research. *Annals of Tourism Research*, 15(1), 63–75.

Priest, N., Armstrong, R., Doyle, J. and Waters, E. (2008) Interventions implemented through sporting organisations for increasing participation in sport. *Cochrane Database of Systematic Reviews*, 3, no pagination.

Prior, L. (2003) *Using Documents in Social Research.* London: Sage.

Project on Disney (1995) *Inside the Mouse: Work and Play at Disney World.* Durham, NC: Duke University Press.

Punch, M. (1994) Politics and ethics in qualitative research. In N. K. Denzin and Y. S. Lincoln (eds) *Handbook of Qualitative Research.* Thousand Oaks. CA: Sage, 83–98.

Rapoport, R. and Rapoport, R. N. (1975) *Leisure and the Family Life Cycle.* London: Routledge.

Reason, P. and Bradbury, H. (eds) (2001) *Handbook of Action Research: Participative Inquiry and Practice.* London: Sage.

Reynolds, F. and Johnson, D. (1978) Validity of focus group findings. *Journal of Advertising Research*, 19(1), 3–24.

Richards, T. J. and Richards, L. (1994) Using computers in qualitative research. In N. K. Denzin and Y. S. Lincoln (eds) *Handbook of Qualitative Research*, Thousand Oaks, CA: Sage, 445–62.

Riddick, C. C. and Russell, R. V. (2008) *Research in Recreation, Parks, Sport, and Tourism*, 2nd edition. Champaign, IL: Sagamore.

Ridley, K., Olds, T. S. and Hill, A. (2006) The multimedia activity recall for children and adolescents (MARCA): development and evaluation. *International Journal of Behavioral Nutrition and Physical Activity*, 3(10), 1–11, available at: www.ijbnpa.org/content/3/1/10.

Riley, R. W. and Love, L. L. (2000) The state of qualitative tourism research. *Annals of Tourism Research*, 27(1), 164–87.

Ritchie, J. R. B. (1994) Tourism research: policy and managerial priorities for the 1990s and beyond. In D. G. Pearce and R. W. Butler (eds) *Tourism Research: Critiques and Challenges.* London: Routledge, 201–16.

Ritchie, J. R. B. and Goeldner, C. R. (eds) (1994) *Travel, Tourism and Hospitality Research*, Second edn. New York: John Wiley.

Roberts, B. (2002) *Biographical Research*. Buckingham, UK: Open University Press.

Robertson, R. W. and Veal, A. J. (1987) *Port Hacking Visitor Use Study*, Sydney: Centre for Leisure and Tourism Studies, University of Technology, Sydney.

Rojek, C. (1989) Leisure and recreation theory. In E. L. Jackson and T.L. Burton (eds) *Understanding Leisure and Recreation: Mapping the Past and Charting the Future*. State College, PA: Venture, 69–88.

Rojek, C. (1993) Disney culture. *Leisure Studies*, 12(2), 121–36.

Rojek, C. (2000) *Leisure and Culture*. Basingstoke, UK: Macmillan.

Rose, D. (ed.) (2000) *Researching Social and Economic Change: the Uses of Household Panel Studies*. London: Routledge.

Rosenthal, R. (1966) *Experimenter Effects in Behavioral Research*. New York: Appleton-Century-Crofts.

Rowe, D. (1995) *Popular Cultures: Rock Music, Sport and the Politics of Pleasure*. London: Sage.

Rowe, D. (ed.) (2004) *Critical Readings: Sport, Culture and the Media*. Maidenhead, UK: Open University Press.

Rowe, D. and Brown, P. (1994) Promoting women's sport: theory, policy and practice. *Leisure Studies*, 13(2), 97–110.

Rowntree, B. S. and Lavers, G. R. (1951) *English Life and Leisure: a Social Study*. London: Longmans, Green and Co.

Ruddell, E. J. and Hammit, W. E. (1987) Prospect refuge theory: a psychological orientation for edge effect in recreation environments. *Journal of Leisure Research*, 19(4), 249–60.

Ryan, C. (1995) *Researching Tourist Satisfaction: Issues, Concepts, Problems*. London: Routledge.

Ryan, C. (2000) Tourist experiences, phenomenographic analysis, post-positivism and neural network software. *International Journal of Tourism Research*, 2(1), 119–31.

Ryan, C. (2005) Ethics in tourism research: objectives and personal perspectives. In B. W. Ritchie, P. Burns and C. Palmer (eds) *Tourism Research Methods: Integrating Theory with Practice*. Wallingford, UK: CABI Publishing, 9–19.

Ryan, C. and Glendon, I. (1998) Application of leisure motivation scale to tourism. *Annals of Tourism Research*, 25(1), 169–84.

Sandiford, P. J. and Ap, J. (1998) The role of ethnographic techniques in tourism planning. *Journal of Travel Research*, 37(1), 3–11.

Saunders, D. M. and Turner, D. E. (1987) Gambling and leisure: the case of racing. *Leisure Studies*, 6(3), 281–300.

Saunders, M., Lewis, P. and Thornhill, A. (2000) *Research Methods for Business Students*. Harlow, UK: Financial Times-Prentice Hall.

Schaeffer, N. C. (2000) Asking questions about threatening topics: a selective overview. In A. A. Stone *et al. The Science of Self-report: Implications for Research and Practice*. Mahwah, NJ: Lawrence Erlbaum, 105–22.

Schimmack, U. and Diener, E. (eds) (2003) Experience sampling method in happiness research: special issue. *Journal of Happiness Studies*, 3(1).

Schneider, B., Ainbinder, A.M. and Csikszentmihalyi, M. (2004) Stress and working parents. In J. T. Haworth and A. J. Veal (eds) *Work and Leisure*. London: Routledge: 145–67.

Scott, D. and U'Ren, R. (1962) *Leisure: a Social Enquiry into Leisure Activities and Needs in an Australian Housing Estate*. Melbourne: F. W. Cheshire.

Scott, N., Baggio, R. and Cooper, C. (2008) *Network Analysis and Tourism*. Clevedon, UK: Channel View.

Searle, M. S., Mahon, M. J., Iso-Ahola, S., Sdrolias, H. A. and Van Dyck J. (1995) Enhancing a sense of independence and psychological well-being among the elderly: a field experiment. *Journal of Leisure Research*, 27(2), 107–24.

Seaton, A. V. (1997) Unobtrusive observational measures as a quality extension of visitor surveys at festivals and events: mass observation revisited. *Journal of Travel Research*, 35(4), 25–30.

Sechrest, L. (1992) Roots: back to our first generations. *Evaluation Practice*, 13(1), 1–7.

Semeonoff, B. (1976) *Projective Techniques*. London: John Wiley and Sons.

Shadish, W. R. Jr., Cook, T. D. and Leviton, L. C. (1991) *Foundations of Program Evaluation: Theories of Practice*. Newbury Park, CA: Sage.

Shelby, B. and Harris, R. (1985) Comparing methods for determining visitor evaluations of ecological impacts: site visits, photographs and written descriptions. *Journal of Leisure Research*, 17(1), 56–67.

Shelby, L. B. and Vaske, J. J. (2008) Understanding meta-analysis: a review of the methodological literature. *Leisure Sciences*, 30(1), 96–110.

Sherrow, V. (ed.) (1996) *Encyclopedia of Women and Sports*. Santa Barbara, CA: ABC-CLIO.

Shih, D. (1986) VALS as a tool of tourism marketing research. *Journal of Travel Research*, 25(1), 2–11.

Shoval, N. and Isaacson, M. (2007) Tracking tourists in the digital age. *Annals of Tourism Research*, 34(1), 141–59.

Shrestha, R. K. and Loomis, J. B. (2003) Meta-analytic benefit transfer of outdoor recreation economic values: testing out-of-sample convergent validity. *Environmental and Resource Economics*, 25(1), 79–100.

Sickler, J. and Fraser, J. (2009) Enjoyment in zoos. *Leisure Studies*, 28(3), 313–32.

Silverman, D. (1993) *Interpreting Qualitative Data: Methods for Analysing Talk, Text and Interaction*. London: Sage.

Skelton, A., Bridgwood, A. *et al.* (2002) *Arts in England: Attendance, Participation and Attitudes in 2001: Findings of A Study Carried Out by Social Survey Division of the Office for National Statistics*. London: Arts Council of England, available at: www.artscouncil.org.uk/information/ publications.html (Accessed Oct. 2004).

Small, J. (2004) Memory work. In J. Phillimore and L. Godson (eds) *Qualitative Research in Tourism: Ontologies, Epistemologies and Methodologies*. London: Routledge: 255–72.

Smith, S. L. J. (1985) *Tourism Analysis: A Handbook*. Harlow, UK: Longman.

Smith, S. L. J. (1995) *Tourism Analysis: A Handbook, Second Edition*. Harlow, UK: Longman.

Smyth, J. M. and Stone, A. A. (2003) Ecological momentary assessment research in behavioral medicine. *Journal of happiness Studies*, 4(1), 35–52.

Snape, R. (2004) The Co-operative Holidays Association and the cultural formation of countryside leisure practice. *Leisure Studies*, 23(2), 143–58.

Snooks and Co. (2002) *Style Manual for Authors, Editors and Printers*, Sixth edn. Milton, Qld: John Wiley and Sons.

Solesbury, W. (2002) The ascendancy of evidence. *Planning Theory and Practice*, 3(1), 90–6.

Sönmez, S., Shinew, K., Marchese, L., Veldkamp, C. and Burnett, G. W. (1993) Leisure corrupted: an artist's portrait of leisure in a changing society. *Leisure Studies*, 12(4), 266–76.

Spatz, C. and Johnston, J. O. (1989) *Basic Statistics: Tales of Distribution*, Fourth edn. Pacific Grove, CA: Brooks/Cole Publishing.

Stake, R. E. (1995) *The Art of Case Study Research*. Thousand Oaks, CA: Sage.

Standing Committee on Recreation and Sport (SCORS) (Annual) *Participation in Exercise, Recreation and Sport: Annual Resport*. Canberra: Australian Sports Commission/ SCORS, available at: www.ausport.gov.au information/scors/ERASS (Accessed March 2010).

Stebbins, R. (1992) *Amateurs, Professionals and Serious Leisure*. Montreal: McGill-Queen's University Press.

Stewart, D. W. and Shamdasani, P. N. (1990) *Focus Groups: Theory and Practice*. Newbury Park, CA: Sage.

Stockdale, J. (1984) People's conceptions of leisure. In A. Tomlinson (ed.) *Leisure: Politics, Planning and People*. London: Leisure Studies Association, 86–115.

Stokowski, P. A. (1994) *Leisure in Society: a Network Structural Perspective*. London: Mansell.

Stokowski, P. A. and Lee, R. G. (1991) The influence of social network ties on recreation and leisure: an exploratory study. *Journal of Leisure Research*, 23(1), 95–113.

Stone, A. A., Turkkan, J. S. *et al.* (2000) *The Science of Self-report: Implications for Research and Practice*. Mahwah, NJ: Lawrence Erlbaum.

Storey, W. K. (2004) *Writing History: A Guide for Students*. New York: Oxford University Press.

Strategic Business Insights (2009) *The VALS Survey*. Menlo Park, CA: Strategic Business Insights, available at: www.strategicbusinessinsights.com/vals/presurvey.shtml.

Strauss, A. and Corbin, J. (1994) Grounded theory methodology. In N. K. Denzin and Y. S. Lincoln (eds) *Handbook of Qualitative Research*. Thousand Oaks, CA: Sage, 273–85.

Strauss, A. L. (1987) *Qualitative Analysis for Social Scientists*. Cambridge: Cambridge University Press.

Straw, W. (1993) Characterising rock music culture: the case of heavy metal. In S. During (ed.) *The Cultural Studies Reader*. London: Routledge, 368–81.

Sust, F. (1995) The sports legacy of the Barcelona Games. In M. De Moragas and M. Botella (eds) *The Keys to Success: The Social, Sporting, Economic and Communications Impact of Barcelona '92*. Barcelona: Centre d'Estudis Olímpics i de l'Esport, Universitat Autonoma de Barcelona, 261–5.

Szalai, A. (ed.) (1972) *The Use of Time: Daily Activities of Urban and Suburban Populations in Twelve Countries*. The Hague: Mouton.

Szarycz, G. S. (2009) Some issues in tourism research phenomenology: a commentary. *Current Issues in Tourism*, 12(1), 47–58.

Tomlinson, A. (ed.) (1990) *Consumption, Identity, and Style: Marketing, Meanings, and the Packaging of Pleasure*. London: Comedia/Routledge.

Toohey, K. (1990) A content analysis of the Australian television coverage of the 1988 Seoul Olympics. Paper to the *Commonwealth and International Conference of Physical Education, Sport, Health, Dance, Recreation and Leisure*, January, Auckland.

Treuren, G. and Lane, D. (2003) The tourism planning process in the context of organised interests, industry structure, state capacity, accumulation and sustainability. *Current Issues in Tourism*, 6(1), 1–22.

Tribe, J. (1997) The indiscipline of tourism. *Annals of Tourism Research*, 24(3), 638–57.

Tyre, G. L. and Siderelis, C. D. (1978) Instant-count sampling – a technique for estimating recreation use in municipal settings. *Journal of Leisure Research*, 10(2), 173–80.

United Nations Intergovernmental Panel on Climate Change (UNIPCC) (2007) *Climate Change 2007: Synthesis Report*. Geneva: UNIPCC, available at: www.ipcc.ch.

Urry, J. (1994) Cultural change and contemporary tourism. *Leisure Studies*, 13(4), 233–8.

Van der Zande, A. N. (1985) Distribution patterns of visitors in large areas: a problem of measurement and analysis. *Leisure Studies*, 4(1), 85–100.

Vanden Heuvel, A. and Conolly, L. (2001) *The Impact of the Olympics on Participation in Australia: Trickle Down Effect, Discouragement Effect or no Effect?* Draft paper, Adelaide: Australian Bureau of Statistics.

Vaske, J. J. (2008) *Survey Research and Analysis: Applications in Parks, Recreation and Human Dimensions*. State College, PA: Venture.

Veal, A. J. (1987) The leisure forecasting tradition. Chapter 7 of *Leisure and the Future*. London: Allen and Unwin, 125–56.

Veal, A. J. (1993) The concept of lifestyle: a review. *Leisure Studies*, 12(4), 233–52.

Veal, A. J. (1994) Intersubjectivity and the transatlantic divide: a comment on Glancy (and Ragheb and Tate). *Leisure Studies*, 13(3), 211–16.

Veal, A. J. (1995) Leisure studies: frameworks for analysis. In H. Ruskin and A. Sivan (eds) *Leisure Education: Towards the 21st Century*. Provo, Utah: Brigham Young University Press, 124–36.

Veal, A. J. (1997) *Recreational Use of Beaches: Bibliography*. School of Leisure and Tourism Studies, University of Technology, Sydney, On-line Bibliography 1, available at: www.business.uts.edu.au/lst/research/publications/bibliographies/index.html.

Veal, A. J. (2000) *Lifestyle and Leisure: A Bibliography and Review*. School of Leisure and Tourism Studies, University of Technology, Sydney, On-line Bibliography 8, available at: www.business.uts.edu.au/lst/research/publications/bibliographies/index.html.

Veal, A. J. (2002) Leisure studies at the millennium: intellectual crisis or mature complacency? *Journal of Hospitality and Tourism Management*, 9(1), 37–45.

Veal, A. J. (2003) Tracking change: leisure participation and policy in Australia, 1985–2002. *Annals of Leisure Research*, 6(3), 246–78.

Veal, A. J. (2004) *Urban Parks and Open Space Planning and Management: A Bibliography*. School of Leisure and Tourism Studies, University of Technology, Sydney, On-line Bibliography 9, available at: www.business.uts.edu.au/lst/research/publications/bibliographies/index.html (Accessed March 2005).

Veal, A. J. (2005) Australia. In G. Cushman, A. J. Veal and J. Zuzanek (eds) *Free Time and Leisure Participation: International Perspectives*. Wallingford, UK: CABI Publishing, 17–40.

Veal, A. J. (2006) 25 years of *Leisure Studies*. Presentation to the *Leisure Studies Association Conference: Making Space: Leisure, Tourism & Renewal*, University of Western England, Bristol, July, PowerPoint presentation available under 'Other papers' at: www.leisuresource.net.

Veal, A. J. (2009) *Leisure and the Concept of Need: U-Plan Project Paper 4*. School of Leisure, Sport and Tourism Working Paper 14, University of Technology, Sydney, Lindfield, NSW, available at: www.leisuresource.net under 'U-Plan'.

Veal, A. J. (2010a) *Leisure, Sport and Tourism: Politics, Policy and Planning*. Wallingford, UK: CABI Publishing.

Veal, A. J. (2010b) *Leisure Needs Studies: A Review: U-Plan Project Paper 7*. School of Leisure, Sport and Tourism Working Paper 17, Lindfied, NSW: University of Technology, Sydney, available at: www.leisuresource.net.

Veal, A. J. and Frawley, S. (2009) *'Sport For All' and Major Sporting Events: Trends in Sport Participation and the Sydney 2000 Olympic Games, the 2003 Rugby World Cup and the Melbourne 2006 Commonwealth Games*. School of Leisure, Sport and Tourism Working Paper 6, Sydney: UTS. available under 'Other papers' at: www.leisuresource.net.

Veal, A. J. and Toohey, K. (2009) *The Olympic Games: A Bibliography*. School of Leisure and Tourism Studies, University of Technology, Sydney, On-line Bibliography 5, available at: www.business.uts.edu.au/lst/research/bibs.html (Accessed March 2010).

Wade, G. (1982) The relationship between landscape preference and looking time: a methodological investigation. *Journal of Leisure Research*, 14(3), 217–22.

Waldren, J. (1996) *Insiders and Outsiders: Paradise and Reality in Mallorca*. Providence, RI: Berghahn.

Waldren, J. (1997) We are not tourists – we live here. In S. Abram, J. Waldren and D. V. L. Macleod (eds) *Tourists and Tourism: Identifying with People and Places*. Oxford: Berg, 51–70.

Walker, J. C. (1988) *Louts and Legends*. Sydney: Allen and Unwin.

Walker, J. R. and Taylor, T. (1998) *The Columbia Guide to Online Style*. New York: Columbia University Press.

Walle, A. (1997) Quantitative versus qualitative tourism research. *Annals of Tourism Research*, 24(3), 524–36.

Walmsley, D. J. and Jenkins, J. M. (1991) Mental maps, locus of control, and activity: a study of business tourists in Coffs Harbour. *Journal of Tourism Studies*, 2(2), 36–42.

Ware, J. E., Kosinski, M. and Keller, S. D. (1994) *SF 36 Physical and Mental Health Summary Scales: A User's Manual*. Boston, MA: The Health Institute, New England Medical Centre.

Wearing, B. (1998) *Leisure and Feminist Theory*. London: Sage.

Weaver, D. (ed.) (2000) *Encyclopedia of Ecotourism*. Wallingford, UK: CABI Publishing.

Wells, W. D. (ed.) (1974) *Life Style and Psychographics*. Chicago: American Marketing Assn.

West, P. (1989) Urban regional parks and black minorities: subculture, marginality, and interracial relations in park use in the Detroit metropolitan area. *Leisure Sciences*, 11(1), 11–28.

White, J. (2004) Gender, work and leisure. In J. T. Haworth and A. J. Veal (eds) *Work and Leisure*. London: Routledge, 67–84.

Whyte, W. F. (1982) Interviewing in field research. In R. G. Burgess (ed.) *Field Research: A Sourcebook and Field Manual*. London: Allen and Unwin, 111–22.

Wilkinson, R. and Pickett, K. (2009) *The Spirit Level: Why More Equal Societies Almost Always do Better*. London: Allen Lane.

Williams, A. M. and Shaw, G. (1988) *Tourism and Economic Development: Western European Experience*. London: Belhaven.

Williams, C. (1998) Is the SERVQUAL model an appropriate management tool for measuring service delivery quality in the UK leisure industry? *Managing Leisure*, 3(2), 98–110.

Williams, R. C. (2003) *The Historian's Toolbox: A Student's Guide to the Theory and Craft of History*. Armonk, NY: M. E. Sharpe.

Witt, C. A. and Wright, P. L. (1992) Tourist motivation: life after Maslow. In P. Johnston and B. Thomas (eds) *Choice and Demand in Tourism*. London: Mansell, 33–55.

Witt, P. and Ellis, G. (1987) *The Leisure Diagnostic Battery: User's Manual*. State College, PA: Venture.

Woodside, A. G., and Ronkainen, I. A. (1994) Improving advertising conversion studies. In J. R. B. Ritchie and C. R. Goeldner (eds) *Travel, Tourism and Hospitality Research,* Second edn. New York: John Wiley, 481–7.

Woodside, A. G., Crouch, G. I., Mazanec, J. A., Oppermann, M. and Sakai, M. (eds) (2000) *Consumer Psychology of Tourism, Hospitality and Leisure*. Wallingford, UK: CAB International.

Wuellner, L. H. (1981) The adult inhibition and peer disinhibition of preschool group play. *Journal of Leisure Research*, 13(2), 159–73.

Wynne, D. (1986) Living on 'The Heath'. *Leisure Studies*, 5(1), 109–16.

Wynne, D. (1990) Leisure, lifestyle and the construction of social position. *Leisure Studies*, 9(1), 21–34.

Wynne, D. (1998) *Leisure, Lifestyle and the New Middle Class: a Case Study*. London: Routledge.

Xiao, H. and Smith, S. L. J. (2005) Case studies in tourism research: a state-of-the-art analysis. *Tourism Management*, 27(4), 738–49.

Yin, R. K. (2009) *Case Study Research: Design and Methods*, Fourth edition. Thousand Oaks, CA: Sage.

Young, C. H., Savola, K. L. and Phelps, E. (1991) *Inventory of Longitudinal Studies in the Social Sciences*. Newbury Park, CA: Sage.

Young, M. (1999) Cognitive maps of nature-based tourists. *Annals of Tourism Research*, 26(4), 817–39.

Zikmund, W. G. (1997) *Business Research Methods*, Fifth edn. Orlando, FL: Dryden Press.

Zuzanek, J. and Veal, A. J. (eds) (1998) Time pressure, stress, leisure participation and well-being. Special issue of *Loisir et Société/Society and Leisure*, 21(2).

Index

academic research 15
ACORN – A Classification of Residential Neighbourhoods 139
action research 133–4, 150, 337
Active People survey (UK) 139, 190–91, 193, 204
Adler, P. 229
aerial photography 226
age as a variable 291–2
Aitchison, C. 171
Albers, P. 253
Allen, L. 100, 151, 232, 234–5, 236
American Psychological Association 167, 168
Anderson, R. 170, 173
Andrews, D. 253
Annals of Leisure Research 20
Annals of Tourism Research 20
Annear, M. 151
anonymity of research subjects 112–15
anthropology 28–29
Ap, J. 253
applied vs theoretical research 31, 37–38
Archer, B. 26
Arensberg, C. 143
Arnberger, A. 229
arts, the 178
arts participation 205, 290
Association for Time Use 150
Atkinson, R. 253
attitude measurement 298–303, 316, 339
attitude statements 298–9
attitudes in questionnaire surveys 298–300
Australian Bureau of Statistics (ABS) 17, 95, 190, 194, 196, 205, 206, 310, 316, 385

Australian Longitudinal Study on Women's Health 151
Australian Research Council 19
Australian Sports Commission 95, 190
Australian Research Council 120
author/date system 170–72
authorship ethics 117
autobiography 249
autoethnography 126
automatic counters 225, 229

Bachman, J. 309, 316
Balmer, K. 14
Baretje, R. 177
Barry, P. 248
Batty, A. 134, 339
Bazeley, P. 401, 416
BBC – British Broadcasting Corporation 195
beaches 177, 216, 230
Beaman, J. 309, 316
Beard, J. 137, 151
Bell, E. 49, 151, 152, 229
Bella, L. 170, 172, 173
Bennet, T. 83, 452
Bertaux, D. 253
bibliographies 154–5, 157, 160, 177–8
Bialeschki, M. 25, 170, 173
Billings, A. 152
biographical methods 126, 239, 249–50, 253
Birenbaum, A. 215, 230
Bitgood, S. 230
Black, N. 338
Blackshaw, T. 26
Blamey, A. 328

Boothby, J. 192
Borman, K. 49
Botkin, M. 150, 316, 339
Botterill, T. 151, 316
Bourdieu, P. 352, 452
Bower, R. 334
Bradbury, H. 150
brainstorming 57
Bramham, P. 353
Brandenburg, J. 100, 393
briefs for research 11, 96–97
Bromley, D. 353
Brown, P. 53, 57, 151, 202, 248
Brown, W. 151
Brownson, R. 57, 100
Brukner, P. 158
Bruner, G. 137–8, 152
Bryman, A. 49, 151, 152, 229
budget 78
Burdge, R. 163
Burch, W. 229
Burgess, R. 253
Burkart, A. 206
Burns, P. 248
Burns, R. 49, 353, 496
Burton, T. 62, 170, 172, 173, 316, 329, 339
Butler, R. 25

CACI Ltd 139, 151
Calatone, R. 162, 178
Caltabiano, M. 309
Calder, B. 253
Campbell, D. 339
Campbell, F. 153
Cannibal Tours 248
captive group surveys 108, 278
Carlson, J. 57
Carty, V. 152
Carver 452
case-study method 128, 341–53
    analysis 348
    definition 342
    design 346–8
    examples 349–53
    merits 346
    scale 343
    in leisure 353
    in tourism 353
    unit of analysis 346
    validity and reliability 344–5
Cashman, R. 95
catchment areas 275, 388

causality 418–9
census of population 200
Centre for Leisure & Sport Research 528
Centre for Time Use Research 152, 316
Chadwick, R. 100
Chartered Institute of Public Finance and
    Accountancy (CIPFA) 205
Chase, D. 192, 310, 316
checklist
    for in-depth interview 241
    for research proposals 93, 98
Cherem, G. 333
Child, E. 230
children's
    play 230, 335–6, 375–6
    play equipment 335–6, 375–6
    play experiments 335–6
    leisure participation 194–5
Chisnall, P. 25
Christensen, J. 105, 119–20, 331
Christensen, K. 158
cinema demand – case-study 380–84
Clarke, J. 59
class – see social class
Claxton, J. 14
climate change 3
Coakes, S. 452
Coalter, F. 328
coding of questionnaires 303–5
Cohen, E. 249, 253
Collins, M. 353
commercial research 19
communication of findings 80
community studies 143–4, 150
computer-aided qualitative data analysis
    software (CAQDAS) 400
computer-aided telephone interviewing
    (CATI) 266
concept maps 62–72, 100
concepts 62–67, 100
conceptual framework 62–72, 100
    as models 67, 69
conference papers/presentations 21
confirmatory research 31
confidence intervals 362–7, 372
conjoint analysis 14, 140, 150
Connell, L. 95, 253
Connor, T. 131, 151
consultants 18
content analysis 126, 135, 164
contingent valuation 178
continuous counts 217–8

control groups 318
conversion studies 129, 150, 316
Corbin, J. 253
Cordell, H. 189
cordon surveys 129
Coshall, J. 151
Cosper, R. 150, 324, 339
counting heads 145, 150, 183–5, 209–10,
    229, 230
  by automatic counters 225, 229
countryside recreation observation
    research 230
coupon surveys 129, 150, 316
Crawford, G. 26
Critcher, C. 59, 202
critical approach 30–32
Crompton, J. 157
Cross, R. 334
cross-disciplinary research 28
Crouch, G. 151, 178, 323, 324, 339
crowdedness 89
Csiksentmihayli, M. 53, 131, 151
cultural studies 28–29
Cunneeen, C. 213, 230, 248, 253
Cushman, G. 17, 189, 192, 193, 206, 316,
    452

Dann, G. 25
Darcy, S. 178
data
  access to 146
  bases 156
  analysis approaches 77–78
  recording sheet
  storage 80–81, 112–13
Davies, B. 253
Davies, C. 38, 49, 253
Dawson, J. 229
Dayton, T. 141
Dean 243
DeCrop, C. 49
deduction vs induction 39–42
Deem, R. 170, 172
Delphi technique 135, 150
Denison, J. 54
Denzin, N. 35, 253
Department for Communities and Local
    Government (DCLG, UK) 190
Department for Culture, Media and Sport
    (DCMS, UK) 190, 204, 329
dependent variable 318, 464–
descriptive research 5–6, 418

Diener, E. 151
Dillman, D. 270, 316
disability 178
disciplines 16, 27–29, 49, 61
  vs field of study 28
  multi-disciplinary research 28
  inter-disciplinary research 28
  cross-disciplinary research 28
discrete choice experiments 323–6, 339
Disney 248, 249, 350
documentary sources 202
Donne, K. 49, 105
Donohue, H. 135, 150
Douglas, J. 230
Driscol, A. 330
Driver, B. 137, 151, 333
Drogin, E. 271, 272, 331, 339
drug use 259, 309
Duffield, B.
Duffy, M. 143
dummy questions 308
Dunford, R. 253
Dunne, S. 253
Dupuis, S. 35, 49, 151, 237, 397
Dyer, R. 249

Echtner, C. 100
Economic and Social Research Council
    (ESRC) 19
economic
  data 199
  status 292
  surveys 199
economics 28–29
eco-tourism 325
Eder, R. 229
education 28
Edwards, A. 206
electronically activated recorder (EAR) 131
Elias, N. 4
Ellis, G. 152
Ely, M. 229
empirical research 31, 38
en route surveys 129, 150, 229
endnote system – see footnote system
Endnote program 160
Environment, Department of 133, 326, 339
environmental appraisal 11, 21
environmental studies 28–29
epistemology 30–31
Ernst and Young 18
e-surveys 272–4, 316

ethics 78, 101–120
  captive group surveys and 278
  codes of 101–2
  committees 103
ethnic groups 178, 296
ethnography 31, 35, 126, 239, 253
Euro-Disney 350
Eurobarometer 378
evaluating recreation services (case study) 88–91
evaluative research 5, 8, 25, 33, 62, 345, 419
events
  cultural 324
  observational research on 230
evidence-based policy 17, 25
Exercise, Recreation and Sport Survey (ERASS, Aust.) 96, 190–91, 193–4, 205
expenditure 182
experience sampling method (ESM) 131–2, 150, 151, 334
experimental method 31, 42–44, 49, 128, 317–39
  action research and 337
  children's play and 335–6
  classic design 318–9, 339
  dependent and independent variables 318
  discrete choice experiments 323–6
  mental mapping and 338
  physical models and 338
  policy/management-related 326–9
  psychological/perceptual 332, 333–4
  Q methodology 139–40, 150, 51, 337
  qualitative methods and 337
  quasi-experimental design 321–3
  and research methods 329–32
  sport-related 332, 334–5
  training-related 337
  treatments/experimental and control groups 318
  validity 319–20
explanatory research 5, 7, 33, 62
exploratory research 6

facility utilisation (case study) 83–88
facility catchment area (case study) 388
facility demand (case study) 380–4
factor analysis 42
fast leisure 84
Faulkner, B. 57
feasibility studies 22

Fenn, C. 290
fieldwork planning 310–3
film as text 248
Finn, M. 342
Fiske, J. 216, 230
Fleming, S. 120
focus groups 126, 239, 245–6, 253
football fans 216, 230
footnote system 172–4
Ford, R. 151
forecasting 23, 384
Foucault, M. 55
Fox, K. 190
Frawley, S. 94–95, 203
Frazer, J. 151
Frechtling, D. 151, 206
Frow, J. 83
functionalism 31

Garrod, B. 229
Gartner, W. 150, 229
Geary, C. 178
General Household Survey (GHS, UK) 189–90, 193–4, 263
generalisability 147
geography 28–29
George, D. 452
Gerring, J. 342, 344
Gershuny, J. 206, 316
Getz, D. 132, 151
Gobbs, G. 416
Gibson, H. 253
Giddens, A. 316
Gitelson, R. 271, 272, 331, 339
Glancy, M. 38, 49, 253
Glaser, B. 238, 253
Glass, G. 142, 178
Glendon, I. 133, 151
global positioning systems (GPS) 132, 226, 229
Glyptis, S. 230
goals in planning 11
Godbey, G. 49, 192, 253, 316
Goeldner, C. 25, 169, 206, 235
Goffman, I. 215
Goodson, L. 33, 235, 237, 253
Google Scholar 157
Gramza, A. 336
Grant, D. 216, 230
Gratton, C. 100, 190, 192
Gray, H. 25, 26

Green, H. 150
Green Space 229, 230
Greenbaum, T. 253
Greenwood, D. 133–4, 150
Grichting, W. 309
Griffin, C. 253
Groningen Growth & Development
    Centre 378
grounded theory 238, 253
group interviews – see focus groups
group type
Guba, E. 32, 37, 43, 47, 49
Gunn, C. 169
Gushiken, T.
Guy, B. 151

Hagedorn, R. 33, 34
Hall, S.
Hamilton-Smith, E.
Hammitt, W. 272, 331, 339
Hanley, N. 151
Harada, M. 192, 310, 316
harm to research subjects, risk of 112–16
Harmonised European Time Use Survey
    196, 205, 316, 378
Harper, W. 14, 248
Harris, R. 332, 353
Hartman, R. 152
Harvard Business School cases 341
Harvard referencing system 170–72
Hatry, H. 88–91
Havitz, M. 49, 323, 339
Hawthorne effect 320
Hayllar, B. 353
Hedges, B. 250, 253
Hektner, J. 151
Henderson, K. 25, 32, 36, 47, 49, 62–63,
    151, 170, 173, 234, 253, 353
Henley Centre for Forecasting 26
Henry, I. 353
Hensel, G. 137–8, 152
hermeneutics 126, 135, 164
Heywood, L. 334
Hillier, J. 229
Hindson, A. 95
history 28–29, 124, 151
Hodder, I. 249
Hogan, K. 95
Hollands, R. 253
Hollinshead, K. 235, 237
honesty in reporting results 116

Hornery, A. 169
household expenditure 199–205
household surveys 262–4
household type 294–5
housing tenure 297
housing type 297
Howard, A. 335
Howard, K. 100
Howat, G. 72
Howe, C. 49
Huberman, A. 62, 100, 237, 416
Hudson, S. 229, 316
Huh, C. 132, 151
Hultsman, J. 248
Humberstone, B. 32
Hung, P. 151
Hunt, J. 150, 229
Hurst, F. 129, 150
hypotheses 72–73
hypothetical-deductive model 31, 34–35

Iacocca, L. 249
ideology 58–59
idiographic research 131
importance-performance analysis 14, 72,
    100
income 293–4
independent variable 318, 464–5
in-depth interviews 126, 239–45
    standardised 243
    informal/unstructured 243–4
induction vs deduction 39–42
inequality, socio-economic 377–9
informal interviews 126
information requirements 75
information sources 155–9
informed consent 109–12
intercept surveys 129
inter-disciplinary research 28
inter-library loans 159
International Passenger Survey (UK) 198,
    205
International Visitor Survey (Aust.) 198,
    205
internet references 168
internet searching 157
interpretive approach 30–32
intersubjectivity 31
interview checklist 241
interviewer vs respondent completion
    260–1

interviewer recruitment and training 313
interviewing process 242–4
introductory remarks in questionnaires
    300–1
Isaacson, M. 229, 330
ISBN – International Standard Book
    Number 509
ISI Web of Knowledge 156
Iso-Ahola, S. 152

Jackson, E. 162, 170, 172, 173
Jafari, J. 158
James, W. 253
Jenkins, J. 151, 158, 338
Jennings, G. 100, 241–2, 253
Johnson, D. 253
Johnston, J. 371, 496
Jones, I. 100
Jones, R. 105, 150
Jordan, F. 120, 253
journal articles 20
    refereeing of 20
journals 20, 36, 163
Journal of Leisure Research 20, 35, 36, 496
Journal of Park & Recreation Administration
    36
Journal of Travel Research 20

Kamphorst, T. 49, 253
Kanning, M. 334
Kasprzyk, D. 151
Keirle, I. 230
Kellehear, A. 124, 206, 207, 229
Kelly, G. 136, 151, 316
Kelly, Joe 324, 325, 339
Kelly, John 26, 49, 151, 235–6, 257
Kelsey, C. 25, 26
key performance indicators (KPIs) 71
Kidder, L. 371
Kinsley, B. 150, 324, 339
Kleiber, D. 151
Kline, R. 42, 496
Klugman, K. 249
Kraus, R. 100, 232, 234–5, 236
Krenz, C. 49, 151
Krueger, R. 253

Labovitz, S. 33, 34
Ladkin, A. 253
Lainsbury, A. 350
landscape perception 333

Lane, D. 25
Lankford, S. 100
LaPage, W. 105, 132, 151
Larson, R. 131, 151
Latin abbreviations in referencing 176
Lavers, B. 144, 232–4, 349, 353
Lavrakas, P. 316
Lawson, P.
Lawson, R. 330
Lee, R. 142
Leiper, N. 49, 353
leisure:
    definition of 4
    expenditure 182
    measurement- of 181–2
    needs studies 22
    time 182, 379
Leisure, Recreation and Tourism Abstracts
    156
Leisure Boredom Scale 152, 333
Leisure and the Quality of Life study 133,
    326
Leisure Satisfaction Scale 137
Leisure Sciences 20, 36
Leisure Studies 20, 35, 37
Leisure Tourism Database 156
length of stay 224
Lepkowski, J. 316
Lester, J. 248
Levenson, H. 152
Levin, M. 133–4, 150
Levionson, D. 158
library catalogues 155
libraries 160
life cycle 294, 296, 316
Life Satisfaction Index 152, 333
lifestyle 162–3, 178, 316 – see also
    psychographics
Likert scales 298–9
Lincoln, Y. 32, 35, 37, 43, 47, 49, 59, 103,
    120, 237, 253
literature
    review 153–78
    analysis 163
    as basis for research 60
    conduct 61, 164–7
    roles of 154
Litvin, S. 152
Locus of Control Scale 152, 333
Lofland, J. 253
logical empiricism 31